2014 Annual Indices for Expatriates and Ordinary Residents on Cost of Living, Wages and Purchasing Power for World's Major Cities

Lee Kuan Yew School of Public Policy
ASIA COMPETITIVENESS INSTITUTE

NUS National University of Singapore

About ACI

The Asia Competitiveness Institute (ACI) was established in August 2006 as a research centre at the Lee Kuan Yew School of Public Policy (LKYSPP), National University of Singapore (NUS). It aims to build the intellectual leadership and network for understanding and developing competitiveness in the Asia region. ACI seeks to contribute to the enhancement of inclusive growth, living standards and institutional governance through competitiveness research on sub-national economies in Asia. It identifies mitigating issues and challenges for potential public policy interventions through close collaboration with regional governments, business corporations, policy think-tanks and academics.

The ACI's value proposition may be encapsulated in an acronym:

Analytical inputs to initiate policies for policy-makers and business leaders in Asia

Capacity building to enable others through improvement in productivity and efficiency

Intellectual leadership to create pragmatic models of competitiveness and inclusive growth.

The Institute's core research competencies can also be encapsulated in this acronym describing our evidence-based assessments conducted on public policies for **A**SEAN in the context of the rise of **C**HINA and **I**NDIA.

Vision and Mission

- The over-arching vision of ACI is to build up its research credibility with policy impact, contributing as a professional think-tank.
- The mission is to establish our niche as a leading policy think-tank in Asia by identifying competitiveness, promoting competition and synergising complementarities amongst Asian economies and business corporations.
- We will articulate, entice discourse and shape agendas in the arena of public policies amongst Asian governments.
- We will undertake evidence-based assessments of public policy outcomes, their effectiveness and impact on inclusivity.

Asia Competitiveness Institute | Lee Kuan Yew School of Public Policy | National University of Singapore
469A Bukit Timah Road, Level 2 Tower Block, Singapore 259770
Tel: (65) 6516 5025 Fax: (65) 6467 8714 http://spp.nus.edu.sg/ACI

2014 Annual Indices for Expatriates and Ordinary Residents on Cost of Living, Wages and Purchasing Power for World's Major Cities

Tan Khee Giap
Co-Director, Asia Competitiveness Institute
Lee Kuan Yew School of Public Policy
National University of Singapore

Tan Kong Yam
Co-Director, Asia Competitiveness Institute
Lee Kuan Yew School of Public Policy
National University of Singapore

Yuan Randong
Research Associate, Asia Competitiveness Institute
Lee Kuan Yew School of Public Policy
National University of Singapore

Nguyen Le Phuong Anh
Research Associate, Asia Competitiveness Institute
Lee Kuan Yew School of Public Policy
National University of Singapore

- Reviewers -

Cledan Mandri-Perrott
Head of Infrastructure Finance & Public-Private Partnerships
The World Bank Group

Vu Minh Khuong
Associate Professor, Lee Kuan Yew School of Public Policy
National University of Singapore

Lee Kuan Yew School of Public Policy
Asia Competitiveness Institute

NUS National University of Singapore

World Scientific

Published by

World Scientific Publishing Co. Pte. Ltd.
5 Toh Tuck Link, Singapore 596224
USA office: 27 Warren Street, Suite 401-402, Hackensack, NJ 07601
UK office: 57 Shelton Street, Covent Garden, London WC2H 9HE

British Library Cataloguing-in-Publication Data
A catalogue record for this book is available from the British Library.

2014 ANNUAL INDICES FOR EXPATRIATES AND ORDINARY RESIDENTS ON COST OF LIVING, WAGES AND PURCHASING POWER FOR WORLD'S MAJOR CITIES

ISBN 978-981-4583-56-5
ISBN 978-981-4583-57-2 (pbk)

Typeset by Stallion Press
Email: enquiries@stallionpress.com

Printed in Singapore

Contents

Foreword

This publication by Asia Competitiveness Institute (ACI) compiling annual indices of cost of living, wages and purchasing power of the world's major cities is extremely timely.

The issues that have been raised regarding these matters have been of critical concern among policy-makers, employers, ordinary citizens as well as expatriates. They are also kcy indicators that affect a country's standard of living. While cost of living has been routinely measured at the national level by the annual Consumer Price Index, there is as yet no reliable index for tracking and comparing costs of living and purchasing power at the sub-national levels. There are some published surveys done by commercial research organizations but they are mainly used by companies to decide on compensation levels for expatriate professionals. Most do not adequately take into account differences in consumption patterns across cities. Such surveys also lack scientific rigour which make their results less than satisfactory for policy discourse.

This publication is ACI's attempt at meeting this need. It will be useful for policy-makers because it goes beyond expatriate living and takes into account wages and purchasing power of ordinary residents, thus enabling comparisons of standard of living across cities. ACI has made great efforts to ensure that its computation of the indices are transparent, to reinforce confidence in the findings.

ACI's work should help provide useful inputs to the discussion on standards of living and quality of life in cities across the globe. I hope it will continue its outstanding work and contribute to public discussion on these important issues.

Mr Han Fook Kwang
Editor-at-Large
The Straits Times

Preface

This research by the Asia Competitiveness Institute (ACI) at Lee Kuan Yew School of Public Policy (LKYSPP), National University of Singapore (NUS), compares cost of living for expatriates and ordinary residents in 103 major cities in the world. It is an important undertaking for three reasons.

Firstly, the pace of urbanisation has accelerated remarkably across the globe. Since 2008, more than half of humanity has been living in urban areas. According to the United Nations, by 2050, 66 per cent of the world's population will be living in cities. The overwhelming majority of economic activity now takes place in cities. The World Bank has estimated that more than 80 per cent of global GDP is currently generated in cities. This speed and scale of urbanisation not only drives human history but will also have critical implications for governments around the world, as well as for the environment.

Secondly, we live in the age of globalisation. Never before have businesses and talents been as mobile as they are today. The proliferation of global production networks and the emergence of new markets means that competition is now global instead of national. New York is no longer just competing with San Francisco or Chicago, Frankfurt is no longer just competing with Berlin and Munich, and Beijing is no longer competing with just Shanghai and Guangzhou. As a result, international benchmarks for major cities are crucial if individuals and companies are to make informed decisions.

Finally, it is difficult to obtain reliable and comprehensive analyses on such a wide range of cities. ACI's research examines cost of living in the world's major cities for both expatriates and ordinary residents, as well as the wages and purchasing power of ordinary residents. This study therefore contributes a more nuanced understanding of cities than existing indices do. In fact, this is the only benchmark which provides comparable data on city-level cost of living for both expatriates and residents. Consequently, this publication contains invaluable information not only for individuals and corporations, but also for policy-makers and scholars. In short, the value of this study should not be underestimated.

Evidence-based public policy assessment is central to our work at ACI, LKY School. Cutting-edge research methods have been rigorously applied in this study to gain new insights into the world we are living in. I am therefore proud to present this latest study from ACI.

Professor Kishore Mahbubani
Dean
Lee Kuan Yew School of Public Policy
National University of Singapore

Acknowledgements

We from the Asia Competitiveness Institute (ACI) at Lee Kuan Yew School of Public Policy (LKYSPP), National University of Singapore (NUS) have combined leading-edge research methodologies with extensive data collection effort to evaluate and track the economic competitiveness since 2000 at both national and sub-national level for over 100 Asian economies including Greater China, India, Indonesia and ASEAN-10. Building upon our previous works, in 2014 we extended our study to include various published volumes on *2014 Annual Provincial and Regional Competitiveness Analysis for Greater China Economies: Development Strategies under the New Normal, 2014 Regional Competitiveness Analysis and a Master Plan on Regional Development Strategies for India, 2014 Provincial and Inaugural Regional Competitiveness Analysis: Safeguarding Indonesia's Growth Momentum, 2014 Annual Competitiveness Analysis and Development Strategies for Indonesian Provinces* and *2014 Annual Competitiveness Ranking and Simulation Study for ASEAN-10 and Development Strategies to Enhance Asia Economic Connectivity.*

In this book *2014 Annual Indices for Expatriates and Ordinary Residents on Cost of Living, Wages and Purchasing Power for World's Major Cities*, we have constructed annual indices and rankings from 2005 to 2013 for cost of living, wages and purchasing power for major cities around the world, which we intend to update annually. This is also the only publication that provides comparable data for both expatriates and ordinary residents who tend to be very different in their consumption patterns. Cost of living, wages and purchasing power are important benchmarks for monitoring and assessing basic living standard. We therefore believe this compendium is an important reference for not only multinational corporations, human resources managers and expatriates, but also policy-makers, researchers and analysts who are concerned with the cost of living, wages and purchasing power at the city level.

We wish to record our deepest gratitude for the time and effort invested by the following reviewers who evaluated and gave their constructive comments on the research as incorporated in this book:

Dr Cledan Mandri-Perrott
Head of Infrastructure Finance & Public-Private Partnerships,
The World Bank Group

Dr Vu Minh Khuong
Associate Professor,
Lee Kuan Yew School of Public Policy, National University of Singapore

We would also like to place on record our heartfelt appreciation for the support and encouragement from Dean Kishore Mahbubani; Associate Professor Eduardo Araral, Vice Dean

(Research); Mr Donald Low, Associate Dean (Research and Executive Education) and Senior Fellow; and other colleagues at LKYSPP. This book would not have been possible without the dedicated effort of all research and administrative staff at ACI. Thus we note with tremendous appreciation the high team spirit of ACI staff including Sangiita Yoong Wei Cher, Nie Tongxin, Linda Low, Luu Nguyen Trieu Duong, Yap Xin Yi and Tracy Cai.

Tan Khee Giap
Tan Kong Yam
Yuan Randong
Nguyen Le Phuong Anh
Asia Competitiveness Institute
Lee Kuan Yew School of Public Policy
National University of Singapore

About the Authors

Tan Khee Giap is a Co-Director of the Asia Competitiveness Institute (ACI) and Associate Professor at the Lee Kuan Yew School of Public Policy, National University of Singapore. He is also the Chairman of the Singapore National Committee for Pacific Economic Cooperation. Upon graduating with a PhD from University of East Anglia, England, in 1987 under the Overseas Research Scheme awarded by the Committee of Vice-Chancellors and Principals of the Universities of the United Kingdom. He joined the banking sector as a treasury manager and served as secretary to the Assets and Liabilities Committee for three years. Thereafter he taught at the Department of Economics and Statistics, National University of Singapore (NUS), 1990–1993. Dr Tan joined Nanyang Technological University in 1993 and was Associate Dean, Graduate Studies Office, 2007–2009. Dr Tan has consulted extensively with the various government ministries, statutory boards and government linked companies of the Singapore government. He has also served as a consultant to international agencies such as the Asian Development Bank, Asian Development Bank Institute, United Nations Industrial Development Group, World Gold Council, ASEAN Secretariat, Central Policy Unit of Hong Kong, Kerzner International, Las Vegas Sands and Marina Bay Sands. Dr Tan is the lead author for eight books and published widely in international refereed journals. His current research interests include econometric forecasting, Cost of Living Index, Global Liveable Cities Index and competitiveness analysis on 31 provinces in China, 35 states in India and ASEAN-10 economies. Dr Tan was Deputy President of the Singapore Economic Society, 2004. He served in the 2002 Economic Review Committee (ERC), served as Chairman of the Task Force on Portable Medical Benefits (PMB), served as the Deputy Chairman of the IPS Forum for Economic Restructuring (IFER) in 2003 and served as a member of the Resource Panel of the Government Parliamentary Committee for Transport and Government Parliamentary Committee for Finance and Trade since 2007. Dr Tan has extensively advised and guided multinational corporations leading to public listings especially those companies from Mainland China and Taiwan. He is also currently an Independent Director of the publicly listed Artivision, BreadTalk Group, Boustead Projects and TEE Land.

Tan Kong Yam is presently a Co-Director of the Asia Competitiveness Institute. He is also Professor of Economics at the Nanyang Technological University. From 1985–1989, he was the chief assistant to the late Dr Goh Keng Swee on his consultancy to Mr Deng Xiaoping on China's development strategy. From June 2002 to June 2005, he was a senior economist at the World Bank office in Beijing. In 2004, he was a member of the World Bank expert group on the eleventh five-year plan (2006–2010) for the State Council in China. The expert group provided analysis and policy recommendations on urbanisation, regional inequality, innovation policy, energy and water policy as well as strategy on banking reform to the Chinese government. Prior to that, he was the chief economist of the Singapore government (1999–2002), and Head of the Department of Strategy and Policy, Faculty of Business Administration at the National University of Singapore (NUS). He is a graduate of Princeton (1975–1979, class of 1931 scholar, Paul Volcker Thesis prize) and Stanford University (1980–1983), where he completed his Master's and PhD in three years. Prior to joining NUS, he worked at the Hoover Institution at Stanford University, World Bank, the Monetary Authority of Singapore, and was the Director of Research at the Ministry of Trade and Industry in Singapore. His research interests are in international trade and finance, economic and business trends in the Asia Pacific region and economic reforms in China. He has published ten books and numerous articles in major international journals including American Economic Review, World Bank Economic Review, etc on economic and business issues in the Asia Pacific region. He served as board member at the Singapore Central Provident Fund Board (1984–1996) and the National Productivity Board (1989–1990). He has also consulted for many organisations including Temasek, GIC, Citigroup, IBM, ATT, BP, ABN-AMRO, Ikea, Bank of China, China Construction Bank, People's Bank of China, EDB, Areva, Capitaland, Samsung, Mobil, amongst others.

Yuan Randong is a Research Associate at the Asia Competitiveness Institute (ACI) at the Lee Kuan Yew School of Public Policy (LKYSPP), National University of Singapore (NUS). He obtained a joint degree from NUS and Australian National University (ANU) in Economics and Actuarial studies with First Class Honours in 2012. At ACI, he focuses on data analysis and competitiveness studies of the Greater China economies. Yuan Randong's research interests include financial economics, econometric modeling, and economic development and competitiveness of Greater China economies. As a co-author, he published an editorial opinion on public policy in Singapore, a journal paper in International Journal of Chinese Culture and Management, and two books titled "Annual Analysis of Competitiveness, Simulation Studies and Development Perspective for 34 Greater China Economies" and "2014 Annual Provincial and Regional Competitiveness Analysis for Greater China Economies: Development Strategies under the New Normal".

Nguyen Le Phuong Anh is a Research Associate at the Asia Competitiveness Institute (ACI) at the Lee Kuan Yew School of Public Policy (LKYSPP), National University of Singapore (NUS). Phuong Anh received her Bachelor (Honors) degree in Economics from Nanyang Technological University (NTU), Singapore, and a Master of Science degree in Development Studies from London School of Economics and Political Science (LSE), United Kingdom. Prior to joining ACI, she gained extensive experience working in the financial sector with OCBC, DBS and Bloomberg L.P. in Singapore, and additionally held a research internship position at the Mekong Institute in Khon Kaen, Thailand. At ACI, she co-authored a book titled "2014 Annual Indices for Expatriates and Ordinary Residents on Cost of Living, Wages and Purchasing Power for World's Major Cities". She is currently coordinating the competitiveness ranking and simulation studies for the ASEAN-10 economies. Phuong Anh's research interests include economic development policy, international political economy, ASEAN economies and applied econometrics.

List of Cities

	City	Country	Region
1	Adelaide	Australia	Australasia
2	Amman	Jordan	Asia
3	Amsterdam	Netherlands	Western Europe
4	Asuncion	Paraguay	South America
5	Athens	Greece	Western Europe
6	Atlanta	United States	North America
7	Auckland	New Zealand	Australasia
8	Baku	Azerbaijan	Asia
9	Bangkok	Thailand	Asia
10	Barcelona	Spain	Western Europe
11	Beijing	China	Asia
12	Berlin	Germany	Western Europe
13	Bogota	Colombia	South America
14	Boston	United States	North America
15	Bratislava	Slovakia	Eastern Europe
16	Brisbane	Australia	Australasia
17	Brussels	Belgium	Western Europe
18	Bucharest	Romania	Eastern Europe
19	Budapest	Hungary	Eastern Europe
20	Buenos Aires	Argentina	South America
21	Cairo	Egypt	Africa
22	Calgary	Canada	North America
23	Caracas	Venezuela	South America
24	Chicago	United States	North America
25	Cleveland	United States	North America
26	Colombo	Sri Lanka	Asia
27	Copenhagen	Denmark	Western Europe
28	Dalian	China	Asia

	City	Country	Region
29	Detroit	United States	North America
30	Doha	Qatar	Asia
31	Dubai	United Arab Emirates	Asia
32	Dublin	Ireland	Western Europe
33	Frankfurt	Germany	Western Europe
34	Geneva	Switzerland	Western Europe
35	Guangzhou	China	Asia
36	Helsinki	Finland	Western Europe
37	Hong Kong	Hong Kong, China	Asia
38	Honolulu	United States	North America
39	Houston	United States	North America
40	Istanbul	Turkey	Asia
41	Jakarta	Indonesia	Asia
42	Johannesburg	South Africa	Africa
43	Kiev	Ukraine	Eastern Europe
44	Kuala Lumpur	Malaysia	Asia
45	Kuwait	Kuwait	Asia
46	Lexington	United States	North America
47	Lima	Peru	South America
48	Lisbon	Portugal	Western Europe
49	London	Great Britain	Western Europe
50	Los Angeles	United States	North America
51	Luxembourg	Luxembourg	Western Europe
52	Lyon	France	Western Europe
53	Madrid	Spain	Western Europe
54	Manila	Philippines	Asia
55	Melbourne	Australia	Australasia
56	Mexico City	Mexico	North America
57	Miami	United States	North America
58	Milan	Italy	Western Europe
59	Minneapolis	United States	North America
60	Montevideo	Uruguay	South America
61	Montreal	Canada	North America
62	Moscow	Russia	Eastern Europe

	City	Country	Region
63	Mumbai	India	Asia
64	Munich	Germany	Western Europe
65	Nairobi	Kenya	Africa
66	New Delhi	India	Asia
67	New York	United States	North America
68	Osaka/Kobe	Japan	Asia
69	Oslo	Norway	Western Europe
70	Paris	France	Western Europe
71	Perth	Australia	Australasia
72	Pittsburgh	United States	North America
73	Prague	Czech Republic	Eastern Europe
74	Pretoria	South Africa	Africa
75	Qingdao	China	Asia
76	Quito	Ecuador	South America
77	Reykjavik	Iceland	Western Europe
78	Rio de Janeiro	Brazil	South America
79	Rome	Italy	Western Europe
80	San Francisco	United States	North America
81	Santiago	Chile	South America
82	Sao Paulo	Brazil	South America
83	Seattle	United States	North America
84	Seoul	South Korea	Asia
85	Shanghai	China	Asia
86	Shenzhen	China	Asia
87	Singapore	Singapore	Asia
88	Sofia	Bulgaria	Eastern Europe
89	St Petersburg	Russia	Eastern Europe
90	Stockholm	Sweden	Western Europe
91	Suzhou	China	Asia
92	Sydney	Australia	Australasia
93	Taipei	Taiwan, China	Asia
94	Tel Aviv	Israel	Asia
95	Tianjin	China	Asia
96	Tokyo	Japan	Asia

	City	Country	Region
97	Toronto	Canada	North America
98	Vancouver	Canada	North America
99	Vienna	Austria	Western Europe
100	Warsaw	Poland	Eastern Europe
101	Washington DC	United States	North America
102	Wellington	New Zealand	Australasia
103	Zurich	Switzerland	Western Europe

List of Abbreviations

ACI	Asia Competitiveness Institute
BLS	United States Bureau of Labour Statistics
CPF	Central Provident Fund
CSRWs	Clerical, Sales & Services Workers
EIU	Economist Intelligence Unit
ICP	International Comparison Programme
ILO	International Labour Organisation
LKYSPP	Lee Kuan Yew School of Public Policy
NUS	National University of Singapore
PMETs	Professionals, Managers, Executives & Technicians
PPP	Purchasing Power Parity
PTOGLs	Production, Transportation Operators and General Labours
US	United States
USD	United States dollar

List of Boxes, Figures and Tables

Chapter 5

Chapter 6

Discussant Notes 2

Chapter 1

Understanding and Tracking Cost of Living, Wages and Purchasing Power for Ordinary Residents and Expatriates for City Dwellers: Figures, Facts and Fallacies

1.1 Introductory Notes: Research Motivation and Literature Review

There has been broad-based growth in wealth for cities all over the world, albeit increasingly unequal within and across cities. Some cities tend to grow faster than others, especially emerging cities in Asia. Due to external shocks, longer period of economic expansions compared to downturns has resulted in greater volatility in growth as cities are also increasingly open and interconnected. Such volatility would mean a less stable macroeconomic environment for cities leading to fluctuations in prices, employment as well as varying shares between private and public consumption.

Cost of living, wages and hence purchasing power therefore become important key benchmark indicators to track and monitor basic living standard for cities, not just by employers and employees; they matter even more for policy-makers, multinational corporations and the government of the day.

While changes in the cost of living over time can be measured by the Consumer Price Index, there is yet a reliable and consistent index for comparing the cost of living across different major cities to guide policy analysis. Commercial cost of living surveys, while very useful for compensation decisions for expatriate managers, are inadequate as they do not accommodate for differences in consumption patterns among cities and also do not take into account differences in lifestyles between ordinary residents and expatriates across the cities.

This book with annual updates since 2005 is thus a valuable compendium report on 103 major cities around the world whereby indices on cost of living, wages and purchasing power were tracked and monitored systematically, for both ordinary residents and expatriates who tend to be vastly different in their lifestyles. In fact this is currently the only publication that provides comparable data on cost of living across cities for both ordinary residents and expatriates, which is of critical significance as cost of living analysis on the latter is often mistaken or confused as the former!

We are first attracted by the highly demanded reports and eyeball catching headlines on cost of living, wages and purchasing power for city dwellers. Existing major related studies on cost of living index for expatriates are as follows:

- *UBS Prices and Earnings* is the report prepared by the Wealth Management Research Department of UBS located in Zurich, Switzerland. The Report is updated every year by offering indices on price levels for expatriates. The basket of goods and services used to calculate indices is based on a European family of three. The same basket assumes common consumer preferences across all cities regardless of geography, lifestyle, culture, etc. Our case study on the UBS Report in Section 1.2 will discuss features of the UBS study in greater detail and depth.

Prices and earnings

CIO Wealth Management Research
September 2012

Prices and earnings iPhone App

Edition 2012

A comparison of purchasing power around the globe

Price comparison

Asia is the region with the greatest variation in prices

Food costs five times as much in Tokyo as in Mumbai

Domestic purchasing power

Buying an iPhone in Zurich requires 22 hours of work

In Manila this takes around 20 times longer

Wage comparison

Highest net wages in Zurich, Geneva and Luxembourg

Shortest working hours in Paris, Lyon and Copenhagen

UBS

■ Economist Intelligent Unit (EIU): *Worldwide Cost of Living* is updated annually and includes only the cost of living index for expatriates. The study is based on a single weight for the basket of goods and services which is geared towards Western consumption patterns. We suspect the ranking of the EIU study is sensitive to the choice of base city as in reply to our enquiry, EIU said "the reality is that the availability of goods and services and factors like rounding of numbers means that rebasing a city will produce slightly different results" which the Asia Competitiveness Institute (ACI) approach would not!

- Mercer: *Cost-of-Living Information Services* which is updated annually provides only the ranking of cities according to cost of living for expatriates with no index value. The Report offers the key to designing accurate expatriate compensation packages.

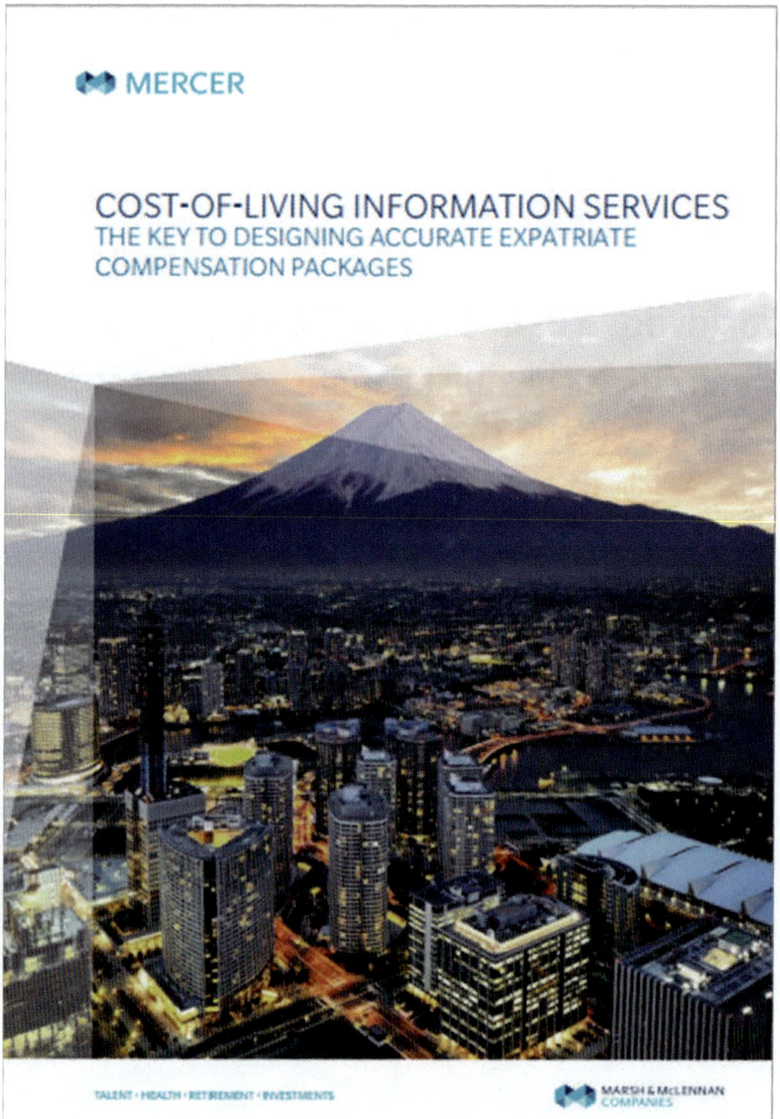

1.2 A Case Study on the UBS Prices and Earnings Report: Figures, Facts and Fallacies

Most of us are aware that figures are like games, you can play with them. Facts speak for themselves and are not susceptible to distortion. Misrepresentation and misreading of figures can result in policy fallacies and can lead to seemingly correct but erroneous conclusions.

Such problems can be exacerbated by findings published by reputable institutions which may have handled figures with insufficient qualifications on methodology and assumptions, and worse, using inaccurately defined figures. For a piece of serious research work, rigorous checks on data sources and verification of figures used are thus paramount.

For all good intents and purposes, a fruitful policy analysis can be misplaced and meaningful policy outcomes denied due to lack of robustness in research discipline, especially for studies which have far-reaching social, political and economic implications. A recent study, *Prices and Earnings,* by the Wealth Management Research Department of UBS AG is a case in point which we will elaborate further.

The *UBS Prices and Earnings Report 2009 — A Global Purchasing Power Comparison* attempts to compare and rank the purchasing power of average wages and relative cost of living across 73 global cities using New York as the benchmark. According to the UBS Wealth Management Research Department, the *Prices and Earnings Comparison* report was first published in 1971 and has generated "high level of interests" based on "frequent inquires received". The UBS Report was updated in August 2010.

We are indeed surprised by UBS Report's over-simplification on differences amongst cities, lack of rigour in the adopted methodology and inaccuracy of the data employed. One should be cautious, as we attempt to show, in using the findings of the UBS Report to undertake policy analysis and draw conclusions. At least we found their various findings on Singapore, and we believe for many other cities too, are markedly different from studies conducted by ACI at the Lee Kuan Yew School of Public Policy, National University of Singapore.

While UBS is one of the world's largest financial institutions, it appears to have only limited resources to prepare the report. UBS said that it has included "more than 30,000 data points". However, the report covers 75 cities with 154 items of goods and services and 14 separate occupations. This meant that the occupational wages and prices in the UBS Report are not representative, since only approximately 3 data points per item or occupation are collected for each city.

To conduct international comparisons, UBS had to use a number of simplifying assumptions and standardisations, which do not accurately reflect the true situation since cities are very different one from another. One of the major flaws in the UBS Report is its assumption that the occupation profile is the same across cities. In this assumption, this employment structure in Singapore is similar to those of the cities in developing countries. The global comparison was made worse by "limited selection of goods and services with adjustments to individual components based on the weighting in the European consumer price index" or the "Western European consumer preferences"!

Upon examining the UBS case on Singapore, we found some of the assumptions made inevitably resulted in a significant downward bias in the purchasing power of our wages.

Firstly, the UBS Report understates wages in Singapore:

a. UBS uses a common occupational profile, based on global averages, to derive the average wage of each city. This occupation profile, however, severely understates the percentage of Professionals, Managers, Executives and Technicians (PMETs) in Singapore, thus resulting in an average wage that is much lower than the true average wage in Singapore. The percentage of PMETs in our resident workforce in 2009 was 54%, way higher than the 9% assumed by UBS which was not mentioned in the report but kindly made available upon request. The downward bias is more severe in Singapore's case compared to some of our other Asian neighbours which have relatively fewer PMETs in their workforce. Singapore's percentage of Production, Transportation Operators and General Labours (PTOGLs) and Clerical, Sales & Service Workers (CSRWs) are respectively 21% and 25%, way lower than the 58% and 33% assumed by the UBS Report, thus again resulting in an average wage much lower than the true average wage in Singapore.

b. UBS appears to have excluded Central Provident Fund (CPF) contributions from the calculation of net wages for Singapore. However, our CPF system is in fact a defined contribution system with individual accounts where the CPF contributions, apart from providing for retirement, are also extensively used for housing, medical and educational expenses prior to retirement. It is different from the typical Western social security system which involves transfers from one group to another. Therefore, CPF contributions should be included as part of wages and not be considered as tax payments.

Secondly, price levels constructed by UBS overstate the cost of living in Singapore:

a. The Report uses a common European basket of goods and services to reflect cost of living across all cities. This would have caused an upward bias in the cost of living in Singapore as Western consumption goods tend to be more expensive in Asian cities. In the case of Singapore, we found that weights on basket of goods and services for food, clothing and household appliances are quite different from the European baskets commonly adopted in the UBS Report, which again can lead to significant distortions.
b. UBS uses rents of private housing in the construction of the price levels (including rental). In Singapore's case, however, the majority of our population stay in public housing and median rents in public housing are more than 30% lower than the figure used in the UBS Report.
c. There appears to be some discrepancies in the price levels of specific categories. For example, prices of home electronics and household appliances: the UBS Report puts Singapore's price level above that of Mumbai, which is counterintuitive since we know anecdotally that visitors from India spend much on electronics in Singapore. On restaurants, UBS Report puts Singapore's price level slightly above that of many Western European cities including Paris, which are known for their expensive restaurant meals. The discrepancies may have resulted from the small number of data points for each city.

In the following empirical exercise, which was published as editorial opinions in *Lianhe Zaobao* and *The Straits Times* in 2011 (see Tan and Gu, 2011; Tan and Vu, 2011), we attempted to revise estimates of the UBS study by having a "correct" set of data used with appropriate assumptions made in order to reveal how misleading empirical findings can be if one is not careful and thorough in research. Such exercise is of course quite different from the pioneering research effort by ACI as exhibited throughout the rest of the chapters in this book.

1.2.1 Price Level Index and Cost of Living of Six Economies: UBS Study and Revised Estimates by ACI

Estimating the purchasing power of wages in an economy requires reliable and internationally comparable information on costs of living and nominal wages. In this attempt, the statistics provided by the World Bank International Comparison Programme (ICP) on costs of living and from the International Labour Organisation (ILO) and the US Bureau of Labour Statistics (BLS) on nominal wages are our main sources for research and policy analysis.

According to the World Bank ICP data, for the consumption expenditure by the average household, using the US as the 100% benchmark, Singapore's overall price level of 88.6% is lower than that of the US, and comparatively lower than Hong Kong's 93%. Switzerland and Japan are significantly higher respectively at 150% and 129.8%. Although South Korea and Taiwan's overall price levels are lower at 86% and 70.2%, respectively, note that they include many cities and towns other than Seoul and Taipei. In particular, Singapore's cost of expenditure is notably low in education, healthcare, and communications, which are equal to 31%, 33% and 55%, respectively, compared to the US level, and lower than the prices in Hong Kong and South Korea.

Singapore, however, is significantly more expensive than the benchmark countries on two consumption categories, namely alcoholic beverages and transportation, both public and private modes included. Relative to the US, Singapore's price level is 261% for alcoholic beverages and 120% for transport as shown in Table 1.1.

1.2.2 Wages amongst Six Major Cities: UBS Study and Revised Estimates by ACI

We attempted our own comparison of city-level prices and earnings. We focused on a few cities — London, Tokyo, Taipei, Hong Kong, Singapore and the US metropolitan area of New York–North-eastern New Jersey — as few have published data. Data definitions may be slightly different across countries and cities so we had to make some adjustments to make them more comparable with each other. The key point is that because the wage data are from official sources, they do not suffer from the small sample size problem that UBS Report has.

We similarly created a purchasing power index by adjusting wages for price differences using two methods: (i) UBS's method and price indices and (ii) using Purchasing Power Parity (PPP) rates, i.e., market exchange rates, adjusted for price differences between countries. Table 1.2 exhibits similar results. Even using UBS's price indices, Singapore's purchasing power-adjusted wages are higher than, if not comparable to, those of Taipei and Hong Kong.

The discussion above shows that we need to be careful in the use and interpretation of data. The UBS Report is targeted towards its investment banking, asset management and wealth management clients to aid decisions on travel and relocation, which is why UBS had picked a Western basket of goods and services to construct the price index. However, it would be inappropriate to compare a Western consumption pattern against an assumed workforce composition with only 9% PMETs, as they pull in contradictory directions. It is also important to consider country-specific issues, such as the differences between our CPF system and Western social security systems.

Table 1.1: Price Levels and Costs of Living*

Economy	USA	Singapore	Hong Kong	Japan	South Korea	Taiwan	Switzerland
Individual consumption expenditure by households	100	88.6	93.0	129.8	86.0	70.2	150.0
Food and non-alcoholic beverages	100	106.3	113.4	215.2	147.3	108.0	166.1
Alcoholic beverages, tobacco and narcotics	100	260.8	130.0	87.5	83.3	70.8	100.0
Clothing and footwear	100	96.1	78.6	152.4	110.7	67.0	138.8
Housing with imputed rentals, water, electricity, gas and other fuels	100	98.4	117.2	116.4	76.6	76.6	164.1
Furnishings, household equipment and maintenance	100	103.9	98.1	152.4	75.7	97.1	134.0
Healthcare	100	33.3	37.6	59.1	34.9	18.3	104.3
Public and private transportation	100	120.5	121.6	147.7	108.0	88.6	176.1
Communications	100	55.1	88.2	115.7	56.7	50.4	127.6
Recreation and culture	100	69.3	67.3	109.9	91.1	56.4	144.6
Education	100	30.6	41.9	82.7	46.8	23.8	110.1
Restaurants and hotels	100	101.1	114.9	162.1	127.6	79.3	178.2
Miscellaneous goods and services	100	69.4	72.1	120.7	74.8	58.6	147.7

Note: *The ICP coordinated by the World Bank during 2003–2007 covered 146 economies and nearly 1,000 items of goods and services
Source: Computed from World Bank (2008, pp. 38–47, Table 2)

The difficulty in the interpretation of the results and various technical and data shortfalls mean that readers should not over-rely on the UBS Report, which has understated wage levels and overstated price levels in Singapore. Hence, UBS unjustifiably ranked Singapore at the bottom one-third amongst the 73 cities, which cannot be correct.

Using more representative data from the World Bank and government statistical agencies, we have shown that purchasing power of wages in Singapore is better than what the UBS Report suggested. The UBS Report is indeed a classic case of comparing not even between apples and oranges, but a mistaken case of treating a highly valuable jewel as stones.

1.3 Expected Contributions of ACI's Studies and Chapter Organisation of the Book

This book provides annual indices and rankings of cost of living since 2005 for ordinary residents of cities, and we believe ACI's pioneering attempt is the first ever comprehensive study of this kind available today. As for expatriates, cost of living studies, though widely available, were done less rigorously as compared to the ACI approach. ACI studies also provide annual indices and rankings of wages and purchasing power since 2005 for ordinary residents.

The publication of this book represents a colossal undertaking combining leading-edge research with rigorous methodology and datasets which are disclosed openly. Weights employed

Table 1.2: Wage Levels and Purchasing Power

	UBS Report on gross wage, USD/hr	**ACI estimates of monthly wage, USD**	
		Method (i)	**Method (ii)**
	Converted to USD using market exchange rates, and divided by UBS's cost of entire basket of commodities excluding rent	**Converted to USD using market exchange rates, and divided by UBS's cost of entire basket of commodities excluding rent**	**Converted to USD using PPP rates# to take into account price differences across economies**
New York*	100.0	100.0	100.0
London	81.5	106.7	88.3
Tokyo	72.6	105.8	88.1
Taipei	47.9	63.8	76.6
Hong Kong	41.6	63.3	74.0
Singapore	32.7	70.1	79.1
Rankings			
New York*	1	3	1
London	2	1	2
Tokyo	3	2	3
Taipei	4	5	5
Hong Kong	5	6	6
Singapore	6	4	4

Notes:
*UBS Report refers to New York City; our estimates are based on New York–North-eastern New Jersey metropolitan area
PPP rates are market exchange rates, adjusted for price differences between economies. The rates used here are from the International Monetary Fund World Economic Outlook, April 2011. As PPP rates are only available at country level and price levels tend to be higher in cities, Method (ii) is biased in favour of New York, London, Tokyo and Taipei. Monthly wage data for countries are based on national statistics, with some adjustments to make them more comparable due to slightly different data definitions
Source: English version of the table which appears in Tan and Gu (2011, p. 20)

for consumption baskets are justified across different continents and stated explicitly, and all assumptions made are also laid down in a transparent manner.

This book provides the ingredients to analyse questions pertaining to differences in the cost of living in cities across the globe for ordinary residents in the city they are residing or cities they may intend to relocate to, for multinational corporations which deal with professionals who work abroad and paramount of all for public policy-makers who try to render a better city for ordinary residents. It is thus important to understand factors or policies which contribute to these changes, especially on whether earnings and purchasing powers have been keeping up with cost of living, more importantly so for ordinary residents of cities.

For transparency and consistency, unless assumptions, methodology and data sources are disclosed publicly for open scrutiny, non-rigorous studies can lead to spurious or misleading results for cities. For policy-makers, poverty statistics can be measured differently by taking into account cost of living of ordinary residents. Differences between ordinary residents and expatriates, which were previously hidden by a national index, are now made salient, which should be welcomed by all interested parties.

For academics, more accurate depictions of price levels for each city are now made available. Distinction made between ordinary residents and expatriates opens up more tools for social research. For multinational corporations, employers can review and adjust compensation packages according to cities for expatriates. This allows employers to adopt more competitive compensation packages for their staff being dispatched to work abroad, given the differences in cost of living between expatriates and ordinary residents in a given city, a comparison now made possible by ACI's pioneering research effort.

The world's major 103 cities are covered by the ACI Annual Indices on Cost of Living, Wages and Purchasing Power, spreading across six continents including Asia, Australasia, Europe, Africa, North and South America as shown in Table 1.3.

Table 1.3: List of Cities covered by the ACI Annual Indices on Cost of Living, Wages and Purchasing Power

	City	Country	Region
1	Adelaide	Australia	Australasia
2	Amman	Jordan	Asia
3	Amsterdam	Netherlands	Western Europe
4	Asuncion	Paraguay	South America
5	Athens	Greece	Western Europe
6	Atlanta	United States	North America
7	Auckland	New Zealand	Australasia
8	Baku	Azerbaijan	Asia
9	Bangkok	Thailand	Asia
10	Barcelona	Spain	Western Europe
11	Beijing	China	Asia
12	Berlin	Germany	Western Europe
13	Bogota	Colombia	South America
14	Boston	United States	North America
15	Bratislava	Slovakia	Eastern Europe
16	Brisbane	Australia	Australasia
17	Brussels	Belgium	Western Europe
18	Bucharest	Romania	Eastern Europe
19	Budapest	Hungary	Eastern Europe
20	Buenos Aires	Argentina	South America
21	Cairo	Egypt	Africa
22	Calgary	Canada	North America

(Continued)

Table 1.3: (*Continued*)

	City	Country	Region
23	Caracas	Venezuela	South America
24	Chicago	United States	North America
25	Cleveland	United States	North America
26	Colombo	Sri Lanka	Asia
27	Copenhagen	Denmark	Western Europe
28	Dalian	China	Asia
29	Detroit	United States	North America
30	Doha	Qatar	Asia
31	Dubai	United Arab Emirates	Asia
32	Dublin	Ireland	Western Europe
33	Frankfurt	Germany	Western Europe
34	Geneva	Switzerland	Western Europe
35	Guangzhou	China	Asia
36	Helsinki	Finland	Western Europe
37	Hong Kong	Hong Kong, China	Asia
38	Honolulu	United States	North America
39	Houston	United States	North America
40	Istanbul	Turkey	Asia
41	Jakarta	Indonesia	Asia
42	Johannesburg	South Africa	Africa
43	Kiev	Ukraine	Eastern Europe
44	Kuala Lumpur	Malaysia	Asia
45	Kuwait	Kuwait	Asia
46	Lexington	United States	North America
47	Lima	Peru	South America
48	Lisbon	Portugal	Western Europe
49	London	Great Britain	Western Europe
50	Los Angeles	United States	North America
51	Luxembourg	Luxembourg	Western Europe
52	Lyon	France	Western Europe
53	Madrid	Spain	Western Europe
54	Manila	Philippines	Asia
55	Melbourne	Australia	Australasia
56	Mexico City	Mexico	North America
57	Miami	United States	North America

(*Continued*)

Table 1.3: (*Continued*)

	City	Country	Region
58	Milan	Italy	Western Europe
59	Minneapolis	United States	North America
60	Montevideo	Uruguay	South America
61	Montreal	Canada	North America
62	Moscow	Russia	Eastern Europe
63	Mumbai	India	Asia
64	Munich	Germany	Western Europe
65	Nairobi	Kenya	Africa
66	New Delhi	India	Asia
67	New York	United States	North America
68	Osaka/Kobe	Japan	Asia
69	Oslo	Norway	Western Europe
70	Paris	France	Western Europe
71	Perth	Australia	Australasia
72	Pittsburgh	United States	North America
73	Prague	Czech Republic	Eastern Europe
74	Pretoria	South Africa	Africa
75	Qingdao	China	Asia
76	Quito	Ecuador	South America
77	Reykjavik	Iceland	Western Europe
78	Rio de Janeiro	Brazil	South America
79	Rome	Italy	Western Europe
80	San Francisco	United States	North America
81	Santiago	Chile	South America
82	Sao Paulo	Brazil	South America
83	Seattle	United States	North America
84	Seoul	South Korea	Asia
85	Shanghai	China	Asia
86	Shenzhen	China	Asia
87	Singapore	Singapore	Asia
88	Sofia	Bulgaria	Eastern Europe
89	St. Petersburg	Russia	Eastern Europe
90	Stockholm	Sweden	Western Europe
91	Suzhou	China	Asia
92	Sydney	Australia	Australasia

(*Continued*)

Table 1.3: (*Continued*)

	City	Country	Region
93	Taipei	Taiwan, China	Asia
94	Tel Aviv	Israel	Asia
95	Tianjin	China	Asia
96	Tokyo	Japan	Asia
97	Toronto	Canada	North America
98	Vancouver	Canada	North America
99	Vienna	Austria	Western Europe
100	Warsaw	Poland	Eastern Europe
101	Washington DC	United States	North America
102	Wellington	New Zealand	Australasia
103	Zurich	Switzerland	Western Europe

Source: Asia Competitiveness Institute

The organisation of this book is as follows: Chapter 2 discusses at length the methodology on cost of living for expatriates, revealing data sources including prices and weights used where assumptions made were also being explicitly stated. The construction method on the cost of living index and ranking for expatriates was also spelt out in detail including indices for 10 ACI consumption categories.

Chapter 3 discusses in detail the methodology on cost of living, wages and purchasing power for ordinary residents where components of adjustment factors such as inflation rates, nominal expenditure and real expenditure per capita were highlighted. The construction of the cost of living index and ranking for ordinary residents was painstakingly elaborated including indices for 10 ACI consumption categories. The computation of the wage index and ranking for ordinary residents involving gross average nominal monthly wages and mean weekly hours actually worked was illustrated step-by-step. Finally, through cost of living index and wage index, the purchasing power index and ranking for ordinary residents were constructed and reported.

Chapter 4 analyses findings pertaining to the cost of living rankings for expatriates in the 103 cities over the years since 2005. The results are presented in alphabetical order of the cities' names. Each city's results are presented in the figure titled "Cost of Living and 10 Consumption Categories Rankings for Expatriates". The horizontal axis denotes the years in the study period while the vertical axis shows the rankings of a particular city. Rankings range from first to 103rd with first meaning the highest cost and 103rd indicating the lowest cost.

Chapter 5 analyses findings pertaining to the cost of living, wages and purchasing power for ordinary residents in the 103 cities across the years since 2005. The results are presented in alphabetical order of the cities' names. Three figures were computed for each city. The Cost of Living and 10 Consumption Categories Rankings for Ordinary Residents are captured in Figure a. The horizontal axis denotes the years in the study period while the vertical axis shows the rankings of a particular city. Rankings range from first to 103rd with first meaning the highest cost and 103rd indicating the lowest cost.

Figure b is the Gross Hourly Wages in USD and Wages Ranking for Ordinary Residents. Similarly, the horizontal axis denotes the years in the study period. There are two vertical axes in this figure. The left axis shows the wages ranking of a particular city, which ranges from first to 103rd with first meaning the highest wage level and 103rd indicating the lowest level. The right axis indicates the dollar value (USD) of gross hourly wages in that city.

Figure c is the Cost of Living, Wages and Purchasing Power Indices and Purchasing Power Ranking for Ordinary Residents. Likewise, the horizontal axis denotes the years in the study period. There are two vertical axes in this figure. The left axis shows the purchasing power ranking of a particular city, which ranges from first to 103rd with first meaning the highest purchasing power and 103rd indicating the lowest. The right axis indicates the values of the cost of living, wages and purchasing power indices for that city.

Chapter 6 examines factors and attributes on cities' costs of living. In the first case study, Hong Kong and Singapore were employed to simulate the effects of currency appreciation on expatriates and ordinary residents who were found to have experienced different impacts respectively. In the second case study, an interesting observation emerged when we compared the costs of living in different cities across geographical regions. Cities in the Western world tend to have higher costs of living for ordinary residents than cities elsewhere. There is, however, no similar pattern in the geographical distribution of the cities according to their costs of living for expatriates.

References

Tan K. G. 陈企业 and Gu Q. 顾清扬 2011. "Shu ju, shi shi he miu wu", 数据、事实和谬误 [Figures, facts and fallacies]. *Lianhe Zaobao* 联合早报, 3 May, p. 20.

Tan K. G. and Vu M. K. 2011. "Figures, facts and fallacies". *The Straits Times*, 3 May, p. A35.

World Bank. 2008. *Global Purchasing Power Parities and Real Expenditures: 2005 International Comparison Program.* http://siteresources.worldbank.org/ICPINT/Resources/icp-final.pdf.

Chapter 2
Methodology on Cost of Living for Expatriates

2.1 Introduction

This chapter outlines the framework employed by the Asia Competitiveness Institute (ACI) in tracking the cost of living for expatriates in world's major 103 cities[1] from 2005 to 2013. More than 280 individual prices of 165 goods and services have been compiled for each city to form the basis of calculating the Cost of Living Index for Expatriates. For the purpose of this study, the expatriates are assumed to follow Western consumption preferences and gear towards high-end and lifestyle products.

The ACI cost of living for expatriates framework, with its 10 Consumption Categories, is an overarching, comprehensive and systematic way of examining cost of living in each city. ACI has defined cost of living for expatriates according to 10 Consumption Categories: (1) Food & Non-alcoholic Beverages, (2) Alcohol & Tobacco, (3) Clothing, (4) Housing Rents & Utilities, (5) Household Supplies & Domestic Help, (6) Health, (7) Transport, (8) Recreation, (9) Education, and (10) Miscellaneous Goods & Services (see Figure 2.1).

New York has been chosen as the base city for the study, with other cities being benchmarked against it. This is because apart from being a city globally known, similar studies on cost of living have also used New York as the benchmark. The index values of New York are always 100.00.

As a summary measure of the overall cost of living in each city for the expatriates, we have derived the Cost of Living Index for Expatriates which is made up of the 10 ACI Consumption Categories. A larger Cost of Living Index for Expatriates implies that the city is more expensive for the expatriates to live in. In contrast, a smaller Cost of Living Index denotes lower cost of living. Furthermore, expatriates who live in cities with Cost of Living Index larger (smaller) than 100.00 face higher (lower) cost as compared to their counterparts in New York. In our study, we also produce a ranking on the cost of living for expatriates by arranging the Cost of Living Index for Expatriates in each city in a descending order. In other words, cities which rank at the top of the ranking are more expensive than those at the bottom.

The rest of Chapter 2 is organised as follows. Section 2.2 introduces the sources of data used in the study, followed by Section 2.3 on the major assumptions adopted in the calculation of Cost of Living Index for Expatriates. Section 2.4 describes the price data for all items included under the various ACI Consumption Categories and the treatment of missing data, while Section 2.5 explains the weights data employed. By piecing together the prices and weights data, Section 2.6 details the algorithm for constructing the Cost of Living Index and Ranking for Expatriates. Lastly, Section 2.7 demonstrates the algorithm used to construct the 10 ACI Consumption Categories Indices and Rankings for Expatriates.

[1]See Table 1.3 of Chapter 1 for the complete list of 103 cities covered in this study.

Figure 2.1: The 10 ACI Consumption Categories

Source: Asia Competitiveness Institute

2.2 Data Sources

The construction of Cost of Living Index for Expatriates requires data on prices, exchange rates as well as weights. The respective sources and descriptions are summarised below. Price data are mainly obtained from the Economist Intelligence Unit (EIU) CityData, which are available in local currency every year over the period studied, from 2005 to 2013. The only exception is the price data for Miscellaneous Goods & Services, reported in US dollar, which are acquired from the Services category in UBS Prices and Earnings study. This UBS study is conducted every three years, therefore data from 2003, 2006, 2009 and 2012 reports are used in our study.

All price data reported in local currency need to be converted into a common currency for comparison. Therefore, in order to smooth the effects of daily fluctuations in the currency market, we use the yearly average exchange rate which is calculated based on the daily average exchange rate retrieved from the Bloomberg Terminal. All exchange rates used in this study are expressed in local currency against US dollar and they are listed in Appendix 3.

Weights are derived based on the World Bank International Comparison Programme (ICP) survey and household expenditure surveys from various countries. The World Bank ICP survey is implemented every six years. Thus, the 2005 and 2011 round of the ICP survey are referenced. The list of items and corresponding weights are detailed in Section 2.5 of this chapter. The value of all weights data ranges from zero to one and together they sum to unity.

2.3 Assumptions Made

Partly due to data limitations, we have made the following four key assumptions when developing the Cost of Living Index and thus Ranking as well as the Indices and Rankings for each ACI Consumption Category for Expatriates.

Firstly, expatriates are assumed to follow Western consumption preferences and gear towards high-end and lifestyle products. For example, the consumption basket of expatriates includes wine, Burberry raincoat and international schools.

Secondly, the consumption pattern of expatriates is also assumed to be the same across all 103 cities. For example, expatriates living in New York will have the same consumption pattern as their counterparts in Amsterdam, Beijing or Buenos Aires.

Thirdly, the consumption pattern for expatriates is assumed to reflect the consumption patterns of 24 industrialised countries, which are Australia, Austria, Belgium, Canada, Denmark, Finland, France, Germany, Great Britain, Greece, Iceland, Ireland, Israel, Italy, Japan, Luxembourg, the Netherlands, New Zealand, Norway, Portugal, Spain, Sweden, Switzerland and the United States.

Finally, consumption pattern for expatriates is assumed to change over time. The change in spending preference of expatriates partially affected by the variation in prices and quality of goods and services is reflected in different sets of weights being used for expatriates for each year.

2.4 Price Data

The consumption basket for expatriates proposed by ACI comprises 10 Consumption Categories, which are in turn made up of various products and services. This section will provide details on the items included under the various consumption categories and treatment of items with missing price data.

There are in total 165 different products and services under the 10 ACI Consumption Categories. The number of items under each ACI Consumption Category is not the same. For example, the Food & Non-alcoholic Beverages contains 56 different items covering a wide range of products including bread (1kg), olive oil (1l), potatoes (2kg), apples (1kg), sliced pineapples (canned, 500g), beef (filet mignon, 1kg), fresh fish (1kg), instant coffee (125g), orange juice (1l) and etc. On the other hand, the Alcohol & Tobacco contains 13 products including wine (common table, 1l), beer (top quality, 330ml), and cigarettes (Marlboro, pack of 20). The complete list of items under each ACI Consumption Category and their respective weights are shown in Table 2.2 of Section 2.5.

The price data for most items are obtained from the EIU CityData except for the Miscellaneous Goods & Services. In some cases, a single item may have multiple prices in the EIU CityData, which are collected from different locations such as supermarket, mid-priced store, branded store, chain store and etc. Under such circumstances, the average value of all the prices available will be used as the price of that item in the computation. For instance, the prices of white bread (1kg) in each city are collected from two different locations, namely supermarket and mid-priced store. We will use the average of these two prices as the price of white bread for that city in the computation. As such, for the 165 items in the study, we use 283 price data entries.

We adopt a simple method to proxy for the missing data entry in EIU CityData. The proxy value is assumed to be the average of all available data in the rest of the cities for that particular price data entry in the year. In addition, the proxy for the missing data entry will be carried out before the computation of the average price at different sales locations mentioned above. For example, the price of white bread (1kg) collected from supermarket is available while the price of white bread (1kg) collected from mid-priced store is unavailable for city m. The proxy for the price of white bread (1kg) collected from mid-priced store for city m will be the average of all available prices of white bread (1kg) collected from mid-priced store in the rest of the cities in that particular year. After the proxy, the price of white bread (1kg) in city m will be computed as the average of actual price of white bread (1kg) collected from supermarket and the price of white bread (1kg) from mid-priced store by proxy.

However, the price data for Miscellaneous Goods & Services are obtained from the Services category in UBS Prices and Earnings study, which is conducted every three years. Thus, we have to proxy the data for intermediate years as well as some other missing data based on the reports available in 2003, 2006, 2009 and 2012. The proxy adopts the following principles:

i. For years with missing data, we will adopt linear interpolation and extrapolation. If (i) is not applicable, then,
ii. For cities with missing data and data for other cities of the same country are available, we will use the average of all the other cities in that particular country. If neither (i) nor (ii) is applicable, then,
iii. For cities with missing data and no data for other cities of the same country is available, we will use the average of all the cities of the country which has the closest Gross Domestic Product (GDP) per capita by country to that particular country of the city.

However, these general proxy principles may produce some unreasonable proxies in some special cases, which have to be handled on a case-by-case basis. There are four such special cases in total:

a. For 2003 Beijing data, the proxy follows principle (ii) instead of principle (i). Subsequently, this proxy value for 2003 is used to proxy the values for 2004 and 2005 according to principle (i).
b. For 2003 Cairo data, the proxy follows principle (iii) instead of principle (i). This proxy value for 2003 is also used to proxy the values for 2004, 2005, 2006, 2007 and 2008 according to principle (i).
c. For 2003 Doha data, the proxy follows principle (iii) instead of principle (i). This proxy value for 2003 is also used to proxy the values for 2004, 2005, 2006, 2007 and 2008 according to principle (i).
d. For 2012 Sao Paulo data, the proxy follows principle (ii) instead of principle (i). This proxy value for 2012 is also used to proxy the values for 2007, 2008, 2009, 2010, 2011 and 2013 according to principle (i).

2.5 Weights Data

As mentioned in the third assumption of Section 2.3, the weight of each item in the consumption basket for expatriates reflects the consumption pattern of 24 industrialised countries. This set of weights is geared toward Western consumption preferences and it reflects the tendency of expatriates to purchase high-end and lifestyle products. By analysing the findings of ICP surveys conducted by the World Bank and household expenditure surveys published by the various relevant census departments and statistical bureaus of different countries across the years, we have derived a unique set of weights for every year covered under our study period (i.e., from 2005 to 2013). Details on steps involved in this exercise of deriving weights for expatriates can be found in the unpublished ACI Technical Working Paper 10/2015 titled *Methodology on Weights in the Cost of Living Study for Expatriates and Ordinary Residents*.

We will now compare the differences between consumption categories as defined by the World Bank ICP survey and that of the ACI Consumption Categories. ICP study has 12 categories while our study has 10. Thus, the 12 ICP categories are rearranged to match the 10 ACI Consumption Categories as shown in Table 2.1.

The first nine ACI Consumption Categories can be matched one-to-one to the categories in ICP data notwithstanding some slight differences in naming. For example, the fourth ACI Consumption Category is Housing Rents & Utilities, while its counterpart in ICP data is (4) Housing, Water, Electricity, Gas and Other Fuels. The only exception is the last ACI Consumption Category, the Miscellaneous Goods & Services, which is defined with a broader scope corresponding to the sum of three categories in ICP data, namely (8) Communication, (11) Restaurants and Hotels, and (12) Miscellaneous Goods and Services.

Lastly, the weight of each item within the Cost of Living Index for Expatriates from 2005 to 2013 is shown in Table 2.2. It is worth noting that this set of weights is applied uniformly across 103 cities in the study, in accordance with the second assumption listed in Section 2.3.

Table 2.1: Matching the 12 ICP Categories to the 10 ACI Consumption Categories

ACI consumption categories	ICP categories
(1) Food & Non-alcoholic Beverages	(1) Food & Non-alcoholic Beverages
(2) Alcohol & Tobacco	(2) Alcoholic Beverages, Tobaccos, and Narcotics
(3) Clothing	(3) Clothing and Footwear
(4) Housing Rents & Utilities	(4) Housing, Water, Electricity, Gas and Other Fuels
(5) Household Supplies & Domestic Help	(5) Furnishings, Household Equipment and Maintenance
(6) Health	(6) Health
(7) Transport	(7) Transport
(8) Recreation	(9) Recreation and Culture
(9) Education	(10) Education
(10) Miscellaneous Goods & Services	(8) Communication; (11) Restaurants and Hotels; (12) Miscellaneous Goods and Services

Source: Asia Competitiveness Institute

Table 2.2: Weight of Each Item within the Cost of Living Index for Expatriates from 2005 to 2013

ACI Consumption Category	Item	Weight (in percentages)								
		2005	2006	2007	2008	2009	2010	2011	2012	2013
(1) Food & Non-alcoholic Beverages	White bread (1kg)	1.6998	1.6762	1.6588	1.6128	1.5368	1.6167	1.6503	1.6431	1.6293
	Butter (500g)	1.1309	1.1280	1.1155	1.0991	1.0898	1.0699	1.0968	1.1138	1.0911
	Margarine (500g)	2.1325	2.1336	2.1721	2.1455	2.0330	2.0874	2.1890	2.1415	2.1404
	White rice (1kg)	0.6391	0.6367	0.6397	0.6343	0.5728	0.5877	0.6203	0.6337	0.6403
	Spaghetti (1kg)	0.4922	0.4979	0.5030	0.4857	0.4375	0.4416	0.4601	0.4681	0.4669
	Flour, white (1kg)	0.3667	0.3600	0.3649	0.3343	0.3157	0.3276	0.3412	0.3383	0.3324
	Sugar, white (1kg)	1.8564	1.8227	1.8274	1.8465	1.8450	1.8409	1.8921	1.8732	1.8081
	Cheese, imported (500g)	0.0825	0.0849	0.0876	0.0912	0.0893	0.0942	0.1038	0.1052	0.1048
	Cornflakes (375g)	0.7839	0.7971	0.8022	0.8279	0.8322	0.8351	0.8787	0.9183	0.9090
	Yoghurt, natural (150g)	3.7564	3.7828	3.7358	3.8110	3.6661	3.7648	3.9339	3.8346	3.7792
	Milk, pasteurised (1l)	8.3570	8.3241	8.0523	7.8008	8.0612	8.3333	8.8138	8.8686	8.9561
	Olive oil (1l)	0.1272	0.1158	0.1147	0.1180	0.1183	0.1221	0.1313	0.1425	0.1375
	Peanut or corn oil (1l)	0.4322	0.4401	0.4472	0.4162	0.3877	0.3976	0.4070	0.4042	0.4116
	Potatoes (2kg)	0.8543	0.8110	0.8078	0.7819	0.7889	0.7927	0.8336	0.9147	0.8604
	Onions (1kg)	1.2517	1.1490	1.1066	1.0856	1.0436	0.9828	1.0387	1.1555	1.1134
	Mushrooms (1kg)	0.1955	0.1900	0.1942	0.2040	0.1913	0.1966	0.2073	0.2128	0.2140
	Tomatoes (1kg)	0.4984	0.4939	0.4989	0.5159	0.5431	0.5237	0.5248	0.5759	0.5641
	Carrots (1kg)	1.0306	1.0234	1.0105	1.0693	1.0442	1.0807	1.1150	1.1636	1.1149
	Oranges (1kg)	1.0813	1.0555	1.0243	1.0382	1.0147	1.0242	1.1544	1.2365	1.1559
	Apples (1kg)	0.9203	0.9085	0.8889	0.8696	0.9025	0.9610	0.9981	1.0478	1.0035
	Lemons (1kg)	0.4295	0.4350	0.4367	0.4045	0.3998	0.3938	0.4266	0.4600	0.4172
	Bananas (1kg)	1.3773	1.3348	1.3778	1.4187	1.3514	1.3832	1.4558	1.5251	1.5595
	Lettuce (one)	1.0859	1.0470	1.0807	1.1566	1.1573	1.1428	1.1951	1.2781	1.2963
	Eggs (12)	1.7521	1.7643	1.7402	1.5920	1.5820	1.6004	1.6340	1.6033	1.5576

(Continued)

Table 2.2: (*Continued*)

ACI Consumption Category	Item	Weight (in percentages)								
		2005	**2006**	**2007**	**2008**	**2009**	**2010**	**2011**	**2012**	**2013**
	Peas, canned (250g)	1.7116	1.6932	1.6479	1.6767	1.6737	1.6560	1.6948	1.6926	1.6864
	Tomatoes, canned (250g)	1.4132	1.4194	1.4201	1.4329	1.3130	1.2989	1.3766	1.4074	1.3966
	Peaches, canned (500g)	0.4880	0.4952	0.4833	0.4937	0.4745	0.4882	0.5133	0.4958	0.4916
	Sliced pineapples, canned (500g)	0.7583	0.7613	0.7708	0.7784	0.7374	0.7568	0.7995	0.8138	0.8110
	Beef: filet mignon (1kg)	0.1066	0.1033	0.1044	0.1063	0.1067	0.1068	0.1139	0.1135	0.1128
	Beef: steak, entrecote (1kg)	0.2080	0.2031	0.1982	0.2017	0.1933	0.1954	0.2109	0.2090	0.2080
	Beef: stewing, shoulder (1kg)	0.1965	0.1946	0.1986	0.1967	0.1975	0.1964	0.2047	0.1978	0.1965
	Beef: roast (1kg)	0.1725	0.1643	0.1703	0.1689	0.1680	0.1742	0.1804	0.1752	0.1699
	Beef: ground or minced (1kg)	0.2450	0.2361	0.2374	0.2393	0.2306	0.2327	0.2432	0.2415	0.2406
	Veal: chops (1kg)	0.0675	0.0655	0.0656	0.0684	0.0676	0.0681	0.0703	0.0733	0.0724
	Veal: fillet (1kg)	0.0557	0.0532	0.0522	0.0547	0.0523	0.0542	0.0582	0.0582	0.0568
	Veal: roast (1kg)	0.1325	0.1264	0.1247	0.1285	0.1224	0.1297	0.1329	0.1368	0.1300
	Lamb: leg (1kg)	0.0659	0.0634	0.0629	0.0657	0.0633	0.0634	0.0653	0.0640	0.0612
	Lamb: chops (1kg)	0.0718	0.0705	0.0689	0.0729	0.0696	0.0719	0.0768	0.0735	0.0752
	Lamb: Stewing (1kg)	0.0398	0.0390	0.0389	0.0393	0.0379	0.0379	0.0398	0.0386	0.0386
	Pork: chops (1kg)	0.0418	0.0413	0.0412	0.0429	0.0425	0.0449	0.0474	0.0488	0.0484
	Pork: loin (1kg)	0.0461	0.0453	0.0446	0.0468	0.0454	0.0484	0.0520	0.0524	0.0514
	Ham: whole (1kg)	0.0641	0.0635	0.0649	0.0686	0.0702	0.0676	0.0714	0.0700	0.0680
	Bacon (1kg)	0.0352	0.0342	0.0351	0.0374	0.0356	0.0358	0.0385	0.0385	0.0389
	Chicken: frozen (1kg)	0.4203	0.4164	0.4124	0.4192	0.4063	0.3997	0.4053	0.4014	0.3848
	Chicken: fresh (1kg)	0.3494	0.3490	0.3411	0.3298	0.3211	0.3298	0.3566	0.3414	0.3334
	Frozen fish fingers (1kg)	0.1435	0.1420	0.1405	0.1465	0.1395	0.1402	0.1486	0.1564	0.1563
	Fresh fish (1kg)	0.0474	0.0447	0.0436	0.0458	0.0451	0.0446	0.0466	0.0475	0.0474

(*Continued*)

Table 2.2: (*Continued*)

ACI Consumption Category	Item	Weight (in percentages)								
		2005	2006	2007	2008	2009	2010	2011	2012	2013
	Instant coffee (125g)	0.2664	0.2661	0.2710	0.2711	0.2732	0.2892	0.2969	0.2810	0.2848
	Ground coffee (500g)	0.3200	0.3057	0.3005	0.3121	0.3005	0.3177	0.3267	0.3096	0.3144
	Tea bags (25 bags)	0.2395	0.2397	0.2445	0.2498	0.2450	0.2374	0.2436	0.2388	0.2451
	Cocoa (250g)	0.1341	0.1318	0.1346	0.1447	0.1469	0.1528	0.1567	0.1553	0.1558
	Drinking chocolate (500g)	0.5850	0.5911	0.5960	0.6026	0.5697	0.5597	0.5827	0.5851	0.5765
	Coca-Cola (1l)	1.2039	1.1847	1.1782	1.1577	1.1025	1.1244	1.1992	1.2016	1.2153
	Tonic water (200ml)	2.5505	2.5706	2.5804	2.6647	2.6409	2.7229	2.8117	2.9170	2.8555
	Mineral water (1l)	0.8706	0.8509	0.8978	0.8939	0.8714	0.9166	0.9869	0.9918	0.9869
	Orange juice (1l)	0.4354	0.4313	0.4250	0.4469	0.4394	0.4579	0.4589	0.4519	0.4573
(2) Alcohol & Tobacco	Wine, common table (1l)	0.1342	0.1327	0.1367	0.1434	0.1399	0.1430	0.1430	0.1500	0.1485
	Wine, superior quality (700ml)	0.1054	0.1039	0.1075	0.1094	0.1054	0.1048	0.1066	0.1044	0.1040
	Wine, fine quality (700ml)	0.0395	0.0394	0.0407	0.0424	0.0407	0.0414	0.0414	0.0406	0.0395
	Beer, local brand (1l)	0.7311	0.7241	0.7243	0.7599	0.7122	0.7208	0.7156	0.7449	0.7418
	Beer, top quality (330ml)	1.6557	1.5989	1.6158	1.6488	1.5883	1.6317	1.6369	1.6875	1.6903
	Scotch whisky, six years old (700ml)	0.1299	0.1285	0.1314	0.1356	0.1310	0.1315	0.1318	0.1372	0.1371
	Gin, Gilbey's or equivalent (700ml)	0.1723	0.1705	0.1762	0.1853	0.1758	0.1796	0.1800	0.1802	0.1780
	Vermouth, Martini & Rossi (1l)	0.1612	0.1597	0.1576	0.1624	0.1577	0.1592	0.1569	0.1597	0.1559
	Cognac, French VSOP (700ml)	0.0393	0.0390	0.0414	0.0430	0.0420	0.0437	0.0441	0.0470	0.0471
	Liqueur, Cointreau (700ml)	0.0597	0.0606	0.0632	0.0668	0.0655	0.0680	0.0687	0.0728	0.0727
	Cigarettes, Marlboro (pack of 20)	1.5524	1.5240	1.5301	1.5447	1.4327	1.4158	1.3642	1.3337	1.2920
	Cigarettes, local brand (pack of 20)	0.5726	0.5570	0.5574	0.5680	0.5240	0.5175	0.5030	0.4827	0.4658
	Pipe tobacco (50g)	0.3272	0.3186	0.3179	0.3336	0.3140	0.3167	0.3151	0.3082	0.2887

(*Continued*)

Table 2.2: (*Continued*)

ACI Consumption Category	Item	Weight (in percentages)								
		2005	2006	2007	2008	2009	2010	2011	2012	2013
(3) Clothing	Business suit, two piece, medium weight	0.0063	0.0063	0.0066	0.0070	0.0066	0.0067	0.0062	0.0064	0.0064
	Business shirt, white	0.0308	0.0303	0.0316	0.0327	0.0298	0.0304	0.0273	0.0262	0.0263
	Men's shoes, business wear	0.0126	0.0129	0.0133	0.0143	0.0133	0.0135	0.0123	0.0124	0.0121
	Men's raincoat, Burberry type	0.0043	0.0045	0.0047	0.0050	0.0048	0.0049	0.0045	0.0047	0.0046
	Socks, wool mixture	0.0264	0.0260	0.0269	0.0281	0.0277	0.0280	0.0252	0.0259	0.0252
	Dress, ready to wear, daytime	0.0267	0.0269	0.0276	0.0302	0.0287	0.0296	0.0271	0.0278	0.0280
	Women's shoes, town	0.0223	0.0223	0.0234	0.0246	0.0222	0.0219	0.0204	0.0204	0.0198
	Women's cardigan sweater	0.0156	0.0158	0.0163	0.0183	0.0171	0.0182	0.0162	0.0156	0.0154
	Women's raincoat, Burberry type	0.0065	0.0066	0.0070	0.0078	0.0071	0.0069	0.0062	0.0061	0.0058
	Tights, panty hose	0.0309	0.0305	0.0308	0.0321	0.0290	0.0275	0.0251	0.0246	0.0245
	Child's jeans	0.0526	0.0518	0.0534	0.0561	0.0550	0.0553	0.0496	0.0497	0.0497
	Child's shoes, dresswear	0.0496	0.0506	0.0522	0.0554	0.0530	0.0526	0.0483	0.0488	0.0484
	Child's shoes, sportswear	0.0398	0.0398	0.0407	0.0425	0.0417	0.0432	0.0386	0.0405	0.0402
	Girl's dress	0.0747	0.0770	0.0798	0.0836	0.0768	0.0764	0.0693	0.0720	0.0690
	Boy's jacket, smart	0.0425	0.0428	0.0442	0.0466	0.0459	0.0450	0.0407	0.0402	0.0400
	Boy's dress trousers	0.0325	0.0322	0.0336	0.0351	0.0355	0.0352	0.0323	0.0315	0.0307
(4) Housing Rents & Utilities	Telephone and line, monthly rental	0.3622	0.3625	0.3631	0.3833	0.3734	0.3771	0.4280	0.4335	0.4363
	Electricity, monthly bill	0.1163	0.1147	0.1152	0.1207	0.1224	0.1278	0.1428	0.1459	0.1453
	Gas, monthly bill	0.0246	0.0232	0.0229	0.0237	0.0238	0.0258	0.0291	0.0293	0.0298
	Furnished residential apartment: 1 bedroom	0.0186	0.0183	0.0183	0.0181	0.0174	0.0178	0.0199	0.0200	0.0199
	Furnished residential apartment: 2 bedrooms	0.0140	0.0138	0.0140	0.0136	0.0131	0.0136	0.0154	0.0153	0.0149
	Unfurnished residential apartment: 2 bedrooms	0.0158	0.0159	0.0160	0.0159	0.0155	0.0159	0.0179	0.0178	0.0175
	Unfurnished residential apartment: 3 bedrooms	0.0122	0.0121	0.0118	0.0120	0.0117	0.0118	0.0134	0.0136	0.0131
	Unfurnished residential apartment: 4 bedrooms	0.0090	0.0088	0.0089	0.0088	0.0089	0.0090	0.0103	0.0105	0.0105

(*Continued*)

Table 2.2: *(Continued)*

ACI Consumption Category	Item	Weight (in percentages)								
		2005	2006	2007	2008	2009	2010	2011	2012	2013
	Furnished residential house: 3 bedrooms	0.0087	0.0088	0.0089	0.0090	0.0087	0.0087	0.0099	0.0098	0.0101
	Unfurnished residential house: 4 bedrooms	0.0075	0.0076	0.0077	0.0077	0.0076	0.0076	0.0084	0.0082	0.0081
(5) Household Supplies & Domestic Help	Soap (100g)	2.0765	2.0046	1.9863	2.0145	1.9245	1.9591	1.7968	1.8361	1.8592
	Laundry detergent (3l)	0.2775	0.2847	0.2928	0.3109	0.2782	0.2607	0.2374	0.2358	0.2283
	Toilet tissue (two rolls)	2.7107	2.6581	2.7462	2.7966	2.7559	2.7507	2.4668	2.5800	2.5767
	Dishwashing liquid (750ml)	1.1876	1.2098	1.2269	1.3023	1.2243	1.2633	1.1309	1.1206	1.1100
	Insect-killer spray (330g)	0.2893	0.2816	0.2956	0.3187	0.2985	0.2960	0.2758	0.2892	0.2868
	Light bulbs (two, 60 watts)	1.7848	1.8420	1.9280	2.0864	1.9700	1.8715	1.7071	1.4479	1.2808
	Batteries (two, size D/LR20)	0.3037	0.2969	0.3096	0.3268	0.3292	0.3354	0.3070	0.3034	0.3069
	Frying pan (Teflon or good equivalent)	0.0501	0.0495	0.0502	0.0528	0.0514	0.0514	0.0452	0.0447	0.0459
	Electric toaster (for two slices)	0.0359	0.0375	0.0389	0.0424	0.0397	0.0402	0.0365	0.0370	0.0369
	Laundry (one shirt)	0.4479	0.4414	0.4429	0.4629	0.4569	0.4622	0.4265	0.4137	0.4077
	Dry cleaning, man's suit	0.1618	0.1629	0.1654	0.1688	0.1654	0.1626	0.1435	0.1439	0.1447
	Dry cleaning, woman's dress	0.3966	0.3935	0.3946	0.4053	0.3988	0.3954	0.3580	0.3511	0.3468
	Dry cleaning, trousers	0.3206	0.3156	0.3250	0.3350	0.3249	0.3255	0.2950	0.2934	0.2954
	Hourly rate for domestic cleaning help	0.5527	0.5459	0.5327	0.5310	0.5082	0.5064	0.4508	0.4593	0.4591
	Maid's monthly wages (full time)	0.0060	0.0060	0.0060	0.0063	0.0064	0.0064	0.0058	0.0060	0.0059
	Babysitter's rate per hour	0.2693	0.2688	0.2652	0.2715	0.2632	0.2643	0.2362	0.2397	0.2355
(6) Health	Aspirins (100 tablets)	0.6956	0.7156	0.7468	0.7822	0.7610	0.8017	0.9091	0.8869	0.8956
	Razor blades (five pieces)	1.3706	1.3220	1.3197	1.3007	1.2084	1.1810	1.2706	1.2332	1.1806
	Toothpaste with fluoride (120g)	3.6480	3.6723	3.6641	3.7387	3.4723	3.3820	3.7446	3.9280	4.0022
	Facial tissues (box of 100)	1.0758	1.0432	1.0474	1.0837	1.0055	1.0540	1.1658	1.1343	1.1173
	Hand lotion (125ml)	1.4692	1.4978	1.5244	1.5393	1.5569	1.5615	1.7376	1.7210	1.7533
	Shampoo & conditioner in one (400ml)	0.5097	0.5270	0.5408	0.5729	0.5682	0.5884	0.6651	0.6912	0.7035
	Lipstick (deluxe type)	0.1038	0.1042	0.1055	0.1124	0.1093	0.1091	0.1224	0.1227	0.1208

(Continued)

Table 2.2: (*Continued*)

ACI Consumption Category	Item	Weight (in percentages)								
		2005	2006	2007	2008	2009	2010	2011	2012	2013
	Man's haircut (tips included)	0.3020	0.3015	0.2990	0.3133	0.3002	0.3058	0.3393	0.3369	0.3347
	Woman's cut & blow dry (tips included)	0.2344	0.2331	0.2313	0.2372	0.2233	0.2213	0.2423	0.2418	0.2387
	Routine checkup at family doctor	0.2789	0.2660	0.2631	0.2808	0.2788	0.2670	0.2934	0.2859	0.2858
	One X-ray at doctor's office or hospital	0.2412	0.2427	0.2402	0.2518	0.2458	0.2417	0.2623	0.2476	0.2447
	Visit to dentist (one X-ray and one filling)	0.1459	0.1412	0.1501	0.1531	0.1406	0.1367	0.1496	0.1508	0.1472
(7) Transport	Low priced car (900–1299 cc)	0.0008	0.0008	0.0009	0.0009	0.0009	0.0009	0.0009	0.0009	0.0009
	Compact car (1300–1799 cc)	0.0007	0.0007	0.0007	0.0008	0.0008	0.0008	0.0008	0.0008	0.0008
	Family car (1800–2499 cc)	0.0004	0.0004	0.0004	0.0005	0.0005	0.0005	0.0005	0.0005	0.0005
	Deluxe car (2500 cc upwards)	0.0001	0.0001	0.0001	0.0001	0.0001	0.0001	0.0001	0.0002	0.0002
	Yearly road tax or registration fee	0.0234	0.0234	0.0233	0.0243	0.0237	0.0263	0.0282	0.0282	0.0278
	Cost of a tune up (but no major repairs)	0.0811	0.0817	0.0844	0.0883	0.0846	0.0833	0.0852	0.0819	0.0788
	Annual premium for car insurance	0.0036	0.0036	0.0038	0.0043	0.0045	0.0047	0.0048	0.0051	0.0050
	Regular unleaded petrol (1l)	12.163	13.044	12.882	11.717	14.462	13.778	11.837	11.337	12.186
	Taxi: initial meter charge	0.6261	0.6038	0.5941	0.6098	0.5797	0.5757	0.5877	0.6024	0.6079
	Taxi rate per additional kilometre	3.1301	2.9995	2.9811	2.9633	2.8929	2.9070	2.9811	3.0513	3.0628
(8) Recreation	Compact disc album	0.2654	0.2786	0.2936	0.3245	0.3221	0.3347	0.3374	0.3548	0.3723
	Television, colour (66 cm)	0.0084	0.0083	0.0082	0.0085	0.0088	0.0098	0.0101	0.0120	0.0134
	Kodak colour film (36 exposures)	0.5175	0.5260	0.5526	0.5742	0.5650	0.5782	0.5670	0.5877	0.5854
	Cost of developing 36 colour pictures	0.2635	0.2764	0.2941	0.3165	0.3153	0.3380	0.3404	0.3597	0.3660
	International foreign daily newspaper	1.6195	1.6178	1.6171	1.6229	1.5064	1.5490	1.5225	1.5434	1.5471
	Daily local newspaper	3.9402	3.8443	3.9762	4.1434	3.8133	3.6069	3.4733	3.0985	2.9841
	International weekly news magazine (Time)	1.2192	1.2209	1.1669	1.2340	1.1808	1.1792	1.1539	1.2079	1.1919
	Paperback novel (at bookstore)	0.2892	0.2869	0.2938	0.3010	0.2902	0.2919	0.2869	0.2884	0.2868
	Three course dinner for four people	0.0286	0.0282	0.0290	0.0308	0.0304	0.0306	0.0299	0.0302	0.0302

(*Continued*)

Table 2.2: (*Continued*)

ACI Consumption Category	Item	Weight (in percentages)								
		2005	2006	2007	2008	2009	2010	2011	2012	2013
	Personal computer	0.0043	0.0046	0.0050	0.0057	0.0062	0.0069	0.0071	0.0082	0.0088
	Four best seats at theatre or concert	0.0129	0.0124	0.0126	0.0129	0.0126	0.0126	0.0125	0.0127	0.0122
	Four best seats at cinema	0.1383	0.1356	0.1393	0.1446	0.1372	0.1364	0.1299	0.1294	0.1308
	Green fees on a public golf course	0.1046	0.1031	0.1012	0.1072	0.1029	0.1004	0.0973	0.0963	0.0941
	Hire of tennis court for one hour	0.2802	0.2789	0.2783	0.2843	0.2796	0.2839	0.2790	0.2910	0.2934
	Cost of six tennis balls, e.g., Dunlop, Wilson	0.4401	0.4523	0.4804	0.5204	0.5075	0.5157	0.5019	0.5109	0.5035
	Entrance fee to a public swimming pool	0.8322	0.8099	0.8073	0.8326	0.8296	0.8072	0.7786	0.7895	0.7757
(9) Education	French school: annual tuition, ages 5–12	0.0010	0.0010	0.0010	0.0010	0.0009	0.0009	0.0010	0.0010	0.0010
	French school: annual tuition, ages 13–17	0.0009	0.0009	0.0009	0.0008	0.0008	0.0008	0.0008	0.0008	0.0008
	French school: extra costs, ages 5–12	0.0052	0.0050	0.0052	0.0054	0.0063	0.0062	0.0063	0.0056	0.0084
	French school: extra costs, ages 13–17	0.0048	0.0047	0.0045	0.0050	0.0054	0.0051	0.0052	0.0048	0.0048
	French school: kindergarten annual fees	0.0012	0.0011	0.0012	0.0011	0.0010	0.0010	0.0010	0.0010	0.0010
	German school: annual tuition, ages 5–12	0.0010	0.0009	0.0009	0.0008	0.0008	0.0008	0.0008	0.0008	0.0008
	German school: annual tuition, ages 13–17	0.0009	0.0009	0.0009	0.0008	0.0007	0.0008	0.0008	0.0008	0.0007
	German school: extra costs, ages 5–12	0.0047	0.0050	0.0050	0.0048	0.0043	0.0046	0.0047	0.0050	0.0049
	German school: extra costs, ages 13–17	0.0039	0.0039	0.0040	0.0039	0.0037	0.0040	0.0040	0.0045	0.0045
	German school: kindergarten annual fees	0.0013	0.0012	0.0013	0.0011	0.0010	0.0010	0.0010	0.0010	0.0009
	American/English school: annual tuition, ages 5–12	0.0005	0.0005	0.0005	0.0005	0.0005	0.0004	0.0004	0.0004	0.0004
	American/English school: annual tuition, ages 13–17	0.0005	0.0004	0.0004	0.0004	0.0004	0.0004	0.0004	0.0004	0.0004
	American/English school: extra costs, ages 5–12	0.0045	0.0045	0.0044	0.0045	0.0041	0.0041	0.0041	0.0042	0.0042
	American/English school: extra costs, ages 13–17	0.0040	0.0039	0.0038	0.0038	0.0035	0.0035	0.0035	0.0035	0.0034
	American/English school: kindergarten annual fees	0.0011	0.0012	0.0012	0.0013	0.0012	0.0011	0.0011	0.0011	0.0010
10) Miscellaneous Goods & Services	Miscellaneous Goods & Services	0.4618	0.4285	0.4375	0.4537	0.4091	0.4002	0.4260	0.4107	0.4015

Source: Asia Competitiveness Institute

2.6 Constructing the Cost of Living Index and Ranking for Expatriates

$$\textit{Cost of Living Index for Expatriates in city } m = \frac{\sum_{i=1}^{n} P_{C,m,i} \times W_i}{\sum_{i=1}^{n} P_{US,NY,i} \times W_i} \times 100 \qquad (2.6.1)$$

where
m = city;
C = the country where city m is located in;
NY = New York;
US = United States;
i = item;
n = number of items in the consumption basket;
$P_{C,m,i}$ = average price of item i in city m of country C;
W_i = weight of item i within Cost of Living Index for Expatriates.

The Cost of Living Index for Expatriates is constructed using two inputs, the average prices, $P_{C,m,i}$, and the weights data, W_i (refer to Sections 2.4 and 2.5 for details on price and weights data, respectively). For expatriates, the weights are identical across all cities as we assume expatriates to have a fixed consumption pattern regardless of where they are posted to. Our common basket of goods and services is based on Western consumption preferences and it reflects the tendency of expatriates to purchase high-end and lifestyle products. Also, the weights of all items in the consumption basket that together describe the cost of living in each city will sum up to unity. In mathematical expression, $\sum_{i=1}^{n} W_i = 1$.

We will now describe in greater detail the average price of item i in city m of country C, $P_{C,m,i}$. In the raw data provided by the EIU CityData, several prices might be available for each item in all 103 cities. This is because prices for each item might be collected from various locations, for example from supermarkets, branded stores, chain stores, etc. Therefore, we will first take an average of all available prices for the same item in each city. For instance, bread has two prices in each city, one obtained from the supermarket and the other from mid-priced store. We will then take the average of these two prices to represent the price of bread in that particular city. This average price for each item i in each city m of country C is thus denoted as $P_{C,m,i}$. Note that all $P_{C,m,i}$ need to be converted into a common currency before comparison across countries can be done. Since New York has been chosen as the base city in our study, we convert all prices reported in local currencies into US dollar. As mentioned in Section 2.2, to smooth the effects of daily fluctuations in the currency market, we use the yearly average exchange rate which is calculated based on the daily average exchange rate retrieved from the Bloomberg Terminal. All exchange rates used in this study are listed in Appendix 3.

After calculating the average price of each item in each city m (denominated in US dollar), we can combine these $P_{C,m,i}$ with their respective weights, W_i, to obtain the Cost of Living Index for Expatriates in each city using the Equation 2.6.1. The Cost of Living Index for Expatriates reflects the cost of consuming all goods and services in the consumption basket of expatriates living in city m relative to those in New York. With New York chosen as the base city, the Cost of Living Index for Expatriates in New York will always be 100.00.[2]

Lastly, the Cost of Living Ranking for Expatriates can be generated by arranging the Cost of Living Index for Expatriates in each city in a descending order. A city which is more expensive (cheaper) for the expatriates to live in will have a larger (smaller) Cost of Living Index and thus occupy a higher (lower) position in the Cost of Living Ranking for Expatriates.

A simple numerical example is provided in Box 2.1 to illustrate the process of constructing the Cost of Living Index and Ranking for Expatriates.

Box 2.1: Example for Constructing the Cost of Living Index and Ranking for Expatriates

Consider a hypothetical case whereby the cost of living consists of two ACI Consumption Categories only, Food & Non-alcoholic Beverages as well as Clothing. For Food & Non-alcoholic Beverages, it is made up of two items, white bread and instant coffee. As for Clothing, it also contains two items, daytime dress and men's shoes. The price of each item sold in Adelaide and Sydney of Australia as well as Chicago and New York of the United States are listed as below.

		Price in US$			
Item, i	**Data series**	**Adelaide**	**Chicago**	**Sydney**	**New York**
White bread, 1kg	White bread, 1kg (supermarket)	4.40	5.80	4.00	7.80
	White bread, 1kg (mid-priced store)	4.80	6.20	5.40	8.40
Instant coffee, 125g	Instant coffee, 125g (supermarket)	7.20	4.80	6.60	5.80
	Instant coffee, 125g (mid-priced store)	7.40	5.20	7.40	6.00
Dress, daytime	Dress, daytime (chain store)	164.00	335.00	258.00	330.00
	Dress, daytime (branded store)	278.00	665.00	380.00	405.00
Men's shoes, business wear	Men's shoes, business wear (chain store)	228.00	180.00	236.00	210.00
	Men's shoes, business wear (branded store)	300.00	332.00	350.00	445.00

Assume the weight of each item is as follows.

Item, i	**Weight of item i, W_i**
White bread, 1kg	0.70
Instant coffee, 125g	0.27
Dress, daytime	0.02
Men's shoes, business wear	0.01

(Continued)

[2] If we take the prices in both the selected city and base city, make an average of them, and use this average as the basis for the index comparison, the ranking will be sensitive to the choice of base city. Please refer to the discussion on sensitivity to the choice of base city in Chapter 3, page 45, footnote 5.

Box 2.1: (*Continued*)

Hence the steps involved in the calculation of Cost of Living Index and producing a ranking for expatriates are as follows.

(1) Compute the average price of each item in each city, $P_{C,m,i}$.

$$P_{\text{Australia, Adelaide, White bread}} = \frac{(4.40 + 4.80)}{2} = 4.60,$$

$$P_{\text{Australia, Adelaide, Instant coffee}} = \frac{(7.20 + 7.40)}{2} = 7.30,$$

$$P_{\text{Australia, Adelaide, Dress}} = \frac{(164.00 + 278.00)}{2} = 221.00,$$

$$P_{\text{Australia, Adelaide, Men's shoes}} = \frac{(228.00 + 300.00)}{2} = 264.00,$$

$$P_{\text{United States, Chicago, White bread}} = \frac{(5.80 + 6.20)}{2} = 6.00,$$

$$P_{\text{United States, Chicago, Instant coffee}} = \frac{(4.80 + 5.20)}{2} = 5.00,$$

$$P_{\text{United States, Chicago, Dress}} = \frac{(335.00 + 665.00)}{2} = 500.00,$$

$$P_{\text{United States, Chicago, Men's shoes}} = \frac{(180.00 + 332.00)}{2} = 256.00,$$

$$P_{\text{Australia, Sydney, White bread}} = \frac{(4.00 + 5.40)}{2} = 4.70,$$

$$P_{\text{Australia, Sydney, Instant coffee}} = \frac{(6.60 + 7.40)}{2} = 7.00,$$

$$P_{\text{Australia, Sydney, Dress}} = \frac{(258.00 + 380.00)}{2} = 319.00,$$

$$P_{\text{Australia, Sydney, Men's shoes}} = \frac{(236.00 + 350.00)}{2} = 293.00,$$

$$P_{\text{United States, New York, White bread}} = \frac{(7.80 + 8.40)}{2} = 8.10,$$

(*Continued*)

Box 2.1: (*Continued*)

$$P_{\text{United States, New York, Instant coffee}} = \frac{(5.80 + 6.00)}{2} = 5.90,$$

$$P_{\text{United States, New York, Dress}} = \frac{(330.00 + 405.00)}{2} = 367.50,$$

$$P_{\text{United States, New York, Men's shoes}} = \frac{(210.00 + 445.00)}{2} = 327.50.$$

(2) Compute the Cost of Living Index for Expatriates in each city.

Cost of Living Index for Expatriates in Adelaide =

$$\frac{(4.60 \times 0.70 + 7.30 \times 0.27 + 221.00 \times 0.02 + 264.00 \times 0.01)}{(8.10 \times 0.70 + 5.90 \times 0.27 + 367.50 \times 0.02 + 327.50 \times 0.01)} \times 100 = 68.49,$$

Cost of Living Index for Expatriates in Chicago =

$$\frac{(6.00 \times 0.70 + 5.00 \times 0.27 + 500.00 \times 0.02 + 256.00 \times 0.01)}{(8.10 \times 0.70 + 5.90 \times 0.27 + 367.50 \times 0.02 + 327.50 \times 0.01)} \times 100 = 101.24,$$

Cost of Living Index for Expatriates in Sydney =

$$\frac{(4.70 \times 0.70 + 7.00 \times 0.27 + 319.00 \times 0.02 + 293.00 \times 0.01)}{(8.10 \times 0.70 + 5.90 \times 0.27 + 367.50 \times 0.02 + 327.50 \times 0.01)} \times 100 = 81.00,$$

Cost of Living Index for Expatriates in New York =

$$\frac{(8.10 \times 0.70 + 5.90 \times 0.27 + 367.50 \times 0.02 + 327.50 \times 0.01)}{(8.10 \times 0.70 + 5.90 \times 0.27 + 367.50 \times 0.02 + 327.50 \times 0.01)} \times 100 = 100.00,$$

(3) Generate the Cost of Living Ranking for Expatriates.

Rank	City	Country	Cost of Living Index for Expatriates
1	Chicago	United States	101.24
2	New York	United States	100.00
3	Sydney	Australia	81.00
4	Adelaide	Australia	68.49

Source: Asia Competitiveness Institute

2.7 Constructing the 10 ACI Consumption Categories Indices and Rankings for Expatriates

Besides the Cost of Living Index and Ranking for Expatriates, our study also constructs indices and rankings for each of the 10 ACI Consumption Categories. This allows us to not only look at the overall cost of living in a particular city, but also to examine the cost of certain consumption categories, for example Food & Non-alcoholic Beverages, Transport or Housing Rents & Utilities. The ACI Consumption Category *j* Index for Expatriates in city m, is defined as Equation 2.7.1.

$$\textit{ACI Consumption Category j Index for Expatriates in city m} = \frac{\sum_{i=1}^{n_j} P_{C,m,i} \times \omega_i}{\sum_{i=1}^{n_j} P_{US,NY,i} \times \omega_i} \times 100 \tag{2.7.1}$$

where
m = city;
C = the country where city *m* is located in;
NY = New York;
US = United States;
i = item;
j = ACI Consumption Category of which item i is in;
n_j = number of items in ACI Consumption Category j;
$P_{C,m,i}$ = average price of item i in city m of country C;
ω_i = normalised weight of item i based on its ACI Consumption Category.

Similar to the Cost of Living Index for Expatriates, the consumption category indices for expatriates are made up of two inputs, prices and weights. The average price of item i in city m of country C, $P_{C,m,i}$, used in the calculation of these indices are the same as those described in Section 2.6.

As for the weights data, normalised weight of each item based on its respective ACI Consumption Category, ω_i, are employed instead. ω_i is obtained by dividing the weight as shown in Table 2.2 of Section 2.5 with the sum of all the weights of items belonging to the same consumption category. In mathematical form, $\omega_i = \frac{W_i}{\sum_{i \in j} W_i}$. For instance, there are only two items within the Food & Non-alcoholic Beverages consumption category, bread and coffee. The normalised weight of bread will therefore equal to the weight of bread (as shown in Table 2.2) divided by the sum of weights of bread and coffee (as shown in Table 2.2). As a result, the normalised weights of all items within the same consumption category will sum to unity (i.e., $\sum_{i=1}^{n_j} \omega_i = 1$).

We can then combine these $P_{C,m,i}$ with their respective normalised weights, ω_i, to obtain the Consumption Category j Index for Expatriates in each city using the Equation 2.7.1. The ACI Consumption Category j Index for Expatriates reflects the cost of consuming all goods and services included under that particular consumption category by expatriates living in city m relative to their counterparts in New York. For example, the Transport Index for Expatriates in city m illustrates the transport cost for expatriates living in city m relative to their counterparts in New York. With New York chosen as the base city, the ACI Consumption Category j Index for Expatriates in New York are always 100.00.

Similar to the Cost of Living Ranking for Expatriates, the ACI Consumption Category j Ranking for Expatriates is obtained by arranging its corresponding ACI Consumption Category j Indices in a descending order. Cities which are ranked at the top of the ranking are more expensive than those at the bottom. A simple numerical example is provided in Box 2.2 to illustrate the process of constructing the 10 ACI Consumption Categories Indices and Rankings for Expatriates.

Box 2.2: Example for Constructing the 10 ACI Consumption Categories Indices and Rankings for Expatriates

Following the example provided in Box 2.1 of Section 2.6, we could calculate the cost indices for two ACI Consumption Categories, namely the Food & Non-alcoholic Beverages and Clothing, for Adelaide, Chicago, Sydney and New York. Based on the calculations in Box 2.1, the average price for each item in each city, $P_{C,m,i}$, are as follows.

$P_{\text{Australia,Adelaide,White bread}} = 4.60,$
$P_{\text{Australia,Adelaide,Instant coffee}} = 7.30,$
$P_{\text{Australia,Adelaide,Dress}} = 221.00,$
$P_{\text{Australia,Adelaide,Men's shoes}} = 264.00,$
$P_{\text{United States,Chicago,White bread}} = 6.00,$
$P_{\text{United States,Chicago,Instant coffee}} = 5.00,$
$P_{\text{United States,Chicago,Dress}} = 500.00,$
$P_{\text{United States,Chicago,Men's shoes}} = 256.00,$
$P_{\text{Australia Sydney,White bread}} = 4.70,$
$P_{\text{Australia Sydney,Instant coffee}} = 7.00,$
$P_{\text{Australia Sydney,Dress}} = 319.00,$
$P_{\text{Australia Sydney,Men's shoes}} = 293.00,$
$P_{\text{United States,New York,White bread}} = 8.10,$
$P_{\text{United States,New York,Instant coffee}} = 5.90,$
$P_{\text{United States,New York,Dress}} = 367.50,$
$P_{\text{United States,New Men's shoes}} = 327.50.$

Also, the weight of each item is as follows.

Item, i	**Weight of item i, W_i**
White bread, 1kg	0.70
Instant coffee, 125g	0.27
Dress, daytime	0.02
Men's shoes, business wear	0.01

(Continued)

Box 2.2: (*Continued*)

Hence the steps involved in the calculation of indices for each ACI Consumption Category and producing rankings for expatriates are as follows.

(1) Compute the normalised weight of each item based on its respective ACI Consumption Category.

$$\omega_{\text{White bread}} = \frac{0.70}{(0.70+0.27)} = 0.72,$$

$$\omega_{\text{Instant coffee}} = \frac{0.27}{(0.70+0.27)} = 0.28,$$

$$\omega_{\text{Dress}} = \frac{0.02}{(0.02+0.01)} = 0.67,$$

$$\omega_{\text{Men's shoes}} = \frac{0.01}{(0.02+0.01)} = 0.33.$$

(2) Compute the ACI Consumption Categories Indices for Expatriates in each city.
Food & Non-alcoholic Beverages Index for Expatriates in Adelaide =

$$= \frac{(4.60\times 0.72+7.30\times 0.28)}{(8.10\times 0.72+5.90\times 0.28)}\times 100 = 71.47,$$

Food & Non-alcoholic Beverages Index for Expatriates in Chicago =

$$= \frac{(6.00\times 0.72+5.00\times 0.28)}{(8.10\times 0.72+5.90\times 0.28)}\times 100 = 76.41,$$

Food & Non-alcoholic Beverages Index for Expatriates in Sydney =

$$= \frac{(4.70\times 0.72+7.00\times 0.28)}{(8.10\times 0.72+5.90\times 0.28)}\times 100 = 71.32,$$

Food & Non-alcoholic Beverages Index for Expatriates in New York =

$$= \frac{(8.10\times 0.72+5.90\times 0.28)}{(8.10\times 0.72+5.90\times 0.28)}\times 100 = 100.00,$$

Clothing Index for Expatriates in Adelaide =

$$= \frac{(221.00\times 0.67+264.00\times 0.33)}{(367.50\times 0.67+327.50\times 0.33)}\times 100 = 66.45,$$

Clothing Index for Expatriates in Chicago =

$$= \frac{(500.00\times 0.67+256.00\times 0.33)}{(367.50\times 0.67+327.50\times 0.33)}\times 100 = 118.21,$$

(*Continued*)

Box 2.2: (*Continued*)

Clothing Index for Expatriates in Sydney =

$$= \frac{(319.00 \times 0.67 + 293.00 \times 0.33)}{(367.50 \times 0.67 + 327.50 \times 0.33)} \times 100 = 87.62,$$

Clothing Index for Expatriates in New York =

$$= \frac{(367.50 \times 0.67 + 327.50 \times 0.33)}{(367.50 \times 0.67 + 327.50 \times 0.33)} \times 100 = 100.00.$$

(3) Generate the ACI Consumption Categories Rankings for Expatriates.
Food & Non-alcoholic Beverages Ranking

Rank	City	Country	Food & Non-alcoholic Beverages Index for Expatriates
1	New York	United States	100.00
2	Chicago	United States	76.41
3	Adelaide	Australia	71.47
4	Sydney	Australia	71.32

Clothing Ranking

Rank	City	Country	Clothing Index for Expatriates
1	Chicago	United States	118.21
2	New York	United States	100.00
3	Sydney	Australia	87.62
4	Adelaide	Australia	66.45

Source: Asia Competitiveness Institute

Chapter 3

Methodology on Cost of Living, Wages and Purchasing Power for Ordinary Residents

3.1 Introduction

This chapter outlines the framework employed by the Asia Competitiveness Institute (ACI) in tracking the cost of living, wages and purchasing power for ordinary residents in the world's major 103 cities from 2005 to 2013. For the purpose of this study, the ordinary residents are assumed to follow local consumption preferences which differ from country to country.

The ACI cost of living for ordinary residents framework, with its 10 Consumption Categories, is an overarching, comprehensive and systematic way of examining cost of living in each city. ACI has defined cost of living for ordinary residents according to 10 Consumption Categories: (1) Food & Non-alcoholic Beverages, (2) Alcohol & Tobacco, (3) Clothing, (4) Housing Rents & Utilities, (5) Household Supplies & Domestic Help, (6) Health, (7) Transport, (8) Recreation, (9) Education, and (10) Miscellaneous Goods & Services (see Figure 3.1). Note that similar consumption categories are also employed in the cost of living for expatriates framework (refer to Section 2.1 in Chapter 2 for more details).

New York has been chosen as the base city for the study, with other cities being benchmarked against it. Apart from being a city globally known, New York is made the base city to facilitate comparison as similar studies on cost of living, wages and purchasing power have also used New York as the benchmark.[1] The index values of New York are always 100.00.

As a summary measure of the overall cost of living in each city for the ordinary residents, we have derived the Cost of Living Index for Ordinary Residents which is made up of the 10 ACI Consumption Categories. A larger Cost of Living Index for Ordinary Residents implies that the city is more expensive for the ordinary residents. In contrast, a smaller Cost of Living Index denotes lower cost of living. Furthermore, ordinary residents who live in cities with Cost of Living Index larger (smaller) than 100.00 face higher (lower) cost as compared to their counterparts in New York. In our study, we also produce a ranking on the cost of living for ordinary residents by arranging the Cost of Living Index for Ordinary Residents in each city in a descending order. In other words, cities which rank at the top of the ranking are more expensive than those at the bottom.

After analysing the costs borne by ordinary residents living in various cities, we explore the wages earned by them. Specifically, we have computed the gross hourly wages received by ordinary residents in 103 cities. Similar to cost of living, this information is also transformed into an index, namely the Wages Index for Ordinary Residents. Cities in which ordinary residents receive higher (lower) hourly wages are awarded with higher (lower) Wages Indices. Additionally,

[1] See, for example, the Worldwide Cost of Living Index and Ranking annually published by the Economist Intelligence Unit (EIU), and the Cost of Living City Rankings annually published by Mercer.

Figure 3.1: The 10 ACI Consumption Categories

Source: Asia Competitiveness Institute

larger (smaller) than 100.00 Wages Index for Ordinary Residents implies that ordinary residents in those cities earn more (less) than their counterparts in New York for an hour's work. We also generate a ranking on the hourly wages of ordinary residents by arranging the Wages Index for Ordinary Residents in each city in a descending order. Hence, cities which rank at the top of the ranking have higher wages than those at the bottom.

Having examined the cost of living in certain cities and their level of remuneration, it is useful to compare these two figures to see the buying power of ordinary residents in these cities. We have thus devised a Purchasing Power Index for Ordinary Residents which measures the number of baskets of goods and services that ordinary residents in a given city can enjoy if they work for an hour relative to that of their counterparts in New York. Cities in which ordinary residents are able to afford more (less) goods and service for every hour worked have higher (lower) Purchasing Power Index. Also, larger (smaller) than 100.00 Purchasing Power Index for Ordinary Residents implies that ordinary residents in those cities have higher (lower) buying power than their counterparts in New York. The Purchasing Power Index in each city is then arranged in a descending order, cities which rank at the top of the ranking have higher purchasing power than those at the bottom.

The rest of Chapter 3 is organised as follows. Section 3.2 introduces the sources of data and describes the data used in the study. Section 3.3 discusses major assumptions in the computation of Cost of Living, Wages and Purchasing Power Indices for Ordinary Residents. Both Section 3.4 and 3.5 are dedicated to the discussions on cost of living for ordinary residents in each of the

103 city. While Section 3.4 focuses on the methodology for overall Cost of Living Index and Ranking in each city, Section 3.5 concentrates on that of each ACI Consumption Category and its respective rankings. This is followed by Section 3.6 on the methodology for Wages Index and Ranking for Ordinary Residents. Finally, Section 3.7 shows the algorithm used to construct the Purchasing Power Index and Ranking for Ordinary Residents.

3.2 Data Sources

The construction of the three indices, namely Cost of Living Index for Ordinary Residents, Wages Index for Ordinary Resident and Purchasing Power Index for Ordinary Residents, requires data on prices, weights, inflation rates, nominal expenditure per capita, real expenditure per capita, wages, working hours and exchange rates.

Price data for all 10 ACI Consumption Categories except for Miscellaneous Goods & Services are acquired from the Economist Intelligence Unit (EIU) CityData, which are available in local currency every year over the study period from 2005 to 2013. On the other hand, the price data for Miscellaneous Goods & Services, reported in US dollar, are obtained and estimated from the 2003, 2006, 2009 and 2012 UBS Prices and Earnings study (refer to Section 2.2 and 2.4 in Chapter 2 for more details on the price data).

Weights data are derived based on International Comparison Programme (ICP) survey conducted by the World Bank and household expenditure surveys in various countries. As the World Bank ICP survey is implemented every six years, the 2005 and 2011 round of the ICP survey are referenced. The value of all weights data ranges from zero to one and together they sum to unity.

The data on inflation rates, nominal expenditure per capita and real expenditure per capita are used to construct the Cost of Living Index for Ordinary Residents as part of the adjustment factors, which will be explained in detail in Section 3.4.1, 3.4.2 and 3.5 of this chapter. The annual inflation rates are mainly obtained from the World Bank World Development Indicators over the study period. On the other hand, the data on nominal expenditure per capita and real expenditure per capita are acquired from the World Bank ICP survey. As mentioned earlier, we only use two rounds of ICP survey whose timeframe is relevant to our study period, namely the 2005 and 2011 ICP survey.

Wages and working hours data are obtained from International Labour Organisation (ILO). As the data are compiled by ILO from various sources, the availability and definition of data may differ across countries. In general, the national level data on both the gross average nominal monthly wages (reported in local currency) and mean weekly hours actually worked are used in this study. The details on data and proxy will be discussed in Sections 3.6.1 and 3.6.2 of this chapter.

As some price data and all wage data are reported in local currency, exchange rates are needed to convert those data into a common currency for comparison. In order to smooth the effects of daily fluctuations in the currency market, we use the yearly average exchange rates which are calculated based on the daily average exchange rates retrieved from the Bloomberg Terminal. All exchange rates used in this study are expressed in local currency against US dollar and they are listed in Appendix 3.

3.3 Assumptions Made

Partly due to data limitations, we have made several strong but plausible assumptions when constructing the Cost of Living, Wages and Purchasing Power Indices for Ordinary Residents.

Firstly, ordinary residents living in different cities of the same country are assumed to have the same consumption pattern, which varies from country to country and is different from that of the expatriates. In contrast to the expatriates who tend to enjoy Western consumption preferences and gear towards high-end and lifestyle products, the consumption pattern of ordinary residents is influenced by geographical location, social values and cultural affiliation in the respective countries.

Secondly, consumption pattern of ordinary residents is assumed to change over time. The change in spending preference of ordinary residents partially affected by the variation in prices and quality of goods and services is reflected in different sets of weights being used for ordinary residents in each year.

Thirdly, as ICP survey is conducted every six years, proxy for the nominal expenditure per capita and real expenditure per capita in years not covered under the study will be made based on exchange rates and inflation rates. The details can be found in Section 3.4.1 and 3.4.2 of this chapter.

Finally, as the data for inflation rates, nominal expenditure per capita, real expenditure per capita, nominal monthly wages and mean weekly working hours are not available at the city level, the national level data will be used as the proxy.

3.4 Constructing the Cost of Living Index and Ranking for Ordinary Residents

This section details the data and methodology used to construct the Cost of Living Index and Ranking for Ordinary Residents in 103 cities. Prices data have already been discussed in Chapter 2 (see Section 2.2 and 2.4 for more details). As mentioned in the first assumption of Section 3.3, ordinary residents follow country-specific weights, which are influenced by geographical locations, social values and cultural affiliation in the respective countries. These country-specific weights are derived by analysing the World Bank ICP surveys and household expenditure surveys conducted by relevant census departments and statistical agencies in various countries across the years. In every year over the study period from 2005 to 2013, a unique set of weights is derived for each country according to the detailed steps as documented in the unpublished ACI Technical Working Paper 10/2015 titled *Methodology on Weights in the Cost of Living Study for Expatriates and Ordinary Residents*.

A separate section, Section 3.4.1, is dedicated to describing the components of the adjustment factors used when constructing the Cost of Living Index for Ordinary Residents, namely inflation rates, nominal expenditure per capita and real expenditure per capita, followed by Section 3.4.2, which explains the steps involved in computing the Cost of Living Index and producing the Cost of Living Ranking for Ordinary Residents. A numerical example is also provided in Section 3.4.2 to illustrate the methodology used.

3.4.1 Components of Adjustment Factors: Inflation Rates, Nominal Expenditure per Capita and Real Expenditure per Capita

The computation of the Cost of Living Index and Ranking for Ordinary Residents, which will be discussed in detail in Section 3.4.2, requires data on inflation rates, nominal expenditure per capita and real expenditure per capita as part of the adjustment factors.

Most of the inflation rate data are acquired from the World Bank World Development Indicators with the following exceptions:

a. The inflation rates for Argentina from 2005 to 2013, Chile from 2005 to 2009 and Venezuela from 2005 to 2008 are retrieved from International Financial Statistics.
b. The inflation rates for Taiwan from 2005 to 2013 are retrieved from Taiwan Directorate General of Budget, Accounting and Statistics, PC-AXIS database.
c. The inflation rates for United Arab Emirates from 2005 to 2007 and 2012 to 2013 are retrieved from United Arab Emirates National Bureau of Statistics.

The nominal expenditure per capita and real expenditure per capita on the 10 ACI Consumption Categories for each country and the world are obtained from the World Bank ICP survey. The overall nominal (or real) expenditure per capita is the sum of the nominal (or real) expenditure per capita on the 10 ACI Consumption Categories. Refer to Table 2.1 in Section 2.5 of Chapter 2 for details on the rearrangement of 12 ICP categories to match 10 ACI Consumption Categories. This dataset is almost complete except for two countries:

a. The data for United Arab Emirates are missing in 2005 round of ICP survey. Qatar data are used as the proxy.
b. The data for Argentina are missing in 2011 round of ICP survey. Brazil data are used as the proxy.

3.4.2 Computation of Cost of Living Index and Ranking for Ordinary Residents

$$\textit{Cost of Living Index for Ordinary Residents in city } m = \frac{CP^{EIU}_{C,m} \times \dfrac{NP^{ICP}_{C}}{NP^{EIU}_{C}}}{CP^{EIU}_{US,NY} \times \dfrac{NP^{ICP}_{US}}{NP^{EIU}_{US}}} \quad (3.4.1)$$

where
m = city;
C = the country where city m is located in;
NY = New York;
US = United States;
$CP^{EIU}_{C,m} = \sum_{i=1}^{n} P_{C,m,i} \times W_{C,i}$ (3.4.2);

i = item;
n = number of items in the consumption basket;
$P_{C,m,i}$ = average price of item i in city m of country C;
$W_{C,i}$ = weight of item i within Cost of Living Index for Ordinary Residents in country C;

$$NP_{C}^{ICP} = \frac{\text{index of nominal expenditure per capita for country C}}{\text{index of real expenditure per capita for country C}} \quad (3.4.3);$$

index of nominal expenditure per capita for country C

$$= \frac{\text{nominal expenditure per capita for country C}}{\text{nominal expenditure per capita of the world}};$$

index of real expenditure per capita for country C

$$= \frac{\text{real expenditure per capita for country C}}{\text{real expenditure per capita of the world}};$$

NP_{C}^{EIU} = mean $CP_{C,m}^{EIU}$ from all cities within country C.

The Cost of Living Index for Ordinary Residents is made up of three main components, namely $CP_{C,m}^{EIU}$, NP_{C}^{ICP}, and NP_{C}^{EIU}. Firstly, $CP_{C,m}^{EIU}$ is constructed using the average price of each item, $P_{C,m,i}$, and its respective weight. For ordinary residents, the weight of each item, $W_{C,i}$, is country-specific as it reflects the different consumption patterns of ordinary residents in each country. These baskets of goods and services tend to follow the local patterns of consumption. Also, the weights of all items that together describe the total cost of living in each city will sum up to unity. In mathematical expression, $\sum_{i=1}^{n} W_{C,i} = 1$. As for prices, data treatment is the same as described in Section 2.4 and 2.6 of Chapter 2 (i.e. first, take an average of all prices collected from the various sales locations for the same item in each city, followed by converting the average prices which are reported in local currencies to US dollar). The prices and weights are then combined using Equation 3.4.2 to obtain $CP_{C,m}^{EIU}$.

$$CP_{C,m}^{EIU} = \sum_{i=1}^{n} P_{C,m,i} \times W_{C,i} \qquad (3.4.2)$$

where
m = city;
C = the country where city m is located in;
i = item;
n = number of items in the consumption basket;
$P_{C,m,i}$ = average price of item i in city m of country C;
$W_{C,i}$ = weight of item i within Cost of Living Index for Ordinary Residents in country C.

Notice that Equation 3.4.2 takes a similar form as the numerator of the equation for Cost of Living Index for Expatriates.[2] We can understand $CP_{C,m}^{EIU}$ as the cost of living index for ordinary

[2]Refer to Equation 2.6.1 in Section 2.6 of Chapter 2 on the Cost of Living Index for Expatriates.

residents who purchase goods and services consumed by expatriates but with their own consumption patterns.

As the EIU data are reflective of the prices and consumption behaviours of the expatriates at the city level while World Bank ICP data are indicative of that of ordinary residents at the national level, some adjustment factors need to be introduced to $CP_{C,m}^{EIU}$ in order to construct the Cost of Living Index for Ordinary Residents. We thus use two adjustment factors, namely NP_{C}^{ICP} and NP_{C}^{EIU}.

For the first adjustment factor, NP_{C}^{ICP}, it is constructed using data from the ICP which include both the nominal expenditure per capita and real expenditure per capita for each country as well as the world. All data used are denominated in US dollar and NP_{C}^{ICP} is as defined in Equation 3.4.3.

$$NP_{C}^{ICP} = \frac{\text{index of nominal expenditure per capita for country C}}{\text{index of real expenditure per capita for country C}} \tag{3.4.3}$$

where
C = country;

$$\text{index of nominal expenditure per capita for country C} = \frac{\text{nominal expenditure per capita for country C}}{\text{nominal expenditure per capita of the world}};$$

$$\text{index of real expenditure per capita for country C} = \frac{\text{real expenditure per capita for country C}}{\text{real expenditure per capita of the world}};$$

The NP_{C}^{ICP} can be understood as the price level per unit real consumption for ordinary residents living in country C. In other words, it is the cost of living for ordinary residents in country C based on the ICP survey. This adjustment factor is multiplied to $CP_{C,m}^{EIU}$ to introduce the cost of living for ordinary residents based on ICP survey. The constraint of this adjustment factor is that it is available at national level only.

Since the ICP survey is conducted every six years, we construct NP_{C}^{ICP} for 2006 to 2010 and 2012 to 2013 by taking into account extra information about exchange rates and inflation rates, which reflect the key factors affecting the comparison of cost of living for ordinary residents across countries. The NP_{C}^{ICP} from 2006 to 2010 are thus constructed as Equation 3.4.4.

$$NP_{C,T}^{ICP} = NP_{C,2005}^{ICP} \times \frac{\text{Exchange Rate}_{C,2005}}{\text{Exchange Rate}_{C,T}} \times \prod_{t=2006}^{T} \left(1 + \text{Inflation rate}_{C,t}\right) \forall T \in (2006, 2007, 2008, 2009, \text{and } 2010) \tag{3.4.4}$$

where
C = country;
T = year;
$NP_{C,T}^{ICP} = NP_{C}^{ICP}$ in year T;

Inflation rate$_{C,t}$ = yearly average inflation rate for country C in year t;
Exchange Rate$_{C,T}$ = yearly average exchange rate between country C and the United States in year T (expressed as local currency unit per US dollar).

Take for example, if we want to construct $NP_{C,2007}^{ICP}$ (i.e. the NP_{C}^{ICP} for country C in 2007), we will first need to multiply $NP_{C,2005}^{ICP}$ by the 2005 exchange rate between country C and the United States (expressed as local currency unit per US dollar), then multiply it with the cumulative inflation rate between 2005 to 2007, and lastly divide it by the 2007 exchange rate between country C and the United States (expressed as local currency unit per US dollar). As mentioned above, we can understand NP_{C}^{ICP} as the cost of living for ordinary residents living in country C based on the ICP survey. As such, $NP_{C,2005}^{ICP}$ can be understood as the cost of living for ordinary residents in 2005, calculated based on US dollar, so that we have a common basis for comparison. This figure is thus subjected to the 2005 exchange rate between country C and the United States. In order for us to construct $NP_{C,2007}^{ICP}$, we will need to remove the effect of exchange rate in 2005 and at the same time introduce the effect of exchange rate in 2007. Also, during the 2005 to 2007 period, inflation rates will affect the cost of living for ordinary residents. We have therefore incorporated the cumulative inflation rate into the equation as well.

By applying the same rationale, NP_{C}^{ICP} in 2012 and 2013 can be constructed using the following Equation 3.4.5.

$$NP_{C,T}^{ICP} = NP_{C,2011}^{ICP} \times \frac{\text{Exchange Rate}_{C,2011}}{\text{Exchange Rate}_{C,T}} \times \prod_{t=2012}^{T} \left(1 + \text{Inflation rate}_{C,t}\right) \forall T \in \text{(2012 and 2013)} \tag{3.4.5}$$

where
C = country;
T = year;
$NP_{C,T}^{ICP} = NP_{C}^{ICP}$ in year T;

Inflation rate$_{C,t}$ = yearly average inflation rate for country C in year t;
Exchange Rate$_{C,T}$ = yearly average exchange rate between country C and the United States in year T (expressed as local currency unit per US dollar).

Since the NP_{C}^{ICP} for the period 2006–2010 are calculated based on $NP_{C,2005}^{ICP}$, while the NP_{C}^{ICP} for the period 2012–2013 are calculated based on $NP_{C,2011}^{ICP}$, we might expect to see some break in trend for results between 2010 and 2011. Indeed, the "Purchasing Power Parities and Real Expenditures of World Economies: Summary of Results and Findings of the 2011 International Comparison Program" by the World Bank has cautioned us against comparing data from the 2005 survey to that of the 2011.[3] One of the main reasons cited was the change in methodology used for these two rounds of surveys. As such, ACI has segmented the findings of our study on Cost of Living for Ordinary Residents based on two sub-periods, 2005 to 2010 and 2011 to 2013.[4] This is one of the constraints of our study.

As for the second adjustment factor, NP_C^{EIU}, it is constructed based on $CP_{C,m}^{EIU}$ as defined in Equation 3.4.2 using the following Equation 3.4.6.

$$NP_C^{EIU} = \frac{1}{N_C} \sum_{m \in C} CP_{C,m}^{EIU} \qquad (3.4.6)$$

where
m = city;
C = the country where city m is located in;
N_C = number of cities in country C;
$CP_{C,m}^{EIU}$ is as defined in Equation 3.4.2.

NP_C^{EIU} is the mean value of $CP_{C,m}^{EIU}$ from all cities within country C. It can be understood as a proxy for the general level of $CP_{C,m}^{EIU}$ in country C. In other words, it reflects the cost incurred by ordinary residents living in country C based on the EIU data. In the calculation of Cost of Living Index for Ordinary Residents, this adjustment factor is used to divide $CP_{C,m}^{EIU}$. This will serve to offset the effect of using expatriates' consumption basket as well as the effect of using national level data.

Therefore, the two adjustment factors, NP_C^{ICP} and NP_C^{EIU}, are applied to the $CP_{C,m}^{EIU}$ using Equation 3.4.1 to construct the Cost of Living Index for Ordinary Residents in each city.

$$\textit{Cost of Living Index for Ordinary Residents city}\, m = \frac{CP_{C,m}^{EIU} \times \dfrac{NP_C^{ICP}}{NP_C^{EIU}}}{CP_{US,NY}^{EIU} \times \dfrac{NP_{US}^{ICP}}{NP_{US}^{EIU}}} \qquad (3.4.1)$$

There is an alternative approach to parse Equation 3.4.1 and interpret its structure, which will offer another vantage point from which we can gain a clearer view on the issue of controlling for utility in constructing the Cost of Living Index and Ranking for Ordinary Residents. As mentioned previously, the term NP_C^{ICP} can be understood as the price level per unit real consumption for ordinary residents living in country C based on data from ICP surveys, which is standardised against the world level as defined by Equation 3.4.3. Since the term NP_C^{ICP} can

[3]The "Purchasing Power Parities and Real Expenditures of World Economies: Summary of Results and Findings of the 2011 International Comparison Program" is obtained from the World Bank website, http://siteresources.worldbank.org/ICPINT/Resources/270056-1183395201801/Summary-of-Results-and-Findings-of-the-2011-International-Comparison-Program.pdf, on May 19th, 2015.

[4]See Chapter 5 for research findings on Cost of Living, Wages and Purchasing Power for Ordinary Residents.

be construed as the standardised price per unit real consumption of goods and services for ordinary residents in a country, it actually by itself forms a measure of the cost of living for ordinary residents while controlling for the utility level, or standard of living, across the countries for which NP_C^{ICP} is calculated, as it pins down the level of such consumption at a fixed amount across countries.

Had the ICP achieved a finer degree of granularity by conducting their surveys and compiling the data at the city level (at least in the representative cities in our study per each country with each city being a statistical unit), we could have been able to exclusively use the ICP data to construct a cost of living index for ordinary residents in cities around the world. Since the ICP data are only available at national level in reality, we can still make use of such data by incorporating them into the construction of the index for the cost of living for ordinary residents, as reflected in the inclusion of the term NP_C^{ICP} into Equation 3.4.1, while integrating it with some relevant factors to arrive at a practical proxy for the variations among cities within each country in terms of the cost of living for ordinary residents. The inclusion of the ratio between $CP_{C,m}^{EIU}$ and NP_C^{EIU} into Equation 3.4.1 can be viewed as providing such a proxy for generating the city level variations in a specific country C.

As defined by Equation 3.4.2, $CP_{C,m}^{EIU}$ gives a measure of the cost of living index for ordinary residents with their own consumption patterns but using the prices of the consumption items for expatriates as in the EIU data, assuming such data for prices will generally correlate with the data for prices of the counterpart items in the consumption basket for ordinary residents in each city. As defined by Equation 3.4.6, NP_C^{EIU} is simply the average of the values of $CP_{C,m}^{EIU}$ for all the cities within country C. Thus, the ratio between $CP_{C,m}^{EIU}$ and NP_C^{EIU}, i.e. the former divided by the latter, can be viewed as an indicator of how high the cost of living is for ordinary residents in a particular city as compared to the national average, as a value of one for this ratio will mean that city m is on par with the national average level of country C in terms of the cost of living for ordinary residents, and a value above or below one will imply that city m has higher or lower cost of living for ordinary residents as compared to the national average level of country C respectively. Combining this ratio with the term NP_C^{ICP} as in Equation 3.4.1, therefore, will provide an assessment of the cost of living for ordinary residents for each city, utilising the available relevant datasets from both ICP at the national level and EIU at the city level.

To the extent that the term NP_C^{ICP} controls for utility across countries as it is in essence a standardised price index for per unit real consumption, and that the introduction of the ratio between $CP_{C,m}^{EIU}$ and NP_C^{EIU} proxies for the variations among cities within a country while maintaining such controlling for utility, the Cost of Living Index for Ordinary Residents constructed in Equation 3.4.1 to allow for the comparison of cost of living for ordinary residents across cities around the world also controls for utility. It is extremely important to put in explicit efforts to control for utility or standard of living when conceptualising a framework and designing a methodology for comparing cost of living, as in essence the notion of cost of living should directly relate to the amount of monetary expenses required for maintaining a certain standard of living or generating a certain level of utility for the person who spends that amount.

A cost of living index or ranking constructed without controlling for utility would be meaningless, as a higher or lower index value for the cost of living may be mostly a result of higher or lower utility and better or worse standard of living associated with such level of living expenses, or in other words, one could never ascertain whether he is comparing apple to apple. Hence, without controlling for utility the results of any cost of living analysis will be of limited usefulness as the resultant ranking or comparison can only be done on an inherently unfair basis. Some may argue that such attempts to control for utility can never be perfect, as utility is affected by the natural endowment of the city such as climate, landscape, natural scenery and so on, which may not be able to be captured by monetary data in terms of prices in the markets for goods and services. While that statement is certainly true as those factors do affect a person's utility level or standard of living, we should bear in mind that it is not the total utility level or overall standard of living that is of our concern here. Rather, we are focusing on a subset of the total utility or overall standard of living that is underpinned by the results of consuming goods and services. Some may point out that controlling for the utility generated by the consumption of goods and services still cannot be perfect, as the quality of services may differ and so do the types of goods available in different regions of the world. Nevertheless, we should strive, as conceptually examined in the analysis framework and concretely reflected in the methodology, to control for utility by making explicit efforts in order to make the comparison of cost of living meaningful.

The Cost of Living Index for Ordinary Residents reflects the cost of consuming all goods and services in the consumption basket of ordinary residents living in city m relative to those in New York. With New York chosen as the base city, the Cost of Living Index for Ordinary Residents in New York will always be 100.00.

Lastly, the Cost of Living Ranking for Ordinary Residents can be generated by arranging the Cost of Living Index for Ordinary Residents in each city in a descending order. A city which is more expensive (cheaper) for the ordinary residents will have a larger (smaller) Cost of Living Index and thus occupy a higher (lower) position in the Cost of Living Ranking for Ordinary Residents.

One advantage of the ACI methodology lies in the fact that the Cost of Living Ranking for Ordinary Residents will not be sensitive to the choice of base city. Whether the base city is chosen to be New York, Beijing, Tokyo or any other city, the ranking will remain the same.[5] This property of the ranking methodology for cost of living analysis is crucial for the objectivity of the research, because one does not know *a priori* the order of the ranking prior to conducting the calculation to arrive at the results and one's subjective choice of the base city should not interfere with the order of the ranking. If, for example, using New York as the base city will yield a different sequence in the ranking for cost of living as compared to the case where London is used as the base city, such inconsistency will be a sign of dubious results and no claims of such ranking being internationally valid and a source of valuable reference to a global audience should ever be made.

A simple numerical example is provided in Box 3.1 to illustrate the process of constructing the Cost of Living Index and Ranking for Ordinary Residents.

---

[5]If we take the prices in both the selected city and base city, make an average of them, and use this average as the basis for the index comparison, the ranking will be sensitive to the choice of base city.

Box 3.1: Example for Constructing the Cost of Living Index and Ranking for Ordinary Residents

Consider a case whereby the cost of living consists of two consumption categories only, Food & Non-alcoholic Beverages and Clothing. For Food & Non-alcoholic Beverages, it is made up of two items, white bread and instant coffee. As for Clothing, it contains two items, daytime dress and men's shoes. The prices of each item sold in Adelaide and Sydney of Australia as well as Chicago and New York of the United States are listed as below. These prices are the same as those shown in Box 2.1 of Section 2.6 in Chapter 2.

		Price in US$			
Item, i	**Data Series**	**Adelaide**	**Chicago**	**Sydney**	**New York**
White bread, 1kg	White bread, 1kg (supermarket)	4.40	5.80	4.00	7.80
	White bread, 1kg (mid-priced store)	4.80	6.20	5.40	8.40
Instant coffee, 125g	Instant coffee, 125g (supermarket)	7.20	4.80	6.60	5.80
	Instant coffee, 125g (mid-priced store)	7.40	5.20	7.40	6.00
Dress, daytime	Dress, daytime (chain store)	164.00	335.00	258.00	330.00
	Dress, daytime (branded store)	278.00	665.00	380.00	405.00
Men's shoes, business wear	Men's shoes, business wear (chain store)	228.00	180.00	236.00	210.00
	Men's shoes, business wear (branded store)	300.00	332.00	350.00	445.00

Assume the weight of each item for Ordinary Residents in Australia and United States is as follows.

Item, i	**Weight of item i in Australia, $W_{Australia,i}$**	**Weight of item i in United States, $W_{United\ States,i}$**
White bread, 1kg	0.30	0.20
Instant coffee, 125g	0.05	0.06
Dress, daytime	0.45	0.50
Men's shoes, business wear	0.20	0.24

The nominal and real expenditure per capita in Australia, United States and the world are as follows.

	In US$		
Data Series	**Australia**	**United States**	**World**
Nominal expenditure per capita	4,824.00	3,411.00	1,198.00
Real expenditure per capita	2,937.00	3,411.00	1,370.00

Based on the calculations in Box 2.1 of Section 2.6 in Chapter 2, the average price of item i in city m of country C, $P_{C,m,i}$, is as follows (refer to step (1) of Box 2.1 for details on how to calculate $P_{C,m,i}$).

$P_{Australia,Adelaide,White\ bread} = 4.60$

$P_{Australia,Adelaide,Instant\ coffee} = 7.30$

(Continued)

Box 3.1: (*Continued*)

$P_{\text{Australia, Adelaide, Dress}} = 221.00$
$P_{\text{Australia, Adelaide, Men's shoes}} = 264.00$
$P_{\text{United States, Chicago, White bread}} = 6.00$
$P_{\text{United States, Chicago, Instant coffee}} = 5.00$
$P_{\text{United States, Chicago, Dress}} = 500.00$
$P_{\text{United States, Chicago, Men's shoes}} = 256.00$
$P_{\text{Australia, Sydney, White bread}} = 4.70$
$P_{\text{Australia, Sydney, Instant coffee}} = 7.00$
$P_{\text{Australia, Sydney, Dress}} = 319.00$
$P_{\text{Australia, Sydney, Men's shoes}} = 293.00$
$P_{\text{United States, New York, White bread}} = 8.10$
$P_{\text{United States, New York, Instant coffee}} = 5.90$
$P_{\text{United States, New York, Dress}} = 367.50$
$P_{\text{United States, New York, Men's shoes}} = 327.50$

Hence the steps involved in the calculation of Cost of Living Index and producing a ranking for ordinary residents are as follows.

(1) Compute $CP^{EIU}_{C,m}$ for each city.

$$CP^{EIU}_{\text{Australia,Adelaide}} = 4.60 \times 0.30 + 7.30 \times 0.05 + 221.00 \times 0.45 + 264.00 \times 0.20 = 154.00$$

$$CP^{EIU}_{\text{United States,Chicago}} = 6.00 \times 0.20 + 5.00 \times 0.06 + 500.00 \times 0.50 + 256.00 \times 0.24 = 312.94$$

$$CP^{EIU}_{\text{Australia,Sydney}} = 4.70 \times 0.30 + 7.00 \times 0.05 + 319.00 \times 0.45 + 293.00 \times 0.20 = 203.91$$

$$CP^{EIU}_{\text{United States,New York}} = 8.10 \times 0.20 + 5.90 \times 0.06 + 367.50 \times 0.50 + 327.50 \times 0.24 = 264.32$$

(2) Compute the indices for nominal and real expenditure per capita in each country.

$$\text{Index of nominal expenditure per capita for Australia} = \frac{4{,}824.00}{1{,}198.00} = 4.0267$$

(*Continued*)

Box 3.1: (*Continued*)

$$\text{Index of nominal expenditure per capita for United States} = \frac{3{,}411.00}{1{,}198.00} = 2.8472$$

$$\text{Index of real expenditure per capita for Australia} = \frac{2{,}937.00}{1{,}370.00} = 2.1438$$

$$\text{Index of real expenditure per capita for United States} = \frac{3{,}411.00}{1{,}370.00} = 2.4898$$

(3) Compute the first adjustment factor, $\text{NP}_{\text{C}}^{\text{ICP}}$, for each country.

$$\text{NP}_{\text{Australia}}^{\text{ICP}} = \frac{4.0267}{2.1438} = 1.8783$$

$$\text{NP}_{\text{United States}}^{\text{ICP}} = \frac{2.8472}{2.4898} = 1.1436$$

(4) Compute the second adjustment factor, $\text{NP}_{\text{C}}^{\text{EIU}}$, for each country.

$$\text{NP}_{\text{Australia}}^{\text{EIU}} = \frac{1}{2} \times (154.00 + 203.91) = 178.95$$

$$\text{NP}_{\text{United States}}^{\text{EIU}} = \frac{1}{2} \times (312.94 + 264.32) = 288.63$$

(5) Compute the Cost of Living Index for Ordinary Residents in each city.

$$\text{Cost of Living Index for Ordinary Residents in Adelaide} = \frac{154.00 \times \frac{1.8783}{178.95}}{264.32 \times \frac{1.1436}{288.63}} \times 100 = 154.34$$

$$\text{Cost of Living Index for Ordinary Residents in Chicago} = \frac{312.94 \times \frac{1.1436}{288.63}}{264.32 \times \frac{1.1436}{288.63}} \times 100 = 118.39$$

$$\text{Cost of Living Index for Ordinary Residents in Sydney} = \frac{203.91 \times \frac{1.8783}{178.95}}{264.32 \times \frac{1.1436}{288.63}} \times 100 = 204.37$$

$$\text{Cost of Living Index for Ordinary Residents in New York} = \frac{264.32 \times \frac{1.1436}{288.63}}{264.32 \times \frac{1.1436}{288.63}} \times 100 = 100.00$$

(*Continued*)

Box 3.1: (*Continued*)

(6) Generate the Cost of Living Ranking for Ordinary Residents.

Rank	City	Country	Cost of Living Index for Ordinary Residents
1	Sydney	Australia	204.37
2	Adelaide	Australia	154.34
3	Chicago	United States	118.39
4	New York	United States	100.00

Source: Asia Competitiveness Institute

3.5 Constructing the 10 ACI Consumption Categories Indices and Rankings for Ordinary Residents

Besides the Cost of Living Index and Ranking for Ordinary Residents, our study also constructs indices and rankings for each of the 10 ACI Consumption Categories. This allows us to not only look at the overall cost of living in a particular city, but also to examine the cost of certain Consumption Categories, for example Food & Non-alcoholic Beverages, Transport or Housing Rents & Utilities. The ACI Consumption Category j Index for Ordinary Residents in city m is defined as Equation 3.5.1.

ACI Consumption Category j Index for Ordinary Residents in city m =

$$\frac{CP^{EIU}_{C,m,j} \times \dfrac{NP^{ICP}_{C,j}}{NP^{EIU}_{C,j}}}{CP^{EIU}_{US,NY,j} \times \dfrac{NP^{ICP}_{US,j}}{NP^{EIU}_{US,j}}} \qquad (3.5.1)$$

where

m = city;

C = the country where city m is located in;

NY = New York;

US = United States;

$$CP^{EIU}_{C,m,j} = \sum_{i=1}^{n_j} P_{C,m,i} \times \omega_{C,i} \qquad (3.5.2);$$

i = item;

j = ACI Consumption Category of which item i is in;

n_j = number of items in ACI Consumption Category j;

$P_{C,m,i}$ = average price of item i in city m of country C;

$\omega_{C,i}$ = normalised weight of item i based on its ACI Consumption Category for country C;

$$NP^{ICP}_{C,j} = \frac{\text{index of nominal expenditure per capita on ACI Consumption Category j for country C}}{\text{index of real expenditure per capita on ACI Consumption Category j for country C}} \qquad (3.5.3);$$

index of nominal expenditure per capita on ACI Consumption Category j for country C=

$$\frac{\text{nominal expenditure per capita on ACI Consumption Category j for country C}}{\text{nominal expenditure per capita on ACI Consumption Category j of the world}};$$

index of real expenditure per capita on ACI Consumption Category j for country C=

$$\frac{\text{real expenditure per capita on ACI Consumption Category j for country C}}{\text{real expenditure per capita on ACI Consumption Category j of the world}};$$

$NP^{EIU}_{C,j}$ = mean $CP^{EIU}_{C,m,j}$ from all cities within country C.

Similar to the Cost of Living Index for Ordinary Residents, the ACI Consumption Category j Index for Ordinary Residents is made up of three parts, namely $CP^{EIU}_{C,m,j}$, $NP^{ICP}_{C,j}$, and $NP^{EIU}_{C,j}$. Firstly, $CP^{EIU}_{C,m,j}$ is constructed using two inputs, prices and weights. The average price of item i in city m of country C, $P_{C,m,i}$, used in the calculation of these indices are the same as those described in Sections 2.4 and 2.6 of Chapter 2.

As for the weights data, normalised weight of each item based on its respective ACI Consumption Category, $\omega_{C,i}$, is employed instead. $\omega_{C,i}$ is obtained by dividing the weight as described in Section 3.4.2 with the sum of all the weights of items belonging to the same consumption category. In mathematical form, $\omega_{C,i} = \frac{w_{C,i}}{\sum_{i \in j} w_{C,i}}$. In the example in Box 3.1, there are only two items within the Food & Non-alcoholic Beverages consumption category, bread and coffee. The normalised weight of bread will therefore be equal to the weight of bread divided by the sum of weights of bread and coffee. As a result, the normalised weights of all items within the same consumption category will sum to unity $\left(\text{i.e.,} \sum_{i=1}^{n_j} \omega_{C,i} = 1\right)$. Note that the normalised weight of each item, $\omega_{C,i}$, is also country-specific as the weights reflect the different consumption patterns of ordinary residents in each country. We can then combine $P_{C,m,i}$ with their respective normalised weights, $\omega_{C,i}$, to obtain $CP^{EIU}_{C,m,j}$ using Equation 3.5.2.

$$CP^{EIU}_{C,m,j} = \sum_{i=1}^{n_j} P_{C,m,i} \times \omega_{C,i} \tag{3.5.2}$$

where

m = city;

C = the country where city m is located in;

i = item;

j = ACI Consumption Category of which item i is in;

n_j = number of items in ACI Consumption Category j;

$P_{C,m,i}$ = average price of item i in city m of country C;

$\omega_{C,i}$ = normalised weight of item i based on its ACI Consumption Category for country C.

We can understand $CP^{EIU}_{C,m,j}$ as the cost of consuming all goods and services enjoyed by the expatriates that are under that particular ACI Consumption Category j by ordinary residents but with ordinary residents' own consumption patterns.

As the EIU data are reflective of the prices and consumption behaviours of the expatriates at the city level while World Bank ICP data are indicative of that of ordinary residents at the national level, some adjustment factors need to be introduced to $CP_{C,m,j}^{EIU}$ in order to construct the ACI Consumption Category j Index for Ordinary Residents. We thus use two adjustment factors, namely $NP_{C,j}^{ICP}$ and $NP_{C,j}^{EIU}$.

For the first adjustment factor, $NP_{C,j}^{ICP}$, it is constructed using data from the ICP which include both the nominal expenditure per capita and real expenditure per capita for each country as well as the world. All data used are denominated in US dollar and $NP_{C,j}^{ICP}$ is defined in Equation 3.5.3.

$$NP_{C,j}^{ICP} = \frac{\text{index of nominal expenditure per capita on ACI Consumption Category j for country C}}{\text{index of real expenditure per capita on ACI Consumption Category j for country C}} \tag{3.5.3}$$

where

C = country;

$$\text{index of nominal expenditure per capita on ACI Consumption Category j for country C} = \frac{\text{nominal expenditure per capita on ACI Consumption Category j for country C}}{\text{nominal expenditure per capita on ACI Consumption Category j of the world}};$$

$$\text{index of real expenditure per capita on ACI Consumption Category j for country C} = \frac{\text{real expenditure per capita on ACI Consumption Category j for country C}}{\text{real expenditure per capita on ACI Consumption Category j of the world}}.$$

$NP_{C,j}^{ICP}$ can be understood as the price level per unit real consumption of ACI Consumption Category j for ordinary residents living in country C. In other words, it is the cost of consuming ACI Consumption Category j for ordinary residents in country C based on the ICP survey. This adjustment factor is multiplied to $CP_{C,m,j}^{EIU}$ to introduce the cost of consuming ACI Consumption Category j for ordinary residents based on ICP survey. The constraint of this adjustment factor is that it is available at national level only.

Since the ICP survey is conducted every six years, we construct $NP_{C,j}^{ICP}$ for 2006 to 2010 and 2012 to 2013 by taking into account extra information about exchange rates and inflation rates, which reflect the key factors affecting the comparison of the costs of various ACI Consumption Categories for ordinary residents living in different countries. $NP_{C,j}^{ICP}$ in 2006 to 2010 are thus constructed in Equation 3.5.4.

$$NP_{C,T}^{ICP} = NP_{C,2005}^{ICP} \times \frac{\text{Exchange Rate}_{C,2005}}{\text{Exchange Rate}_{C,T}} \times \prod_{t=2006}^{T} \left(1 + \text{Inflation rate}_{C,t}\right) \forall T \in (2006, 2007, 2008, 2009, \text{and } 2010) \tag{3.5.4}$$

where

C = country;

T = year;

$NP^{ICP}_{C,j,T} = NP^{ICP}_{C,j}$ in year T;

Inflation rate$_{C,t}$ = yearly average inflation rate for country C in year t;
Exchange Rate$_{C,T}$ = yearly average exchange rate between country C and the United States in year T (expressed as local currency unit per US dollar).

For example, if we want to construct $NP^{ICP}_{C,j,2007}$ (i.e. the $NP^{ICP}_{C,j}$ for country C in 2007), we will first need to multiply $NP^{ICP}_{C,j,2005}$ by the 2005 exchange rate between country C and the United States (expressed as local currency unit per US dollar), then multiply it with the cumulative inflation rate between 2005 to 2007, and lastly divide it by the 2007 exchange rate between country C and the United States (expressed as local currency unit per US dollar). As mentioned above, we can understand $NP^{ICP}_{C,j}$ as the cost of consuming ACI Consumption Category j for ordinary residents in country C based on the ICP survey. As such, $NP^{ICP}_{C,j,2005}$ can be understood as the cost of consuming ACI Consumption Category j for ordinary residents in 2005, calculated based on US dollar, so that we have a common basis for comparison. This figure is thus subjected to the 2005 exchange rate between country C and the United States. In order for us to construct $NP^{ICP}_{C,j,2007}$, we will need to remove the effect of exchange rate in 2005 and at the same time introduce the effect of exchange rate in 2007. Also, during the 2005 to 2007 period, inflation rates will affect the cost of consuming ACI Consumption Category j for ordinary residents. We have therefore incorporated the cumulative inflation rate into the equation as well. The inflation rates, nominal expenditure per capita on ACI Consumption Category j and real expenditure per capita on ACI Consumption Category j used are described in Section 3.4.1.

By applying the same rationale, $NP^{ICP}_{C,j}$ in 2012 and 2013 can be constructed using the following Equation 3.5.5.

$$NP^{ICP}_{C,j,T} = NP^{ICP}_{C,j,2011} \times \frac{\text{Exchange Rate}_{C,2011}}{\text{Exchange Rate}_{C,T}} \times \prod_{t=2012}^{T} \left(1 + \text{Inflation rate}_{C,t}\right) \forall T \in (2012 \text{ and } 2013) \tag{3.5.5}$$

where
C = country;
T = year;
$NP^{ICP}_{C,j,T} = NP^{ICP}_{C,j}$ in year T;

Inflation rate$_{C,t}$ = yearly average inflation rate for country C in year t;
Exchange Rate$_{C,T}$ = yearly average exchange rate between country C and the United States in year T (expressed as local currency unit per US dollar).

Since the $NP^{ICP}_{C,j}$ for the period 2006–2010 are calculated based on $NP^{ICP}_{C,j,2005}$, while the $NP^{ICP}_{C,j}$ for the period 2012–2013 are calculated based on $NP^{ICP}_{C,j,2011}$, we might expect to see some break in trend for the results between 2010 and 2011. The reasons for this observation have been discussed in the earlier Section 3.4.2 of this chapter.

As for the second adjustment factor, $NP^{EIU}_{C,j}$, it is constructed based on $CP^{EIU}_{C,m,j}$ as defined in Equation 3.5.2 using the following Equation 3.5.6.

$$NP^{EIU}_{C,j} = \frac{1}{N_C} \sum_{m \in c} CP^{EIU}_{C,m,j} \tag{3.5.6}$$

where
m = city;
C = the country where city m is located in;
N_C = number of cities in country C;
$CP^{EIU}_{C,m,j}$ is as defined in Equation 3.5.2.

$NP^{EIU}_{C,j}$ is the mean value of $CP^{EIU}_{C,m,j}$ from all cities within country C. It can be understood as a proxy for the general level of $CP^{EIU}_{C,m,j}$ in country C. In other words, the cost incurred by ordinary residents living in country C for consuming all goods and services under that particular consumption category based on the EIU data. In the calculation of ACI Consumption Category j Index for Ordinary Residents, this adjustment factor is used to divide $CP^{EIU}_{C,m,j}$. This will serve to offset the effect of using expatriates' consumption basket as well as the effect of using national level data.

Therefore, the two adjustment factors, $NP^{ICP}_{C,j}$ and $NP^{EIU}_{C,j}$, are applied to $CP^{EIU}_{C,m,j}$ using Equation 3.5.1 to construct the ACI Consumption Category j Index for Ordinary Residents in each city.

ACI Consumption Category j Index for Ordinary Residents in city m =

$$\frac{CP^{EIU}_{C,m,j} \times \dfrac{NP^{ICP}_{C,j}}{NP^{EIU}_{C,j}}}{CP^{EIU}_{US,NY,j} \times \dfrac{NP^{ICP}_{US,j}}{NP^{EIU}_{US,j}}} \tag{3.5.1}$$

Similar to the previous section on constructing the Cost of Living Index and Ranking for Ordinary Residents, there is also an alternative approach to parse Equation 3.5.1 and interpret its structure, which will offer another vantage point from which we can gain a clearer view on the issue of controlling for utility in constructing the 10 ACI Consumption Categories Indices and Rankings for Ordinary Residents. As mentioned previously, the term $NP^{ICP}_{C,j}$ can be understood as the price level per unit real consumption in consumption category j for ordinary residents living in country C based on data from ICP surveys, which is standardised against the world level as defined by Equation 3.5.3. Since the term $NP^{ICP}_{C,j}$ can be construed as the standardised price per unit real consumption of goods and services in consumption category j for ordinary residents in country C, it actually in itself forms a measure of the cost of living for ordinary residents in consumption category j while controlling for the utility level, or standard of living, across the countries for which $NP_{C,j}^{ICP}$ is calculated, as it pins down the level of such consumption in consumption category j at a fixed amount across countries.

Had the ICP achieved a finer degree of granularity by conducting their surveys and compiling the data at the city level (at least in the representative cities in our study per each country with each city being a statistical unit), we could have been able to exclusively use the ICP data to construct the 10 ACI Consumption Categories Indices for Ordinary Residents in cities around the world. Since the ICP data are only available at national level in reality, we can still make use of such data by incorporating them into the construction of the 10 ACI Consumption Categories Indices for Ordinary Residents, as reflected in the inclusion of the term $NP_{C,j}^{ICP}$ into Equation 3.5.1, while integrating it with some relevant factors to arrive at a practical proxy for the variations among cities within each country in terms of the cost of living for each consumption category for ordinary residents. The inclusion of the ratio between $CP_{C,m,j}^{EIU}$ and $NP_{C,j}^{EIU}$ into Equation 3.5.1 can be viewed as providing such a proxy for generating the city level variations in a specific country C.

As defined by Equation 3.5.2, $CP_{C,m,j}^{EIU}$ gives a measure of the cost of living index for consumption category j for ordinary residents with their own consumption patterns but using the prices of the consumption items for expatriates as in the EIU data, assuming such data for prices will generally correlate with the data for prices of the counterpart items in that category of the consumption basket for ordinary residents in each city. As defined by Equation 3.5.6, $NP_{C,j}^{EIU}$ is simply the average of the values of $CP_{C,m,j}^{EIU}$ for all the cities within country C. Thus, the ratio between $CP_{C,m,j}^{EIU}$ and $NP_{C,j}^{EIU}$, i.e. the former divided by the latter, can be viewed as an indicator of how high the cost of living in terms of consumption category j is for ordinary residents in a particular city as compared to the national average, as a value of one for this ratio will mean that city m is on par with the national average level of country C in terms of the cost of living in consumption category j for ordinary residents, and a value above or below one will imply that city m has higher or lower cost of living in terms of consumption category j for ordinary residents as compared to the national average level of country C respectively. Combining this ratio with the term $NP_{C,j}^{ICP}$ as in Equation 3.5.1, therefore, will provide an assessment of the cost of living in terms of each consumption category for ordinary residents for each city, utilising the available relevant datasets from both ICP at the national level and EIU at the city level.

To the extent that the term $NP_{C,j}^{ICP}$ controls for utility across countries as it is in essence a standardised price index for per unit real consumption in consumption category j, and that the introduction of the ratio between $CP_{C,m,j}^{EIU}$ and $NP_{C,j}^{EIU}$ proxies for the variations among cities within a country while maintaining such controlling for utility, the 10 ACI Consumption Categories Indices for Ordinary Residents as constructed in Equation 3.5.1 to allow for the comparison of cost of living for ordinary residents in each consumption category across cities around the world also controls for utility. Putting in explicit efforts to control for utility or standard of living when conceptualising a framework and designing a methodology for comparing cost of living is of vital importance no matter whether such cost of living comparison is done at the overall level or consumption category level. The reasons for such importance have already been discussed in the previous section, which are all relevant for the methodology for constructing the 10 ACI Consumption Categories Indices for Ordinary Residents and will not be repeated here.

The ACI Consumption Category j Index for Ordinary Residents reflects the cost of consuming a specific Consumption Category by ordinary residents living in city m relative to those in New York. For example, the Transport Index for Ordinary Residents in city m illustrates the transport cost for ordinary residents living in city m relative to their counterparts in New York. With New York chosen as the base city, the ACI Consumption Category j Index for Ordinary Residents in New York will always be 100.00.

Likewise, the ACI Consumption Category j Ranking for Ordinary Residents is obtained by arranging its corresponding ACI Consumption Category j Index in a descending order. Cities which rank at the top of the ranking are more expensive than those at the bottom. A simple numerical example is provided in Box 3.2 to illustrate the process of constructing the 10 ACI Consumption Categories Indices and Rankings for Ordinary Residents.

As in the case of constructing the Cost of Living Index and Ranking for Ordinary Residents, the ACI methodology in constructing the 10 ACI Consumption Categories Indices and Rankings for Ordinary Residents has the same advantage that the rankings generated will not be sensitive to the choice of base city. Whether the base city is chosen to be New York, Beijing, Tokyo or any other city, the rankings for each consumption category will remain the same. The importance of the insensitivity of rankings to the choice of base city lies in the fact that it underpins the objectivity of the research and is based on the same reasons as discussed in the previous section, and therefore will not be restated here.

Box 3.2: Example for Constructing the 10 ACI Consumption Categories Indices and Rankings for Ordinary Residents

Following the example provided in Box 3.1 of Section 3.4.2, we could calculate the indices for two ACI Consumption Categories, namely Food & Non-alcoholic Beverages and Clothing, for Adelaide, Chicago, Sydney and New York.

The nominal and real expenditure per capita for each ACI Consumption Category in Australia, United States and the world are as follows.

Consumption Category	Data Series	In US$		
		Australia	United States	World
Food & Non-alcoholic Beverages	Nominal expenditure per capita	3,643.00	2,238.00	912.00
	Real expenditure per capita	2,164.00	2,238.00	1,018.00
Clothing	Nominal expenditure per capita	1,181.00	1,173.00	286.00
	Real expenditure per capita	773.00	1,173.00	352.00

(*Continued*)

Box 3.2: (*Continued*)

Based on the calculations in Box 2.1 of Section 2.6 in Chapter 2, the average price of item i in city m of country C, $P_{C,m,i}$, is as follows (refer to step (1) of Box 2.1 for details on how to calculate $P_{C,m,i}$).

$$P_{\text{Australia, Adelaide, White bread}} = 4.60$$

$$P_{\text{Australia, Adelaide, Instant coffee}} = 7.30$$

$$P_{\text{Australia, Adelaide, Dress}} = 221.00$$

$$P_{\text{Australia, Adelaide, Men's shoes}} = 264.00$$

$$P_{\text{United States, Chicago, White bread}} = 6.00$$

$$P_{\text{United States, Chicago, Instant coffee}} = 5.00$$

$$P_{\text{United States, Chicago, Dress}} = 500.00$$

$$P_{\text{United States, Chicago, Men's shoes}} = 256.00$$

$$P_{\text{Australia, Sydney, White bread}} = 4.70$$

$$P_{\text{Australia, Sydney, Instant coffee}} = 7.00$$

$$P_{\text{Australia, Sydney, Dress}} = 319.00$$

$$P_{\text{Australia, Sydney, Men's shoes}} = 293.00$$

$$P_{\text{United States, New York, White bread}} = 8.10$$

$$P_{\text{United States, New York, Instant coffee}} = 5.90$$

$$P_{\text{United States, New York, Dress}} = 367.50$$

$$P_{\text{United States, New York, Men's shoes}} = 327.50$$

Also, the weight of each item for ordinary residents in Australia and United States is as follows.

Item, i	**Weight of item i in Australia, $W_{\text{Australia},i}$**	**Weight of item i in United States, $W_{\text{United States},i}$**
White bread, 1kg	0.30	0.20
Instant coffee, 125g	0.05	0.06
Dress, daytime	0.45	0.50
Men's shoes, business wear	0.20	0.24

Hence, the steps involved in the calculation of indices for each ACI Consumption Category and producing rankings for ordinary residents are as follows.

(1) Compute the normalised weight of each item based on its respective ACI Consumption Category.

$$\omega_{\text{Australia, White bread}} = \frac{0.30}{(0.30+0.05)} = 0.86$$

(*Continued*)

Box 3.2: (*Continued*)

$$\omega_{\text{Australia,Instant coffee}} = \frac{0.05}{(0.30+0.05)} = 0.14$$

$$\omega_{\text{Australia,Dress}} = \frac{0.45}{(0.45+0.20)} = 0.69$$

$$\omega_{\text{Australia,Men's shoes}} = \frac{0.20}{(0.45+0.20)} = 0.31$$

$$\omega_{\text{United States, White bread}} = \frac{0.20}{(0.20+0.06)} = 0.77$$

$$\omega_{\text{United States, Instant coffee}} = \frac{0.06}{(0.20+0.06)} = 0.23$$

$$\omega_{\text{United States, Dress}} = \frac{0.50}{(0.50+0.24)} = 0.68$$

$$\omega_{\text{United States, Men's shoes}} = \frac{0.24}{(0.50+0.24)} = 0.32$$

(2) Compute the $CP^{EIU}_{C,m,j}$ for each city.

$$CP^{EIU}_{\text{Australia, Adelaide, Food \& Non-alcoholic Beverages}} = 4.60\times0.86+7.30\times0.14 = 4.99$$

$$CP^{EIU}_{\text{Australia, Adelaide, Clothing}} = 221.00\times0.69+264.00\times0.31 = 234.23$$

$$CP^{EIU}_{\text{United States, Chicago, Food \& Non-alcoholic Beverages}} = 6.00\times0.77+5.00\times0.23 = 5.77$$

$$CP^{EIU}_{\text{United States, Chicago, Clothing}} = 500.00\times0.68+256.00\times0.32 = 420.86$$

$$CP^{EIU}_{\text{Australia, Sydney, Food \& Non-alcoholic Beverages}} = 4.70\times0.86+7.00\times0.14 = 5.03$$

$$CP^{EIU}_{\text{Australia, Sydney, Clothing}} = 319.00\times0.69+293.00\times0.31 = 311.00$$

$$CP^{EIU}_{\text{United States, New York, Food \& Non-alcoholic Beverages}} = 8.10\times0.77+5.90\times0.23 = 7.59$$

$$CP^{EIU}_{\text{United States, New York, Clothing}} = 367.50\times0.68+327.50\times0.32 = 354.53$$

(3) Compute the indices for nominal and real expenditure per capita on each ACI Consumption Category in each country.

Index of nominal expenditure per capita on Food & *Non-alcoholic Beverages for Australia*

$$= \frac{3,643.00}{912.00} = 3.9945$$

Index of real expenditure per capita on Food & *Non-alcoholic Beverages for Australia*

$$= \frac{2,164.00}{1,018.00} = 2.1257$$

(*Continued*)

Box 3.2: (*Continued*)

Index of nominal expenditure per capita on Food & *Non-alcoholic Beverages for United States*

$$= \frac{2,238.00}{912.00} = 2.4539$$

Index of real expenditure per capita on Food & *Non-alcoholic Beverages for United States*

$$= \frac{2,238.00}{1,018.00} = 2.1984$$

$$\text{Index of nominal expenditure per capita on Clothing for Australia} = \frac{1,181.00}{286.00} = 4.1294$$

$$\text{Index of real expenditure per capita on Clothing for Australia} = \frac{773.00}{352.00} = 2.1960$$

$$\text{Index of nominal expenditure per capita on Clothing for United States} = \frac{1,173.00}{286.00} = 4.1014$$

$$\text{Index of real expenditure per capita on Clothing for United States} = \frac{1,173.00}{352.00} = 3.3324$$

(4) Compute the first adjustment factor, $NP^{ICP}_{C,j}$, for each ACI Consumption Category in each country.

$$NP^{ICP}_{\text{Australia, Food \& Non-alcoholic Beverages}} = \frac{3.9945}{2.1257} = 1.8791,$$

$$NP^{ICP}_{\text{United States, Food \& Non-alcoholic Beverages}} = \frac{2.4539}{2.1984} = 1.1162,$$

$$NP^{ICP}_{\text{Australia, Clothing}} = \frac{4.1294}{2.1960} = 1.8804,$$

$$NP^{ICP}_{\text{United States, Clothing}} = \frac{4.1014}{3.3324} = 1.2308.$$

(5) Compute the second adjustment factor, $NP^{EIU}_{C,j}$, for each ACI Consumption Category in each country.

$$NP^{EIU}_{\text{Australia, Food \& Non-alcoholic Beverages}} = \frac{1}{2} \times (4.99 + 5.03) = 5.01$$

$$NP^{EIU}_{\text{United States, Food \& Non-alcoholic Beverages}} = \frac{1}{2} \times (5.77 + 7.59) = 6.68$$

$$NP^{EIU}_{\text{Australia, Clothing}} = \frac{1}{2} \times (234.23 + 311.00) = 272.62$$

$$NP^{EIU}_{\text{United States, Clothing}} = \frac{1}{2} \times (420.86 + 354.53) = 387.70$$

(*Continued*)

Box 3.2: (*Continued*)

(6) Compute the ACI Consumption Categories Indices for Ordinary Residents in each city.

Food & Non-alcoholic Beverages index for Ordinary Residents in Adelaide

$$= \frac{4.99 \times \frac{1.8791}{5.01}}{7.59 \times \frac{1.1162}{6.68}} \times 100 = 147.50,$$

Food & Non-alcoholic Beverages index for Ordinary Residents in Chicago

$$= \frac{5.77 \times \frac{1.1162}{6.68}}{7.59 \times \frac{1.1162}{6.68}} \times 100 = 75.99,$$

Food & Non-alcoholic Beverages index for Ordinary Residents in Sydney

$$= \frac{5.03 \times \frac{1.8791}{5.01}}{7.59 \times \frac{1.1162}{6.68}} \times 100 = 148.77,$$

Food & Non-alcoholic Beverages index for Ordinary Residents in New York

$$= \frac{7.59 \times \frac{1.1162}{6.68}}{7.59 \times \frac{1.1162}{6.68}} \times 100 = 100.00,$$

Clothing Index for Ordinary Residents in Adelaide

$$= \frac{234.23 \times \frac{1.8804}{272.62}}{354.53 \times \frac{1.2308}{387.70}} \times 100 = 143.55,$$

Clothing Index for Ordinary Residents in Chicago

$$= \frac{420.86 \times \frac{1.2308}{387.70}}{354.53 \times \frac{1.2308}{387.70}} \times 100 = 118.71,$$

Clothing Index for Ordinary Residents in Sydney

$$= \frac{311.00 \times \frac{1.8804}{272.62}}{354.53 \times \frac{1.2308}{387.70}} \times 100 = 190.60,$$

(*Continued*)

Box 3.2: (*Continued*)

Clothing Index for Ordinary Residents in New York

$$= \frac{354.53 \times \frac{1.2308}{387.70}}{354.53 \times \frac{1.2308}{387.70}} \times 100 = 100.00.$$

(7) Generate the ACI Consumption Categories Rankings for Ordinary Residents.
Food & Non-alcoholic Beverages Ranking

Rank	City	Country	Food & Non-alcoholic Beverages Index for Ordinary Residents
1	Sydney	Australia	148.77
2	Adelaide	Australia	147.50
3	New York	United States	100.00
4	Chicago	United States	75.99

Clothing Ranking

Rank	City	Country	Clothing Index for Ordinary Residents
1	Sydney	Australia	190.60
2	Adelaide	Australia	143.55
3	Chicago	United States	118.71
4	New York	United States	100.00

Source: Asia Competitiveness Institute

3.6 Constructing the Wages Index and Ranking for Ordinary Residents

This section details the methodology and data used to derive the Wages Index and Ranking for Ordinary Residents in 103 cities. Both Section 3.6.1 and 3.6.2 provide detailed descriptions of the raw data and data processing which are relevant to the calculation of the index. In particular, the gross average nominal monthly wages received by ordinary residents in the 103 cities are discussed in Section 3.6.1 while Section 3.6.2 focuses on the mean weekly hours actually worked. This is followed by Section 3.6.3 which describes the steps involved in computing the Wages Index and producing the Ranking for Ordinary Residents. A numerical example is also provided in Section 3.6.3 to illustrate the methodology used.

3.6.1 Gross Average Nominal Monthly Wages

The gross average nominal monthly wages in local currency units are retrieved from the ILO database.[6] As the ILO database compiles data from various agencies, multiple sources might be available for the same data. In such cases, the average value of all available sources will be calculated and used in the computation of Wages Index for Ordinary Residents. The proxy for missing data are projected based on the average wages growth rates of all years with available data.

3.6.2 Mean Weekly Hours Actually Worked

The mean weekly hours actually worked are retrieved from the ILO database. As several series may be available for one data at the same time, the selection of series is based on the following priority:

i. Aggregate categories of economic activities;
ii. Broad sector;
iii. International Standard Industrial Classification of all economic activities, Revision 4 (ISIC Rev.4)
iv. International Standard Industrial Classification of all economic activities, Revision 3.1 (ISIC Rev.3.1)
v. International Standard Industrial Classification of all economic activities, Revision 2 (ISIC Rev.2)
vi. Mean weekly working hours for various economic activities (subject to data availability) will be collected and the average of these data will be computed.

However, some data are still missing in the ILO database. For countries with at least one year of data, the proxies for the missing years are based on the closest year with available data. In the case that the missing data is sandwiched equally in terms of time distance between two years with available data, the more recent value is adopted as the proxy. Data for Kuwait and Kenya are unavailable throughout the years from 2005 to 2013. United Arab Emirates data are used as the proxy for Kuwait. This is because United Arab Emirates is an Arab state with the closest Gross Domestic Product (GDP) per capita (based on 2012 data from World Bank) to that of Kuwait. On the other hand, South Africa data are used as the proxy for Kenya since South Africa has the closest GDP per capita (based on 2012 data from World Bank) to that of Kenya within Africa.

3.6.3 Computation of Wages Index and Ranking for Ordinary Residents

$$\textit{Wages Index for Ordinary Residents in city } m = \frac{\text{gross hourly wage}_{\text{C,m}}}{\text{gross hourly wage}_{\text{US,NY}}} \times 100 \qquad (3.6.1)$$

[6]The gross average nominal monthly wages in local currency units are retrieved from the ILO database on July 16th, 2012. This data may be subject to revision.

where
m = city;
C = the country where city m is located in;
NY = New York;
US = United States;

$$\text{gross hourly wage}_{C,m} = \frac{\text{monthly wages}_C \times 12}{\text{mean weekly hours actually worked}_C \times 52} \quad (3.6.2);$$

monthly wages$_C$ = monthly wages in country C;
mean weekly hours actually worked$_C$ = mean weekly hours actually worked in country C.

The Wages Index for Ordinary Residents is constructed using two inputs, the monthly wages and the mean weekly hours actually worked. The data for the first input, the gross average nominal monthly wages, are obtained from the ILO database. Similar to the prices of individual items which are employed in the calculations of the Cost of Living Index for Ordinary Residents, the monthly wages are converted from their respective local currencies to US dollar. As mentioned in Section 3.2 of this chapter, to smooth the effects of daily fluctuations in the currency market, we use the yearly average exchange rate which is calculated based on the daily average exchange rates retrieved from the Bloomberg Terminal. All exchange rates used in this study are listed in Appendix 3.

As for the second input for the Wages Index for Ordinary Residents, namely the mean weekly hours actually worked, it is also obtained from the ILO database. In particular, the "mean weekly hours actually worked per employed person by sex and economic activity" data series is employed in our study. The constraint of these two sets of data is that it is available at national level only. Hence, all the cities of the same country share a common value.

The monthly wages and mean weekly hours actually worked are combined using the following Equation 3.6.2 to compute the gross hourly wage in each city.

$$\text{gross hourly wage}_{C,m} = \frac{\text{monthly wages}_C \times 12}{\text{mean weekly hours actually worked}_C \times 52} \quad (3.6.2)$$

The gross hourly wage of each city is then divided by the gross hourly wage of New York to obtain the Wages Index for Ordinary Residents as shown in Equation 3.6.1.

$$\textit{Wages Index for Ordinary Residents in city } m = \frac{\text{gross hourly wage}_{C,m}}{\text{gross hourly wage}_{US,NY}} \times 100 \quad (3.6.1)$$

The Wages Index for Ordinary Residents, as shown in Equation 3.6.1, reflects the gross hourly wage earned by ordinary residents in the city of interest relative to that of their counterparts in the base city. With New York chosen as the base city, the Wages Index for Ordinary Residents in New York will always be 100.00.

Lastly, the Wages Ranking for Ordinary Residents can be generated by arranging the Wages Index for Ordinary Residents in each city in a descending order. A city whereby ordinary residents receive higher (lower) wage will have a larger (smaller) Wages Index and thus occupy a higher (lower) position in the Wages Ranking for Ordinary Residents.

A simple numerical example is provided in Box 3.3 to illustrate the process of constructing the Wages Index and Ranking for Ordinary Residents.

Box 3.3: Example for Constructing the Wages Index and Ranking for Ordinary Residents

Continuing the example provided in Box 3.1 of Section 3.4.2, we will now illustrate the computations of Wages Indices and thus Ranking for Ordinary Residents in Adelaide, Chicago, Sydney and New York. Assume the monthly wages and mean weekly hours actually worked of ordinary residents in Australia and United States are as follows.

	Australia	**United States**
Monthly wages in US$	5,120.00	3,300.00
Mean weekly hours actually worked	33.9	38.6

Hence, the steps involved in the calculation of Wages Index and producing a ranking for ordinary residents are as follows.

(1) Compute the gross hourly wage in each city.

$$\text{gross hourly wage}_{\text{Australia, Adelaide}} = \frac{5{,}120.00 \times 12}{33.9 \times 52} = 34.85,$$

$$\text{gross hourly wage}_{\text{United States, Chicago}} = \frac{3{,}300.00 \times 12}{38.6 \times 52} = 19.73,$$

$$\text{gross hourly wage}_{\text{Australia, Sydney}} = \frac{5{,}120.00 \times 12}{33.9 \times 52} = 34.85,$$

$$\text{gross hourly wage}_{\text{United States, New York}} = \frac{3{,}300.00 \times 12}{38.6 \times 52} = 19.73.$$

(2) Compute the Wages Index for Ordinary Residents in each city.

$$\text{Wages Index for Ordinary Residents in Adelaide} = \frac{34.85}{19.73} \times 100 = 176.66,$$

$$\text{Wages Index for Ordinary Residents in Chicago} = \frac{19.73}{19.73} \times 100 = 100.00,$$

$$\text{Wages Index for Ordinary Residents in Sydney} = \frac{34.85}{19.73} \times 100 = 176.66,$$

$$\text{Wages Index for Ordinary Residents in New York} = \frac{19.73}{19.73} \times 100 = 100.00.$$

(*Continued*)

Box 3.3: (*Continued*)

(3) Generate the Wages Ranking for Ordinary Residents.

Rank	City	Country	Wages Index for Ordinary Residents
1	Adelaide	Australia	176.66
1	Sydney	Australia	176.66
3	Chicago	United States	100.00
3	New York	United States	100.00

Source: Asia Competitiveness Institute

3.7 Constructing the Purchasing Power Index and Ranking for Ordinary Residents

$$\textit{Purchasing Power Index for Ordinary Residents in city } m = \frac{\text{Wages Index for Ordinary Residents}_{C,m}}{\text{Cost of Living Index for Ordinary Residents}_{C,m}} \times 100 \tag{3.7.1}$$

where
m = city;
C = the country where city m is located in;
Wages Index for Ordinary Residents$_{C,m}$ is as defined in Equation 3.6.1;
Cost of Living Index for Ordinary Residents$_{C,m}$ is as defined in Equation 3.4.1.

The Purchasing Power Index for Ordinary Residents is constructed using two inputs, the Wages Index for Ordinary Residents as defined in Equation 3.6.1 of Section 3.6.3 and the Cost of Living Index for Ordinary Residents as defined in Equation 3.4.1 in Section 3.4.2 of this chapter. It can be obtained by simply dividing the Wages Index with the Cost of Living Index, as shown in Equation 3.7.1.

We can understand the purchasing power as the number of baskets of goods and services that the ordinary residents can enjoy if they work for an hour. A higher purchasing power is thus more desirable as ordinary residents are able to enjoy more goods and services given that they work for an hour. The Purchasing Power Index for Ordinary Residents reflects the purchasing power of ordinary residents in the city of interest relative to that of their counterparts in the base city. With New York chosen as the base city, the Purchasing Power Index for Ordinary Residents in New York will always be 100.00.

Lastly, the Purchasing Power Ranking for Ordinary Residents can be generated by arranging the Purchasing Power Index for Ordinary Residents in each city in a descending order. A city whereby ordinary residents have higher (lower) purchasing power will have a larger (smaller)

Purchasing Power Index and thus occupy a higher (lower) position in the Purchasing Power Ranking for Ordinary Residents.

A simple numerical example is provided in Box 3.4 to illustrate the process of constructing the Purchasing Power Index and Ranking for Ordinary Residents.

Box 3.4: Example for Constructing the Purchasing Power Index and Ranking for Ordinary Residents

Following the example provided in Boxes 3.1 and 3.3 of Section 3.4.2 and 3.6.3, respectively, we will now illustrate the computations of Purchasing Power Indices and thus Ranking for Ordinary Residents in Adelaide, Chicago, Sydney and New York.

Based on the calculations in Box 3.1 of Section 3.4.2, we know that the Cost of Living Indices for Ordinary Residents in various cities are as follows.

Cost of Living Index for Ordinary Residents in Adelaide = 154.34,
Cost of Living Index for Ordinary Residents in Chicago = 118.39,
Cost of Living Index for Ordinary Residents in Sydney = 204.37,
Cost of Living Index for Ordinary Residents in New York = 100.00.

Also, based on computations done in Box 3.3 of Section 3.6.3, the Wages Indices for Ordinary Residents in these four cities are as follows.

Wages Index for Ordinary Residents in Adelaide = 176.66,
Wages Index for Ordinary Residents in Chicago = 100.00,
Wages Index for Ordinary Residents in Sydney = 176.66,
Wages Index for Ordinary Residents in New York = 100.00.

Therefore, the steps involved in the calculation of Purchasing Power Index and producing a ranking for ordinary residents are as follows.

(1) Compute the Purchasing Power Index for Ordinary Residents in each city.

Purchasing Power Index for Ordinary Residents in Adelaide

$$= \frac{176.66}{154.34} \times 100 = 114.46,$$

Purchasing Power Index for Ordinary Residents in Chicago

$$= \frac{100.00}{118.39} \times 100 = 84.46,$$

Purchasing Power Index for Ordinary Residents in Sydney

$$= \frac{176.66}{204.37} \times 100 = 86.44,$$

Purchasing Power Index for Ordinary Residents in New York

$$= \frac{100.00}{100.00} \times 100 = 100.00.$$

(Continued)

Box 3.4: (*Continued*)

(2) Generate the Purchasing Power Ranking for Ordinary Residents.

Rank	City	Country	Wages Index for Ordinary Residents
1	Adelaide	Australia	114.46
2	New York	United States	100.00
3	Sydney	Australia	86.44
4	Chicago	United States	84.46

Source: Asia Competitiveness Institute

References

World Bank. 2014. *Purchasing Power Parities and Real Expenditures of World Economies: Summary of Results and Findings of the 2011 International Comparison Program.* http://siteresources.worldbank.org/ICPINT/Resources/270056-1183395201801/Summary-of-Results-and-Findings-of-the-2011-International-Comparison-Program.pdf (accessed May 19, 2015).

Chapter 4
Findings on Cost of Living for Expatriates

In this chapter, we discuss the findings on the cost of living rankings for expatriates in the 103 cities over the years from 2005 to 2013. The results are presented in alphabetical order of the cities' names. Each city's results are presented in the figure titled "Cost of Living and 10 Consumption Categories Rankings for Expatriates". The horizontal axis denotes the years in the study period while the vertical axis shows the rankings of a particular city. Rankings range from first to 103rd with first meaning the highest cost and 103rd indicating the lowest cost.

ADELAIDE
Australia

Figure 4.1: Cost of Living and 10 Consumption Categories Rankings for Expatriates in Adelaide, Australia

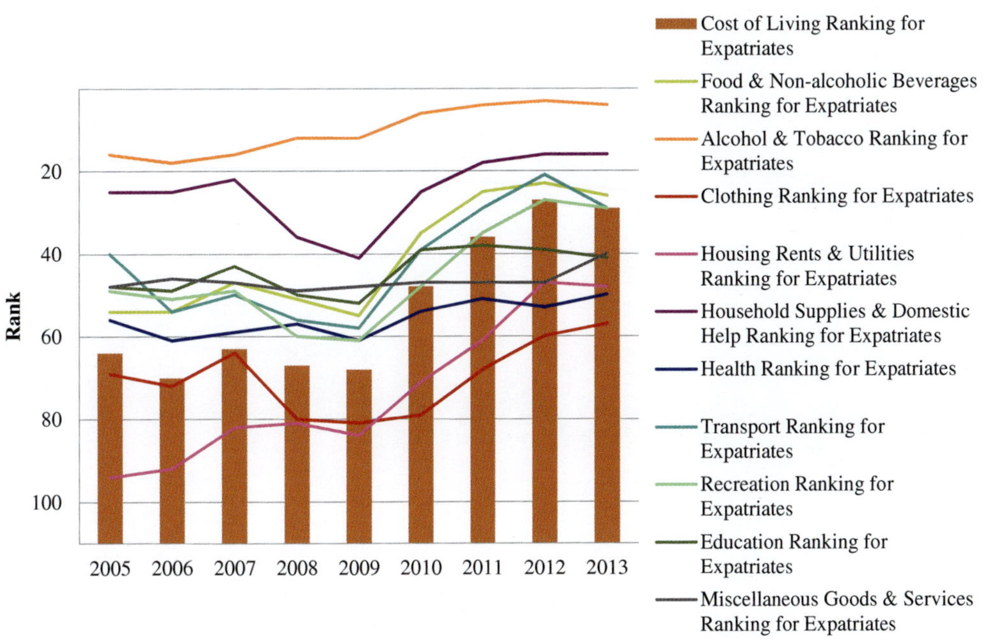

Source: Asia Competitiveness Institute

Adelaide is Australia's fifth most populous city with approximately 1.3 million people. As the capital of South Australia and home to a sizeable manufacturing sector, it saw a significant rise in its Cost of Living Ranking for Expatriates, as denoted by the orange bars, from 64th to 29th between 2005 and 2013 (see Figure 4.1).

Over this period, Adelaide's Housing Rents & Utilities Ranking went up most dramatically from 94th in 2005 to 48th in 2013 although this upward trend appears to be levelling off as good news. Likewise, Food & Non-alcoholic Beverages Ranking jumped 28 places from 54th to 26th over the same period, making it the third highest ranked category in 2013. Transport moved up from 40th to 29th place between 2005 and 2013. Education and Health Ranking climbed seven and six places from 48th to 41st and 56th to 50th, respectively, over the study period. Alcohol & Tobacco Ranking has risen steadily over the years. Consequently in 2013, Adelaide became the fourth most expensive in this category among the 103 cities.

AMMAN
Jordan

Figure 4.2: Cost of Living and 10 Consumption Categories Rankings for Expatriates in Amman, Jordan

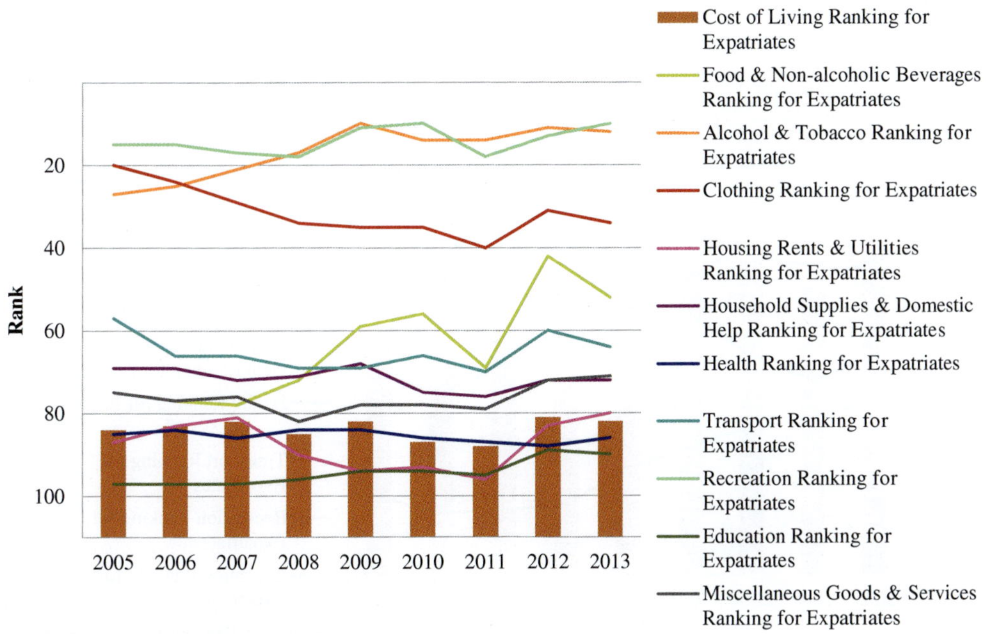

Source: Asia Competitiveness Institute

As the capital of Jordan and one of the most popular locations for multinational corporations to set up their regional offices in the Middle East and North Africa region, it comes as a surprise that Amman's Cost of Living Ranking for Expatriates, as represented by the orange bars, experienced a slight decline from 84th in 2005 to 82nd in 2013 (see Figure 4.2).

In particular, Transport Ranking slipped seven places from 57th to 64th between 2005 and 2013. Health Ranking went down slightly from 85th in 2005 to 86th in 2013, making it the second lowest ranked category in 2013.

Food & Non-alcoholic Beverages Ranking, in contrast, climbed 23 spots from 75th to 52nd over the study period. Housing Rents & Utilities climbed seven places from 87th in 2005 to 80th in 2013. Nonetheless, this category has still remained as one of the more affordable among the 103 cities studied. Education also saw a modest rise in its ranking from 97th to 90th between 2005 and 2013 but it became Amman's lowest ranked category in 2013. Recreation Ranking moved up from 15th in 2005 to 10th in 2013, making it the highest ranked category in 2013.

AMSTERDAM
The Netherlands

Figure 4.3: Cost of Living and 10 Consumption Categories Rankings for Expatriates in Amsterdam, Netherlands

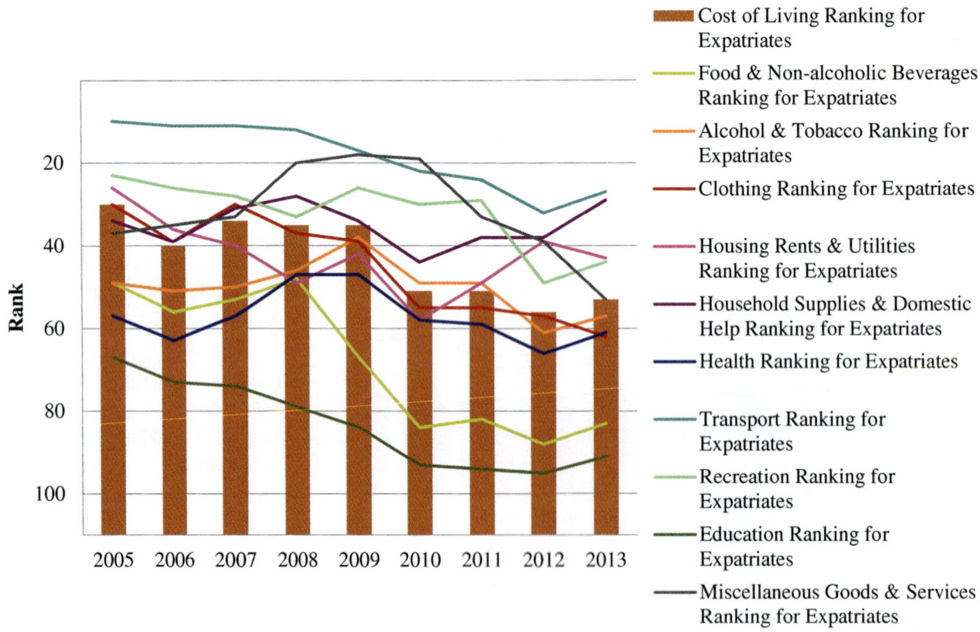

Source: Asia Competitiveness Institute

Known for its picturesque canals and distinct architecture, Amsterdam has been the commercial centre of the Netherlands for centuries and is one of the financial hubs in Europe. The city's Cost of Living Ranking for expatriates, as shown in the orange bars, dropped 23 places from 30th in 2005 to 53rd in 2013 (see Figure 4.3).

Food & Non-alcoholic Beverages and Clothing experienced the most dramatic decline in their rankings among all categories between 2005 and 2013. Food & Non-alcoholic Beverages Ranking slipped 34 spots from 49th to 83rd, while Clothing Ranking fell 32 places from 30th to 62nd over the study period. Education has consistently been the lowest ranked category for Amsterdam, having dropped 24 places from 67th in 2005 to 91st in 2013. Housing Rents & Utilities and Transport Rankings both went down 17 spots from 26th to 43rd and 10th to 27th, respectively, between 2005 and 2013. Nonetheless, Transport became the highest ranked category in 2013.

Household Supplies & Domestic Help was the only category that rose in ranking from 34th in 2005 to 29th in 2013. Consequently, it became the second highest ranked category after Transport in 2013.

ASUNCION
Paraguay

Figure 4.4: Cost of Living and 10 Consumption Categories Rankings for Expatriates in Asuncion, Paraguay

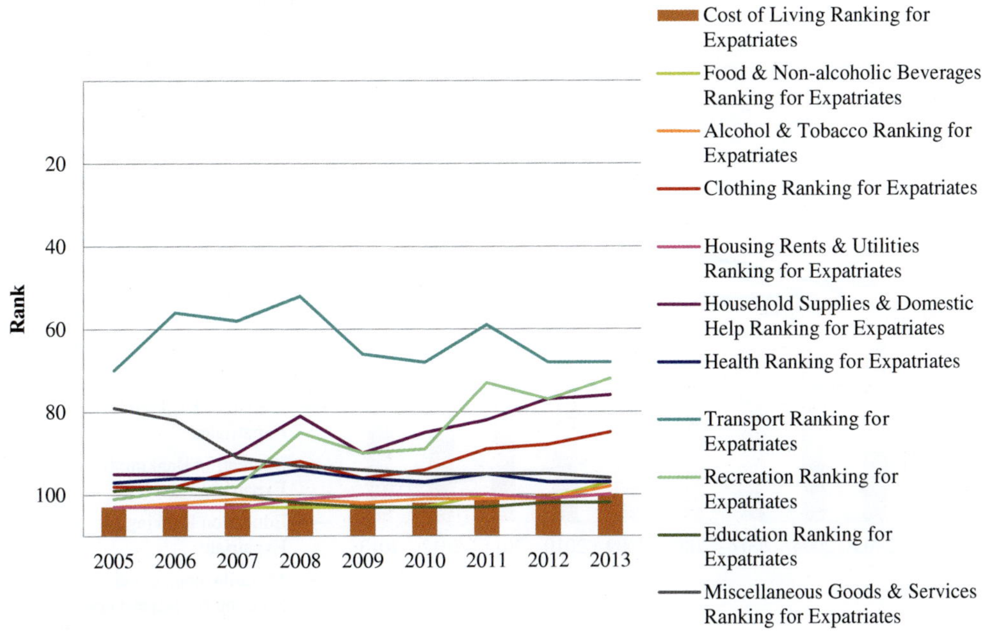

Source: Asia Competitiveness Institute

Asuncion, the capital, and the industrial and cultural centre of Paraguay, has consistently been one of the cheapest for expatriates among the 103 cities studied, despite a slight rise in its Cost of Living Ranking for Expatriates from 103rd in 2005 to 100th in 2013, as denoted by the orange bars (see Figure 4.4).

Education became the lowest ranked category in 2013 as its ranking slipped three places from 99th to 102nd between 2005 and 2013, making Asuncion the second most affordable in this category among the 103 cities studied. While Housing Rents & Utilities Ranking rose from 103rd in 2005 to 100th in 2013, it was the second lowest ranked category in 2013 for Asuncion. Food & Non-alcoholic Beverages Ranking also saw a modest rise from 103rd to 97th over the study period. Health Ranking remained largely unchanged at the 97th place in both 2005 and 2013. Transport has consistently remained as the highest ranked category as its ranking moved up two places from 70th in 2005 to 68th in 2013. Recreation registered the most remarkable rise in ranking as it climbed 29 spots from 101st to 72nd over the study period and consequently became the second highest ranked category in 2013.

ATHENS
Greece

Figure 4.5: Cost of Living and 10 Consumption Categories Rankings for Expatriates in Athens, Greece

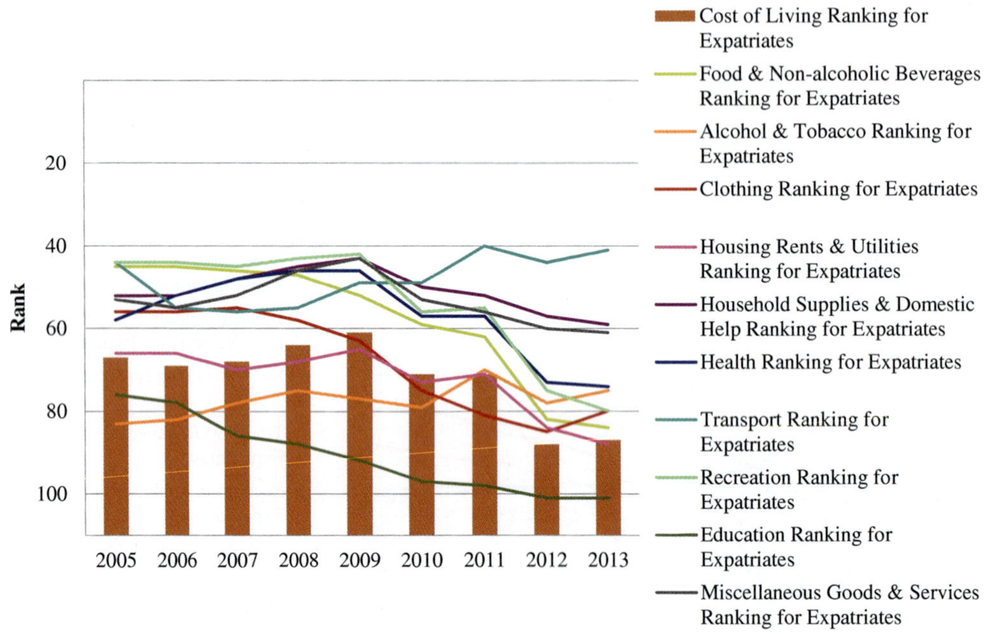

Source: Asia Competitiveness Institute

Widely referred to as the cradle of Western civilisation and the birthplace of democracy, Athens is one of the most fascinating cities in the world. Modern Athens is a cosmopolitan metropolis and the political, cultural and economic centre of Greece. Nonetheless, the city's Cost of Living Ranking for Expatriates, as represented by the orange bars, saw a decline from 67th in 2005 to 87th in 2013 (see Figure 4.5).

Food & Non-alcoholic Beverages saw the most dramatic drop in ranking as it fell 39 places from 45th to 84th between 2005 and 2013. Recreation Ranking slipped 36 spots from 44th to 80th over the same period. Education consistently remained as the lowest ranked category since 2007 as its ranking went down from 76th in 2005 to 101st in 2013, making Athens the third cheapest city in this category in 2013. Housing Rents & Utilities was the second lowest ranked category in 2013 as its ranking fell 22 places from 66th to 88th over the study period. Health Ranking declined from 58th in 2005 to 74th in 2013.

Alcohol & Tobacco and Transport were the only two categories that rose in rankings between 2005 and 2013. Transport became Athens's highest ranked category in 2013 as its ranking jumped to 41st from 44th in 2005. Alcohol & Tobacco Ranking climbed eight places from 83rd in 2005 to 75th in 2013.

ATLANTA
United States

Figure 4.6: Cost of Living and 10 Consumption Categories Rankings for Expatriates in Atlanta, United States

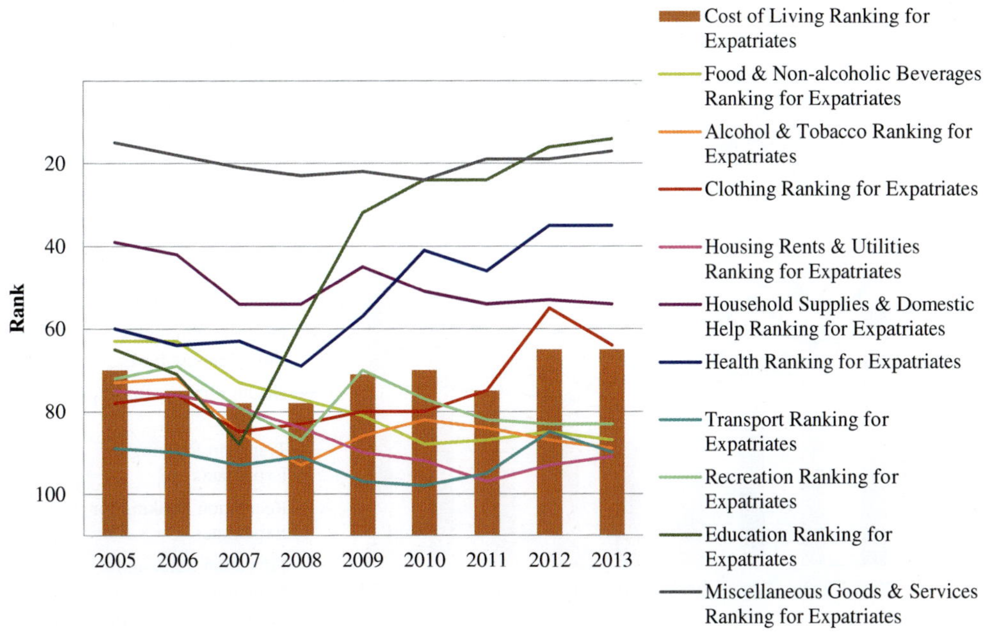

Source: Asia Competitiveness Institute

The Cost of Living Ranking for Expatriates in Atlanta, the ninth largest metropolitan area in the United States, jumped five places from 70th in 2005 to 65th in 2013, as shown in the orange bars (see Figure 4.6).

Education registered the most dramatic rise in ranking as it climbed 51 spots from 65th to 14th between 2005 and 2013 and consequently became Atlanta's highest ranked category in 2013. Health Ranking went up 25 places from 60th to 35th over the same period. Clothing Ranking rose from 78th in 2005 to 64th in 2013.

In contrast, Food & Non-alcoholic Beverages Ranking slipped 24 spots from 63rd to 87th over the study period. Housing Rents & Utilities became the lowest ranked category in 2013 as its ranking fell 16 places from 75th in 2005 to 91st in 2013. Household Supplies & Domestic Help Ranking declined from 39th to 54th over the same period. Recreation Ranking dropped 11 spots from 72nd in 2005 to 83rd Transport Ranking went down slightly from 89th to 90th between 2005 and 2013, making it the second lowest ranked category in 2013.

AUCKLAND
New Zealand

Figure 4.7: Cost of Living and 10 Consumption Categories Rankings for Expatriates in Auckland, New Zealand

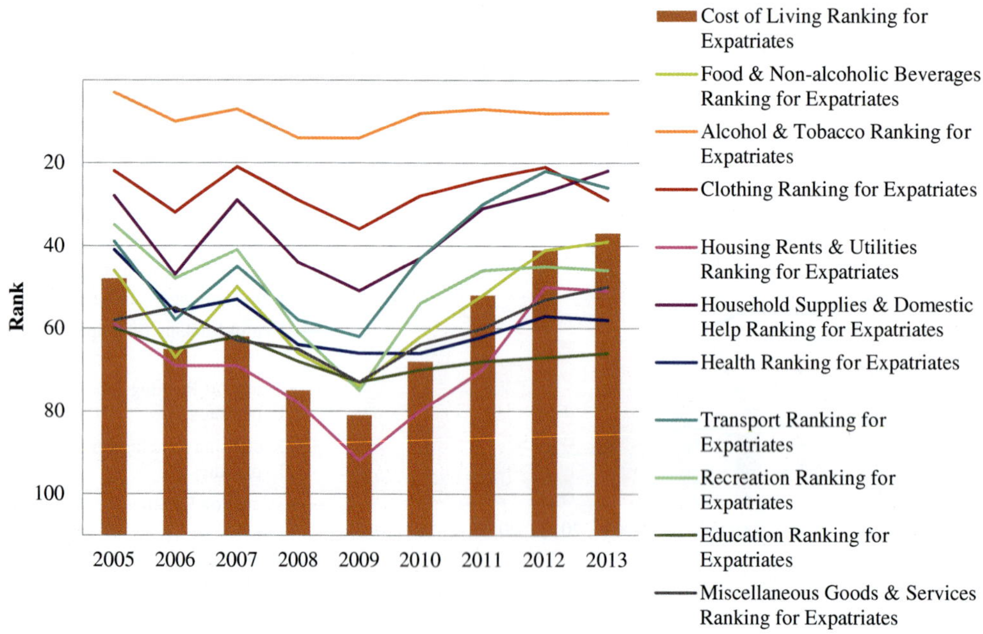

Source: Asia Competitiveness Institute

The Cost of Living for Expatriates in Auckland, the largest and most populous city in New Zealand, rose from 48th to 37th between 2005 and 2013 despite the sharp decline to 81st in 2009, as denoted by the orange bars (see Figure 4.7).

Transport recorded the most significant rise in ranking as it climbed 13 places from 39th in 2005 to 26th in 2013 and consequently became the third highest ranked category in 2013. Housing Rents & Utilities Ranking jumped from 59th to 51st over the same period although this upward trend appears to be levelling off. Food & Non-alcoholic Beverages Ranking moved up seven spots from 46th to 39th between 2005 and 2013. Likewise, Household Supplies & Domestic Help saw its ranking rise from 28th to 22nd over the same period.

In contrast, Health Ranking slipped 17 places from 41st in 2005 to 58th in 2013. Education Ranking fell six spots from 60th to 66th over the study period, making it the lowest ranked category for Auckland in 2013.

BAKU
Azerbaijan

Figure 4.8: Cost of Living and 10 Consumption Categories Rankings for Expatriates in Baku, Azerbaijan

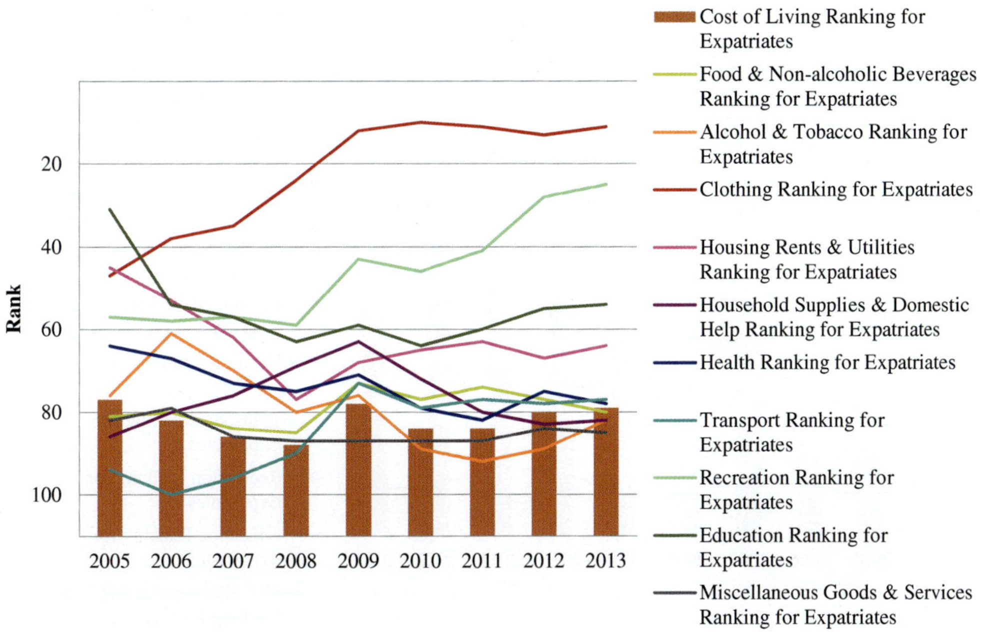

Source: Asia Competitiveness Institute

Nicknamed "the City of Winds", Baku is the cultural, scientific and industrial centre of Azerbaijan. Between 2005 and 2013, the city's Cost of Living Ranking for Expatriates, as represented by the orange bars, saw a slight decline from 77th to 79th (see Figure 4.8).

Education recorded the most dramatic drop in ranking as it fell 23 places from 31st in 2005 to 54th in 2013. Housing Rents & Utilities Ranking also slipped sharply from 45th to 64th over the study period. Health Ranking moved down 14 spots from 64th to 78th between 2005 and 2013.

In contrast, Clothing saw the most significant rise in ranking from 47th in 2005 to 11th in 2013, making it the highest ranked category in 2013. Transport Ranking jumped 17 places from 94th to 77th between 2005 and 2013 while Food & Non-alcoholic Beverages Ranking went up only one spot from 81st to 80th over the same period.

BANGKOK
Thailand

Figure 4.9: Cost of Living and 10 Consumption Categories Rankings for Expatriates in Bangkok, Thailand

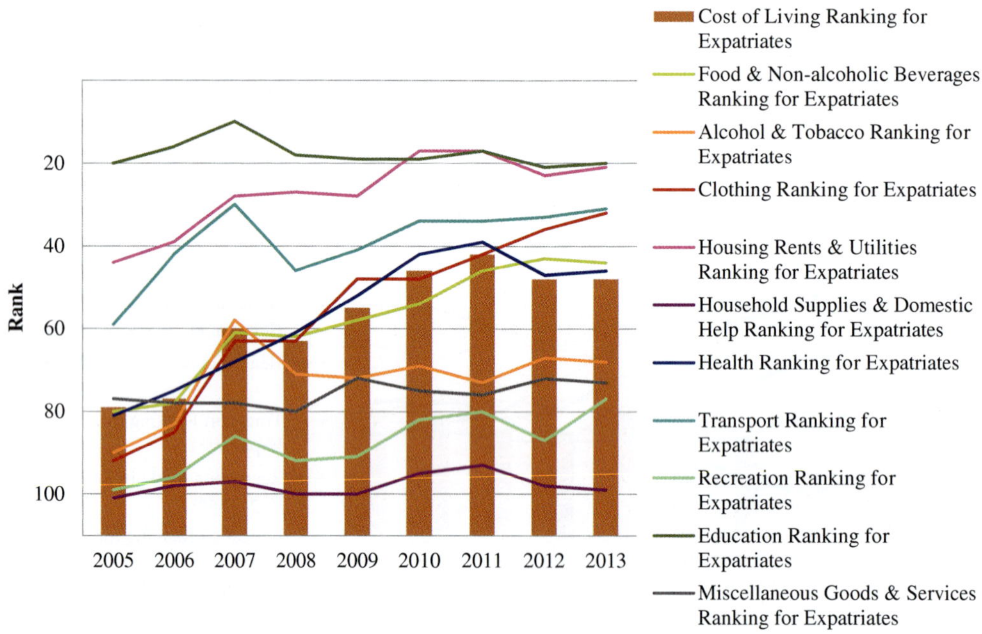

Source: Asia Competitiveness Institute

Known as one of the world's most popular tourist destinations, Bangkok in Thailand is also where many multinational corporations locate their regional headquarters. That said, it is a tad worrisome that the city's Ranking of Cost of Living for Expatriates, as shown in the orange bars, jumped 31 places from 79th in 2005 to 48th in 2013 (see Figure 4.9).

Clothing saw the most significant rise in ranking from 92nd to 32nd over the study period. Food & Non-alcoholic Beverages Ranking also went up sharply from 80th to 44th between 2005 and 2013 although this rising trend appears to be levelling off. Health Ranking jumped 35 places from 81st to 46th over the same period. Transport Ranking climbed 28 spots from 59th in 2005 to 31st in 2013. Housing Rents & Utilities Ranking moved up 23 places from 44th to 21st over the study period, making it the second highest ranked category in 2013. Education was Bangkok's highest ranked category in 2013 as its ranking rose from 20th in 2005 to 10th in 2007 before falling back to 20th in 2013. Household Supplies & Domestic Help remained as the lowest ranked category throughout the entire study period as its ranking went up slightly from 101st in 2005 to 99th in 2013.

BARCELONA
Spain

Figure 4.10: Cost of Living and 10 Consumption Categories Rankings for Expatriates in Barcelona, Spain

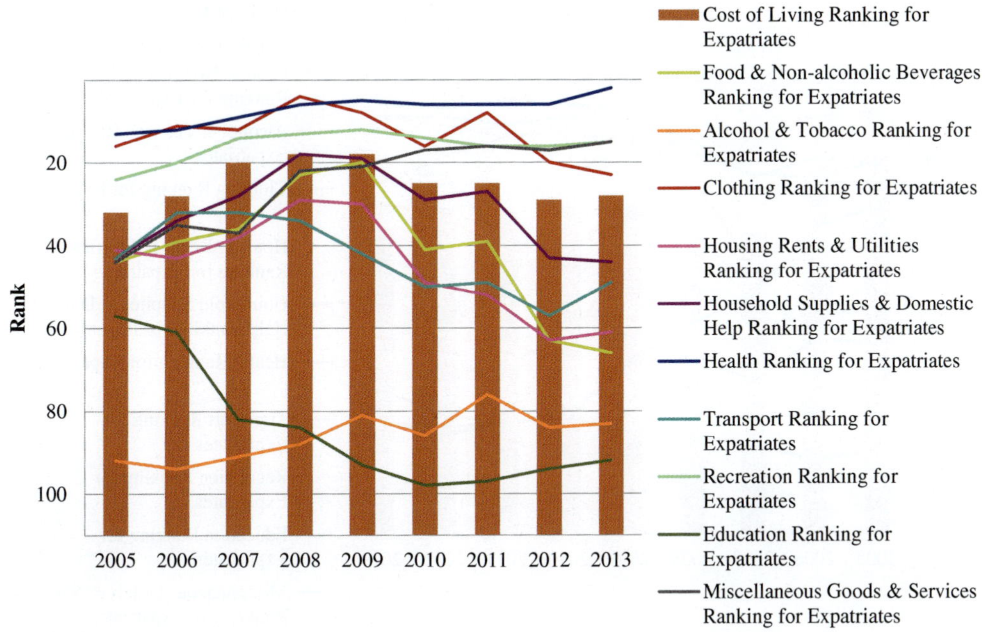

Source: Asia Competitiveness Institute

Known as the largest metropolis on the Mediterranean Sea, Barcelona's Cost of Living Ranking for Expatriates, as denoted by the orange bars, rose from 32nd to 28th between 2005 and 2013 (see Figure 4.10).

In particular, Health Ranking climbed 11 places from 13th in 2005 to second in 2013, making Barcelona the second most expensive city in this category in 2013. Miscellaneous Goods & Services and Recreation were the second highest ranked categories in 2013 as their rankings jumped from 44th to 15th and 24th to 15th, respectively, over the study period.

Education, in contrast, recorded the most significant decline in ranking as it fell 35 places from 57th in 2005 to 92nd in 2013. Food & Non-alcoholic Beverages Ranking also dropped sharply from 44th to 66th between 2005 and 2013. Housing Rents & Utilities Ranking slipped 20 spots from 41st to 61st over the same period. Transport saw a more modest slip in ranking from 43rd in 2005 to 49th in 2013.

BEIJING
China

Figure 4.11: Cost of Living and 10 Consumption Categories Rankings for Expatriates in Beijing, China

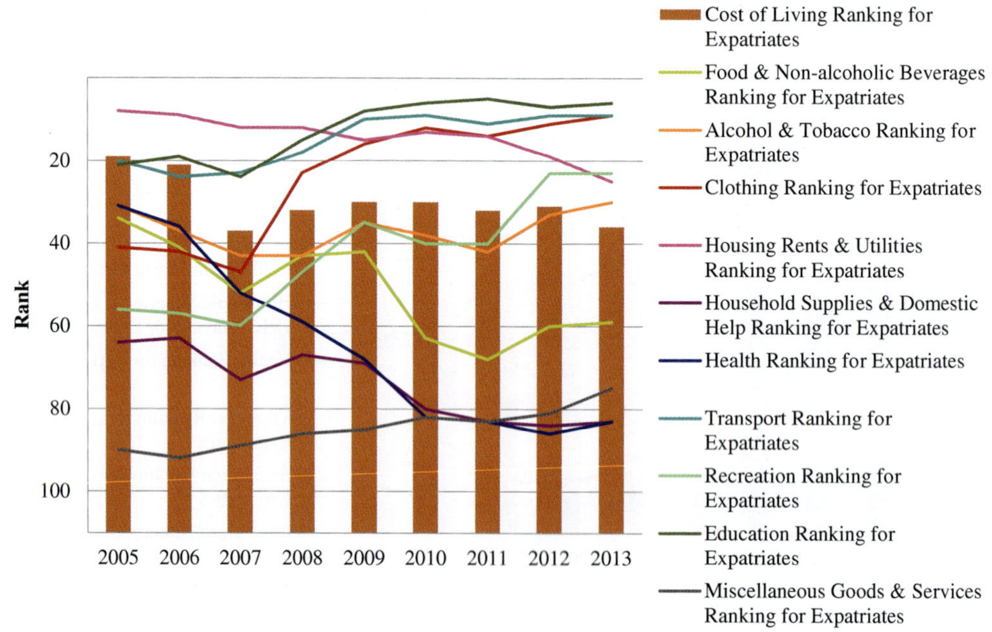

Source: Asia Competitiveness Institute

Home to the headquarters of China's largest state-owned corporations, Beijing is the country's second largest city by urban population after Shanghai. The city's Cost of Living Ranking for Expatriates, as represented by the orange bars, declined from 19th to 36th between 2005 and 2013 (see Figure 4.11).

Health recorded the most dramatic drop in ranking from 31st in 2005 to 83rd in 2013 and consequently became the lowest ranked category in 2013 together with Household Supplies & Domestic Help. Food & Non-alcoholic Beverages Ranking slipped 25 places from 34th to 59th between 2005 and 2013. Housing Rents & Utilities Ranking also fell sharply from eighth to 25th over the same period.

In contrast, Recreation Ranking climbed 33 spots from 56th in 2005 to 23rd in 2013. Clothing Ranking also went up remarkably from 41st to ninth between 2005 and 2013. Transport Ranking jumped 11 places from 20th to ninth over the same period. Nonetheless, Education was the highest ranked category in 2013 as its ranking rose from 21st to sixth over the study period.

BERLIN
Germany

Figure 4.12: Cost of Living and 10 Consumption Categories Rankings for Expatriates in Berlin, Germany

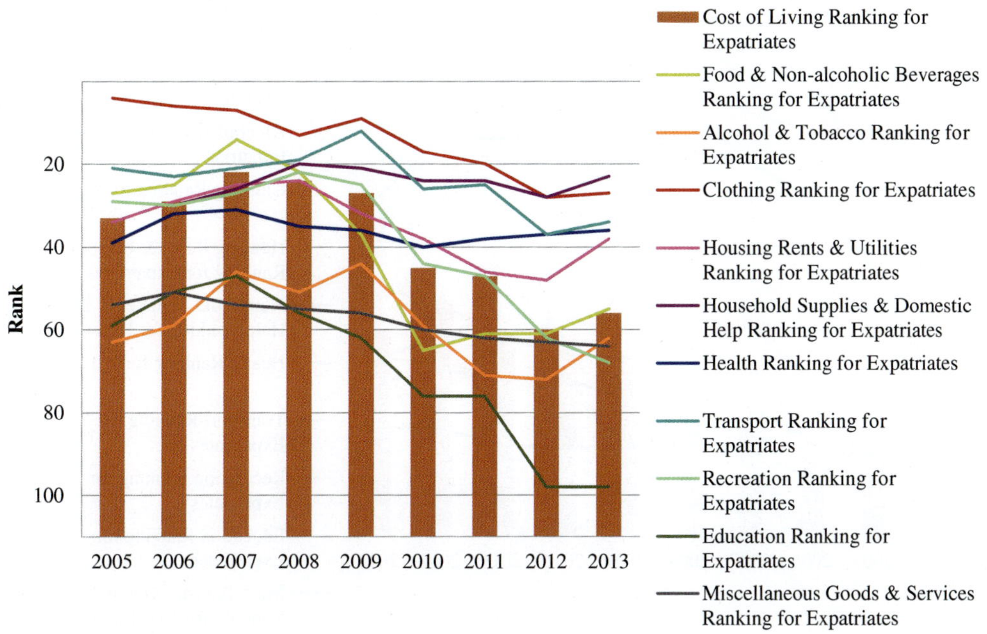

Source: Asia Competitiveness Institute

Home to a sizeable high-technology industry, Berlin is the political, cultural and scientific centre of Germany. The city's Cost of Living Ranking for Expatriates, as shown in the orange bars, saw a sharp decline from 33rd in 2005 to 56th in 2013 (see Figure 4.12).

Education and Recreation registered the most dramatic dip in rankings as they both fell 39 places from 59th to 98th and 29th to 68th, respectively, between 2005 and 2013. Consequently, Education became the lowest ranked category in 2013 although its descending trend appears to be levelling off. Food & Non-alcoholic Beverages Ranking slipped 28 spots from 27th to 55th over the study period. Transport Ranking dropped 13 places from 21st in 2005 to 34th in 2013. Housing Rents & Utilities Ranking fell from 34th to 38th between 2005 and 2013.

Household Supplies & Domestic Help Ranking, in contrast, jumped six spots from 29th to 23rd between 2005 and 2013, making it the highest ranked category in 2013. Health Ranking climbed three places from 39th in 2005 to 36th in 2013.

BOGOTA
Colombia

Figure 4.13: Cost of Living and 10 Consumption Categories Rankings for Expatriates in Bogota, Colombia

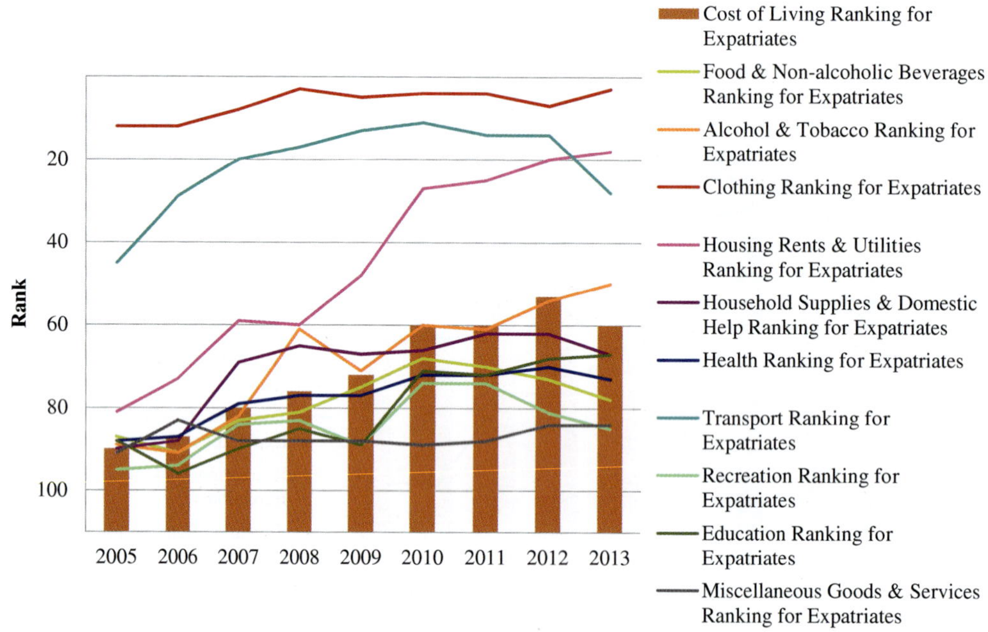

Source: Asia Competitiveness Institute

Bogota, the capital of Colombia, is known for its extensive educational system with more than 100 higher education institutions. The city's Cost of Living Ranking for Expatriates, as denoted by the orange bars, rose dramatically from 90th to 60th between 2005 and 2013 (see Figure 4.13).

All categories rose in rankings over the study period. In particular, Housing Rents & Utilities recorded the sharpest jump in ranking as it climbed 63 places from 81st in 2005 to 18th in 2013, making it the second highest ranked category in 2013. Household Supplies & Domestic Help Ranking went up 23 spots from 90th to 67th, while Education Ranking rose 21 places from 88th to 67th, between 2005 and 2013. Transport and Health Rankings jumped from 45th to 28th and 88th to 73rd, respectively, over the same period. Clothing consistently remained as the highest ranked category as its ranking went up nine spots from 12th in 2005 to third in 2013. Recreation was the lowest ranked category in 2013 although its ranking moved up 10 spots from 95th to 85th over the study period.

BOSTON
United States

Figure 4.14: Cost of Living and 10 Consumption Categories Rankings for Expatriates in Boston, United States

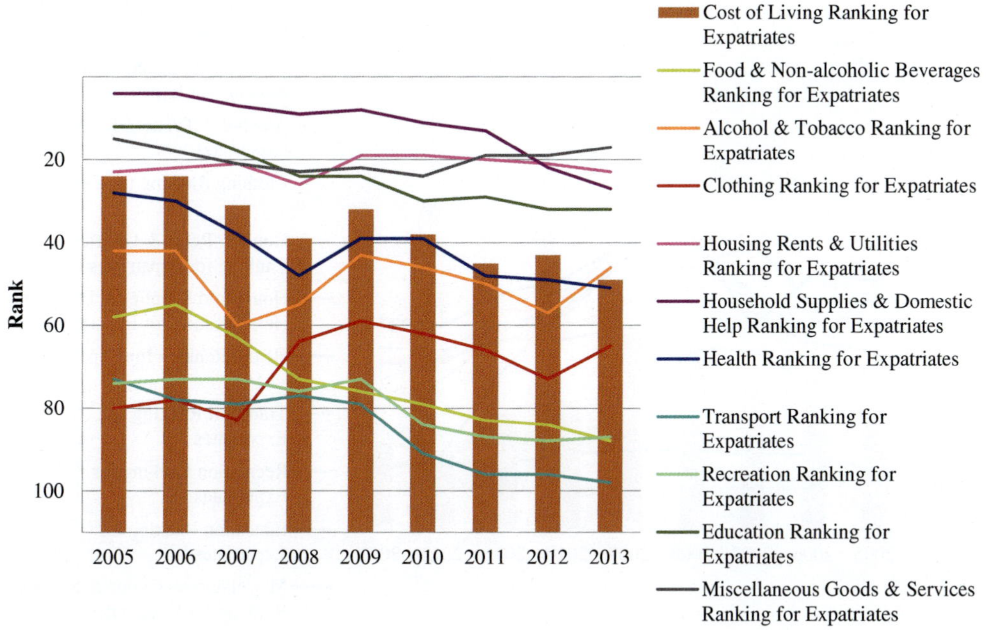

Source: Asia Competitiveness Institute

Home to many world renowned colleges and universities, Boston is widely regarded as an international centre of higher education and innovation. Between 2005 and 2013, the city's Cost of Living Ranking for Expatriates, as represented by the orange bars, slipped 25 places from 24th to 49th (see Figure 4.14).

Food & Non-alcoholic Beverages saw the most remarkable drop in ranking as it fell 30 spots from 58th in 2005 to 88th in 2013. Transport became the lowest ranked category in 2013 as its ranking dropped 25 spots from 73rd to 98th between 2005 and 2013. Health and Household Supplies & Domestic Help Rankings both slipped 23 places from 28th to 51st and fourth to 27th, respectively, over the same period. Education Ranking also declined sharply from 12th in 2005 to 32nd in 2013. Housing Rents & Utilities Ranking went up from 23rd in 2005 to 19th in 2009 and 2010 before falling back to 23rd in 2013. Miscellaneous Goods & Services Ranking fell slightly from 15th in 2005 to 17th in 2013, making it the highest ranked category in 2013. Clothing was the only category that rose in ranking from 80th to 65th over the study period.

BRATISLAVA
Slovakia

Figure 4.15: Cost of Living and 10 Consumption Categories Rankings for Expatriates in Bratislava, Slovakia

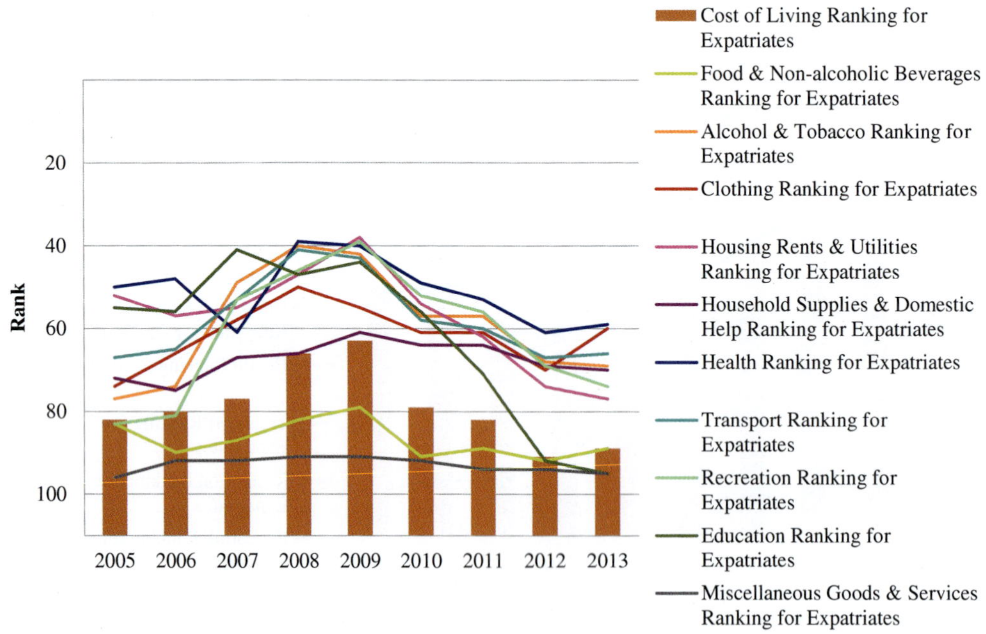

Source: Asia Competitiveness Institute

Bratislava, the capital of Slovakia, is the only national capital that borders two countries, namely Austria and Hungary. The city's Cost of Living Ranking for Expatriates, as denoted by the orange bars, fell seven places from 82nd to 89th between 2005 and 2013 (see Figure 4.15).

Education recorded the sharpest decline in ranking as it fell from 55th in 2005 to 95th in 2013 and consequently became the lowest ranked category in 2013 together with Miscellaneous Goods & Services. Housing Rents & Utilities Ranking also fell sharply from 52nd to 77th between 2005 and 2013. Health and Food & Non-alcoholic Beverages Rankings dropped more modestly from 50th to 59th and 83rd to 89th, respectively, over the same period. Nonetheless, Health became the highest ranked category in 2013.

In contrast, Clothing Ranking climbed 14 places from 74th to 60th over the study period. Recreation Ranking rose from 83rd in 2005 to 74th in 2013. Transport Ranking moved up only one spot from 67th to 66th over the same period.

BRISBANE
Australia

Figure 4.16: Cost of Living and 10 Consumption Categories Rankings for Expatriates in Brisbane, Australia

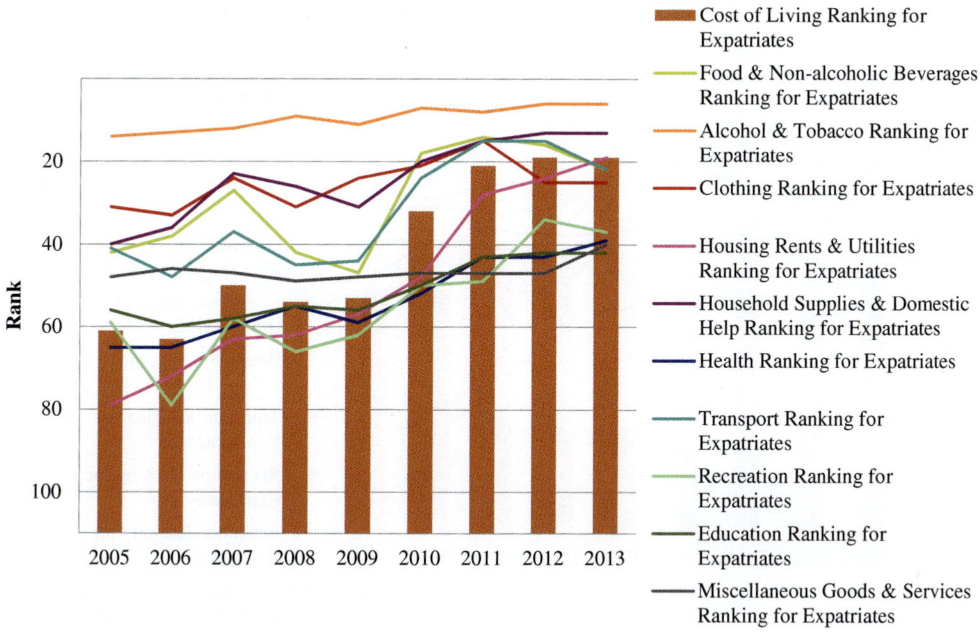

Source: Asia Competitiveness Institute

Brisbane is the third most populous city in Australia and has hosted many large international events including the 1982 Commonwealth Games and the 2014 G-20 Summit. The city's Cost of Living Ranking for Expatriates, as represented by the orange bars, rose dramatically from 61st in 2005 to 19th in 2013 (see Figure 4.16).

All categories rose in rankings between 2005 and 2013. Notably, Housing Rents & Utilities Ranking climbed 60 spots from 79th to 19th over the study period. Household Supplies & Domestic Help Ranking went up 27 places from 40th in 2005 to 13th in 2013, making it the second highest ranked category in 2013 after Alcohol & Tobacco at the sixth place. Health Ranking also rose remarkably from 65th to 39th between 2005 and 2013. Food & Non-alcoholic Beverages Ranking jumped 20 spots from 42nd to 22nd, while Transport Ranking moved up 19 places from 41st to 22nd, over the same period. Education Ranking went up more modestly from 56th in 2005 to 42nd in 2013, making it the lowest ranked category in 2013. Nonetheless, the rankings of Food & Non-alcoholic Beverages, Transport and Education reached their peaks in 2011 and have been declining ever since.

BRUSSELS
Belgium

Figure 4.17: Cost of Living and 10 Consumption Categories Rankings for Expatriates in Brussels, Belgium

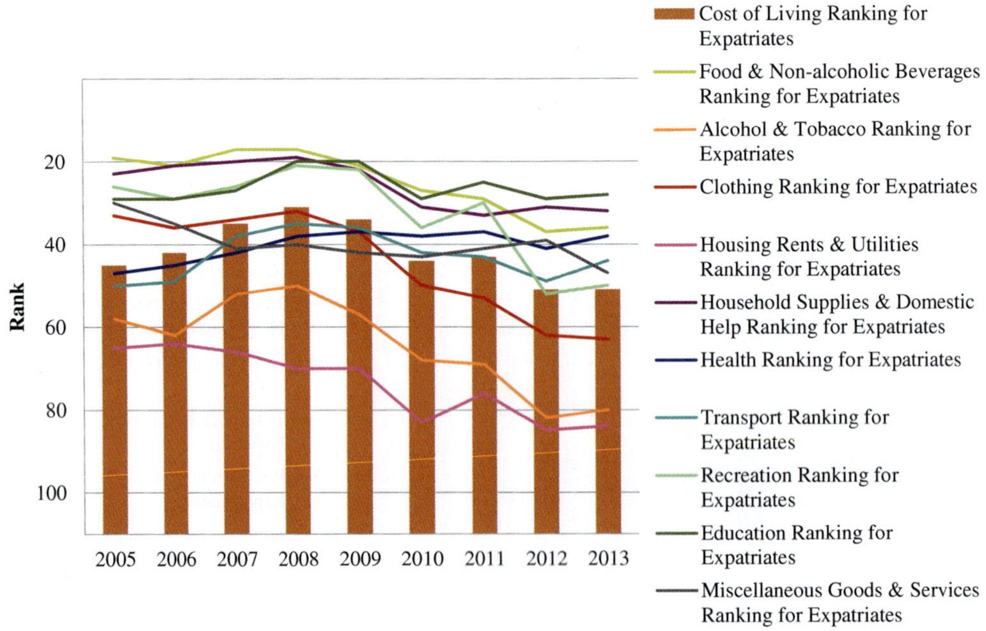

Source: Asia Competitiveness Institute

Since the end of the Second World War, Brussels has become a major centre of international politics, hosting principal European Union (EU) institutions and the headquarter of the North Atlantic Treaty Organisation (NATO). The city's Cost of Living Ranking for Expatriates, as shown in the orange bars, fell six places from 45th to 51st between 2005 and 2013 (see Figure 4.17).

Clothing saw the most remarkable decline in ranking as it slipped 30 spots from 33rd in 2005 to 63rd in 2013. Recreation Ranking also dropped sharply from 26th to 50th over the study period. Housing Rents & Utilities consistently remained as the lowest ranked category as its ranking went down 19 places from 65th in 2005 to 84th in 2013. Food & Non-alcoholic Beverages Ranking slipped 17 spots from 19th to 36th over the same period.

In contrast, Health Ranking jumped nine places from 47th to 38th between 2005 and 2013. Transport Ranking moved up from 50th to 44th over the same period. Education became the highest ranked category in 2013 as its ranking went up slightly from 29th in 2005 to 28th in 2013.

BUCHAREST
Romania

Figure 4.18: Cost of Living and 10 Consumption Categories Rankings for Expatriates in Bucharest, Romania

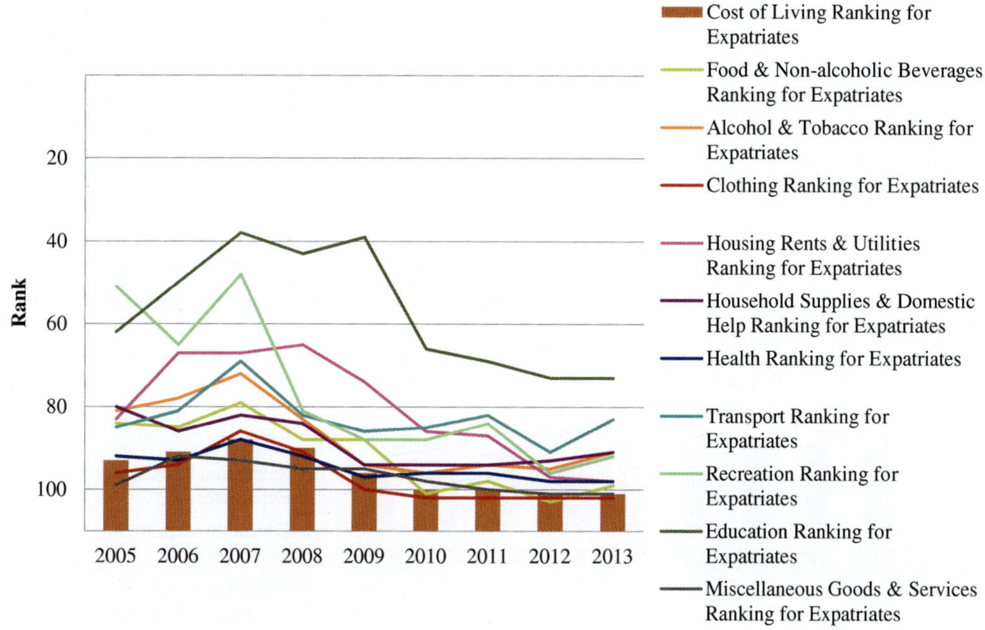

Source: Asia Competitiveness Institute

Bucharest, the capital of Romania, is not only the country's cultural, industrial and financial centre but also one of the main industrial centres and transportation hubs of Eastern Europe. The city's Cost of Living Ranking for Expatriates, as denoted by the orange bars, dropped eight places from 93rd in 2005 to 101st in 2013, making it the third most affordable among the 103 cities studied (see Figure 4.18).

Recreation recorded the sharpest decline in ranking as it fell 41 spots from 51st to 92nd between 2005 and 2013. Housing Rents & Utilities and Food & Non-alcoholic Beverages Rankings both slipped 15 places from 83rd to 98th and 84th to 99th, respectively, over the study period. Health Ranking declined more modestly from 92nd in 2005 to 98th in 2013. Education remained the highest ranked category since 2006 although its ranking dropped from 62nd in 2005 to 73rd in 2013. Clothing became the lowest ranked category as its ranking went down from 96th to 102nd over the same period. Transport was the only category that rose in ranking from 85th in 2005 to 83rd in 2013.

BUDAPEST
Hungary

Figure 4.19: Cost of Living and 10 Consumption Categories Rankings for Expatriates in Budapest, Hungary

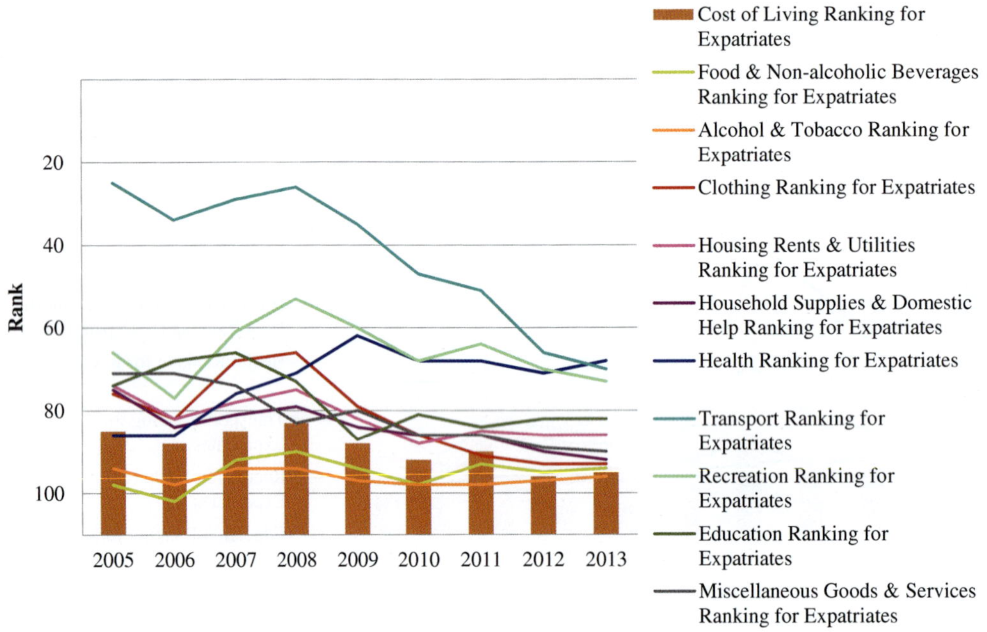

Source: Asia Competitiveness Institute

Straddling on both banks of the river Danube, Budapest in Hungary is widely regarded as one of the most beautiful cities in Europe. The city's Cost of Living Ranking for Expatriates, as represented by the orange bars, declined from 85th to 95th between 2005 and 2013 (see Figure 4.19).

In particular, Transport saw the most dramatic dip in ranking as it fell 45 places from 25th in 2005 to 70th in 2013. Miscellaneous Goods & Services Ranking dropped 19 spots from 71st to 90th over the study period. Clothing and Household Supplies & Domestic Help Rankings both went down 17 places from 76th to 93rd and 75th to 92nd, respectively, between 2005 and 2013. Housing Rents & Utilities Ranking slipped 12 spots from 74th to 86th over the same period. Education Ranking fell more modestly from 74th in 2005 to 82nd in 2013.

In contrast, Health Ranking climbed 18 places from 86th to 68th over the study period, making it the highest ranked category in 2013. Food & Non-alcoholic Beverages Ranking went up four spots from 98th in 2005 to 95th in 2013. Nonetheless, it was the second lowest ranked category in 2013 after Alcohol & Tobacco at 96th.

BUENOS AIRES
Argentina

Figure 4.20: Cost of Living and 10 Consumption Categories Rankings for Expatriates in Buenos Aires, Argentina

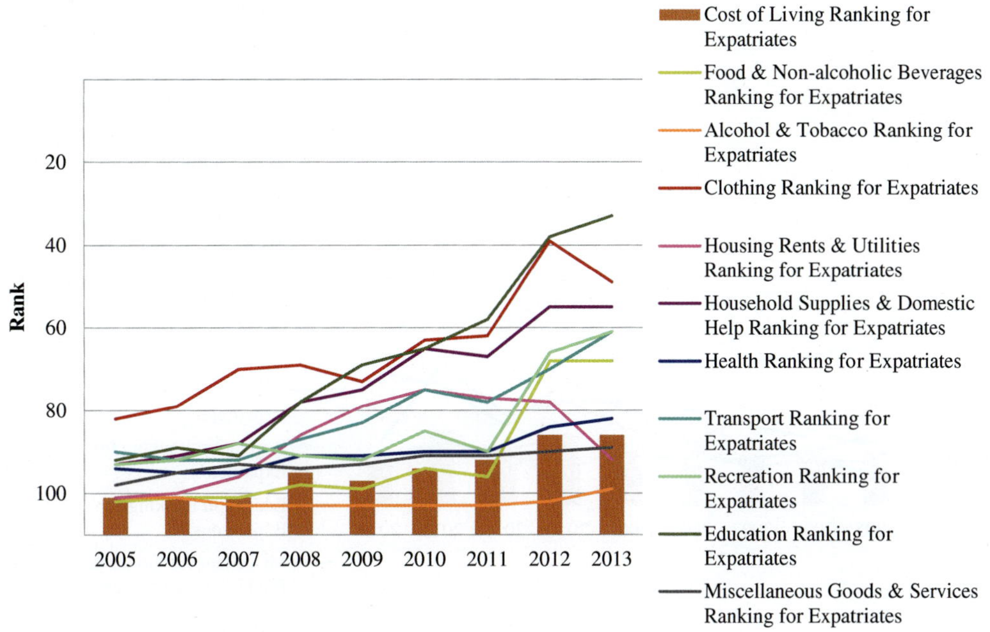

Source: Asia Competitiveness Institute

Known as the capital and largest city in Argentina, Buenos Aires is also the second largest metropolitan area in South America after Great São Paulo. The city's Cost of Living Ranking for Expatriates, as shown in the orange bars, went up 15 places from 101st in 2005 to 86th in 2013 (see Figure 4.20).

All categories rose in rankings over the study period. Notably, Education recorded the most significant rise in ranking from 92nd to 33rd between 2005 and 2013 and consequently became the highest ranked category in 2013. Household Supplies & Domestic Help Ranking climbed 38 spots from 93rd to 55th over the study period. Food & Non-alcoholic Beverages Ranking jumped 34 places from 102nd in 2005 to 68th in 2013. Transport Ranking moved up 29 spots from 90th to 61st over the same period. Health Ranking went up more modestly from 94th in 2005 to 82nd in 2013. Likewise, Housing Rents & Utilities Ranking jumped nine places from 101st to 92nd between 2005 and 2013. Nonetheless, it was the second lowest ranked category in 2013 after Alcohol & Tobacco at 99th.

CAIRO
Egypt

Figure 4.21: Cost of Living and 10 Consumption Categories Rankings for Expatriates in Cairo, Egypt

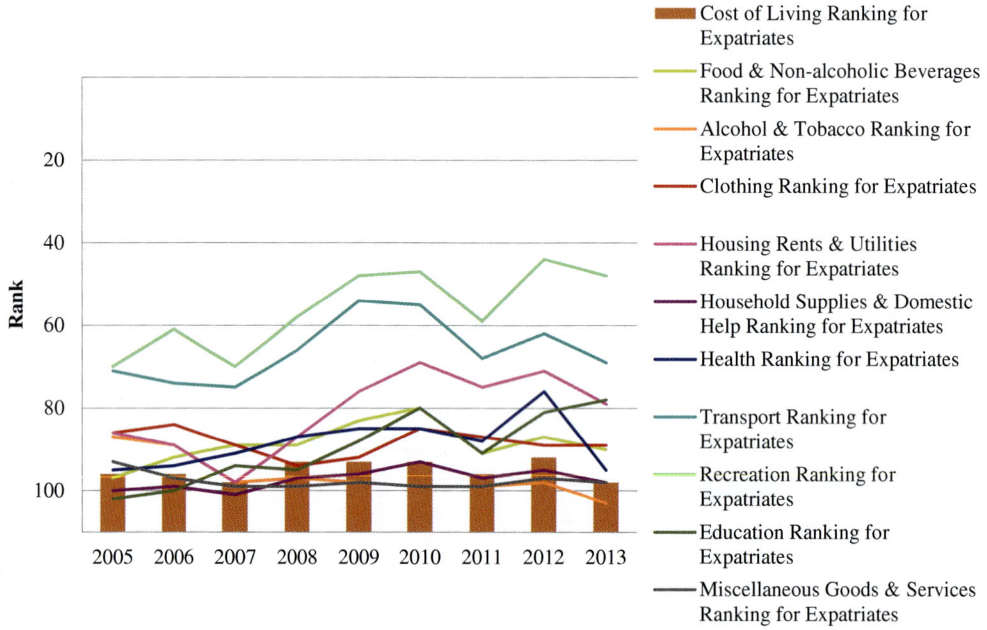

Source: Asia Competitiveness Institute

Known for its proximity to the Great Sphinx and the pyramids of Giza, Cairo is the capital of Egypt and the most populous city in the Middle East. The city's Cost of Living Ranking for Expatriates, as denoted by the orange bars, declined slightly from 96th to 98th between 2005 and 2013 (see Figure 4.21).

Education saw the sharpest jump in ranking from 102nd in 2005 to 78th in 2013. Nonetheless, Recreation consistently remained as the highest ranked category throughout the study period as its ranking climbed 22 places from 70th to 48th between 2005 and 2013. Food & Non-alcoholic Beverages and Housing Rents & Utilities Rankings rose more modestly from 97th to 90th and 86th to 79th, respectively, over the same period. Transport Ranking went up two spots from 71st in 2005 to 69th in 2013. Health Ranking moved up from 95th in 2005 to 85th in 2009 and 2010 before falling back to 95th in 2013.

In contrast, Alcohol & Tobacco Ranking slipped 16 places from 87th to 103rd between 2005 and 2013, making Cairo the cheapest city in this category in 2013. Miscellaneous Goods & Services Ranking fell five spots from 93rd in 2005 to 98th in 2013. Clothing Ranking dropped three places from 86th to 89th over the same period.

CALGARY
Canada

Figure 4.22: Cost of Living and 10 Consumption Categories Rankings for Expatriates in Calgary, Canada

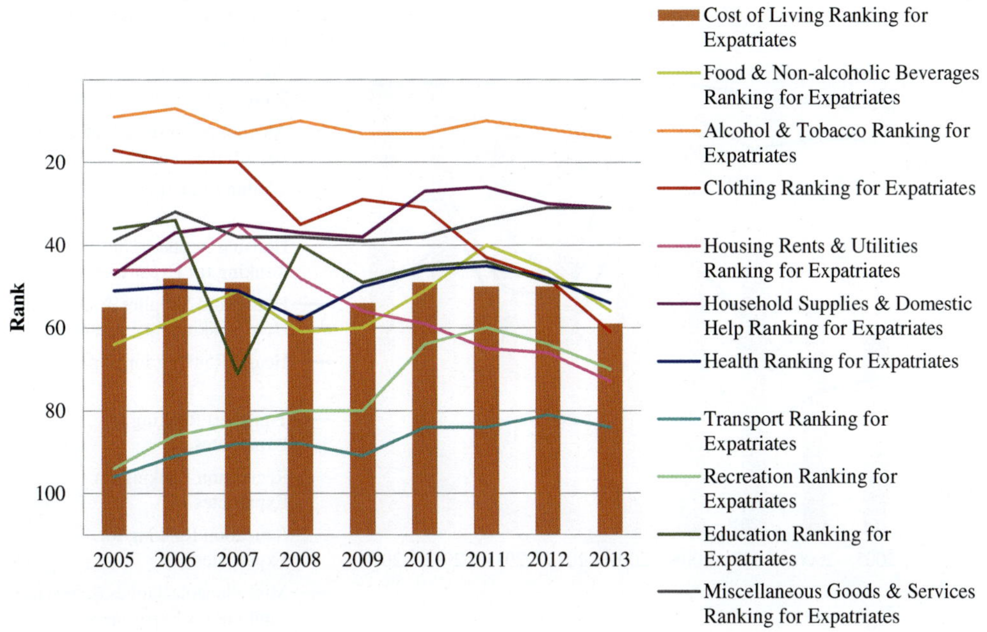

Source: Asia Competitiveness Institute

Home to a sizeable energy industry, Calgary is the third largest municipality in Canada. The city's Cost of Living Ranking for Expatriates, as represented by the orange bars, moved up four places from 55th in 2005 to 59th in 2013 (see Figure 4.22).

Recreation saw the sharpest rise in ranking as it climbed 24 spots from 94th to 70th between 2005 and 2013. Household Supplies & Domestic Help jumped 16 places from 47th to 31st over the study period. Transport consistently remained as the lowest ranked category throughout the study period although its ranking went up from 96th in 2005 to 84th in 2013. Food & Non-alcoholic Beverages Ranking rose eight spots from 64th to 56th over the same period.

In contrast, Clothing registered the most dramatic drop in ranking as it fell 44 places from 17th to 61st between 2005 and 2013. Housing Rents & Utilities Ranking slipped 27 spots from 46th in 2005 to 73rd in 2013. Education Ranking dropped 14 places from 36th to 50th while Health Ranking declined more modestly from 51st to 54th over the study period.

CARACAS
Venezuela

Figure 4.23: Cost of Living and 10 Consumption Categories Rankings for Expatriates in Caracas, Venezuela

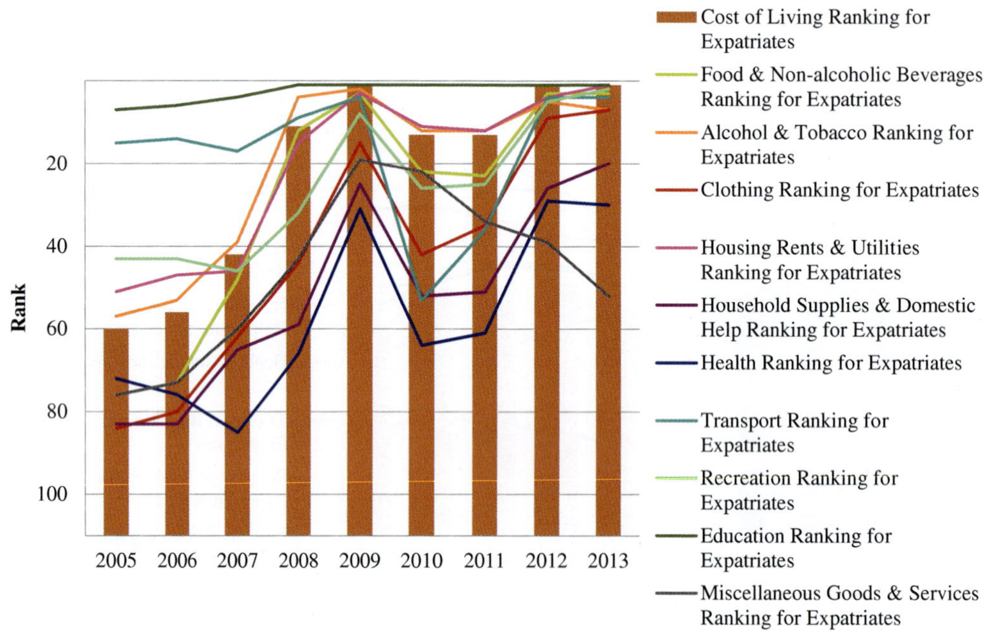

Source: Asia Competitiveness Institute

Caracas is the capital and largest city of Venezuela and home to one of the largest financial districts in Latin America. The city's Cost of Living Ranking for Expatriates, as shown in the orange bars, saw a dramatic rise from 60th to first between 2005 and 2013 (see Figure 4.23), which can be attributed to the "inflation-depreciation" spiral that has plagued Venezuela, particular since 2010.

In particular, Clothing Ranking climbed 77 places from 84th in 2005 to seventh in 2013. Food & Non-alcoholic Beverages Ranking jumped 73 spots from 76th to third over the study period. Household Supplies & Domestic Help Ranking moved up 63 places from 83rd to 20th between 2005 and 2013. Housing Rents & Utilities Ranking rose from 51st to first over the same period, making Caracas the most expensive among the 103 cities studied in this category in 2013. Health Ranking jumped 42 spots from 72nd in 2005 to 30th in 2013. Nonetheless, it was the second lowest ranked category in 2013 after Miscellaneous Goods & Services at 52nd. Transport Ranking rose more modestly from 15th to fourth between 2005 and 2013. Education consistently remained as the highest ranked category for Caracas throughout the study period as its ranking went up six places from seventh in 2005 to first in 2013.

CHICAGO
United States

Figure 4.24: Cost of Living and 10 Consumption Categories Rankings for Expatriates in Chicago, United States

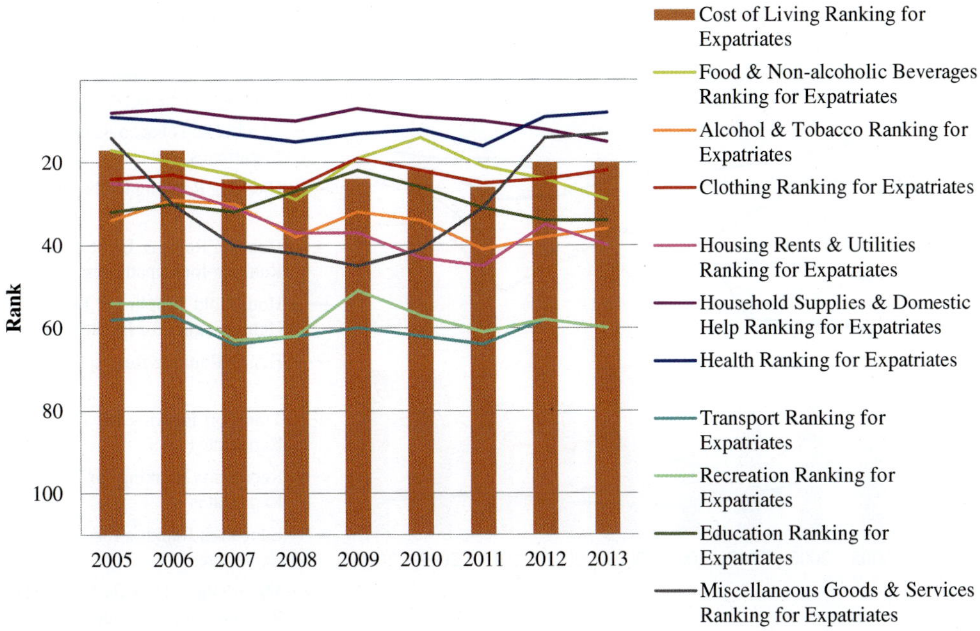

Source: Asia Competitiveness Institute

Chicago is the third most populous city in the United States with approximately 2.7 million residents. The city's Cost of Living Ranking for Expatriates, as denoted by the orange bars, declined from 17th to 20th between 2005 and 2013 (see Figure 4.24).

Housing Rents & Utilities saw the most remarkable dip in ranking as it fell 15 places from 25th in 2005 to 40th in 2013. Food & Non-alcoholic Beverages Ranking slipped 12 spots from 17th to 29th over the study period. Household Supplies & Domestic Help Ranking dropped seven places from eighth to 15th, while Recreation Ranking moved down six spots from 54th to 60th between 2005 and 2013. Education and Transport Rankings both went down two spots from 32nd to 34th and 58th to 60th, respectively, over the same period. Consequently, Recreation and Transport became the lowest ranked categories in 2013.

In contrast, Clothing Ranking jumped two places from 24th in 2005 to 22nd in 2013. Health and Miscellaneous Goods & Services Rankings both moved up one spot from ninth to eighth and 14th to 13th, respectively, over the same period, making them the highest and second highest ranked category in 2013.

CLEVELAND
United States

Figure 4.25: Cost of Living and 10 Consumption Categories Rankings for Expatriates in Cleveland, United States

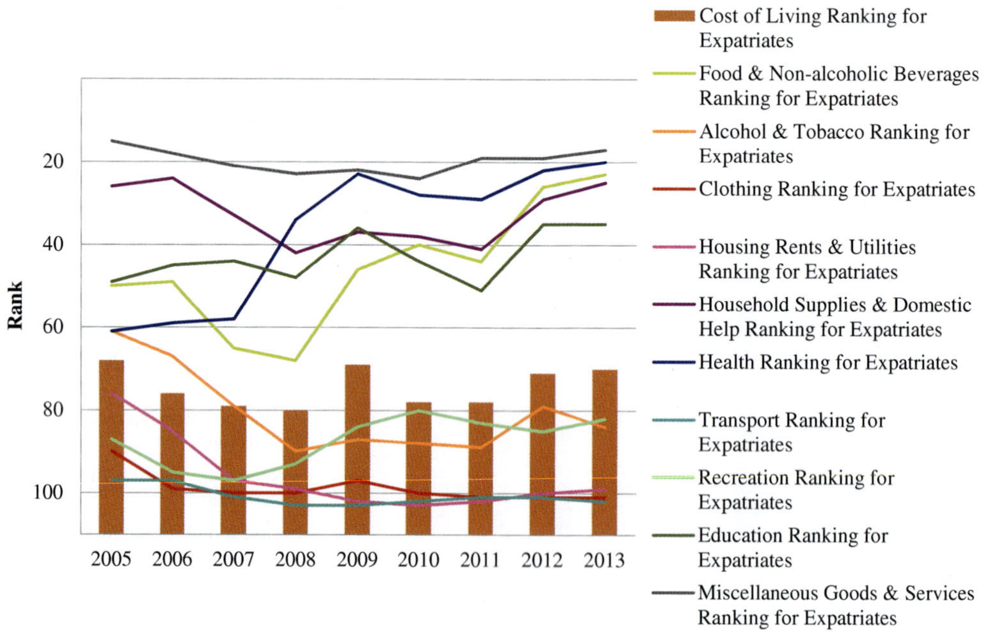

Source: Asia Competitiveness Institute

Located in Northeastern Ohio with connection to numerous canals and railroad lines, Cleveland is one of the country's leading manufacturing centres. The city's Cost of Living Ranking for Expatriates, as represented by the orange bars, dropped slightly from 68th in 2005 to 70th in 2013 (see Figure 4.25).

Housing Rents & Utilities and Alcohol & Tobacco saw the most significant decline in rankings as they both slipped 23 places from 76th to 99th and 61st to 84th, respectively, between 2005 and 2013. Clothing Ranking fell 11 spots from 90th to 101st over the study period. Transport Ranking declined from 97th in 2005 to 102nd in 2013, making Cleveland the second cheapest city in this category in 2013.

In contrast, Health recorded the sharpest rise in ranking from 61st to 20th between 2005 and 2013 and consequently became the second highest ranked category in 2013 after Miscellaneous Goods & Services at 17th. Food & Non-alcoholic Beverages Ranking climbed 27 places from 50th to 23rd over the same period.

COLOMBO
Sri Lanka

Figure 4.26: Cost of Living and 10 Consumption Categories Rankings for Expatriates in Colombo, Sri Lanka

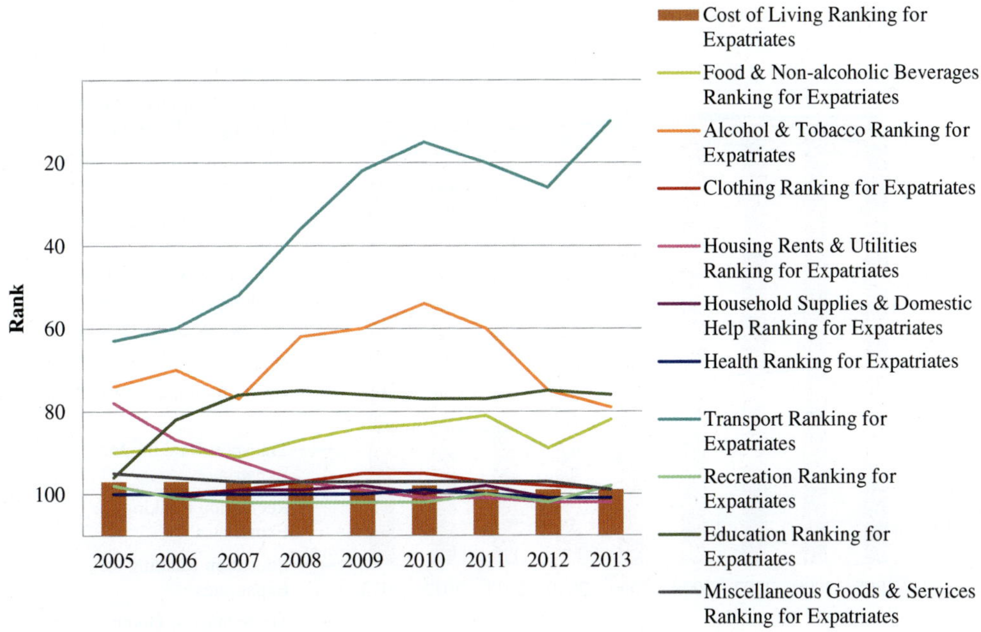

Source: Asia Competitiveness Institute

Known for its strategic position along the East–West maritime routes, Colombo is the commercial capital and largest city of Sri Lanka. The city's Cost of Living Ranking for Expatriates, as shown in the orange bars, declined slightly from 97th to 99th between 2005 and 2013 (see Figure 4.26).

Notably, Housing Rents & Utilities Ranking fell 24 places from 78th in 2005 to 102nd in 2013, making Colombo the second cheapest city in this category in 2013. Colombo was also the third most affordable among 103 cities studied in terms of Health and Household Supplies & Domestic Help in 2013 as their rankings went down from 100th to 101st and 98th to 101st, respectively, between 2005 and 2013.

In contrast, Transport Ranking climbed 53 places from 63rd to 10th, while Education Ranking jumped 20 spots from 96th to 76th over the study period. Consequently, they became the highest and second highest ranked category for Colombo in 2013. Food & Non-alcoholic Beverages saw a more modest rise in ranking from 90th in 2005 to 82nd in 2013.

COPENHAGEN
Denmark

Figure 4.27: Cost of Living and 10 Consumption Categories Rankings for Expatriates in Copenhagen, Denmark

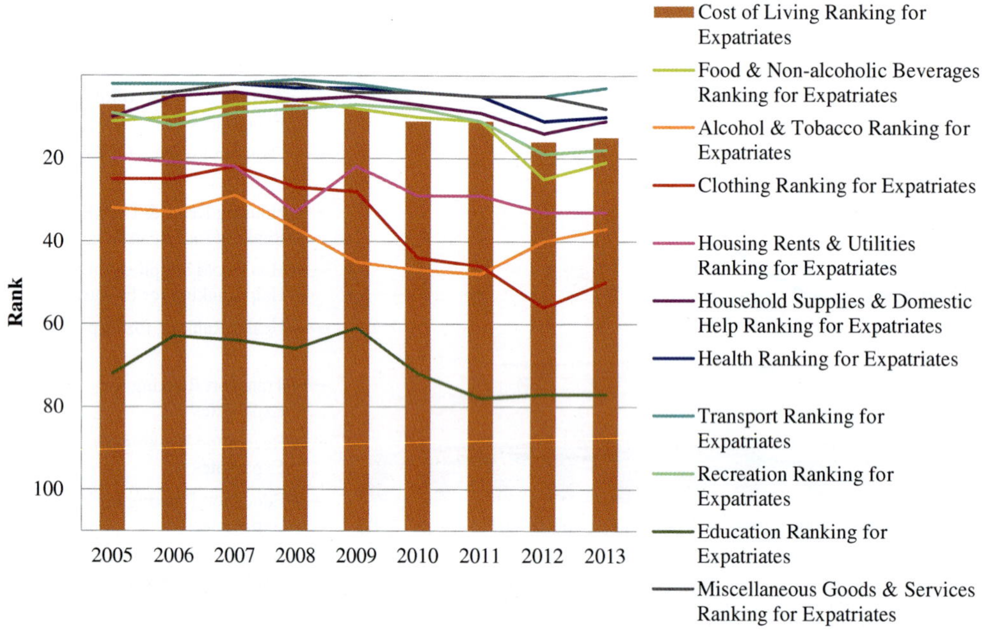

Source: Asia Competitiveness Institute

Copenhagen is not only Denmark's political, cultural and financial centre but also widely known as one of the world leaders in clean technology. The city's Cost of Living Ranking for Expatriates, as denoted by the orange bars, slipped eight places from seventh to 15th between 2005 and 2013 (see Figure 4.27).

The rankings of all 10 categories went down over the study period. Clothing registered the sharpest decline in ranking from 25th in 2005 to 50th in 2013. Housing Rents & Utilities Ranking dropped 13 places from 20th to 33rd between 2005 and 2013. Food & Non-alcoholic Beverages Ranking slipped 10 spots from 11th to 21st over the same period. Health Ranking went down from second to tenth between 2005 and 2013. Education consistently remained as the lowest ranked category throughout the study period as its ranking slipped from 72nd in 2005 to 77th in 2013. Transport became the highest ranked category in 2013 although its ranking moved down from second to third over the same period.

DALIAN
China

Figure 4.28: Cost of Living and 10 Consumption Categories Rankings for Expatriates in Dalian, China

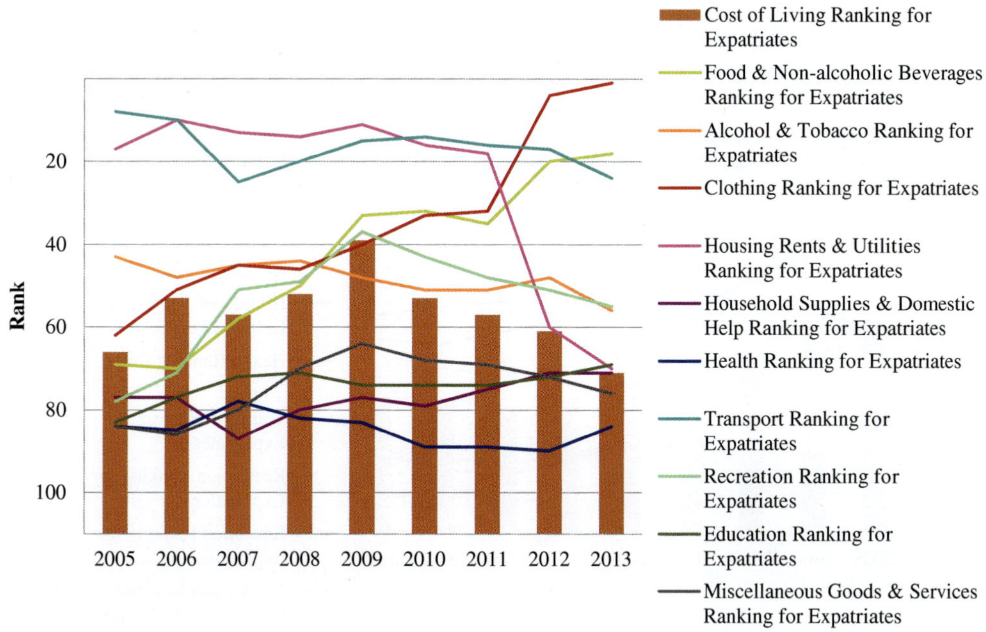

Source: Asia Competitiveness Institute

Located in the south of Liaoning province of China, Dalian is the financial, shipping and logistics hub of Northeast Asia. The city's Cost of Living Ranking for Expatriates, as represented by the orange bars, declined from 66th in 2005 to 71st in 2013 (see Figure 4.28).

Housing Rents & Utilities recorded the most dramatic drop in ranking as it fell 53 places from 17th to 70th between 2005 and 2013. Transport Ranking slipped more modestly from eighth to 24th over the study period. Health Ranking declined from 84th in 2005 to 90th in 2012 before rising back to 84th in 2013. However, Health consistently remained as the lowest ranked category since 2008.

In contrast, Clothing Ranking climbed 61 spots from 62nd in 2005 to first in 2013, making Dalian the most expensive city in this category in 2013. Food & Non-alcoholic Beverages became the second highest ranked category in 2013 after Clothing as its ranking jumped 51 places from 69th to 18th between 2005 and 2013. Education Ranking moved up 14 spots from 83rd to 69th over the same period. Household Supplies & Domestic Help Ranking went up six places from 77th to 71st over the study period.

DETROIT
United States

Figure 4.29: Cost of Living and 10 Consumption Categories Rankings for Expatriates in Detroit, United States

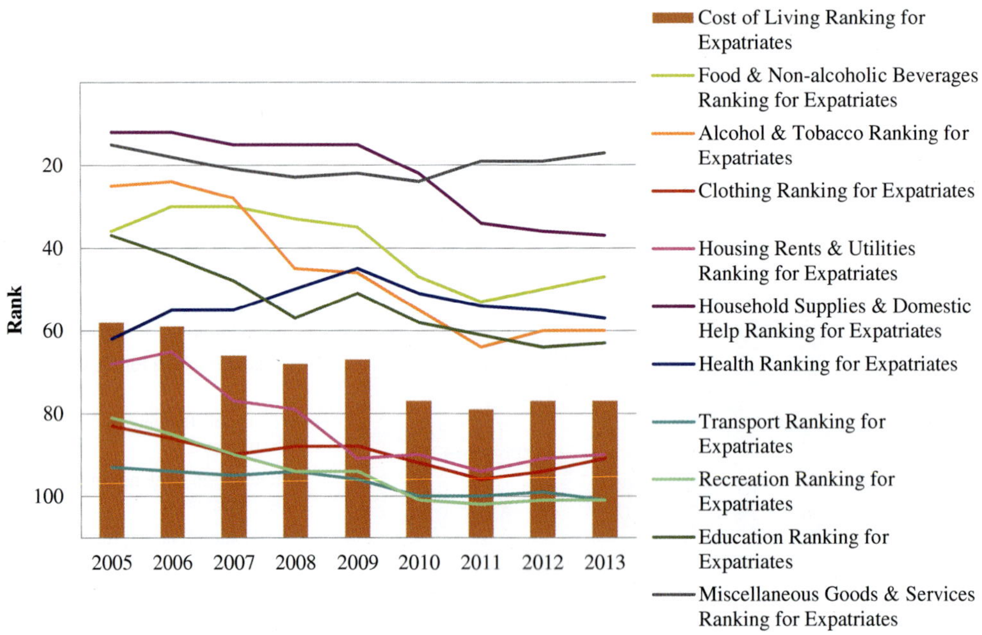

Source: Asia Competitiveness Institute

Known as the world's traditional automotive centre, Detroit has suffered from a major economic and demographic decline in recent years as the automobile companies moved production out, including offshore. The city's Cost of Living Ranking for Expatriates, as shown in the orange bars, fell 19 places from 58th to 77th between 2005 and 2013 (see Figure 4.29).

Health was the only category that rose in ranking from 62nd in 2005 to 57th in 2013. In contrast, Recreation and Transport Rankings both declined to 101st in 2013 from 81st and 93rd, respectively, in 2005, making Detroit the third most affordable city in these categories in 2013. Education Ranking slipped 26 places from 37th to 63rd over the study period. Housing Rents & Utilities Ranking went down 22 spots from 68th in 2005 to 90th in 2013. Food & Non-alcoholic Beverages Ranking dropped 11 places from 36th to 47th between 2005 and 2013. Clothing Ranking fell eight spots from 83rd to 91st over the same period. Miscellaneous Goods & Services became the highest ranked category in 2013 as its ranking slipped two places from 15th to 17th over the study period.

DOHA
Qatar

Figure 4.30: Cost of Living and 10 Consumption Categories Rankings for Expatriates in Doha, Qatar

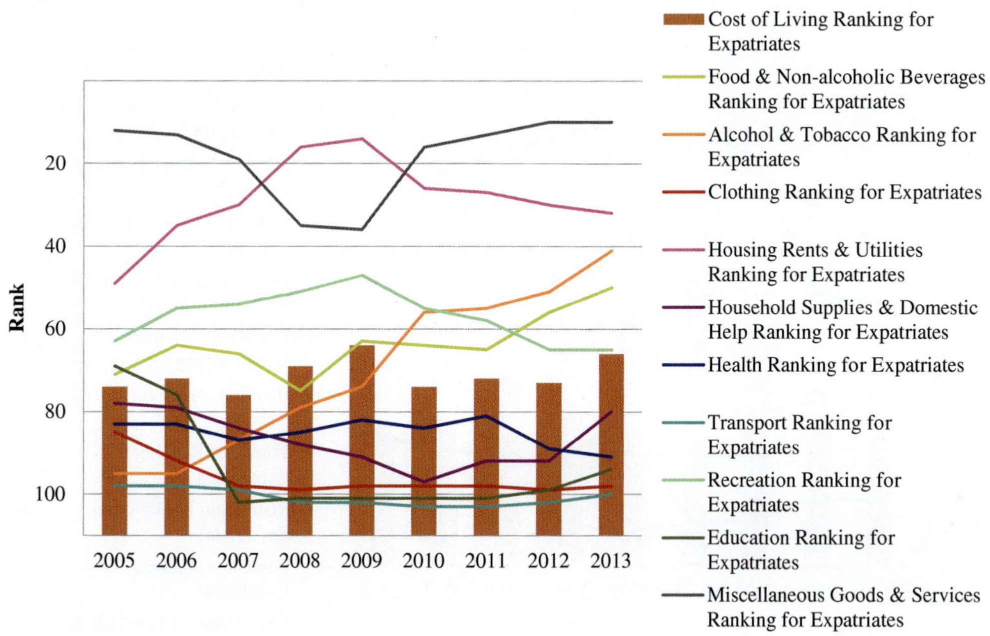

Source: Asia Competitiveness Institute

Doha, the capital and largest city of Qatar, is best known for hosting the first ministerial meeting of the Doha Development Round of the World Trade Organisation (WTO). The city's Cost of Living Ranking for Expatriates, as denoted by the orange bars, jumped eight places from 74th to 66th between 2005 and 2013 (see Figure 4.30).

Alcohol & Tobacco registered the most dramatic rise in ranking as it climbed 54 spots from 95th in 2005 to 41st in 2013. Food & Non-alcoholic Beverages Ranking also went up sharply from 71st to 50th over the study period. Housing Rents & Utilities Ranking jumped 17 spots from 49th in 2005 to 32nd in 2013, making it the second highest ranked category in 2013 after Miscellaneous Goods & Services at 10th.

In contrast, Education saw the sharpest decline in ranking from 69th to 94th between 2005 and 2013. Health Ranking dropped more modestly from 83rd in 2005 to 91st in 2013. Transport became the lowest ranked category in 2013 as its ranking slipped two places from 98th to 100th over the study period.

DUBAI
United Arab Emirates

Figure 4.31: Cost of Living and 10 Consumption Categories Rankings for Expatriates in Dubai, United Arab Emirates

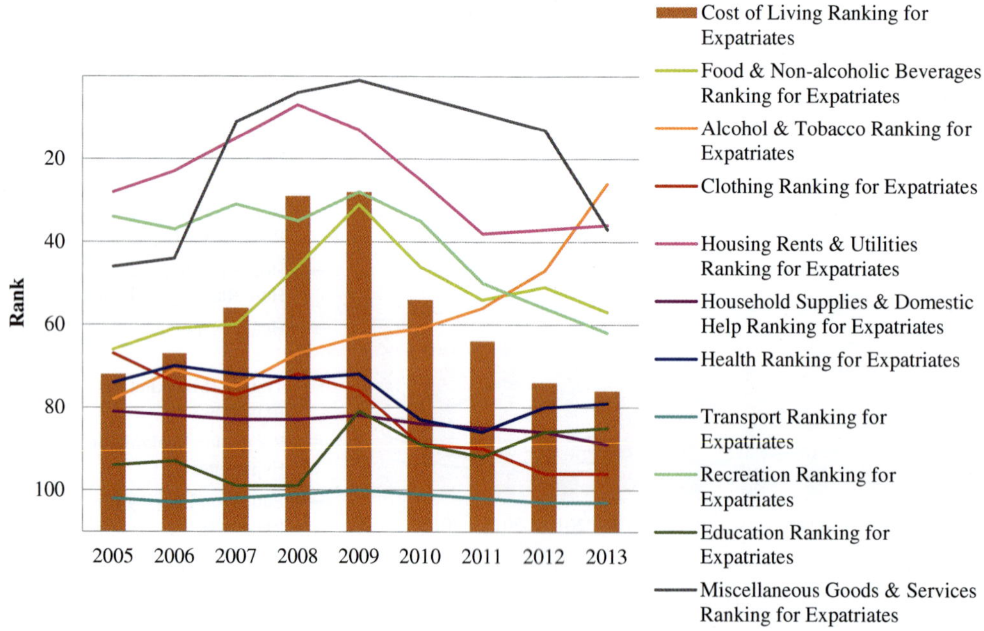

Source: Asia Competitiveness Institute

Famous for its skyscrapers, in particular the world's tallest building, the Burj Khalifa, Dubai in the United Arab Emirates is one of the major business hubs of the Middle East. The city's Cost of Living Ranking for Expatriates, as represented by the orange bars, declined from 72nd to 76th between 2005 and 2013 (see Figure 4.31).

Clothing recorded the most significant drop in ranking as it fell 29 places from 67th in 2005 to 96th in 2013. Recreation Ranking also went down sharply from 34th to 62nd over the study period. Housing Rents & Utilities Ranking slipped eight places from 28th to 36th, while Health Ranking moved down five spots from 74th to 79th between 2005 and 2013. Transport remained the lowest ranked category throughout the study period as its ranking dropped slightly from 102nd in 2005 to 103rd in 2013, making Dubai the cheapest city in this category in 2013.

In contrast, Alcohol & Tobacco saw the sharpest jump in ranking from 78th to 26th between 2005 and 2013 and consequently became the highest ranked category in 2013. Food & Non-alcoholic Beverages and Education Rankings both went up nine places from 66th to 57th and 94th to 85th, respectively, over the same period.

DUBLIN
Ireland

Figure 4.32: Cost of Living and 10 Consumption Categories Rankings for Expatriates in Dublin, Ireland

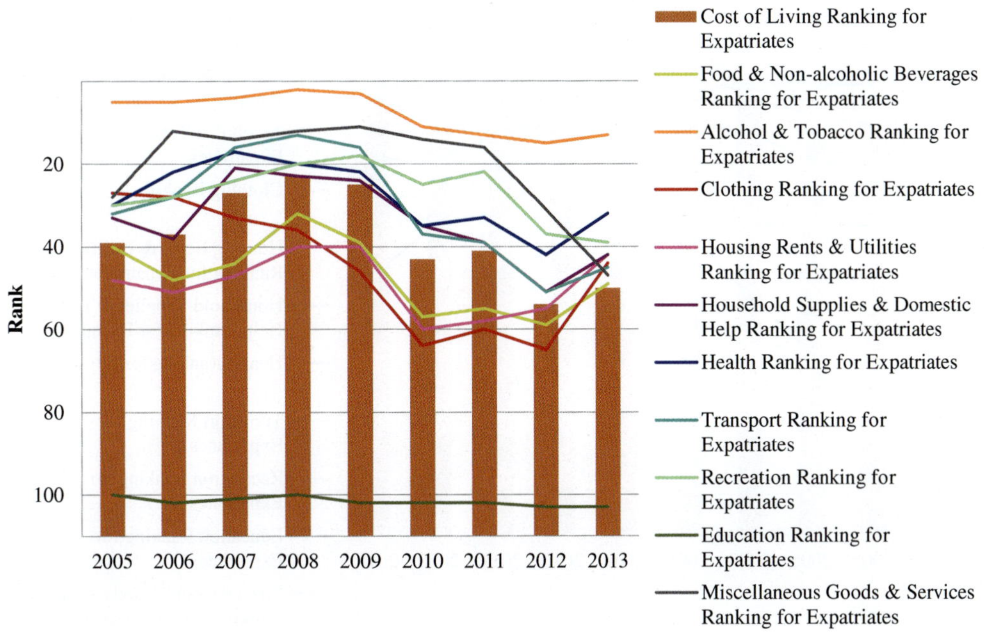

Source: Asia Competitiveness Institute

Dublin, the capital and largest city of Ireland, is home to the European headquarters of many global information technology companies including Microsoft, Google, Amazon, Facebook, Twitter. The city's Cost of Living Ranking for Expatriates, as shown in the orange bars, slipped 11 places from 39th in 2005 to 50th in 2013 (see Figure 4.32).

In particular, Clothing Ranking fell 17 spots from 27th in 2005 to 44th in 2013. Transport Ranking went down 13 places from 32nd to 45th over the study period. Food & Non-alcoholic Beverages and Recreation Rankings both slipped nine spots from 40th to 49th and 30th to 39th, respectively, between 2005 and 2013. Alcohol & Tobacco remained the highest ranked category throughout the study period although its ranking dropped from fifth in 2005 to 13th in 2013. Health Ranking declined slightly from 30th to 32nd over the same period. Education was consistently the lowest ranked category as its ranking slipped three places from 100th to 103rd between 2005 and 2013. Consequently, Dublin became the most affordable among the 103 cities studied in terms of Education in 2013. Housing Rents & Utilities was the only category that rose in ranking from 48th in 2005 to 42nd in 2013.

FRANKFURT
Germany

Figure 4.33: Cost of Living and 10 Consumption Categories Rankings for Expatriates in Frankfurt, Germany

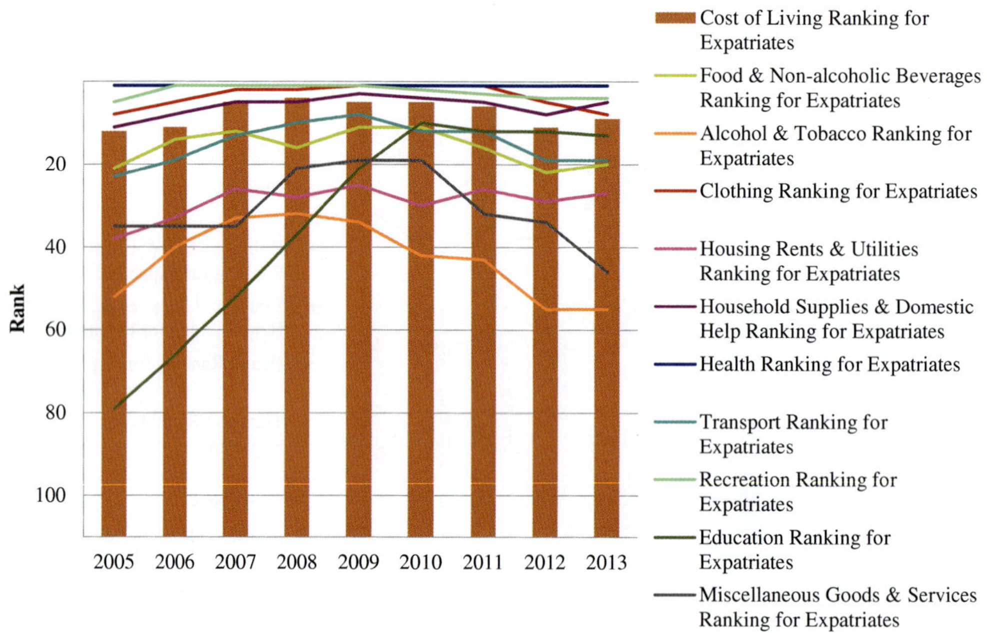

Source: Asia Competitiveness Institute

Frankfurt, the fifth largest city in Germany, is the largest financial centre in continental Europe and home to the European Central Bank. The city's Cost of Living Ranking for Expatriates, as denoted by the orange bars, moved up from 12th in 2005 to ninth in 2013 (see Figure 4.33).

Education recorded the most dramatic rise in ranking as it climbed 66 places from 79th to 13th between 2005 and 2013. Nonetheless, this upward trend appears to be levelling off as good news. Housing Rents & Utilities Ranking jumped more modestly from 38th to 27th over the study period. Transport Ranking went up four spots from 23rd in 2005 to 19th in 2013. Food & Non-alcoholic Beverages Ranking rose slightly from 21st to 20th over the same period. Health Ranking remained unchanged at the top spot for the entire study period, making Frankfurt the most expensive city in this category throughout the period. Alcohol & Tobacco and Miscellaneous Goods & Services were the lowest and second lowest ranked category in 2013 as their rankings dropped from 52nd to 55th and 35th to 46th, respectively, between 2005 and 2013.

GENEVA
Switzerland

Figure 4.34: Cost of Living and 10 Consumption Categories Rankings for Expatriates in Geneva, Switzerland

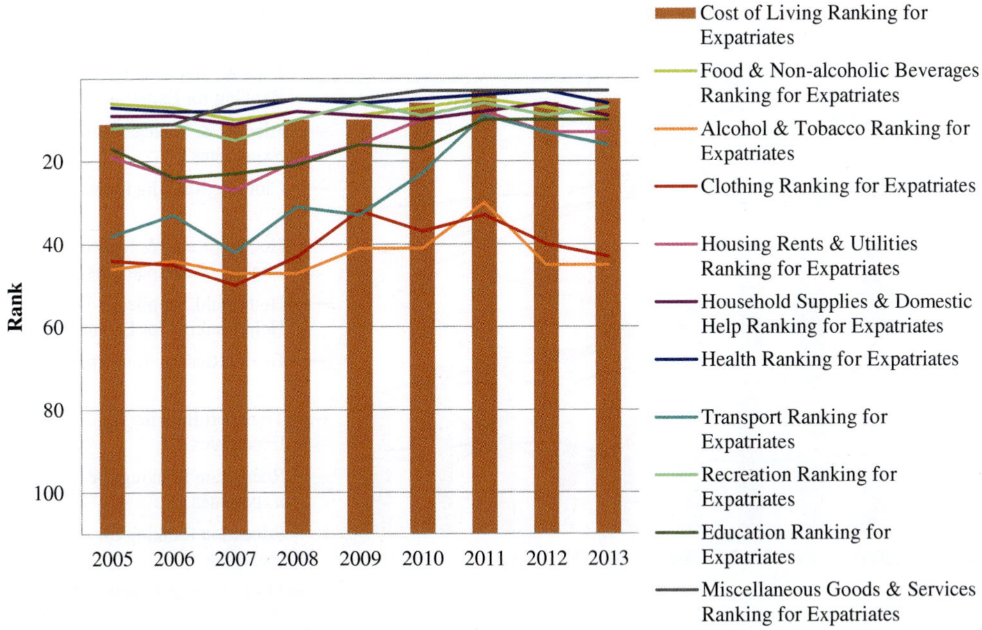

Source: Asia Competitiveness Institute

Geneva, the second most populous city in Switzerland, is widely renowned as the global centre of diplomacy as it hosts the highest number of international organisations in the world, including many agencies of the United Nations and the Red Cross. The city's Cost of Living Ranking for Expatriates, as represented by the orange bars, rose from 11th to fifth between 2005 and 2013 (see Figure 4.34).

In particular, Transport Ranking registered the sharpest rise in ranking as it climbed 22 places from 38th in 2005 to 16th in 2013. Miscellaneous Goods & Services became the highest ranked category in 2013 as its ranking went up from 11th to third between 2005 and 2013. Education Ranking jumped seven spots from 17th to 10th over the study period. Housing Rents & Utilities Ranking moved up six places from 19th in 2005 to 13th in 2013. Health Ranking rose slightly from seventh to sixth over the same period. Alcohol & Tobacco and Clothing were the lowest and second lowest ranked category in 2013 as their rankings jumped one spot from 46th to 45th and 44th to 43rd, respectively, between 2005 and 2013. Food & Non-alcoholic Beverages was the only category that slipped in ranking from sixth in 2005 to 10th in 2013.

GUANGZHOU
China

Figure 4.35: Cost of Living and 10 Consumption Categories Rankings for Expatriates in Guangzhou, China

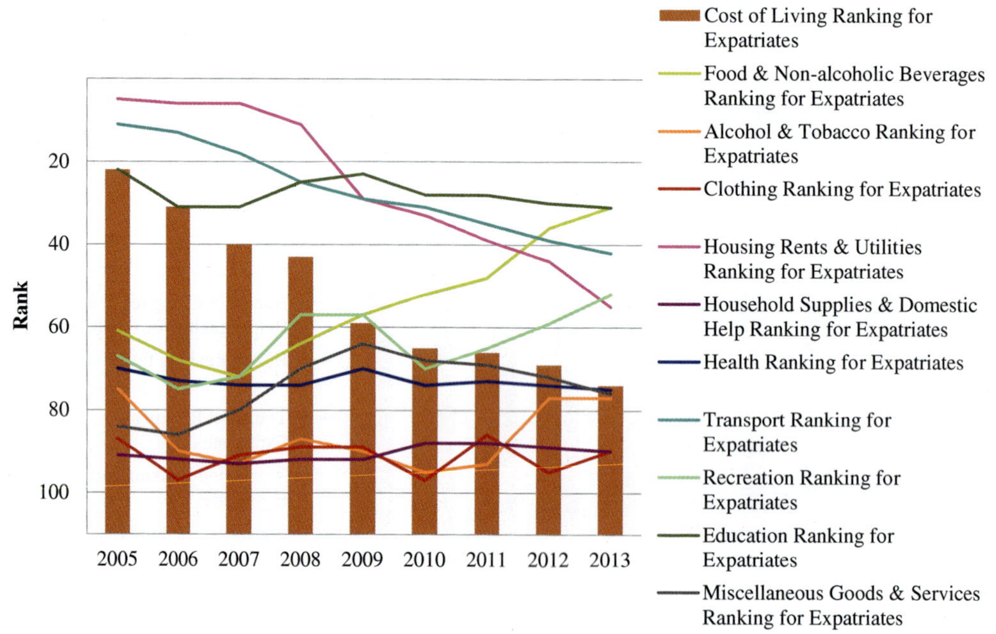

Source: Asia Competitiveness Institute

Guangzhou, the capital of Guangdong province, is the third largest city in China with a population of approximately 12.7 million. The city's Cost of Living Ranking for Expatriates, as shown in the orange bars, declined sharply from 22nd in 2005 to 74th in 2013 (see Figure 4.35).

Housing Rents & Utilities saw the most significant drop in ranking as it fell 50 places from fifth to 55th between 2005 and 2013. Transport Ranking slipped 31 spots from 11th in 2005 to 42nd in 2013. Education and Health Rankings declined more modestly from 22nd to 31st and 70th to 75th, respectively, over the study period.

In contrast, Food & Non-alcoholic Beverages Ranking climbed 30 places from 61st to 31st between 2005 and 2013, making it the highest ranked category in 2013 together with Education. Recreation Ranking jumped 15 spots from 67th in 2005 to 52nd in 2013. Miscellaneous Goods & Services Ranking went up eight places from 84th to 76th over the same period. Household Supplies & Domestic Help Ranking rose slightly from 91st in 2005 to 90th in 2013, making it the lowest ranked category in 2013 together with Clothing.

HELSINKI
Finland

Figure 4.36: Cost of Living and 10 Consumption Categories Rankings for Expatriates in Helsinki, Finland

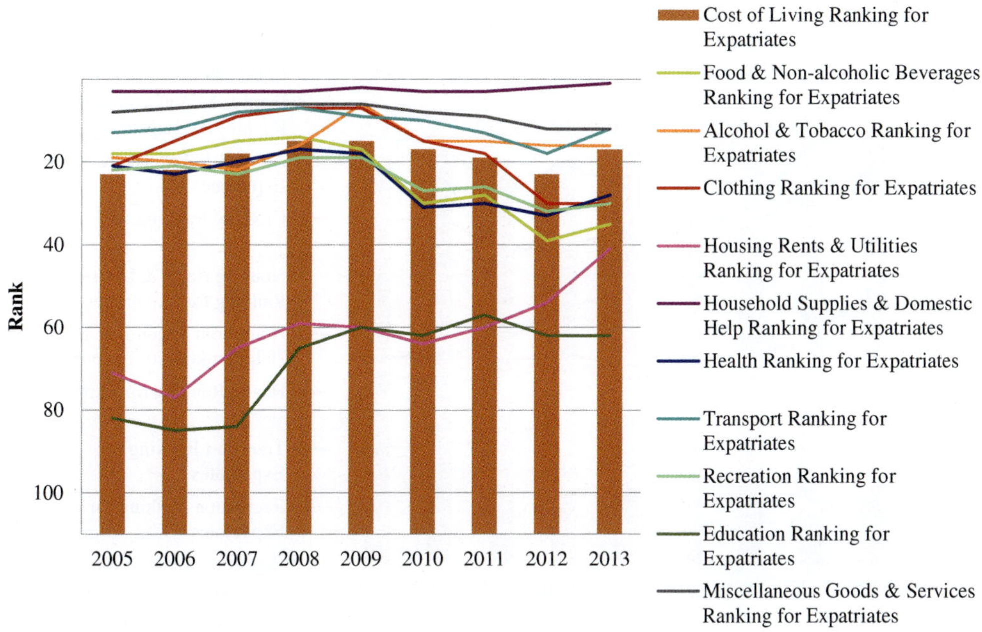

Source: Asia Competitiveness Institute

Helsinki, the capital and educational, financial and research centre of Finland, is the third largest Nordic city after Stockholm and Oslo. The city's Cost of Living Ranking for Expatriates, as denoted by the orange bars, moved up from 23rd to 17th between 2005 and 2013 (see Figure 4.36).

Housing Rents & Utilities registered the most significant rise in ranking as it climbed 30 places from 71st in 2005 to 41st in 2013. Education Ranking also went up sharply from 82nd to 62nd between 2005 and 2013. Nonetheless, Education and Housing Rents & Utilities were the lowest and second lowest ranked category in 2013. Household Supplies & Domestic Help consistently remained as the highest ranked category throughout the study period as its ranking jumped from third in 2005 to first in 2013, making Helsinki the most expensive city in this category in 2013. Transport Ranking rose slightly from 13th to 12th over the same period.

In contrast, Food & Non-alcoholic Beverages Ranking slipped 17 places from 18th in 2005 to 35th in 2013. Clothing Ranking fell nine spots from 21st to 30th between 2005 and 2013. Health Ranking declined from 21st to 28th over the same period.

HONG KONG
Hong Kong, China

Figure 4.37: Cost of Living and 10 Consumption Categories Rankings for Expatriates in Hong Kong, Hong Kong, China

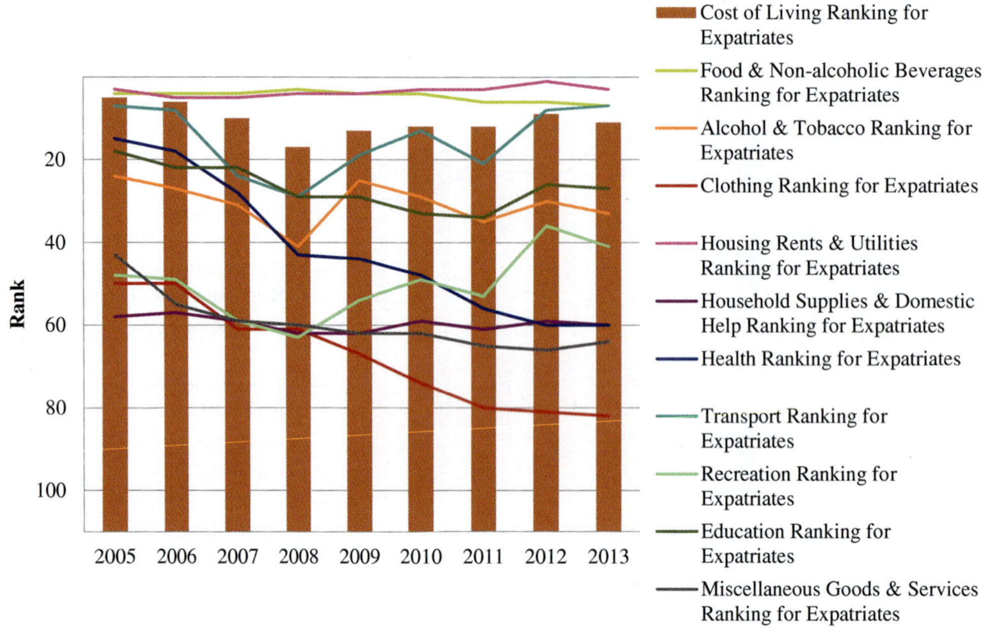

Source: Asia Competitiveness Institute

Known for its expansive skyline, Hong Kong is one of the most important international financial centres in the world as well as a global hub for trade and logistics. The city's Cost of Living Ranking for Expatriates, as represented by the orange bars, declined from fifth to 11th between 2005 and 2013 (see Figure 4.37).

Health registered the most dramatic dip in ranking as it fell 45 places from 15th in 2005 to 60th in 2013. Clothing Ranking also dropped sharply from 50th to 82nd between 2005 and 2013, making it the lowest ranked category in 2013. Miscellaneous Goods & Services Ranking slipped 21 spots from 43rd to 64th over the same period. Education Ranking went down more modestly from 18th in 2005 to 27th in 2013. Food & Non-alcoholic Beverages Ranking slipped three places from fourth to seventh between 2005 and 2013. Housing Rents & Utilities overtook Food & Non-alcoholic Beverages to become the highest ranked category since 2010 as its ranking remained largely stable at third over the study period. Transport Ranking fell from seventh in 2005 to 29th in 2008 before jumping back to seventh in 2013. Recreation was the only category that rose in ranking from 48th to 41st between 2005 and 2013.

HONOLULU
United States

Figure 4.38: Cost of Living and 10 Consumption Categories Rankings for Expatriates in Honolulu, United States

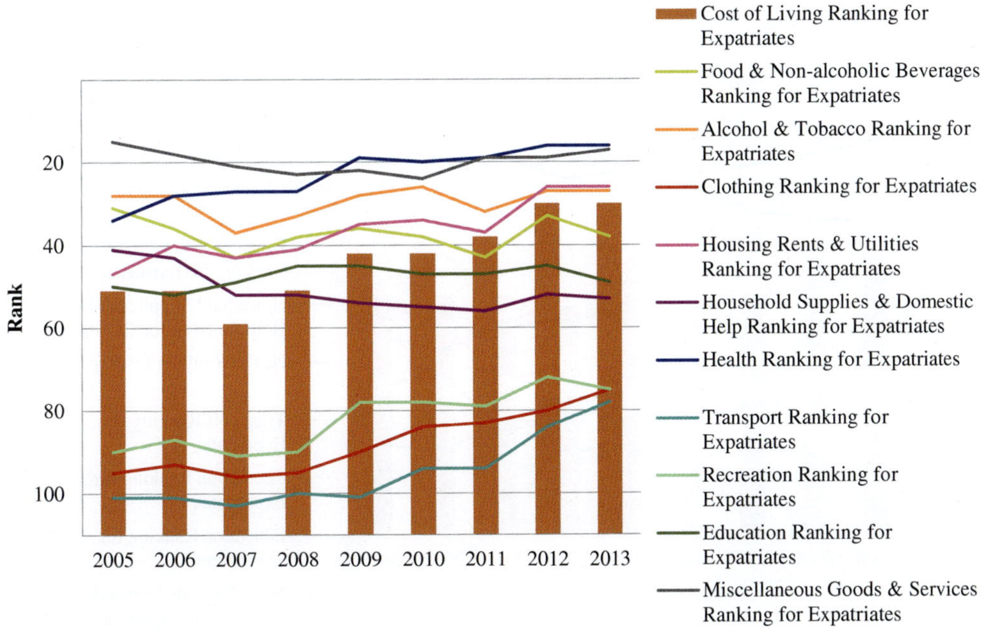

Source: Asia Competitiveness Institute

Known as a popular tourist destination, Honolulu is also a major U.S. hub for international business and military defense. The city's Cost of Living Ranking for Expatriates, as shown in the orange bars, jumped 21 places from 51st in 2005 to 30th in 2013 (see Figure 4.38).

Transport recorded the sharpest rise in ranking as it climbed 23 spots from 101st to 78th between 2005 and 2013. Nonetheless, it remained as the lowest ranked category throughout the study period. Housing Rents & Utilities Ranking went up 21 places from 47th in 2005 to 26th in 2013. Health overtook Miscellaneous Goods & Services to become the highest ranked category in 2013 as its ranking rose from 34th to 16th over the study period. Recreation Ranking moved up 15 spots from 90th in 2005 to 75th in 2013. Education Ranking jumped only one place from 50th to 49th between 2005 and 2013.

In contrast, Household Supplies & Domestic Help Ranking fell 12 spots from 41st to 53rd over the study period. Food & Non-alcoholic Beverages Ranking slipped seven places from 31st in 2005 to 38th in 2013. Miscellaneous Goods & Services Ranking dropped slightly from 15th to 17th over the same period.

HOUSTON
United States

Figure 4.39: Cost of Living and 10 Consumption Categories Rankings for Expatriates in Houston, United States

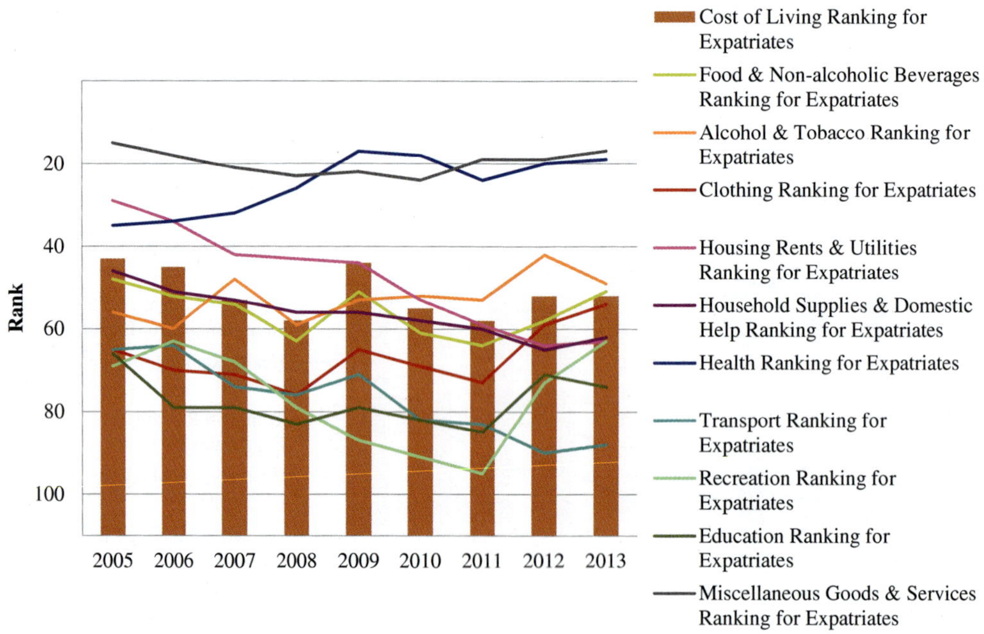

Source: Asia Competitiveness Institute

Widely known for its sizeable energy industry and biomedical research, Houston is the fourth most populous city in the United States with a population of approximately 2.2 million. The city's Cost of Living Ranking for Expatriates, as denoted by the orange bars, declined from 43rd to 52nd between 2005 and 2013 (see Figure 4.39).

Housing Rents & Utilities registered the most significant dip in ranking as it fell 34 places from 29th in 2005 to 63rd in 2013. Transport Ranking slipped 23 spots from 65th to 88th over the same period, making it the lowest ranked category in 2013. Household Supplies & Domestic Help Ranking went down 16 spots from 46th to 62nd between 2005 and 2013. Education Ranking declined more modestly from 66th to 74th over the study period. Food & Non-alcoholic Beverages Ranking dropped slightly from 48th in 2005 to 51st in 2013.

In contrast, Health Ranking jumped 16 places from 35th to 19th between 2005 and 2013. Consequently, Health became the second highest ranked category in 2013 after Miscellaneous Goods & Services at 17th. Clothing Ranking went up 11 spots from 65th in 2005 to 54th in 2013. Recreation Ranking rose from 69th to 63rd over the same period.

ISTANBUL
Turkey

Figure 4.40: Cost of Living and 10 Consumption Categories Rankings for Expatriates in Istanbul, Turkey

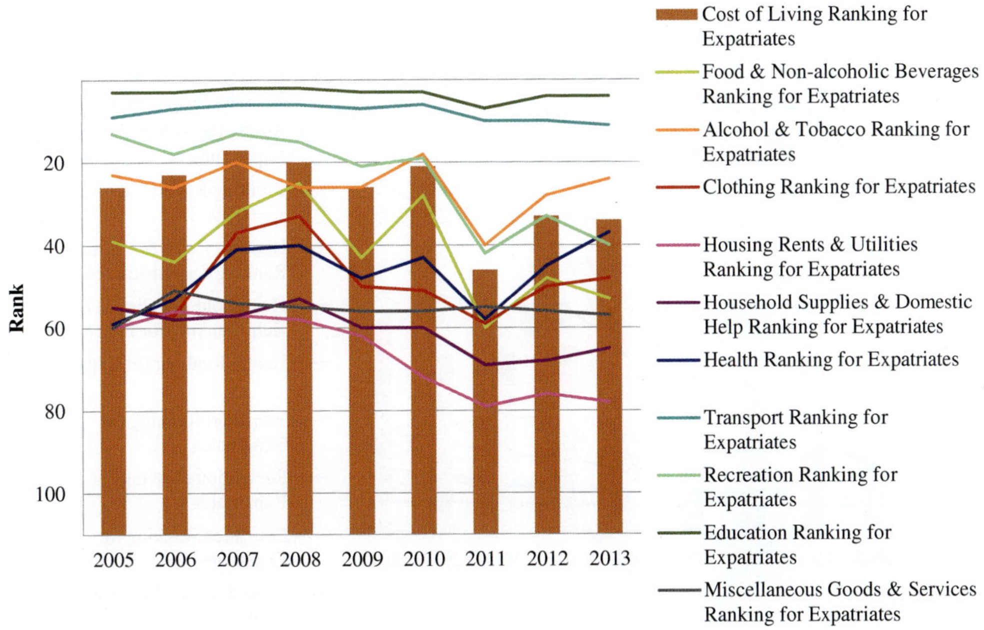

Source: Asia Competitiveness Institute

Best known as a transcontinental city in Eurasia, Istanbul is the largest city in Turkey and accounts for more than a quarter of the country's GDP. The city's Cost of Living Ranking for Expatriates, as represented by the orange bars, declined from 26th in 2005 to 34th in 2013 (see Figure 4.40).

Recreation saw the most remarkable drop in ranking as it slipped 27 places from 13th to 40th between 2005 and 2013. Housing Rents & Utilities Ranking fell 18 spots from 60th to 78th over the study period, making it the lowest ranked category since 2009. Food & Non-alcoholic Beverages Ranking went down 14 places from 39th in 2005 to 53rd in 2013. Household Supplies & Domestic Help was the second lowest ranked category in 2013 as its ranking dropped 10 spots from 55th to 65th over the same period. Education and Transport consistently remained as the highest and second highest ranked category throughout the study period as their rankings declined slightly from third to fourth and ninth to 11th, respectively, between 2005 and 2013.

In contrast, Health Ranking climbed 22 places from 59th in 2005 to 37th in 2013. Clothing Ranking jumped seven spots from 55th to 48th over the same period.

JAKARTA
Indonesia

Figure 4.41: Cost of Living and 10 Consumption Categories Rankings for Expatriates in Jakarta, Indonesia

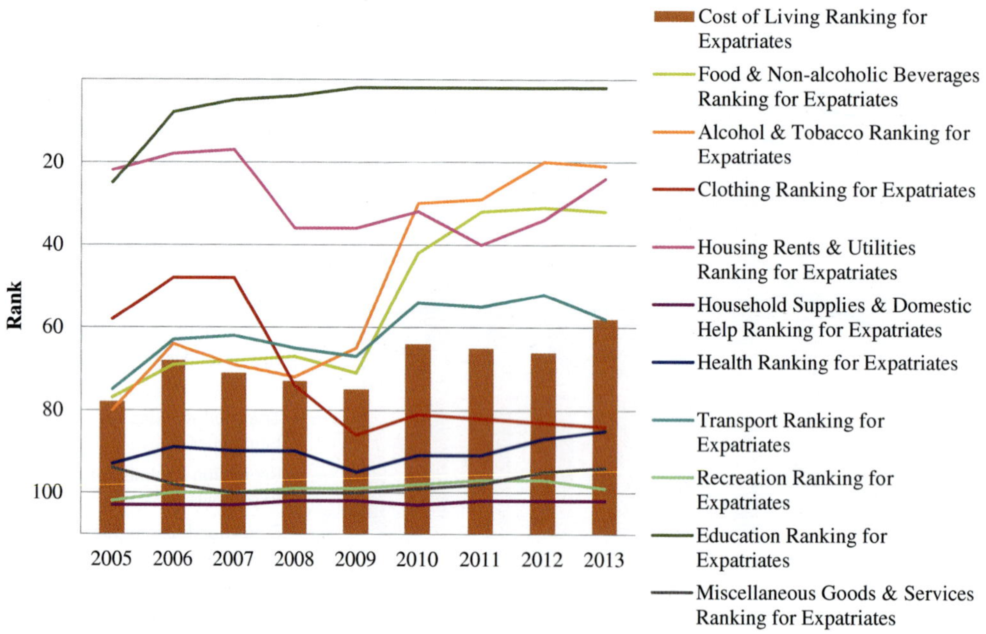

Source: Asia Competitiveness Institute

Located on the northwest coast of Java, Jakarta is the capital of Indonesia and also the most populous city in Southeast Asia with a population of 9.8 million. The city's Cost of Living Ranking for Expatriates, as shown in the orange bars, rose from 78th to 28th between 2005 and 2013 (see Figure 4.41).

Alcohol & Tobacco saw the sharpest rise in ranking as it climbed 59 places from 80th in 2005 to 21st in 2013. Food & Non-alcoholic Beverages Ranking jumped 45 spots from 77th to 32nd over the study period. Education consistently remained as the highest ranked category since 2006 as its ranking went up 23 places from 25th to second between 2005 and 2013. Consequently, Jakarta was the second most expensive among the 103 cities studied in terms of Education in 2013. Transport Ranking moved up 17 spots from 75th in 2005 to 58th in 2013. Health Ranking rose more modestly from 93rd to 85th over the same period. Household Supplies & Domestic Help was the lowest ranked category throughout the study period as its ranking jump slightly from 103rd to 102nd between 2005 and 2013, making Jakarta the second cheapest city in this category in 2013.

In contrast, Clothing Ranking fell 26 places from 58th in 2005 to 84th in 2013. Housing Rents & Utilities Ranking declined slightly from 22nd to 24th between 2005 and 2013.

JOHANNESBURG
South Africa

Figure 4.42: Cost of Living and 10 Consumption Categories Rankings for Expatriates in Johannesburg, South Africa

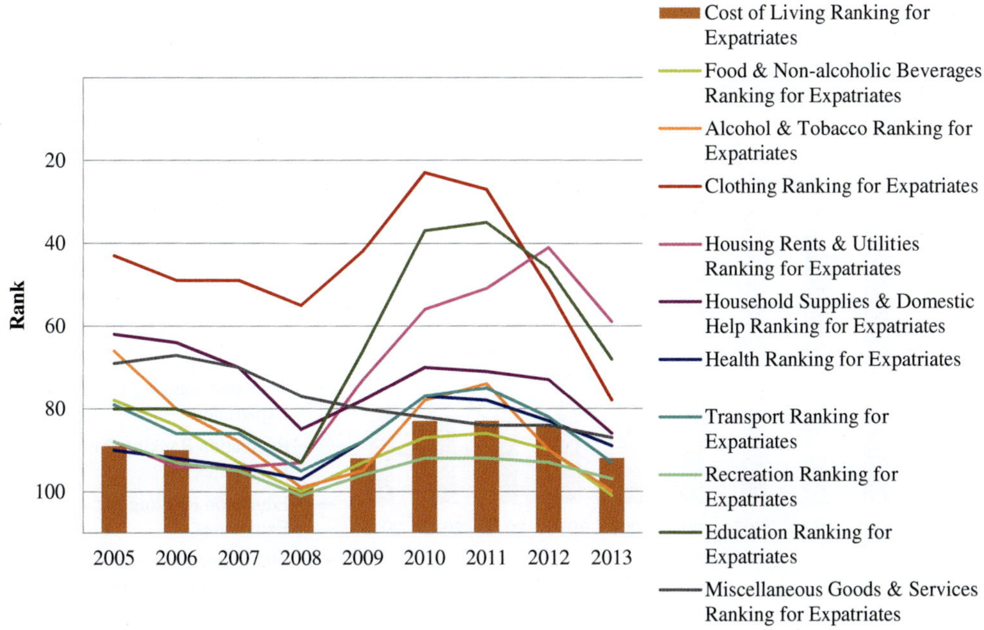

Source: Asia Competitiveness Institute

With a population of approximately 4.4 million, Johannesburg is the largest city and economic centre of South Africa. The city's Cost of Living Ranking for Expatriates, as denoted by the orange bars, declined from 89th to 92nd between 2005 and 2013 (see Figure 4.42).

Clothing recorded the most remarkable dip in ranking as it fell 35 places from 43rd in 2005 to 78th in 2013. Household Supplies & Domestic Help Ranking slipped 24 spots from 62nd to 86th over the study period. Food & Non-alcoholic Beverages Ranking also dropped sharply from 78th to 101st between 2005 and 2013, making Johannesburg the third cheapest city in this category in 2013. Transport Ranking went down 14 places from 79th in 2005 to 93rd in 2013.

In contrast, Housing Rents & Utilities became the highest ranked category in 2013 as its ranking climbed 29 spots from 88th to 59th between 2005 and 2013. Education Ranking jumped 12 places from 80th in 2005 to 68th in 2013. Health Ranking rose slightly from 90th to 89th over the study period.

KIEV
Ukraine

Figure 4.43: Cost of Living and 10 Consumption Categories Rankings for Expatriates in Kiev, Ukraine

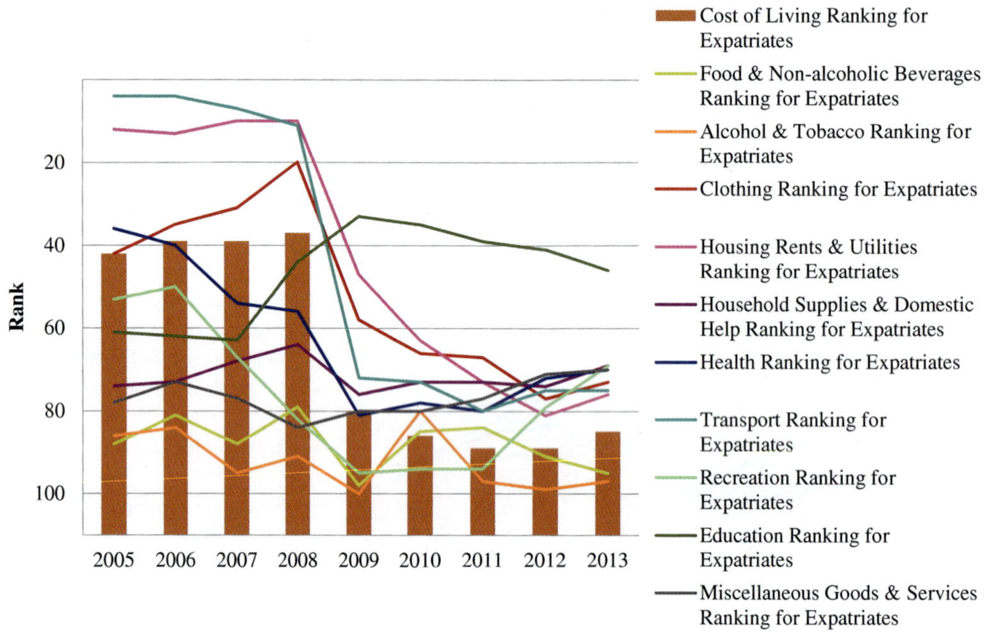

Source: Asia Competitiveness Institute

Kiev, the capital and largest city of Ukraine, is a major industrial, scientific, educational and cultural centre of Eastern Europe. The city's Cost of Living Ranking for Expatriates, as represented by the orange bars, declined sharply from 42nd in 2005 to 85th in 2013 (see Figure 4.43).

Transport registered the most dramatic dip in ranking as it fell 71 places from fourth to 75th between 2005 and 2013. Housing Rents & Utilities Ranking slipped 64 spots from 12th to 76th over the study period. Health Ranking went down 34 places from 36th in 2005 to 70th in 2013. Food & Non-alcoholic Beverages Ranking dropped more modestly from 88th to 95th over the same period, making it the second lowest ranked category in 2013 after Alcohol & Tobacco at 97th.

In contrast, Education Ranking jumped 15 spots from 61st to 46th between 2005 and 2013. Consequently, Education became the highest ranked category for Kiev since 2009. Miscellaneous Goods & Services Ranking went up eight places from 78th to 70th over the study period. Housing Supplies & Domestic Help Ranking rose from 74th in 2005 to 69th in 2013.

KUALA LUMPUR
Malaysia

Figure 4.44: Cost of Living and 10 Consumption Categories Rankings for Expatriates in Kuala Lumpur, Malaysia

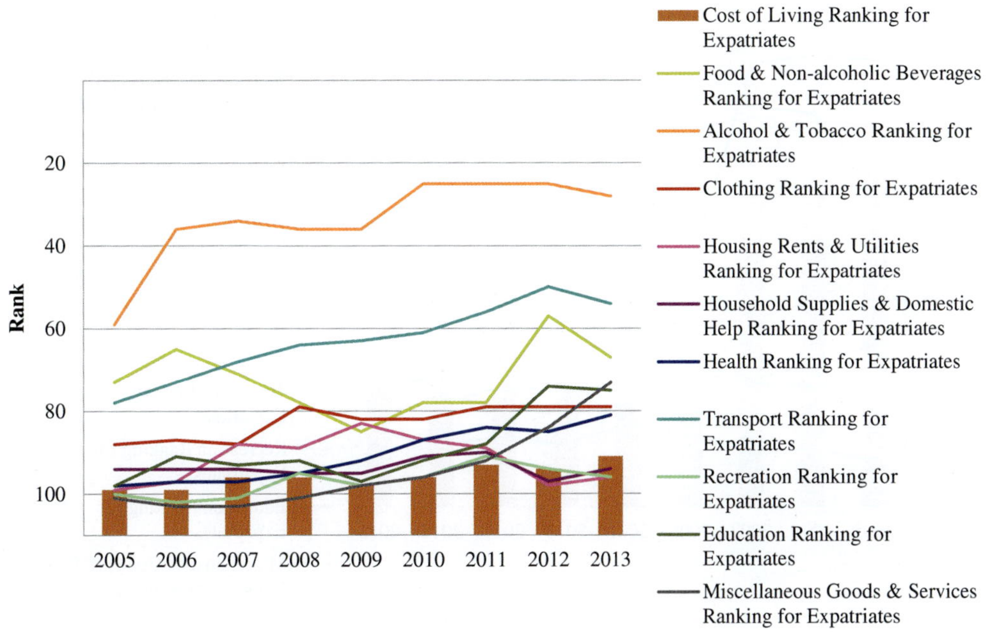

Source: Asia Competitiveness Institute

Kuala Lumpur, the federal capital and the most populous city in Malaysia, is poised to become a global Islamic financing hub with increasing presence of Islamic financial institutions. The city's Cost of Living Ranking for Expatriates, as shown in the orange bars, moved up from 99th to 91st between 2005 and 2013 (see Figure 4.44).

Alcohol & Tobacco saw the most significant rise in ranking as it climbed 31 places from 59th in 2005 to 28th in 2013. Consequently, it remained the highest ranked category throughout the study period. Transport overtook Food & Non-alcoholic Beverages to become the second highest ranked category since 2008 as its ranking jumped 24 spots from 78th to 54th between 2005 and 2013. Education Ranking also rose sharply from 98th to 75th over the same period. Health Ranking moved up 17 places from 98th in 2005 to 81st in 2013. Food & Non-alcoholic Beverages Ranking went up more modestly from 73rd to 67th over the study period. Housing Rents & Utilities Ranking jumped three spots from 99th to 96th between 2005 and 2013, making it the second lowest ranked category in 2013 after Recreation at 96th. Household Supplies & Domestic Help Ranking declined from 94th in 2005 to 97th in 2012 before rising back to 94th in 2013.

KUWAIT CITY
Kuwait

Figure 4.45: Cost of Living and 10 Consumption Categories Rankings for Expatriates in Kuwait, Kuwait

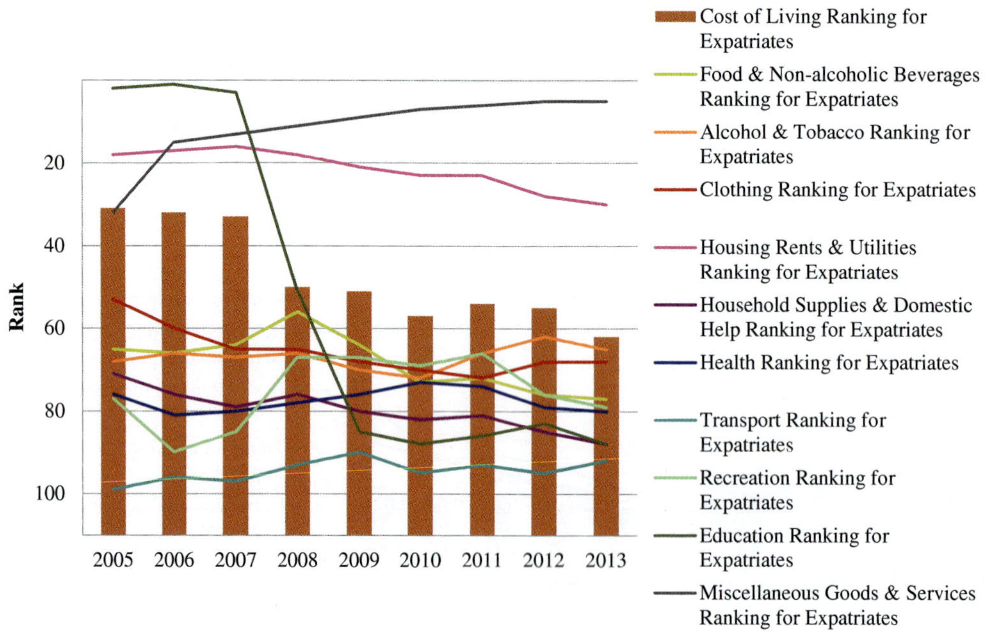

Source: Asia Competitiveness Institute

Known for its petroleum-based economy, Kuwait City is the capital and largest city of Kuwait. The city's Cost of Living Ranking for Expatriates, as denoted by the orange bars, slipped 31 places from 31st to 62nd between 2005 and 2013 (see Figure 4.45).

Education registered the most dramatic dip in ranking as it fell 86 spots from second in 2005 to 88th in 2013. Household Supplies & Domestic Help Ranking declined more modestly from 71st to 88th between 2005 and 2013. Housing Rents & Utilities and Food & Non-alcoholic Beverages Rankings both dropped 12 places from 18th to 30th and 65th to 77th, respectively, over the study period. Health Ranking went down four spots from 76th in 2005 to 80th in 2013.

In contrast, Miscellaneous Goods & Services Ranking jumped 27 places from 32nd to fifth between 2005 and 2013, making it the highest ranked category since 2008. Transport Ranking went up seven spots from 99th in 2005 to 92nd in 2013. However, it remained the lowest ranked category throughout the study period.

LEXINGTON
United States

Figure 4.46: Cost of Living and 10 Consumption Categories Rankings for Expatriates in Lexington, United States

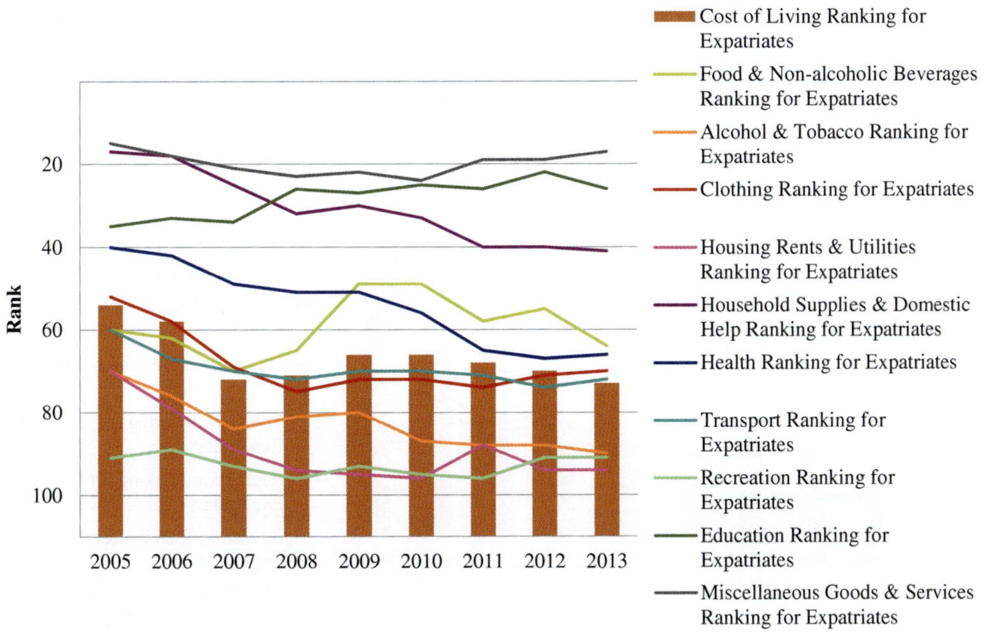

Source: Asia Competitiveness Institute

Lexington, the second largest city in Kentucky, is among the most educated cities in the United States with more than one-third of residents having at least a bachelor's degree. The city's Cost of Living Ranking for Expatriates, as represented by the orange bars, dropped 19 places from 54th to 73rd between 2005 and 2013 (see Figure 4.46).

In particular, Health Ranking slipped 26 spots from 40th in 2005 to 66th in 2013. Housing Rents & Utilities overtook Recreation to become the lowest ranked category since 2012 as its ranking fell 24 places from 70th to 94th over the study period. Clothing Ranking declined from 52nd to 70th between 2005 and 2013. Transport Ranking moved down 12 spots from 60th to 72nd over the same period. Food & Non-alcoholic Beverages Ranking dropped more modestly from 60th in 2005 to 64th in 2013. Miscellaneous Goods & Services remained the highest ranked category throughout the study period as its ranking went down slightly from 15th to 17th between 2005 and 2013. In contrast, Education was the only category that rose in ranking as it jumped nine places from 35th in 2005 to 26th in 2013. Consequently, it became the second highest ranked category since 2008.

LIMA
Peru

Figure 4.47: Cost of Living and 10 Consumption Categories Rankings for Expatriates in Lima, Peru

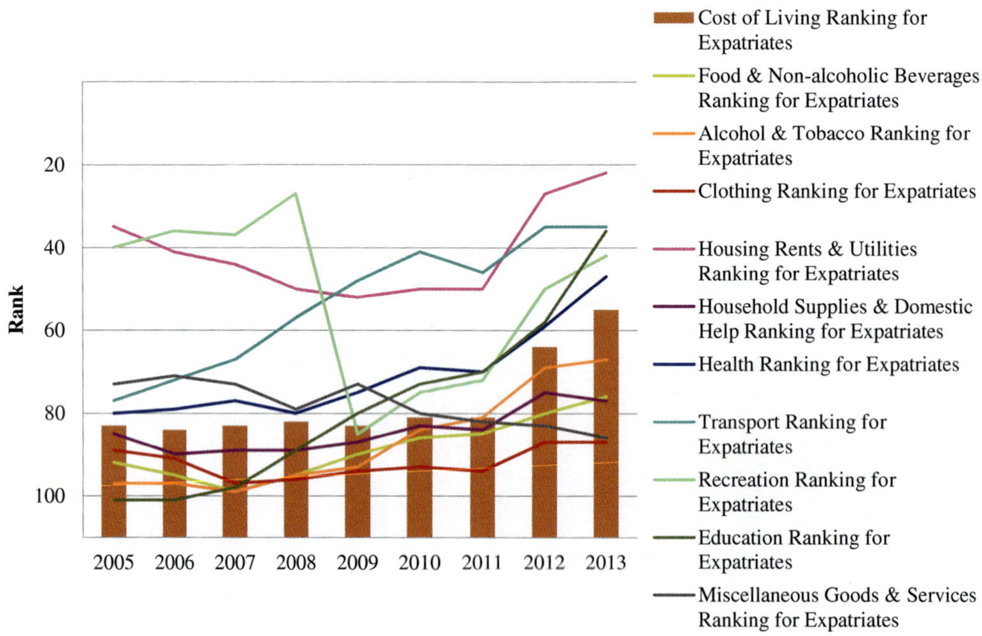

Source: Asia Competitiveness Institute

Lima, the capital and largest city of Peru, is one of the most important financial centres in Latin America. The city's Cost of Living Ranking for Expatriates, as shown in the orange bars, rose from 83rd in 2005 to 55th in 2013 (see Figure 4.47).

Education registered the most remarkable rise in ranking as it climbed 65 places from 101st to 36th between 2005 and 2013. Transport Ranking jumped 42 spots from 77th to 35th over the study period. Health Ranking went up 33 spots from 80th in 2005 to 47th in 2013. Food & Non-alcoholic Beverages Ranking rose from 92nd to 76th over the same period. Housing Rents & Utilities became the highest ranked category since 2012 as its ranking jumped 13 places from 35th in 2005 to 22nd in 2013.

In contrast, Miscellaneous Goods & Services Ranking slipped 13 spots from 73rd to 86th between 2005 and 2013, making it the second lowest ranked category in 2013 after Clothing at 87th. Recreation Ranking dropped slightly from 40th in 2005 to 42nd in 2013.

LISBON
Portugal

Figure 4.48: Cost of Living and 10 Consumption Categories Rankings for Expatriates in Lisbon, Portugal

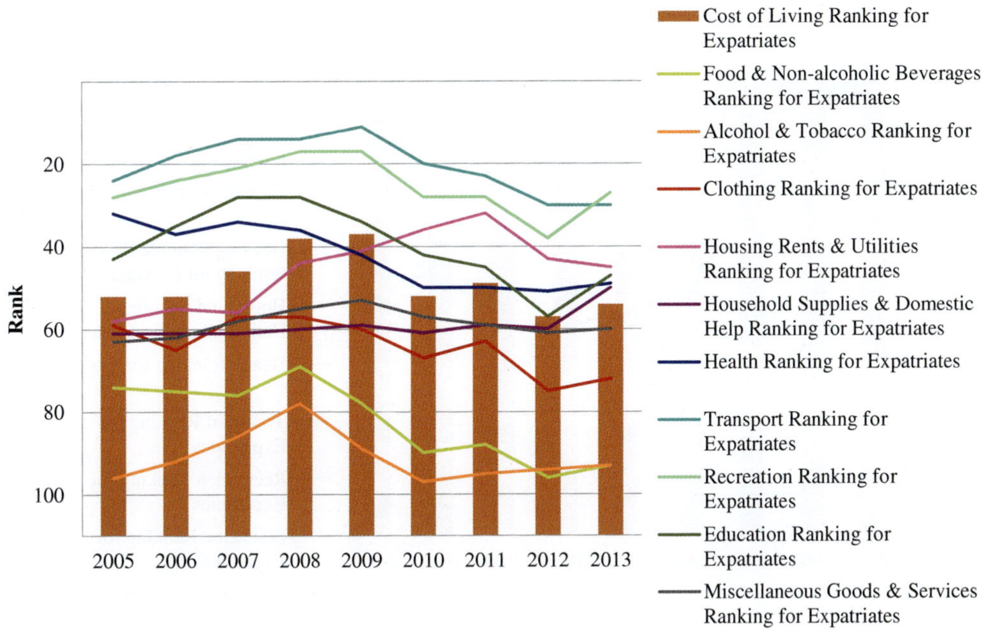

Source: Asia Competitiveness Institute

Home to one of the largest container ports on Europe's Atlantic coast, Lisbon in Portugal is one of the major economic centres of the continent. The city's Cost of Living Ranking for Expatriates, as denoted by the orange bars, declined slightly from 52nd to 54th between 2005 and 2013 (see Figure 4.48).

Food & Non-alcoholic Beverages saw the most remarkable dip in ranking as it fell 19 places from 74th in 2005 to 93rd in 2013, making it the lowest ranked category in 2013 together with Alcohol & Tobacco. Health Ranking slipped 17 spots from 32nd to 49th over the study period. Transport Ranking dropped six places from 24th to 30th between 2005 and 2013. Education Ranking went down four places from 43rd in 2005 to 47th in 2013.

In contrast, Housing Rents & Utilities Ranking climbed 13 spots from 58th to 45th over the study period. Household Supplies & Domestic Help Ranking jumped 11 places from 61st in 2005 to 50th in 2013. Recreation Ranking rose slightly from 28th to 27th between 2005 and 2013, making it the highest ranked category in 2013.

LONDON
Great Britain

Figure 4.49: Cost of Living and 10 Consumption Categories Rankings for Expatriates in London, Great Britain

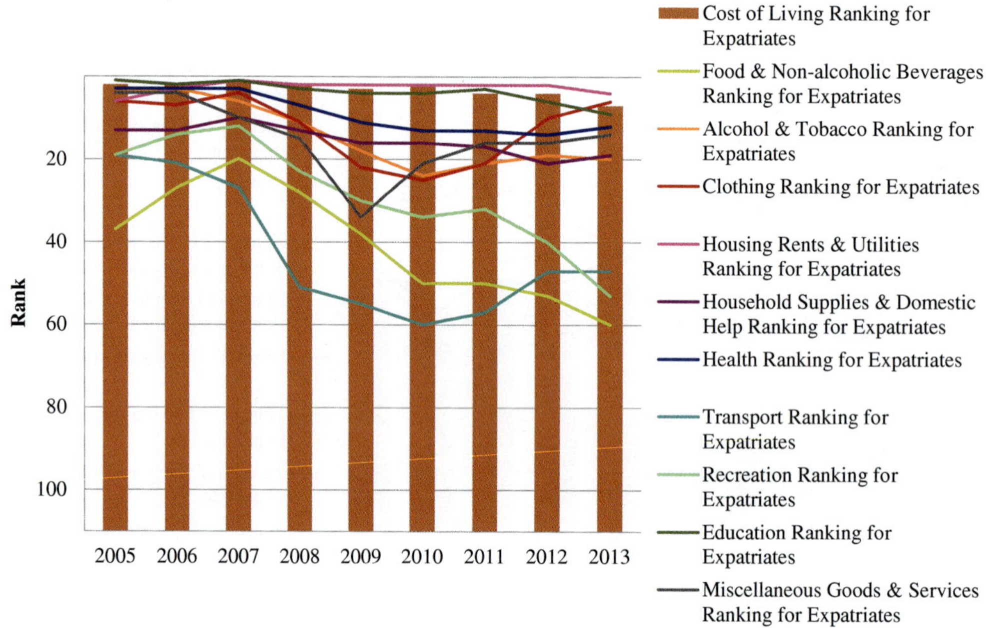

Source: Asia Competitiveness Institute

Widely renowned as the world's leading financial centre and cultural capital, London, Great Britain, is one of the largest cities in the world in terms of GDP. The city's Cost of Living Ranking for Expatriates, as represented by the orange bars, declined from second to seventh between 2005 and 2013 (see Figure 4.49).

Recreation recorded the most significant dip in ranking as it fell 34 places from 19th in 2005 to 53rd in 2013. Transport Ranking dropped 28 spots from 19th to 47th over the study period. Food & Non-alcoholic Beverages became the lowest ranked category in 2013 as its ranking went down 23 places from 37th in 2005 to 60th in 2013. Health and Education Rankings declined from third to 12th and first to ninth, respectively, over the same period. Household Supplies & Domestic Help Ranking moved down six spots from 13th to 19th between 2005 and 2013.

Housing Rents & Utilities was the only category that rose in ranking from sixth to fourth over the study period. Consequently, it consistently remained as the highest ranked category since 2008. Clothing Ranking fell from sixth in 2006 to 25th in 2010 before jumping back to sixth in 2013, making it the second highest ranked category in 2013.

LOS ANGELES
United States

Figure 4.50: Cost of Living and 10 Consumption Categories Rankings for Expatriates in Los Angeles, United States

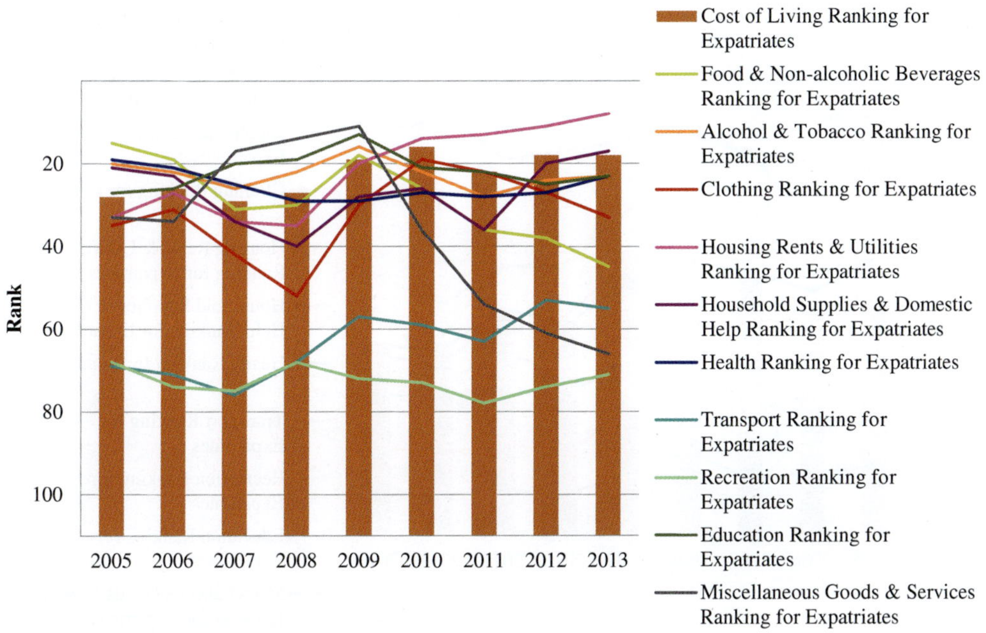

Source: Asia Competitiveness Institute

Nicknamed the "City of Angels" and home to the world renowned Hollywood, Los Angeles is the second largest city in the United States and best known for its vibrant film and television industry. The city's Cost of Living Ranking for Expatriates, as shown in the orange bars, rose from 28th to 18th between 2005 and 2013 (see Figure 4.50).

Housing Rents & Utilities saw the most remarkable rise in ranking as it climbed 25 places from 33rd in 2005 to eighth in 2013 and consequently became the highest ranked category since 2010. Transport Ranking jumped 14 spots from 69th to 55th over the study period. Education Ranking went up four places from 27th in 2005 to 23rd in 2013.

In contrast, Miscellaneous Goods & Services Ranking slipped 33 spots from 33rd to 66th between 2005 and 2013, making it the second lowest ranked category in 2013 after Recreation at 71st. Food & Non-alcoholic Beverages Ranking fell 30 places from 15th to 45th over the study period. Health Ranking declined more modestly from 19th in 2005 to 23rd in 2013.

LUXEMBOURG
Luxembourg

Figure 4.51: Cost of Living and 10 Consumption Categories Rankings for Expatriates in Luxembourg, Luxembourg

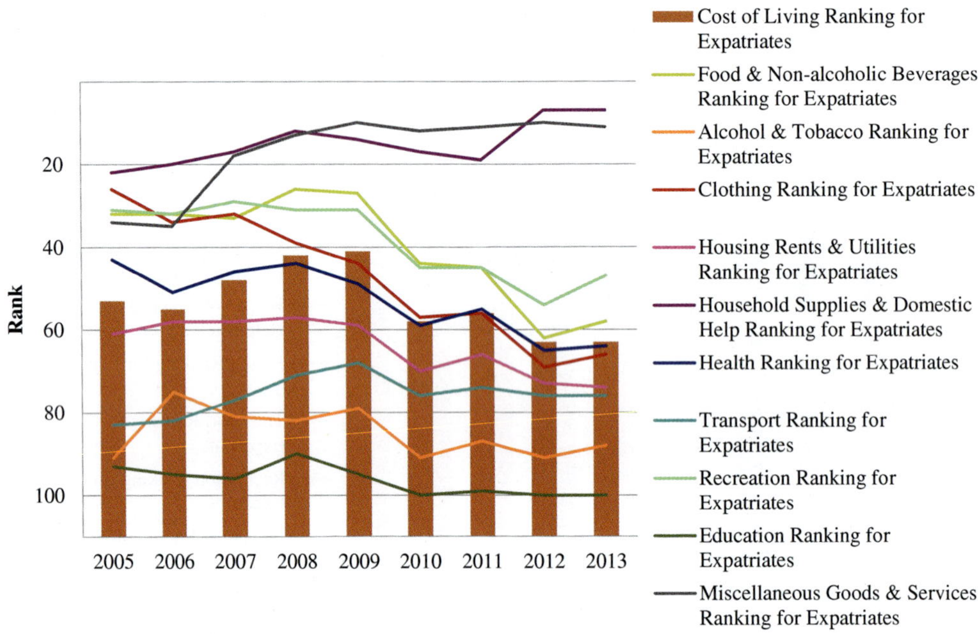

Source: Asia Competitiveness Institute

Situated at the heart of Western Europe, Luxembourg is best known for having one of the highest per capita GDP in the world. The city's Cost of Living Ranking for Expatriates, as shown in the orange bars, declined from 53rd to 63rd between 2005 and 2013 (see Figure 4.51).

Clothing registered the most significant dip in ranking as it fell 40 places from 26th in 2005 to 66th in 2013. Food & Non-alcoholic Beverages Ranking slipped 26 spots from 32nd to 58th over the study period. Health Ranking went down 21 places from 43rd to 64th between 2005 and 2013. Housing Rents & Utilities Ranking dropped 13 spots from 61st to 74th over the same period. Education saw a more modest decline in ranking from 93rd in 2005 to 100th in 2013, making Luxembourg the fourth cheapest city in this category in 2013.

In contrast, Household Supplies & Domestic Help became the highest ranked category in 2013 as its ranking jumped 15 places from 22nd to seventh between 2005 and 2013. Transport Ranking went up seven spots from 83rd to 76th over the study period.

LYON
France

Figure 4.52: Cost of Living and 10 Consumption Categories Rankings for Expatriates in Lyon, France

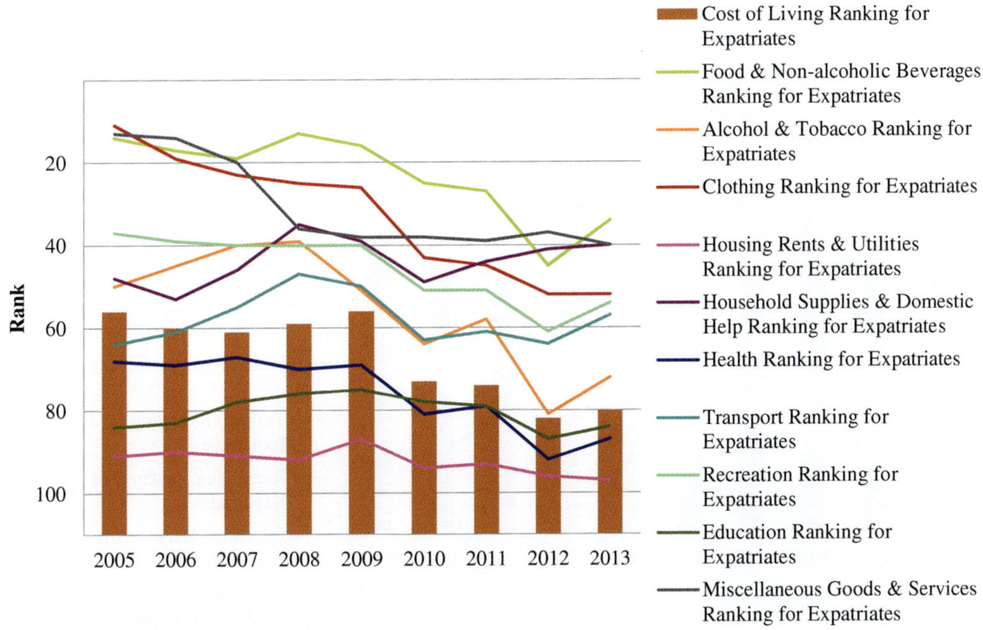

Source: Asia Competitiveness Institute

Lyon is a major centre for banking in France and also home to high-technology industries including biotechnology and software. The city's Cost of Living Ranking for Expatriates, as denoted by the orange bars, declined sharply from 56th to 80th between 2005 and 2013 (see Figure 4.52).

Clothing recorded the most remarkable dip in ranking as it slipped 41 places from 11th in 2005 to 52nd in 2013. Food & Non-alcoholic Beverages was the highest ranked category in 2013 although its ranking fell 20 spots from 14th to 34th over the study period. Health Ranking dropped 19 places from 68th to 87th between 2005 and 2013, making it the second lowest ranked category in 2013. Housing Rents & Utilities consistently remained as the lowest ranked category throughout the study period as its ranking went down six spots from 91st in 2005 to 97th in 2013. Education Ranking rose from 84th in 2005 to 75th in 2009 before falling back to 84th in 2013.

In contrast, Household Supplies & Domestic Help Ranking jumped eight places from 48th to 40th between 2005 and 2013. Transport Ranking went up from 64th in 2005 to 57th in 2013.

MADRID
Spain

Figure 4.53: Cost of Living and 10 Consumption Categories Rankings for Expatriates in Madrid, Spain

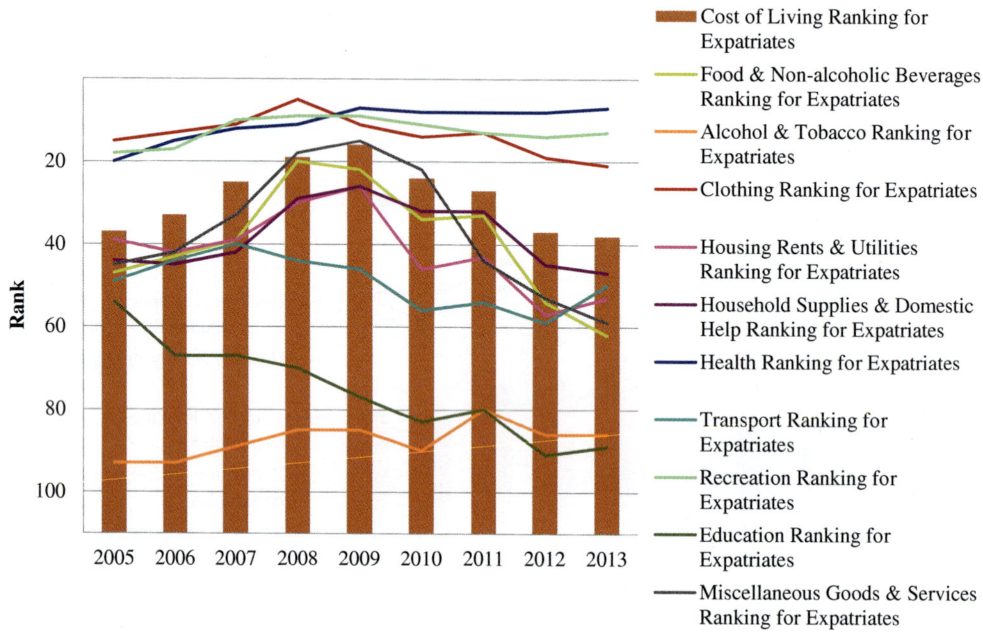

Source: Asia Competitiveness Institute

Madrid, the capital and largest city of Spain, is the country's second most important industrial centre (after Barcelona) specialising in high-technology production. The city's Cost of Living Ranking for Expatriates, as represented by the orange bars, declined slightly from 37th to 38th between 2005 and 2013 (see Figure 4.53).

Education saw the most remarkable dip in ranking as it fell 35 places from 54th in 2005 to 89th in 2013. Consequently, Education overtook Alcohol & Tobacco to become the lowest ranked category since 2012. Food & Non-alcoholic Beverages Ranking slipped 15 spots from 47th to 62nd between 2005 and 2013. Housing Rents & Utilities Ranking went down 14 places from 39th to 53rd over the study period. Transport Ranking dropped slightly from 49th in 2005 to 50th in 2013.

In contrast, Health became the highest ranked category since 2009 as its ranking jumped 13 spots from 20th to seventh between 2005 and 2013. Recreation Ranking went up five places from 18th to 13th over the same period, making it the second highest ranked category in 2013.

MANILA
Philippines

Figure 4.54: Cost of Living and 10 Consumption Categories Rankings for Expatriates in Manila, Philippines

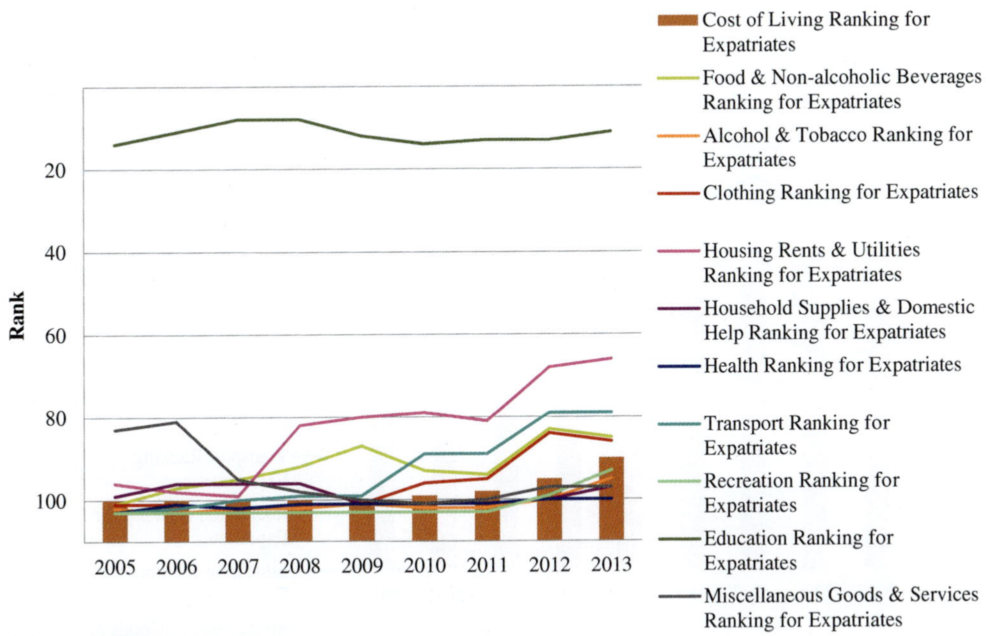

Source: Asia Competitiveness Institute

Manila, the capital and second largest city in the Philippines, is home to the Port of Manila, the country's largest seaport and important international shipping gateway. The city's Cost of Living Ranking for Expatriates, as shown in the orange bars, moved up from 100th in 2005 to 90th in 2013 (see Figure 4.54).

Housing Rents & Utilities registered the most significant rise in ranking as it jumped 30 places from 96th to 66th between 2005 and 2013, making it the second highest ranked category since 2008. Transport Ranking climbed 24 spots from 103rd to 79th over the study period. Clothing Ranking also rose sharply from 101st in 2005 to 86th in 2013. Food & Non-alcoholic Beverages Ranking went up 16 places from 101st in 2005 to 85th in 2013. Health and Education Rankings both moved up three spots from 103rd to 100th and 14th to 11th, respectively, over the same period. Nonetheless, Education consistently remained as the highest ranked category throughout the study period while Health became the lowest ranked category in 2013. Household Supplies & Domestic Help Ranking rose slightly from 99th to 97th between 2005 and 2013.

MELBOURNE
Australia

Figure 4.55: Cost of Living and 10 Consumption Categories Rankings for Expatriates in Melbourne, Australia

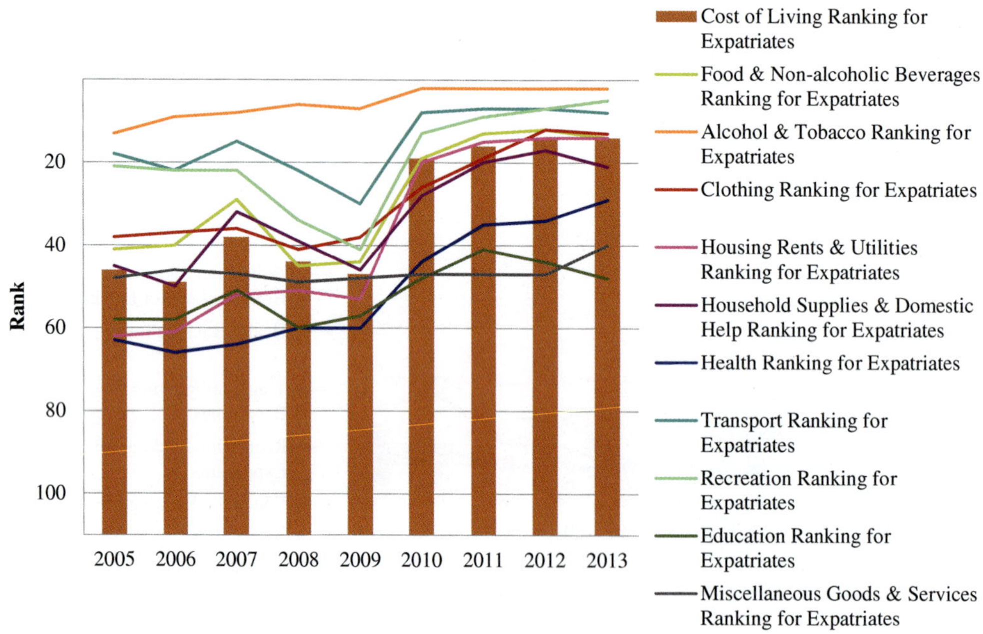

Source: Asia Competitiveness Institute

Home to the world's largest urban tram network, Melbourne is often referred to as the cultural capital of Australia. The city's Cost of Living Ranking for Expatriates, as denoted by the orange bars, rose from 46th to 14th between 2005 and 2013 (see Figure 4.55).

Housing Rents & Utilities saw the most dramatic rise in ranking as it climbed 48 places from 62nd in 2005 to 14th in 2013. Health Ranking jumped 34 spots from 63rd to 29th over the study period. Food & Non-alcoholic Beverages Ranking moved up 27 places from 41st to 14th between 2005 and 2013. Alcohol & Tobacco consistently remained as the highest ranked category throughout the study period as its ranking rose from 13th in 2005 to second in 2013, making Melbourne the second most expensive city in this category in 2013. Recreation became the second highest ranked category in 2013 as its ranking jumped from 21st to fifth over the study period. Education and Transport Rankings both went up ten spots from 58th to 48th and 18th to eighth, respectively, between 2005 and 2013. Nonetheless, Education was the lowest ranked category in 2013.

MEXICO CITY
Mexico

Figure 4.56: Cost of Living and 10 Consumption Categories Rankings for Expatriates in Mexico City, Mexico

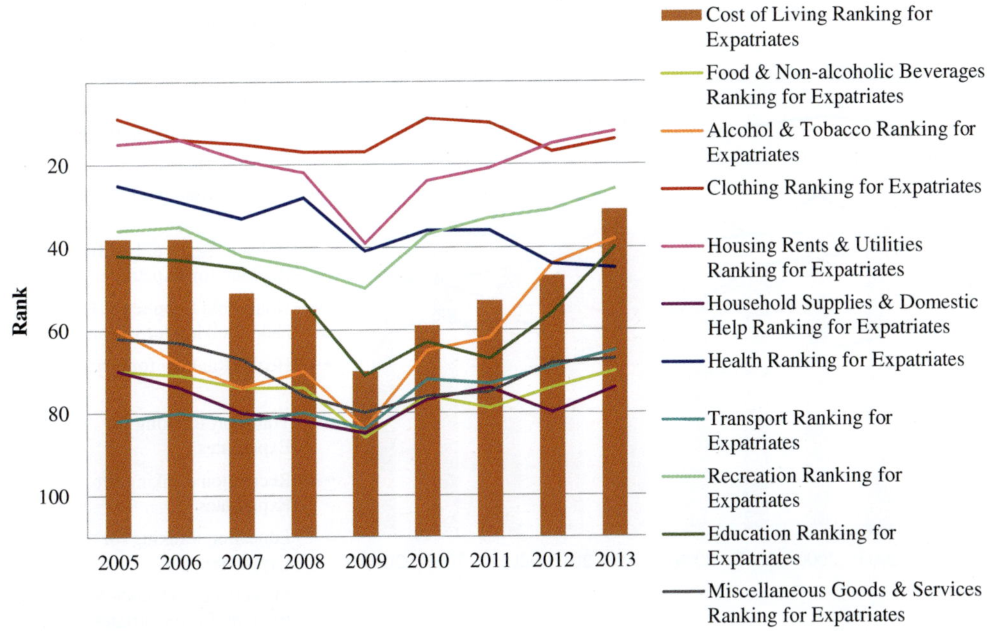

Source: Asia Competitiveness Institute

Mexico City, the capital of Mexico, is the largest Spanish-speaking city in the world with an estimated population of 8.8 million. The city's Cost of Living Ranking for Expatriates, as represented by the orange bars, moved up from 38th to 31st between 2005 and 2013 (see Figure 4.56).

Alcohol & Tobacco registered the most significant rise in ranking as it climbed 22 places from 60th in 2005 to 38th in 2013. Transport Ranking jumped 17 spots from 82nd to 65th over the study period. Recreation Ranking went up 10 places from 36th to 26th between 2005 and 2013. Housing Rents & Utilities became the highest ranked category in 2013 as its ranking rose from 15th to 12th over the same period. Education Ranking moved up two spots from 42nd in 2005 to 40th in 2013. Food & Non-alcoholic Beverages Ranking declined from 70th in 2005 to 86th in 2009 before rising back to 70th in 2013.

In contrast, Health Ranking slipped 20 places from 25th to 45th over the study period. Household Supplies & Domestic Help Ranking fell four spots from 70th in 2005 to 74th in 2013, making it the lowest ranked category in 2013.

MIAMI
United States

Figure 4.57: Cost of Living and 10 Consumption Categories Rankings for Expatriates in Miami, United States

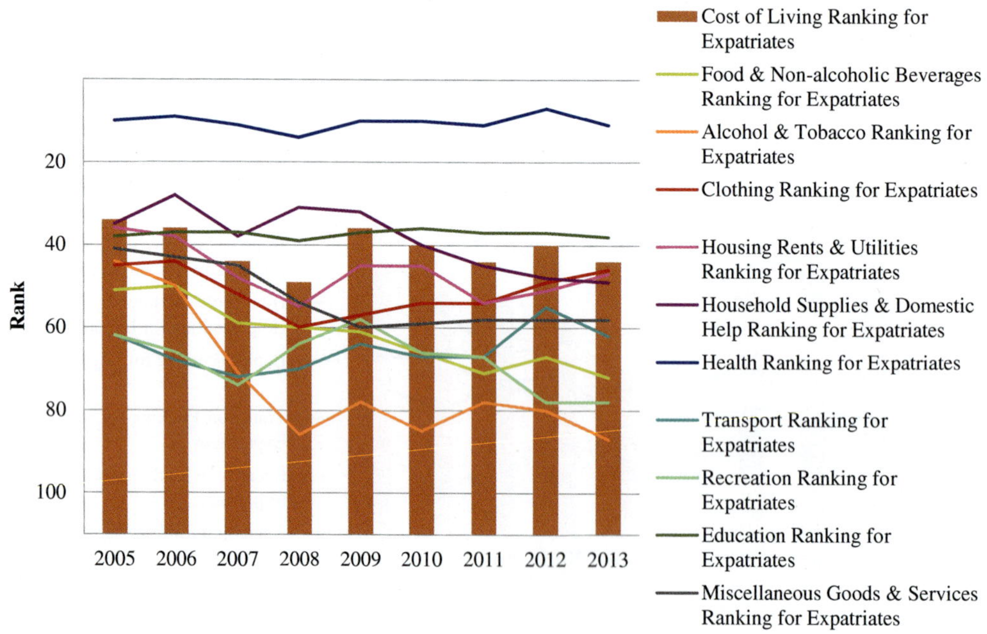

Source: Asia Competitiveness Institute

Known for its beautiful beaches, Miami is also a major centre of commerce, finance and media in the United States. The city's Cost of Living Ranking for Expatriates, as shown in the orange bars, declined from 34th to 44th between 2005 and 2013 (see Figure 4.57).

Alcohol & Tobacco saw the most dramatic dip in ranking as it fell 43 places from 44th in 2005 to 87th in 2013, making it the lowest ranked category since 2008. Food & Non-alcoholic Beverages Ranking slipped 21 spots from 51st to 72nd over the study period. Recreation was the second lowest ranked category in 2013 as its ranking declined sharply from 62nd in 2005 to 78th in 2013. Housing Rents & Utilities Ranking dropped 11 places from 36th to 47th between 2005 and 2013. Education Ranking remained largely stable at 38th over the same period. Transport Ranking went down from 62nd in 2005 to 72nd in 2007 before rising back to 62nd in 2013. Clothing Ranking declined from 45th to 46th between 2005 and 2013. Likewise, Health Ranking moved down one spot from 10th in 2005 to 11th in 2013. Nonetheless, Health consistently remained as the highest ranked category throughout the study period.

MILAN
Italy

Figure 4.58: Cost of Living and 10 Consumption Categories Rankings for Expatriates in Milan, Italy

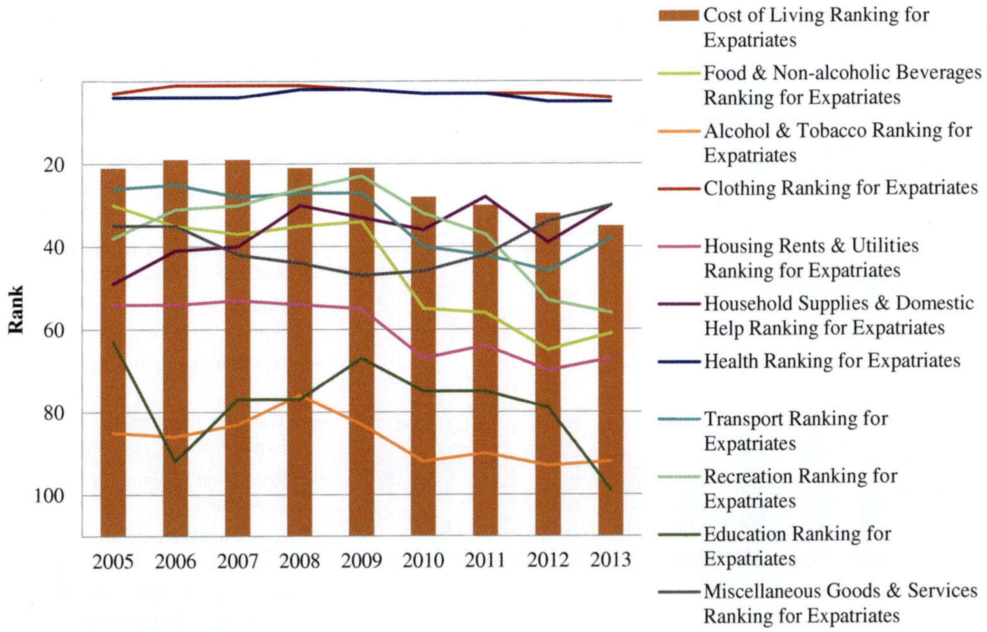

Source: Asia Competitiveness Institute

Widely referred to as the world's fashion and design capital, Milan is also one of the major industrial, commercial and financial centres of Italy. The city's Cost of Living Ranking for Expatriates, as denoted by the orange bars, declined from 21st to 35th between 2005 and 2013 (see Figure 4.58).

Education recorded the most remarkable dip in ranking as it slipped 36 places from 63rd in 2005 to 99th in 2013, making it the lowest ranked category in 2013. Food & Non-alcoholic Beverages Ranking fell 31 spots from 30th to 61st over the study period. Housing Rents & Utilities Ranking dropped 13 places from 54th in 2005 to 67th in 2013. Transport Ranking went down 12 spots from 26th to 38th between 2005 and 2013. Clothing and Health Rankings declined slightly from third to fourth and fourth to fifth, respectively, over the study period, making them the highest and second highest ranked category in 2013. Milan has therefore been consistently among the top five most expensive cities in terms of Clothing and Health throughout the study period.

In contrast, Household Supplies & Domestic Help Ranking jumped 19 places from 49th in 2005 to 30th in 2013. Miscellaneous Goods & Services Ranking went up five spots from 35th to 30th over the same period.

MINNEAPOLIS
United States

Figure 4.59: Cost of Living and 10 Consumption Categories Rankings for Expatriates in Minneapolis, United States

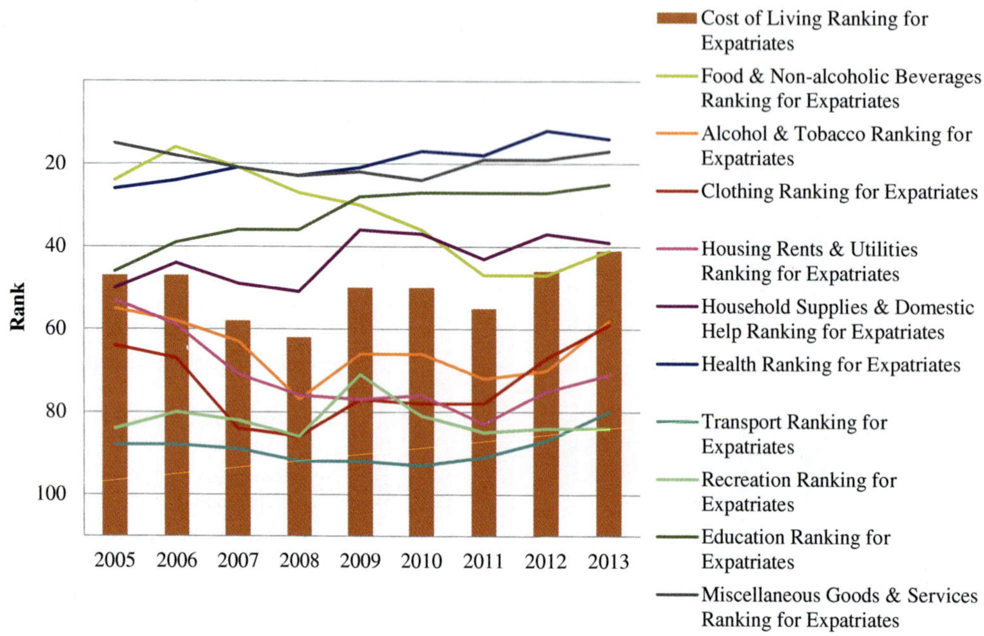

Source: Asia Competitiveness Institute

Once a hub for flour milling and timber, Minneapolis today is a primary economic centre in the American Midwest. The city's Cost of Living Ranking for Expatriates, as represented by the orange bars, rose from 47th to 41st between 2005 and 2013 (see Figure 4.59).

In particular, Education Ranking climbed 21 places from 46th in 2005 to 25th in 2013. Health became the highest ranked category in 2013 as its ranking jumped 12 spots from 26th to 14th over the study period. Household Supplies & Domestic Help Ranking moved up 11 places from 50th to 39th between 2005 and 2013. Transport Ranking rose from 88th in 2005 to 80th in 2013, making it the second lowest ranked category in 2013 after Recreation at 84th.

In contrast, Housing Rents & Utilities registered the most significant dip in ranking as it fell 18 spots from 53rd to 71st between 2005 and 2013. Food & Non-alcoholic Beverages Ranking slipped 17 places from 24th to 41st over the same period.

MONTEVIDEO
Uruguay

Figure 4.60: Cost of Living and 10 Consumption Categories Rankings for Expatriates in Montevideo, Uruguay

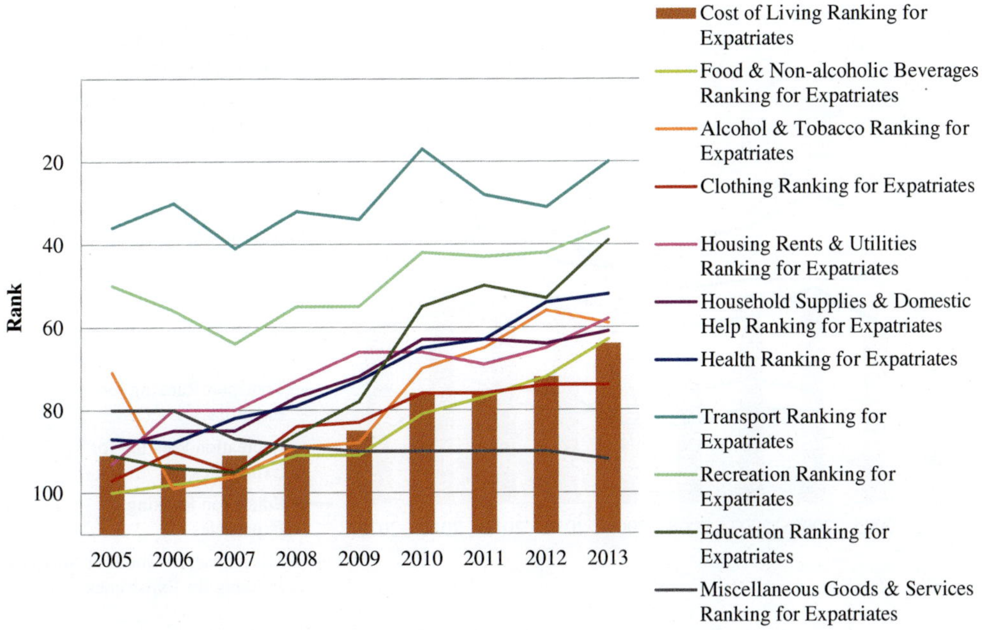

Source: Asia Competitiveness Institute

Montevideo, the capital and largest city of Uruguay, is the country's centre of finance, commerce and higher education. The city's Cost of Living Ranking for Expatriates, as shown in the orange bars, rose sharply from 91st to 64th between 2005 and 2013 (see Figure 4.60).

Education saw the most dramatic rise in ranking as it climbed 52 places from 91st in 2005 to 39th in 2013. Food & Non-alcoholic Beverages Ranking jumped 37 spots from 100th to 63rd over the study period. Housing Rents & Utilities and Health Rankings both moved up 35 places from 93rd to 58th and 87th to 52nd, respectively, between 2005 and 2013. Household Supplies & Domestic Help Ranking rose from 89th in 2005 to 61st in 2013. Transport consistently remained as the highest ranked category throughout the study period as its ranking jumped 16 spots from 36th to 20th between 2005 and 2013. Miscellaneous Goods & Services was the only category that declined in ranking from 80th to 92nd over the period studied, making it the lowest ranked category since 2010.

MONTREAL
Canada

Figure 4.61: Cost of Living and 10 Consumption Categories Rankings for Expatriates in Montreal, Canada

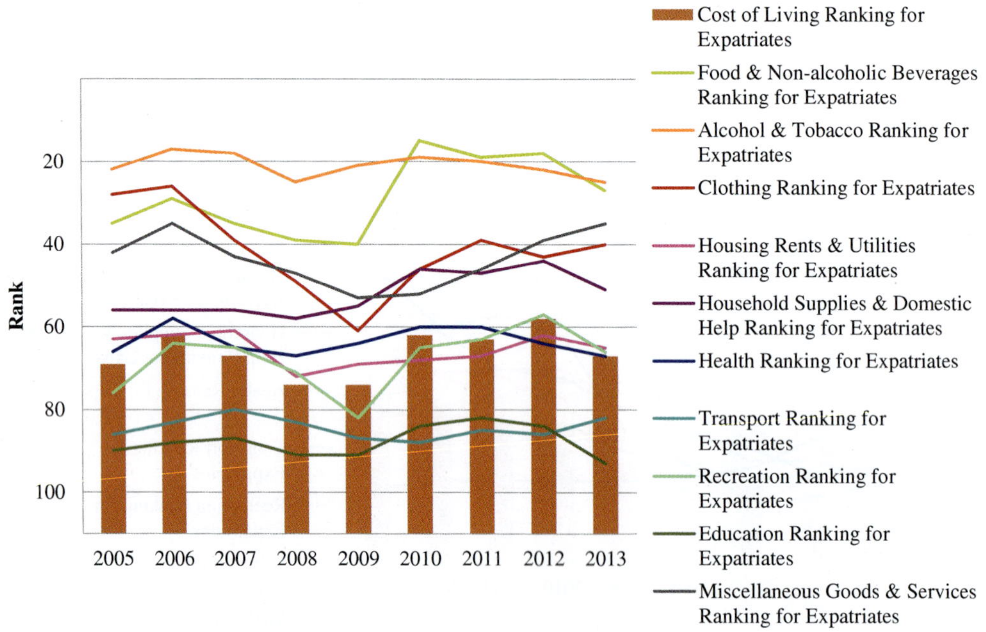

Source: Asia Competitiveness Institute

Montreal is the second largest among Canadian cities in terms of GDP after Toronto. The city's Cost of Living Ranking for Expatriates, as denoted by the orange bars, moved up from 69th to 67th between 2005 and 2013 (see Figure 4.61).

In particular, Recreation Ranking jumped 10 places from 76th in 2005 to 66th in 2013. Food & Non-alcoholic Beverages Ranking climbed eight spots from 35th to 27th over the study period, making it the second highest ranked category in 2013 after Alcohol & Tobacco at 25th. Household Supplies & Domestic Help Ranking went up five places from 56th to 51st between 2005 and 2013. Transport Ranking rose from 86th in 2005 to 82nd in 2013.

In contrast, Clothing Ranking fell 12 spots from 28th to 40th between 2005 and 2013. Education became the lowest ranked category in 2013 as its ranking slipped three places from 90th in 2005 to 93rd in 2013. Health Ranking declined slightly from 66th to 67th over the study period.

MOSCOW
Russia

Figure 4.62: Cost of Living and 10 Consumption Categories Rankings for Expatriates in Moscow, Russia

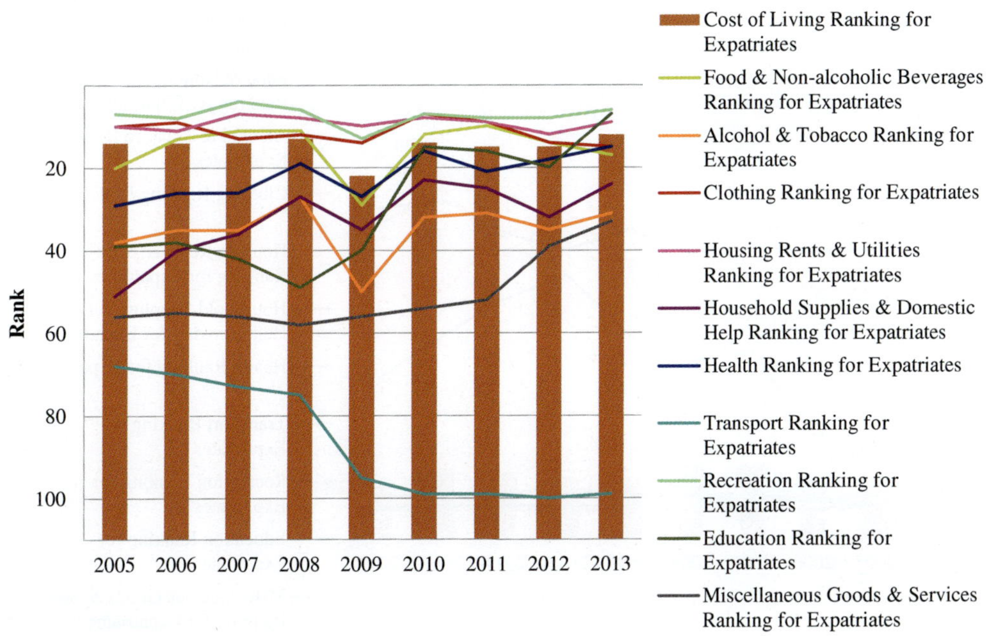

Source: Asia Competitiveness Institute

Moscow, the capital city of Russia, is the most populous city in Europe with a population of approximately 12 million. The city's Cost of Living Ranking for Expatriates, as represented by the orange bars, went up from 14th to 12th between 2005 and 2013 (see Figure 4.62).

Education recorded the most significant rise in ranking as it climbed 32 places from 39th in 2005 to seventh in 2013, making it the second highest ranked category in 2013 after Recreation at sixth. Household Supplies & Domestic Help Ranking jumped 27 spots from 51st to 24th over the study period. Health Ranking moved up 14 places from 29th to 15th between 2005 and 2013. Food & Non-alcoholic Beverages and Housing Rents & Utilities Rankings rose more modestly from 20th to 17th and 10th to ninth, respectively, over the same period.

In contrast, Transport consistently remained as the lowest ranked category throughout the study period as its ranking fell 31 places from 68th in 2005 to 99th in 2013. Clothing Ranking slipped five spots from 10th to 15th between 2005 and 2013.

MUMBAI
India

Figure 4.63: Cost of Living and 10 Consumption Categories Rankings for Expatriates in Mumbai, India

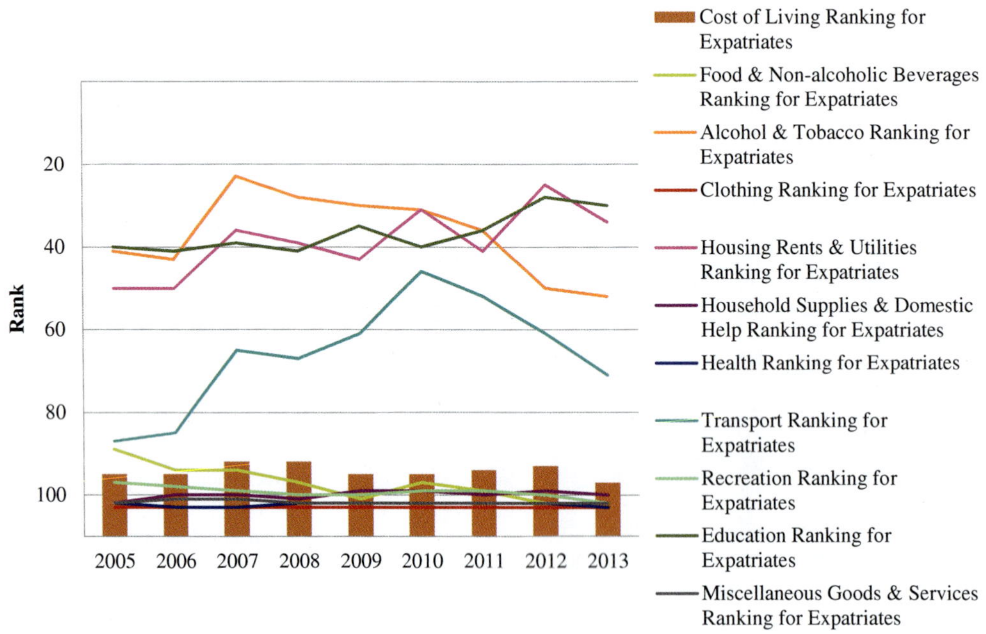

Source: Asia Competitiveness Institute

Situated on the west coast of India with a deep natural harbour, Mumbai is the country's most populous city, and financial and commercial capital. The city's Cost of Living Ranking for Expatriates, as shown in the orange bars, declined from 95th in 2005 to 97th in 2013 (see Figure 4.63).

In particular, Food & Non-alcoholic Beverages Ranking slipped 14 places from 89th in 2005 to 103rd in 2013, making Mumbai the cheapest among the 103 cities studied in this category in 2013. Health Ranking fell one spot from 102nd to 103rd over the study period. Miscellaneous Goods & Services and Clothing Rankings largely remained stable at 102nd and 103rd, respectively, between 2005 and 2013.

In contrast, Housing Rents & Utilities and Transport Rankings both jumped 16 places from 50th to 34th and 87th to 71st, respectively, over the study period. Education became the highest ranked category in 2013 as its ranking moved up 10 spots from 40th in 2005 to 30th in 2013. Household Supplies & Domestic Help Ranking went up slightly from 102nd to 100th over the same period.

MUNICH
Germany

Figure 4.64: Cost of Living and 10 Consumption Categories Rankings for Expatriates in Munich, Germany

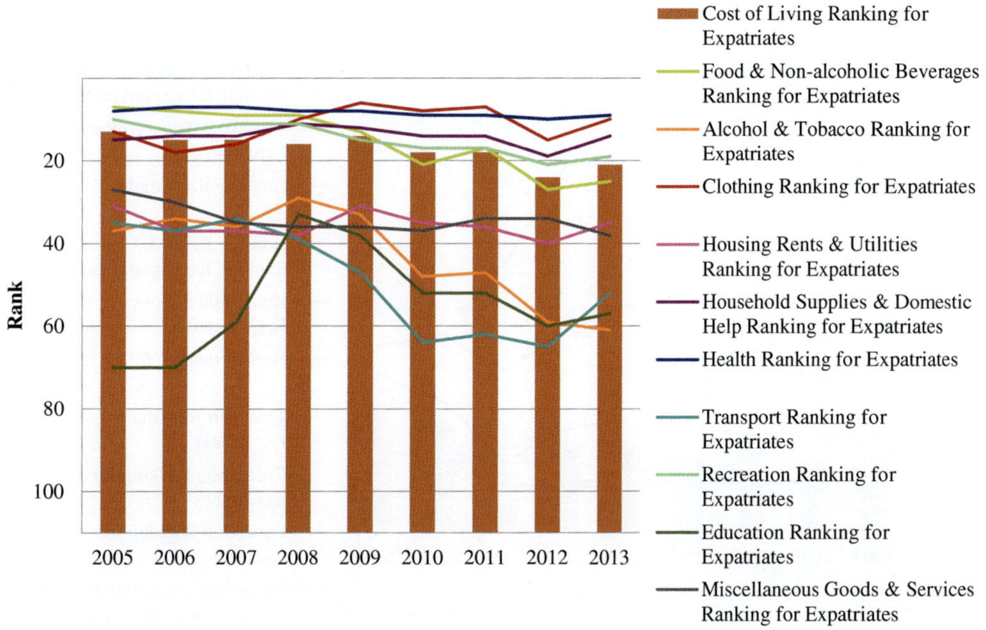

Source: Asia Competitiveness Institute

Home to Oktoberfest, the world's largest annual funfair, Munich is Germany's third largest city and centre of publishing and advanced technologies. The city's Cost of Living Ranking for Expatriates, as denoted by the orange bars, declined from 13th to 21st between 2005 and 2013 (see Figure 4.64).

Alcohol & Tobacco registered the most remarkable dip in ranking as it fell 24 places from 37th in 2005 to 61st in 2013, making it the lowest ranked category in 2013. Food & Non-alcoholic Beverages Ranking slipped 18 spots from seventh to 25th over the study period. Transport Ranking also declined sharply from 35th to 52nd between 2005 and 2013. Housing Rents & Utilities Ranking went down four places from 31st in 2005 to 35th in 2013. Health became the highest ranked category in 2013 as its ranking moved down one spot from eighth to ninth over the same period.

In contrast, Education Ranking jumped 13 places from 70th to 57th between 2005 and 2013. However, it was the second lowest ranked category in 2013. Clothing and Household Supplies & Domestic Help Rankings went up from 13th to 10th and 15th to 14th, respectively, over the study period.

NAIROBI
Kenya

Figure 4.65: Cost of Living and 10 Consumption Categories Rankings for Expatriates in Nairobi, Kenya

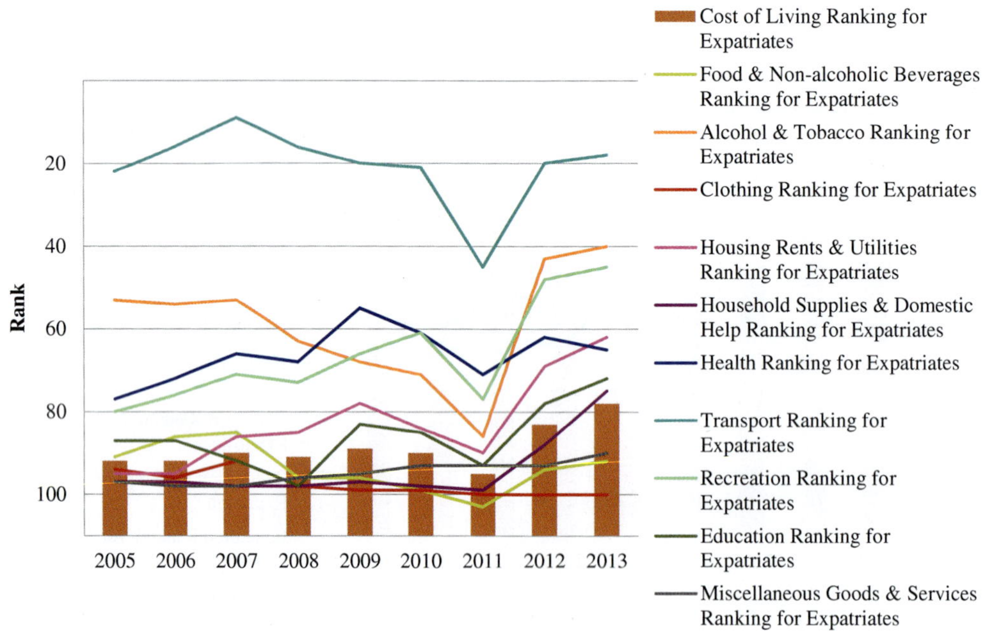

Source: Asia Competitiveness Institute

Nairobi, the capital and largest city of Kenya, is known for hosting the headquarters for the United Nations in Africa, the United Nations Environment Programme (UNEP) and the United Nations Human Settlements Programme (UN-Habitat). The city's Cost of Living Ranking for Expatriates, as represented by the orange bars, rose from 92nd in 2005 to 78th in 2013 (see Figure 4.65).

In particular, Recreation Ranking climbed 35 places from 80th to 45th between 2005 and 2013. Housing Rents & Utilities Ranking jumped 33 spots from 95th in 2005 to 62nd in 2013. Education and Health Rankings went up from 87th to 72nd and 77th to 65th, respectively, over the study period. Transport consistently remained as the highest ranked category throughout the study period as its ranking rose from 22nd in 2005 to 18th in 2013.

In contrast, Clothing Ranking slipped six places from 94th to 100th between 2005 and 2013, making it the lowest ranked category since 2012. Food & Non-alcoholic Beverages Ranking dropped slightly from 91st to 92nd over the same period.

NEW DELHI
India

Figure 4.66: Cost of Living and 10 Consumption Categories Rankings for Expatriates in New Delhi, India

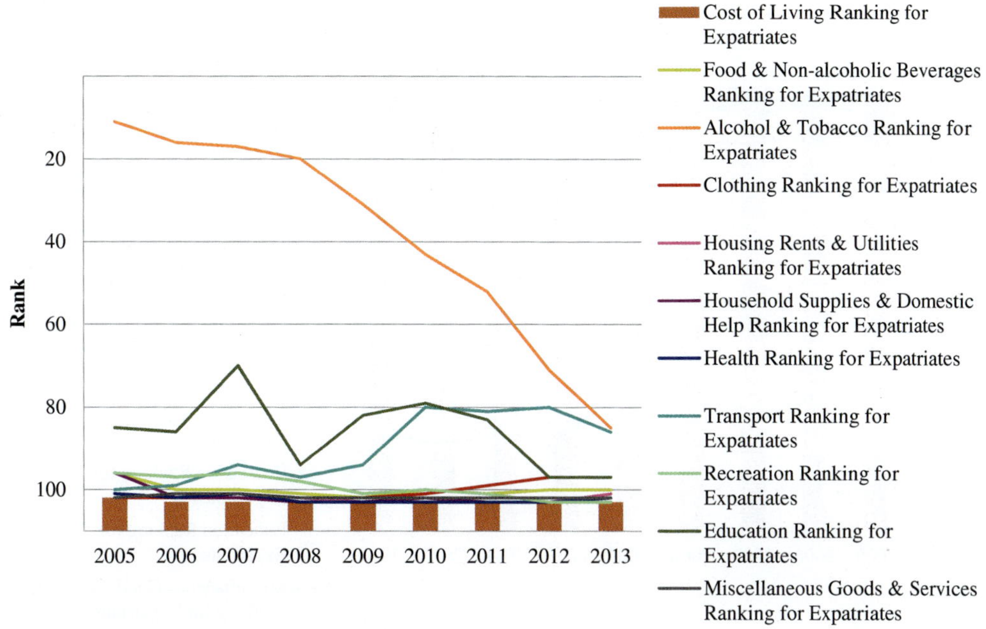

Source: Asia Competitiveness Institute

New Delhi, the capital of India, is home to a sizeable tertiary sector that includes information technology, telecommunications, hotels, banking and media. The city's Cost of Living Ranking for Expatriates, as shown in the orange bars, declined from 102nd in 2005 to 103rd in 2013, making New Delhi the most affordable among the 103 cities studied in 2013 (see Figure 4.66).

Alcohol & Tobacco recorded the most dramatic dip in ranking as it fell 74 places from 11th to 85th between 2005 and 2013. Nonetheless, it remained as the highest ranked category throughout the study period. Education Ranking slipped 12 spots from 85th in 2005 to 97th in 2013. Recreation and Household Supplies & Domestic Help Rankings both dropped seven places from 96th to 103rd over the same period. Food & Non-alcoholic Beverages Ranking went down from 96th in 2005 to 100th in 2013. Health Ranking moved down one spot from 101st to 102nd between 2005 and 2013.

In contrast, Transport Ranking jumped 14 places from 100th in 2004 to 86th in 2013, making it the second highest ranked category in 2013. Clothing Ranking moved up five spots from 102nd to 97th between 2005 and 2013. Housing Rents & Utilities Ranking rose slightly from 102nd to 101st over the same period.

NEW YORK
United States

Figure 4.67: Cost of Living and 10 Consumption Categories Rankings for Expatriates in New York, United States

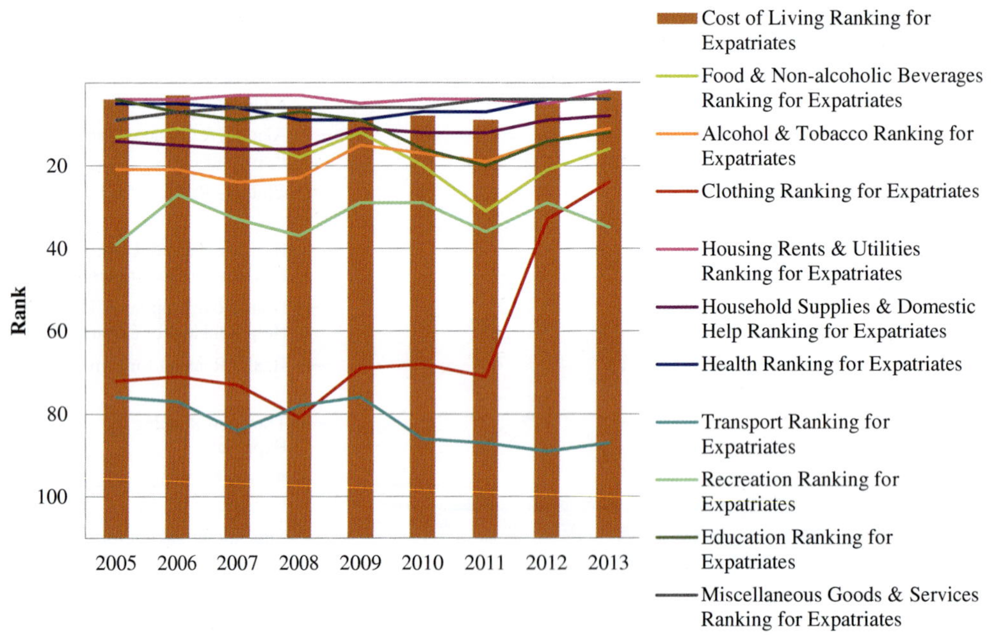

Source: Asia Competitiveness Institute

Home to the United Nations Headquarters, New York is an important centre for international diplomacy as well as one of the world's leading financial capitals. The city's Cost of Living Ranking for Expatriates, as denoted by the orange bars, moved up from fourth to second between 2005 and 2013 (see Figure 4.67).

Clothing recorded the most dramatic rise in ranking as it climbed 48 places from 72nd in 2005 to 24th in 2013. Alcohol & Tobacco Ranking jumped 10 spots from 21st to 11th over the study period. Household Supplies & Domestic Help Ranking rose from 14th to eighth between 2005 and 2013. Housing Rents & Utilities remained the highest ranked category for most of the study period as its ranking moved up two places from fourth in 2005 to second in 2013, making New York the second most expensive among the 103 cities studied in this category. Health Ranking went up from fifth in 2005 to fourth in 2013.

In contrast, Transport Ranking slipped 11 places from 76th in 2005 to 87th in 2013 although this downward trend appears to be levelling off. Consequently, Transport overtook Clothing to become the lowest ranked category since 2009. Education Ranking fell eight places from fourth to 12th between 2005 and 2013. Food & Non-alcoholic Beverages Ranking declined from 13th to 16th over the same period.

OSAKA & KOBE
Japan

Figure 4.68: Cost of Living and 10 Consumption Categories Rankings for Expatriates in Osaka–Kobe, Japan

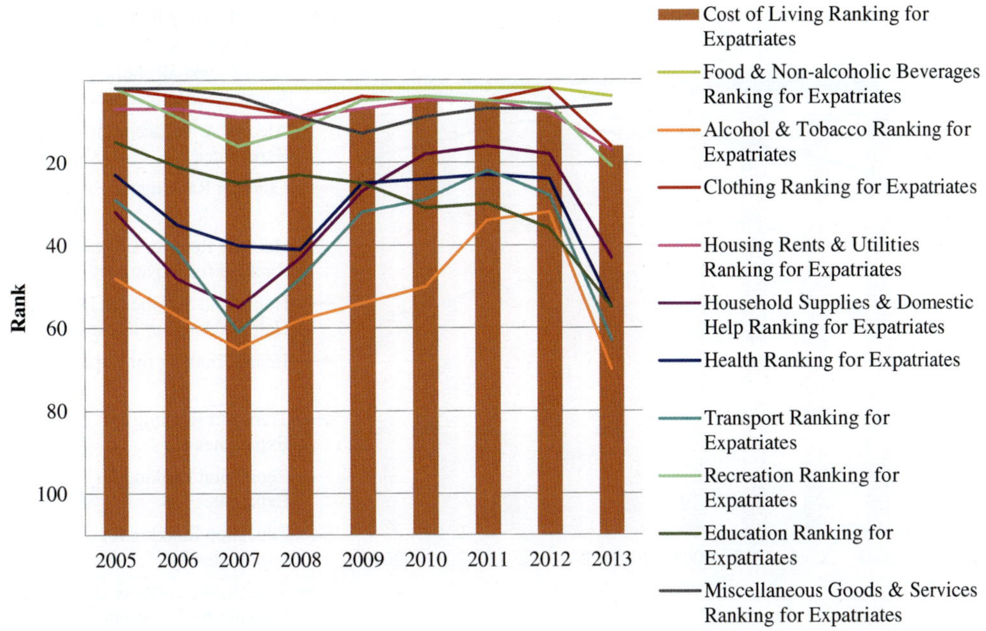

Source: Asia Competitiveness Institute

Osaka is Japan's third largest city by population and a leading centre of commerce, while Kobe is the sixth largest city and home to the fourth busiest port in the country. The cities' Cost of Living Ranking for Expatriates, as represented by the orange bars, declined from third to 13th between 2005 and 2013 (see Figure 4.68).

The rankings of all 10 categories went down over the study period. In particular, Education Ranking slipped 40 places from 15th in 2005 to 55th in 2013. Transport Ranking fell 34 spots from 29th to 63rd between 2005 and 2013, making it the second lowest ranked category in 2013 after Alcohol & Tobacco at 70th. Health Ranking dropped 32 places from 23rd to 55th over the study period. Clothing Ranking declined more modestly from second to 16th between 2005 and 2013. Household Supplies & Domestic Help Ranking went down from 32nd in 2005 to 43rd in 2013. Housing Rents & Utilities Ranking moved down 10 spots from seventh to 17th over the same period. Food & Non-alcoholic Beverages remained as the highest ranked category for most of the study period as its ranking fell two places from second in 2005 to fourth in 2013. Miscellaneous Goods & Services was the second highest ranked category in 2013 as its ranking moved down from second to sixth over the study period.

OSLO
Norway

Figure 4.69: Cost of Living and 10 Consumption Categories Rankings for Expatriates in Oslo, Norway

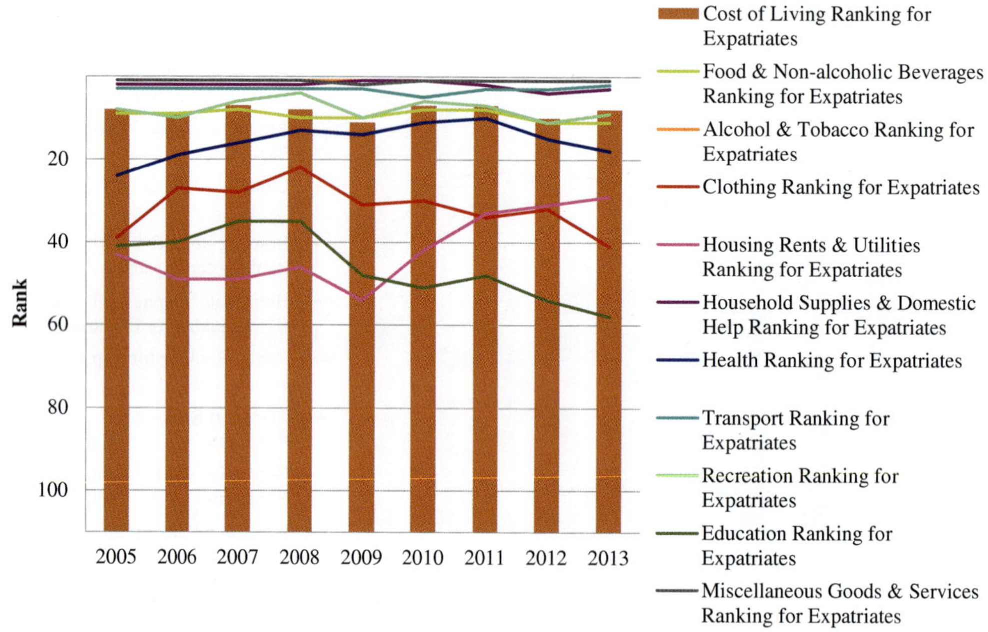

Source: Asia Competitiveness Institute

Oslo, the capital and most populous city in Norway, is an important centre for maritime industries and maritime trade in Europe. The city's Cost of Living Ranking for Expatriates, as shown in the orange bars, went down from eighth in 2005 to 11th in 2009 before rising back to eighth in 2013 (see Figure 4.69).

Housing Rents & Utilities registered the most significant rise in ranking as it jumped 14 places from 43rd to 29th between 2005 and 2013. Health Ranking moved up six spots from 24th to 18th over the study period. Transport became the second highest ranked category in 2013 as its ranking rose from third in 2005 to second in 2013. Alcohol & Tobacco and Miscellaneous Goods & Services remained the highest ranked categories throughout the study period as their rankings largely stayed at the top spot.

In contrast, Education overtook Housing Rents & Utilities to become the lowest ranked category since 2010 as its ranking slipped 17 places from 41st in 2005 and 58th in 2013. Food & Non-alcoholic Beverages and Clothing Rankings both fell two spots from ninth to 11th and 39th to 41st, respectively, over the study period.

PARIS
France

Figure 4.70: Cost of Living and 10 Consumption Categories Rankings for Expatriates in Paris, France

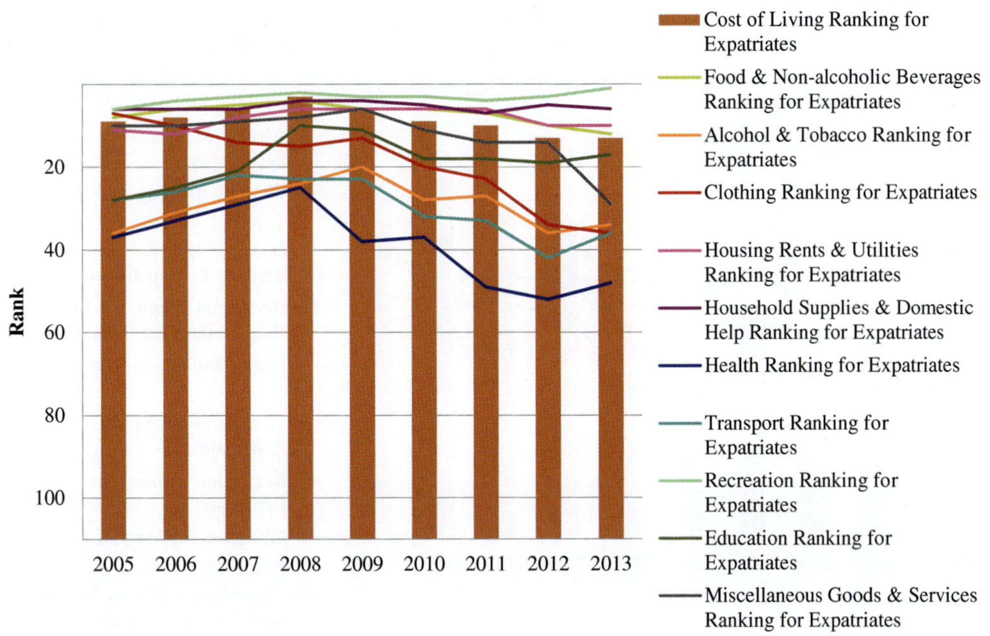

Source: Asia Competitiveness Institute

Nicknamed "the City of Light", Paris, the capital and most populous city of France, is one of the major tourist destinations in the world and home to many notable architectural landmarks. The city's Cost of Living Ranking for Expatriates, as denoted by the orange bars, declined from ninth to 13th between 2005 and 2013 (see Figure 4.70).

Clothing saw the most significant dip in ranking as it fell 29 places from seventh in 2005 to 36th in 2013. Health consistently remained as the lowest ranked category throughout the study period as its ranking slipped 11 spots from 37th to 48th between 2005 and 2013. Transport Ranking dropped eight places from 28th to 36th over the study period. Food & Non-alcoholic Beverages Ranking went down from eighth in 2005 to 12th in 2013.

In contrast, Education Ranking jumped 11 places from 28th to 17th between 2005 and 2013. Recreation Ranking moved up five spots from sixth to first over the same period, making Paris the most expensive city in this category in 2013. Housing Rents & Utilities Ranking rose slightly from 11th in 2005 to 10th in 2013.

PERTH
Australia

Figure 4.71: Cost of Living and 10 Consumption Categories Rankings for Expatriates in Perth, Australia

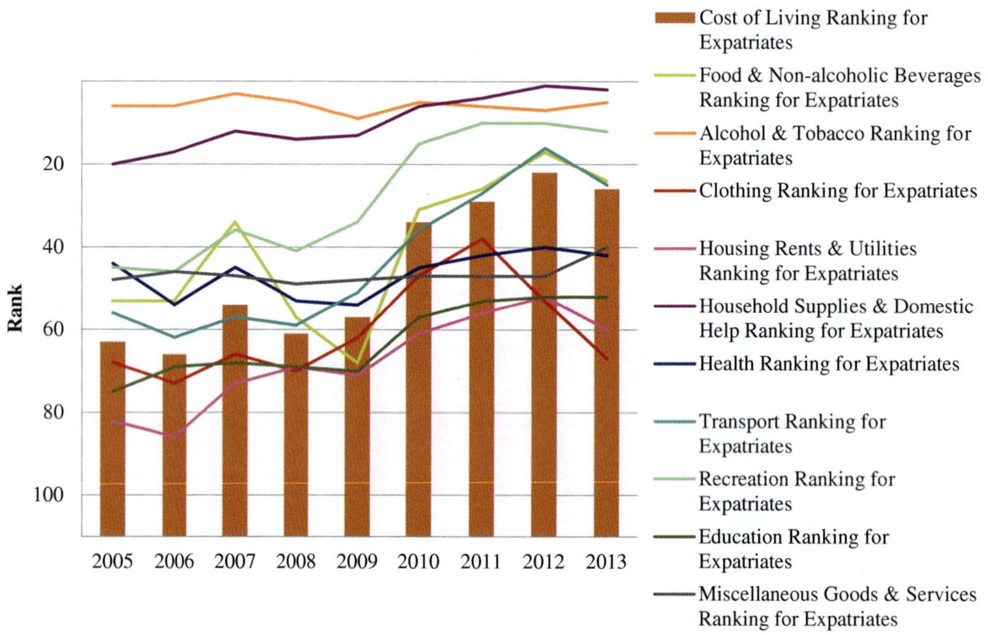

Source: Asia Competitiveness Institute

Home to a sizeable mining industry, Perth is the fourth most populous city in Australia with a population of approximately 2 million. The city's Cost of Living Ranking for Expatriates, as represented by the orange bars, rose sharply from 63rd to 26th between 2005 and 2013 (see Figure 4.71).

All categories rose in rankings over the study period. Recreation registered the most remarkable rise in ranking as it climbed 33 places from 45th in 2005 to 12th in 2013. Transport Ranking jumped 31 spots from 56th to 25th over the study period. Food & Non-alcoholic Beverages Ranking moved up 29 places from 53rd to 24th between 2005 and 2013. Education and Housing Rents & Utilities Rankings also rose sharply from 75th to 52nd and 82nd to 60th, respectively, over the same period. Household Supplies & Domestic Help overtook Alcohol & Tobacco to become the highest ranked category since 2011 as its ranking went up 18 spots from 20th in 2005 to second in 2013, making Perth the second most expensive city in this category in 2013. Health and Clothing Rankings rose more modestly from 44th to 42nd and 68th to 67th, respectively, over the study period. Consequently, Clothing became the lowest ranked category in 2013.

PITTSBURGH
United States

Figure 4.72: Cost of Living and 10 Consumption Categories Rankings for Expatriates in Pittsburgh, United States

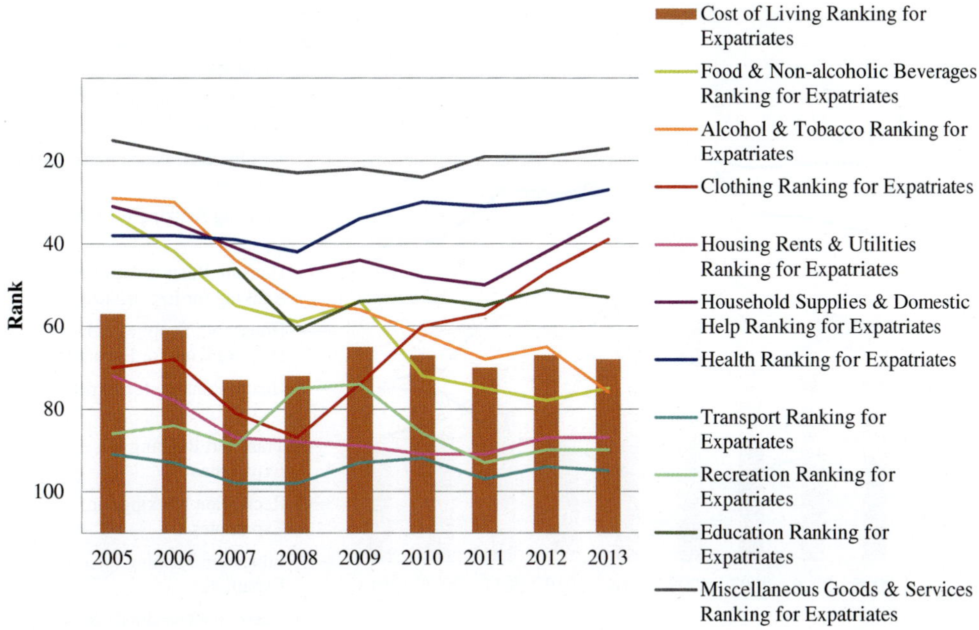

Source: Asia Competitiveness Institute

Known as "the Steel City" for its more than 300 steel-related businesses, Pittsburgh, the second largest city in the state of Pennsylvania, USA is also famous for hosting technology giants including Google, Intel, IBM and Apple. The city's Cost of Living Ranking for Expatriates, as shown in the orange bars, declined from 57th to 68th between 2005 and 2013 (see Figure 4.72).

In particular, Food & Non-alcoholic Beverages Ranking fell 42 places from 33rd in 2005 to 75th in 2013. Housing Rents & Utilities Ranking slipped 15 spots from 72nd to 87th over the study period. Education Ranking dropped six places from 47th to 53rd between 2005 and 2013. Transport and Recreation Rankings both went down four places from 91st to 95th and 86th to 90th, respectively, over the same period, making them the lowest and second lowest ranked category in 2013. Miscellaneous Goods & Services consistently remained as the highest ranked category throughout the study period as its ranking slipped slightly from 15th in 2005 to 17th in 2013.

In contrast, Clothing Ranking climbed 31 places from 70th to 39th between 2005 and 2013. Health became the second highest ranked category since 2008 as its ranking jumped 11 spots from 38th to 27th over the study period.

PRAGUE
Czech Republic

Figure 4.73: Cost of Living and 10 Consumption Categories Rankings for Expatriates in Prague, Czech Republic

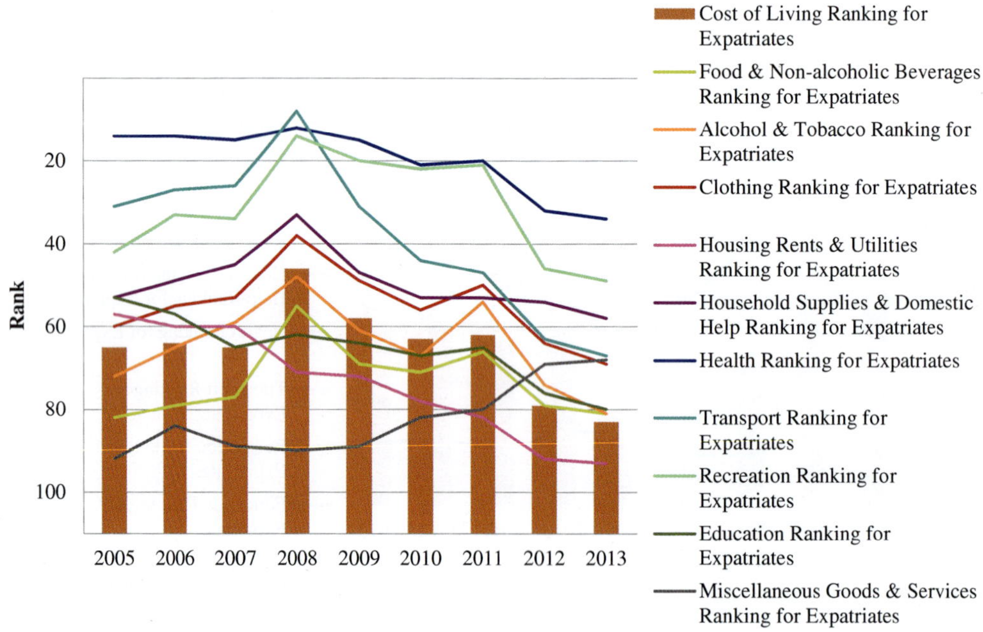

Source: Asia Competitiveness Institute

Known for its rich history and distinct architecture, Prague is the capital and largest city of the Czech Republic and also a cultural and economic centre of central Europe. The city's Cost of Living Ranking for Expatriates, as denoted by the orange bars, declined from 65th in 2005 to 83rd in 2013 (see Figure 4.73).

Housing Rents & Utilities and Transport saw the most dramatic dip in rankings as they both fell 36 places from 57th to 93rd and 31st to 67th, respectively, between 2005 and 2013. Consequently, Housing Rents & Utilities became the lowest ranked category since 2011. Education Ranking slipped 27 spots from 53rd to 80th over the same period. Health was the highest ranked category in 2013 although its ranking moved down 20 places from 14th in 2005 to 34th in 2013.

In contrast, Miscellaneous Goods & Services Ranking jumped 24 spots from 92nd to 68th between 2005 and 2013. Food & Non-alcoholic Beverages Ranking moved up one place from 82nd to 81st over the same period.

PRETORIA
South Africa

Figure 4.74: Cost of Living and 10 Consumption Categories Rankings for Expatriates in Pretoria, South Africa

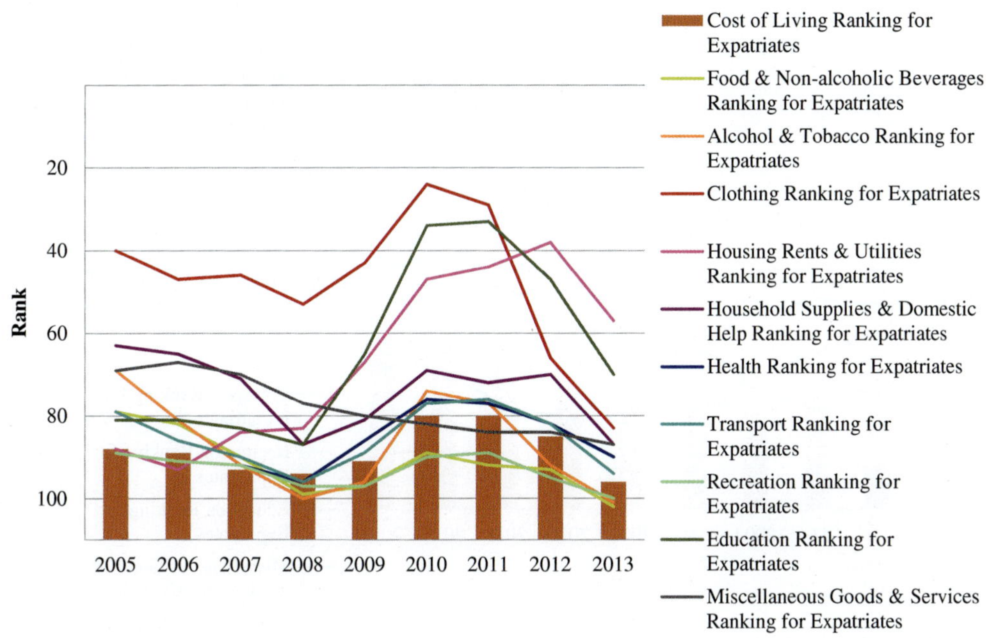

Source: Asia Competitiveness Institute

Situated in northern South Africa, Pretoria is the country's administrative capital and the seat of the President and Cabinet. The city's Cost of Living Ranking for Expatriates, as represented by the orange bars, went down from 88th in 2005 to 96th in 2013 (see Figure 4.74).

Clothing recorded the most significant dip in ranking as it fell 43 places from 40th to 83rd between 2005 and 2013. Household Supplies & Domestic Help Ranking slipped 24 spots from 63rd to 87th over the study period. Food & Non-alcoholic Beverages became the lowest ranked category in 2013 as its ranking moved down 23 places from 79th in 2005 to 102nd in 2013, making Pretoria the second cheapest city in this category in 2013. Transport Ranking went down 15 spots from 79th to 94th between 2005 and 2013. Health Ranking declined slightly from 89th to 90th over the same period.

In contrast, Housing Rents & Utilities Ranking climbed 31 places from 88th to 57th over the study period. Consequently, it was the highest ranked category since 2012. Education was the second highest ranked category since 2012 as its ranking jumped 11 spots from 81st in 2005 to 70th in 2013.

QINGDAO
China

Figure 4.75: Cost of Living and 10 Consumption Categories Rankings for Expatriates in Qingdao, China

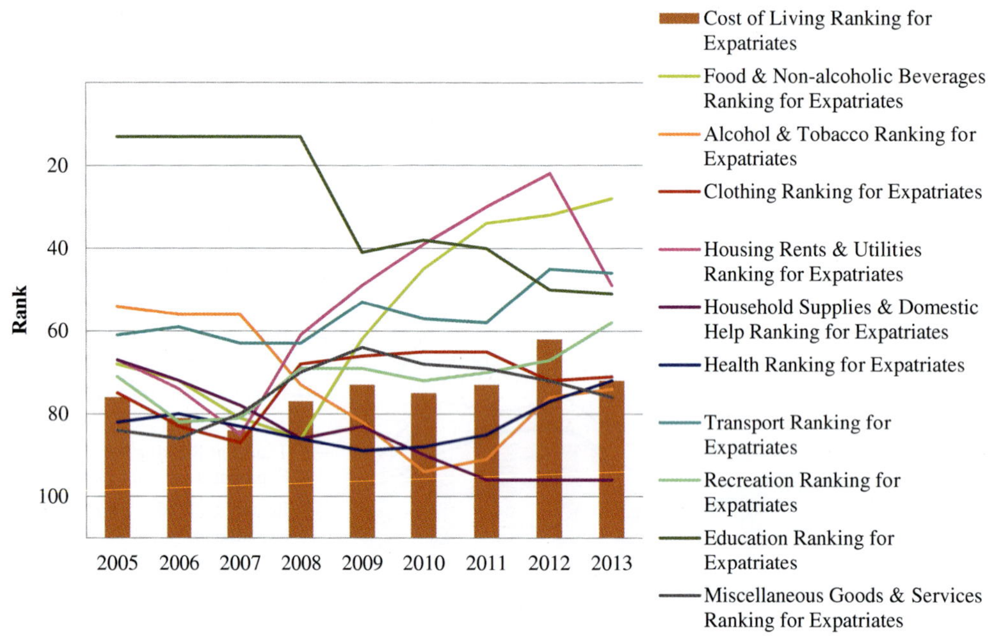

Source: Asia Competitiveness Institute

Home to the world's longest sea bridge, the Jiaozhou Bay Bridge, Qingdao is an important seaport, naval base and industrial centre in China. The city's Cost of Living Ranking for Expatriates, as shown in the orange bars, moved up from 76th to 72nd between 2005 and 2013 (see Figure 4.75).

Food & Non-alcoholic Beverages saw the most significant rise in ranking as it climbed 40 places from 68th in 2005 to 28th in 2013 and consequently became the highest ranked category in 2013. Housing Rents & Utilities Ranking jumped 18 spots from 67th to 49th over the study period. Transport Ranking moved up 15 places from 61st to 46th between 2005 and 2013.

In contrast, Education Ranking fell 38 spots from 13th in 2005 to 51st in 2013. Household Supplies & Domestic Help Ranking slipped 29 places from 67th to 96th over the study period, making it the lowest ranked category since 2011. Alcohol & Tobacco Ranking also declined sharply from 54th to 74th between 2005 and 2013.

QUITO
Ecuador

Figure 4.76: Cost of Living and 10 Consumption Categories Rankings for Expatriates in Quito, Ecuador

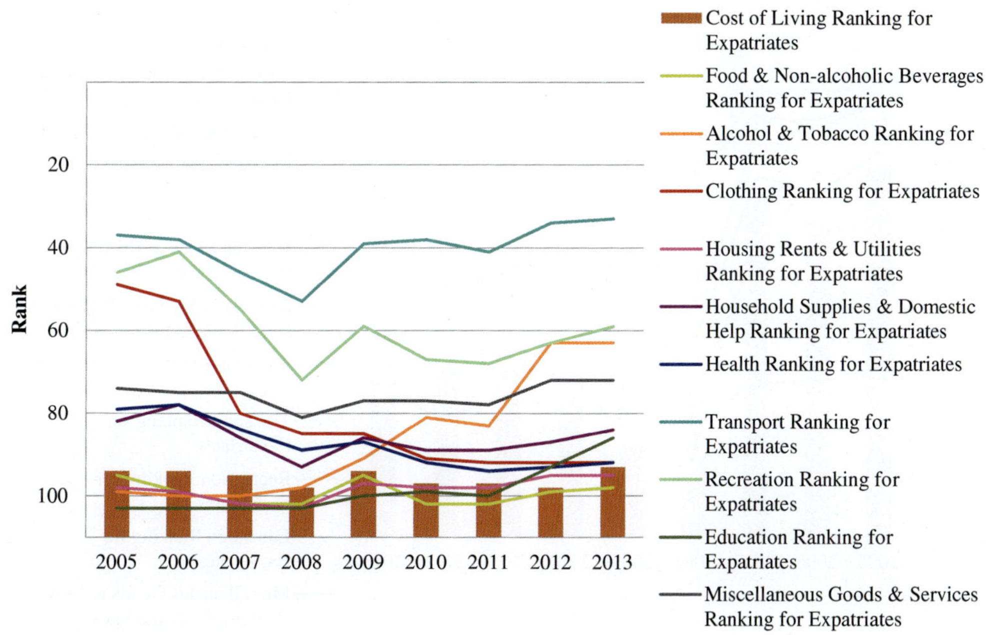

Source: Asia Competitiveness Institute

Quito, the capital city of Ecuador, is the highest official city in the world at 2,800 metres above sea level. The city's Cost of Living Ranking for Expatriates, as denoted by the orange bars, rose from 94th to 93rd between 2005 and 2013 (see Figure 4.76).

Alcohol & Tobacco registered the most remarkable rise in ranking as it climbed 36 places from 99th in 2005 to 63rd in 2013. Education Ranking jumped 17 spots from 103rd to 86th between 2005 and 2013. Transport consistently remained as the highest ranked category throughout the study period as its ranking moved up four places from 37th in 2005 to 33rd in 2013. Housing Rents & Utilities Ranking went up from 98th to 95th over the same period, making it the second lowest ranked category in 2013.

In contrast, Clothing saw the most significant dip in ranking as it fell 43 places from 49th to 92nd between 2005 and 2013. Health Ranking slipped 13 spots from 79th in 2005 to 92nd in 2013. Food & Non-alcoholic Beverages was the lowest ranked category since 2010 as its ranking declined from 95th to 98th over the study period.

REYKJAVIK
Iceland

Figure 4.77: Cost of Living and 10 Consumption Categories Rankings for Expatriates in Reykjavik, Iceland

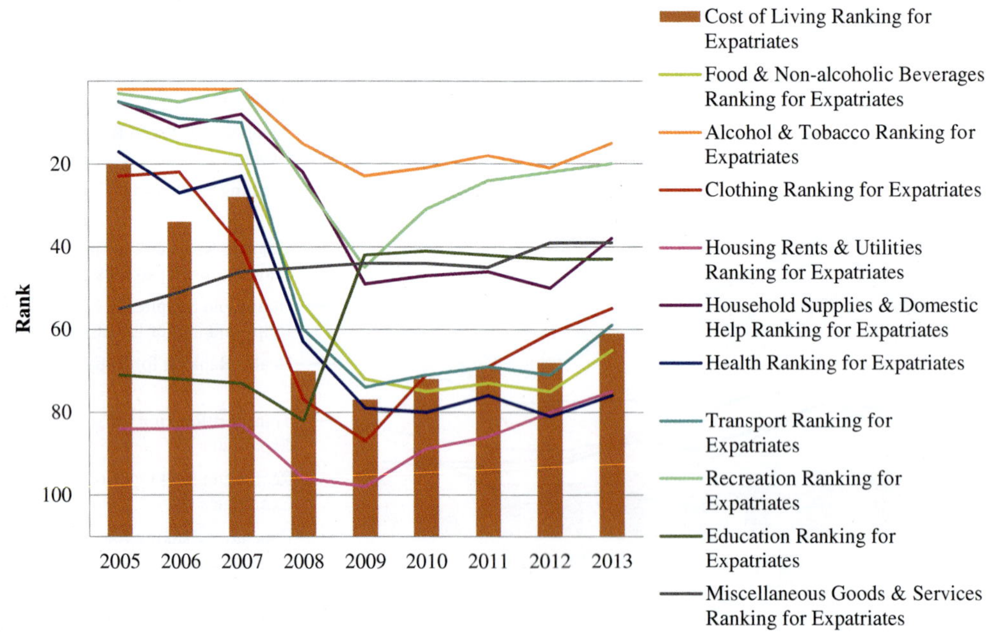

Source: Asia Competitiveness Institute

Reykjavik, the capital and largest city of Iceland, is the world's northernmost capital and a major tourist destination. The city's Cost of Living Ranking for Expatriates, as represented by the orange bars, declined sharply from 20th in 2005 to 61st in 2013 (see Figure 4.77).

Health recorded the most dramatic dip in ranking as it slipped 59 places from 17th to 76th between 2005 and 2013, making it the lowest ranked category in 2013. Food & Non-alcoholic Beverages Ranking fell 55 spots from 10th to 65th over the study period. Transport Ranking moved down 54 places from fifth in 2005 to 59th in 2013. Household Supplies & Domestic Ranking dropped 33 spots from fifth to 38th over the same period. Alcohol & Tobacco remained the highest ranked category for the entire study period although its ranking declined from second to 15th between 2005 and 2013.

In contrast, Education Ranking jumped 28 places from 71st in 2005 to 43rd in 2013. Housing Rents & Utilities Ranking moved up nine spots from 84th to 75th over the same period. However, it was the second lowest ranked category in 2013.

RIO DE JANEIRO
Brazil

Figure 4.78: Cost of Living and 10 Consumption Categories Rankings for Expatriates in Rio de Janeiro, Brazil

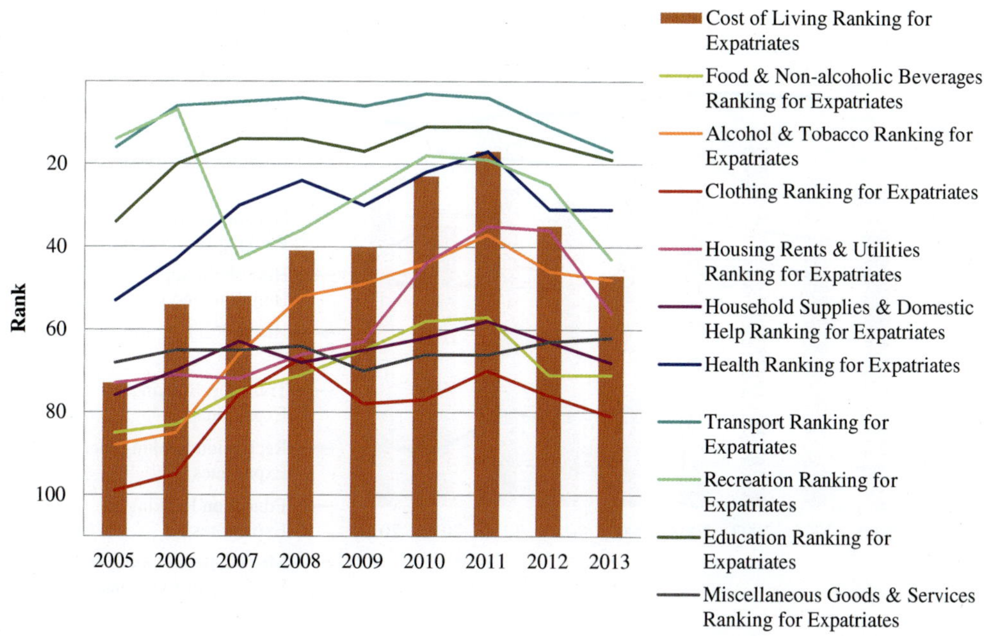

Source: Asia Competitiveness Institute

Rio de Janeiro is the second largest city in terms of GDP in Brazil. The city's Cost of Living Ranking for Expatriates, as shown in the orange bars, moved up from 73rd to 47th between 2005 and 2013 (see Figure 4.78).

In particular, Health Ranking jumped 22 places from 53rd in 2005 to 31st in 2013. Clothing was the lowest ranked category since 2009 although its ranking climbed 18 spots from 99th to 81st over the study period. Housing Rents & Utilities Ranking moved up 17 places from 73rd to 56th between 2005 and 2013. Education Ranking rose from 34th in 2005 to 19th in 2013, making it the second highest ranked category since 2007. Food & Non-alcoholic Beverages became the second lowest ranked category in 2013 although its ranking jumped 14 places from 85th to 71st over the study period.

In contrast, Recreation Ranking fell 29 places from 14th in 2005 to 43rd in 2013. Transport overtook Recreation to become the highest ranked category since 2007 as its ranking moved down only one spot from 16th to 17th over the same period.

ROME
Italy

Figure 4.79: Cost of Living and 10 Consumption Categories Rankings for Expatriates in Rome, Italy

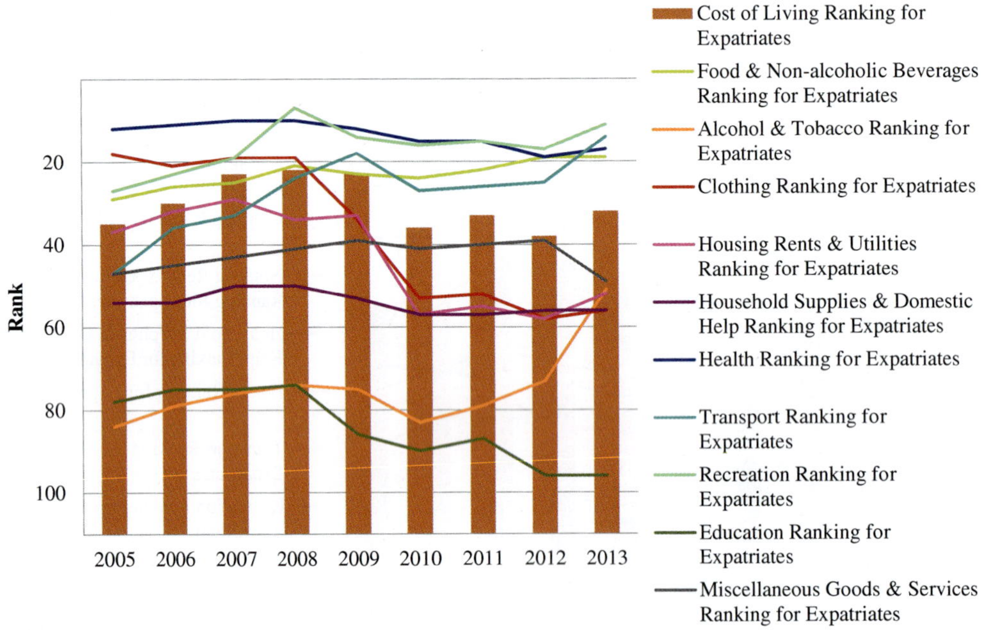

Source: Asia Competitiveness Institute

Known for its history spanning more than 2,500 years, Rome, the capital of Italy, is one of the oldest cities in Europe and the country's most popular tourist destination. The city's Cost of Living Ranking for Expatriates, as denoted by the orange bars, rose from 35th to 32nd between 2005 and 2013 (see Figure 4.79).

Transport and Alcohol & Tobacco recorded the most significant rise in rankings as they both climbed 33 places from 47th to 14th and 84th to 51st, respectively, over the study period. Consequently, Transport became the second highest ranked category in 2013. Recreation Ranking jumped 16 spots from 27th in 2005 to 11th in 2013, making it the highest ranked category in 2013. Food & Non-alcoholic Beverages Ranking moved up 10 places from 29th to 19th over the same period.

In contrast, Clothing Ranking fell 38 spots from 18th to 56th over the study period. Education became the lowest ranked category since 2009 as its ranking slipped 18 places from 78th in 2005 to 96th in 2013. Housing Rents & Utilities Ranking moved down 15 spots from 37th to 52nd over the same period. Health Ranking dropped five places from 12th in 2005 to 17th in 2013.

SAN FRANCISCO
United States

Figure 4.80: Cost of Living and 10 Consumption Categories Rankings for Expatriates in San Francisco, United States

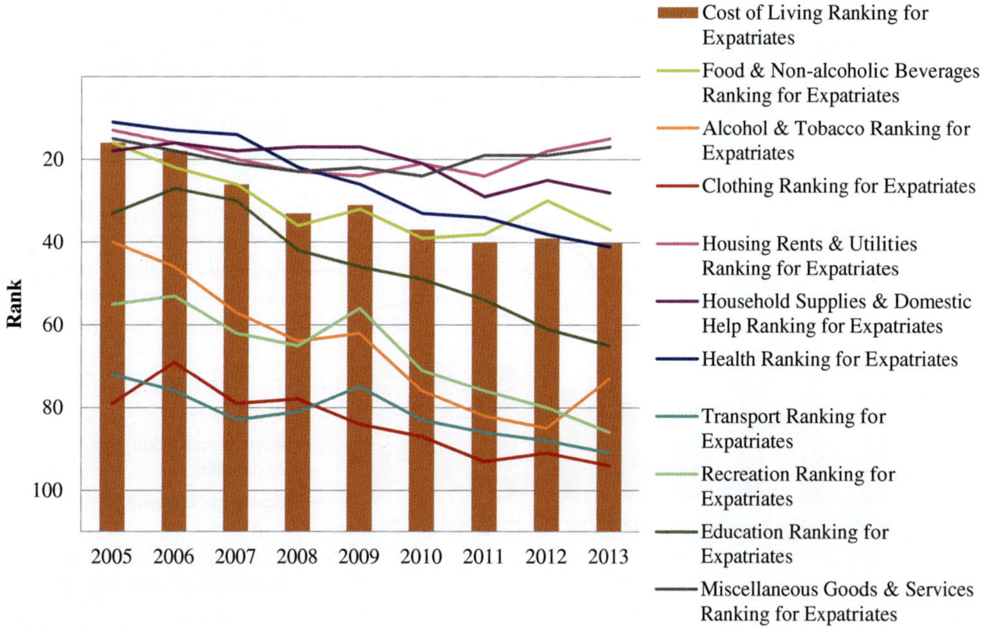

Source: Asia Competitiveness Institute

Home to a sizeable financial services industry, San Francisco is the cultural, commercial and financial centre of northern California. The city's Cost of Living Ranking for Expatriates, as represented by the orange bars, declined from 16th to 40th between 2005 and 2013 (see Figure 4.80).

The rankings of all 10 categories went down over the study period. In particular, Education Ranking fell 32 places from 33rd in 2005 to 65th in 2013. Health Ranking slipped 30 spots from 11th to 41st over the same period. Food & Non-alcoholic Beverages Ranking moved down 21 places from 16th to 37th between 2005 and 2013. Clothing and Transport Rankings declined from 79th to 94th and 72nd to 91st, respectively, over the study period, making them the lowest and second lowest ranked category in 2013. Household Supplies & Domestic Help Ranking fell 10 spots from 18th in 2005 to 28th in 2013. Housing Rents & Utilities was the highest ranked category in 2013 as its ranking slipped two places from 13th to 15th between 2005 and 2013. Likewise, Miscellaneous Goods & Services Ranking dropped from 15th to 17th over the same period.

SANTIAGO
Chile

Figure 4.81: Cost of Living and 10 Consumption Categories Rankings for Expatriates in Santiago, Chile

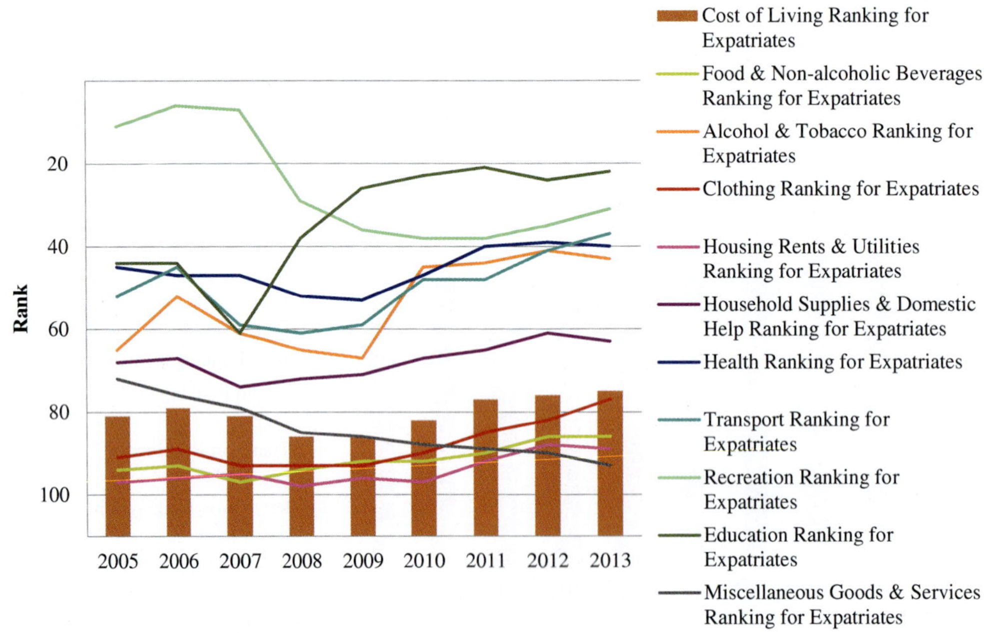

Source: Asia Competitiveness Institute

Santiago, the capital of Chile, is the country's industrial and financial centre and home to the United Nations Economic Commission for Latin America and the Caribbean (ECLA). The city's Cost of Living Ranking for Expatriates, as shown in the orange bars, moved up from 81st in 2005 to 75th in 2013 (see Figure 4.81).

In particular, Education Ranking climbed 22 places from 44th to 22nd between 2005 and 2013, making it the highest ranked category since 2009. Transport Ranking jumped 15 spots from 52nd to 37th between 2005 and 2013. Housing Rents & Utilities and Food & Non-alcoholic Beverages Rankings both moved up eight places from 97th to 89th and 94th to 86th, respectively, over the same period. Health Ranking went up five spots from 45th in 2005 to 40th in 2013.

In contrast, Miscellaneous Goods & Services Ranking fell 21 places from 72nd to 93rd over the study period. Consequently, it became the lowest ranked category in 2013. Recreation Ranking slipped 20 spots from 11th in 2005 to 31st in 2013.

SAO PAULO
Brazil

Figure 4.82: Cost of Living and 10 Consumption Categories Rankings for Expatriates in Sao Paulo, Brazil

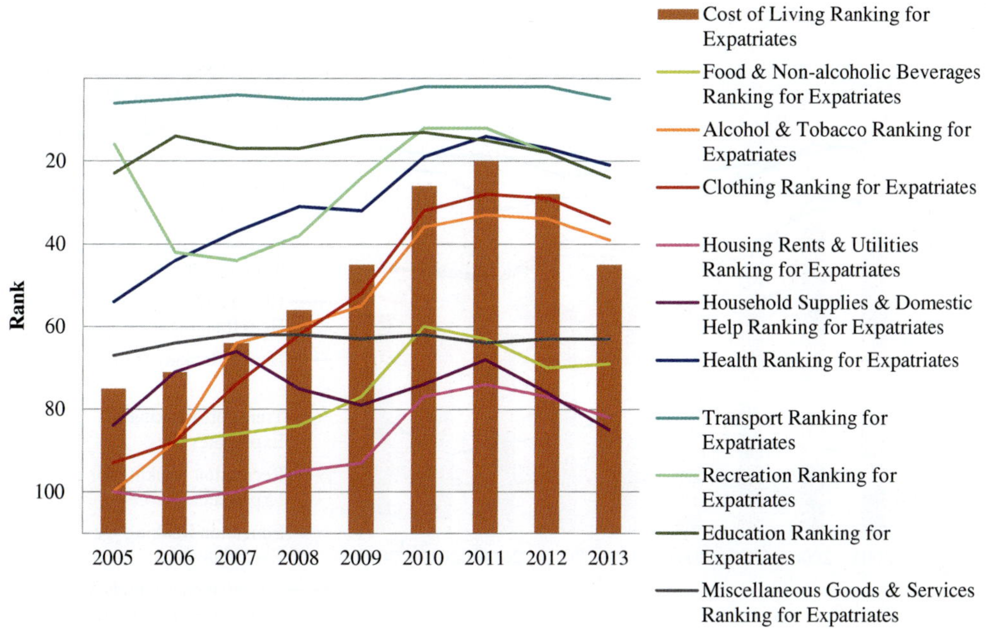

Source: Asia Competitiveness Institute

Often referred to as the largest city by GDP in Latin America, Sao Paulo is the centre for finance and science and technology in Brazil. The city's Cost of Living for Expatriates, as denoted by the orange bars, rose sharply from 75th to 45th between 2005 and 2013 (see Figure 4.82).

Alcohol & Tobacco saw the most dramatic rise in ranking as it climbed 61 places from 100th in 2005 to 39th in 2013. Clothing Ranking jumped 58 spots from 93rd to 35th over the study period. Health Ranking moved up 33 places from 54th to 21st between 2005 and 2013. Food & Non-alcoholic Beverages Ranking also rose sharply from 93rd in 2005 to 69th in 2013. Housing Rents & Utilities Ranking went up from 100th to 82nd over the same period. Nonetheless, it was the second lowest ranked category in 2013 after Household Supplies & Domestic Help at 85th. Transport consistently remained as the highest ranked category throughout the study period as its ranking moved up one spot from sixth to fifth between 2005 and 2013. Consequently, Sao Paulo was among the top five most expensive cities in terms of Transport in 2013.

In contrast, Recreation Ranking fell eight places from 16th in 2005 to 24th in 2013. Education and Household Supplies & Domestic Help Rankings slipped one spot from 23rd to 24th and 84th to 85th, respectively, over the study period.

SEATTLE
United States

Figure 4.83: Cost of Living and 10 Consumption Categories Rankings for Expatriates in Seattle, United States

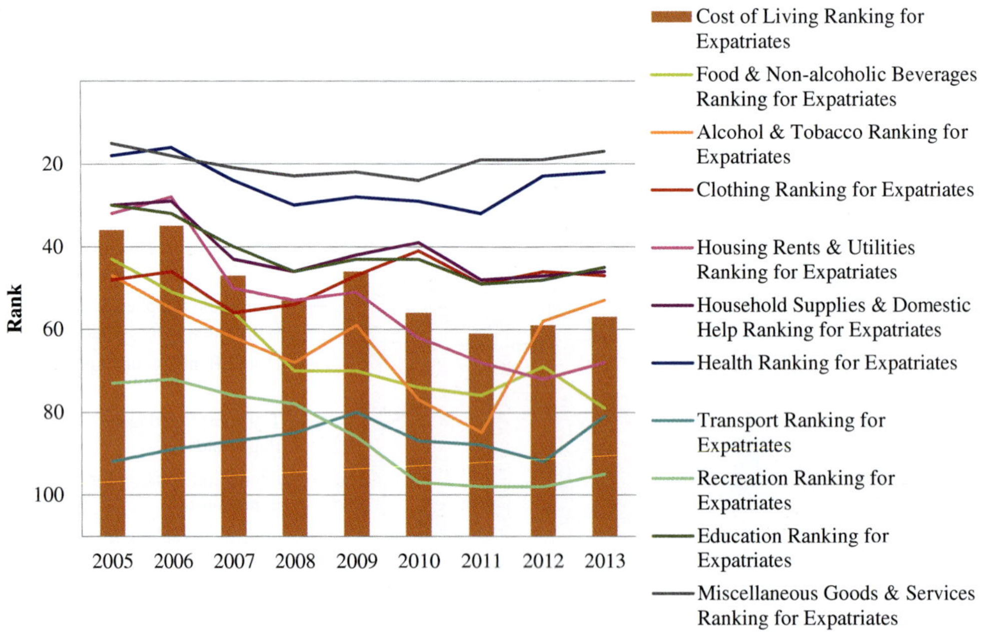

Source: Asia Competitiveness Institute

Known as a technology centre with companies like Microsoft, Amazon and T-Mobile located in the area, Seattle is the largest city in the Pacific Northwest region of the United States. The city's Cost of Living Ranking for Expatriates, as represented by the orange bars, declined from 36th in 2005 to 57th in 2013 (see Figure 4.83).

Housing Rents & Utilities and Food & Non-alcoholic Beverages registered the most significant dip in rankings as they fell 36 places from 32nd to 68th and 43rd to 79th, respectively, between 2005 and 2013. Recreation became the lowest ranked category since 2009 as its ranking slipped 22 spots from 73rd to 95th over the study period. Education Ranking moved down 15 places from 30th in 2005 to 45th in 2013. Miscellaneous Goods & Services and Health Rankings declined more modestly from 15th to 17th and 18th to 22nd, respectively, over the same period, making them the highest and second highest ranked category in 2013.

In contrast, Transport Ranking jumped 11 places from 92nd to 81st between 2005 and 2013. Nonetheless, it was the second lowest ranked category in 2013. Clothing Ranking moved up one spot from 48th to 47th over the study period.

SEOUL
South Korea

Figure 4.84: Cost of Living and 10 Consumption Categories Rankings for Expatriates in Seoul, South Korea

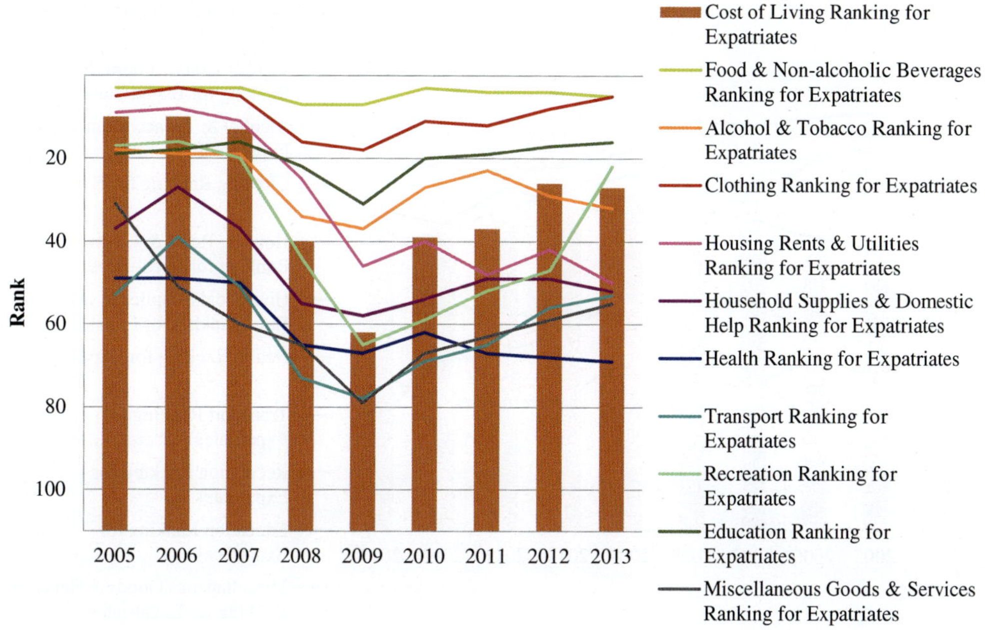

Source: Asia Competitiveness Institute

Seoul, the capital of South Korea, is widely known as one of the world's technological hubs with high-technology companies such as Samsung and LG based in the city. The city's Cost of Living Ranking for Expatriates, as shown in the orange bars, declined from 10th to 27th between 2005 and 2013 (see Figure 4.84).

Education was the only category that rose in ranking from 19th to 16th over the study period. Housing Rents & Utilities recorded the most dramatic dip in ranking as it fell 41 places from ninth in 2005 to 50th in 2013. Miscellaneous Goods & Services Ranking dropped 24 spots from 31st to 55th between 2005 and 2013. Health became the lowest ranked category since 2011 as its ranking slipped 20 spots from 49th in 2005 to 69th in 2013. Household Supplies & Domestic Help Ranking moved down 15 places from 37th to 52nd over the same period. Food & Non-alcoholic Beverages Ranking declined more modestly from third in 2005 to fifth in 2013, making it the highest ranked category in 2013 together with Clothing. Transport Ranking fell from 53rd in 2005 to 78th in 2009 before rising back to 53rd in 2013.

SHANGHAI
China

Figure 4.85: Cost of Living and 10 Consumption Categories Rankings for Expatriates in Shanghai, China

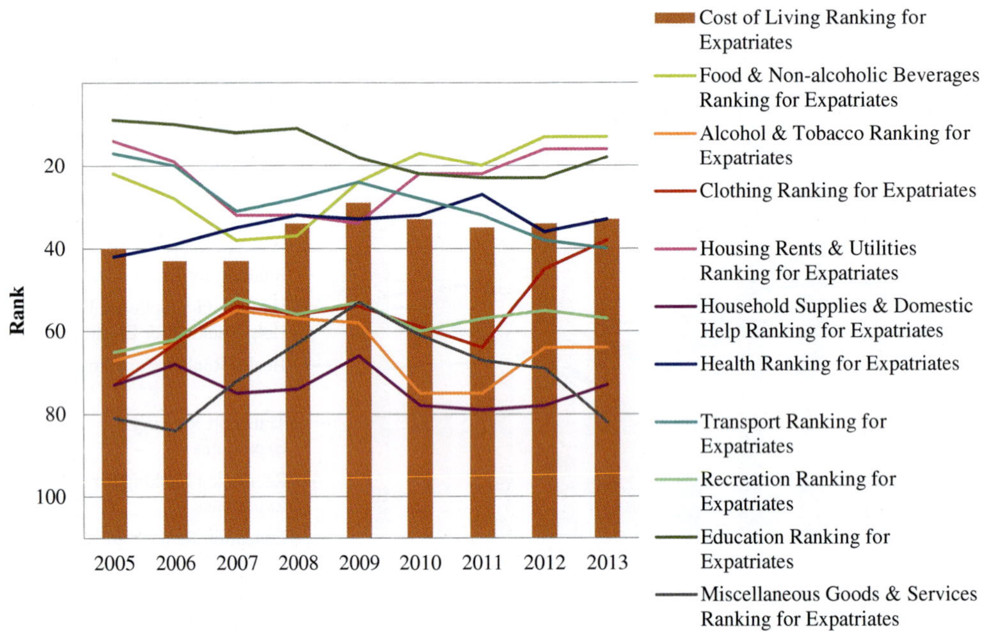

Source: Asia Competitiveness Institute

With a population of approximately 24 million, Shanghai is the largest Chinese city by population and home to a sizeable financial industry and the country's largest free trade zone. The city's Cost of Living Ranking for Expatriates, as denoted by the orange bars, rose from 40th in 2005 to 33rd in 2013 (see Figure 4.85).

Clothing saw the most significant rise in ranking as it climbed 35 places from 73rd to 38th between 2005 and 2013. Food & Non-alcoholic Beverages and Health Rankings both jumped nine spots from 22nd to 13th and 42nd to 33rd, respectively, over the same period. Consequently, Food & Non-alcoholic Beverages became the highest ranked category since 2010. Recreation Ranking moved up eight spots from 65th in 2005 to 57th in 2013.

In contrast, Education Ranking fell nine places from ninth to 18th over the study period. Housing Rents & Utilities Ranking slipped two spots from 14th in 2005 to 16th in 2013, making it the second highest ranked category since 2011. Miscellaneous Goods & Services overtook Household Supplies & Domestic Help to become the lowest ranked category in 2013 as its ranking moved down one place to 82nd from 81st in 2005. Household Supplies & Domestic Help Ranking rose from 73rd in 2005 to 66th in 2009 before falling back to 73rd in 2013.

SHENZHEN
China

Figure 4.86: Cost of Living and 10 Consumption Categories Rankings for Expatriates in Shenzhen, China

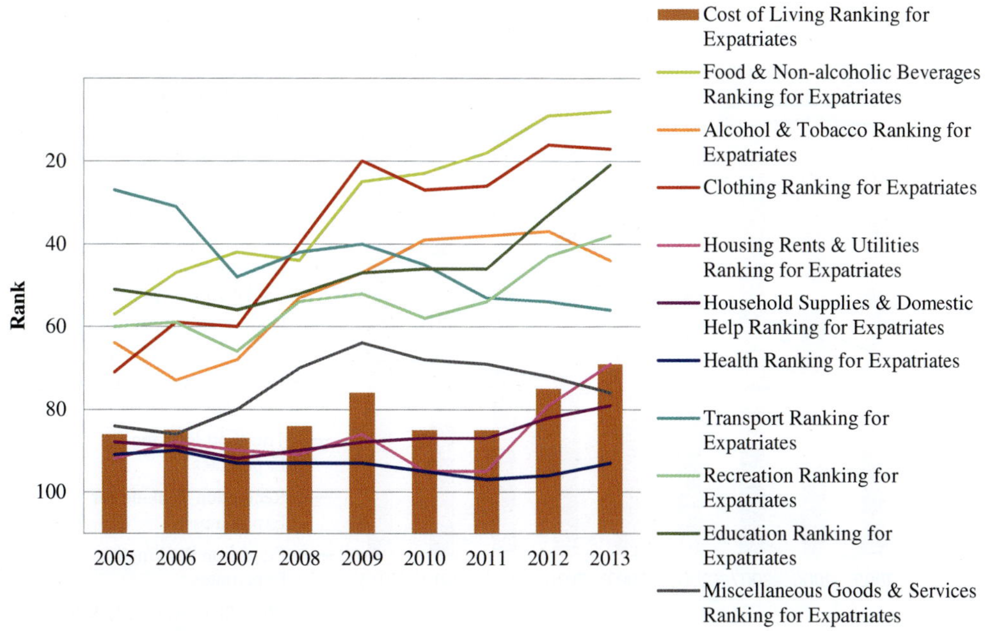

Source: Asia Competitiveness Institute

Situated immediately north of Hong Kong, Shenzhen is China's first and one of the most successful special economic zones. The city's Cost of Living Ranking for Expatriates, as represented by the orange bars, moved up from 86th to 69th between 2005 and 2013 (see Figure 4.86).

Clothing registered the most dramatic rise in ranking as it climbed 54 places from 71st in 2005 to 17th in 2013, making it the second highest ranked category since 2010. Food & Non-alcoholic Beverages became the highest ranked category since 2010 as its ranking jumped 49 spots from 57th to eighth over the study period. Education Ranking moved up 30 places from 51st in 2005 to 21st in 2013. Housing Rents & Utilities Ranking climbed 23 spots from 92nd to 69th over the same period. Household Supplies & Domestic Help Ranking went up from 88th in 2005 to 79th in 2013. Nonetheless, it was the second lowest ranked category in 2012 and 2013.

In contrast, Transport Ranking slipped 29 places from 27th to 56th between 2005 and 2013. Health remained the lowest ranked category for most of the study period as its ranking fell two spots from 91st in 2005 to 93rd in 2013.

SINGAPORE
Singapore

Figure 4.87: Cost of Living and 10 Consumption Categories Rankings for Expatriates in Singapore, Singapore

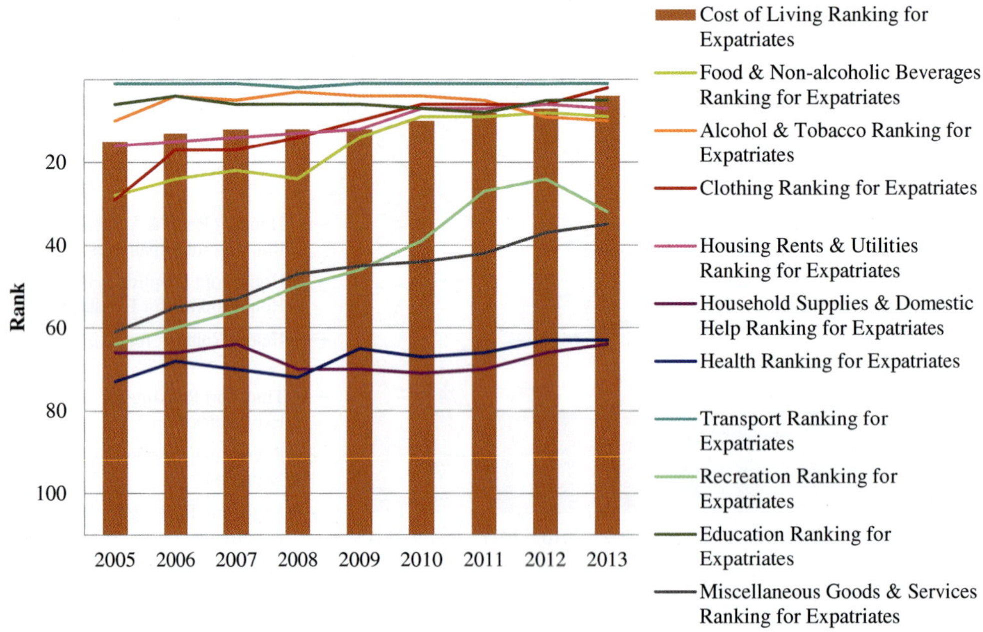

Source: Asia Competitiveness Institute

Located off the southern tip of the Malay Peninsula, the city–state Singapore is a major commercial hub and international financial centre with one of the highest per capita income levels in the world. The city's Cost of Living Ranking for Expatriates, as shown in the orange bars, rose from 15th to fourth between 2005 and 2013 (see Figure 4.87). Singapore thus entered the top five most expensive cities for expatriates for the first time in 2013.

Recreation registered the most significant rise in ranking as it climbed 32 places from 64th in 2005 to 32nd in 2013. Clothing Ranking jumped 27 spots from 29th to second over the study period, making Singapore the second most expensive city in this category in 2013. Miscellaneous Goods & Services Ranking moved up 26 places from 61st to 35th between 2005 and 2013. Food & Non-alcoholic Beverages Ranking also rose sharply from 28th to ninth over the same period. Housing Rents & Utilities Ranking went up nine spots from 16th in 2005 to seventh in 2013. Health became the second lowest ranked category since 2009 although its ranking jumped from 73rd to 63rd over the study period. Nonetheless, these upward trends appear to be levelling off as good news. Household Supplies & Domestic Help overtook Health to become the lowest ranked category since 2009 as its ranking moved up two places from 66th to 64th between 2005 and 2013. Education Ranking moved up one spot from sixth to fifth over the same period.

Transport remained as the highest ranked category for the entire study period as its ranking fell from first in 2005 to second in 2008 before rising back to first in 2013. Singapore was therefore the most expensive city in this category for five consecutive years from 2009 to 2013.

SOFIA
Bulgaria

Figure 4.88: Cost of Living and 10 Consumption Categories Rankings for Expatriates in Sofia, Bulgaria

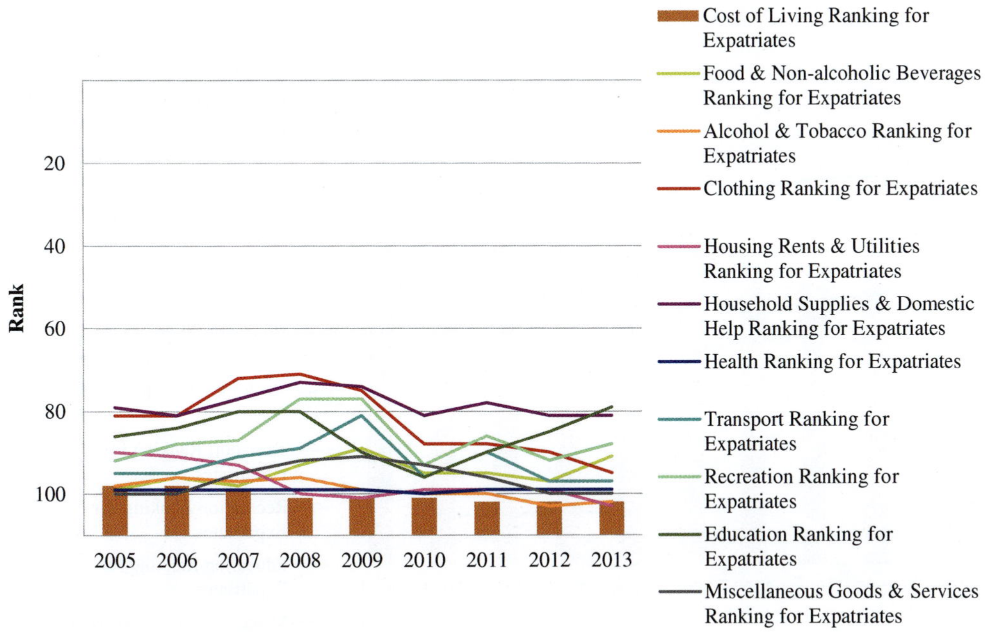

Source: Asia Competitiveness Institute

Sofia, the capital and largest city of Bulgaria, is increasingly becoming an outsourcing destination for multinational high-technology companies including IBM, Hewlett-Packard and Siemens. The city's Cost of Living Ranking for Expatriates, as denoted by the orange bars, declined from 98th to 102nd between 2005 and 2013 (see Figure 4.88). Sofia therefore became the second cheapest among the 103 cities studied in 2013.

In particular, Housing Rents & Utilities Ranking fell 13 places from 90th in 2005 to 103rd in 2013, making Sofia the most affordable city in this category in 2013. Alcohol & Tobacco Ranking slipped four spots from 98th to 102nd over the study period. Transport and Household Supplies & Domestic Help Rankings both moved down two places from 95th to 97th and 79th to 81st, respectively, between 2005 and 2013. Health Ranking fell from 99th in 2005 to 100th in 2010 before rising back to 99th in 2013.

In contrast, Food & Non-alcoholic Beverages Ranking jumped eight places from 99th in 2005 to 91st in 2013. Education became the highest ranked category in 2013 as its ranking moved up seven spots from 86th to 79th over the same period. Recreation Ranking climbed four places from 92nd to 88th between 2005 and 2013.

ST PETERSBURG
Russia

Figure 4.89: Cost of Living and 10 Consumption Categories Rankings for Expatriates in St Petersburg, Russia

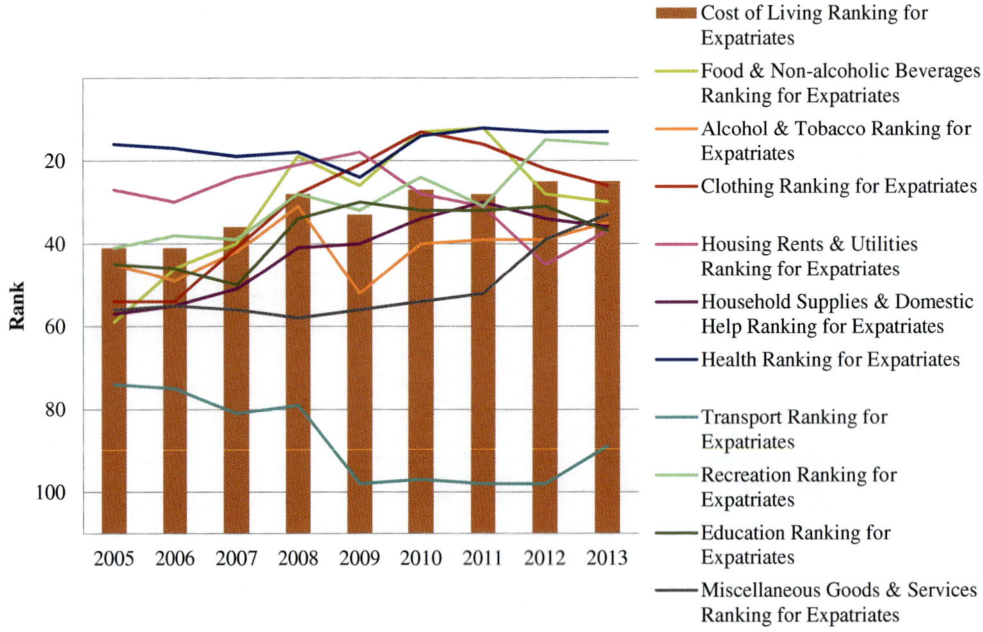

Source: Asia Competitiveness Institute

St Petersburg, the second largest city in Russia, is the country's hub for heavy industries including aerospace, shipbuilding and machinery among others. The city's Cost of Living Ranking for Expatriates, as represented by the orange bars, moved up from 41st to 25th between 2005 and 2013 (see Figure 4.89).

Eight out of 10 categories rose in rankings over the study period. In particular, Food & Non-alcoholic Beverages Ranking climbed 29 places from 59th in 2005 to 30th in 2013. Clothing Ranking jumped 28 spots from 54th to 26th between 2005 and 2013. Recreation Ranking moved up 25 places from 41st to 16th over the same period. Household Supplies & Domestic Help Ranking also rose sharply from 57th in 2005 to 36th in 2013. Education Ranking went up more modestly from 45th to 37th over the study period. Health Ranking jumped three spots from 16th to 13th between 2005 and 2013, making it the highest ranked category in 2013.

In contrast, Transport consistently remained as the lowest ranked category throughout the study period as its ranking fell 15 places from 74th in 2005 to 89th in 2013. Housing Rents & Utilities Ranking slipped 10 spots from 27th to 37th over the same period.

STOCKHOLM
Sweden

Figure 4.90: Cost of Living and 10 Consumption Categories Rankings for Expatriates in Stockholm, Sweden

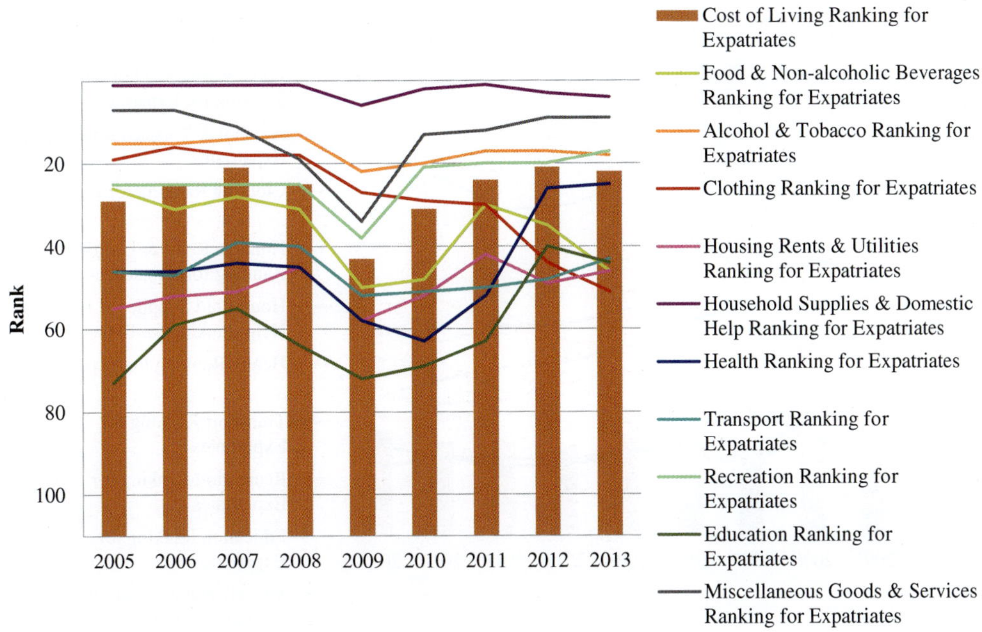

Source: Asia Competitiveness Institute

Known for hosting the annual Nobel Prize ceremonies, Stockholm, the capital of Sweden, is the country's political, cultural and economic centre. The city's Cost of Living Ranking for Expatriates, as denoted by the orange bars, rose from 29th to 22nd between 2005 and 2013 (see Figure 4.90).

Education recorded the most significant rise in ranking as it climbed 29 places from 73rd in 2005 to 44th in 2013. Health Ranking jumped 21 spots from 46th to 25th over the study period. Housing Rents & Utilities Ranking rose more modestly from 55th to 46th between 2005 and 2013. Recreation Ranking went up from 25th to 17th over the same period. Transport Ranking moved up three places from 46th in 2005 to 43rd in 2013.

In contrast, Clothing Ranking fell 32 places from 19th to 51st between 2005 and 2013, making it the lowest ranked category in 2013. Food & Non-alcoholic Beverages Ranking slipped 20 spots from 26th in 2005 to 46th in 2013. Household Supplies & Domestic Help consistently remained as the highest ranked category for the entire study period as its ranking moved down three places from first in 2005 to fourth in 2013. Miscellaneous Goods & Services Ranking declined from seventh to ninth between 2005 and 2013. Consequently, it became the second highest ranked category since 2010.

SUZHOU China

Figure 4.91: Cost of Living and 10 Consumption Categories Rankings for Expatriates in Suzhou, China

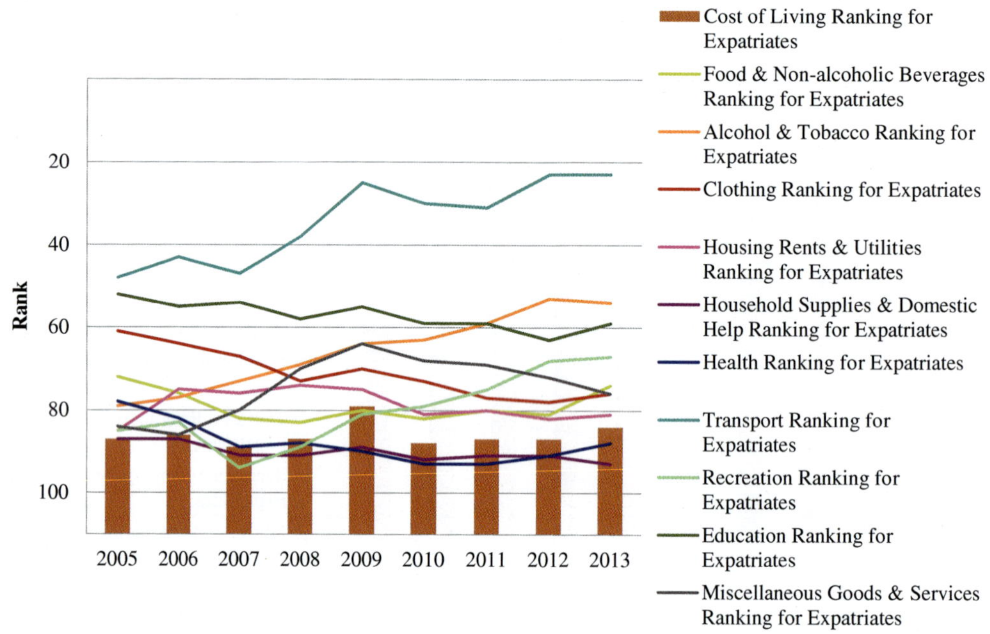

Source: Asia Competitiveness Institute

With a history spanning over 2,500 years, Suzhou is not only one of China's top tourist attractions but also one of the most economically developed cities in the Chinese mainland. The city's Cost of Living Ranking for Expatriates, as represented by the orange bars, moved up from 87th to 84th between 2005 and 2013 (see Figure 4.91).

In particular, Transport consistently remained as the highest ranked category for the entire study period as its ranking climbed 25 places from 48th in 2005 to 23rd in 2013. Likewise, Alcohol & Tobacco Ranking jumped 25 spots from 79th to 54th over the study period, making it the second highest ranked category in 2012 and 2013. Recreation Ranking moved up 18 places from 85th to 67th between 2005 and 2013. Housing Rents & Utilities Ranking rose more modestly from 85th in 2005 to 81st in 2013.

In contrast, Clothing Ranking fell 15 spots from 61st to 76th between 2005 and 2013. Health Ranking slipped 10 places from 78th to 88th over the study period. Education Ranking declined from 52nd in 2005 to 59th in 2013. Household Supplies & Domestic Help became the lowest ranked category in 2013 as its ranking moved down six spots from 87th to 93rd over the same period. Food & Non-alcoholic Beverages Ranking fell two places from 72nd in 2005 to 74th in 2013.

SYDNEY
Australia

Figure 4.92: Cost of Living and 10 Consumption Categories Rankings for Expatriates in Sydney, Australia

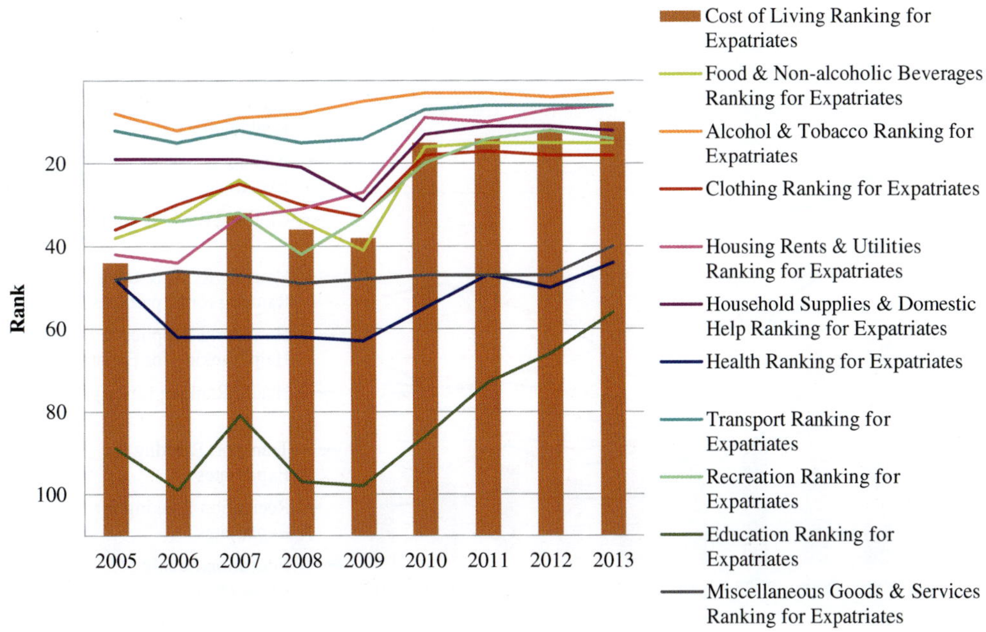

Source: Asia Competitiveness Institute

Sydney is the most populous city in Australia with an estimated population of 4.8 million and one of the leading financial hubs in Asia Pacific with a significant concentration of multinational banks. The city's Cost of Living Ranking for Expatriates, as shown in the orange bar, climbed 34 places from 44th in 2005 to 10th in 2013 (see Figure 4.92).

The rankings of all 10 categories went up over the study period. In particular, Housing Rents & Utilities saw the most dramatic rise in ranking as it jumped 36 places from 42nd to sixth between 2005 and 2013, making it the second highest ranked category in 2013 together with Transport. Education Ranking moved up 33 spots from 89th to 56th over the study period. Nonetheless, it remained as the lowest ranked category throughout the study period. Food & Non-alcoholic Beverages Ranking climbed 23 places from 38th in 2005 to 15th in 2013. Recreation and Clothing Rankings rose from 33rd to 14th and 36th to 18th, respectively, over the same period. Transport Ranking went up more modestly from 12th to sixth between 2005 and 2013. Alcohol & Tobacco was consistently the highest ranked category for the entire study period as its ranking climbed five places from eighth in 2005 to third in 2013. Health Ranking jumped four spots from 48th to 44th between 2005 and 2013, making it the second lowest ranked category in 2013.

TAIPEI
Taiwan, China

Figure 4.93: Cost of Living and 10 Consumption Categories Rankings for Expatriates in Taipei, Taiwan, China

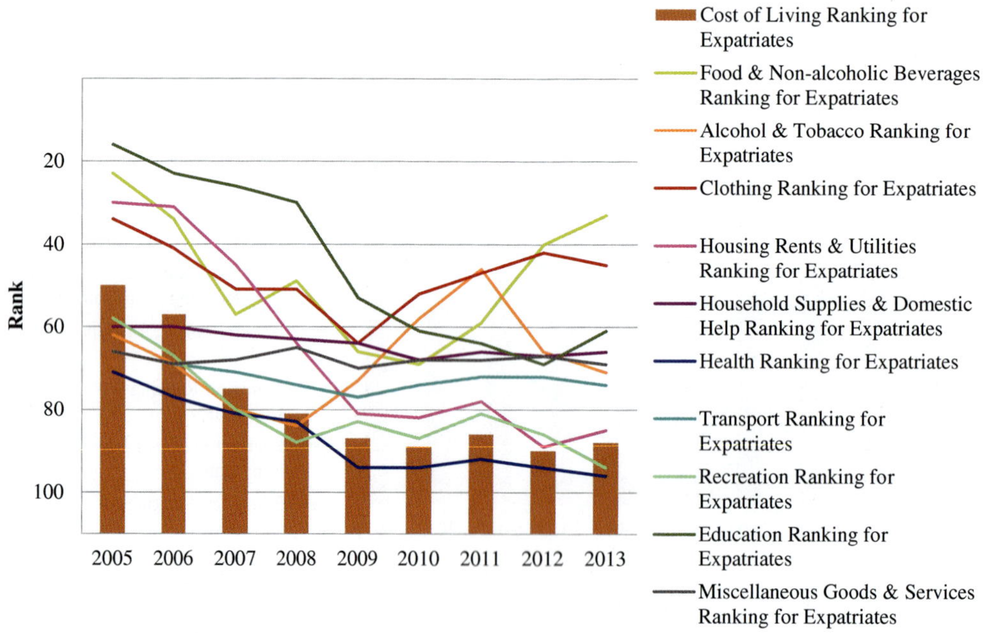

Source: Asia Competitiveness Institute

Taipei, the capital city of Taiwan, has long been the country's foremost industrial centre with high concentration of both secondary and tertiary sectors. The city's Cost of Living Ranking for Expatriates, as denoted by the orange bars, declined sharply from 50th to 88th between 2005 and 2013 (see Figure 4.93).

The rankings of all 10 categories went down over the study period. Housing Rents & Utilities registered the most dramatic dip in ranking as it fell 55 places from 30th in 2005 to 85th in 2013. Education Ranking slipped 45 spots from 16th to 61st between 2005 and 2013. Recreation Ranking dropped 36 places from 58th in 2005 to 94th in 2013. Health Ranking moved down 25 spots from 71st to 96th over the study period, making it the lowest ranked category since 2009. Food & Non-alcoholic Beverages Ranking fell 10 places from 23rd to 33rd over the same period. Nonetheless, it became the highest ranked category in 2013. Transport Ranking slipped eight spots from 66th in 2005 to 74th in 2013.

TEL AVIV
Israel

Figure 4.94: Cost of Living and 10 Consumption Categories Rankings for Expatriates in Tel Aviv, Israel

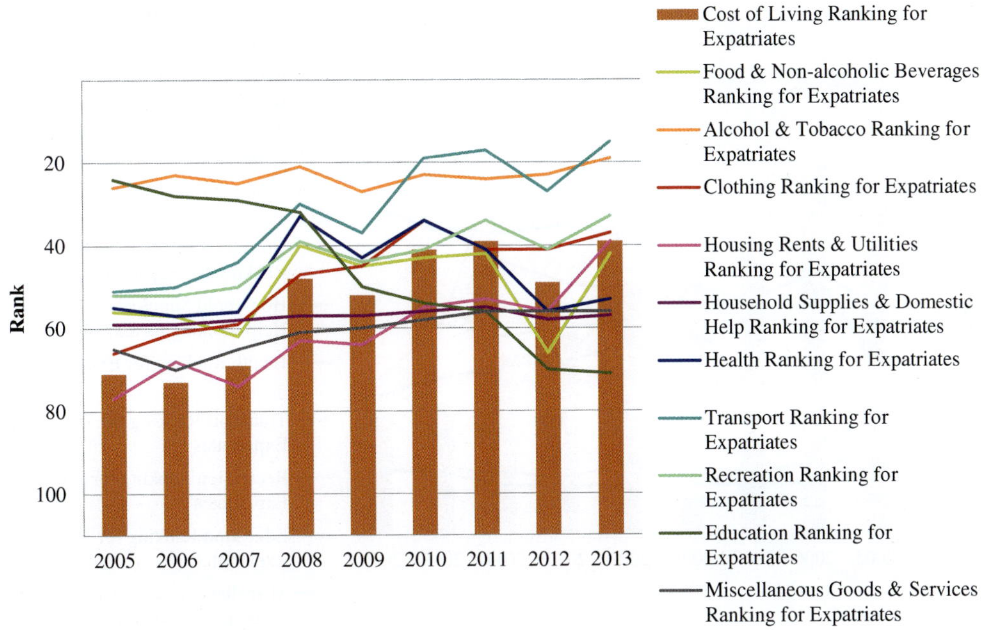

Source: Asia Competitiveness Institute

Tel Aviv, the second most populous city in Israel, is the country's economic and technological hub and the second largest economy in the Middle East after Dubai. The city's Cost of Living Ranking for Expatriates, as represented by the orange bars, rose sharply from 71st in 2005 to 39th in 2013 (see Figure 4.94).

In particular, Housing Rents & Utilities Ranking climbed 38 places from 77th to 39th between 2005 and 2013. Transport Ranking jumped 36 places from 51st to 15th over the study period, making it the highest ranked category in 2013. Clothing Ranking moved up 29 places from 66th in 2005 to 37th in 2013. Recreation Ranking climbed 19 spots from 52nd to 33rd over the same period. Food & Non-alcoholic Beverages Ranking rose from 56th in 2005 to 42nd in 2013. Health and Household Supplies & Domestic Help Rankings went up more modestly from 55th to 53rd and 59th to 57th, respectively, between 2005 and 2013.

Education was the only category that declined in ranking as it fell 47 places from 24th in 2005 to 71st in 2013. Consequently, it became the lowest ranked category in 2013.

TIANJIN
China

Figure 4.95: Cost of Living and 10 Consumption Categories Rankings for Expatriates in Tianjin, China

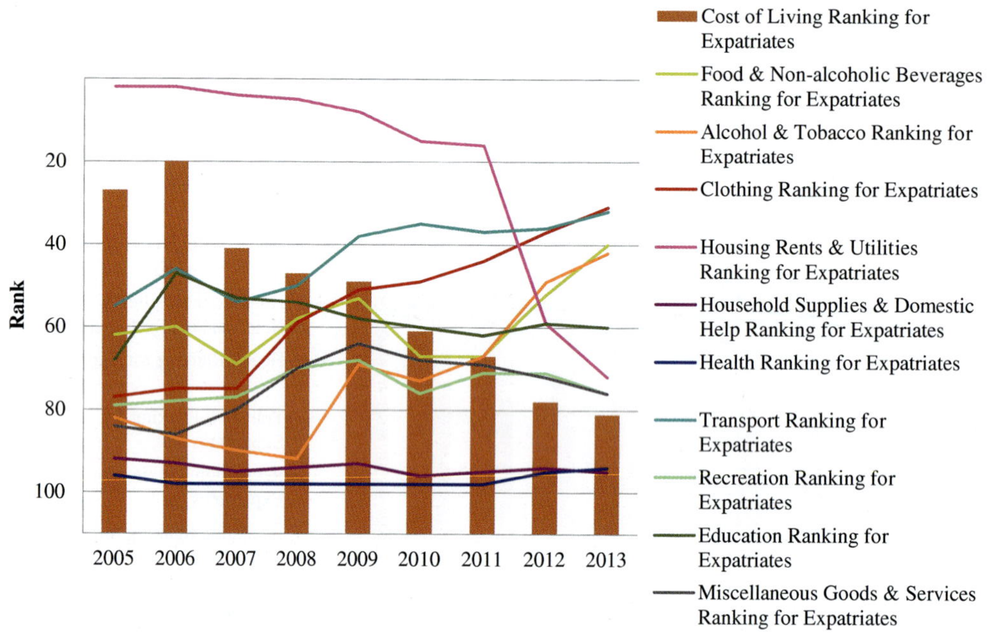

Source: Asia Competitiveness Institute

Tianjin, the fourth largest city in China in terms of urban population, is the country's centre for international shipping and logistics, modern manufacturing and research and development. The city's Cost of Living Ranking for Expatriates, as shown in the orange bars, fell 54 places from 27th to 81st between 2005 and 2013 (see Figure 4.95).

Housing Rents & Utilities saw the most dramatic dip in ranking as it slipped 70 places from second in 2005 to 72nd in 2013. Household Supplies & Domestic Help Ranking declined more modestly from 92nd to 95th over the same period, making it the lowest ranked category in 2013.

In contrast, the rankings of the remaining eight categories went up over the study period. In particular, Clothing became the highest ranked category in 2013 as its ranking climbed 46 spots from 77th to 31st between 2005 and 2013. Transport Ranking jumped 23 places from 55th to 32nd over the same period. Food & Non-alcoholic Beverages Ranking also rose sharply from 62nd in 2005 to 40th in 2013. Education Ranking went up more modestly from 68th to 60th over the study period. Health Ranking moved up two places from 96th to 94th between 2005 and 2013.

TOKYO
Japan

Figure 4.96: Cost of Living and 10 Consumption Categories Rankings for Expatriates in Tokyo, Japan

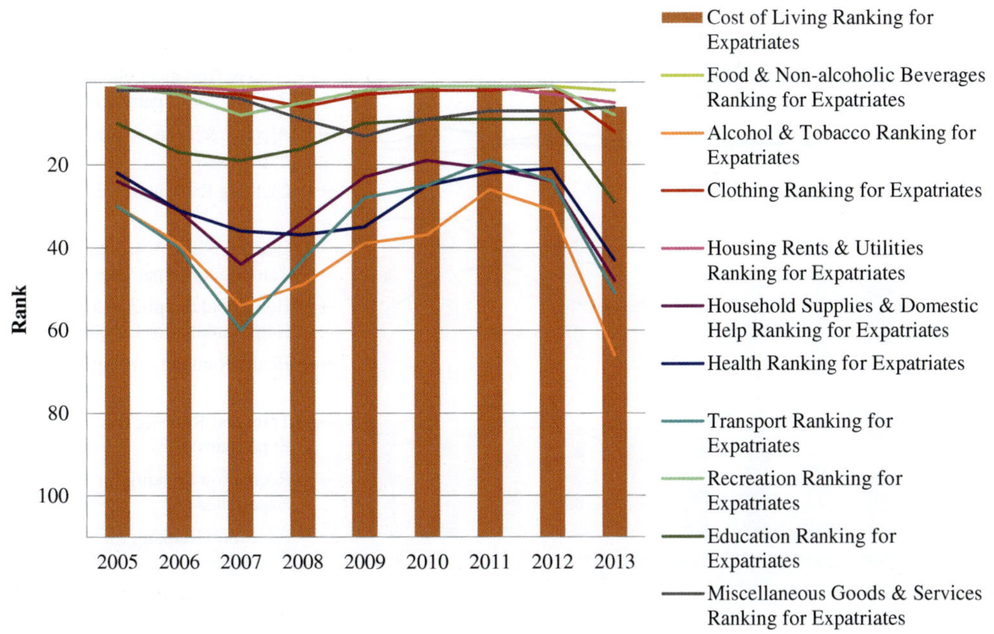

Source: Asia Competitiveness Institute

Tokyo, the capital city of Japan, has the largest metropolitan economy in the world and home to one of the world's largest financial centres. The city's Cost of Living Ranking for Expatriates, as denoted by the orange bars, declined from first to sixth between 2005 and 2013 (see Figure 4.96).

The rankings of all 10 categories went down over the study period. In particular, Alcohol & Tobacco saw the most dramatic dip in ranking as it fell 36 places from 30th in 2005 to 66th in 2013, making it the lowest ranked category since 2008. Household Supplies & Domestic Help Ranking slipped 24 spots from 24th to 48th between 2005 and 2013. Health and Transport Rankings both moved down 21 places from 22nd to 43rd and 30th to 51st, respectively, over the same period. Education Ranking also declined sharply from 10th in 2005 to 29th in 2013. Clothing Ranking fell 11 spots from first to 12th over the study period. Recreation Ranking slipped from first to eighth between 2005 and 2013. Housing Rents & Utilities Ranking moved down from first to fifth over the same period. Likewise, Miscellaneous Goods & Services Ranking fell four places from second to sixth between 2005 and 2013. Food & Non-alcoholic Beverages registered a slight decline in ranking from first in 2005 to second in 2013. Tokyo has therefore remained in the top two most expensive cities in terms of Food & Non-alcoholic Beverages for the entire study period.

TORONTO
Canada

Figure 4.97: Cost of Living and 10 Consumption Categories Rankings for Expatriates in Toronto, Canada

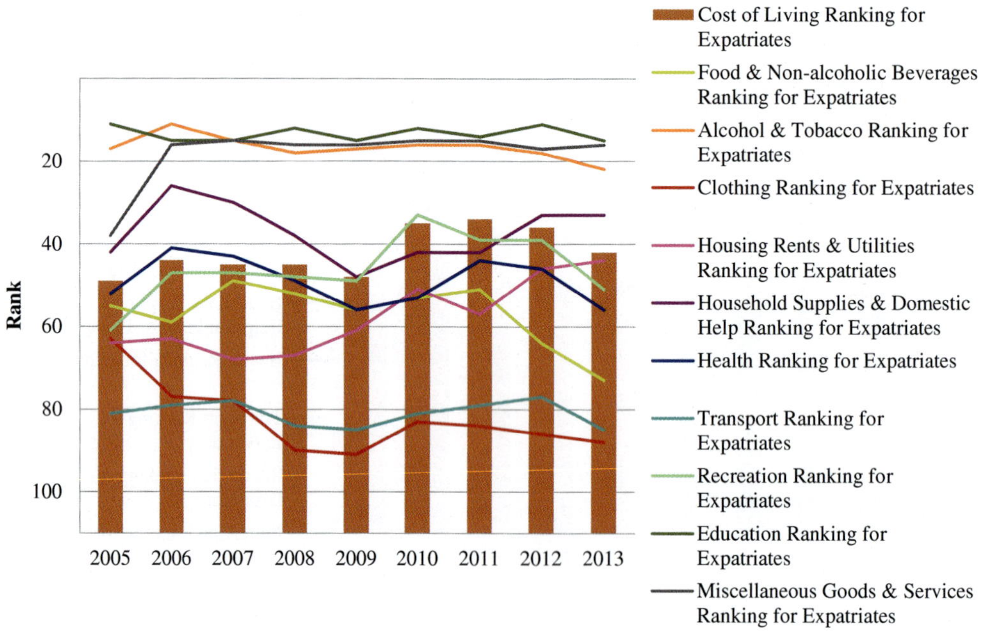

Source: Asia Competitiveness Institute

Toronto is the most populous city in Canada with an estimated population of 2.6 million and the country's financial capital. The city's Cost of Living Ranking for Expatriates, as represented by the orange bars, moved up from 49th to 42nd between 2005 and 2013 (see Figure 4.97).

In particular, Miscellaneous Goods & Services Ranking moved up 22 places from 38th in 2005 to 16th in 2013, making it the second highest ranked category in 2013. Housing Rents & Utilities Ranking climbed 20 spots from 64th in 2005 to 44th in 2013. Recreation Ranking jumped 10 places from 61st to 51st over the same period.

The rankings of the remaining seven categories went down over the study period. Clothing saw the most remarkable dip in ranking as it fell 25 places from 63rd to 88th between 2005 and 2013 and consequently became the lowest ranked category since 2007. Food & Non-alcoholic Beverages Ranking slipped 18 spots from 55th in 2005 to 73rd in 2013. Transport Ranking moved down four places from 81st to 85th over the same period. Likewise, Health Ranking declined from 52nd to 56th between 2005 and 2013. Education consistently remained as the highest ranked category since 2007 although its ranking dropped from 11th to 15th over the study period.

VANCOUVER
Canada

Figure 4.98: Cost of Living and 10 Consumption Categories Rankings for Expatriates in Vancouver, Canada

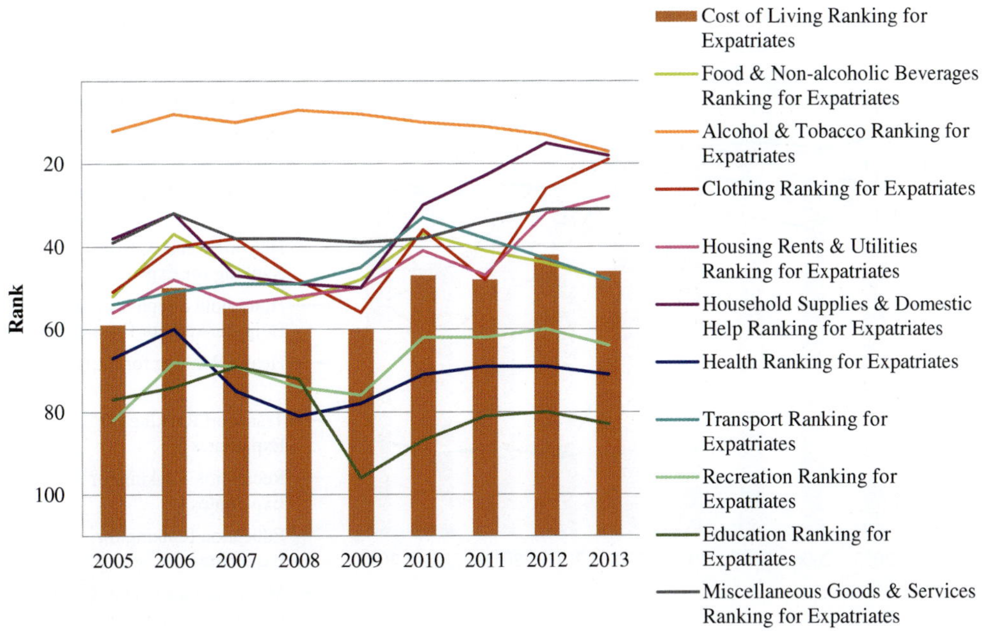

Source: Asia Competitiveness Institute

Home to Port Metro Vancouver, Canada's largest port, Vancouver is the country's centre for forestry and mining as well as high-technology industries including software, biotechnology and aerospace. The city's Cost of Living Ranking for Expatriates, as shown in the orange bars, rose from 59th to 46th between 2005 and 2013 (see Figure 4.98).

Clothing registered the most significant rise in ranking as it climbed 32 places from 51st in 2005 to 19th in 2013. Housing Rents & Utilities Ranking jumped 28 spots from 56th to 28th over the study period. Household Supplies & Domestic Help Ranking moved up 20 places from 38th to 18th between 2005 and 2013, making it the second highest ranked category since 2010 after Alcohol & Tobacco. Recreation Ranking also rose sharply from 82nd in 2005 to 64th in 2013. Transport and Food & Non-alcoholic Beverages Rankings went up more modestly from 54th to 48th and 52nd to 48th, respectively, over the same period.

In contrast, Education consistently remained as the lowest ranked category since 2009 as its ranking fell six places from 77th in 2005 to 83rd in 2013. Health Ranking slipped four spots from 67th to 71st over the study period, making it the second lowest ranked category since 2009.

VIENNA
Austria

Figure 4.99: Cost of Living and 10 Consumption Categories Rankings for Expatriates in Vienna, Austria

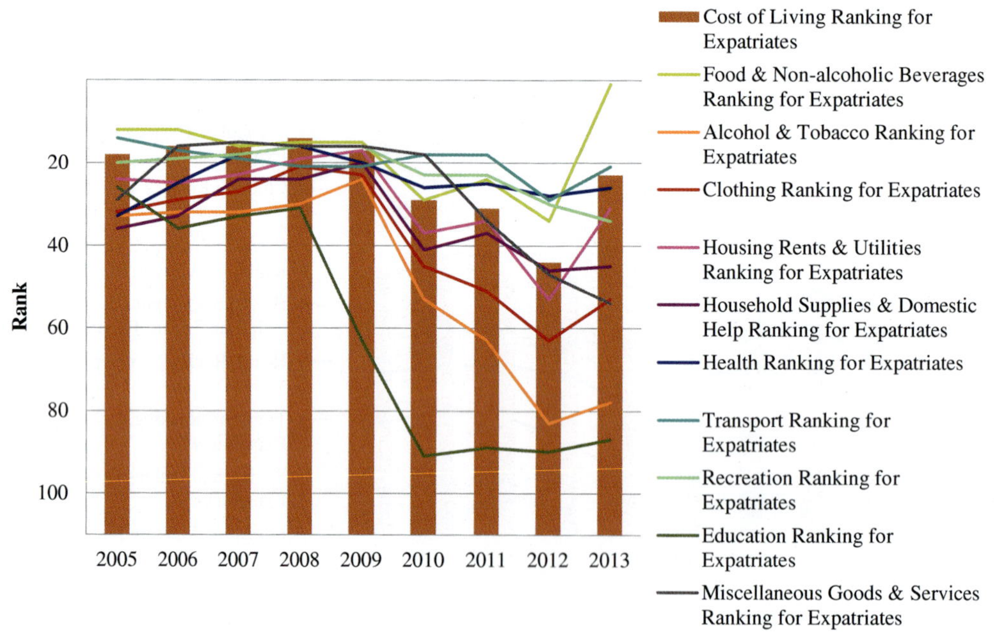

Source: Asia Competitiveness Institute

Home to musical prodigies including Mozart and Beethoven, Vienna is the capital and largest city of Austria and one of Europe's leading cultural centres. The city's Cost of Living Ranking for Expatriates, as denoted by the orange bars, declined from 18th to 23rd between 2005 and 2013 (see Figure 4.99).

Education saw the most dramatic dip in ranking as it fell 61 places from 26th in 2005 to 87th in 2013, making it the lowest ranked category since 2006. Alcohol & Tobacco Ranking slipped 45 spots from 33rd to 78th over the study period. Miscellaneous Goods & Services Ranking moved down 25 places from 29th in 2005 to 54th in 2013. Clothing Ranking dropped 21 spots from 32nd to 53rd between 2005 and 2013. Housing Rents & Utilities and Transport Rankings declined more modestly from 24th to 31st and 14th to 21st, respectively, over the study period.

In contrast, Food & Non-alcoholic Beverages Ranking jumped 11 places from 12th to first between 2005 and 2013, making Vienna the most expensive city in this category in 2013. Health Ranking moved up seven spots from 33rd to 26th over the same period.

WARSAW
Poland

Figure 4.100: Cost of Living and 10 Consumption Categories Rankings for Expatriates in Warsaw, Poland

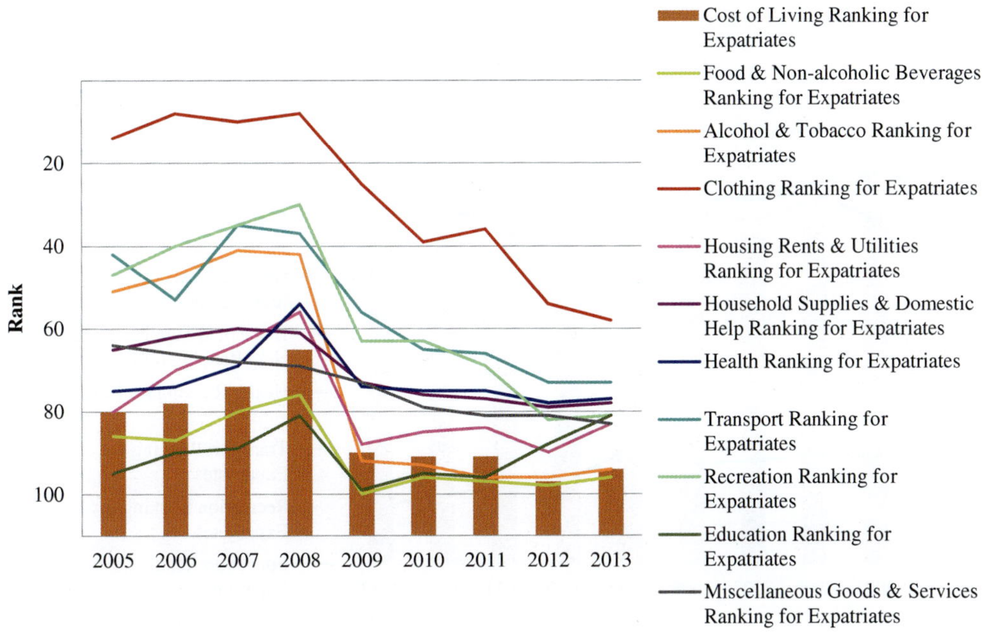

Source: Asia Competitiveness Institute

Warsaw, the capital and largest city of Poland, is home to the country's electronics and high-technology industries. The city's Cost of Living Ranking for Expatriates, as represented by the orange bars, declined from 80th to 94th between 2005 and 2013 (see Figure 4.100).

In particular, Clothing registered the most dramatic dip in ranking as it fell 44 places from 14th in 2005 to 58th in 2013. Nonetheless, it remained as the highest ranked category for the entire study period. Recreation Ranking slipped 34 spots from 47th to 81st between 2005 and 2013. Transport Ranking dropped 31 places from 42nd to 73rd over the same period. Household Supplies & Domestic Help Ranking moved down 13 spots from 65th in 2005 to 78th in 2013. Food & Non-alcoholic Beverages overtook Education to become the lowest ranked category since 2009 as its ranking fell 10 places from 86th to 96th over the study period. Housing Rents & Utilities and Health Rankings went down more modestly from 80th to 83rd and 75th to 77th, respectively, between 2005 and 2013. Education was the only category that saw a rise in ranking from 95th in 2005 to 81st in 2013.

WASHINGTON DC
United States

Figure 4.101: Cost of Living and 10 Consumption Categories Rankings for Expatriates in Washington DC, United States

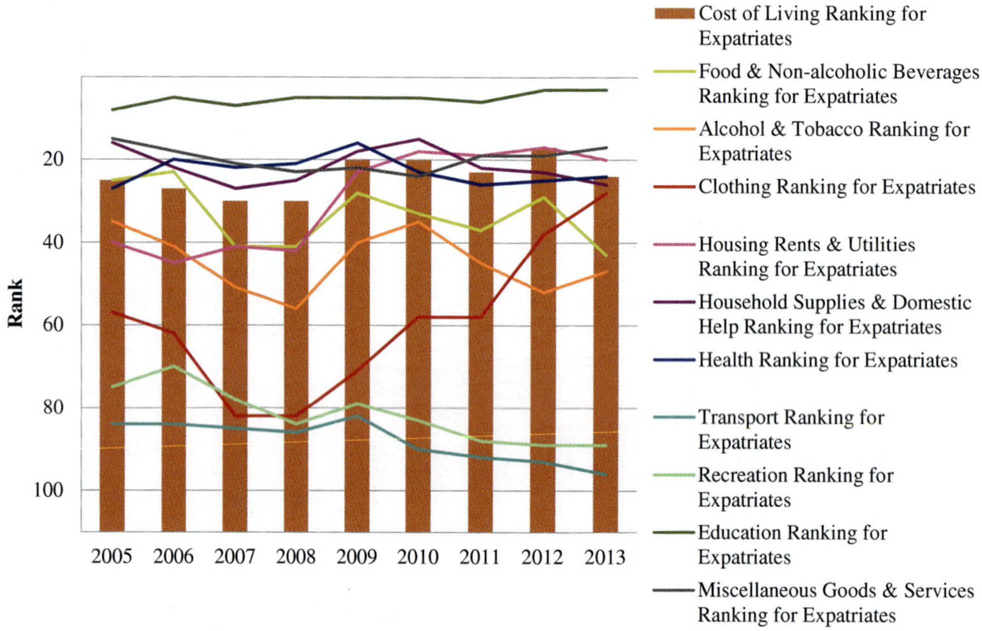

Source: Asia Competitiveness Institute

Washington DC, the capital of the United States, is widely known for hosting major international organizations including the World Bank and the International Monetary Fund (IMF). The city's Cost of Living Ranking for Expatriates, as shown in the orange bars, moved up from 25th in 2005 to 24th in 2013 (see Figure 4.101).

Clothing recorded the most significant rise in ranking as it climbed 29 places from 57th to 28th between 2005 and 2013. Housing Rents & Utilities Ranking jumped 20 spots from 40th in 2005 to 20th in 2013. Education consistently remained as the highest ranked category for the entire study period as its ranking moved up five places from eighth to third between 2005 and 2013, making Washington DC the third most expensive city in this category in 2013. Health Ranking went up three spots from 27th in 2005 to 24th in 2013.

In contrast, Food & Non-alcoholic Ranking fell 18 places from 25th to 43rd over the study period. Recreation Ranking slipped 14 spots from 75th in 2005 to 89th in 2013. Transport was the lowest ranked category throughout the study period as its ranking dropped 12 places from 84th to 96th between 2005 and 2013. Household Supplies & Domestic Help Ranking moved down 10 spots from 16th in 2005 to 26th in 2013. Miscellaneous Goods & Services Ranking declined slightly from 15th to 17th over the same period, making it the second highest ranked category in 2013.

WELLINGTON
New Zealand

Figure 4.102: Cost of Living and 10 Consumption Categories Rankings for Expatriates in Wellington, New Zealand

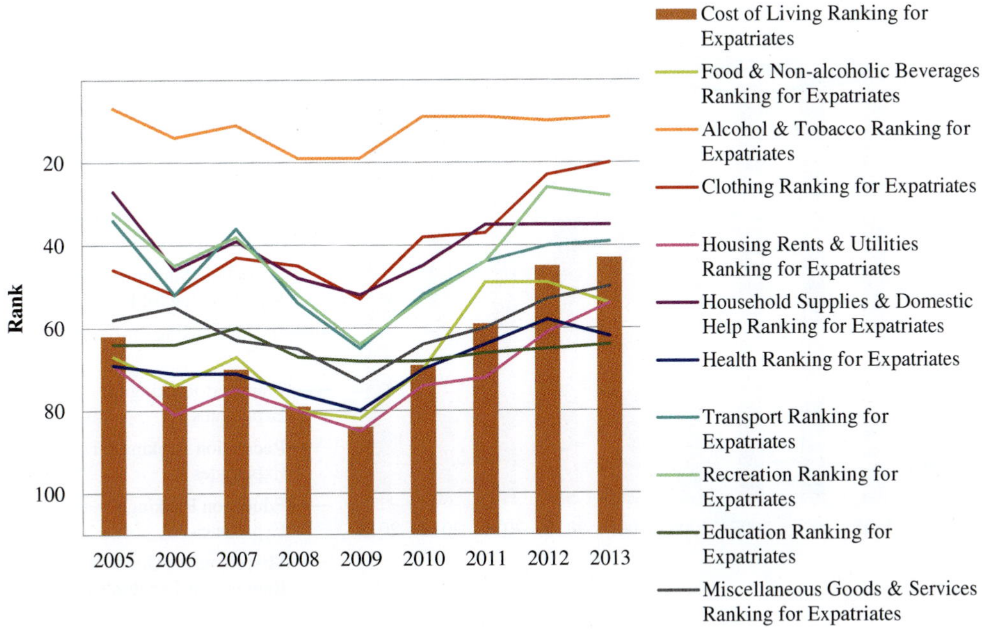

Source: Asia Competitiveness Institute

Wellington, the capital and second most populous city of New Zealand, is the world's southernmost capital city. The city's Cost of Living Ranking for Expatriates, as denoted by the orange bars, rose from 62nd to 43rd between 2005 and 2013 (see Figure 4.102).

Clothing saw the most remarkable rise in ranking as it climbed 26 places from 46th in 2005 to 20th in 2013, making it the second highest ranked category in 2013 after Alcohol & Tobacco at ninth. Housing Rents & Utilities Ranking jumped 15 spots from 69th to 54th over the study period. Health Ranking moved up seven places from 69th to 62nd between 2005 and 2013. Recreation Ranking rose from 32nd in 2005 to 28th in 2013. Education was the lowest ranked category in 2013 as its ranking went down from 64th in 2005 to 68th in 2009 and 2010 before rising back to 64th in 2013.

In contrast, Household Supplies & Domestic Help Ranking fell eight places from 27th to 35th between 2005 and 2013. Transport Ranking slipped five spots from 34th to 39th over the same period.

ZURICH
Switzerland

Figure 4.103: Cost of Living and 10 Consumption Categories Rankings for Expatriates in Zurich, Switzerland

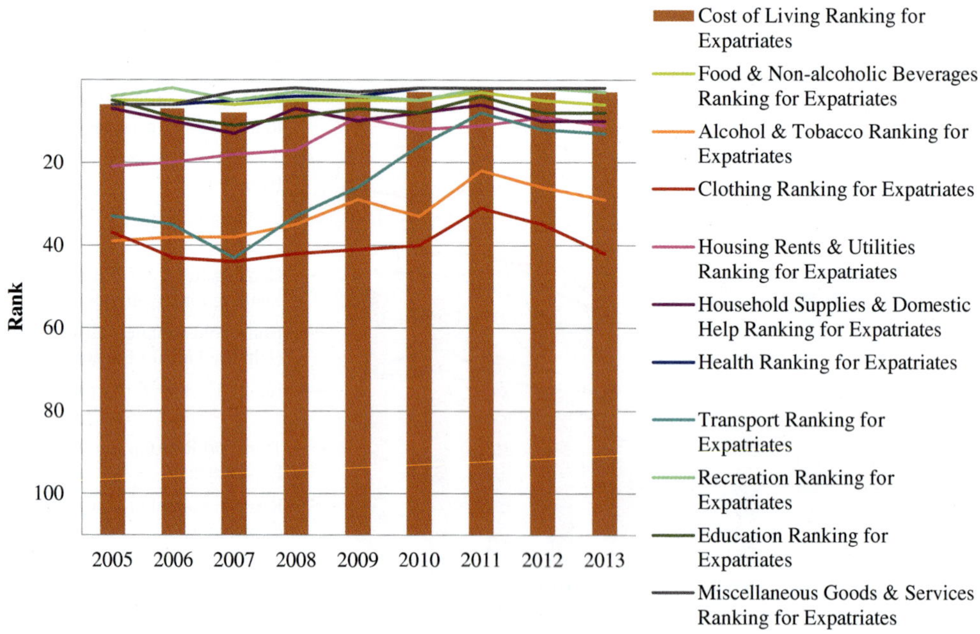

Source: Asia Competitiveness Institute

Home to the headquarters of most Swiss banks and numerous foreign banks, Zurich is the financial capital of Switzerland notwithstanding its small population of approximately 380,000. The city's Cost of Living Ranking for Expatriates, as shown in the orange bars, moved up from sixth to third between 2005 and 2013 (see Figure 4.103).

In particular, Transport registered the most significant rise in ranking as its climbed 20 places from 33rd in 2005 to 13th in 2013. Housing Rents & Utilities Ranking jumped 10 spots from 21st to 11th over the study period. Miscellaneous Goods & Services became the highest ranked category in 2013 as its ranking moved up four places from sixth to second between 2005 and 2013, making Zurich the second most expensive city in this category in 2013. Health Ranking rose from sixth in 2005 to third in 2013. Recreation Ranking went up one spot from fourth to third over the same period. Nonetheless, these upward trends appear to be levelling off as good news.

In contrast, Clothing Ranking fell five places from 37th to 42nd over the study period. Consequently, Clothing remained as the lowest ranked category since 2006. Education and Household Supplies & Domestic Help Rankings both slipped three spots from fifth to eighth and seventh to 10th, respectively, between 2005 and 2013. Food & Non-alcoholic Beverages Ranking declined slightly from fifth in 2005 to sixth in 2013.

Chapter 5

Findings on Cost of Living, Wages and Purchasing Power for Ordinary Residents

In this chapter, we discuss the findings on cost of living, wages and purchasing power for ordinary residents in the 103 cities across the years from 2005 to 2013. The results are presented in alphabetical order of the cities' names. For each city, there are three figures, namely a, b and c.

Figure a is the Cost of Living and 10 Consumption Categories Rankings for Ordinary Residents. The horizontal axis denotes the years in the study period while the vertical axis shows the rankings of a particular city. Rankings range from first to 103rd with first meaning the highest cost and 103rd indicating the lowest cost.

Figure b is the Gross Hourly Wages in USD and Wages Ranking for Ordinary Residents. Similarly, the horizontal axis denotes the years in the study period. There are two vertical axes in this figure. The left axis shows the wages ranking of a particular city, which ranges from first to 103rd with first meaning the highest wage level and 103rd indicating the lowest level. The right axis indicates the dollar value (USD) of gross hourly wages in that city.

Figure c is the Cost of Living, Wages and Purchasing Power Indices and Purchasing Power Ranking for Ordinary Residents. Likewise, the horizontal axis denotes the years in the study period. There are two vertical axes in this figure. The left axis shows the purchasing power ranking of a particular city, which ranges from first to 103rd with first meaning the highest purchasing power and 103rd indicating the lowest. The right axis indicates the values of cost of living, wages and purchasing power indices for that city.

ADELAIDE
Australia

Figure 5.1a: Cost of Living and 10 Consumption Categories Rankings for Ordinary Residents in Adelaide, Australia

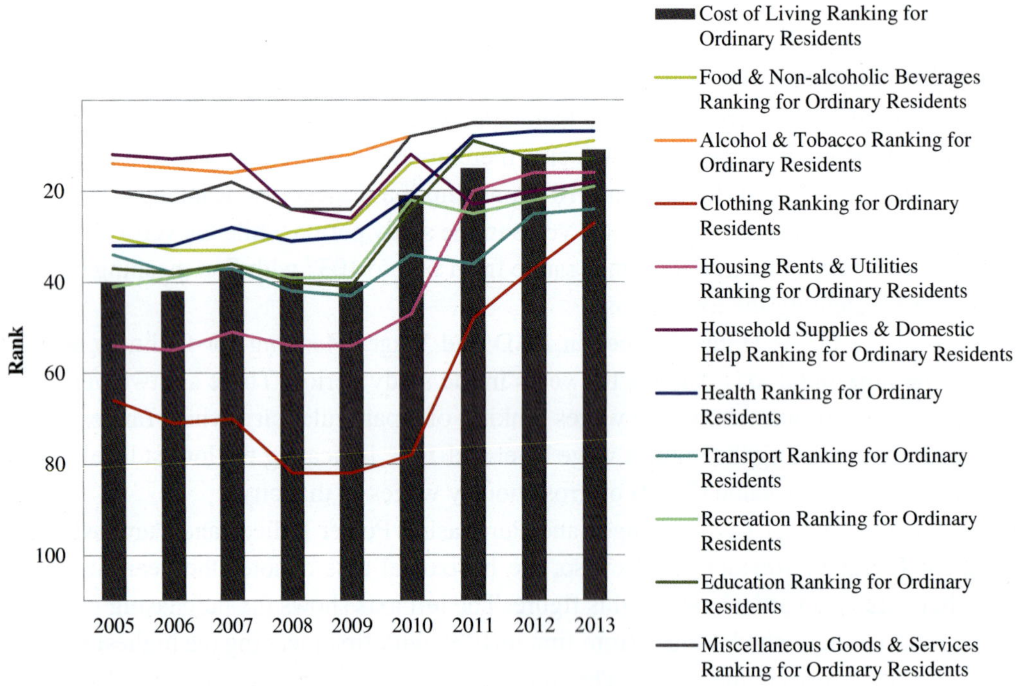

Source: Asia Competitiveness Institute

Figure 5.1b: Gross Hourly Wages in USD and Wages Ranking for Ordinary Residents in Adelaide, Australia

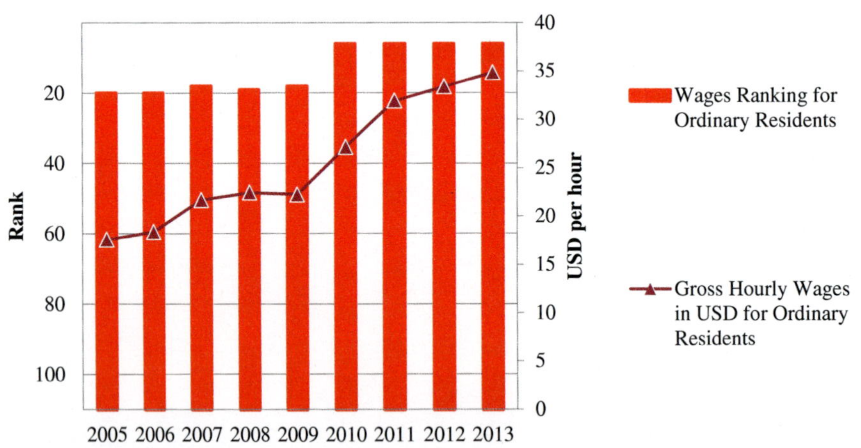

Source: Asia Competitiveness Institute

ADELAIDE
Australia

Figure 5.1c: Cost of Living, Wages and Purchasing Power Indices and Purchasing Power Ranking for Ordinary Residents in Adelaide, Australia

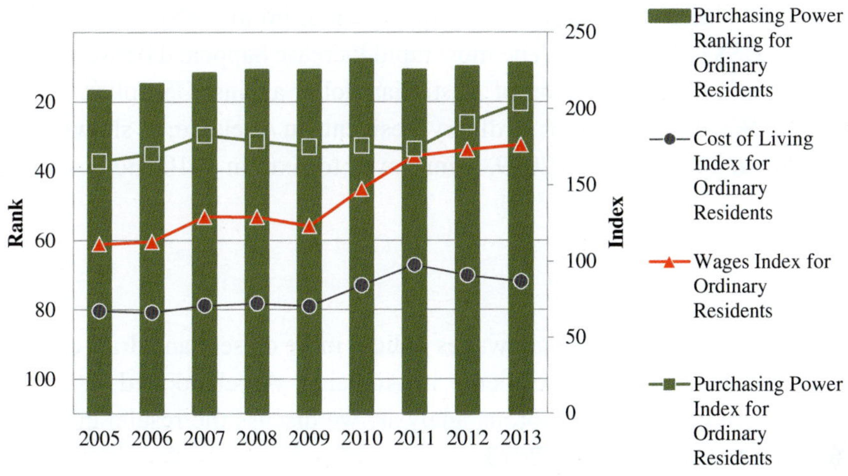

Source: Asia Competitiveness Institute

Figure 5.1a

Famous for its warm, Mediterranean climate and beautiful beachfronts, Adelaide is also the most vibrant city in South Australia where many governmental, commercial and financial institutions are situated. The city's Cost of Living Ranking for Ordinary Residents, as denoted by the grey bars, rose from 40th to 21st between 2005 and 2010, and from 15th to 11th between 2011 and 2013 (see Figure 5.1a). As explained in Section 3.4.2 of Chapter 3, for a more precise comparison of rankings, we have split the analysis into two sub-periods.

In the first sub-period from 2005 to 2010, Recreation saw the most remarkable rise in ranking as it climbed 19 places from 41st to 22nd. Food & Non-alcoholic Beverages Ranking jumped 16 spots from 30th in 2005 to 14th in 2010. Education Ranking moved up 13 places from 37th to 24th over the first sub-period. Health Ranking rose from 32nd in 2005 to 21st in 2010. Housing Rents & Utilities Ranking jumped seven spots from 54th to 47th over the same sub-period. Transport Ranking fell from 34th in 2005 to 43rd in 2009 before rising back to 34th in 2010.

In the second sub-period between 2011 and 2013, Clothing registered the most significant jump in ranking from 48th to 27th. Nonetheless, Clothing consistently remained as the lowest ranked category for the entire study period. Transport Ranking climbed 12 places from 36th in 2011 to 24th in 2013. Housing Rents & Utilities Ranking and Food & Non-alcoholic Beverages Ranking rose more modestly from 20th to 16th and 12th to ninth, respectively, over the second sub-period. Health Ranking moved up one spot from eighth to seventh between 2011 and 2013. Miscellaneous Goods & Services and Alcohol & Tobacco Rankings remained unchanged at fifth from 2011 to 2013, making them the highest ranked categories throughout the second sub-period.

ADELAIDE
Australia

Figure 5.1b

The Gross Hourly Wages in USD for Ordinary Residents in Adelaide, as denoted by the red line in Figure 5.1b, have almost doubled over the study period. From US$17.56 in 2005, Adelaide's wage level rose to US$34.83 in 2013. The most rapid increase happened between 2009 and 2011. This was partly due to the appreciation of Australian dollar against US dollar.

Meanwhile, the Wages Ranking for Ordinary Residents in Adelaide, as shown by the red bars, first rose from 20th in 2005 to 18th in 2009. It improved to sixth in 2010 and has remained at that level thereafter.

Figure 5.1c

Let us now analyse the cost of living and wages indices more closely and draw conclusions about the purchasing power of ordinary residents in Adelaide. As elaborated in Section 3.4.2 of Chapter 3, for a more precise and rigorous analysis, we discuss the results in two sub-periods: from 2005 to 2010 and from 2011 to 2013.

The Cost of Living Index and the Wages Index for Ordinary Residents in Adelaide are represented respectively by the grey and red line in Figure 5.1c. Between 2005 and 2010, the Cost of Living Index for Ordinary Residents increased substantially. In 2005, the cost of living for ordinary residents in Adelaide was roughly 67.23% of that for their counterparts in New York (the base city). In 2010, this rose to 83.94%. Over the same sub-period, the Wages Index for Ordinary Residents also increased, rising from 111.21 in 2005 to 147.34 in 2010.

Over the first sub-period, wages rose faster than cost of living. Thus, ordinary residents in Adelaide were able to afford more goods and services over time during these years. This is reflected in the Purchasing Power Index for Ordinary Residents, which is represented by the green line in Figure 5.1c. Between 2005 and 2010, this index rose from 165.40 in 2005 to 175.54 in 2010. Meanwhile, the Purchasing Power Ranking for Ordinary Residents in Adelaide, as represented by the green bars, also improved. It rose from 17th to eighth between 2005 and 2010.

Over the second sub-period (2011–2013), the Cost of Living Index for Ordinary Residents has steadily declined. In 2011, the cost of living for ordinary residents in Adelaide was 97.41% of that for their counterparts in New York. It dropped over the years to 86.54%. Meanwhile, the Wages Index for Ordinary Residents has increased, rising from 168.86 in 2011 to 176.22 by 2013.

The combined trends of decreasing cost of living and increasing wages have allowed ordinary residents in Adelaide to afford higher consumption level over time throughout the second sub-period. Evidently, the Purchasing Power Index for Ordinary Residents in Adelaide has risen from 173.35 in 2011 to 203.64 by 2013. Ranking-wise, the Purchasing Power Ranking for Ordinary Residents has improved from 11th in 2011 to ninth in 2013.

Finally, we note that throughout the entire study period (2005–2013), the Purchasing Power Index for Ordinary Residents in Adelaide has always been above 100.00 — the base index value. This indicates that ordinary residents in Adelaide have always been able to afford a higher level of consumption than their counterparts in New York, given the same number of working hours.

AMMAN
Jordan

Figure 5.2a: Cost of Living and 10 Consumption Categories Rankings for Ordinary Residents in Amman, Jordan

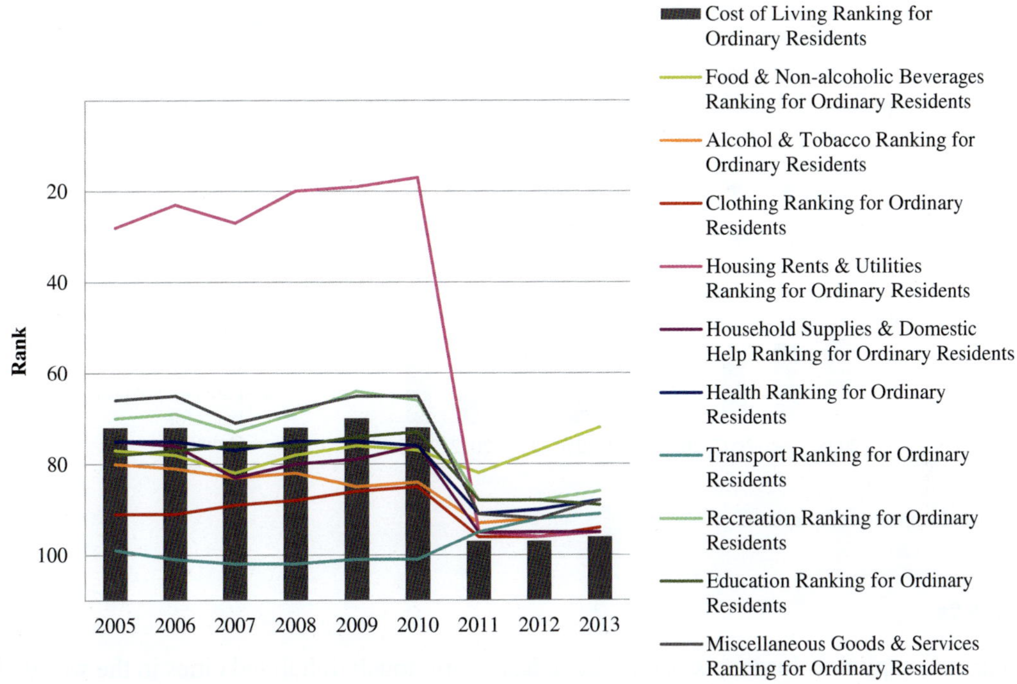

Source: Asia Competitiveness Institute

Figure 5.2b: Gross Hourly Wages in USD and Wages Ranking for Ordinary Residents in Amman, Jordan

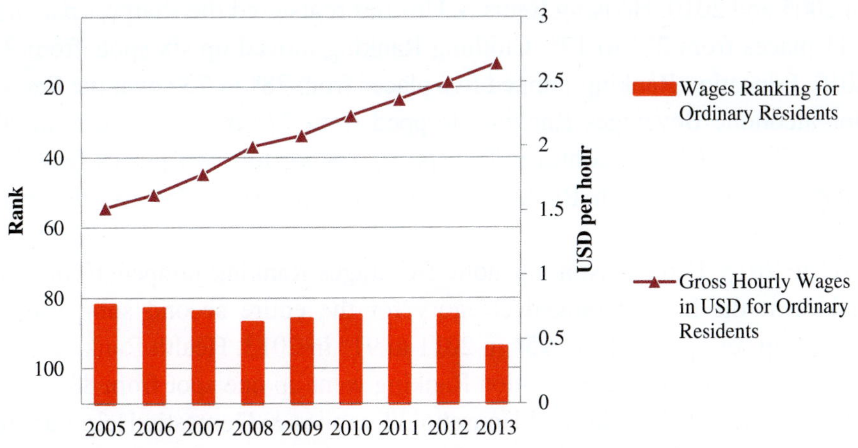

Source: Asia Competitiveness Institute

AMMAN
Jordan

Figure 5.2c: Cost of Living, Wages and Purchasing Power Indices and Purchasing Power Ranking for Ordinary Residents in Amman, Jordan

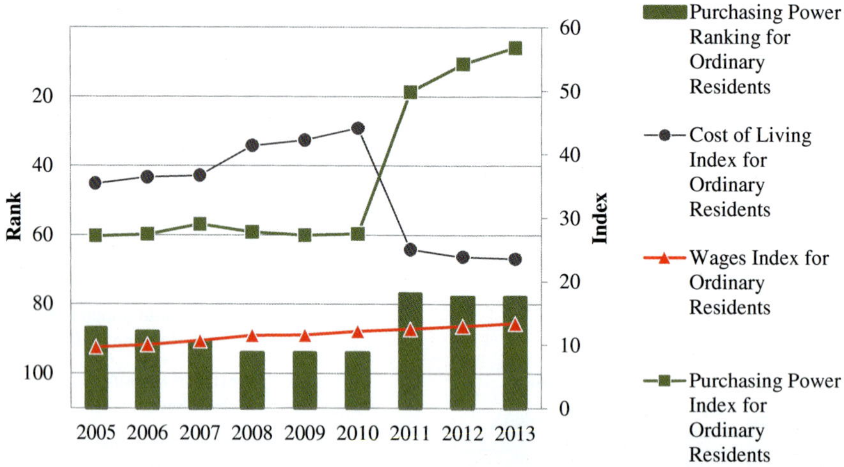

Source: Asia Competitiveness Institute

Figure 5.2a

Amman, the capital of Jordan, is one of the oldest continuously inhabited cities in the world. The city's Cost of Living Ranking for Ordinary Residents, as represented by the grey bars, fell from 72nd in 2005 to 75th in 2007 before rising back to 72nd in 2010, and rose from 97th to 96th between 2011 and 2013 (see Figure 5.2a). As elaborated in Section 3.4.2 of Chapter 3, for a more rigorous comparison of rankings, we have split the analysis into two sub-periods: from 2005 to 2010 and from 2011 to 2013.

Between 2005 and 2010, Housing Rents & Utilities registered the sharpest rise in ranking as it climbed 11 places from 28th to 17th. Clothing Ranking moved up six spots from 91st in 2005 to 85th in 2010. Education Ranking jumped five places from 78th to 73rd over the first sub-period. Food & Non-alcoholic Beverages Ranking dropped from 77th in 2005 to 82nd in 2007 before rising back to 77th in 2010. In contrast, Transport Ranking fell two places from 99th to 101st between 2005 and 2010. Health Ranking slipped one spot from 75th to 76th over the same sub-period.

From 2011 to 2013, Food & Non-alcoholic Beverages Ranking jumped 10 places from 82nd to 72nd, making it the highest ranked category for the entire second sub-period. Transport Ranking moved up four places from 95th in 2011 to 91st in 2013. Health Ranking rose from 91st to 88th over the same sub-period. Education Ranking went up one spot from 88th in 2011 to 89th in 2013. Housing Rents & Utilities and Household Supplies & Domestic Help Rankings largely remained at 95th between 2011 and 2013, making them the lowest ranked categories throughout the second sub-period.

AMMAN
Jordan

Figure 5.2b

The Gross Hourly Wages in USD for Ordinary Residents in Amman, as represented by the red line in Figure 5.2b, increased steadily from US$1.51 in 2005 to US$2.64 in 2013.

Meanwhile, the Wages Ranking for Ordinary Residents in Amman, as denoted by the red bars, did not demonstrate the same trend. It deteriorated from 82nd in 2005 to 87th in 2008 before it slipped back to 85th in 2012. The ranking then dropped to 94th in 2013. This plunge happened mainly because the wage level in Amman fell below the wage level in the Chinese cities. As explained in Section 3.3 of Chapter 3, cities in the same country are assumed to share a common Gross Hourly Wages in USD for Ordinary Residents. Consequently, the eight Chinese cities also share the same Wages Ranking for Ordinary Residents and form a cluster on the wage ranking table. In 2013, this cluster surpassed Amman, causing the significant drop in the latter's ranking as observed.

Figure 5.2c

Let us now analyse the cost of living and wages indices more closely and draw conclusions about the purchasing power of ordinary residents in Amman. As elaborated in Section 3.4.2 of Chapter 3, for a more precise and rigorous analysis, we discuss the results in two sub-periods: from 2005 to 2010 and from 2011 to 2013.

The Cost of Living Index and the Wages Index for Ordinary Residents in Amman are represented respectively by the grey and red line in Figure 5.2c. Between 2005 and 2010, the Cost of Living Index for Ordinary Residents followed an increasing trend. In 2005, the cost of living for ordinary residents in Amman was roughly 35.37% of that for their counterparts in New York (the base city). In 2010, this rose to 44.09%. Over the same sub-period, the Wages Index for Ordinary Residents also increased, rising from 9.59 in 2005 to 12.11 in 2010.

Wages could keep up with cost of living so throughout the first sub-period, ordinary residents in Amman were able to consume similar amount of goods and services over time despite the rise in prices. This is reflected in the relative stability of the Purchasing Power Index for Ordinary Residents, which is represented by the green line in Figure 5.2c. Between 2005 and 2010, this index only fluctuated around 27.65. However, the Purchasing Power Ranking for Ordinary Residents in Amman, which is represented by the green bars, dropped from 87th in 2005 to 94th in 2010.

Over the second sub-period (2011–2013), the Cost of Living Index for Ordinary Residents has been on a decreasing trend, albeit marginally. In 2011, the cost of living for ordinary residents in Amman was 25.04% of that for their counterparts in New York. It dropped slightly to 23.51% in 2013. In contrast, the Wages Index for Ordinary Residents has been increasing, rising marginally from 12.48 to 13.35.

The combined trends of decreasing cost of living and increasing wages have allowed ordinary residents in Amman to afford a higher consumption level over time throughout the second sub-period. Evidently, the Purchasing Power Index for Ordinary Residents in Amman rose from

AMMAN
Jordan

49.82 in 2011 to 56.78 in 2013. Ranking-wise, the Purchasing Power Ranking for Ordinary Residents has also improved marginally, rising from 77th in 2011 to 78th in 2013.

Finally, we note that throughout the entire study period (2005–2013), the Purchasing Power Index for Ordinary Residents in Amman has never been higher than 100.00 — the base index value. This means that ordinary residents in Amman have only been able to consume fewer goods and services than their counterparts in New York, given the same number of working hours.

AMSTERDAM
Netherlands

Figure 5.3a: Cost of Living and 10 Consumption Categories Rankings for Ordinary Residents in Amsterdam, Netherlands

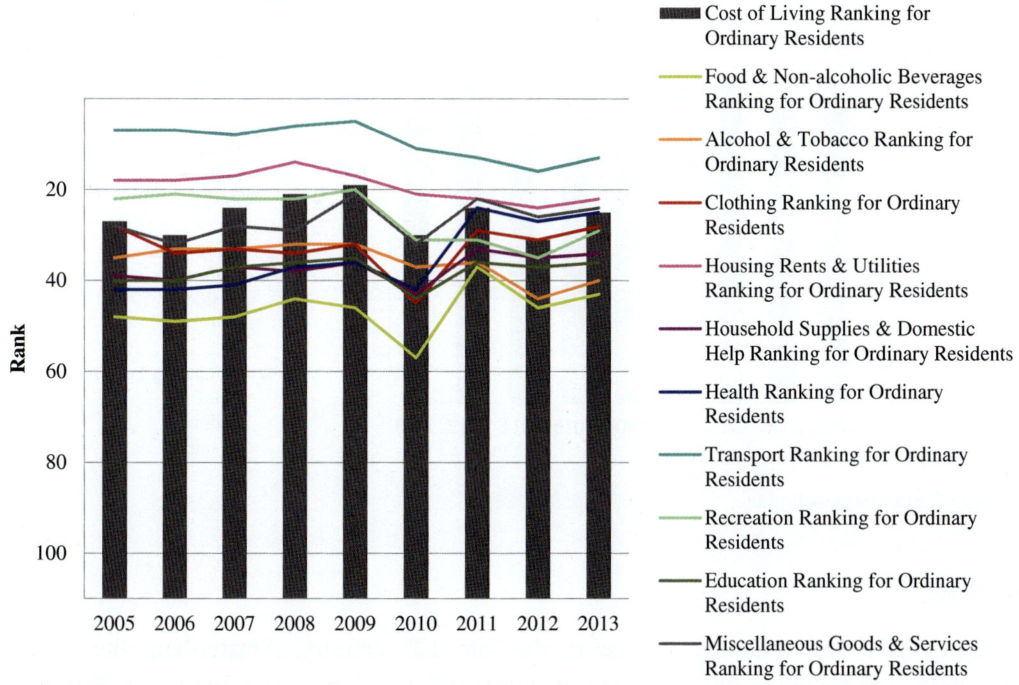

Source: Asia Competitiveness Institute

Figure 5.3b: Gross Hourly Wages in USD and Wages Ranking for Ordinary Residents in Amsterdam, Netherlands

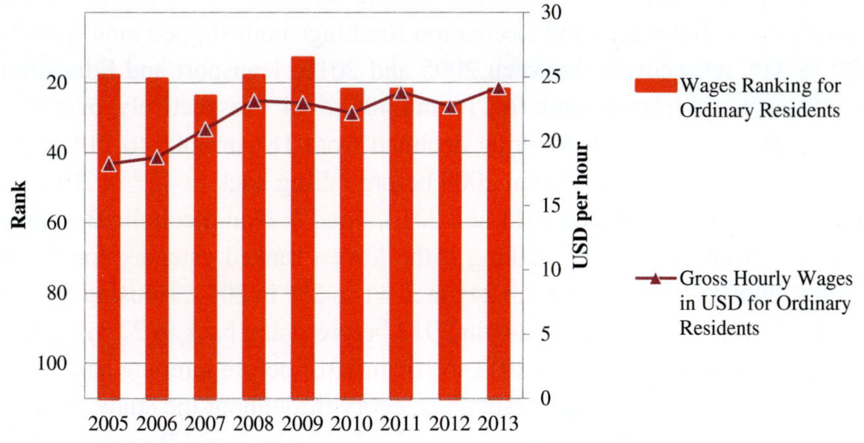

Source: Asia Competitiveness Institute

AMSTERDAM
Netherlands

Figure 5.3c: Cost of Living, Wages and Purchasing Power Indices and Purchasing Power Ranking for Ordinary Residents in Amsterdam, Netherlands

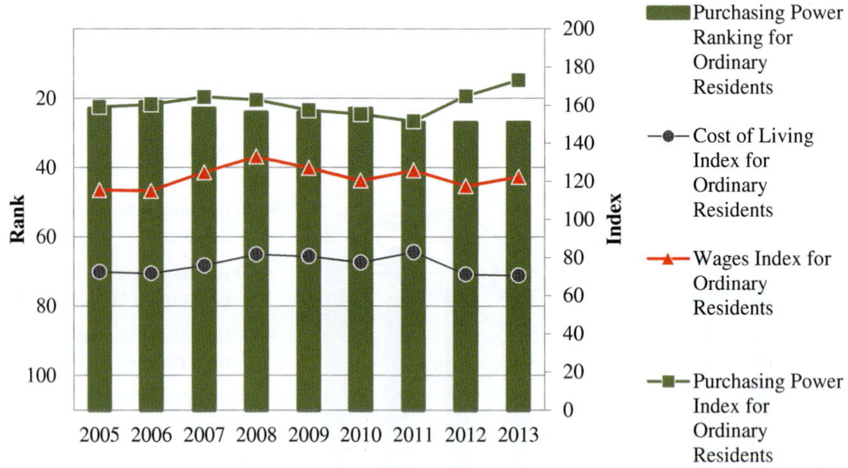

Source: Asia Competitiveness Institute

Figure 5.3a

Originating as a small fishing village in the late 12th century, Amsterdam, the capital of Netherlands, has become one of the major commercial and financial centres in Europe. The city's Cost of Living Ranking for Ordinary Residents, as shown in the grey bars, declined from 27th to 30th between 2005 and 2010, and from 24th to 25th between 2011 and 2013 (see Figure 5.3a). As explained in Section 3.4.2 of Chapter 3, for a more precise comparison of rankings, we have split the analysis into two sub-periods.

In the first sub-period from 2005 to 2010, Clothing Ranking fell 17 places from 28th to 45th. Food & Non-alcoholic Beverages and Recreation Rankings both slipped nine spots from 48th to 57th and 22nd to 31st, respectively, between 2005 and 2010. Transport and Education Rankings moved down four places from seventh to 11th and 40th to 44th, respectively, over the same sub-period. Housing Rents & Utilities Ranking declined from 18th in 2005 to 21st in 2010. Health Ranking rose from 42nd in 2005 to 36th in 2009 before falling back to 42nd in 2010.

In the second sub-period between 2011 and 2013, Food & Non-alcoholic Beverages Ranking slipped six places from 37th to 43rd, making it the lowest ranked category for the entire study period. Health Ranking fell one spot from 24th in 2011 to 25th in 2013. Housing Rents & Utilities Ranking declined from 22nd in 2011 to 24th in 2012 before rising back to 22nd in 2013. Likewise, Transport Ranking slipped from 13th in 2011 to 16th in 2012 before jumping back to 13th in 2013. Transport thus remained as the highest ranked category throughout the study period. Education Ranking largely stayed at 36th between 2011 and 2013. Clothing and Recreation Rankings rose from 29th to 28th and 31st to 29th, respectively, over the same sub-period.

AMSTERDAM
Netherlands

Figure 5.3b

The Gross Hourly Wages in USD for Ordinary Residents in Amsterdam, as denoted by the red line in Figure 5.3b, have generally exhibited an upward trend over the study period. From US$18.22 in 2005, Amsterdam's wage level rose to US$24.16 in 2013.

Meanwhile, the Wages Ranking for Ordinary Residents in Amsterdam, as shown by the red bars, has fluctuated considerably over the study period. The highest ranking was 13th (in 2009) and the lowest was 26th (in 2012). Amsterdam's ranking in 2013 was 22nd.

Figure 5.3c

Let us now analyse the cost of living and wages indices more closely and draw conclusions about the purchasing power of ordinary residents in Amsterdam. As elaborated in Section 3.4.2 of Chapter 3, for a more precise and rigorous analysis, we discuss the results in two sub-periods: from 2005 to 2010 and from 2011 to 2013.

The Cost of Living Index and the Wages Index for Ordinary Residents in Amsterdam are represented respectively by the grey and red line in Figure 5.3c. Between 2005 and 2010, the Cost of Living Index for Ordinary Residents exhibited moderate fluctuations. In 2005, the cost of living for ordinary residents in Amsterdam was about 72.51% of that for their counterparts in New York (the base city). It first rose to peak at 81.64% in 2008 before embarking on a decreasing trend to reach 77.44% in 2010. Over the same sub-period, the Wages Index for Ordinary Resident also tracked a similar pattern. This index rose from 115.40 in 2005 to peak at 132.89 in 2008 and then dropped steadily to 120.31 in 2010.

Not only did wages and cost of living follow similar patterns but they also generally changed at similar rates. Thus, ordinary residents in Amsterdam were able to maintain their consumption level over time throughout the first sub-period. This is reflected in the Purchasing Power Index for Ordinary Residents in Amsterdam, which is represented by the green line in Figure 5.3c. Overall, this index only fluctuated around 159.89 during the first sub-period. Ranking-wise, the Purchasing Power Ranking for Ordinary Residents in Amsterdam, which is represented by the green bars, was also stable. It fluctuated between 23rd and 24th over 2005–2010, with a one-off improvement to 21st in 2006.

Over the second sub-period (2011–2013), the Cost of Living Index for Ordinary Residents has been on a decreasing trend. In 2011, the cost of living for ordinary residents in Amsterdam was 82.93% of that for their counterparts in New York. It dropped over the years to 70.62% in 2013. Meanwhile, the Wages Index for Ordinary Residents has also been decreasing, dropping from 125.73 in 2011 to 122.23 in 2013.

Wages have decreased at a slower rate than cost of living. Thus, ordinary residents in Amsterdam have been able to afford a higher consumption level over time throughout the second sub-period. Evidently, the Purchasing Power Index for Ordinary Residents rose from 151.62 in 2011 to 173.08 in 2013. Despite the positive showing of the index, Amsterdam saw its Purchasing Power Ranking for Ordinary Residents stagnate at 27th over the sub-period.

AMSTERDAM
Netherlands

Finally, we note that throughout the entire study period (2005–2013), the Purchasing Power Index for Ordinary Residents in Amsterdam has always been higher than 100.00 — the base index value. This indicates that ordinary residents in Amsterdam have consistently been able to consume more goods and services than their counterparts in New York, given the same number of working hours.

ASUNCION
Paraguay

Figure 5.4a: Cost of Living and 10 Consumption Categories Rankings for Ordinary Residents in Asuncion, Paraguay

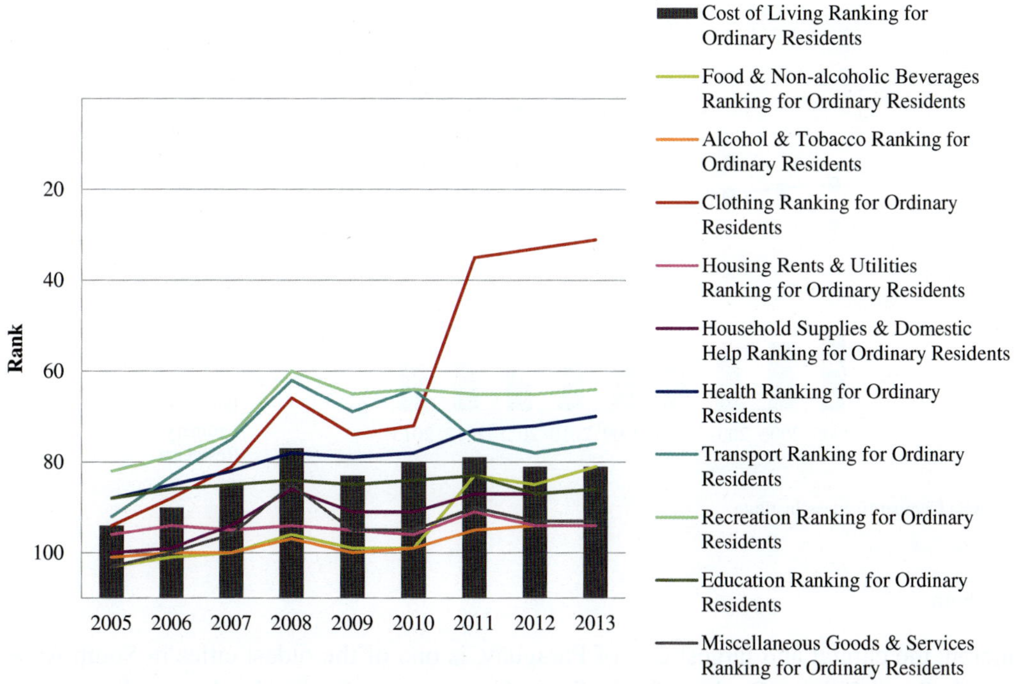

Source: Asia Competitiveness Institute

Figure 5.4b: Gross Hourly Wages in USD and Wages Ranking for Ordinary Residents in Asuncion, Paraguay

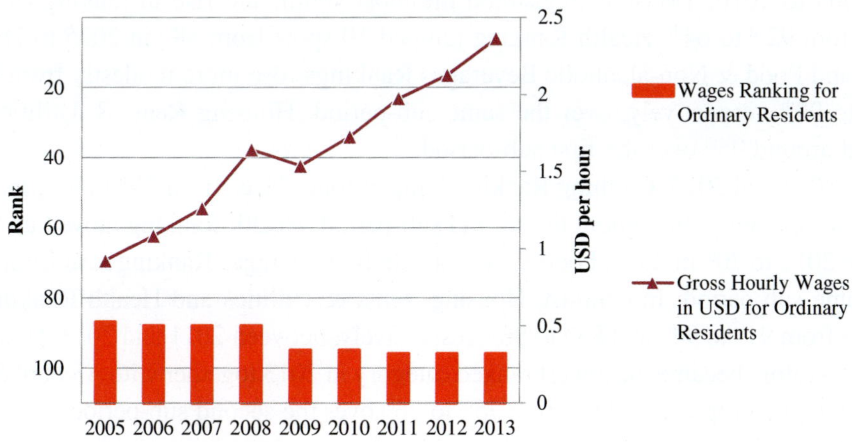

Source: Asia Competitiveness Institute

ASUNCION
Paraguay

Figure 5.4c: Cost of Living, Wages and Purchasing Power Indices and Purchasing Power Ranking for Ordinary Residents in Asuncion, Paraguay

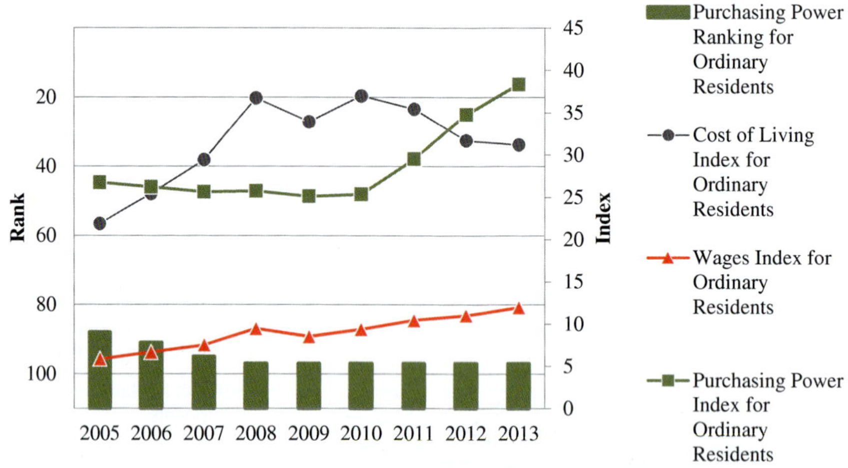

Source: Asia Competitiveness Institute

Figure 5.4a

Asuncion, the capital and largest city of Paraguay, is one of the oldest cities in South America. The city's Cost of Living Ranking for Ordinary Residents, as denoted by the grey bars, rose from 94th to 80th between 2005 and 2010, and from 83rd to 81st between 2011 and 2013 (see Figure 5.4a). As elaborated in Section 3.4.2 of Chapter 3, for a more rigorous comparison of rankings, we have split the analysis into two sub-periods.

From 2005 to 2010, Transport registered the most significant rise in ranking as it climbed 28 places from 92nd to 64th. Health Ranking jumped 10 spots from 88th in 2005 to 78th in 2010. Education and Food & Non-alcoholic Beverages Rankings rose more modestly from 88th to 84th and 103rd to 99th, respectively, over the same sub-period. Housing Rents & Utilities Ranking remained at around 96th over the first sub-period.

Between 2011 and 2013, Clothing Ranking jumped four places from 35th to 31st, making it the highest ranked category throughout the second sub-period. Health Ranking moved up three spots from 73rd in 2011 to 70th in 2013. Food & Non-alcoholic Beverages Ranking rose from 83rd to 81st over the same sub-period. In contrast, Housing Rents & Utilities and Health Rankings slipped three places from 91st to 94th and 83rd to 86th, respectively, between 2011 and 2013. Housing Rents & Utilities therefore became the lowest ranked category in 2013 together with Alcohol & Tobacco. Transport Ranking dropped slightly from 75th to 76th over the second sub-period.

ASUNCION
Paraguay

Figure 5.4b

The Gross Hourly Wages in USD for Ordinary Residents in Asuncion, as depicted by the red line in Figure 5.4b, have generally followed an increasing trend over the study period. Asuncion's wage level more than doubled from US$0.92 in 2005 to US$2.36 in 2013.

Despite the steady growth of the wage level, the Wages Ranking for Ordinary Residents in Asuncion, as represented by the red bars, actually declined from 87th in 2005 to 96th in 2013. This can be partly attributed to the stronger performance of other cities with rankings close to Asuncion, in particular the eight Chinese cities.

Figure 5.4c

Let us now analyse the cost of living and wages indices more closely and draw conclusions about the purchasing power of ordinary residents in Asuncion. As elaborated in Section 3.4.2 of Chapter 3, for a more precise and rigorous analysis, we discuss the results in two sub-periods: from 2005 to 2010 and from 2011 to 2013.

The Cost of Living Index and the Wages Index for Ordinary Residents in Asuncion are represented respectively by the grey and red line in Figure 5.4c. Between 2005 and 2010, the Cost of Living Index for Ordinary Residents increased significantly. In 2005, the cost of living for ordinary residents in Asuncion was about 21.85% of that for their counterparts in New York (the base city). This rose to 36.96% in 2010. Over the same sub-period, the Wages Index for Ordinary Residents also increased considerably, rising from 5.84 in 2005 to 9.36 in 2010.

Wages were generally able to keep up with the cost of living so despite the increase in prices, ordinary residents in Asuncion were able to consume the same amount of goods and services over time during the first sub-period. This is reflected in the Purchasing Power Index for Ordinary Residents in Asuncion, which is represented by the green line in Figure 5.4c. This index only fluctuated around 25.50. Ranking-wise, the Purchasing Power Ranking for Ordinary Residents in Asuncion actually deteriorated over the first sub-period, dropping from 88th in 2005 to 97th in 2010.

Over the second sub-period (2011–2013), the Cost of Living Index for Ordinary Residents has been on a decreasing trend. In 2011, the cost of living for ordinary residents in Asuncion was 35.42% of that for their counterparts in New York while in 2013, it dropped to 31.17%. Meanwhile, the Wages Index for Ordinary Residents has steadily increased. Between 2011 and 2013, this index rose from 10.45 to 11.95.

The combined trends of decreasing cost of living and increasing wages have allowed ordinary residents in Asuncion to increase the amount of goods and services they consume over the second sub-period. The Purchasing Power Index for Ordinary Residents rose from 29.49 in 2011 to 38.34 in 2013. Despite this positive showing of the index, the Purchasing Power Ranking for Ordinary Residents stagnated at 97th for every year between 2011 and 2013.

ASUNCION
Paraguay

Finally, we note that throughout the entire study period (2005–2013), the Purchasing Power Index for Ordinary Residents in Asuncion has always been lower than 100.00 — the base index value. This indicates that ordinary residents in Asuncion have only been able to consume fewer goods and services than their counterparts in New York, given the same number of working hours.

ATHENS
Greece

Figure 5.5a: Cost of Living and 10 Consumption Categories Rankings for Ordinary Residents in Athens, Greece

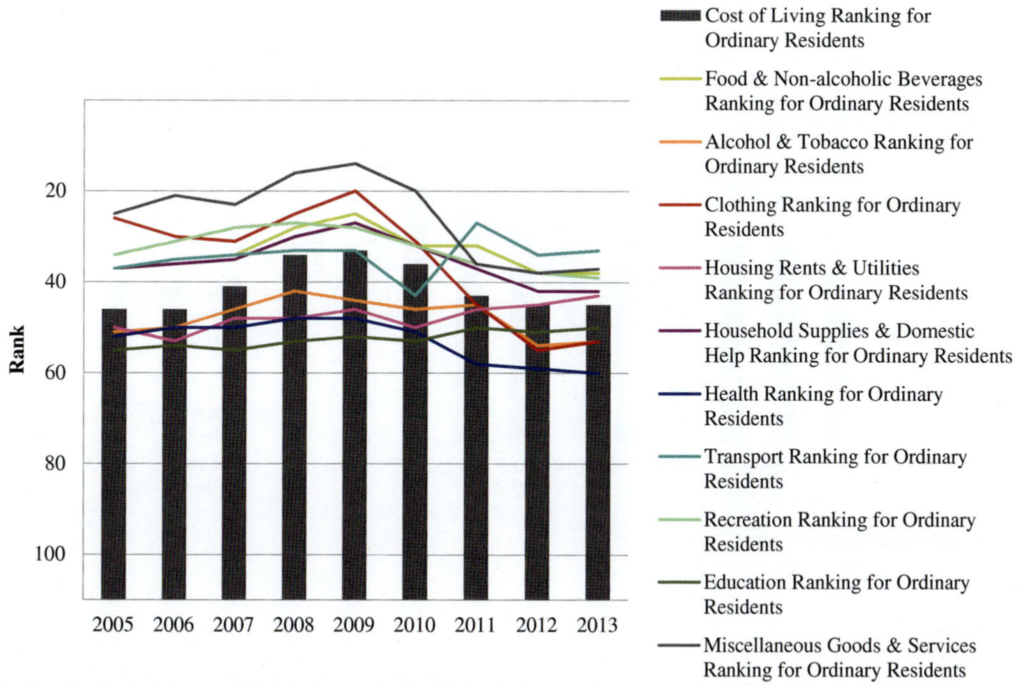

Source: Asia Competitiveness Institute

Figure 5.5b: Gross Hourly Wages in USD and Wages Ranking for Ordinary Residents in Athens, Greece

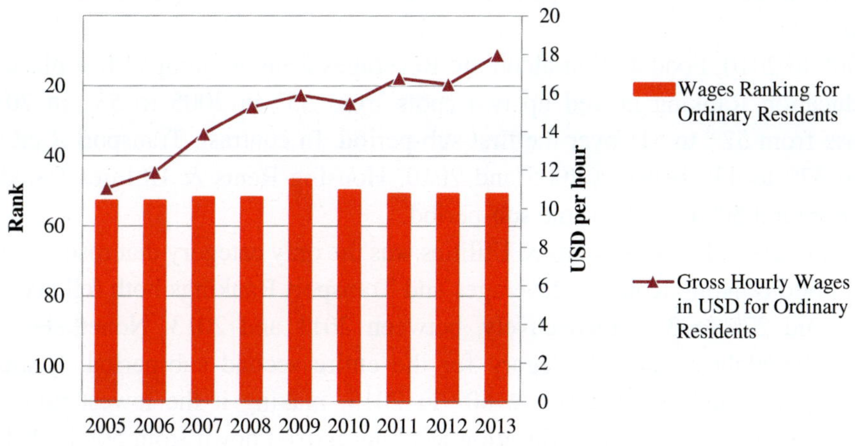

Source: Asia Competitiveness Institute

ATHENS
Greece

Figure 5.5c: Cost of Living, Wages and Purchasing Power Indices and Purchasing Power Ranking for Ordinary Residents in Athens, Greece

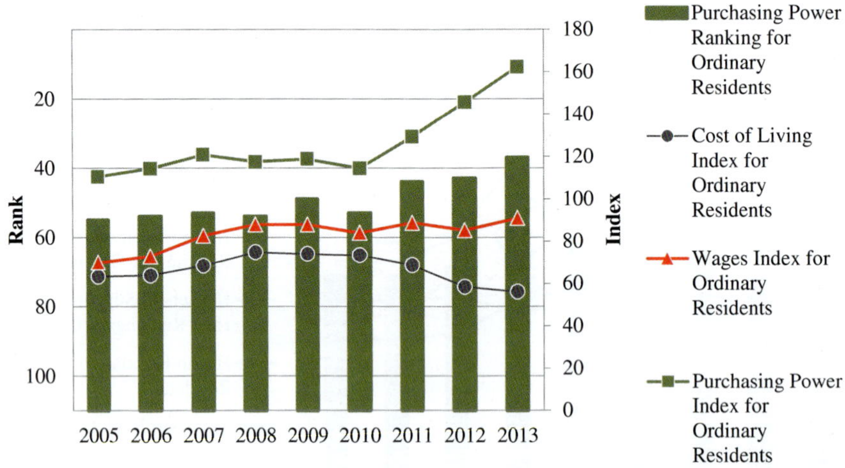

Source: Asia Competitiveness Institute

Figure 5.5a

Athens, the capital and largest city of Greece, is one of the oldest cities in the world with a history spanning 3,400 years. The city's Cost of Living Ranking for Ordinary Residents, as represented by the grey bars, moved up from 46th to 36nd between 2005 and 2010, and declined from 43rd to 45th between 2011 and 2013 (see Figure 5.5a). As explained in Section 3.4.2 of Chapter 3, for a more precise comparison of rankings, we have split the analysis into two sub-periods.

From 2005 to 2010, Food & Non-alcoholic Beverages Ranking jumped five places from 37th to 32nd. Education Ranking moved up two spots from 55th in 2005 to 53rd in 2010. Health Ranking rose from 52nd to 51st over the first sub-period. In contrast, Transport Ranking fell six places from 37th to 43rd between 2005 and 2010. Housing Rents & Utilities Ranking largely remained at around 50th over the same sub-period.

From 2011 to 2013, Housing Rents & Utilities was the only category that rose in ranking from 46th to 43rd. Food & Non-alcoholic Beverages and Transport Rankings both fell six places from 32nd to 38th and 27th to 33rd, respectively, between 2011 and 2013. Nonetheless, Transport remained as the highest ranked category for the entire second sub-period. Health Ranking slipped two spots from 58th in 2011 to 60th in 2013, making it the lowest ranked category throughout the second sub-period. Education Ranking moved down from 50th in 2011 to 51st in 2012 before rising back to 50th in 2013.

ATHENS
Greece

Figure 5.5b

The Gross Hourly Wages in USD for Ordinary Residents in Athens, as denoted by the red line in Figure 5.5b, have generally followed an upward trend between 2005 and 2013. Over these years, Athens's wage level increased from US$11.05 to US$17.96.

Meanwhile, the Wages Ranking for Ordinary Residents in Athens, as shown by the red bars, has remained fairly consistent. From 53rd in 2005, it rose to 51st in 2013, exhibiting minor fluctuations in between. The exception was 2009, when the ranking rose to 47th.

Figure 5.5c

Let us now analyse the cost of living and wages indices more closely and draw conclusions about the purchasing power of ordinary residents in Athens. As elaborated in Section 3.4.2 of Chapter 3, for a more precise and rigorous analysis, we discuss the results in two sub-periods: from 2005 to 2010 and from 2011 to 2013.

The Cost of Living Index and the Wages Index for Ordinary Residents in Athens are represented respectively by the grey and red line in Figure 5.5c. Between 2005 and 2010, the Cost of Living Index for Ordinary Residents was on an increasing trend. In 2005, the cost of living for ordinary residents in Athens was about 63.30% of that for their counterparts in New York (the base city). This rose to 73.38% in 2010. Over the same sub-period, the Wages Index for Ordinary Residents was also increasing. This index rose from 69.96 in 2005 to 83.95 in 2010.

Wages increased at a moderately faster rate than cost of living. As such, ordinary residents in Athens were able to increase the amount of goods and services they consumed over time throughout the first sub-period. This is reflected in the Purchasing Power Index for Ordinary Residents in Athens, which is represented by the green line in Figure 5.5c. From 110.52 in 2005, this index increased to 114.40 in 2010. Meanwhile, the Purchasing Power Ranking for Ordinary Residents in Athens, as represented by the green bars, also slightly improved from 55th in 2005 to 53rd in 2010, with a one-off rise to 49th in 2009.

Over the second sub-period (2011–2013), the Cost of Living Index for Ordinary Residents has been declining. In 2011, the cost of living for ordinary residents in Athens was 68.63% of that for their counterparts in New York while in 2013, it dropped to 55.97%. In contrast, the Wages Index for Ordinary Residents has been rather stable. It only rose slightly from 88.73 in 2011 to 90.86 in 2013.

The combined trends of stable wages and decreasing cost of living have enabled ordinary residents in Athens to afford a higher consumption level over the second sub-period. This is evident in that the Purchasing Power Index for Ordinary Residents steadily increased from 129.29 in 2011 to 162.33 in 2013. The Purchasing Power Ranking for Ordinary Residents has also improved significantly, rising from 44th in 2011 to 37th in 2013.

Finally, we note that over the entire study period (2005–2013), the Purchasing Power Index for Ordinary Residents in Athens has always been above 100.00 — the base index value. This indicates that ordinary residents in Athens have consistently been able to consumer more goods and services than their counterparts in New York, given the same number of working hours.

ATLANTA
United States

Figure 5.6a: Cost of Living and 10 Consumption Categories Rankings for Ordinary Residents in Atlanta, United States

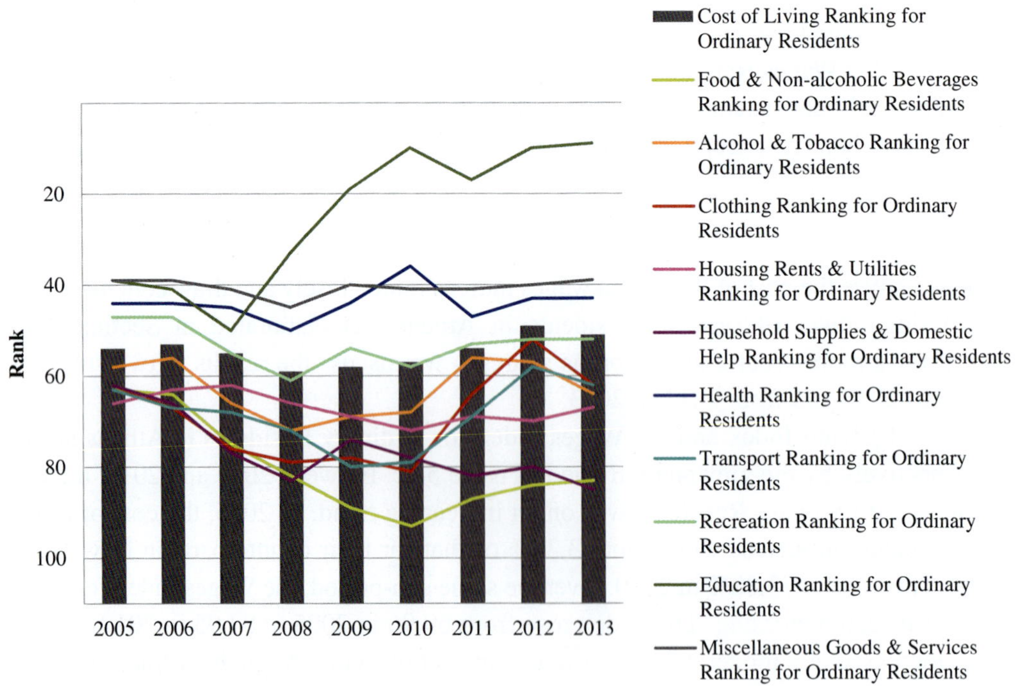

Source: Asia Competitiveness Institute

Figure 5.6b: Gross Hourly Wages in USD and Wages Ranking for Ordinary Residents in Atlanta, United States

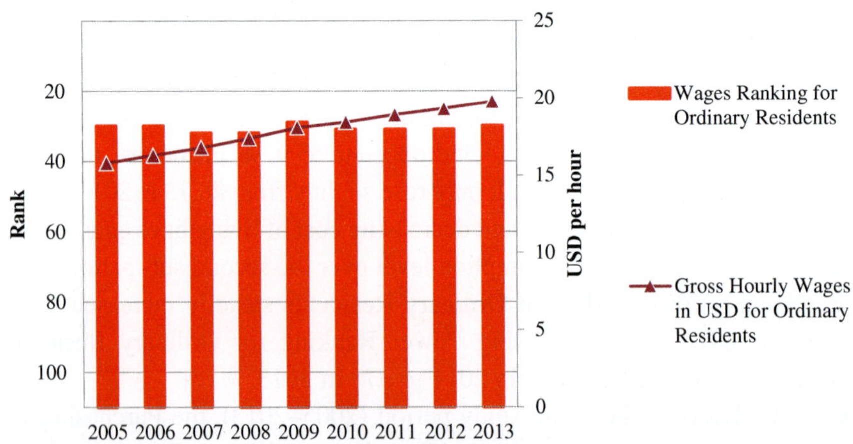

Source: Asia Competitiveness Institute

ATLANTA
United States

Figure 5.6c: Cost of Living, Wages and Purchasing Power Indices and Purchasing Power Ranking for Ordinary Residents in Atlanta, United States

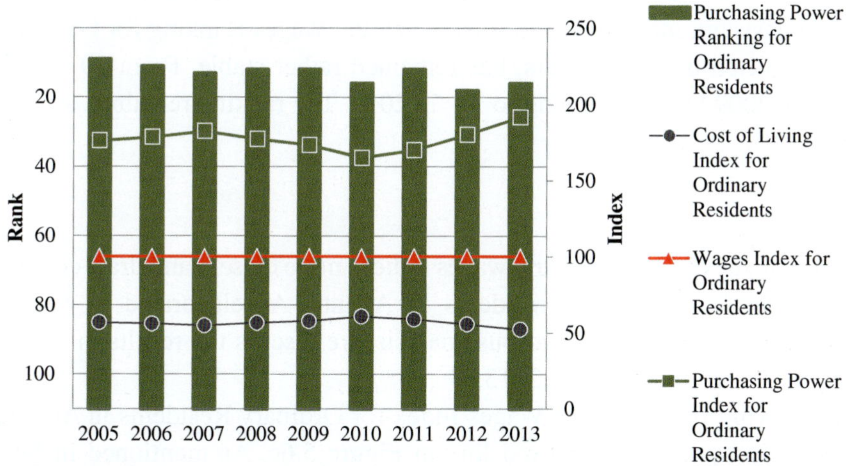

Source: Asia Competitiveness Institute

Figure 5.6a

Established in 1837, Atlanta is the most populous city and the economic and cultural centre of the state of Georgia. The city's Cost of Living Ranking for Ordinary Residents, as shown in the grey bars, declined from 54th to 57th between 2005 and 2010, but rose from 54th to 51st between 2011 and 2013 (see Figure 5.6a). As elaborated in Section 3.4.2 of Chapter 3, for a more rigorous comparison of rankings, we have split the analysis into two sub-periods.

From 2005 to 2010, Health and Education were the only two categories that rose in rankings. Education Ranking climbed 29 places from 39th in 2005 to 10th in 2010. Health Ranking jumped eight spots from 44th to 36th over the first sub-period. In contrast, Food & Non-alcoholic Ranking fell 30 places from 63rd in 2005 to 93rd in 2010. Transport Ranking slipped 16 spots from 63rd to 79th between 2005 and 2010. Housing Rents & Utilities Ranking moved down six places from 66th to 72nd over the same sub-period.

Between 2011 and 2013, Education Ranking jumped eight places from 17th to ninth, making it the highest ranked category throughout the second sub-period. Transport Ranking moved up seven spots from 69th in 2011 to 62nd in 2013. Food & Non-alcoholic Beverages and Health Rankings rose from 87th to 83rd and 47th to 43rd, respectively, between 2011 and 2013. Housing Rents & Utilities Ranking went up from 69th to 67th over the same sub-period. In contrast, Household Supplies & Domestic Help Ranking slipped three places from 82nd in 2011 to 85th in 2013. Consequently, it became the lowest ranked category in 2013.

ATLANTA
United States

Figure 5.6b

The Gross Hourly Wages in USD for Ordinary Residents in Atlanta, as represented by the red line in Figure 5.6b, increased gradually from US$15.79 in 2005 to US$19.77 in 2013.

Despite the consistent increase in the wage level, the Wages Ranking for Ordinary Residents in Atlanta, as depicted by the red bars, has remained rather stable. From 30th in 2005, it rose slightly to 29th in 2009 before dropping to 31st in 2010. The ranking remained at 31st until 2013, when it rose to 30th.

Figure 5.6c

Let us now analyse the cost of living and wages indices more closely and draw conclusions about the purchasing power of ordinary residents in Atlanta. As elaborated in Section 3.4.2 of Chapter 3, for a more precise and rigorous analysis, we discuss the results in two sub-periods: from 2005 to 2010 and from 2011 to 2013.

The Cost of Living Index and the Wages Index for Ordinary Residents in Atlanta are represented respectively by the grey and red line in Figure 5.6c. As mentioned in Section 3.3 of Chapter 3, wage data are only available at the national level and not by cities. Therefore, wages in all cities in the United States are assumed to be the same. As a result, Atlanta, being a city in the United States, shares a common Wages Index for Ordinary Residents with the base city New York (whose index value is 100.00) over the entire study period (2005–2013).

Between 2005 and 2010, the Cost of Living Index for Ordinary Residents in Atlanta was on a slight increasing trend. In 2005, the cost of living for ordinary residents in Atlanta was about 56.79% of that for ordinary residents in New York. It climbed to 60.69% in 2010, with marginal fluctuations in between. Since the Wages Index for Ordinary Residents is constant across the years, the Purchasing Power Index for Ordinary Residents in Atlanta (or any other cities in the United States) depends only on variations in the Cost of Living Index for Ordinary Residents. Thus, the marginal upward trend of the latter caused the Purchasing Power Index for Ordinary Residents, which is represented by the green line in Figure 5.6c, to decline over the first sub-period. There was a period of marginal increase during 2005–2007 but overall, the index dropped from 176.08 in 2005 to 164.78 in 2010. Ranking-wise, the Purchasing Power Ranking for Ordinary Residents in Atlanta, as represented by the green bars, dropped from ninth in 2005 to 16th in 2010.

Over the second sub-period (2011–2013), the Cost of Living Index for Ordinary Residents has been on a decreasing trend. In 2011, the cost of living for ordinary residents in Atlanta was 58.90% of that for their counterparts in New York while in 2013, it dropped to 52.24%. As a result, the Purchasing Power Index for Ordinary Residents in Atlanta steadily increased from 169.78 in 2011 to 191.41 in 2013. Meanwhile, the Purchasing Power Ranking for Ordinary Residents has been deteriorating. It dropped from 12th in 2011 to 16th in 2013.

Finally, we note that over the entire study period (2005–2013), the Purchasing Power Index for Ordinary Residents in Atlanta has always been above 100.00 — the base index value. This indicates that ordinary residents in Atlanta have always been able to consume more goods and services than their counterparts in New York, given the same number of working hours.

AUCKLAND
New Zealand

Figure 5.7a: Cost of Living and 10 Consumption Categories Rankings for Ordinary Residents in Auckland, New Zealand

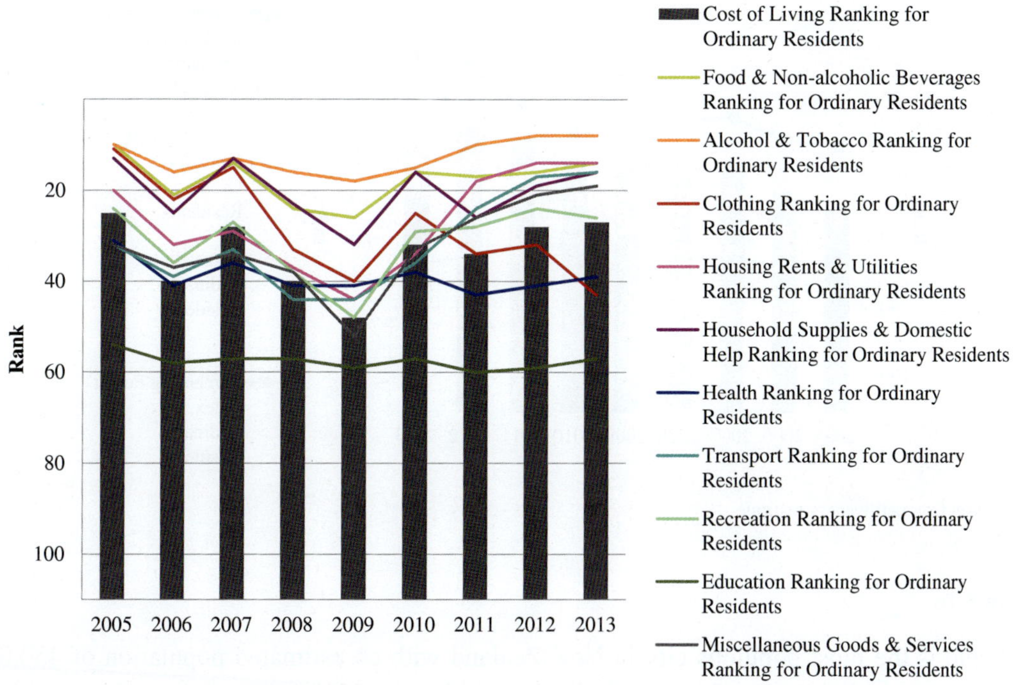

Source: Asia Competitiveness Institute

Figure 5.7b: Gross Hourly Wages in USD and Wages Ranking for Ordinary Residents in Auckland, New Zealand

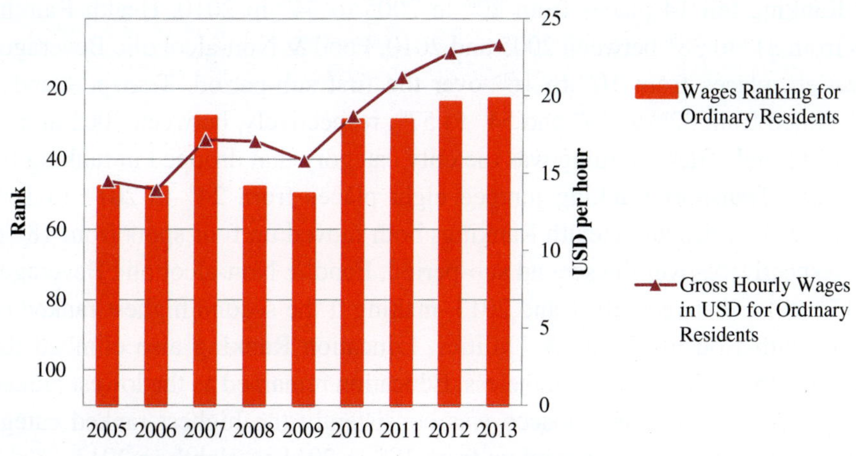

Source: Asia Competitiveness Institute

AUCKLAND
New Zealand

Figure 5.7c: Cost of Living, Wages and Purchasing Power Indices and Purchasing Power Ranking for Ordinary Residents in Auckland, New Zealand

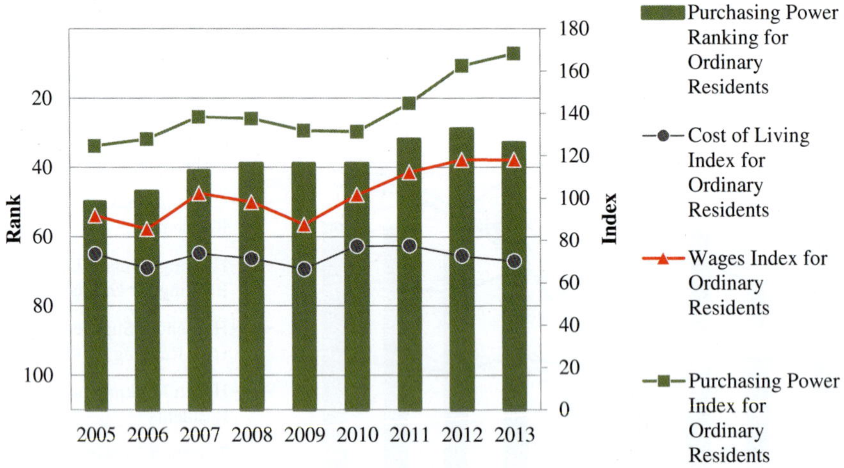

Source: Asia Competitiveness Institute

Figure 5.7a

Auckland is the most populous city in New Zealand with an estimated population of 450,000. The city's Cost of Living Ranking for Ordinary Residents, as denoted by the grey bars, declined from 25th to 32nd between 2005 and 2010, but rose from 34th to 27th between 2011 and 2013 (see Figure 5.7a). As explained in Section 3.4.2 of Chapter 3, for a more precise comparison of rankings, we have split the analysis into two sub-periods.

The rankings of all 10 categories went down from 2005 to 2010. In particular, Housing Rents & Utilities Ranking fell 14 places from 20th in 2005 to 34th in 2010. Health Ranking slipped seven spots from 31st to 38th between 2005 and 2010. Food & Non-alcoholic Beverages Ranking moved down six places from 10th to 16th over the first sub-period. Transport and Education Rankings declined from 32nd to 36th and 54th to 57th, respectively, between 2005 and 2010.

Between 2011 and 2013, Clothing was the only category that dropped in ranking from 34th to 43rd. In contrast, Transport Ranking jumped eight places from 24th in 2011 to 16th in 2013. Housing Rents & Utilities and Health Rankings both moved up four spots from 18th to 14th and 43rd to 39th, respectively, over the second sub-period. Food & Non-alcoholic Beverages Ranking rose from 17th to 14th between 2011 and 2013, making it the second highest ranked category in 2013 together with Housing Rents & Utilities. Education Ranking also climbed three places from 60th in 2011 to 57th in 2013. Nonetheless, Education remained as the lowest ranked category in both sub-periods. Alcohol & Tobacco was consistently the highest ranked category in the second sub-period as its ranking moved up from 10th in 2011 to eighth in 2013.

AUCKLAND
New Zealand

Figure 5.7b

The Gross Hourly Wages in USD for Ordinary Residents in Auckland, as denoted by the red line in Figure 5.7b, fluctuated greatly between 2005 and 2009. Since 2009, however, Auckland's wage level has been on a steady upward trend, reaching US$23.32 in 2013.

Ranking-wise, the Wages Ranking for Ordinary Residents in Auckland, as depicted by the red bars, has generally improved over the study period, reaching 23rd in 2013. However, it has also exhibited considerable fluctuations. For example, from 48th in 2005 and 2006, the ranking jumped to 28th in 2007 before dropping back to 48th in 2008.

Such fluctuations happened because Auckland regularly traded places with the 16 cities in the United States on the ranking table. As mentioned in Section 3.3 of Chapter 3, wage data are only available at the national level. Therefore, all cities in the United States are assumed to have the same Gross Hourly Wages in USD for Ordinary Residents and consequently, the same Wages Ranking for Ordinary Residents. Thus, whenever Auckland surpassed any city in the United States, it overtook the other 15 cities as well. The same would hold in the reverse situation. These were precisely what happened between 2006 and 2008 and the result was the large fluctuations in Auckland's ranking as observed.

Figure 5.7c

Let us now analyse the cost of living and wages indices more closely and draw conclusions about the purchasing power of ordinary residents in Auckland. As elaborated in Section 3.4.2 of Chapter 3, for a more precise and rigorous analysis, we discuss the results in two sub-periods: from 2005 to 2010 and from 2011 to 2013.

The Cost of Living Index and the Wages Index for Ordinary Residents in Auckland are represented respectively by the grey and red line in Figure 5.7c. Between 2005 and 2010, the Cost of Living Index for Ordinary Residents exhibited large fluctuations. However, as compared to its value in 2005, the index in 2010 was higher. In 2005, the cost of living for ordinary residents in Auckland was 73.64% of that for ordinary residents in New York (the base city) while in 2010, it was 77.32%. Over the same period, the Wages Index for Ordinary Residents tracked the Cost of Living Index for Ordinary Residents quite closely. As compared to 2005, wages for ordinary residents in 2010 were also higher: the wages index in 2005 was 91.79 while in 2010, it was 101.47.

Reflecting the fluctuations in the wages and cost of living indices, the Purchasing Power Index for Ordinary Residents in Auckland, which is represented by the green line in Figure 5.7c, also exhibited considerable fluctuations. Overall, however, the index value in 2010 (131.24) was higher than it was in 2005 (124.65). This indicates that ordinary residents in Auckland were able to afford a higher consumption level in 2010 than that in 2005. Meanwhile, the Purchasing Power Ranking for Ordinary Residents in Auckland, as represented by the green bars, steadily improved over the first sub-period, rising from 50th in 2005 to 39th in 2010.

AUCKLAND
New Zealand

Over the second sub-period (2011–2013), the Cost of Living Index for Ordinary Residents has been on a decreasing trend. In 2011, the cost of living for ordinary residents in Auckland was 77.46% of that for their counterparts in New York while in 2013, it dropped to 70.09%. Meanwhile, the Wages Index for Ordinary Residents has been on a moderately increasing trend, rising from 112.13 in 2011 to 117.97 in 2013.

The combined trends of increasing wages and decreasing cost of living have enabled ordinary residents in Auckland to afford a higher consumption level over time throughout the second sub-period. This is evident in that the Purchasing Power Index for Ordinary Residents steadily increased from 144.75 in 2011 to 168.31 in 2013. The Purchasing Power Ranking for Ordinary Residents in Auckland, however, remained relatively stable. It increased to 29th in 2012 from 32nd in 2011 before dropping to 33rd in 2013.

Finally, we note that over the entire study period (2005–2013), the Purchasing Power Index for Ordinary Residents in Auckland has always been above 100.00 — the base index value. This means that ordinary residents in Auckland have consistently been able to consumer more goods and services than their counterparts in New York, given the same number of working hours.

BAKU
Azerbaijan

Figure 5.8a: Cost of Living and 10 Consumption Categories Rankings for Ordinary Residents in Baku, Azerbaijan

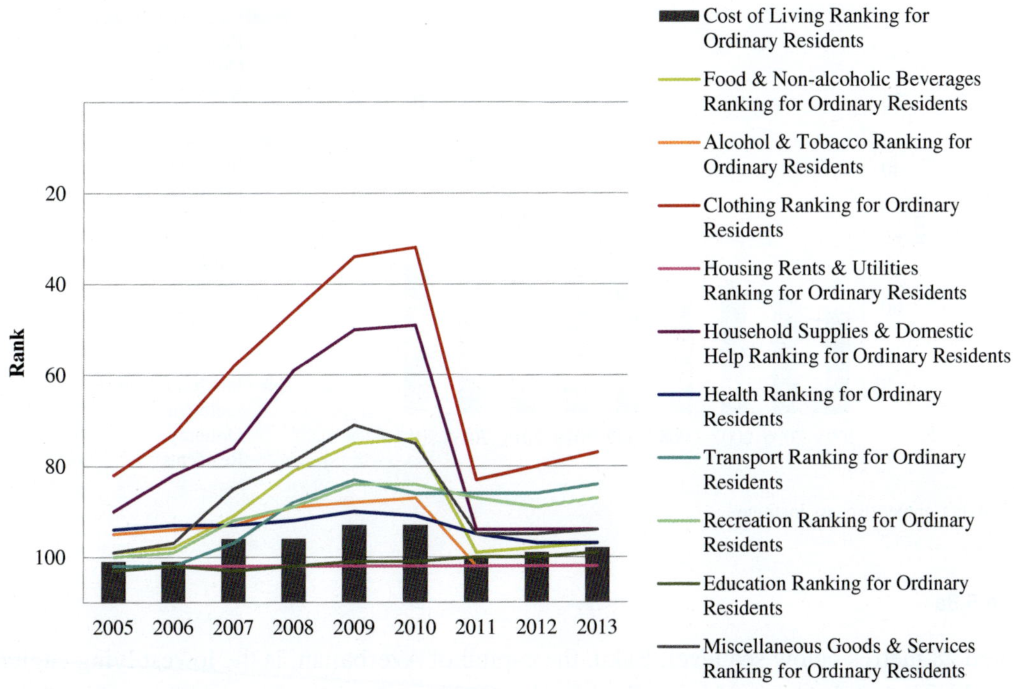

Source: Asia Competitiveness Institute

Figure 5.8b: Gross Hourly Wages in USD and Wages Ranking for Ordinary Residents in Baku, Azerbaijan

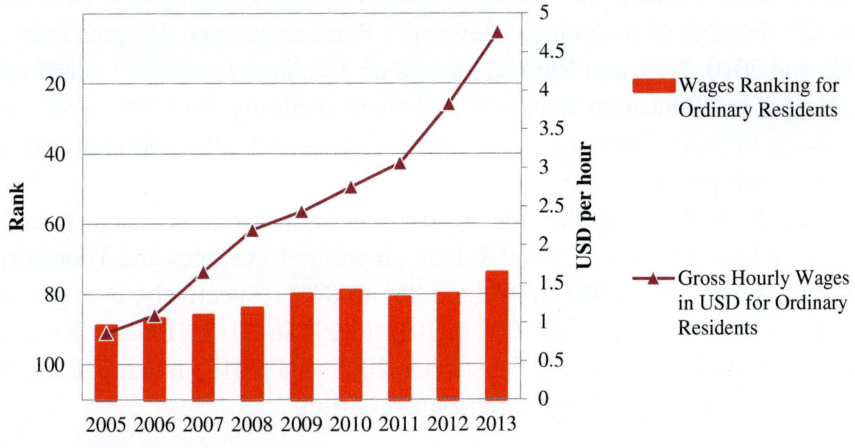

Source: Asia Competitiveness Institute

BAKU
Azerbaijan

Figure 5.8c: Cost of Living, Wages and Purchasing Power Indices and Purchasing Power Ranking for Ordinary Residents in Baku, Azerbaijan

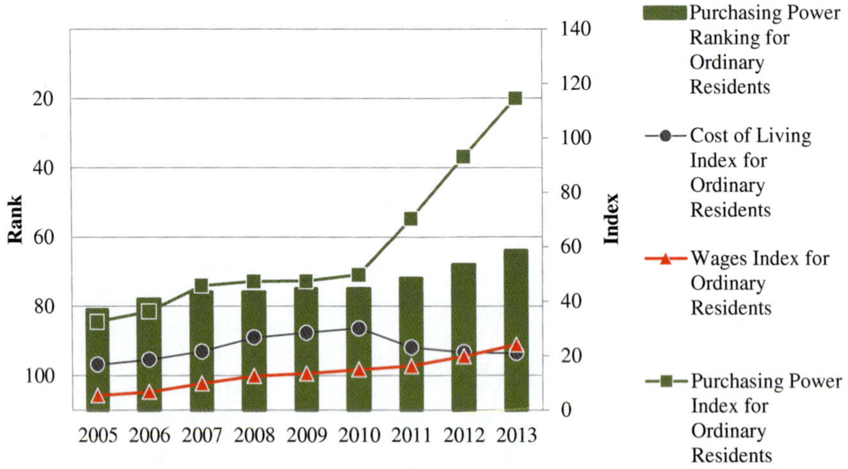

Source: Asia Competitiveness Institute

Figure 5.8a

Located 28 metres below sea level, Baku, the capital of Azerbaijan, is the lowest lying capital in the world. The city's Cost of Living Ranking for Ordinary Residents, as represented by the grey bars, rose from 101st to 93rd between 2005 and 2010, and from 100th to 98th between 2011 and 2013 (see Figure 5.8a). As elaborated in Section 3.4.2 of Chapter 3, for a more rigorous comparison of rankings, we have split the analysis into two sub-periods.

From 2005 to 2010, Clothing saw the most dramatic rise in ranking as it climbed 50 places from 82nd to 32nd. Food & Non-alcoholic Beverages Ranking jumped 25 spots from 99th to 74th between 2005 and 2010. Transport Ranking moved up 16 places from 102nd to 86th over the first sub-period. Health and Education Rankings rose more modestly from 94th to 91st and 103rd to 101st, respectively, between 2005 and 2010. Housing Rents & Utilities Ranking stayed at 102nd for the entire first sub-period.

From 2011 to 2013, Clothing was consistently the highest ranked category as its ranking jumped six places from 83rd to 77th. Food & Non-alcoholic Beverages and Transport Rankings both moved up two spots from 99th to 97th and 86th to 84th, respectively, over the second sub-period. Education Ranking rose from 100th in 2011 to 99th in 2013. Housing Rents & Utilities Ranking remained unchanged at 102nd between 2005 and 2013, making Baku the second cheapest city in this category throughout the study period.

BAKU
Azerbaijan

Figure 5.8b

The Gross Hourly Wages in USD for Ordinary Residents in Baku, as represented by the red line in Figure 5.8b, have been on an increasing trend over the study period. From US$0.86 in 2005, Baku's wage level rose rapidly to US$4.76 in 2013.

Corresponding to the rapid increase in the wage level, the Wages Ranking for Ordinary Residents in Baku, as denoted by the red bars, also substantially increased from 89th in 2005 to 74th in 2013.

Figure 5.8c

Let us now analyse the cost of living and wages indices more closely and draw conclusions about the purchasing power of ordinary residents in Baku. As elaborated in Section 3.4.2 of Chapter 3, for a more precise and rigorous analysis, we discuss the results in two sub-periods: from 2005 to 2010 and from 2011 to 2013.

The Cost of Living Index and the Wages Index for Ordinary Residents in Baku are represented respectively by the grey and red line in Figure 5.8c. Between 2005 and 2010, the Cost of Living Index for Ordinary Residents was on an increasing trend. In 2005, the cost of living for ordinary residents in Baku was 16.77% of that for their counterparts in New York (the base city). In 2010, it increased significantly to 30.03%. Over the same period, the Wages Index for Ordinary Residents also increased significantly, rising from 5.45 in 2005 to 14.94 in 2010.

Wages generally rose faster than cost of living so throughout the first sub-period, ordinary residents in Baku were able to afford more goods and services over time. This is reflected in the Purchasing Power Index for Ordinary Residents in Baku, which is represented by the green line in Figure 5.8c. From 32.48 in 2005, this index rose to 49.74 in 2010. Ranking-wise, the Purchasing Power Ranking for Ordinary Residents in Baku, as represented by the green bars, steadily improved over the first sub-period. It rose from 81st in 2005 to 75th in 2010.

Over the second sub-period (2011–2013), the Cost of Living Index for Ordinary Residents has been on a decreasing trend. In 2011, the cost of living for ordinary residents in Baku was 23.05% of that for their counterparts in New York while in 2013, it dropped slightly to 21.02%. Meanwhile, the Wages Index for Ordinary Residents has been increasing, rising from 16.21 in 2011 to 24.07 in 2013.

The combined trends of increasing wages and decreasing cost of living have enabled ordinary residents in Baku to afford a higher consumption level the second sub-period. This is evident in that the Purchasing Power Index for Ordinary Residents steadily increased from 70.32 in 2011 to 114.51 in 2013. The Purchasing Power Ranking for Ordinary Residents in Baku also improved from 72nd in 2011 to 64th in 2013.

Finally, we note that before 2013, the Purchasing Power Index for Ordinary Residents in Baku had consistently been below 100.00 — the base index value. In other words, it was not until 2013 that ordinary residents in Baku were able to consumer more goods and services than their counterparts in New York, given the same number of working hours. From 2005 to 2012, the consumption level for ordinary residents in Baku had consistently been lower than that for their counterparts in New York.

BANGKOK
Thailand

Figure 5.9a: Cost of Living and 10 Consumption Categories Rankings for Ordinary Residents in Bangkok, Thailand

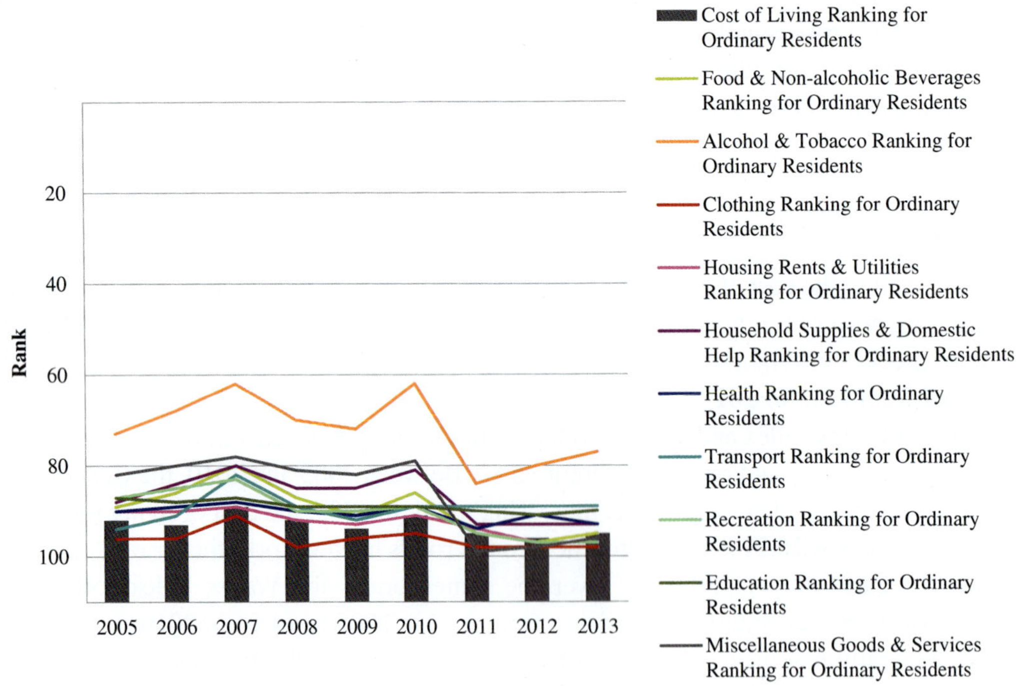

Source: Asia Competitiveness Institute

Figure 5.9b: Gross Hourly Wages in USD and Wages Ranking for Ordinary Residents in Bangkok, Thailand

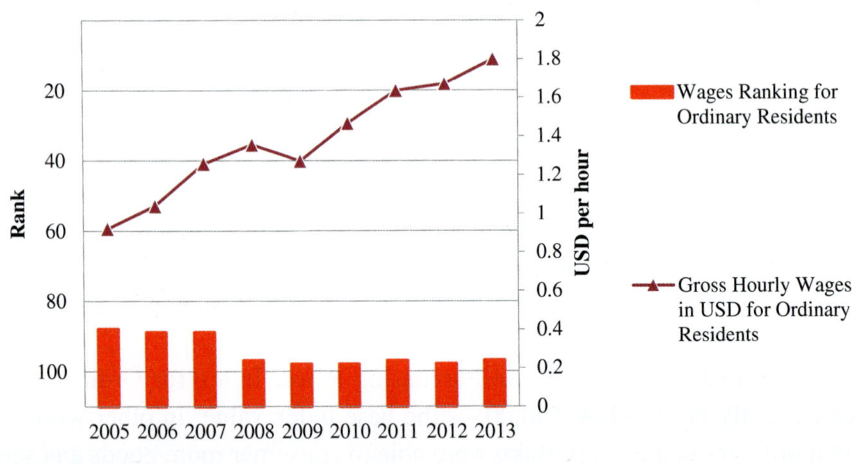

Source: Asia Competitiveness Institute

BANGKOK
Thailand

Figure 5.9c: Cost of Living, Wages and Purchasing Power Indices and Purchasing Power Ranking for Ordinary Residents in Bangkok, Thailand

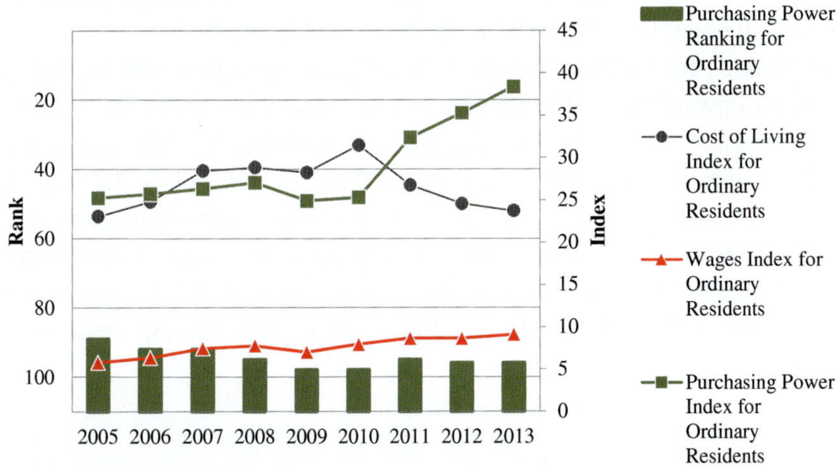

Source: Asia Competitiveness Institute

Figure 5.9a

Known for its vibrant street life and cultural landmarks, Bangkok is the political, cultural and economic centre of Thailand. The city's Cost of Living Ranking for Ordinary Residents, as shown in the grey bars, rose from 92nd to 91st between 2005 and 2010, but largely remained at 95th between 2011 and 2013 (see Figure 5.9a). As explained in Section 3.4.2 of Chapter 3, for a more precise comparison of rankings, we have split the analysis into two sub-periods.

From 2005 to 2010, Transport Ranking jumped five places from 94th to 89th. Food & Non-alcoholic Beverages Ranking moved up three spots from 89th in 2005 to 86th in 2010. Health Ranking rose slightly from 90th to 89th between 2005 and 2010. In contrast, Education Ranking slipped two places from 87th in 2005 to 89th in 2010. Housing Rents & Utilities Ranking fell one spot from 90th to 91st over the first sub-period.

From 2011 to 2013, Clothing Ranking remained at 98th, making it the lowest ranked category in 2013. Likewise, Transport Ranking stayed unchanged at 89th over the second sub-period. Food & Non-alcoholic Beverages Ranking fell from 95th in 2011 to 97th in 2013 before rising back to 95th in 2013. Health Ranking moved up one spot from 94th to 93rd over the second sub-period. In contrast, Housing Rents & Utilities Ranking slipped three places from 94th in 2011 to 97th in 2013. Alcohol & Tobacco consistently remained the highest ranked category for the entire study period as its ranking rose from 73rd in 2005 to 62nd in 2010, and from 84th in 2011 to 77th in 2013.

BANGKOK
Thailand

Figure 5.9b

The Gross Hourly Wages in USD for Ordinary Residents in Bangkok, as represented by the red line in Figure 5.9b, have generally followed an upward trend over the study period. Bangkok's wage level nearly doubled from US$0.92 in 2005 to US$1.80 in 2013.

The Wages Ranking for Ordinary Residents in Bangkok, as depicted by the red bars, has not exhibited a similar upward trend. The ranking at first remained at about 88th between 2005 and 2007. It then dropped to 97th in 2008 and stagnated around that level thereafter. The plunge in 2008 happened mainly because the wage level in Bangkok fell below the wage level in the Chinese cities. As explained in Section 3.3 of Chapter 3, cities in the same country are assumed to share a common Gross Hourly Wages in USD for Ordinary Residents. Consequently, the eight Chinese cities also share the same Wages Ranking for Ordinary Residents and form a cluster on the wage ranking table. In 2008, this cluster surpassed Bangkok, causing the significant drop in the latter's ranking.

Figure 5.9c

Let us now analyse the cost of living and wages indices more closely and draw conclusions about the purchasing power of ordinary residents in Bangkok. As elaborated in Section 3.4.2 of Chapter 3, for a more precise and rigorous analysis, we discuss the results in two sub-periods: from 2005 to 2010 and from 2011 to 2013.

The Cost of Living Index and the Wages Index for Ordinary Residents in Bangkok are represented respectively by the grey and red line in Figure 5.9c. Between 2005 and 2010, the Cost of Living Index for Ordinary Residents was on an increasing trend. In 2005, the cost of living for ordinary residents in Bangkok was 23.08% of that for their counterparts in New York (the base city). In 2010, it increased to 31.44%. Over the same sub-period, the Wages Index for Ordinary Residents also increased, rising from 5.83 in 2005 to 7.95 in 2010.

Wages were generally able to keep up with cost of living so ordinary residents in Bangkok were able to maintain their consumption level over time throughout the first sub-period. This is reflected in the stability of the Purchasing Power Index for Ordinary Residents in Bangkok, which is represented by the green line in Figure 5.9c. Between 2005 and 2010, the index only fluctuated around 25.75. Meanwhile, the Purchasing Power Ranking for Ordinary Residents in Bangkok, as represented by the green bars, deteriorated rather remarkably over the first sub-period. It dropped from 89th in 2005 to 98th in 2010.

Over the second sub-period (2011–2013), the Cost of Living Index for Ordinary Residents has been on a decreasing trend. In 2011, the cost of living for ordinary residents in Bangkok was 26.74% of that for their counterparts in New York while it dropped to 23.72% in 2013. Meanwhile, the Wages Index for Ordinary Residents has been increasing. This index rose from 8.65 in 2011 to 9.10 in 2013.

BANGKOK
Thailand

The combined trends of increasing wages and decreasing cost of living have enabled ordinary residents in Bangkok to afford a higher consumption level time throughout the second sub-period. This is evident in that the Purchasing Power Index for Ordinary Residents steadily increased from 32.35 in 2011 to 38.37 in 2013. Despite the positive showing of the index, the Purchasing Power Ranking for Ordinary Residents in Bangkok remained relatively stable, only fluctuating between 95th and 96th.

Finally, we note that over the entire study period (2005–2013), the Purchasing Power Index for Ordinary Residents in Bangkok has consistently been below 100.00 — the base index value. This means that ordinary residents in Bangkok have only been able to consume fewer goods and services than their counterparts in New York, given the same number of working hours.

BARCELONA
Spain

Figure 5.10a: Cost of Living and 10 Consumption Categories Rankings for Ordinary Residents in Barcelona, Spain

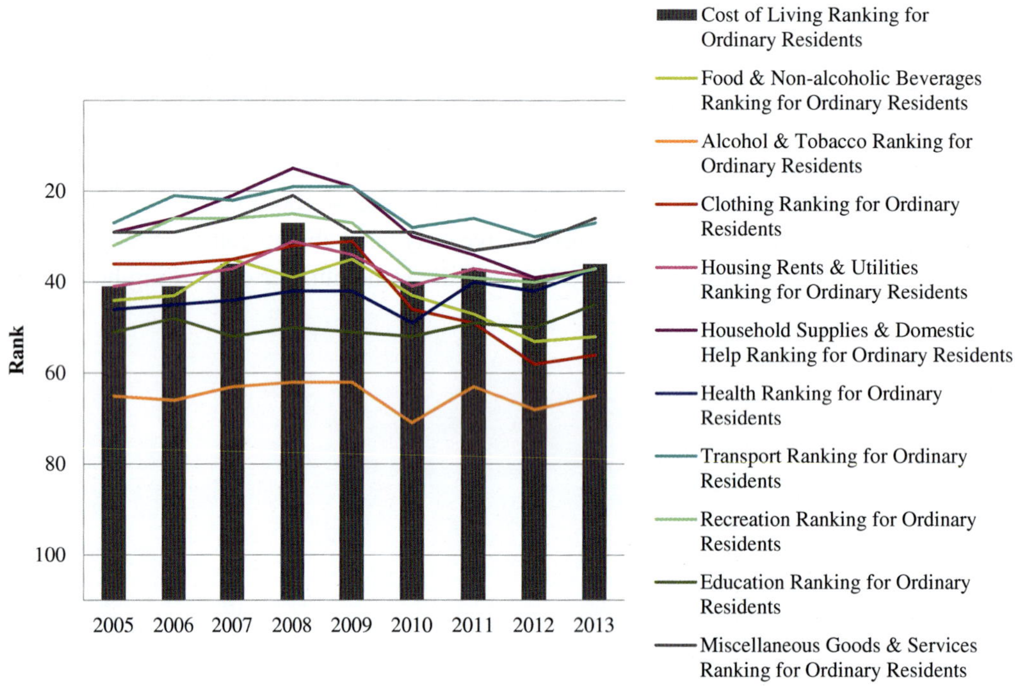

Source: Asia Competitiveness Institute

Figure 5.10b: Gross Hourly Wages in USD and Wages Ranking for Ordinary Residents in Barcelona, Spain

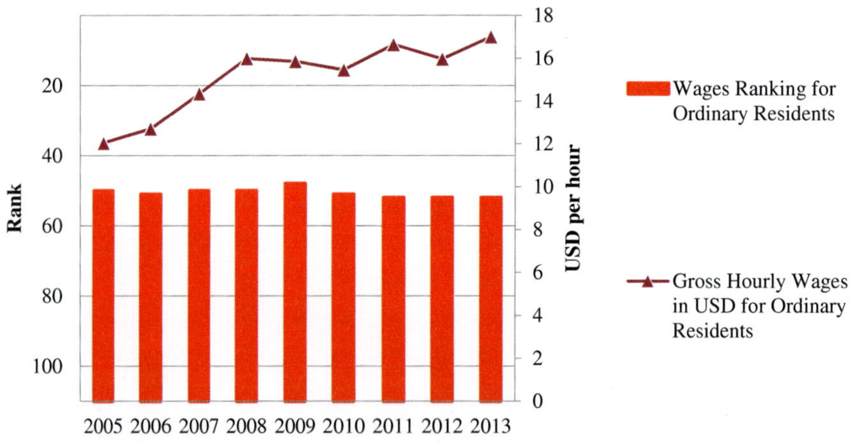

Source: Asia Competitiveness Institute

BARCELONA
Spain

Figure 5.10c: Cost of Living, Wages and Purchasing Power Indices and Purchasing Power Ranking for Ordinary Residents in Barcelona, Spain

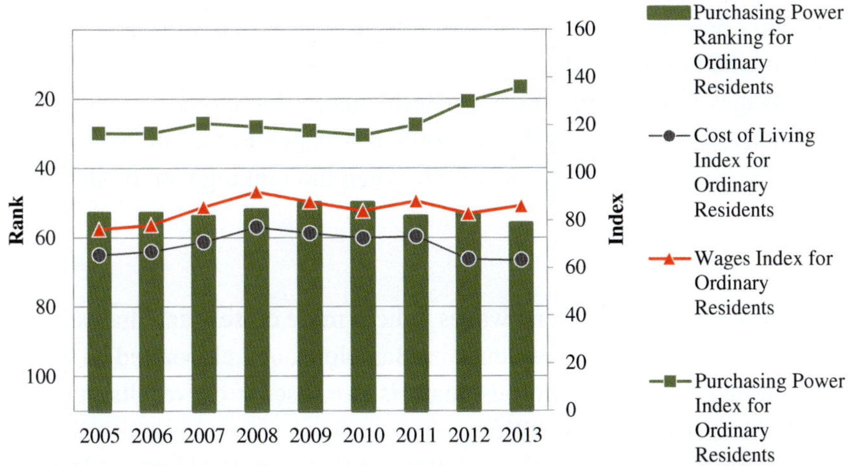

Source: Asia Competitiveness Institute

Figure 5.10a

Renowned for its distinct architecture, Barcelona is the second most populous city in Spain with an estimated population of 1.6 million. The city's Cost of Living Ranking for Ordinary Residents, as denoted by the grey bars, rose from 41st to 40th between 2005 and 2010, and from 37th to 36th between 2011 and 2013 (see Figure 5.10a). As elaborated in Section 3.4.2 of Chapter 3, for a more rigorous comparison of rankings, we have split the analysis into two sub-periods.

From 2005 to 2010, Clothing registered the most remarkable dip in ranking as it fell 10 places from 36th to 46th. Health Ranking slipped three spots from 46th in 2005 to 49th in 2010. Education and Transport Rankings declined slightly from 51st to 52nd and 27th to 28th, respectively, over the first sub-period. Housing Rents & Utilities Ranking rose from 41st in 2005 to 31st in 2008 before falling back to 41st in 2010. Food & Non-alcoholic Beverages Ranking moved up one place from 44th to 43rd between 2005 and 2010.

Between 2011 and 2013, Miscellaneous Goods & Services saw the most significant rise in ranking as it climbed seven places from 33rd to 26th, making it the highest ranked category in 2013. Education Ranking jumped four spots from 49th to 45th. Health Ranking moved up three places from 40th in 2011 to 37th in 2013. In contrast, Food & Non-alcoholic Beverages Ranking fell five spots from 47th in 2011 to 52nd in 2013. Transport Ranking slipped one place from 26th to 27th over the same sub-period. Housing Rents & Utilities Ranking dropped from 37th in 2011 to 39th in 2012 before rising back to 37th in 2013.

BARCELONA
Spain

Figure 5.10b

The Gross Hourly Wages in USD for Ordinary Residents in Barcelona, as denoted by the red line in Figure 5.10b, have been increasing over the study period. From US$12.04 in 2005, Barcelona's wage level rose to US$17.00 in 2013.

However, the Wages Ranking for Ordinary Residents in Barcelona, as represented by the red bars, has been relatively stable. From 50th in 2005, it dropped to 52nd in 2013, exhibiting minor fluctuations in between. The exception was 2009 when the ranking rose to 48th.

Figure 5.10c

Let us now analyse the cost of living and wages indices more closely and draw conclusions about the purchasing power of ordinary residents in Barcelona. As elaborated in Section 3.4.2 of Chapter 3, for a more precise and rigorous analysis, we discuss the results in two sub-periods: from 2005 to 2010 and from 2011 to 2013.

The Cost of Living Index and the Wages Index for Ordinary Residents in Barcelona are represented respectively by the grey and red line in Figure 5.10c. Between 2005 and 2010, the Cost of Living Index for Ordinary Residents exhibited moderate fluctuations. In 2005, the cost of living for ordinary residents in Barcelona was 65.43% of that for their counterparts in New York. It first rose to peak at 77.11% in 2008 before embarking on a decreasing trend to eventually settle at 72.50% in 2010. Over the same period, the Wages Index for Ordinary Residents also followed a similar pattern. This index rose from 76.26 to peak at 91.91 in 2008 and eventually settled at 83.87 in 2010.

Not only did wages and cost of living follow similar patterns but they also generally changed at similar rates. Thus, ordinary residents in Barcelona were able to maintain the same consumption level over time during the first sub-period. This is reflected in the stability of the Purchasing Power Index for Ordinary Residents in Barcelona, which is represented by the green line in Figure 5.10c. Between 2005 and 2010, the index fluctuated around 117.73. Meanwhile, the Purchasing Power Ranking for Ordinary Residents in Barcelona, as represented by the green bars, improved from 53rd in 2005 to 50th in 2010.

Over the second sub-period (2011–2013), the Cost of Living Index for Ordinary Residents has been on a decreasing trend. In 2011, the cost of living for ordinary residents in Barcelona was 73.28% of that for their counterparts in New York while in 2013, it dropped to 63.26%. The Wages Index for Ordinary Residents has also been decreasing. This index dropped from 88.03 in 2011 to 86.00 in 2013.

Wages did not decrease as fast as cost of living so throughout the second sub-period, ordinary residents in Barcelona were actually able to afford a higher consumption level over time. This is evident in the Purchasing Power Index for Ordinary Residents which steadily increased from 120.12 in 2011 to 135.96 in 2013. Despite this positive showing of the index, the Purchasing

BARCELONA
Spain

Power Ranking for Ordinary Residents has been deteriorating. Barcelona's ranking in 2013 (56th) was lower than its ranking in 2011 (54th).

Finally, we note that over the entire study period (2005–2013), the Purchasing Power Index for Ordinary Residents in Barcelona has always been above 100.00 — the base index value. This means that ordinary residents in Barcelona have consistently been able to consumer more goods and services than their counterparts in New York, given the same number of working hours.

BEIJING
China

Figure 5.11a: Cost of Living and 10 Consumption Categories Rankings for Ordinary Residents in Beijing, China

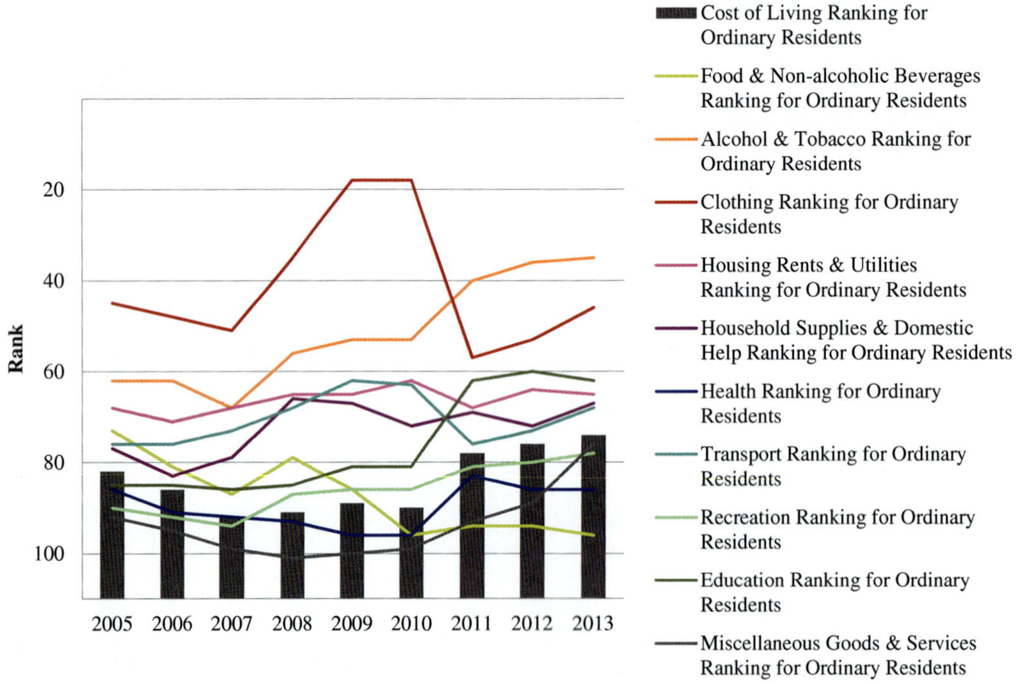

Source: Asia Competitiveness Institute

Figure 5.11b: Gross Hourly Wages in USD and Wages Ranking for Ordinary Residents in Beijing, China

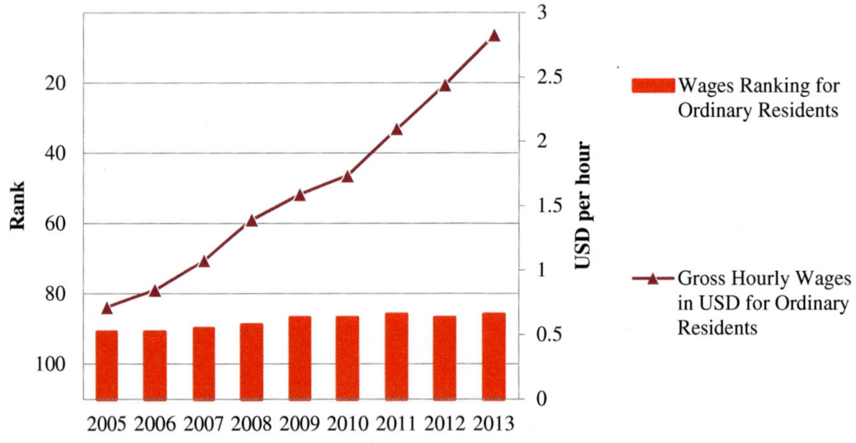

Source: Asia Competitiveness Institute

BEIJING
China

Figure 5.11c: Cost of Living, Wages and Purchasing Power Indices and Purchasing Power Ranking for Ordinary Residents in Beijing, China

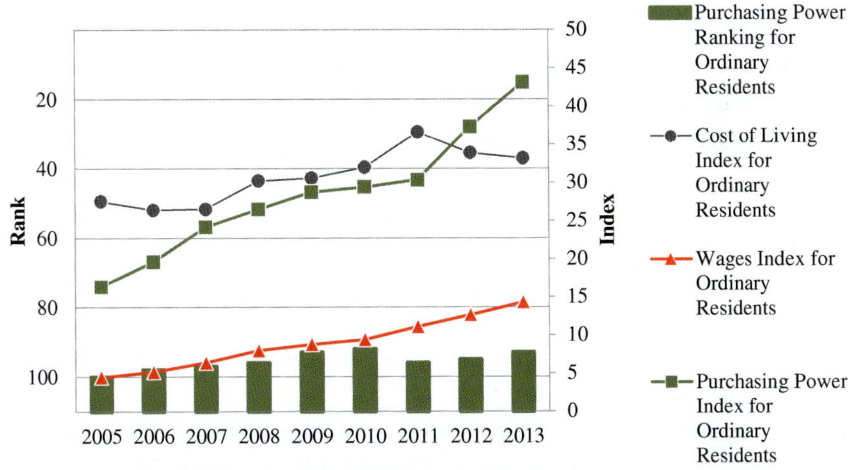

Source: Asia Competitiveness Institute

Figure 5.11a

With a history spanning three millennia, Beijing has been the capital and political centre of China for much of the past eight centuries. The city's Cost of Living Ranking for Ordinary Residents, as represented by the grey bars, declined from 82nd to 90th between 2005 and 2010, but rose from 78th to 74th between 2011 and 2013 (see Figure 5.11a). As explained in Section 3.4.2 of Chapter 3, for a more precise comparison of rankings, we have split the analysis into two sub-periods.

From 2005 to 2010, Food & Non-alcoholic Beverages saw the most dramatic dip in ranking as it fell 23 places from 73rd to 96th. Health Ranking slipped 10 spots from 86th in 2005 to 96th in 2010. In contrast, Clothing Ranking climbed 27 places from 45th to 18th over the first sub-period. Transport Ranking jumped 13 spots from 76th in 2005 to 63rd in 2010. Housing Rents & Utilities and Education Rankings rose more modestly from 68th to 62nd and 85th to 81st, respectively, over the same sub-period.

Between 2011 and 2013, Food & Non-alcoholic Beverages Ranking fell from 94th to 96th, making it the lowest ranked category throughout the second sub-period. Health Ranking slipped three places from 83rd in 2011 to 86th in 2013. In contrast, Transport Ranking jumped eight places from 76th to 68th over the second sub-period. Alcohol & Tobacco was consistently the highest ranked category from 2011 to 2013 as its ranking went up from 40th to 35th over the same sub-period. Housing Rents & Utilities Ranking moved up three spots from 68th to 65th between 2011 and 2013. Education Ranking rose from 62nd in 2011 to 60th in 2012 before falling back to 62nd in 2013.

BEIJING
China

Figure 5.11b

The Gross Hourly Wages in USD for Ordinary Residents in Beijing, as denoted by the red line in Figure 5.11b, have increased significantly over the study period. Beijing's wage level rose almost fourfold from US$0.71 in 2005 to US$2.83 in 2013.

Meanwhile, the Wages Ranking for Ordinary Residents in Beijing, as represented by the red bars, also improved from 91st in 2005 to 86th in 2013.

Figure 5.11c

Let us now analyse the cost of living and wages indices more closely and draw conclusions about the purchasing power of ordinary residents in Beijing. As elaborated in Section 3.4.2 of Chapter 3, for a more precise and rigorous analysis, we discuss the results in two sub-periods: from 2005 to 2010 and from 2011 to 2013.

The Cost of Living Index and the Wages Index for Ordinary Residents in Beijing are represented respectively by the grey and red line in Figure 5.11c. Between 2005 and 2010, the Cost of Living Index for Ordinary Residents was clearly on an increasing trend. In 2005, the cost of living for ordinary residents in Beijing was 27.55% of that for their counterparts in New York (the base city). In 2010, it increased to 31.97%. Over the same period, the Wages Index for Ordinary Residents increased significantly, rising from 4.50 in 2005 to 9.40 in 2010.

Wages generally grew faster than cost of living so throughout the first sub-period, ordinary residents in Beijing were able to afford more goods and services over time. This is reflected in the Purchasing Power Index for Ordinary Residents in Beijing, which is represented by the green line in Figure 5.11c. This index rose steadily to 29.40 in 2010 from 16.34 in 2005. Ranking-wise, the Purchasing Power Ranking for Ordinary Residents in Beijing, as represented by the green bars, also improved remarkably, climbing from 100th in 2005 to 92nd in 2010.

Over the second sub-period (2011–2013), the Cost of Living Index for Ordinary Residents has been on a decreasing trend. In 2011, the cost of living for ordinary residents in Beijing was 36.59% of that for their counterparts in New York while in 2013, it dropped to 33.16%. In contrast, over the same sub-period, the Wages Index for Ordinary Residents has been increasing. Between 2011 and 2013, this index rose from 11.10 to 14.30.

The combined trends of increasing wages and decreasing cost of living have enabled ordinary residents in Beijing to afford a higher consumption level over time during the second sub-period. This is evident in the steady increase of the Purchasing Power Index for Ordinary Residents which rose from 30.33 in 2011 to 43.12 in 2013. The Purchasing Power Ranking for Ordinary Residents has also improved over the sub-period. It rose from 96th in 2011 to 93rd in 2013.

Finally, we note that over the entire study period (2005–2013) the Purchasing Power Index for Ordinary Residents in Beijing has been consistently below 100.00 — the base index value. This means that ordinary residents in Beijing have only been able to consume fewer goods and services than their counterparts in New York, given the same number of working hours.

BERLIN
Germany

Figure 5.12a: Cost of Living and 10 Consumption Categories Rankings for Ordinary Residents in Berlin, Germany

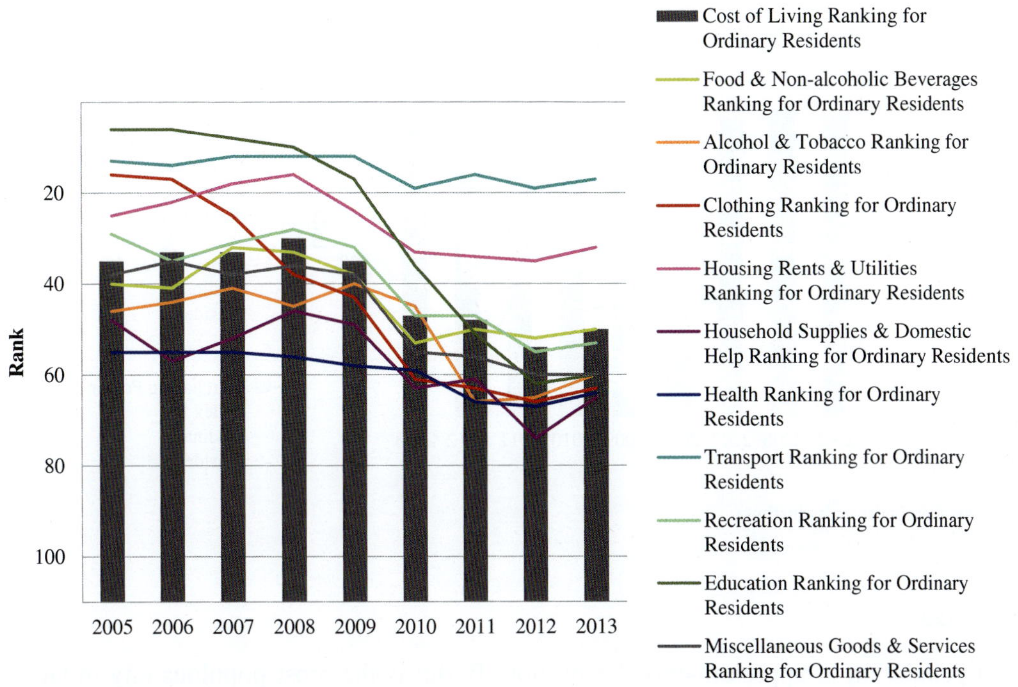

Source: Asia Competitiveness Institute

Figure 5.12b: Gross Hourly Wages in USD and Wages Ranking for Ordinary Residents in Berlin, Germany

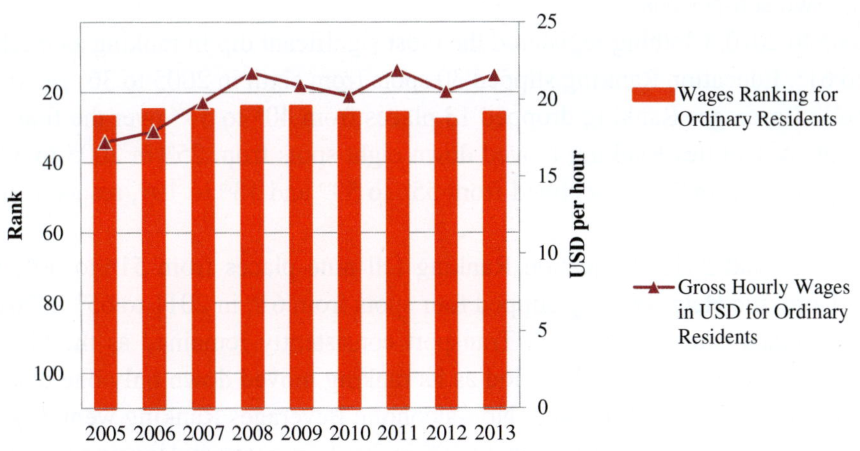

Source: Asia Competitiveness Institute

BERLIN
Germany

Figure 5.12c: Cost of Living, Wages and Purchasing Power Indices and Purchasing Power Ranking for Ordinary Residents in Berlin, Germany

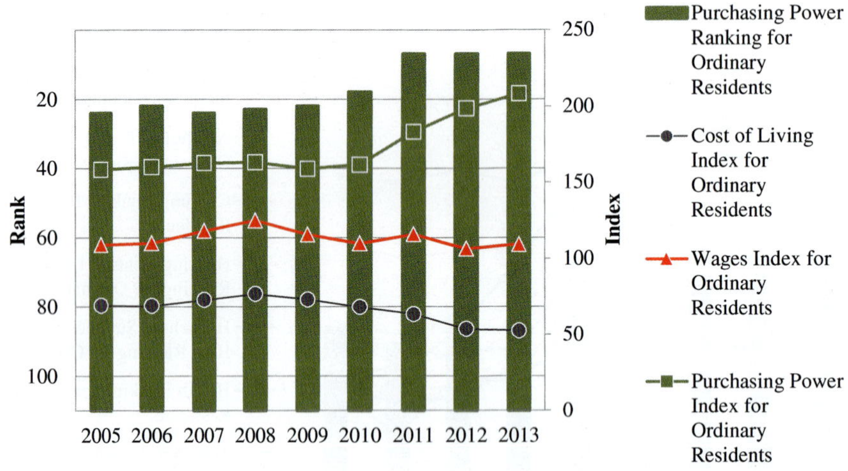

Source: Asia Competitiveness Institute

Figure 5.12a

With a population of approximately 3.5 million, Berlin is the most populous city in Germany and the seventh most populous urban area in the European Union. The city's Cost of Living Ranking for Ordinary Residents, as denoted by the grey bars, declined from 35th to 47th between 2005 and 2010, and from 48th to 50th between 2011 and 2013 (see Figure 5.12a). As elaborated in Section 3.4.2 of Chapter 3, for a more rigorous comparison of rankings, we have split the analysis into two sub-periods.

From 2005 to 2010, Clothing registered the most significant dip in ranking as it fell 45 places from 16th to 61st. Education Ranking slipped 30 spots from sixth in 2005 to 36th in 2010. Food & Non-alcoholic Beverages Ranking dropped 13 places from 40th to 53rd over the first sub-period. Housing Rents & Utilities Ranking moved down eight spots from 25th in 2005 to 33rd in 2010. Health and Transport Rankings declined from 55th to 59th and 13th to 19th, respectively, over the same sub-period.

Between 2011 and 2013, Education Ranking fell nine places from 51st to 60th. Household Supplies & Domestic Help Ranking slipped four spots from 61st in 2011 to 65th in 2013, making it the lowest ranked category in 2013. Transport consistently remained as the highest ranked category throughout the second sub-period as its ranking moved down only one place from 16th to 17th between 2011 and 2013. Food & Non-alcoholic Beverages Ranking went down from 50th in 2011 to 52nd in 2012 before rising back to 50th in 2013. In contrast, Housing Rents & Utilities and Health Rankings both moved up two places from 34th to 32nd and 66th to 64th, respectively, over the second sub-period.

BERLIN
Germany

Figure 5.12b

The Gross Hourly Wages in USD for Ordinary Residents in Berlin, as denoted by the red line in Figure 5.12b, increased consistently from US$17.21 in 2005 to US$21.71 in 2008. From 2008 onwards, Berlin's wage level has fluctuated substantially, reaching US$21.59 in 2013.

The Wages Ranking for Ordinary Residents in Berlin, as represented by the red bars, has mirrored the trend of the wage level. It improved from 27th in 2005 to 24th in 2008. Since then, it has fluctuated between 24th and 28th. Berlin's ranking in 2013 was 26th.

Figure 5.12c

Let us now analyse the cost of living and wages indices more closely and draw conclusions about the purchasing power of ordinary residents in Berlin. As elaborated in Section 3.4.2 of Chapter 3, for a more precise and rigorous analysis, we discuss the results in two sub-periods: from 2005 to 2010 and from 2011 to 2013.

The Cost of Living Index and the Wages Index for Ordinary Residents in Berlin are represented respectively by the grey and red line in Figure 5.12c. Between 2005 and 2010, the Cost of Living Index for Ordinary Residents fluctuated substantially. In 2005, the cost of living for ordinary residents in Berlin was 68.91% of that for their counterparts in New York (the base city). It increased steadily to its peak at 76.56% in 2008 and then began to decrease until it reached 67.94% in 2010. Over the same sub-period, the Wages Index for Ordinary Residents changed in a similar pattern. Overall, from its initial level at 109.01 in 2005, the index reached 109.68 in 2010.

Not only did wages and cost of living fluctuated in similar manners, they also generally changed at similar rates. Thus, throughout the second sub-period, ordinary residents in Berlin were able to at least maintain the same consumption level over time. This is evident in the stability of the Purchasing Power Index for Ordinary Residents in Berlin, which is represented by the green line in Figure 5.12c. Between 2005 and 2010, the index only fluctuated around 160.66. Meanwhile, the Purchasing Power Ranking for Ordinary Residents in Berlin, which is represented by the green bars, was also relatively stable. It fluctuated among 24th, 23rd and 22nd between 2005 and 2009 before rising to 18th in 2010.

Over the second sub-period (2011–2013), the Cost of Living Index for Ordinary Residents has been on a decreasing trend. In 2011, the cost of living for ordinary residents in Berlin was 63.24% of that for their counterparts in New York while in 2013, it dropped to 52.46%. Over the same sub-period, the Wages Index for Ordinary Residents has also been decreasing trend. The index declined from 115.75 in 2011 to 109.22 in 2013.

Wages have decreased at a slower rate than cost of living. Thus, ordinary residents in Berlin have actually been able to afford more goods and services over time throughout the second sub-period. This is evident in the Purchasing Power Index for Ordinary Residents which increased

BERLIN
Germany

from 183.02 in 2011 to 208.19 in 2013. Despite this good showing of the index, the Purchasing Power Ranking for Ordinary Residents in Berlin has remained at seventh throughout the second sub-period.

Finally, we note that over the entire study period (2005–2013), the Purchasing Power Index for Ordinary Residents in Berlin has always been above 100.00 — the base index value. This means that ordinary residents in Berlin have always been able to consume more goods and services than their counterparts in New York, given the same number of working hours.

BOGOTA
Colombia

Figure 5.13a: Cost of Living and 10 Consumption Categories Rankings for Ordinary Residents in Bogota, Colombia

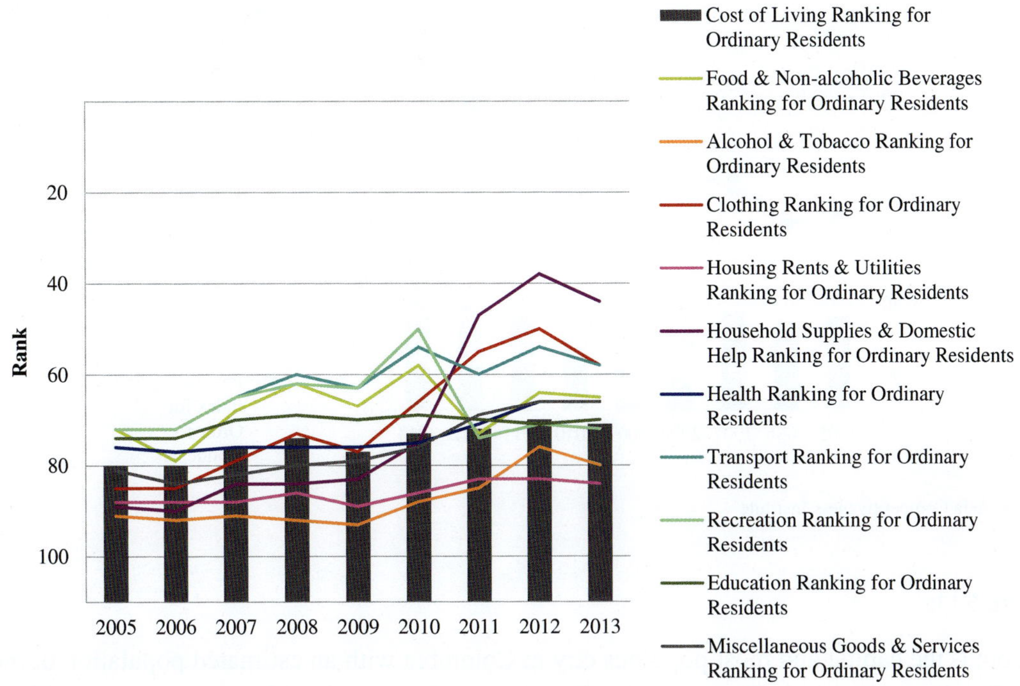

Source: Asia Competitiveness Institute

Figure 5.13b: Gross Hourly Wages in USD and Wages Ranking for Ordinary Residents in Bogota, Colombia

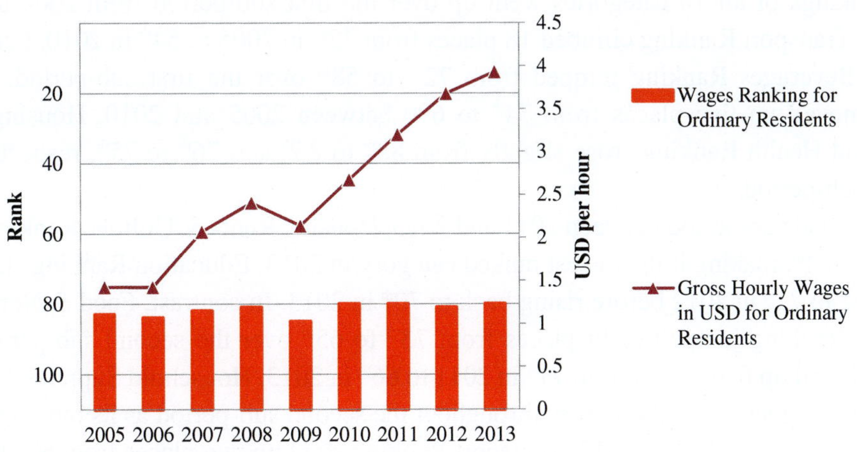

Source: Asia Competitiveness Institute

BOGOTA
Colombia

Figure 5.13c: Cost of Living, Wages and Purchasing Power Indices and Purchasing Power Ranking for Ordinary Residents in Bogota, Colombia

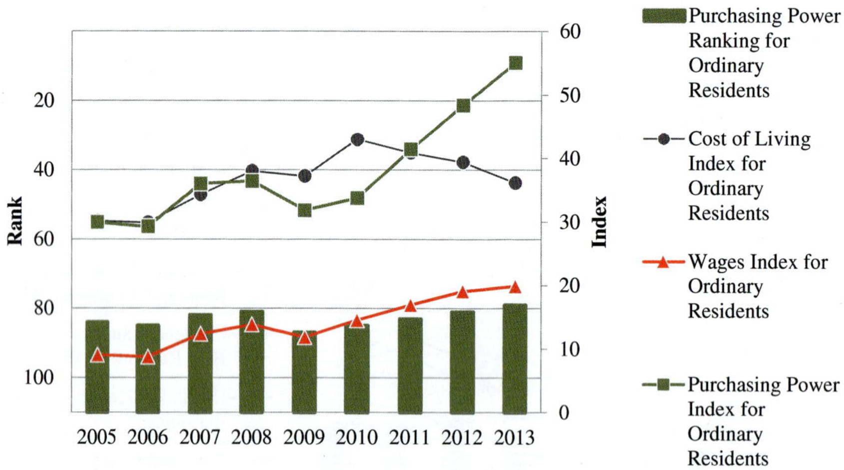

Source: Asia Competitiveness Institute

Figure 5.13a

Bogota is the capital and most populous city in Colombia with an estimated population of more than 7 million. The city's Cost of Living Ranking for Ordinary Residents, as represented by the grey bars, rose from 80th to 73rd between 2005 and 2010, and from 72nd to 71st between 2011 and 2013 (see Figure 5.13a). As explained in Section 3.4.2 of Chapter 3, for a more precise comparison of rankings, we have split the analysis into two sub-periods.

The rankings of all 10 categories went up over the first sub-period from 2005 to 2010. In particular, Transport Ranking climbed 18 places from 72nd in 2005 to 54th in 2010. Food & Non-alcoholic Beverages Ranking jumped from 72nd to 58th over the first sub-period. Education Ranking moved up five places from 74th to 69th between 2005 and 2010. Housing Rents & Utilities and Health Rankings rose slightly from 88th to 86th and 76th to 75th, respectively, over the same sub-period.

In the second sub-period between 2011 and 2013, Housing Rents & Utilities Ranking declined from 83rd to 84th, making it the lowest ranked category in 2013. Education Ranking slipped from 70th in 2011 to 71st in 2012 before rising back to 70th in 2013. In contrast, Food & Non-alcoholic Beverages Ranking jumped eight places from 73rd to 65th over the second sub-period. Health Ranking moved up five places from 71st in 2011 to 66th in 2013. Household Supplies & Domestic Help was the highest ranked category throughout the second sub-period as its ranking rose from 47th to 44th between 2011 and 2013. Transport Ranking went up two places from 60th to 58th over the same sub-period.

BOGOTA
Colombia

Figure 5.13b

The Gross Hourly Wages in USD for Ordinary Residents in Bogota, as shown by the red line in Figure 5.13b, have grown considerably over the study period. Bogota's wage level in 2013 (US$3.93) was about 2.76 times its initial value in 2005 (US$1.42).

Meanwhile, the Wages Ranking for Ordinary Residents in Bogota, has also improved, albeit modestly. From 83rd in 2005, it rose to 80th in 2013.

Figure 5.13c

Let us now analyse the cost of living and wages indices more closely and draw conclusions about the purchasing power of ordinary residents in Bogota. As elaborated in Section 3.4.2 of Chapter 3, for a more precise and rigorous analysis, we discuss the results in two sub-periods: from 2005 to 2010 and from 2011 to 2013.

The Cost of Living Index and the Wages Index for Ordinary Residents in Bogota are represented respectively by the grey and red line in Figure 5.13c. Between 2005 and 2010, the Cost of Living Index for Ordinary Residents was generally on an increasing trend. In 2005, the cost of living for ordinary residents in Bogota was 30.14% of that for their counterparts in New York (the base city). It rose to reach 42.97% in 2010. Over the same sub-period, the Wages Index for Ordinary Residents also increased, rising from 9.02 in 2005 to 14.50 in 2010.

Wages rose faster than cost of living so during the first sub-period, ordinary residents in Bogota were able to afford more goods and services over time. This is evident in the Purchasing Power Index for Ordinary Residents in Bogota, which is represented by the green line in Figure 5.13c. From 29.93 in 2005, the index rose to 33.74 in 2010. Ranking-wise, the Purchasing Power Ranking for Ordinary Residents in Bogota, as represented by the green bars, fluctuated moderately. From 84th in 2005, it improved to 81st in 2008 before slipping to 85th in 2010.

Over the second sub-period (2011–2013), the Cost of Living Index for Ordinary Residents has been on a steady decreasing trend. In 2011, the cost of living for ordinary residents in Bogota was 40.87% of that for their counterparts in New York while in 2013, it dropped to 36.12%. In contrast, the Wages Index for Ordinary Residents has been increasing. It rose from 16.92 in 2011 to 19.88 in 2013.

The combined trends of increasing wages and decreasing cost of living have enabled ordinary residents in Bogota to afford more goods and services over time during the second sub-period. This is evident in the steady increase of the Purchasing Power Index for Ordinary Residents which rose from 41.41 in 2011 to 55.03 in 2013. The Purchasing Power Ranking for Ordinary Residents in Bogota also improved steadily, rising from 83rd in 2011 to 79th in 2013.

Finally, we note that over the entire study period (2005–2013), the Purchasing Power Index for Ordinary Residents in Bogota has consistently been lower than 100.00 — the base index value. This means that ordinary residents in Bogota have only been able to consume fewer goods and services than their counterparts in New York, given the same number of working hours.

BOSTON
United States

Figure 5.14a: Cost of Living and 10 Consumption Categories Rankings for Ordinary Residents in Boston, United States

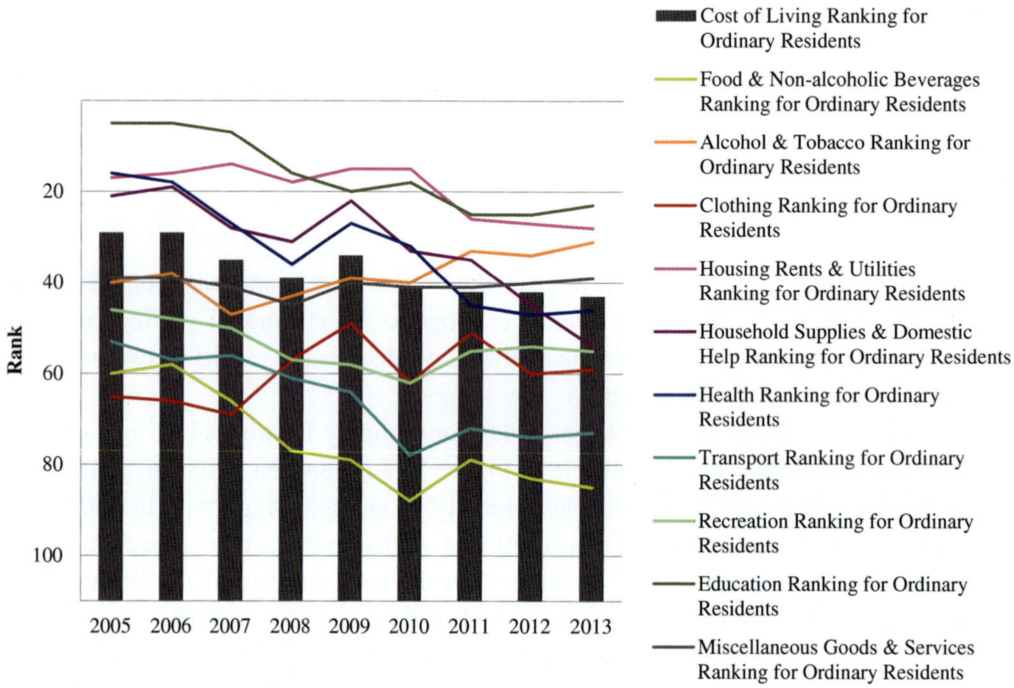

Source: Asia Competitiveness Institute

Figure 5.14b: Gross Hourly Wages in USD and Wages Ranking for Ordinary Residents in Boston, United States

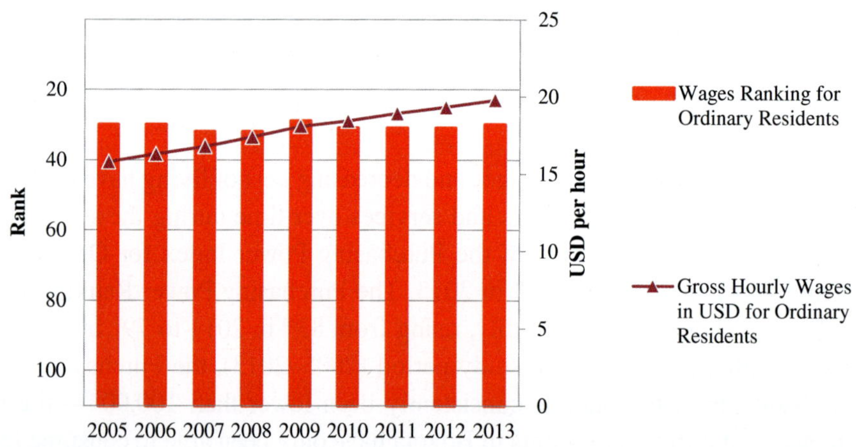

Source: Asia Competitiveness Institute

BOSTON
United States

Figure 5.14c: Cost of Living, Wages and Purchasing Power Indices and Purchasing Power Ranking for Ordinary Residents in Boston, United States

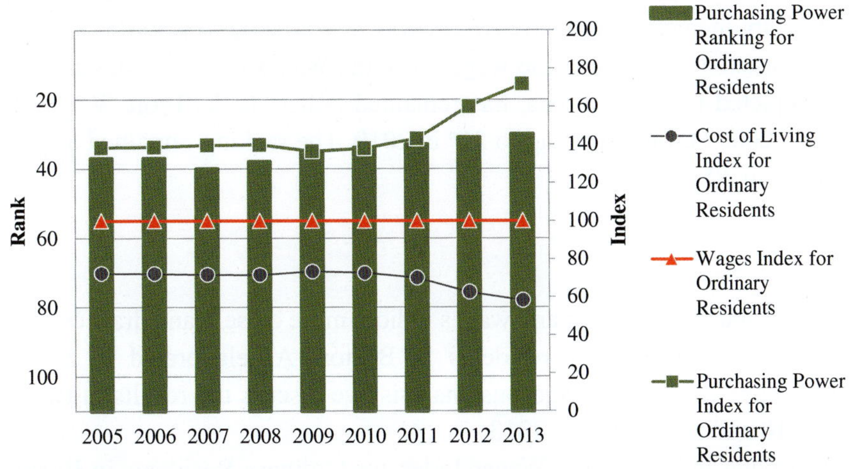

Source: Asia Competitiveness Institute

Figure 5.14a

Founded in 1630, Boston, the capital and largest city of the state of Massachusetts, is one of the oldest cities in the United States. The city's Cost of Living Ranking for Ordinary Residents, as shown in the grey bars, fell from 29th to 41st between 2005 and 2010, and from 42nd to 43rd between 2011 and 2013 (see Figure 5.14a). As elaborated in Section 3.4.2 of Chapter 3, for a more rigorous comparison of rankings, we have split the analysis into two sub-periods.

From 2005 to 2010, Food & Non-alcoholic Beverages saw the most remarkable dip in ranking as it fell 28 places from 60th to 88th. Transport Ranking slipped 25 spots from 53rd in 2005 to 78th in 2010. Health Ranking dropped 16 places from 16th to 32nd over the first sub-period. Education Ranking moved down 13 spots from fifth in 2005 to 18th in 2010. In contrast, Housing Rents & Utilities Ranking climbed two places from 17th to 15th between 2005 and 2010.

From 2011 to 2013, Household Supplies & Domestic Help Ranking fell 19 places from 35th to 54th. Food & Non-alcoholic Beverages Ranking slipped six spots from 79th in 2011 to 85th in 2013, making it the lowest ranked category throughout the second sub-period. Housing Rents & Utilities Ranking moved down two places from 26th to 28th between 2011 and 2013. Health and Transport Rankings declined from 45th to 46th and 72nd to 73rd, respectively over the same sub-period. In contrast, Education became the highest ranked category since 2011 as its ranking jumped two places from 25th to 23rd over the second sub-period.

BOSTON
United States

Figure 5.14b

The Gross Hourly Wages in USD for Ordinary Residents in Boston, as represented by the red line in Figure 5.14b, increased gradually from US$15.79 in 2005 to US$19.77 in 2013.

Despite the consistent increase in the wage level, the Wages Ranking for Ordinary Residents in Boston, as depicted by the red bars, has remained rather stable. From 30th in 2005, it rose slightly to 29th in 2009 before dropping to 31st in 2010. The ranking remained at 31st until 2013, when it rose back to 30th.

Figure 5.14c

Let us now analyse the cost of living and wages indices more closely and draw conclusions about the purchasing power of ordinary residents in Boston. As elaborated in Section 3.4.2 of Chapter 3, for a more precise and rigorous analysis, we discuss the results in two sub-periods: from 2005 to 2010 and from 2011 to 2013.

The Cost of Living Index and the Wages Index for Ordinary Residents in Boston are represented respectively by the grey and red line in Figure 5.14c. As mentioned in Section 3.3 of Chapter 3, wage data are only available at the national level and not by cities. Therefore, wages in all cities in the United States are assumed to be the same. As a result, Boston, being a city in the United States, shares a common Wages Index for Ordinary Residents with the base city New York (whose index value is 100.00) over the entire study period (2005–2013).

Between 2005 and 2010, the Cost of Living Index for Ordinary Residents in Boston was rather stable. During these years, the cost of living for ordinary residents in Boston fluctuated around 72.24% of that for ordinary residents in New York. Since the Wages Index for Ordinary Residents is constant across the years, the Purchasing Power Index for Ordinary Residents in Boston (or any other cities in the United States) depends only on variations in the Cost of Living Index for Ordinary Residents. Thus, the stability of the latter caused the Purchasing Power Index for Ordinary Residents to be stable throughout the first sub-period too. Between 2005 and 2010, the index, which is represented by the green line in Figure 5.14c, only varied around 138.44. Ranking-wise, the Purchasing Power Ranking for Ordinary Residents in Boston, as represented by the green bars, improved from 37th in 2005 to 34th in 2010.

Over the second sub-period (2011–2013), the Cost of Living Index for Ordinary Residents has steadily declined. In 2011, the cost of living for ordinary residents in Boston was 69.92% of that for their counterparts in New York while in 2013, it dropped to 58.22%. As a result, the Purchasing Power Index for Ordinary Residents in Boston has been increasing. The index rose from 143.03 in 2011 to 171.75 in 2013. The Purchasing Power Ranking has also improved, rising from 33rd in 2011 to 30th in 2013.

Finally, we note that over the entire study period (2005–2013), the Purchasing Power Index for Ordinary Residents in Boston has always been above 100.00 — the base index value. Thus, ordinary residents in Boston have always been able to consume more goods and services than their counterparts in New York, given the same number of working hours.

BRATISLAVA
Slovakia

Figure 5.15a: Cost of Living and 10 Consumption Categories Rankings for Ordinary Residents in Bratislava, Slovakia

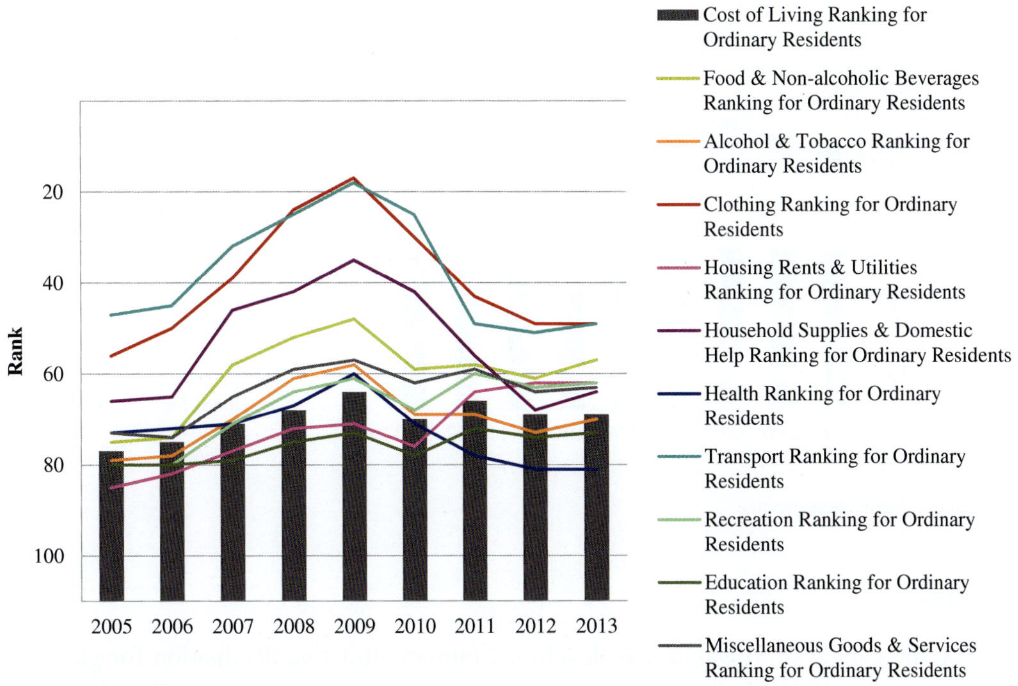

Source: Asia Competitiveness Institute

Figure 5.15b: Gross Hourly Wages in USD and Wages Ranking for Ordinary Residents in Bratislava, Slovakia

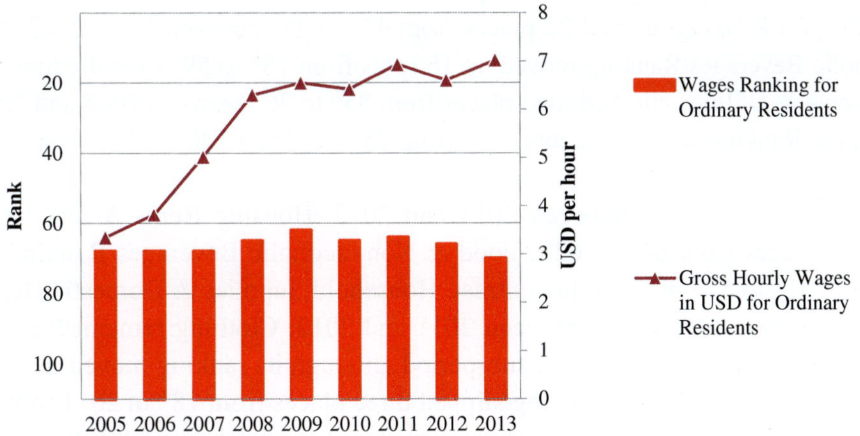

Source: Asia Competitiveness Institute

BRATISLAVA
Slovakia

Figure 5.15c: Cost of Living, Wages and Purchasing Power Indices and Purchasing Power Ranking for Ordinary Residents in Bratislava, Slovakia

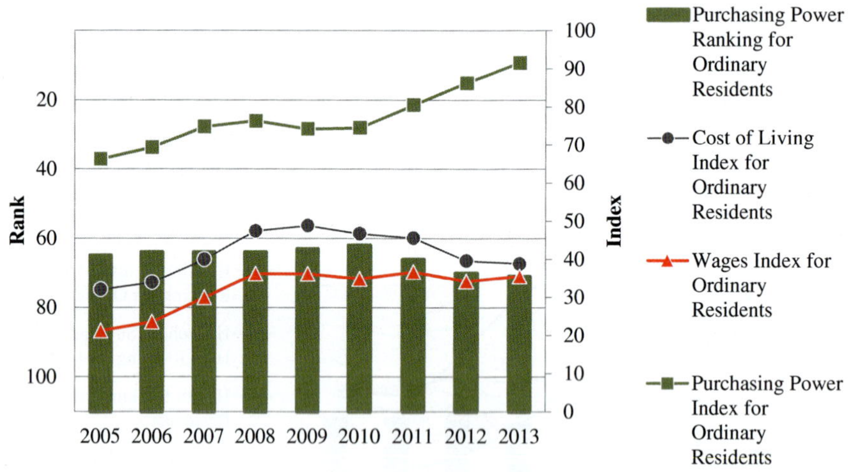

Source: Asia Competitiveness Institute

Figure 5.15a

Bratislava, the capital of Slovakia, has developed into an attractive destination for global high-technology companies including IBM, Dell, Lenovo, SAP and Accenture. The city's Cost of Living Ranking for Ordinary Residents, as denoted by the grey bars, rose from 77th to 70th between 2005 and 2010, but declined from 66th to 69th between 2011 and 2013 (see Figure 5.15a). As explained in Section 3.4.2 of Chapter 3, for a more precise comparison of rankings, we have split the analysis into two sub-periods.

The rankings of all 10 categories went up over the first sub-period from 2005 to 2010. In particular, Transport Ranking jumped 22 places from 47th to 25th between 2005 and 2010. Food & Non-alcoholic Beverages Ranking moved up 16 spots from 75th to 59th over the first sub-period. Housing Rents & Utilities climbed nine places from 85th to 76th between 2005 and 2010. Health and Education Rankings rose more modestly from 73rd to 71st and 80th to 78th, respectively, over the same sub-period.

In the second sub-period between 2011 and 2013, Housing Rents & Utilities Ranking climbed two places from 64th to 62nd. Food & Non-alcoholic Beverages Ranking moved up from 58th in 2011 to 57th in 2013. In contrast, Household Supplies & Domestic Help Ranking fell eight spots from 56th to 64th between 2011 and 2013. Clothing remained as the highest ranked category for the entire second sub-period although its ranking moved down from 43rd in 2011 to 49th in 2013. Health Ranking slipped three places from 78th in 2011 to 81st in 2013, making it the lowest ranked category throughout the second sub-period. Education Ranking declined slightly from 72nd to 73rd over the same sub-period. Transport Ranking largely remained at 49th over the second sub-period. It thus became the highest ranked category in 2013 together with Clothing.

Figure 5.15b

The Gross Hourly Wages in USD for Ordinary Residents in Bratislava, as denoted by the red line in Figure 5.15b, increased rapidly from US$3.34 in 2005 to US$6.55 in 2009. Bratislava's wage level, however, has grown more slowly afterwards, reaching US$7.02 in 2013.

Meanwhile, the Wages Ranking for Ordinary Residents in Bratislava, as shown by the red bars, improved from 68th in 2005 to 62nd in 2009. However, perhaps due to the growth slowdown after 2009, Bratislava's ranking has deteriorated ever since, reaching 70th in 2013.

Figure 5.15c

Let us now analyse the cost of living and wages indices more closely and draw conclusions about the purchasing power of ordinary residents in Bratislava. As elaborated in Section 3.4.2 of Chapter 3, for a more precise and rigorous analysis, we discuss the results in two sub-periods: from 2005 to 2010 and from 2011 to 2013.

The Cost of Living Index and the Wages Index for Ordinary Residents in Bratislava are represented respectively by the grey and red line in Figure 5.15c. Between 2005 and 2010, the Cost of Living Index for Ordinary Residents was generally on an increasing trend. In 2005, the cost of living for ordinary residents in Bratislava was 31.98% of that for their counterparts in New York (the base city). It rose to reach 46.69% in 2010. Over the same sub-period, the Wages Index for Ordinary Residents also increased, rising from 21.18 in 2005 to 34.80 in 2010.

Wages generally rose faster than cost of living so during the first sub-period, ordinary residents in Bratislava were able to afford more goods and services over time. This is reflected in the Purchasing Power Index for Ordinary Residents in Bratislava which is represented by the green line in Figure 5.15c. Between 2005 and 2010, the index rose from 66.24 to 74.54. Meanwhile, the Purchasing Power Ranking for Ordinary Residents in Bratislava, as represented by the green bars, improved from 65th in 2005 to 62nd in 2010.

Over the second sub-period (2011–2013), the Cost of Living Index for Ordinary Residents has been on a decreasing trend. In 2011, the cost of living for ordinary residents in Bratislava was 45.55% of that for their counterparts in New York while in 2013, it dropped to 38.81%. Meanwhile, the Wages Index for Ordinary Residents has been rather stable. The index only declined marginally from 36.66 in 2011 to 35.51 in 2013.

The combined trends of stable wages and decreasing cost of living have enabled ordinary residents in Bratislava to afford more goods and services over time during the second sub-period.

BRATISLAVA
Slovakia

This is evident in the Purchasing Power Index for Ordinary Residents which rose from 80.49 in 2011 to 91.50 in 2013. Despite this positive showing of the index, the Purchasing Power Ranking for Ordinary Residents in Bratislava has actually deteriorated. Between 2011 and 2013, it dropped from 66th to 71st.

Finally, we note that over the entire study period (2005–2013), the Purchasing Power Index for Ordinary Residents in Bratislava has consistently been lower than 100.00 — the base index value. This means that ordinary residents in Bratislava have only been able to afford fewer goods and services than their counterparts in New York, given the same number of working hours.

BRISBANE
Australia

Figure 5.16a: Cost of Living and 10 Consumption Categories Rankings for Ordinary Residents in Brisbane, Australia

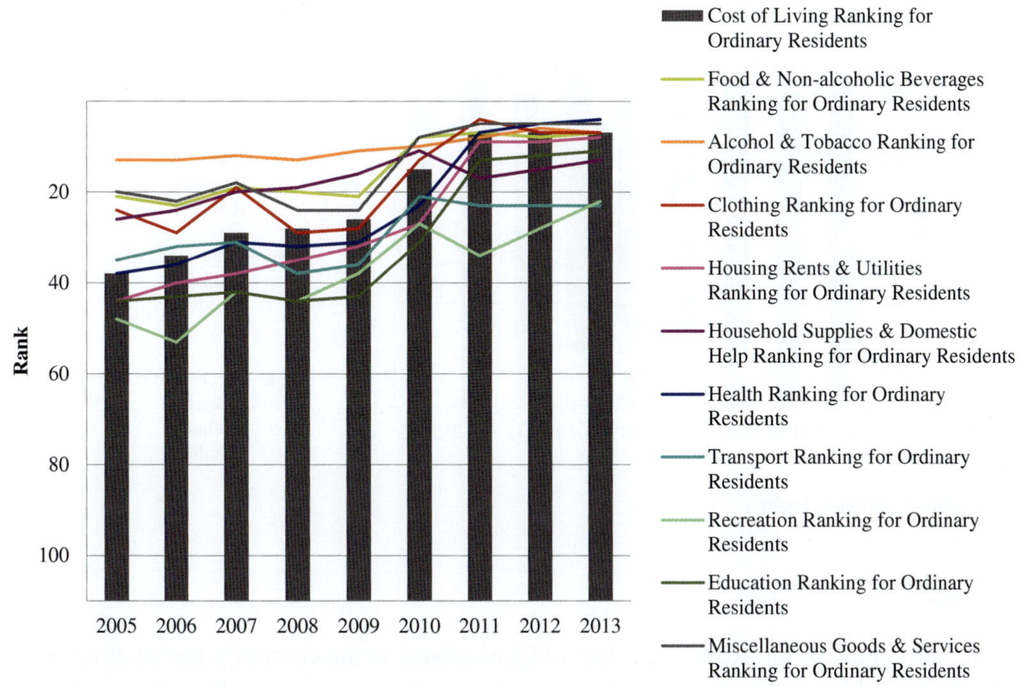

Source: Asia Competitiveness Institute

Figure 5.16b: Gross Hourly Wages in USD and Wages Ranking for Ordinary Residents in Brisbane, Australia

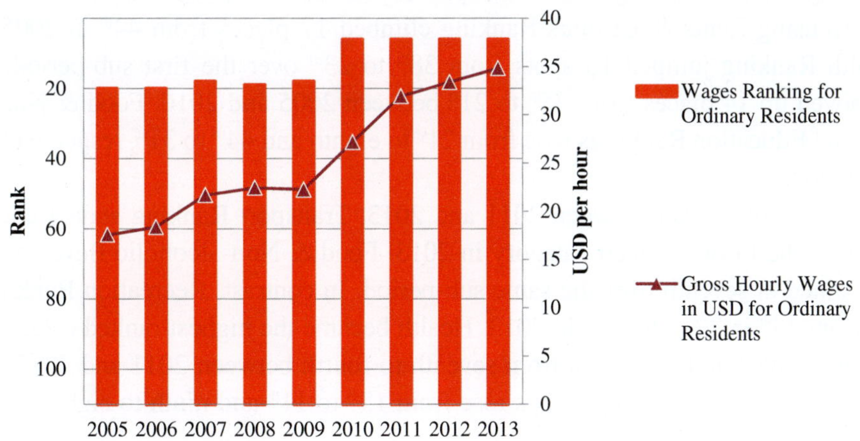

Source: Asia Competitiveness Institute

BRISBANE
Australia

Figure 5.16c: Cost of Living, Wages and Purchasing Power Indices and Purchasing Power Ranking for Ordinary Residents in Brisbane, Australia

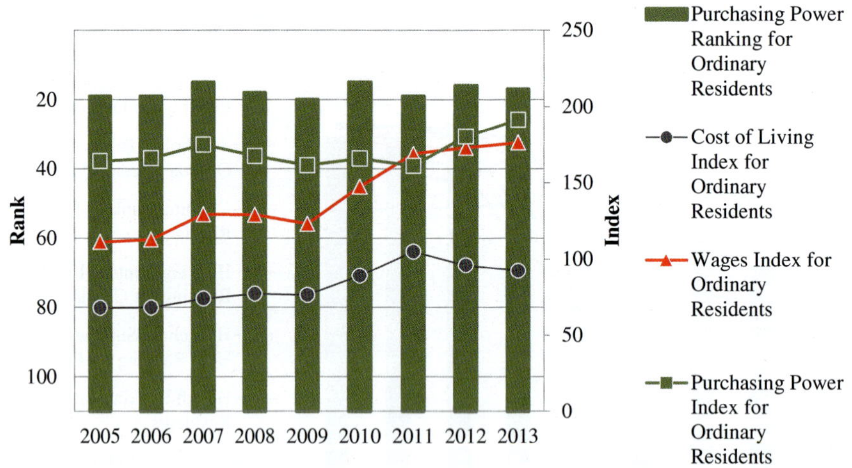

Source: Asia Competitiveness Institute

Figure 5.16a

Brisbane, the capital of the Australian state of Queensland, is the country's centre of oil refinery. The city's Cost of Living Ranking for Ordinary Residents, as represented by the grey bars, rose from 38th to 15th between 2005 and 2010, and remained at seventh between 2011 and 2013 (see Figure 5.16a). As elaborated in Section 3.4.2 of Chapter 3, for a more rigorous comparison of rankings, we have split the analysis into two sub-periods.

The rankings of all 10 categories went up over the first sub-period from 2005 to 2010. In particular, Housing Rents & Utilities Ranking climbed 17 places from 44th in 2005 to 27th in 2010. Health Ranking jumped 15 spots from 38th to 23rd over the first sub-period. Transport Ranking moved up 14 places from 35th to 21st between 2005 and 2010. Food & Non-alcoholic Beverages and Education Rankings rose from 21st to eighth and 44th to 31st, respectively, over the same sub-period.

In the second sub-period between 2011 and 2013, Transport Ranking stayed unchanged at 23rd, making it the lowest ranked category in 2013. Food & Non-alcoholic Beverages Ranking largely remained at seventh over the same sub-period. In contrast, Recreation Ranking jumped 12 places from 34th in 2011 to 22nd in 2013. Health became the highest ranked category in 2013 as its ranking moved up three spots from seventh to fourth between 2011 and 2013. Education and Housing Rents & Utilities Rankings rose from 13th to 11th and ninth to eighth, respectively, over the second sub-period.

BRISBANE
Australia

Figure 5.16b

The Gross Hourly Wages in USD for Ordinary Residents in Brisbane, as denoted by the red line in Figure 5.16b, have almost doubled over the study period. From US$17.56 in 2005, Brisbane's wage level rose to US$34.83 in 2013. The most rapid increase happened between 2009 and 2011. This was partly due to the appreciation of Australian dollar against US dollar.

Meanwhile, the Wages Ranking for Ordinary Residents in Brisbane, as shown by the red bars, first rose from 20th in 2005 to 18th in 2009. It improved to sixth in 2010 and has remained at that level thereafter.

Figure 5.16c

Let us now analyse the cost of living and wages indices more closely and draw conclusions about the purchasing power of ordinary residents in Brisbane. As elaborated in Section 3.4.2 of Chapter 3, for a more precise and rigorous analysis, we discuss the results in two sub-periods: from 2005 to 2010 and from 2011 to 2013.

The Cost of Living Index and the Wages Index for Ordinary Residents in Brisbane are represented respectively by the grey and red line in Figure 5.16c. Between 2005 and 2010, the Cost of Living Index for Ordinary Residents was generally on an increasing trend. In 2005, the cost of living for ordinary residents in Brisbane was 67.79% of that for their counterparts in New York (the base city). It rose to reach 88.91% in 2010. Over the same sub-period, the Wages Index for Ordinary Residents also increased, rising from 111.21 in 2005 to 147.34 in 2010.

Wages generally managed to keep up with cost of living so during the first sub-period, ordinary residents in Brisbane were able to afford the same level of consumption over time. This is reflected in the stability of the Purchasing Power Index for Ordinary Residents in Brisbane, which is represented by the green line in Figure 5.16c. The index generally fluctuated around 166.56, with a one-off spike to 174.84 in 2007. Meanwhile, the Purchasing Power Ranking for Ordinary Residents in Brisbane, which is represented by the green bars, improved from 19th in 2005 to 15th in 2010.

Over the second sub-period (2011–2013), the Cost of Living Index for Ordinary Residents has been on a steady decreasing trend. In 2011, the cost of living for ordinary residents in Brisbane was 104.83% of that for their counterparts in New York while in 2013, it dropped to 92.15%. Meanwhile, the Wages Index for Ordinary Residents has been increasing. The index rose from 168.86 in 2011 to 176.22 in 2013.

The combined trends of increasing wages and decreasing cost of living have enabled ordinary residents in Brisbane to afford more goods and services over time during the second sub-period. This is evident in the Purchasing Power Index for Ordinary Residents which rose from 161.08

BRISBANE
Australia

in 2011 to 191.24 in 2013. The Purchasing Power Ranking for Ordinary Residents in Brisbane has also been improving. It rose from 19th in 2011 to 17th in 2013.

Finally, we note that over the entire study period (2005–2013), the Purchasing Power Index for Ordinary Residents in Brisbane has always been higher than 100.00 — the base index value. This means that ordinary residents in Brisbane have consistently been able to afford a higher consumption level than their counterparts in New York, given the same number of working hours.

BRUSSELS
Belgium

Figure 5.17a: Cost of Living and 10 Consumption Categories Rankings for Ordinary Residents in Brussels, Belgium

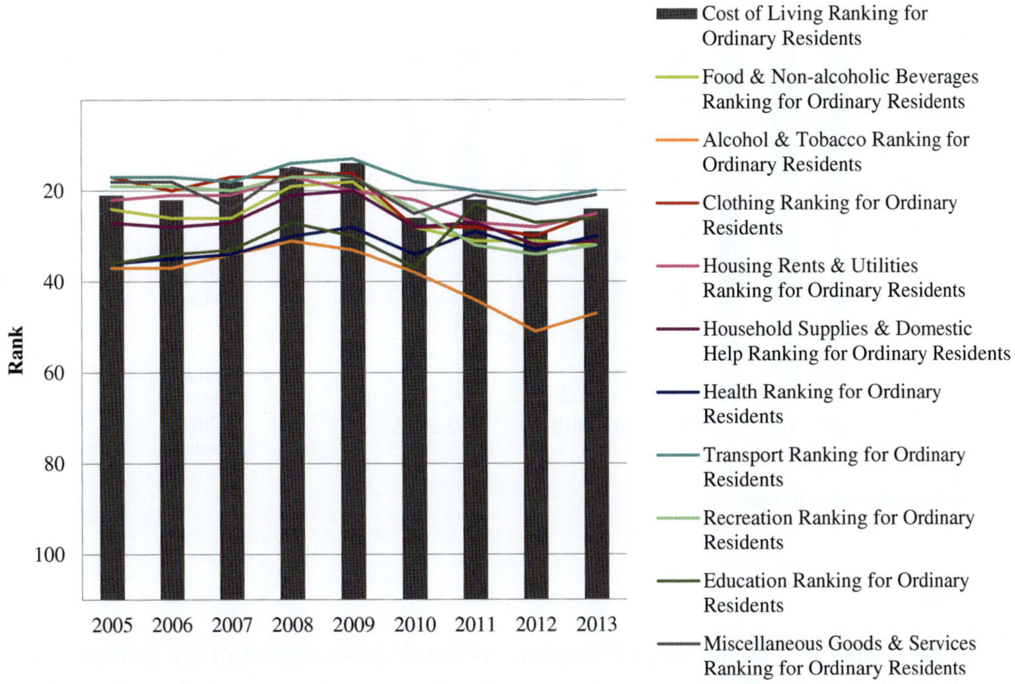

Source: Asia Competitiveness Institute

Figure 5.17b: Gross Hourly Wages in USD and Wages Ranking for Ordinary Residents in Brussels, Belgium

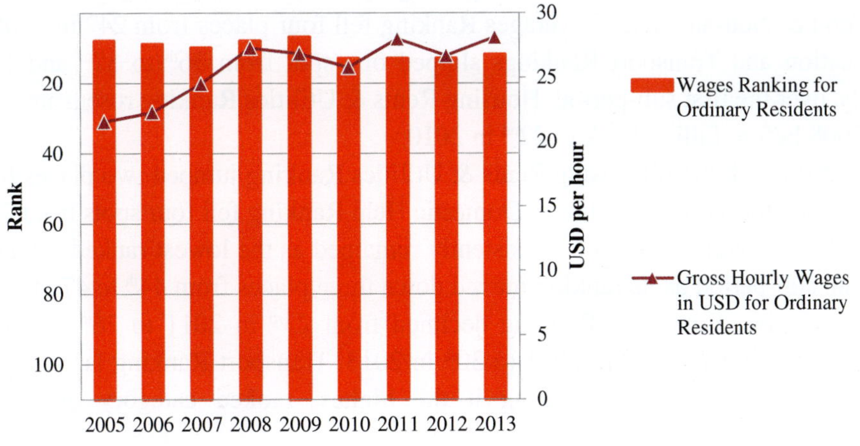

Source: Asia Competitiveness Institute

BRUSSELS
Belgium

Figure 5.17c: Cost of Living, Wages and Purchasing Power Indices and Purchasing Power Ranking for Ordinary Residents in Brussels, Belgium

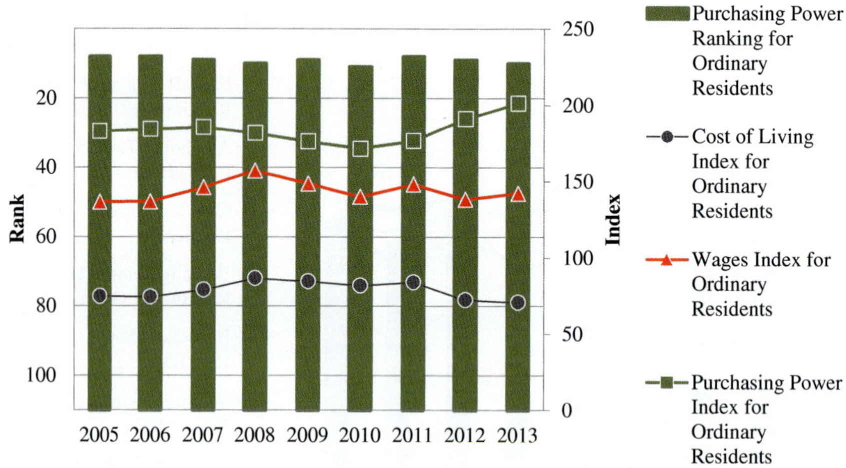

Source: Asia Competitiveness Institute

Figure 5.17a

Brussels, the capital and largest city of Belgium, is the *de facto* capital of the European Union. The city's Cost of Living Ranking for Ordinary Residents, as shown in the grey bars, declined from 21st to 26th between 2005 and 2010, and from 22nd to 24th between 2011 and 2013 (see Figure 5.17a). As explained in Section 3.4.2 of Chapter 3, for a more precise comparison of rankings, we have split the analysis into two sub-periods.

From 2005 to 2010, Health was the only category that rose in ranking from 36th to 34th. In contrast, Food & Non-alcoholic Beverages Ranking fell four places from 24th in 2005 to 28th in 2010. Education and Transport Rankings slipped one spot from 36th to 37th and 17th to 18th, respectively, over the first sub-period. Housing Rents & Utilities Ranking rose from 22nd in 2005 to 17th in 2008 before falling back to 22nd in 2010.

Between 2011 and 2013, Housing Rents & Utilities Ranking jumped two places from 27th to 25th. In contrast, Household Supplies & Domestic Help Ranking fell four spots from 27th in 2011 to 31st in 2013. Alcohol & Tobacco consistently remained as the lowest ranked category for the entire second sub-period as its ranking moved down three places from 44th to 47th between 2011 and 2013. Likewise, Education Ranking declined from 23rd in 2011 to 26th in 2013. Health Ranking fell slightly from 29th in 2011 to 30th in 2013. Transport Ranking largely remained at 20th between 2011 and 2013, making it the highest ranked category over the second sub-period.

BRUSSELS
Belgium

Figure 5.17b

The Gross Hourly Wages in USD for Ordinary Residents in Brussels, as denoted by the red line in Figure 5.17b, grew consistently from US$21.54 in 2005 to US$27.28 in 2008. Since then, Brussels's wage level has exhibited moderate fluctuations, reaching US$28.10 in 2013.

Ranking-wise, the Wages Ranking for Ordinary Residents in Brussels, as shown by the red bars, first rose slightly from eighth in 2005 to seventh in 2009. It then dropped to 13th throughout 2010–2012 before recovering slightly to 12th in 2013.

Figure 5.17c

Let us now analyse the cost of living and wages indices more closely and draw conclusions about the purchasing power of ordinary residents in Brussels. As elaborated in Section 3.4.2 of Chapter 3, for a more precise and rigorous analysis, we discuss the results in two sub-periods: from 2005 to 2010 and from 2011 to 2013.

The Cost of Living Index and the Wages Index for Ordinary Residents in Brussels are represented respectively by the grey and red line in Figure 5.17c. Between 2005 and 2010, the Cost of Living Index for Ordinary Residents exhibited moderate fluctuations. In 2005, the cost of living for ordinary residents in Brussels was 74.61% of that for their counterparts in New York (the base city). It rose steadily to peak at 86.35% in 2008 and then started to decline slightly until it reached 81.63% in 2010. Over the same sub-period, the Wages Index for Ordinary Residents also followed a similar pattern. From 136.43 in 2005, this index also rose to peak at 156.87 in 2008. It then embarked on a decreasing trend until it reached 139.93 in 2010.

Between 2005 and 2008, wages could keep up with the pace of increase of cost of living. Thus, ordinary residents in Brussels were able to afford the same consumption level over time during these years. However, they could no longer do so after 2008, when both wages and cost of living were falling, because wages fell faster than the latter. These trends are reflected in the Purchasing Power Index for Ordinary Residents in Brussels, which is represented by the green line in Figure 5.17c. The index was fairly stable until 2008, after which it declined steadily to reach 171.42 in 2010. Ranking-wise, the Purchasing Power Ranking for Ordinary Resident in Brussels, as represented by the green bars, dropped from eighth to 11th between 2005 and 2010.

Over the second sub-period (2011–2013), the Cost of Living Index for Ordinary Residents has been on a decreasing trend. In 2011, the cost of living for ordinary residents in Brussels was 83.79% of that for their counterparts in New York while in 2013, it dropped to 70.66%. The Wages Index for Ordinary Residents has also been decreasing. The index dropped from 147.96 in 2011 to 142.16 in 2013.

Wages have decreased at a slower rate than cost of living, so ordinary residents in Brussels have actually been able to afford more goods and services over time throughout the second sub-period. This is reflected in the Purchasing Power Index for Ordinary Residents which rose

BRUSSELS
Belgium

steadily from 176.58 in 2011 to 201.18 in 2013. Despite this positive showing of the index, the Purchasing Power Ranking for Ordinary Residents has actually been declining. Between 2011 and 2013, Brussels' rank dropped from eighth to 10th.

Finally, we note that over the entire study period (2005–2013), the Purchasing Power Index for Ordinary Residents in Brussels has always been higher than 100.00 — the base index value. This means that ordinary residents in Brussels have consistently been able to afford a higher consumption level than their counterparts in New York, given the same number of working hours.

BUCHAREST
Romania

Figure 5.18a: Cost of Living and 10 Consumption Categories Rankings for Ordinary Residents in Bucharest, Romania

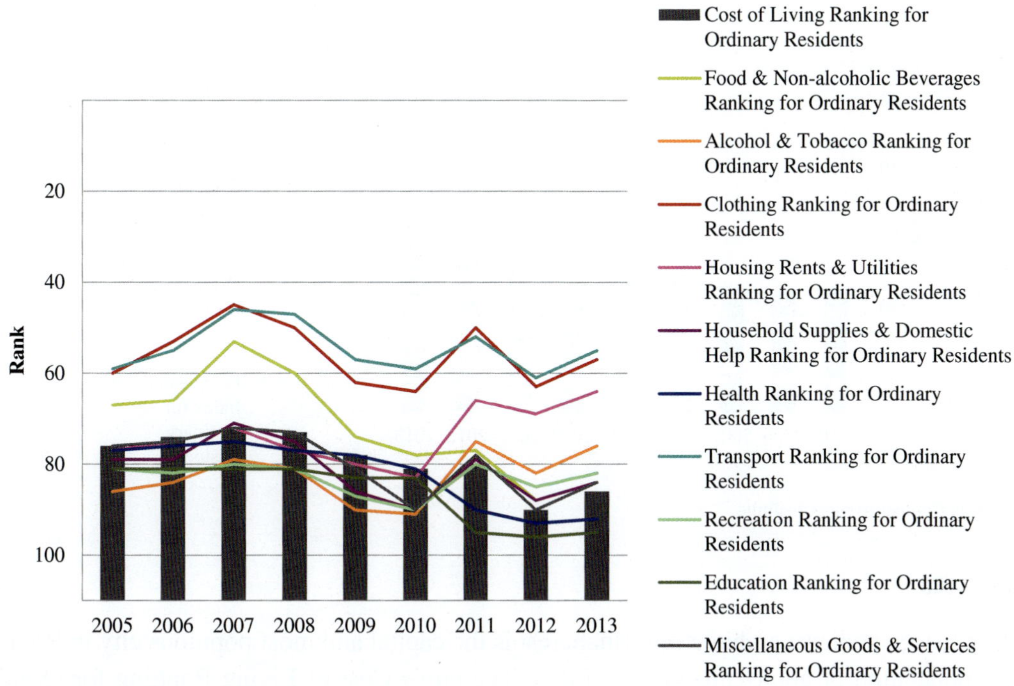

Source: Asia Competitiveness Institute

Figure 5.18b: Gross Hourly Wages in USD and Wages Ranking for Ordinary Residents in Bucharest, Romania

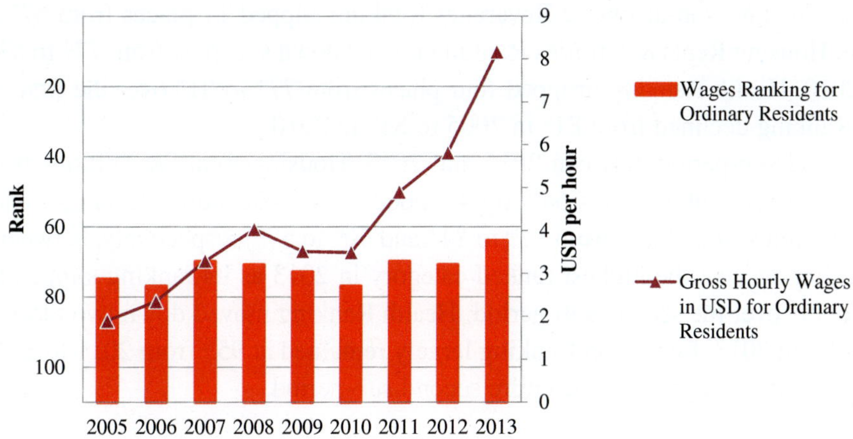

Source: Asia Competitiveness Institute

BUCHAREST
Romania

Figure 5.18c: Cost of Living, Wages and Purchasing Power Indices and Purchasing Power Ranking for Ordinary Residents in Bucharest, Romania

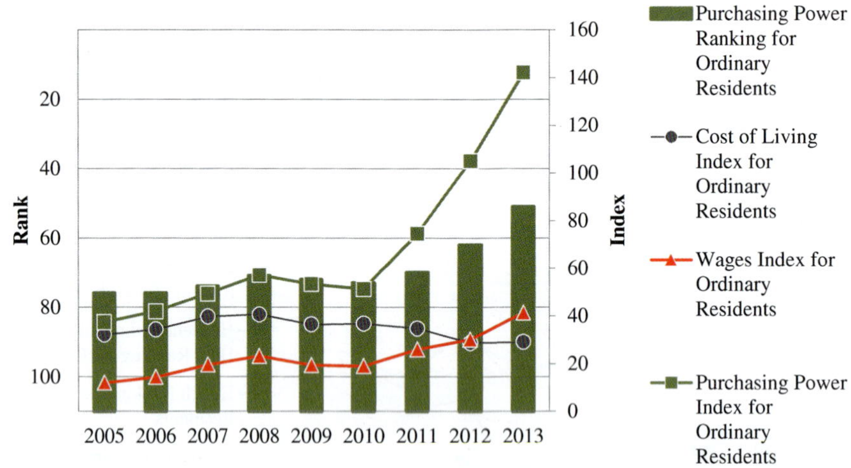

Source: Asia Competitiveness Institute

Figure 5.18a

Famous for its medieval architecture, Bucharest is the capital and most populous city in Romania with a population of approximately 2 million. The city's Cost of Living Ranking for Ordinary Residents, as denoted by the grey bars, fell from 76th to 81st between 2005 and 2010, and from 80th to 86th between 2011 and 2013 (see Figure 5.18a). As elaborated in Section 3.4.2 of Chapter 3, for a more rigorous comparison of rankings, we have split the analysis into two sub-periods.

The rankings of all 10 categories went down over the first sub-period from 2005 to 2010. In particular, Food & Non-alcoholic Beverages Ranking slipped 11 places from 67th in 2005 to 78th in 2010. Housing Rents & Utilities Ranking moved down six spots from 77th to 83rd between 2005 and 2010. Health Ranking dropped four places from 77th to 81st over the first sub-period. Education Ranking declined from 81st in 2005 to 83rd in 2010.

In the second sub-period between 2011 and 2013, Housing Rents & Utilities was the only category that rose in ranking from 66th to 64th. Food & Non-alcoholic Beverages and Clothing Rankings both fell seven places from 77th to 84th and 50th to 57th, respectively, between 2011 and 2013. Transport became the highest ranked category in 2013 as its ranking slipped three spots from 52nd to 55th over the second sub-period. Health Ranking moved down two places from 90th in 2011 to 92nd in 2013. Education Ranking largely remained at 95th from 2011 to 2013, making it the lowest ranked category for the entire second sub-period.

Figure 5.18b

The Gross Hourly Wages in USD for Ordinary Residents in Bucharest, as represented by the red line in Figure 5.18b, initially rose steadily from US$1.89 in 2005 to US$4.03 in 2008.

BUCHAREST
Romania

Bucharest's wage level then declined over 2008–2010 before resuming its upward surge to reach US$8.17 in 2013.

Meanwhile, the Wages Ranking for Ordinary Residents in Bucharest first increased from 75th in 2005 to 70th in 2007. It then steadily deteriorated to 77th in 2010 before gradually picking up over the subsequent years. In 2013, Bucharest's ranking was 64th.

Figure 5.18c

Let us now analyse the cost of living and wages indices more closely and draw conclusions about the purchasing power of ordinary residents in Bucharest. As elaborated in Section 3.4.2 of Chapter 3, for a more precise and rigorous analysis, we discuss the results in two sub-periods: from 2005 to 2010 and from 2011 to 2013.

The Cost of Living Index and the Wages Index for Ordinary Residents in Bucharest are represented respectively by the grey and red line in Figure 5.18c. Between 2005 and 2010, the Cost of Living Index for Ordinary Residents exhibited moderate fluctuations. In 2005, the cost of living for ordinary residents in Bucharest was 32.11% of that for their counterparts in New York (the base city). It rose steadily to peak at 40.59% in 2008 and then started to decrease until it reached 36.83% in 2010. Over the same sub-period, the Wages Index for Ordinary Residents also followed a similar pattern. From 11.99 in 2005, this index reached 18.90 in 2010.

Wages generally increased faster than cost of living so ordinary residents in Bucharest were able to afford more goods and services over time during the first sub-period. This is reflected in the Purchasing Power Index for Ordinary Residents in Bucharest, which is represented by the green line in Figure 5.18c. This index rose from 37.34 in 2005 to 51.32 in 2010. Ranking-wise, the Purchasing Power Ranking for Ordinary Residents in Bucharest, which is represented by the green bars, improved from 76th in 2005 to 73rd in 2010.

Over the second sub-period (2011–2013), the Cost of Living Index for Ordinary Residents has been on decreasing trend. In 2011, the cost of living for ordinary residents in Bucharest was 34.79% of that for their counterparts in New York while in 2013, it dropped to 29.08%. In contrast, the Wages Index for Ordinary Residents has been increasing. Between 2011 and 2013, this index rose from 25.94 to 41.32.

The combined trends of increasing wages and decreasing cost of living have enabled ordinary residents in Bucharest to afford more goods and services over time during the second sub-period. This is reflected in the Purchasing Power Index for Ordinary Residents in Bucharest which rose steadily from 74.57 in 2011 to 142.10 in 2013. The Purchasing Power Ranking for Ordinary Residents in Bucharest has also improved significantly. It rose from 70th in 2011 to 51st in 2013.

Finally, we note that the Purchasing Power Index for Ordinary Residents in Bucharest had consistently been below 100.00 — the base index value — until 2012. This means it was not until 2012 that ordinary residents in Bucharest were able to consume more goods and services than their counterparts in New York, given the same number of working hours. Before 2012, they had only been able to afford a lower consumption level.

BUDAPEST
Hungary

Figure 5.19a: Cost of Living and 10 Consumption Categories Rankings for Ordinary Residents in Budapest, Hungary

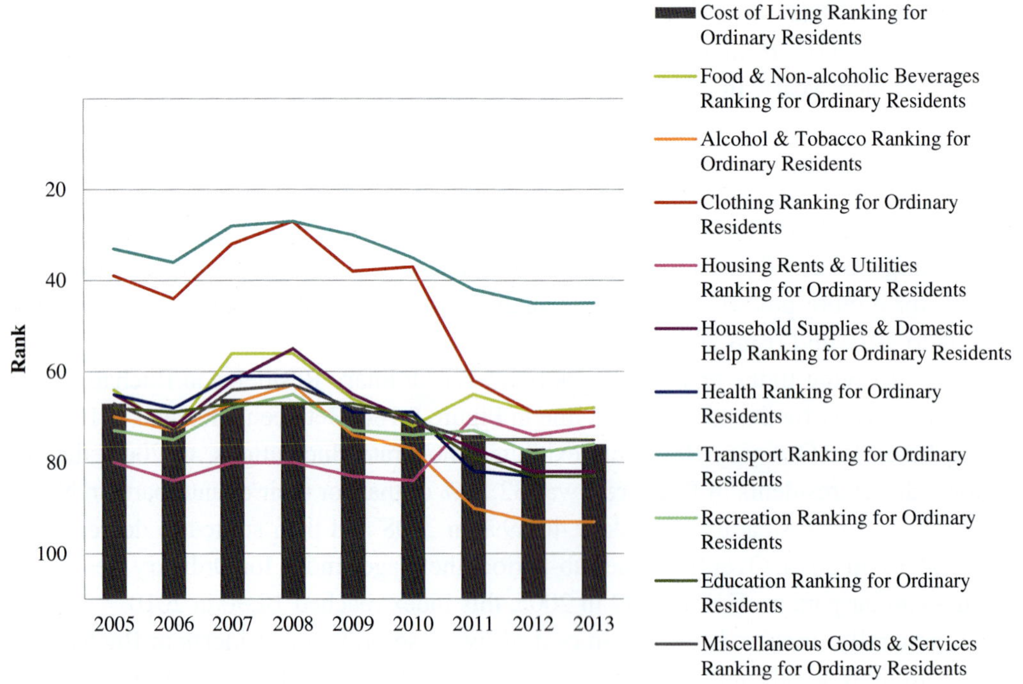

Source: Asia Competitiveness Institute

Figure 5.19b: Gross Hourly Wages in USD and Wages Ranking for Ordinary Residents in Budapest, Hungary

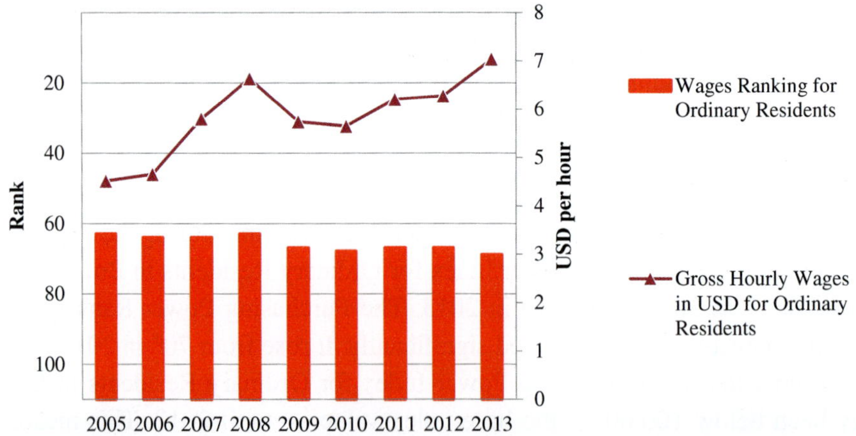

Source: Asia Competitiveness Institute

BUDAPEST
Hungary

Figure 5.19c: Cost of Living, Wages and Purchasing Power Indices and Purchasing Power Ranking for Ordinary Residents in Budapest, Hungary

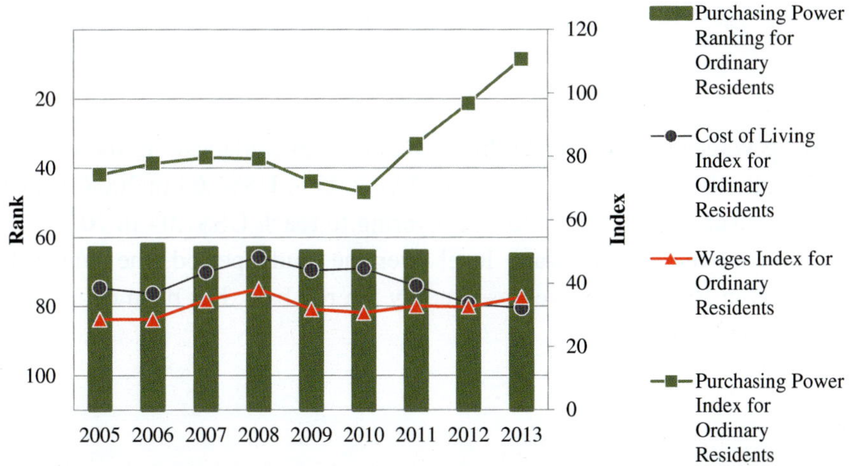

Source: Asia Competitiveness Institute

Figure 5.19a

Known for its diverse architecture, Budapest is the capital and largest city of Hungary. The city's Cost of Living Ranking for Ordinary Residents, as represented by the grey bars, declined from 67th to 71st between 2005 and 2010, and from 74th to 76th between 2011 and 2013 (see Figure 5.19a). As explained in Section 3.4.2 of Chapter 3, for a more precise comparison of rankings, we have split the analysis into two sub-periods.

Clothing was the only category that rose in ranking from 39th to 37th over the first sub-period from 2005 to 2010. Food & Non-alcoholic Beverages Ranking fell eight places from 64th in 2005 to 72nd in 2010. Housing Rents & Utilities and Health Rankings both slipped four spots from 80th to 84th and 65th to 69th, respectively, between 2005 and 2010. Education Ranking moved down two places from 68th to 70th over the same sub-period. Likewise, Transport Ranking declined from 33rd in 2005 to 35th in 2010.

The rankings of all 10 categories went down in the second sub-period between 2011 and 2013. Clothing registered the most significant dip in ranking as it fell seven places from 62nd in 2011 to 69th in 2013. Household Supplies & Domestic Help Ranking moved down five spots from 77th to 82nd over the second sub-period. Education Ranking declined from 79th in 2011 to 83rd in 2013. Transport consistently remained as the highest ranked category for the entire second sub-period as its ranking slipped three places from 42nd to 45th between 2011 and 2013. Food & Non-alcoholic Beverages Ranking also dropped three spots from 65th in 2011 to 68th in 2013. Likewise, Alcohol & Tobacco Ranking fell from 90th to 93rd between 2011 and 2013,

BUDAPEST
Hungary

making it the lowest ranked category over the second sub-period. Housing Rents & Utilities and Health Rankings moved down from 70th to 72nd and 82nd to 83rd, respectively, over the same sub-period.

Figure 5.19b

The Gross Hourly Wages in USD for Ordinary Resident in Budapest, as shown by the red line in Figure 5.19b, initially increased from US$4.52 in 2005 to US$6.64 in 2008. Budapest's wage level then dropped over 2008–2010 before recovering to reach US$7.04 in 2013.

Despite the overall increase in wage level over the study period, the Wages Ranking for Ordinary Residents in Budapest, as represented by the red bars, has been declining. It dropped from 63rd in 2005 to 69th in 2013.

Figure 5.19c

Let us now analyse the cost of living and wages indices more closely and draw conclusions about the purchasing power of ordinary residents in Budapest. As elaborated in Section 3.4.2 of Chapter 3, for a more precise and rigorous analysis, we discuss the results in two sub-periods: from 2005 to 2010 and from 2011 to 2013.

The Cost of Living Index and the Wages Index for Ordinary Residents in Budapest are represented respectively by the grey and red line in Figure 5.19c. Between 2005 and 2010, the Cost of Living Index for Ordinary Residents exhibited moderate fluctuations. In 2005, the cost of living for ordinary residents in Budapest was 38.53% of that for their counterparts in New York. It rose steadily to peak at 48.18% in 2008 and then started to decline until it reached 44.62% in 2010. Over the same sub-period, the Wages Index for Ordinary Residents also followed a similar pattern. In 2005, this index was 28.62 and it reached 30.63 in 2010.

Between 2005 and 2008, wages increased faster than cost of living so during these years, ordinary residents were able to afford a higher consumption level over time. They could no longer do so after 2008; between 2008 and 2010, wages and cost of living were both decreasing and wages decreased faster than the latter. These trends are fully reflected in the Purchasing Power Index for Ordinary Residents in Budapest, which is represented by the green line in Figure 5.19c. From 74.27 in 2005, the index initially followed an upward trend to peak in 2008 before reversing to a decreasing trend until it reached 68.65 in 2010. Ranking-wise, the Purchasing Power Ranking for Ordinary Residents in Budapest, which is represented by the green bars, was rather stable. It only fluctuated between 62nd and 64th during the first sub-period.

Over the second sub-period (2011–2013), the Cost of Living Index for Ordinary Residents has been on a steady decreasing trend. In 2011, the cost of living for ordinary residents in Budapest was 39.14% of that for their counterparts in New York. It dropped over the years to

32.15% in 2013. In contrast, the Wages Index for Ordinary Residents has been on an increasing trend, rising from 32.82 in 2011 to 35.59 in 2013.

The combined trends of increasing wages and decreasing cost of living have enabled ordinary residents in Budapest to afford more goods and services over time during the second sub-period. This is reflected in the Purchasing Power Index for Ordinary Residents in Budapest which rose steadily from 83.87 in 2011 to 110.70 in 2013. The Purchasing Power Ranking for Ordinary Residents has also been stable, fluctuating among 64th, 65th and 66th throughout the second sub-period.

Finally, we note that over the entire study period (2005–2013), the Purchasing Power Index for Ordinary Residents in Budapest had consistently been lower than 100.00 — the base index value — until 2013. This means that not until 2013 were the ordinary residents in Budapest able to afford to consume more goods and services than their counterparts in New York, given the same number of working hours. Before 2013, they had only been able to afford a lower consumption level.

BUENOS AIRES
Argentina

Figure 5.20a: Cost of Living and 10 Consumption Categories Rankings for Ordinary Residents in Buenos Aires, Argentina

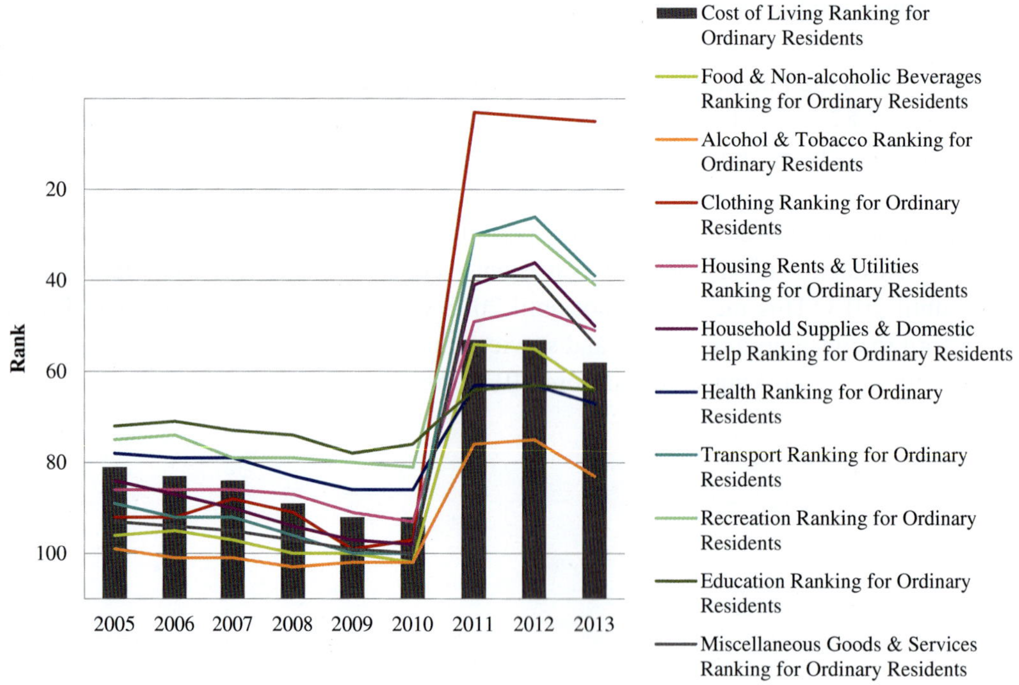

Source: Asia Competitiveness Institute

Figure 5.20b: Gross Hourly Wages in USD and Wages Ranking for Ordinary Residents in Buenos Aires, Argentina

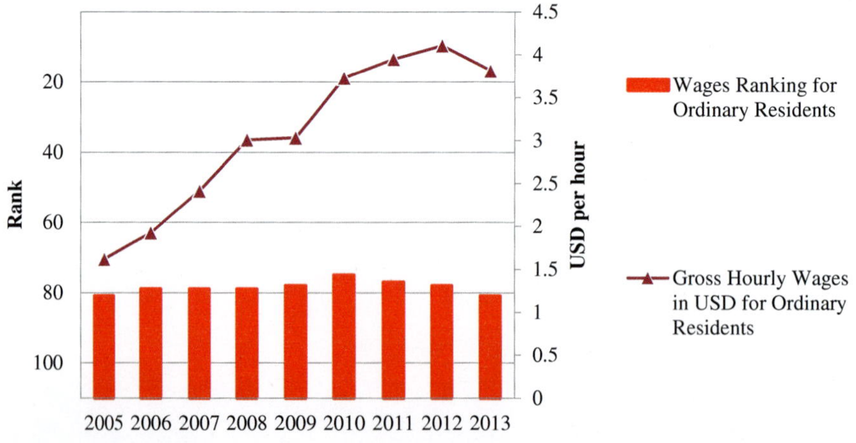

Source: Asia Competitiveness Institute

BUENOS AIRES
Argentina

Figure 5.20c: Cost of Living, Wages and Purchasing Power Indices and Purchasing Power Ranking for Ordinary Residents in Buenos Aires, Argentina

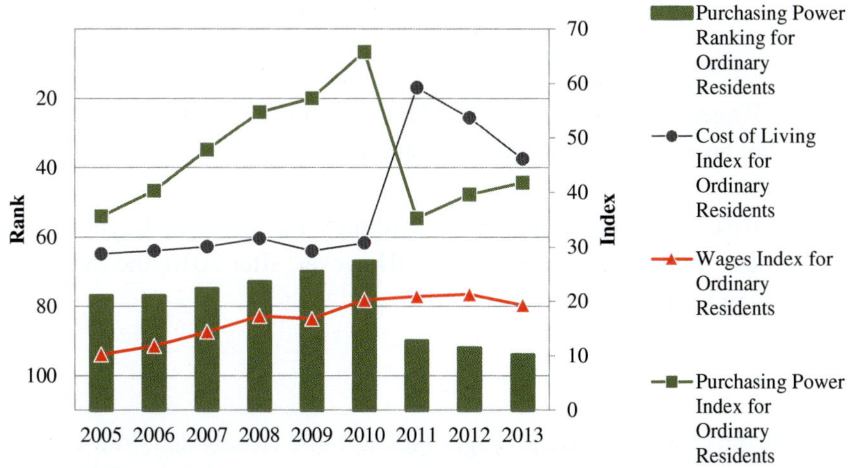

Source: Asia Competitiveness Institute

Figure 5.20a

Renowned for its European-style architecture and the highest concentration of theatres in the world, Buenos Aires is one of the most popular tourist destinations in South America. The city's Cost of Living Ranking for Ordinary Residents, as shown in the grey bars, declined from 81st to 92nd between 2005 and 2010, and from 53rd to 58th between 2011 and 2013 (see Figure 5.20a). As elaborated in Section 3.4.2 of Chapter 3, for a more rigorous comparison of rankings, we have split the analysis into two sub-periods.

From 2005 to 2010, Household Supplies & Domestic Help saw the most remarkable dip in ranking as it fell 14 places from 84th to 98th. Transport Ranking slipped 11 places from 89th in 2005 to 100th in 2010. Health Ranking dropped eight places from 78th to 86th between 2005 and 2010. Housing Rents & Utilities Ranking moved down seven spots from 86th to 93rd over the first sub-period. Food & Non-alcoholic Beverages Ranking declined from 96th in 2005 to 102nd in 2010. Education Ranking fell four places from 72nd to 76th over the same sub-period.

From 2011 to 2013, Food & Non-alcoholic Beverages Ranking slipped 10 places from 54th to 64th. Transport Ranking fell nine spots from 30th in 2011 to 39th in 2013. Health Ranking dropped four places from 63rd to 67th over the second sub-period. Housing Rents & Utilities and Clothing Rankings both moved down two spots from 49th to 51st and third to fifth, respectively, between 2011 and 2013. Clothing was thus the highest ranked category throughout the second sub-period. Education Ranking largely remained at 64th from 2011 to 2013. Alcohol & Tobacco was

BUENOS AIRES
Argentina

consistently the lowest ranked category in both sub-periods as its ranking declined from 99th in 2005 to 102nd in 2010 and from 76th in 2011 to 83rd in 2013.

Figure 5.20b

The Gross Hourly Wages in USD for Ordinary Residents in Buenos Aires, as denoted by the red line in Figure 5.20b, have generally followed an increasing trend, rising from US$1.62 in 2005 to US$3.81 in 2013.

From 2005 to 2010, the Wages Ranking for Ordinary Residents in Buenos Aires, as represented by the red bars, improved from 81st to 75th. However, after 2010, the ranking has steadily deteriorated, dropping back to 81st in 2013.

Figure 5.20c

Let us now analyse the cost of living and wages indices more closely and draw conclusions about the purchasing power of ordinary residents in Buenos Aires. As elaborated in Section 3.4.2 of Chapter 3, for a more precise and rigorous analysis, we discuss the results in two sub-periods: from 2005 to 2010 and from 2011 to 2013.

The Cost of Living Index and the Wages Index for Ordinary Residents in Buenos Aires are represented respectively by the grey and red line in Figure 5.20c. Between 2005 and 2010, the Cost of Living Index for Ordinary Residents was on an increasing trend. In 2005, the cost of living for ordinary residents in Buenos Aires was 28.74% of that for their counterparts in New York (the base city). It rose to reach 30.76% in 2010. Over the same sub-period, the Wages Index for Ordinary Residents also increased, rising from 10.24 in 2005 to 20.23 in 2010.

Wages increased much faster than cost of living so throughout the first sub-period, ordinary residents in Buenos Aires were able to afford more goods and services over time. This is reflected in the Purchasing Power Index for Ordinary Residents in Buenos Aires, which is represented by the green line in Figure 5.20c. Between 2005 and 2010, the index increased significantly from 35.63 to 65.77. Ranking-wise, the Purchasing Power Ranking for Ordinary Residents in Buenos Aires, which is represented by the green bars, also steadily improved, rising from 77th in 2005 to 67th in 2010.

Over the second sub-period (2011–2013), the Cost of Living Index for Ordinary Residents has been on a decreasing trend. In 2011, the cost of living for ordinary residents in Buenos Aires was 59.23% of that for their counterparts in New York while in 2013, it dropped to 46.12%. In contrast, the Wages Index for Ordinary Residents has remained relatively stable, dropping slightly to 19.28 in 2013 from 20.88 in 2011.

The combined trends of stable wages and decreasing cost of have enabled ordinary residents in Buenos Aires to afford more goods and services over time during the second sub-period. This is reflected in the Purchasing Power Index for Ordinary Residents in Buenos Aires which rose steadily from 35.26 in 2011 to 41.80 in 2013. Despite this positive showing of the index, the Purchasing Power Ranking for Ordinary Residents in Buenos Aires has been declining. Between 2011 and 2013, Buenos Aires' rank dropped from 90th to 94th.

Finally, we note that over the entire study period (2005–2013), the Purchasing Power Index for Ordinary Residents in Buenos Aires has consistently been lower than 100.00 — the base index value. This means that ordinary residents in Buenos Aires have only been able to afford a lower consumption level than their counterparts in New York, given the same number of working hours.

CAIRO
Egypt

Figure 5.21a: Cost of Living and 10 Consumption Categories Rankings for Ordinary Residents in Cairo, Egypt

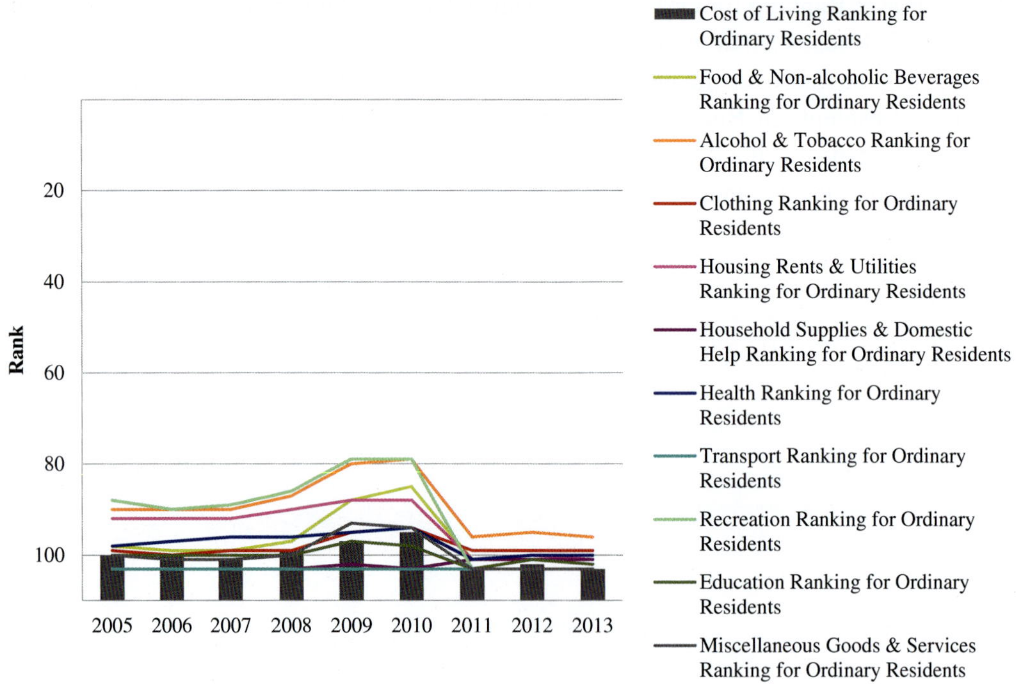

Source: Asia Competitiveness Institute

Figure 5.21b: Gross Hourly Wages in USD and Wages Ranking for Ordinary Residents in Cairo, Egypt

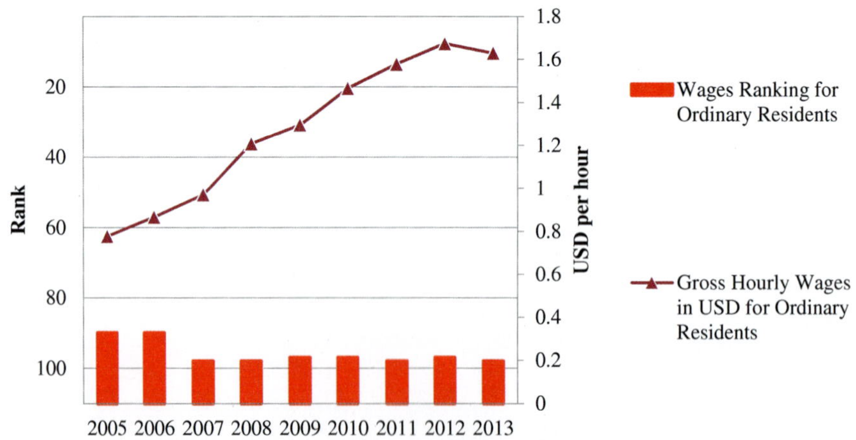

Source: Asia Competitiveness Institute

CAIRO
Egypt

Figure 5.21c: Cost of Living, Wages and Purchasing Power Indices and Purchasing Power Ranking for Ordinary Residents in Cairo, Egypt

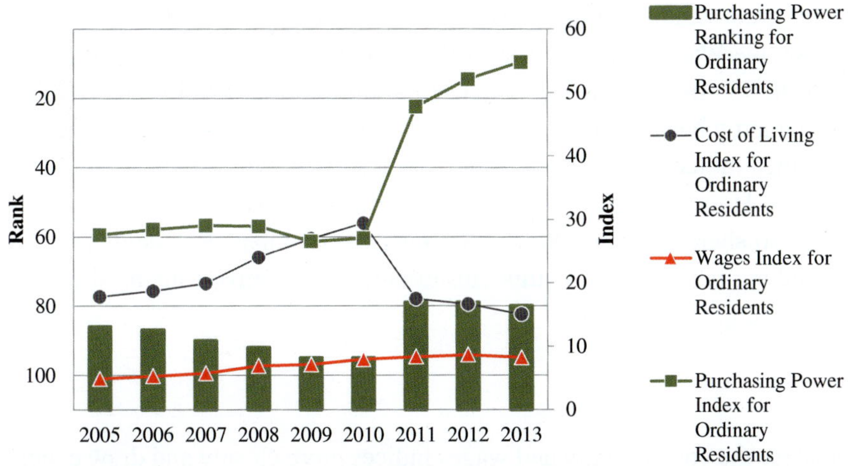

Source: Asia Competitiveness Institute

Figure 5.21a

Founded in 969 AD, Cairo, the capital of Egypt, has long been the country's cultural, political and economic centre. The city's Cost of Living Ranking for Ordinary Residents, as denoted by the grey bars, rose from 100th to 95th between 2005 and 2010, and largely remained at 103rd between 2011 and 2013, making it the cheapest among the 103 cities studied in 2013 (see Figure 5.21a). As explained in Section 3.4.2 of Chapter 3, for a more precise comparison of rankings, we have split the analysis into two sub-periods.

In the first sub-period from 2005 to 2010, Food & Non-alcoholic Beverages Ranking registered the most significant rise in ranking as it climbed 13 places from 98th to 85th. Housing Rents & Utilities and Health Rankings both jumped four spots from 92nd to 88th and 98th to 94th, respectively, between 2005 and 2010. Education Ranking moved up two places from 100th in 2005 to 98th in 2010. Transport Ranking stayed unchanged at 103rd throughout the first sub-period.

In the second sub-period between 2011 and 2013, Health and Education Rankings climbed one place from 101st to 100th and 103rd to 102nd, respectively. The rankings of the remaining eight categories largely remained unchanged. In particular, Housing Rents & Utilities and Food & Non-alcoholic Beverages Rankings both primarily stayed at 101st between 2011 and 2013. Transport, Recreation and Miscellaneous Goods & Services Rankings stayed unchanged at 103rd, making Cairo the most affordable city in these categories throughout the second sub-period.

CAIRO
Egypt

Figure 5.21b

The Gross Hourly Wages in USD for Ordinary Residents in Cairo, as represented by the red line in Figure 5.21b, grew steadily from US$0.78 in 2005 to US$1.63 in 2013.

Ranking-wise, the Wages Ranking for Ordinary Residents in Cairo deteriorated from 90th in 2005 and 2006 to 98th in 2007. It has stagnated at around that level thereafter. The plunge in 2007 happened mainly because the wage level in Cairo fell below the wage level in the Chinese cities. As explained in Section 3.3 of Chapter 3, cities in the same country are assumed to share a common Gross Hourly Wages in USD for Ordinary Residents. Consequently, the eight Chinese cities also share the same Wages Ranking for Ordinary Residents and form a cluster on the wage ranking table. In 2007, this cluster surpassed Cairo, causing the significant drop in the latter's ranking.

Figure 5.21c

Let us now analyse the cost of living and wages indices more closely and draw conclusions about the purchasing power of ordinary residents in Cairo. As elaborated in Section 3.4.2 of Chapter 3, for a more precise and rigorous analysis, we discuss the results in two sub-periods: from 2005 to 2010 and from 2011 to 2013.

The Cost of Living Index and the Wages Index for Ordinary Residents in Cairo are represented respectively by the grey and red line in Figure 5.21c. Between 2005 and 2010, the Cost of Living Index for Ordinary Residents was on an increasing trend. In 2005, the cost of living for ordinary residents in Cairo was 17.82% of that for their counterparts in New York (the base city). It rose to 29.41% in 2010. Over the same sub-period, the Wages Index for Ordinary Residents also increased, rising from 4.92 in 2005 to 7.96 in 2010.

Wages were able to keep up with cost of living throughout the first sub-period. Thus, ordinary residents in Cairo were able to afford the same consumption level over time during these years. This is reflected in the relative stability of the Purchasing Power Index for Ordinary Residents in Cairo, which is represented by the green line in Figure 5.20c. The index only fluctuated around 27.95 over the first sub-period. Meanwhile, the Purchasing Power Ranking for Ordinary Residents in Cairo, as represented by the green bars, steadily deteriorated. It dropped to 95th in 2010 from 86th in 2005.

Over the second sub-period (2011–2013), the Cost of Living Index for Ordinary Residents has been on a decreasing trend. In 2011, the cost of living for ordinary residents in Cairo was 17.47% of that for their counterparts in New York while by 2013, it has dropped to 15.05%. In contrast, the Wages Index for Ordinary Residents has been relatively stable, fluctuating around 8.42.

The combined trends of stable wages and decreasing cost of living have enabled ordinary residents in Cairo to afford more goods and services over time during the second sub-period. This is reflected in the Purchasing Power Index for Ordinary Residents, which rose steadily from 47.79 in 2011 to 54.79 in 2013. Despite this positive showing of the index, the Purchasing Power Ranking for Ordinary Residents has declined, albeit marginally. It dropped from 79th in 2011 and 2012 to 80th in 2013.

Finally, we note that over the entire study period (2005–2013), the Purchasing Power Index for Ordinary Residents in Cairo has consistently been lower than 100.00 — the base index value. This means that ordinary residents in Cairo have only been able to afford a lower consumption level than their counterparts in New York, given the same number of working hours.

CALGARY
Canada

Figure 5.22a: Cost of Living and 10 Consumption Categories Rankings for Ordinary Residents in Calgary, Canada

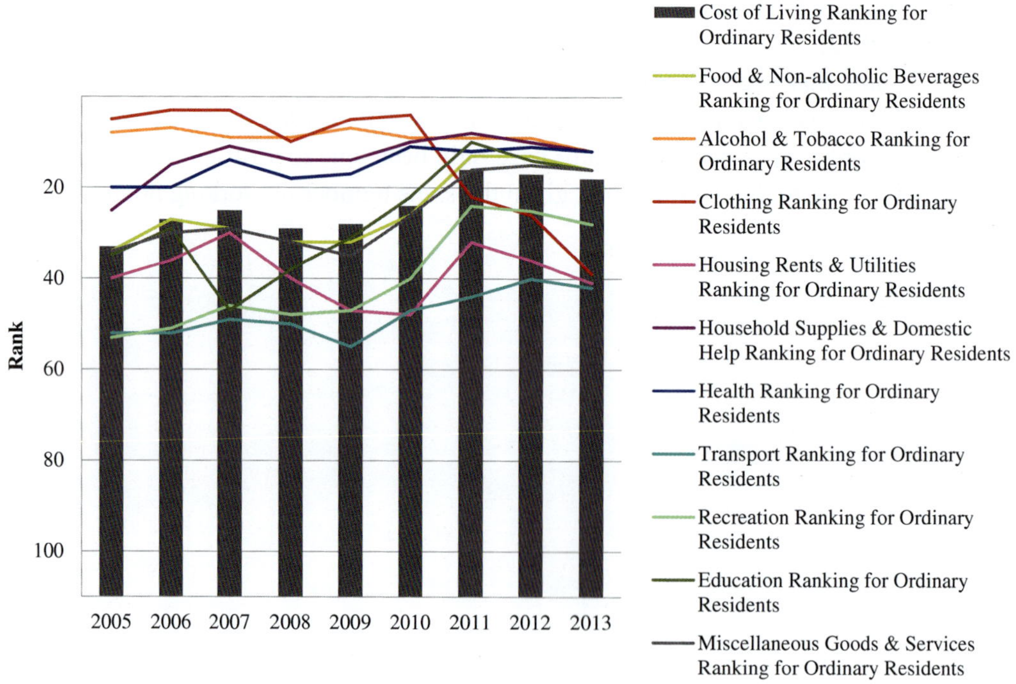

Source: Asia Competitiveness Institute

Figure 5.22b: Gross Hourly Wages in USD and Wages Ranking for Ordinary Residents in Calgary, Canada

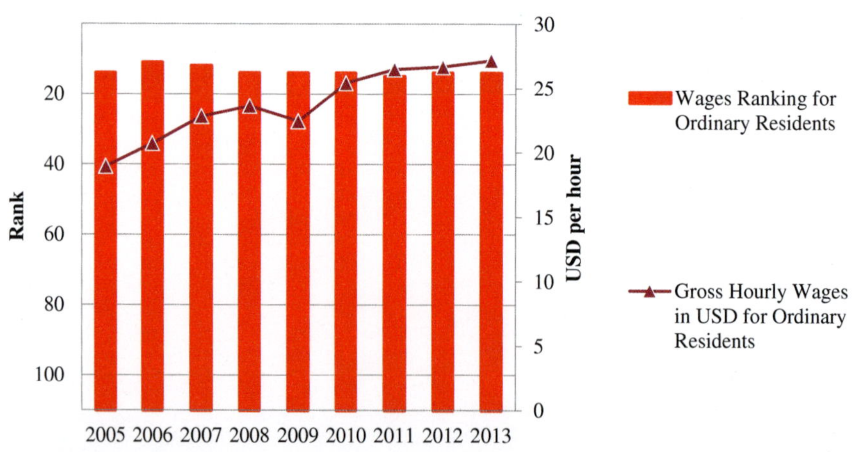

Source: Asia Competitiveness Institute

CALGARY
Canada

Figure 5.22c: Cost of Living, Wages and Purchasing Power Indices and Purchasing Power Ranking for Ordinary Residents in Calgary, Canada

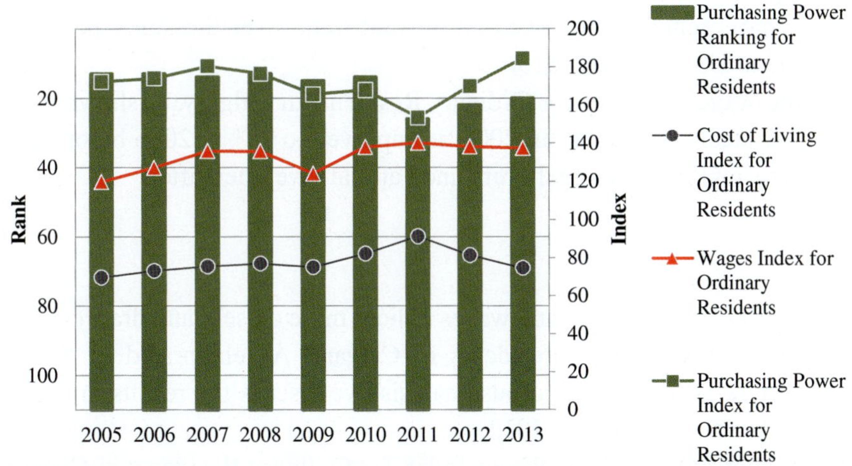

Source: Asia Competitiveness Institute

Figure 5.22a

Calgary, the largest city in the province of Alberta, is Canada's leader in the oil and gas industry. The city's Cost of Living Ranking for Ordinary Residents, as represented by the grey bars, rose from 33rd to 24th between 2005 and 2010, but fell from 16th to 18th between 2011 and 2013 (see Figure 5.22a). As elaborated in Section 3.4.2 of Chapter 3, for a more rigorous comparison of rankings, we have split the analysis into two sub-periods.

From 2005 to 2010, Housing Rents & Utilities Ranking slipped eight places from 40th to 48th. In contrast, Education Ranking jumped 13 spots from 35th in 2005 to 22nd in 2010. Health Ranking moved up nine places from 20th to 11th over the first sub-period. Food & Non-alcoholic Beverages Ranking rose from 34th in 2005 to 26th in 2010. Transport Ranking went up five spots from 52nd to 47th over the same sub-period.

Between 2011 and 2013, Transport was the only category that rose in ranking from 44th to 42nd. Nonetheless, it remained as the lowest ranked category throughout the second sub-period. Health Ranking largely remained at 12th from 2011 to 2013, making it the highest ranked category in 2013 together with Alcohol & Tobacco and Household Supplies & Domestic Help. Clothing registered the most significant dip in ranking as it fell 17 places from 22nd in 2011 to 39th in 2013. Housing Rents & Utilities Ranking slipped nine spots from 32nd to 41st over the second sub-period. Education Ranking moved down six places from 10th in 2011 to 16th in 2013. Food & Non-alcoholic Beverages Ranking declined from 13th to 16th over the same sub-period.

CALGARY
Canada

Figure 5.22b

The Gross Hourly Wages in USD for Ordinary Residents in Calgary, as denoted by the red line in Figure 5.22b, have generally followed an upward trend over the study period, rising from US$18.91 in 2005 to US$27.16 in 2013.

Meanwhile, the Wages Ranking for Ordinary Residents in Calgary, as shown by the red bars, has been relatively stable. From 14th in 2005, it improved to 11th in 2006 before dropping back to 14th in 2008. The ranking has largely remained at that level thereafter.

Figure 5.22c

Let us now analyse the cost of living and wages indices more closely and draw conclusions about the purchasing power of ordinary residents in Calgary. As elaborated in Section 3.4.2 of Chapter 3, for a more precise and rigorous analysis, we discuss the results in two sub-periods: from 2005 to 2010 and from 2011 to 2013.

The Cost of Living Index and the Wages Index for Ordinary Residents in Calgary are represented respectively by the grey and red line in Figure 5.22c. Between 2005 and 2010, the Cost of Living Index for Ordinary Residents was generally on an increasing trend. In 2005, the cost of living for ordinary residents in Calgary was 69.46% of that for their counterparts in New York. It rose to 82.10% in 2010. Over the same sub-period, the Wages Index for Ordinary Residents also increased significantly, rising from 119.76 in 2005 to 137.89 in 2010, with a one-off dip to 124.03 in 2009.

Between 2005 and 2007, wages rose faster than cost of living but thereafter, wages could not keep up with the latter. Thus, ordinary residents in Calgary were initially able to afford to consume more goods and services over time but could no longer do so after 2007. These trends are fully reflected in the Purchasing Power Index for Ordinary Residents in Calgary, which is represented by the green line in Figure 5.22c. The index increased from 172.42 in 2005 to its peak at 180.46 in 2007 and then steadily declined until it reached 137.89 in 2010. Meanwhile, the Purchasing Power Ranking for Ordinary Residents in Calgary, as represented by the green bars, remained rather stable. It only fluctuated between 13th and 15th over the sub-period.

Over the second sub-period (2011–2013), the Cost of Living Index for Ordinary Residents has been on a decreasing trend. In 2011, the cost of living for ordinary residents in Calgary was 91.17% of that for their counterparts in New York while in 2013, it dropped to 74.47%. The Wages Index for Ordinary Residents has also been on a mild decline, dropping to 137.38 in 2013 from 140.07 in 2011.

Wages declined at a slower rate than cost of living so throughout the second sub-period, ordinary residents in Calgary have been able to afford more goods and services over time. This is reflected in the Purchasing Power Index for Ordinary Residents which rose steadily from 153.64 in 2011 to 184.47 in 2013. The Purchasing Power Ranking for Ordinary Residents has also improved over time, rising from 26th in 2011 to 20th in 2013.

Finally, we note that over the entire study period (2005–2013), the Purchasing Power Index for Ordinary Residents in Calgary has always been above 100.00 — the base index value. This means that ordinary residents in Calgary have consistently been able to afford to consume more goods and services than their counterparts in New York, given the same number of working hours.

CARACAS
Venezuela

Figure 5.23a: Cost of Living and 10 Consumption Categories Rankings for Ordinary Residents in Caracas, Venezuela

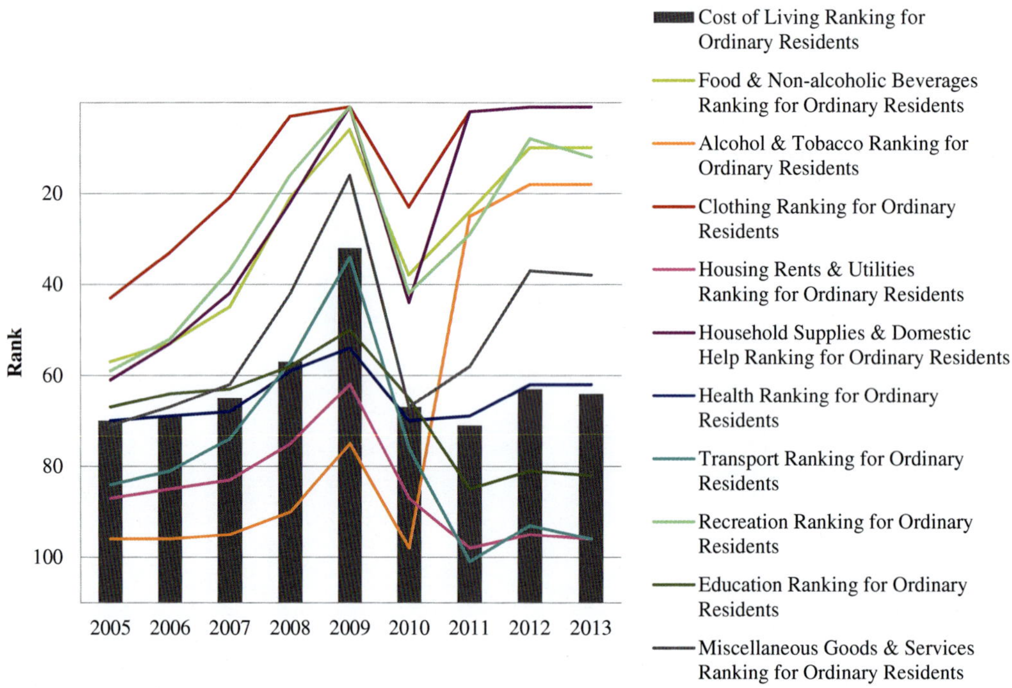

Source: Asia Competitiveness Institute

Figure 5.23b: Gross Hourly Wages in USD and Wages Ranking for Ordinary Residents in Caracas, Venezuela

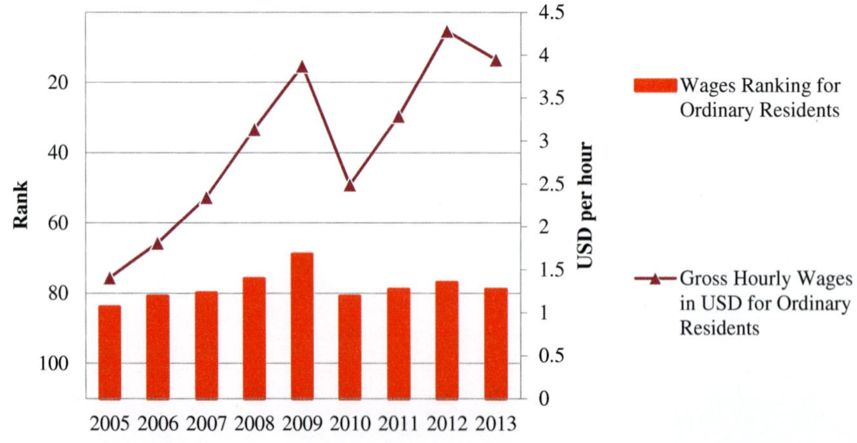

Source: Asia Competitiveness Institute

CARACAS
Venezuela

Figure 5.23c: Cost of Living, Wages and Purchasing Power Indices and Purchasing Power Ranking for Ordinary Residents in Caracas, Venezuela

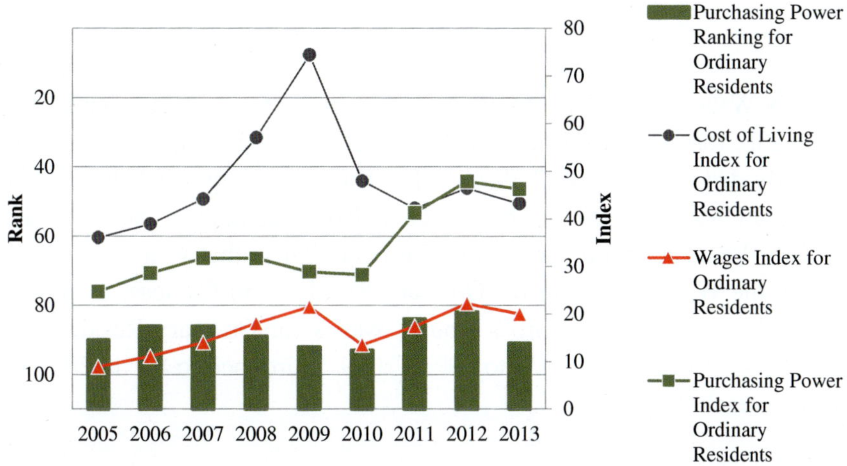

Source: Asia Competitiveness Institute

Figure 5.23a

Located in the northern part of the country, Caracas is the capital and the largest city of Venezuela. The city's Cost of Living Ranking for Ordinary Residents, as shown in the grey bars, rose from 70th to 67th between 2005 and 2010, and from 71st to 64th between 2011 and 2013 (see Figure 5.23a). As explained in Section 3.4.2 of Chapter 3, for a more precise comparison of rankings, we have split the analysis into two sub-periods.

From 2005 to 2010, Clothing registered the most significant rise in ranking as it climbed 20 places from 43rd to 23rd. Food & Non-alcoholic Beverages Ranking jumped 19 spots from 57th in 2005 to 38th in 2010. Household Supplies & Domestic Help and Recreation Rankings both moved up 17 places from 61st to 44th and 59th to 42nd, respectively, over the first sub-period. Transport Ranking rose from 84th in 2005 to 76th in 2010. Education Ranking jumped two spots from 67th to 65th between 2005 and 2010. Housing Rents & Utilities and Health Rankings remained at 87th and 70th, respectively, over the same sub-period.

The rankings of all 10 categories went up over the second sub-period between 2011 and 2013. In particular, Food & Non-alcoholic Beverages Ranking jumped 14 places from 24th in 2011 to 10th in 2013. Transport Ranking moved up five spots from 101st to 96th over the same sub-period. Education Ranking rose from 85th to 82nd between 2011 and 2013. Housing Rents & Utilities Ranking jumped two places from 98th in 2011 to 96th in 2013, making it the lowest ranked category in 2013 together with Transport. Clothing and Household Supplies & Domestic Help

CARACAS
Venezuela

Rankings both moved up one spot from second to first over the second sub-period. Caracas therefore became the most expensive city in these categories in 2013.

Figure 5.23b

The Gross Hourly Wages in USD for Ordinary Residents in Caracas, as represented by the red line in Figure 5.23b, rose steadily from US$1.41 in 2005 to US$3.88 in 2009. Caracas's wage level then abruptly dropped to US$ 2.49 in 2010. The increasing trend then resumed and the wage level reached US$3.95 in 2013. The plunge in 2010 was mainly caused by the significant depreciation of the Venezuelan bolivar against the US dollar in that year.

Ranking-wise, the Wages Ranking for Ordinary Residents in Caracas, as shown by the red bars, has mirrored the trend of the Gross Hourly Wages for Ordinary Residents. The ranking improved consistently from 84th in 2005 to 69th in 2009. It dropped to 81st in 2010 before beginning to recover to reach 79th in 2013.

Figure 5.23c

Let us now analyse the cost of living and wages indices more closely and draw conclusions about the purchasing power of ordinary residents in Caracas. As elaborated in Section 3.4.2 of Chapter 3, for a more precise and rigorous analysis, we discuss the results in two sub-periods: from 2005 to 2010 and from 2011 to 2013.

The Cost of Living Index and the Wages Index for Ordinary Residents in Caracas are represented respectively by the grey and red line in Figure 5.23c. Between 2005 and 2010, the Cost of Living Index for Ordinary Residents exhibited drastic fluctuations. In 2005, the cost of living of ordinary residents in Caracas was 36.06% of that for ordinary residents in New York (the base city). It increased considerably to 74.40% in 2009 before dropping sharply to 47.93% in 2010. The Wages Index for Ordinary Residents also followed a similar pattern, rising from 8.90 in 2005 to 21.44 in 2009 before plunging to 13.51 in 2010. The drastic drops in the cost of living and wages indices were mainly due to extreme exchange rate fluctuations. Between 2009 and 2010, the Venezuelan bolivar depreciated by about 50% against the US dollar. Thus, upon being converted to US dollars, Venezuelan prices and wage levels became drastically lower than they would have been under normal circumstances. The wage and cost of living indices are built on converted wages and prices levels so the indices for Caracas in 2010 picked up this abnormal decline.

Wages grew faster than cost of living between 2005 and 2008 but thereafter, wages could not keep up with the latter. This means that over the first sub-period, ordinary residents in Caracas were initially able to consume more goods and services over time but they could no longer do so after 2008. These trends are reflected in the Purchasing Power Index for Ordinary Residents in Caracas, which is represented by the green line in Figure 5.22c. From 24.69 in 2005, the index rose steadily to 31.65 in 2008 and then began to decline until it reached 28.19 in 2010. Meanwhile, the Purchasing Power Ranking for Ordinary Residents in Caracas, which is represented by the green bars, fluctuated substantially. From 90th in 2005, it first rose to 86th in 2007 and then declined until it reached 93rd in 2010.

Over the second sub-period (2011–2013), the Cost of Living Index for Ordinary Residents has also fluctuated substantially. In 2011, the cost of living for ordinary residents in Caracas was 42.17% of that for their counterparts in New York. This rose to peak at 46.38% in 2012 before declining slightly to 43.19% in 2013. The Wages Index for Ordinary Residents has also followed a similar pattern, rising from 17.40 in 2011 to 22.18 in 2012 before dropping back to 19.97 in 2013.

The Purchasing Power Index for Ordinary Residents in Caracas has fluctuated in the same manner as the cost of living and wages indices. It rose from 41.27 in 2011 to 47.83 in 2012 and then decreased marginally to 46.25 in 2013. That the purchasing power index was higher in 2013 than it was in 2011 indicates that ordinary residents in Caracas have been able to afford a higher consumption level over time during the second sub-period. Ranking-wise, the Purchasing Power Ranking for Caracas also fluctuated substantially. It first improved from 84th to 82nd between 2011 and 2012 but plunged to 91st in 2013.

Finally, we note that throughout the study period (2005–2013), the Purchasing Power Index for Ordinary Residents in Caracas has always been below 100.00 — the base index value. This means that ordinary residents in Caracas have only been able to afford a lower consumption level than their counterparts in New York, given the same number of working hours.

CHICAGO
United States

Figure 5.24a: Cost of Living and 10 Consumption Categories Rankings for Ordinary Residents in Chicago, United States

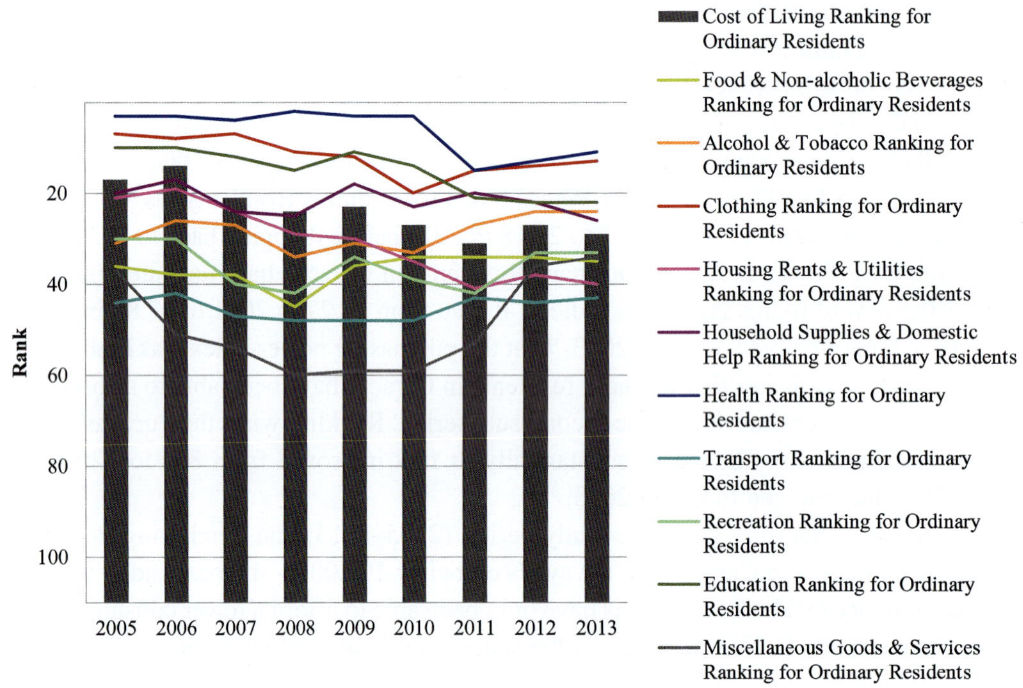

Source: Asia Competitiveness Institute

Figure 5.24b: Gross Hourly Wages in USD and Wages Ranking for Ordinary Residents in Chicago, United States

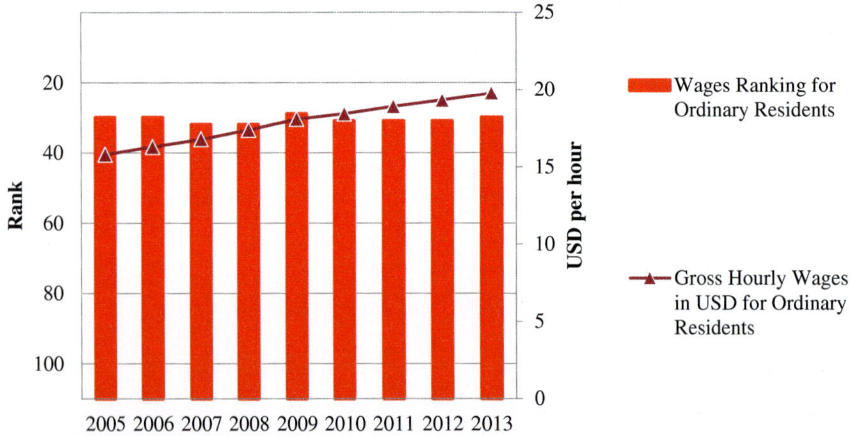

Source: Asia Competitiveness Institute

CHICAGO
United States

Figure 5.24c: Cost of Living, Wages and Purchasing Power Indices and Purchasing Power Ranking for Ordinary Residents in Chicago, United States

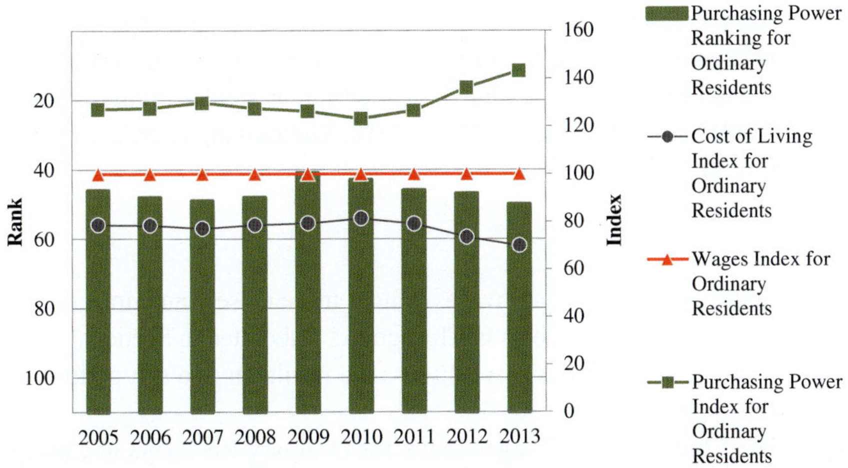

Source: Asia Competitiveness Institute

Figure 5.24a

Chicago, the most populous city of the state of Illinois, is widely known for its cultural heritage in terms of music genres, particularly blues, soul and house music. The city's Cost of Living Ranking for Ordinary Residents, as denoted by the grey bars, declined from 17th to 27th between 2005 and 2010, but rose from 31st to 29th between 2011 and 2013 (see Figure 5.24a). As elaborated in Section 3.4.2 of Chapter 3, for a more rigorous comparison of rankings, we have split the analysis into two sub-periods.

From 2005 to 2010, Food & Non-alcoholic Beverages was the only category that rose in ranking from 36th to 34th. Housing Rents & Utilities Ranking fell 14 places from 21st in 2005 to 35th in 2010. Education and Transport Rankings both moved down four spots from 10th to 14th and 44th to 48th, respectively, over the first sub-period. Health Ranking remained largely at third between 2005 and 2010.

Between 2011 and 2013, Miscellaneous Goods & Services saw the most significant rise in ranking as it climbed 19 places from 53rd to 34th. Health became the highest ranked category since 2012 as its ranking jumped four spots from 15th to 11th. Housing Rents & Utilities Ranking moved up one place from 41st in 2011 to 40th in 2013. In contrast, Household Supplies & Domestic Help Ranking fell six places from 20th to 26th over the second sub-period. Food & Non-alcoholic Beverages and Education Rankings both slipped one spot from 34th to 35th and 21st to 22nd, respectively, between 2011 and 2013. Transport Ranking largely stayed at 43rd from 2011 to 2013, making it the lowest ranked category in 2012 and 2013.

CHICAGO
United States

Figure 5.24b

The Gross Hourly Wages in USD for Ordinary Residents in Chicago, as represented by the red line in Figure 5.24b, increased gradually from US$15.79 in 2005 to US$19.77 in 2013.

Despite the consistent increase in the wage level, the Wages Ranking for Ordinary Residents in Chicago, as depicted by the red bars, has remained rather stable. From 30th in 2005, it rose slightly to 29th in 2009 before dropping to 31st in 2010. The ranking remained at 31st until 2013, when it rose back to 30th.

Figure 5.24c

Let us now analyse the cost of living and wages indices more closely and draw conclusions about the purchasing power of ordinary residents in Chicago. As elaborated in Section 3.4.2 of Chapter 3, for a more precise and rigorous analysis, we discuss the results in two sub-periods: from 2005 to 2010 and from 2011 to 2013.

The Cost of Living Index and the Wages Index for Ordinary Residents in Chicago are represented respectively by the grey and red line in Figure 5.24c. As mentioned in Section 3.3 of Chapter 3, wage data are only available at the national level and not by cities. Therefore, wages in all cities in the United States are assumed to be the same. As a result, Chicago, being a city in the United States, shares a common Wages Index for Ordinary Residents with the base city New York (whose index value is 100.00) over the entire study period (2005–2013).

Between 2005 and 2010, the Cost of Living Index for Ordinary Residents in Chicago was on a slight increasing trend. In 2005, the cost of living for ordinary residents in Chicago was about 78.73% of that for ordinary residents in New York. It climbed to 81.31% in 2010 while also exhibiting marginal fluctuations in between. Since the Wages Index for Ordinary Residents is constant across the years, the Purchasing Power Index for Ordinary Residents in Chicago (or any other cities in the United States) depends only on variations in the Cost of Living Index for Ordinary Residents. Thus, the marginal upward trend of the latter caused the Purchasing Power Index for Ordinary Residents, which is represented by the green line in Figure 5.24c, to generally decrease over the first sub-period. From 127.01 in 2005, the index dropped to 122.99 in 2010. Meanwhile, the Purchasing Power Ranking for Ordinary Residents in Chicago, as represented by the green bars, fluctuated moderately. Overall, Chicago's ranking in 2010 (43rd) was higher than it was in 2005 (46th).

Over the second sub-period (2011–2013), the Cost of Living for Ordinary Residents has steadily declined. In 2011, the cost of living for ordinary residents in Chicago was 79.08% of that for their counterparts in New York. It dropped to 69.86% in 2013. As a result, the Purchasing Power Index for Ordinary Residents in Chicago has been increasing, rising from 126.45 to 143.14 between 2011 and 2013. Ranking-wise, the Purchasing Power Ranking for Ordinary Residents in Chicago has actually deteriorated from 46th in 2011 to 50th in 2013.

Finally, we note that over the entire study period (2005–2013), the Purchasing Power Index for Ordinary Residents in Chicago has always been above 100.00 — the base index value. Thus, ordinary residents in Chicago have consistently been able to afford more goods and services than their counterparts in New York, given the same number of working hours.

CLEVELAND
United States

Figure 5.25a: Cost of Living and 10 Consumption Categories Rankings for Ordinary Residents in Cleveland, United States

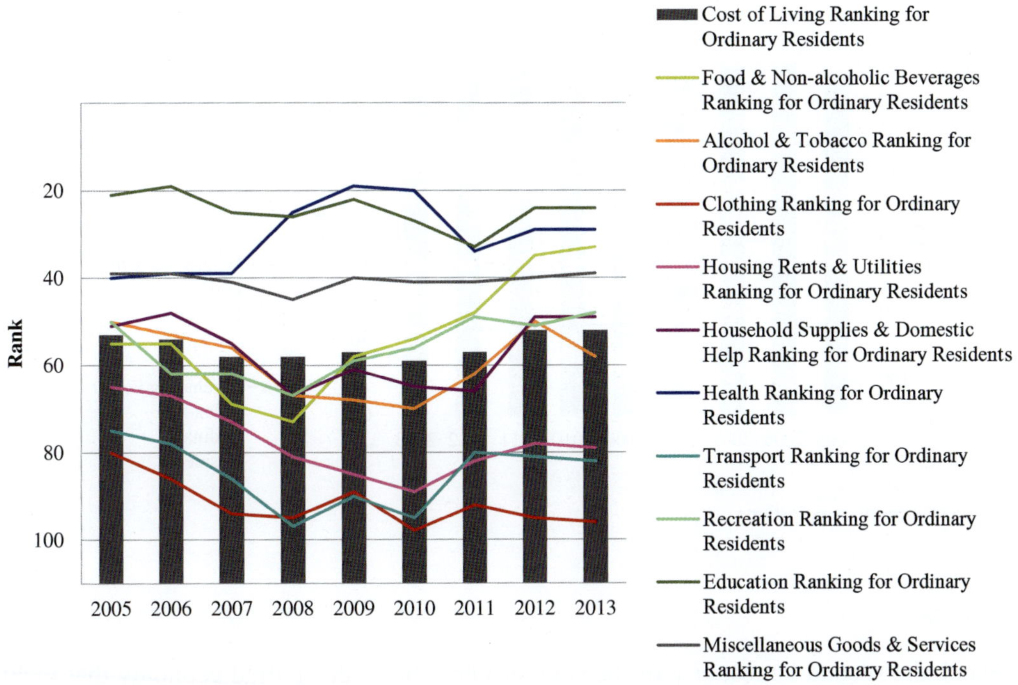

Source: Asia Competitiveness Institute

Figure 5.25b: Gross Hourly Wages in USD and Wages Ranking for Ordinary Residents in Cleveland, United States

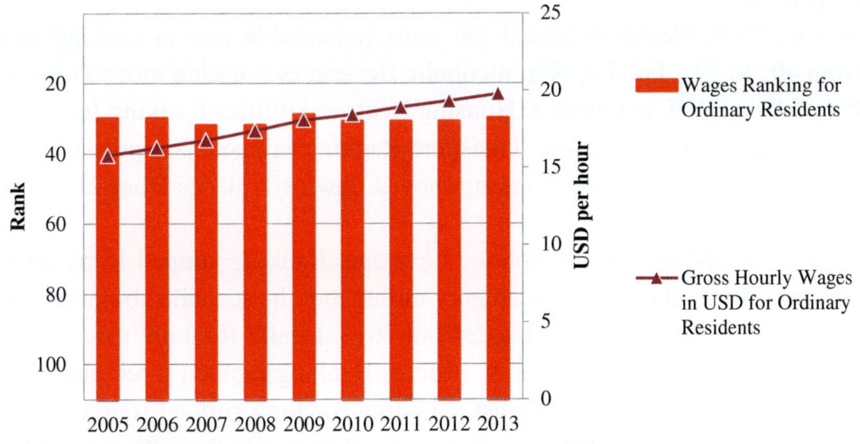

Source: Asia Competitiveness Institute

CLEVELAND
United States

Figure 5.25c: Cost of Living, Wages and Purchasing Power Indices and Purchasing Power Ranking for Ordinary Residents in Cleveland, United States

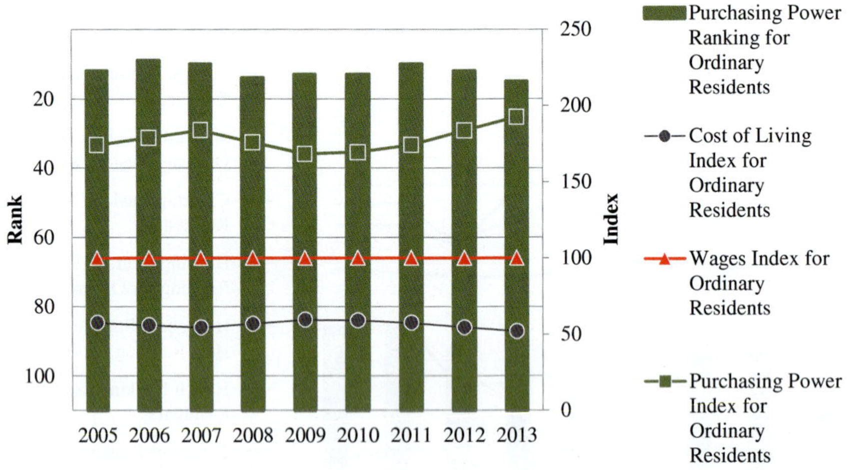

Source: Asia Competitiveness Institute

Figure 5.25a

Cleveland, the second largest city of the state of Ohio, has a diversified economy that includes manufacturing, financial services, biomedical and healthcare. The city's Cost of Living Ranking for Ordinary Residents, as represented by the grey bars, fell from 53rd to 59th between 2005 and 2010, but rose from 57th to 52nd between 2011 and 2013 (see Figure 5.25a). As explained in Section 3.4.2 of Chapter 3, for a more precise comparison of rankings, we have split the analysis into two sub-periods.

From 2005 to 2010, Health recorded the most remarkable rise in ranking as it climbed 20 places from 40th to 20th. Food & Non-alcoholic Beverages Ranking moved up one spot from 55th in 2005 to 54th in 2010. In contrast, Housing Rents & Utilities Ranking fell 24 places from 65th to 89th over the first sub-period. Transport Ranking slipped 20 spots from 75th to 95th between 2005 and 2010. Education Ranking moved down six places from 21st in 2005 to 27th in 2010.

From 2011 to 2013, Food & Non-alcoholic Beverages Ranking jumped 15 places from 48th to 33rd. Education was the highest ranked category throughout the second sub-period as its ranking moved up nine spots from 33rd in 2011 to 24th in 2013. Health Ranking rose from 34th to 29th between 2011 and 2013. Housing Rents & Utilities Ranking jumped three places from 82nd to 79th over the second sub-period. In contrast, Clothing Ranking slipped four spots from 92nd in 2011 to 96th in 2013, making it the lowest ranked category for the entire second sub-period. Transport Ranking fell two places from 80th to 82nd over the same sub-period.

CLEVELAND
United States

Figure 5.25b

The Gross Hourly Wages in USD for Ordinary Residents in Cleveland, as represented by the red line in Figure 5.25b, have been increasing over the study period. From US$15.79 in 2005, Cleveland's wage level rose to US$19.77 in 2013.

Despite the consistent increase in the wage level, the Wages Ranking for Ordinary Residents in Cleveland, as depicted by the red bars, has remained rather stable. From 30th in 2005, it rose slightly to 29th in 2009 before dropping to 31st in 2010. The ranking remained at 31st until 2013, when it rose back to 30th.

Figure 5.25c

Let us now analyse the cost of living and wages indices more closely and draw conclusions about the purchasing power of ordinary residents in Cleveland. As elaborated in Section 3.4.2 of Chapter 3, for a more precise and rigorous analysis, we discuss the results in two sub-periods: from 2005 to 2010 and from 2011 to 2013.

The Cost of Living Index and the Wages Index for Ordinary Residents in Cleveland are represented respectively by the grey and red line in Figure 5.25c. As mentioned in Section 3.3 of Chapter 3, wage data are only available at the national level and not by cities. Therefore, wages in all cities in the United States are assumed to be the same. As a result, Cleveland, being a city in the United States, shares a common Wages Index for Ordinary Residents with the base city New York (whose index value is 100.00) over the entire study period (2005–2013).

Between 2005 and 2010, the Cost of Living Index for Ordinary Residents in Cleveland was on a slight increasing trend. In 2005, the cost of living for ordinary residents in Cleveland was about 57.46% of that for ordinary residents in New York. In 2010, it climbed to 59.05% while also exhibiting marginal fluctuations in between. Since the Wages Index for Ordinary Residents is constant across the years, the Purchasing Power Index for Ordinary Residents in Cleveland (or any other cities in the United States) depends only on variations in the Cost of Living Index for Ordinary Residents. Thus, the upward trend of the latter caused the Purchasing Power Index for Ordinary Residents, which is represented by the green line in Figure 5.25c, to generally decrease over the first sub-period. From 174.03 in 2005, the index dropped to 169.36 in 2010. Meanwhile, the Purchasing Power Ranking for Ordinary Residents in Cleveland, as represented by the green bars, also dropped slightly from 12th in 2005 to 13th in 2010.

Over the second sub-period (2011–2013), the Cost of Living for Ordinary Residents has steadily declined. In 2011, the cost of living for ordinary residents in Cleveland was 57.43% of that for their counterparts in New York. It dropped to 51.97% in 2013. As a result, the Purchasing Power Index for Ordinary Residents in Cleveland has been increasing, rising from 174.12 in

CLEVELAND
United States

2011 to 192.43 in 2013. Despite this positive showing of the index, the Purchasing Power Ranking for Ordinary Residents in Cleveland has been deteriorating. Between 2011 and 2013, it dropped from 10th to 15th.

Finally, we note that over the entire study period (2005–2013), the Purchasing Power Index for Ordinary Residents in Cleveland has always been above 100.00 — the base index value. Thus, ordinary residents in Cleveland have consistently been able to afford more goods and services than their counterparts in New York, given the same number of working hours.

COLOMBO
Sri Lanka

Figure 5.26a: Cost of Living and 10 Consumption Categories Rankings for Ordinary Residents in Colombo, Sri Lanka

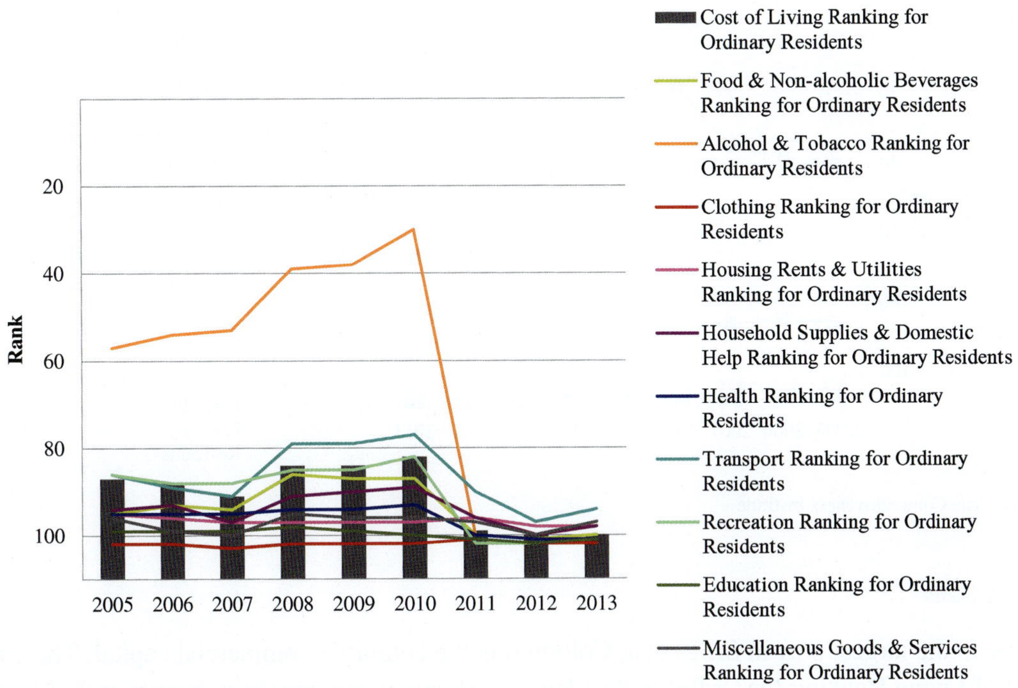

Source: Asia Competitiveness Institute

Figure 5.26b: Gross Hourly Wages in USD and Wages Ranking for Ordinary Residents in Colombo, Sri Lanka

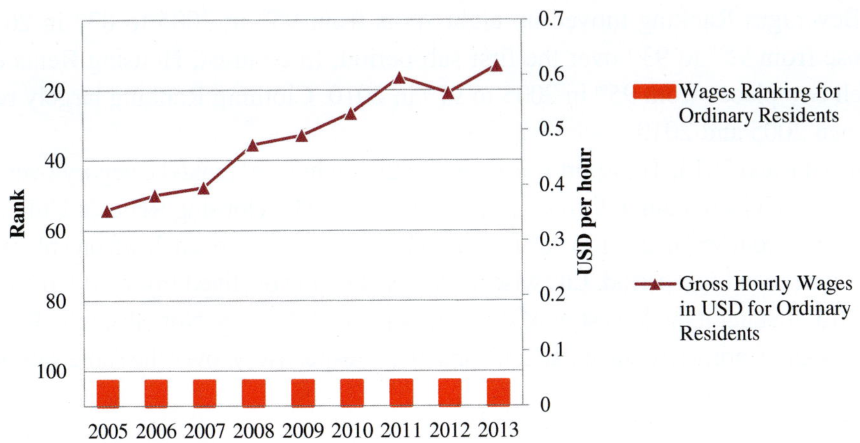

Source: Asia Competitiveness Institute

COLOMBO
Sri Lanka

Figure 5.26c: Cost of Living, Wages and Purchasing Power Indices and Purchasing Power Ranking for Ordinary Residents in Colombo, Sri Lanka

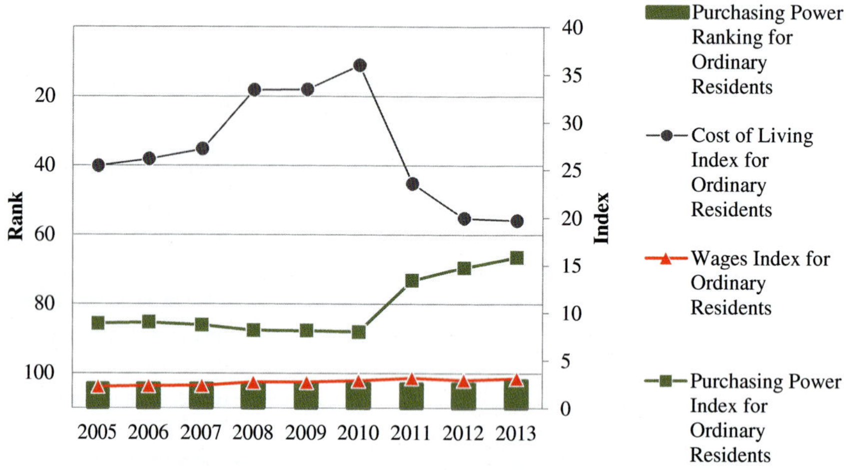

Source: Asia Competitiveness Institute

Figure 5.26a

Home to the largest port in Sri Lanka, Colombo is the country's commercial capital. The city's Cost of Living Ranking for Ordinary Residents, as shown in the grey bars, rose from 87th to 82nd between 2005 and 2010, but fell from 99th to 100th between 2011 and 2013 (see Figure 5.26a). As elaborated in Section 3.4.2 of Chapter 3, for a more rigorous comparison of rankings, we have split the analysis into two sub-periods.

From 2005 to 2010, Transport Ranking jumped nine places from 86th to 77th. Food & Non-alcoholic Beverages Ranking moved up eight spots from 95th in 2005 to 87th in 2010. Health Ranking rose from 95th to 93rd over the first sub-period. In contrast, Housing Rents & Utilities Ranking fell two places from 95th in 2005 to 97th in 2010. Clothing Ranking largely remained at 102nd between 2005 and 2010.

Between 2011 and 2013, Transport was consistently the highest ranked category over the second sub-period although its ranking fell four places from 90th to 94th. Housing Rents & Utilities Ranking slipped two spots from 96th in 2011 to 98th in 2013. Health Ranking moved down one place from 100th to 101st over the second sub-period. Likewise, Clothing Ranking declined from 101st to 102nd between 2011 and 2013, making it the lowest ranked category in 2013. Food & Non-alcoholic Beverages and Education Rankings primarily stayed at 100th and 101st, respectively, over the same sub-period.

Figure 5.26b

The Gross Hourly Wages in USD for Ordinary Residents in Colombo, as denoted by the red line in Figure 5.26b, have been increasing over the study period. From US$0.36 in 2005, Colombo's wage level grew steadily to US$0.62 in 2013.

COLOMBO
Sri Lanka

Despite the growth in wages, the Wages Ranking for Ordinary Residents in Colombo, as depicted by the red bars, has remained at the bottom out of the 103 cities in our study throughout 2005–2013.

Figure 5.26c

Let us now analyse the cost of living and wages indices more closely and draw conclusions about the purchasing power of ordinary residents in Colombo. As elaborated in Section 3.4.2 of Chapter 3, for a more precise and rigorous analysis, we discuss the results in two sub-periods: from 2005 to 2010 and from 2011 to 2013.

The Cost of Living Index and the Wages Index for Ordinary Residents in Colombo are represented respectively by the grey and red line in Figure 5.26c. Between 2005 and 2010, the Cost of Living Index for Ordinary Residents was on an increasing trend. In 2005, the cost of living for ordinary residents in Colombo was 25.39% of that for their counterparts in New York (the base city). It rose significantly to 35.98% in 2010. Over the same sub-period, the Wages Index for Ordinary Residents also increased but at a slower pace. The index marginally rose from 2.25 in 2005 to 2.28 in 2010.

Since wages grew slower than cost of living over the first sub-period, ordinary residents in Colombo could not maintain the same consumption level over time during these years. This is reflected in Purchasing Power Index for Ordinary Residents in Colombo, which is represented by the green line in Figure 5.26c. The index steadily declined from 8.86 in 2005 to 7.99 in 2010. Meanwhile, the Purchasing Power Ranking for Ordinary Residents in Colombo, as represented by the green bars, was stable. It remained at 103rd over the first sub-period.

Over the second sub-period (2011–2013), the Cost of Living Index for Ordinary Residents has been on a decreasing trend. In 2011, the cost of living for ordinary residents in Colombo was 23.55% of that for their counterparts in New York. It dropped to 19.69% in 2013. In contrast, the Wages Index for Ordinary Residents has been relatively stable, fluctuating around 3.07.

The combined trends of stable wages and decreasing cost of living have enabled ordinary residents in Colombo to afford more goods and services over time throughout the second sub-period. This is reflected in the Purchasing Power Index for Ordinary Residents which steadily increased from 13.38 in 2011 to 15.85 in 2013. The Purchasing Power Ranking for Ordinary Residents has also improved, albeit very marginally. It rose from 103rd in 2011 and 2012 to 102nd in 2013.

Finally, we note that over the entire study period (2005–2013), the Purchasing Power Index for Ordinary Residents in Colombo has consistently been lower than 100.00 — the base index value. This means that ordinary residents in Colombo have only been able to afford fewer goods and services than their counterparts in New York, given the same number of working hours.

COPENHAGEN
Denmark

Figure 5.27a: Cost of Living and 10 Consumption Categories Rankings for Ordinary Residents in Copenhagen, Denmark

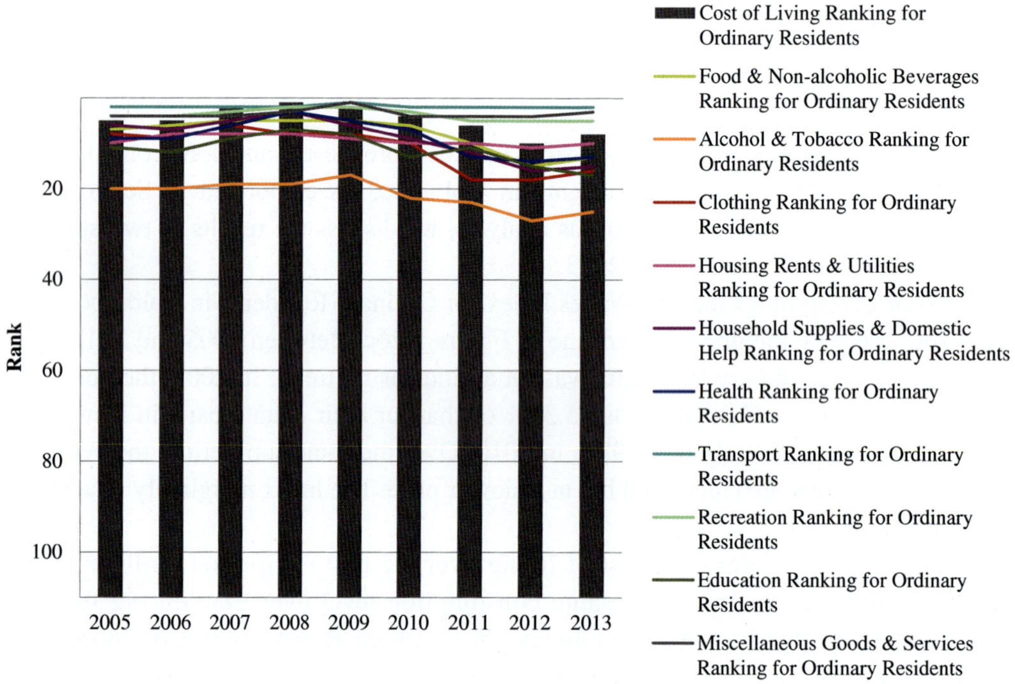

Source: Asia Competitiveness Institute

Figure 5.27b: Gross Hourly Wages in USD and Wages Ranking for Ordinary Residents in Copenhagen, Denmark

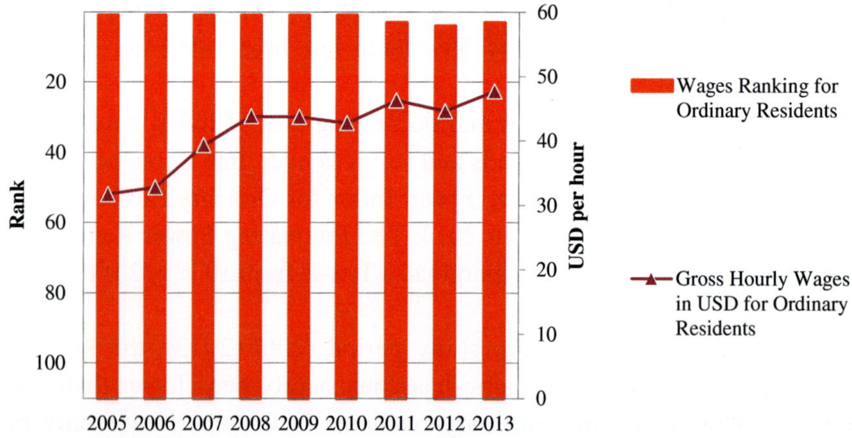

Source: Asia Competitiveness Institute

COPENHAGEN
Denmark

Figure 5.27c: Cost of Living, Wages and Purchasing Power Indices and Purchasing Power Ranking for Ordinary Residents in Copenhagen, Denmark

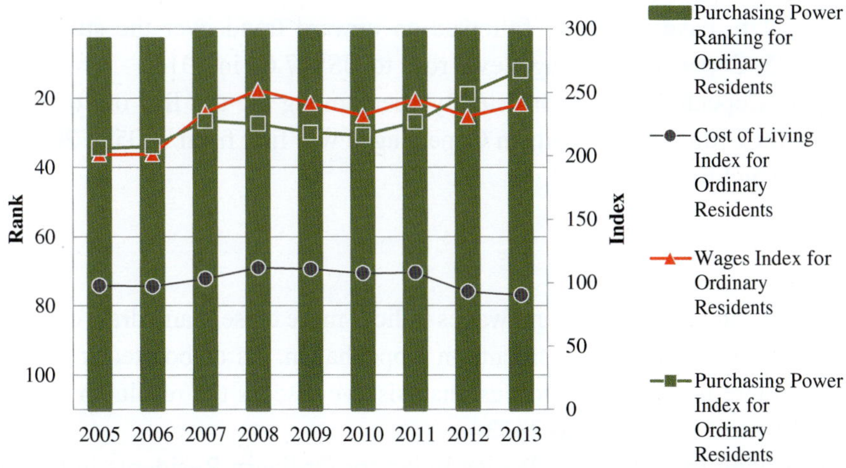

Source: Asia Competitiveness Institute

Figure 5.27a

Known as one of the most bicycle-friendly cities in the world, Copenhagen has been the capital of Denmark since the 15th century. The city's Cost of Living Ranking for Ordinary Residents, as denoted by the grey bars, rose from fifth to fourth between 2005 and 2010, but fell from sixth to eighth between 2011 and 2013 (see Figure 5.27a). As explained in Section 3.4.2 of Chapter 3, for a more precise comparison of rankings, we have split the analysis into two sub-periods.

In the first sub-period from 2005 to 2010, Education Ranking slipped two places from 11th to 13th. Transport and Housing Rents & Utilities Rankings remained at second and 10th, respectively, between 2005 and 2010. In contrast, Health Ranking moved up two spots from ninth in 2005 to seventh in 2011. Food & Non-alcoholic Beverages Ranking jumped one place from seventh to sixth over the first sub-period.

In the second sub-period between 2011 and 2013, Education Ranking fell six places from 11th to 17th. Food & Non-alcoholic Beverages and Household Supplies & Domestic Help Rankings both slipped three spots from 10th to 13th and 12th to 15th, respectively, over the second sub-period. Housing Rents & Utilities and Health Rankings stayed largely unchanged at 10th and 13th, respectively, between 2011 and 2013. Likewise, Transport remained as the highest ranked category from 2011 to 2013 as its ranking remained at second, making Copenhagen the second most expensive city in this category in the second sub-period. Alcohol & Tobacco was consistently the lowest ranked category in both sub-periods as its ranking fell from 20th in 2005 to 22nd in 2010, and 23rd in 2011 to 25th in 2013.

COPENHAGEN
Denmark

Figure 5.27b

The Gross Hourly Wages in USD for Ordinary Residents in Copenhagen, as shown by the red line in Figure 5.27b, have generally followed an upward trend over the study period. From US$31.72 in 2005, Copenhagen's wage level rose to US$47.65 in 2013.

Ranking-wise, Copenhagen has consistently been among the top five out of 103 cities. The Wages Ranking for Ordinary Residents in Copenhagen was first from 2005 to 2010. It was third in 2011 and 2013 and fourth in 2012.

Figure 5.27c

Let us now analyse the cost of living and wages indices more closely and draw conclusions about the purchasing power of ordinary residents in Copenhagen. As elaborated in Section 3.4.2 of Chapter 3, for a more precise and rigorous analysis, we discuss the results in two sub-periods: from 2005 to 2010 and from 2011 to 2013.

The Cost of Living Index and the Wages Index for Ordinary Residents in Copenhagen are represented respectively by the grey and red line in Figure 5.27c. Between 2005 and 2010, the Cost of Living Index for Ordinary Residents exhibited moderate fluctuations. In 2005, the cost of living for ordinary residents in Copenhagen was 97.59% of that for their counterparts in New York (the base city). It rose steadily to peak at 111.71% in 2008 and began to decline until it reached 107.26% in 2010. Over the same sub-period, the Wages Index for Ordinary Residents also followed a similar pattern. The index rose from 200.90 in 2005 to peak at 251.78 in 2008 before declining to reach 231.79 in 2010, a level that was still higher than its initial value in 2005.

Between 2005 and 2008, wages rose faster than cost of living. However, between 2008 and 2010 when both were falling, wages fell faster than the latter. Thus, ordinary residents in Copenhagen were able to afford a higher level of consumption over time between 2005 and 2008 but could not do so thereafter. These trends are reflected in the Purchasing Power Index for Ordinary Residents, which is represented by the green line in Figure 5.27c. From 205.85 in 2005, the index rose to 225.39 in 2008. It then embarked on a decreasing trend until it reached 216.10 in 2010. Meanwhile, the Purchasing Power Ranking for Ordinary Residents in Copenhagen, as represented by the green bars, improved from third in 2005 to first in 2007 and remained at first thereafter.

Over the second sub-period (2011–2013), the Cost of Living Index for Ordinary Residents has been on a decreasing trend. In 2011, the cost of living for ordinary residents in Copenhagen was 107.95% of that for their counterparts in New York. It dropped to 90.23% in 2013. The Wages Index for Ordinary Residents has also decreased, dropping to 241.05 in 2013 from 244.62 in 2011 with a dip to 230.89 in 2012.

COPENHAGEN
Denmark

Wages have declined at a slower rate than cost of living. Thus, during the second sub-period, ordinary residents in Copenhagen have been able to afford more goods and services over time. This is reflected in the Purchasing Power Index for Ordinary Residents which increased from 226.61 in 2011 to 267.16 in 2013. Ranking-wise, the Purchasing Power Ranking for Ordinary Residents has remained first throughout the second sub-period.

Finally, we note that over the entire study period (2005–2013), the Purchasing Power Index for Ordinary Residents in Copenhagen has always been higher than 100.00 — the base index value. This means that ordinary residents in Copenhagen have consistently been able to afford to consume more goods and services than their counterparts in New York, given the same number of working hours.

DALIAN
China

Figure 5.28a: Cost of Living and 10 Consumption Categories Rankings for Ordinary Residents in Dalian, China

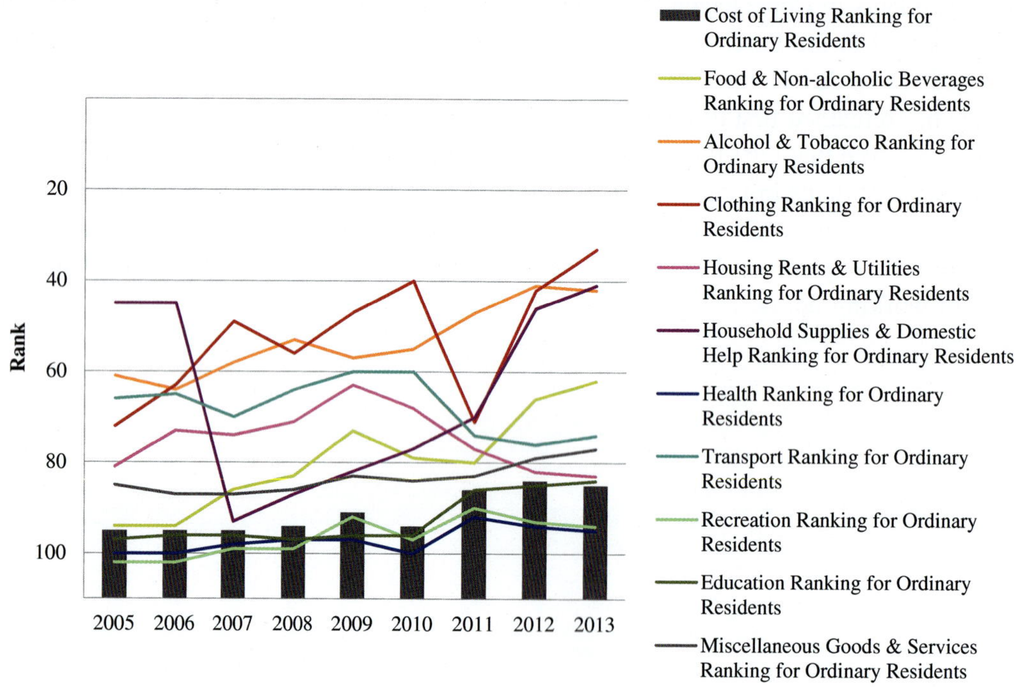

Source: Asia Competitiveness Institute

Figure 5.28b: Gross Hourly Wages in USD and Wages Ranking for Ordinary Residents in Dalian, China

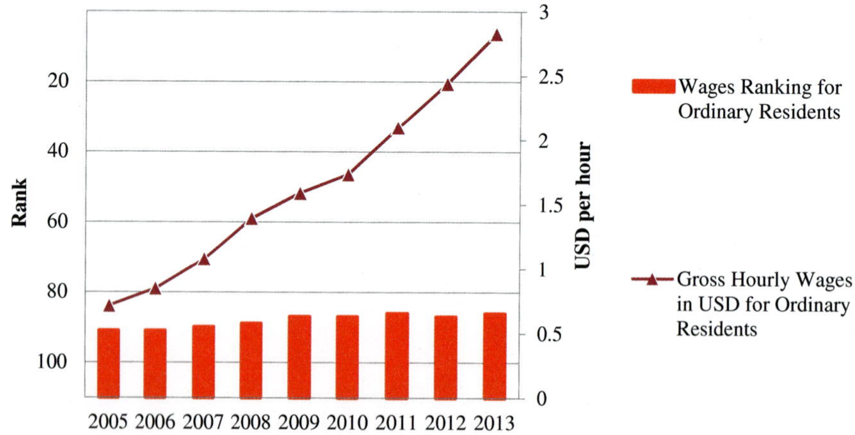

Source: Asia Competitiveness Institute

DALIAN
China

Figure 5.28c: Cost of Living, Wages and Purchasing Power Indices and Purchasing Power Ranking for Ordinary Residents in Dalian, China

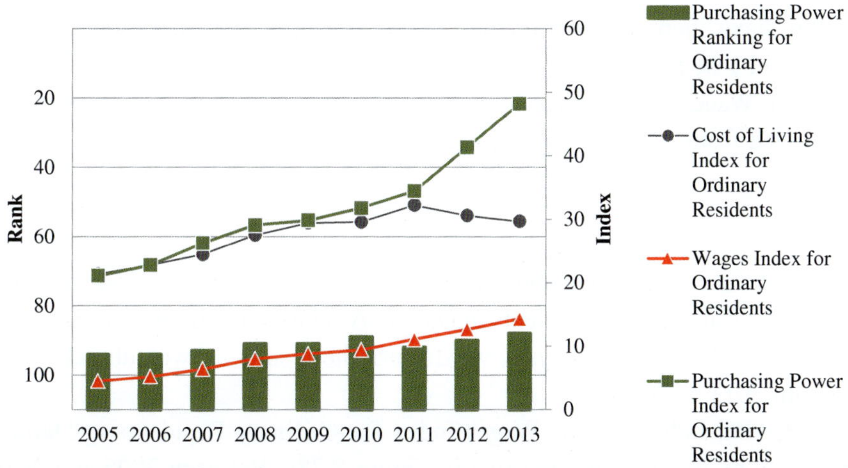

Source: Asia Competitiveness Institute

Figure 5.28a

Dalian, the second largest city of Liaoning province, is the financial centre of Northeast China. The city's Cost of Living Ranking for Ordinary Residents, as represented by the grey bars, rose from 95th to 94th between 2005 and 2010, and from 86th to 85th between 2011 and 2013 (see Figure 5.28a). As elaborated in Section 3.4.2 of Chapter 3, for a more rigorous comparison of rankings, we have split the analysis into two sub-periods.

From 2005 to 2010, Food & Non-alcoholic Beverages Ranking jumped 15 places from 94th to 79th. Housing Rents & Utilities Ranking moved up 13 spots from 81st in 2005 to 68th in 2010. Transport Ranking rose more modestly from 66th to 60th over the first sub-period. Education Ranking went up from 97th in 2005 to 96th in 2010. Health Ranking jumped from 100th in 2005 to 97th in 2008 and 2009 before falling back to 100th in 2010.

From 2011 to 2013, Clothing registered the most dramatic rise in ranking as it climbed 38 places from 71st to 33rd, making it the highest ranked category in 2013. Food & Non-alcoholic Beverages Ranking jumped 18 spots from 80th in 2011 to 62nd in 2013. Education Ranking rose more modestly from 86th to 84th over the second sub-period. In contrast, Housing Rents & Utilities Ranking slipped six places from 77th to 83rd between 2011 and 2013. Health Ranking fell three spots from 92nd to 95th over the same sub-period. Consequently, Health consistently remained as the lowest ranked category over the second sub-period.

DALIAN
China

Figure 5.28b

The Gross Hourly Wages in USD for Ordinary Residents in Dalian, as denoted by the red line in Figure 5.28b, have increased significantly over the study period. From US$0.71 in 2005, Dalian's wage level rose almost fourfold to US$2.83 in 2013.

Meanwhile, the Wages Ranking for Ordinary Residents in Dalian, as represented by the red bars, also improved from 91st in 2005 to 86th in 2013.

Figure 5.28c

Let us now analyse the cost of living and wages indices more closely and draw conclusions about the purchasing power of ordinary residents in Dalian. As elaborated in Section 3.4.2 of Chapter 3, for a more precise and rigorous analysis, we discuss the results in two sub-periods: from 2005 to 2010 and from 2011 to 2013.

The Cost of Living Index and the Wages Index for Ordinary Residents in Dalian are represented respectively by the grey and red line in Figure 5.28c. Between 2005 and 2010, the Cost of Living Index for Ordinary Residents was on an increasing trend. In 2005, the cost of living for ordinary residents in Dalian was 21.35% of that for their counterparts in New York (the base city). It rose steadily to 29.58% in 2010. Over the same sub-period, the Wages Index for Ordinary Residents also increased, rising from 4.50 in 2005 to 9.40 in 2010.

Since wages rose faster than cost of living, ordinary residents in Dalian were able to afford more goods and services over time during the first sub-period. This is reflected in the Purchasing Power Index for Ordinary Residents, which is represented by the green line in Figure 5.28c. From 21.09 in 2005, the index rose to reach 31.78 in 2010. The Purchasing Power Ranking for Ordinary Residents in Dalian, which is represented by the green bars, also improved from 94th in 2005 to 89th in 2010.

Over the second sub-period (2011–2013), the Cost of Living Index for Ordinary Residents has been on a decreasing trend. In 2011, the cost of living for ordinary residents in Dalian was 32.24% of that for their counterparts in New York. It dropped to 29.69% in 2013. In contrast, the Wages Index for Ordinary Residents has been increasing. The index rose from 11.10 in 2011 to 14.30 in 2013.

The combined trends of increasing wages and decreasing cost of living have enabled ordinary residents in Dalian to afford a higher consumption level over time during the second sub-period. This is reflected in the Purchasing Power Index for Ordinary Residents which increased from 34.42 in 2011 to 48.17 in 2013. The Purchasing Power Ranking for Ordinary Residents in Dalian has also been improving. Between 2011 and 2013, it rose from 92nd to 88th.

Finally, we note that over the entire study period (2005–2013), the Purchasing Power Index for Ordinary Residents in Dalian has consistently been lower than 100.00 — the base index value. This means that ordinary residents in Dalian have only been able to afford a lower consumption level than their counterparts in New York, given the same number of working hours.

DETROIT
United States

Figure 5.29a: Cost of Living and 10 Consumption Categories Rankings for Ordinary Residents in Detroit, United States

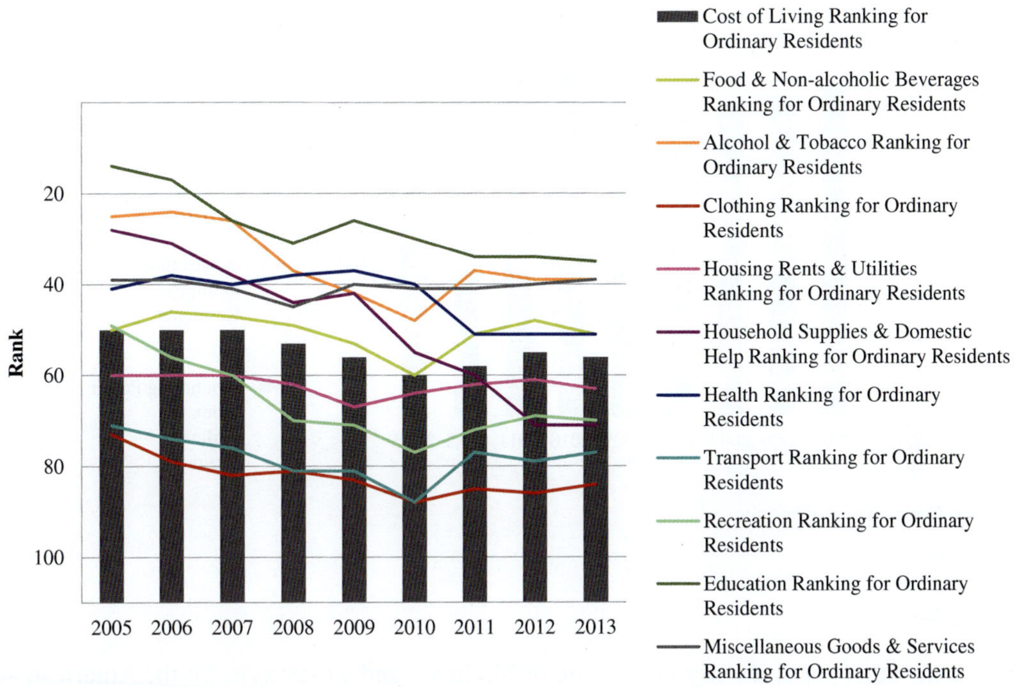

Source: Asia Competitiveness Institute

Figure 5.29b: Gross Hourly Wages in USD and Wages Ranking for Ordinary Residents in Detroit, United States

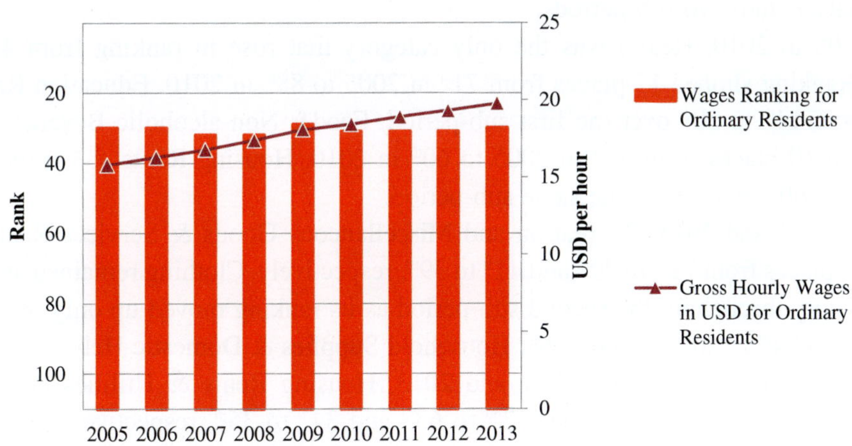

Source: Asia Competitiveness Institute

DETROIT
United States

Figure 5.29c: Cost of Living, Wages and Purchasing Power Indices and Purchasing Power Ranking for Ordinary Residents in Detroit, United States

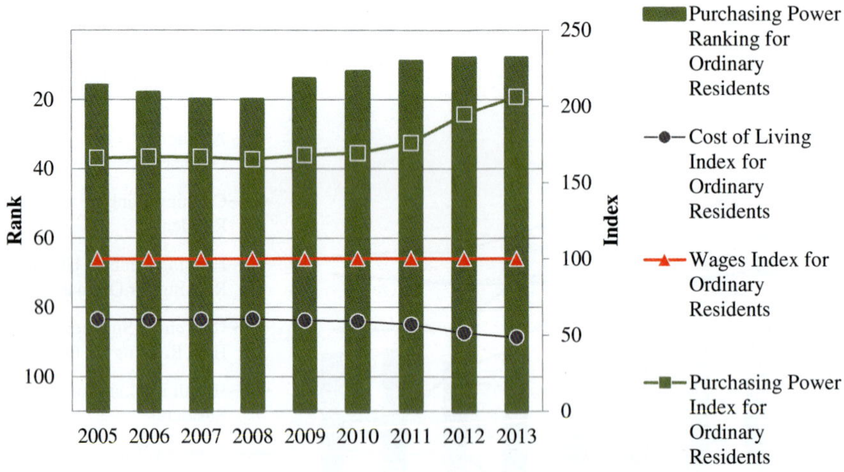

Source: Asia Competitiveness Institute

Figure 5.29a

Detroit is the most populous city in the state of Michigan and a metonym for the American automobile industry. Experiencing an economic and demographic decline since 2000, the city's Cost of Living Ranking for Ordinary Residents, as shown in the grey bars, fell from 50th to 60th between 2005 and 2010, but rose from 58th to 56th between 2011 and 2013 (see Figure 5.29a). As explained in Section 3.4.2 of Chapter 3, for a more precise comparison of rankings, we have split the analysis into two sub-periods.

From 2005 to 2010, Health was the only category that rose in ranking from 41st to 40th. Transport Ranking slipped 17 places from 71st in 2005 to 88th in 2010. Education Ranking fell 16 spots from 14th to 30th over the first sub-period. Food& Non-alcoholic Beverages Ranking moved down 10 places from 50th in 2005 to 60th in 2010. Housing Rents & Utilities Ranking declined from 60th to 64th over the same sub-period.

Between 2011 and 2013, Recreation and Miscellaneous Goods & Services Rankings both jumped two places from 72nd to 70th and 41st to 39th, respectively. Clothing remained as the lowest ranked category throughout the second sub-period as its ranking moved up only one spot from 85th in 2011 to 84th in 2013. In contrast, Household Supplies & Domestic Help Ranking fell 11 places from 60th to 71st between 2011 and 2013. Housing Rents & Utilities and Education Rankings both slipped one spot from 62nd to 63rd and 34th to 35th, respectively, over the same sub-period. Education was thus consistently the highest ranked category for the entire second

DETROIT
United States

sub-period. Health Ranking stayed unchanged at 51st from 2011 to 2013. Likewise, Food & Non-alcoholic Beverages and Transport Rankings largely remained at 51st and 77th, respectively, over the same sub-period.

Figure 5.29b

The Gross Hourly Wages in USD for Ordinary Residents in Detroit, as represented by the red line in Figure 5.29b, grew slightly from US$15.79 in 2005 to US$19.77 in 2013.

Despite the consistent increase in the wage level, the Wages Ranking for Ordinary Residents in Detroit, as depicted by the red bars, has remained rather stable. From 30th in 2005, it rose slightly to 29th in 2009 before dropping to 31st in 2010. The ranking remained at 31st until 2013, when it rose back to 30th.

Figure 5.29c

Let us now analyse the cost of living and wages indices more closely and draw conclusions about the purchasing power of ordinary residents in Detroit. As elaborated in Section 3.4.2 of Chapter 3, for a more precise and rigorous analysis, we discuss the results in two sub-periods: from 2005 to 2010 and from 2011 to 2013.

The Cost of Living Index and the Wages Index for Ordinary Residents in Detroit are represented respectively by the grey and red line in Figure 5.29c. As mentioned in Section 3.3 of Chapter 3, wage data are only available at the national level and not by cities. Therefore, wages in all cities in the United States are assumed to be the same. As a result, Detroit, being a city in the United States, shares a common Wages Index for Ordinary Residents with the base city New York (whose index value is 100.00) over the entire study period (2005–2013).

Between 2005 and 2010, the Cost of Living Index for Ordinary Residents in Detroit was rather stable. The index fluctuated about 59.86, indicating that throughout the first sub-period, the cost of living for ordinary residents in Detroit was about 59.86% of that for their counterparts in New York. Since the Wages Index for Ordinary Residents is constant across the years, the Purchasing Power Index for Ordinary Residents in Detroit (or any other cities in the United States) depends only on variations in the Cost of Living Index for Ordinary Residents. Thus, the stability of the latter also resulted in the Purchasing Power Index for Ordinary Residents, which is represented by the green line in Figure 5.29c, being relatively stable. This index only fluctuated around 167.08 over the first sub-period. However, the Purchasing Power Ranking for Ordinary Residents in Detroit, as represented by the green bars, was not stable. It improved from 16th in 2005 to 12th in 2010 while also fluctuated noticeably in between.

Over the second sub-period (2011–2013), the Cost of Living for Ordinary Residents has steadily declined. In 2011, the cost of living for ordinary residents in Detroit was 56.83% of that

DETROIT
United States

for their counterparts in New York. It dropped to 48.46% in 2013. As a result, the Purchasing Power Index for Ordinary Residents in Detroit has steadily increased from 175.95 in 2011 to 206.36 in 2013. Ranking-wise, the Purchasing Power Ranking for Ordinary Residents in Detroit has also improved, albeit marginally, from ninth in 2011 to eighth in 2013.

Finally, we note that over the entire study period (2005–2013), the Purchasing Power Index for Ordinary Residents in Detroit has always been above 100.00 — the base index value. Thus, ordinary residents in Detroit have consistently been able to afford more goods and services than their counterparts in New York, given the same number of working hours.

DOHA
Qatar

Figure 5.30a: Cost of Living and 10 Consumption Categories Rankings for Ordinary Residents in Doha, Qatar

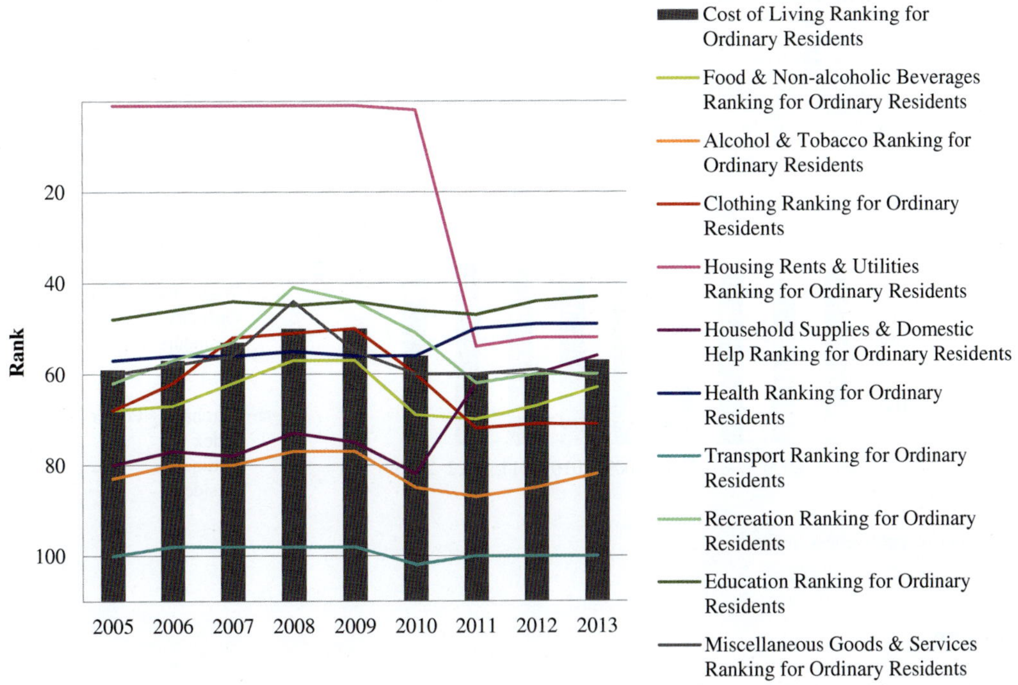

Source: Asia Competitiveness Institute

Figure 5.30b: Gross Hourly Wages in USD and Wages Ranking for Ordinary Residents in Doha, Qatar

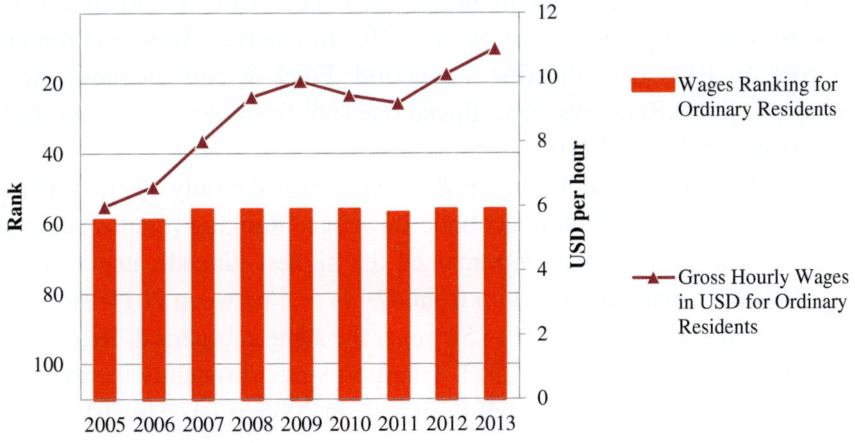

Source: Asia Competitiveness Institute

DOHA
Qatar

Figure 5.30c: Cost of Living, Wages and Purchasing Power Indices and Purchasing Power Ranking for Ordinary Residents in Doha, Qatar

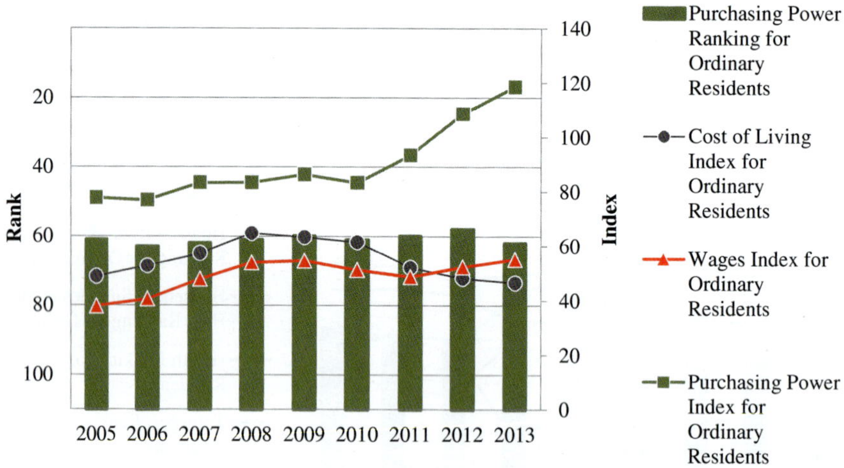

Source: Asia Competitiveness Institute

Figure 5.30a

Doha, the capital city of Qatar, is home to the country's largest oil and gas companies. The city's Cost of Living Ranking for Ordinary Residents, as denoted by the grey bars, rose from 59th to 56th between 2005 and 2010, and from 60th to 57th between 2011 and 2013 (see Figure 5.30a). As elaborated in Section 3.4.2 of Chapter 3, for a more rigorous comparison of rankings, we have split the analysis into two sub-periods.

From 2005 to 2010, Education Ranking jumped two places from 48th to 46th. Health Ranking moved up one spot from 57th in 2005 to 56th in 2010. In contrast, Transport Ranking fell two places from 100th to 102nd over the first sub-period. Food & Non-alcoholic Beverages and Housing Rents & Utilities Rankings both slipped one spot from 68th to 69th and first to second, respectively, between 2005 and 2010.

From 2011 to 2013, Miscellaneous Goods & Services was the only category that declined in ranking from 60th to 61st. Food & Non-alcoholic Beverages Ranking jumped seven places from 70th in 2011 to 63rd in 2013. Education remained the highest ranked category throughout the second sub-period as its ranking moved up from 47th to 43rd between 2011 and 2013. Housing Rents & Utilities Ranking rose from 54th to 52nd over the same sub-period. Health Ranking went up one spot from 50th in 2011 to 49th in 2013. Transport was consistently the lowest ranked category in both sub-periods as its ranking fell from 100th in 2005 to 102nd in 2010 and remained at 100th between 2011 and 2013.

DOHA
Qatar

Figure 5.30b

The Gross Hourly Wages in USD for Ordinary Residents in Doha, as denoted by the red line in Figure 5.30b, initially increased from US$5.98 in 2005 to US$9.88 in 2009. Doha's wage level then decreased over 2009–2011. From 2011 onwards, the upward trend resumed and the wage level reached US$10.89 in 2013.

Meanwhile, the Wages Ranking for Ordinary Residents in Doha, as depicted by the red bars, rose slightly from 59th to 56th between 2005 and 2013.

Figure 5.30c

Let us now analyse the cost of living and wages indices more closely and draw conclusions about the purchasing power of ordinary residents in Doha. As elaborated in Section 3.4.2 of Chapter 3, for a more precise and rigorous analysis, we discuss the results in two sub-periods: from 2005 to 2010 and from 2011 to 2013.

The Cost of Living Index and the Wages Index for Ordinary Residents in Doha are represented respectively by the grey and red line in Figure 5.30c. Between 2005 and 2010, the Cost of Living Index for Ordinary Residents was generally on an increasing trend. In 2005, the cost of living for ordinary residents in Doha was 48.79% of that for their counterparts in New York (the base city). It rose to 61.52% in 2010. Over the same sub-period, the Wages Index for Ordinary Residents also followed a similar pattern, rising from 37.90 in 2005 to 51.23 in 2010.

Wages grew faster than cost of living, so ordinary residents in Doha were able to afford more goods and services over time during the first sub-period. This is reflected in the Purchasing Power Index for Ordinary Residents, which is represented by the green line in Figure 5.30c. From 77.69 in 2005, the index rose to 83.27 in 2010. Meanwhile, the Purchasing Power Ranking for Ordinary Residents in Doha, which is represented by the green bars, was relatively stable. It remained at 61st in 2010 as it was in 2005 and only fluctuated between 60th and 63rd in between.

Over the second sub-period (2011–2013), the Cost of Living Index for Ordinary Residents has been on a decreasing trend. In 2011, the cost of living for ordinary residents in Doha was 52.10% of that for their counterparts in New York. It dropped to 46.48% in 2013. In contrast, the Wages Index for Ordinary Residents has been increasing. The index rose from 48.65 in 2011 to 55.10 in 2013.

The combined trends of increasing wages and decreasing cost of living have enabled ordinary residents in Doha to afford a higher consumption level over time during the second sub-period. This is reflected in the Purchasing Power Index for Ordinary Residents which increased from 93.39 in 2011 to 118.53 in 2013. Ranking-wise, the Purchasing Power Ranking for Ordinary

DOHA
Qatar

Residents in Doha has fluctuated modestly over the second sub-period. From 60th in 2010, it first climbed to 58th in 2012 before dropping to 62nd in 2013.

Finally, we note that over the entire study period (2005–2013), the Purchasing Power Index for Ordinary Residents in Doha had consistently been lower than 100.00 — the base index value — until 2012. This means it was not until 2012 that ordinary residents in Doha were able to afford more goods and services than their counterparts in New York, given the same number of working hours. Before 2012, they had only been able to afford a lower consumption level.

DUBAI
United Arab Emirates

Figure 5.31a: Cost of Living and 10 Consumption Categories Rankings for Ordinary Residents in Dubai, United Arab Emirates

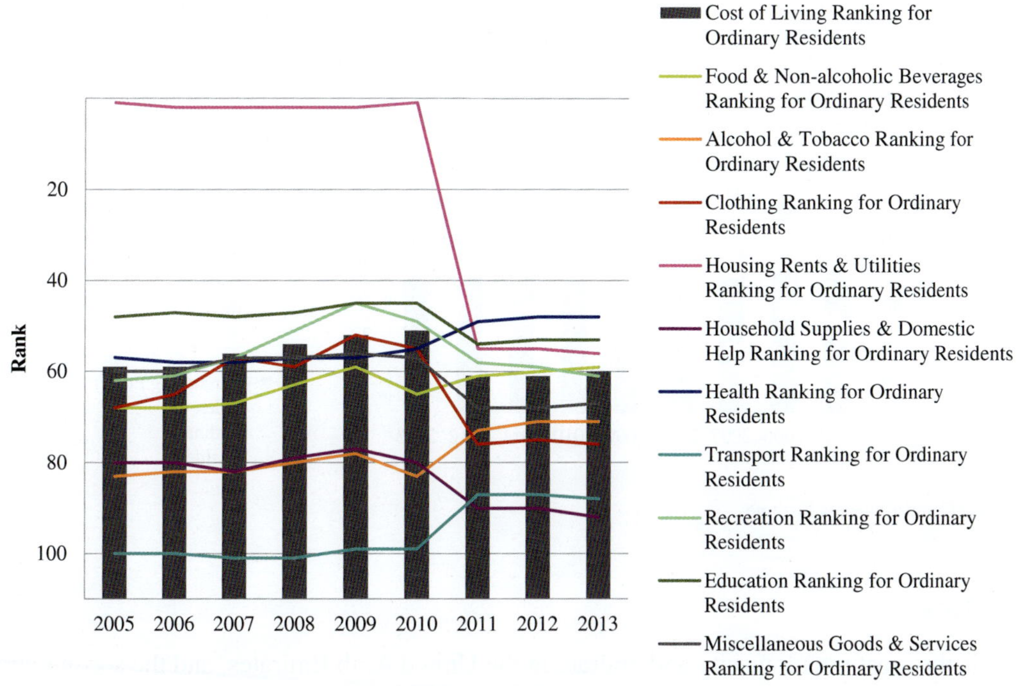

Source: Asia Competitiveness Institute

Figure 5.31b: Gross Hourly Wages in USD and Wages Ranking for Ordinary Residents in Dubai, United Arab Emirates

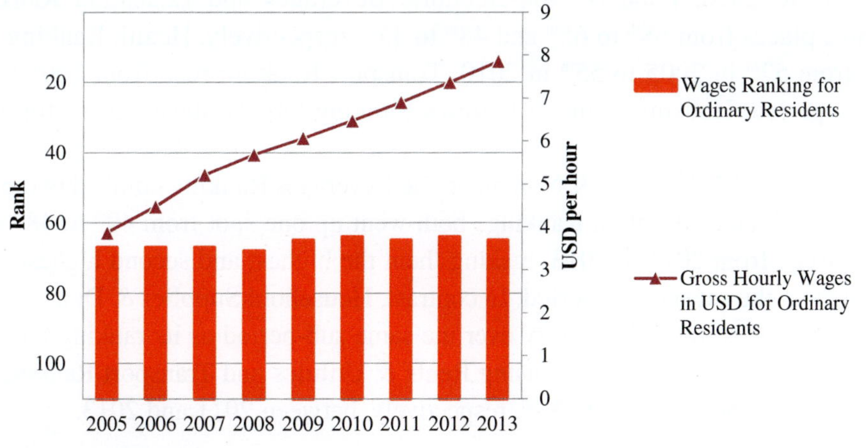

Source: Asia Competitiveness Institute

DUBAI
United Arab Emirates

Figure 5.31c: Cost of Living, Wages and Purchasing Power Indices and Purchasing Power Ranking for Ordinary Residents in Dubai, United Arab Emirates

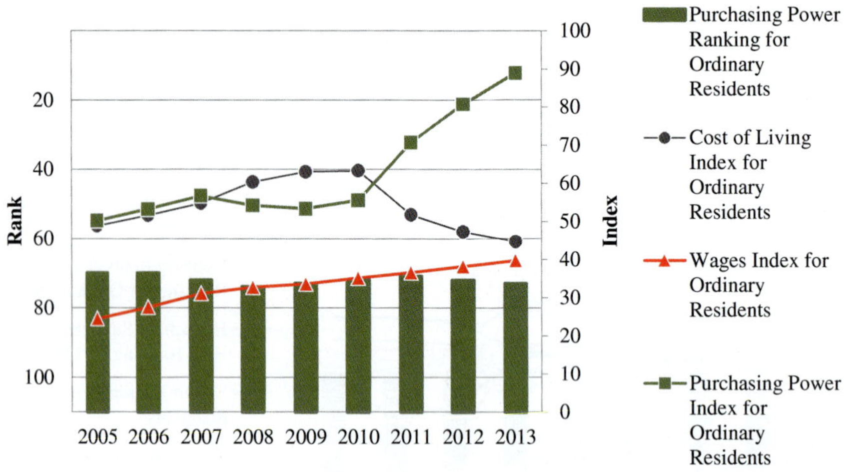

ource: Asia Competitiveness Institute

Figure 5.31a

Dubai is the most populous city and emirate in the United Arab Emirates, and the second largest emirate by land size after the capital, Abu Dhabi. The city's Cost of Living Ranking for Ordinary Residents, as represented by the grey bars, rose from 59th to 51st between 2005 and 2010, and from 61st to 60th, between 2011 and 2013 (see Figure 5.31a). As explained in Section 3.4.2 of Chapter 3, for a more precise comparison of rankings, we have split the analysis into two sub-periods.

From 2005 to 2010, Food & Non-alcoholic Beverages and Education Rankings both jumped three places from 68th to 65th and 48th to 45th, respectively. Health Ranking moved up two spots from 57th in 2005 to 55th in 2010. Transport Ranking rose from 100th to 99th over the first sub-period. Housing Rents & Utilities Ranking largely stayed at the top from 2005 to 2010.

Between 2011 and 2013, Food & Non-alcoholic Beverages Ranking climbed two places from 61st to 59th. Health and Education Rankings both went up one spot from 49th to 48th and 54th to 53rd, respectively, from 2011 to 2013, making them the highest and second highest ranked category throughout the second sub-period. In contrast, Household Supplies & Domestic Help was consistently the lowest ranked category over the same sub-period as its ranking fell two places from 90th in 2011 to 92nd in 2013. Housing Rents & Utilities and Transport Rankings declined slightly from 55th to 56th and 87th to 88th, respectively, between 2011 and 2013.

DUBAI
United Arab Emirates

Figure 5.31b

The Gross Hourly Wages in USD for Ordinary Residents in Dubai, as shown by the red line in Figure 5.31b, have grown considerably over the study period. Dubai's wage level more than doubled from US$3.86 in 2005 to US$7.85 in 2013.

Ranking-wise, the Wages Ranking for Ordinary Residents in Dubai, as represented by the red bars, improved from 67th in 2005 to 65th in 2013.

Figure 5.31c

Let us now analyse the cost of living and wages indices more closely and draw conclusions about the purchasing power of ordinary residents in Dubai. As elaborated in Section 3.4.2 of Chapter 3, for a more precise and rigorous analysis, we discuss the results in two sub-periods: from 2005 to 2010 and from 2011 to 2013.

The Cost of Living Index and the Wages Index for Ordinary Residents in Dubai are represented respectively by the grey and red line in Figure 5.31c. Between 2005 and 2010, the Cost of Living Index for Ordinary Residents was on an increasing trend. In 2005, the cost of living for ordinary residents in Dubai was 48.79% of that for their counterparts in New York (the base city). It rose steadily to reach 63.25% in 2010. Over the same sub-period, the Wages Index for Ordinary Residents also increased significantly, rising from 24.46 in 2005 to 35.12 in 2010.

Wages grew faster than cost of living, so ordinary residents in Dubai were able to afford more goods and services over time during the first sub-period. This is reflected in the Purchasing Power Index for Ordinary Residents, which is represented by the green line in Figure 5.30c. From 50.14 in 2005, the index rose to 55.52 in 2010. Meanwhile, the Purchasing Power Ranking for Ordinary Residents in Dubai, which is represented by the green bars, declined slightly from 70th in 2005 to 72nd in 2010.

Over the second sub-period (2011–2013), the Cost of Living Index for Ordinary Residents has been on a decreasing trend. In 2011, the cost of living for ordinary residents in Dubai was 51.70% of that for their counterparts in New York. It dropped to 44.67% in 2013. In contrast, the Wages Index for Ordinary Residents has been increasing, albeit modestly. The index rose from 36.51 in 2011 to 39.74 in 2013.

The combined trends of increasing wages and decreasing cost of living have enabled ordinary residents in Dubai to afford a higher consumption level over time during the second sub-period. This is reflected in the Purchasing Power Index for Ordinary Residents which increased from 70.63 in 2011 to 88.95 in 2013. Despite this positive showing of the index, the Purchasing Power Ranking for Ordinary Residents in Dubai has actually been deteriorating. It dropped from 71st in 2010 to 73rd in 2013.

Finally, we note that over the entire study period (2005–2013), the Purchasing Power Index for Ordinary Residents in Dubai has consistently been lower than 100.00 — the base index value. This means that ordinary residents in Dubai have only been able to afford a lower consumption level than their counterparts in New York, given the same number of working hours.

DUBLIN
Ireland

Figure 5.32a: Cost of Living and 10 Consumption Categories Rankings for Ordinary Residents in Dublin, Ireland

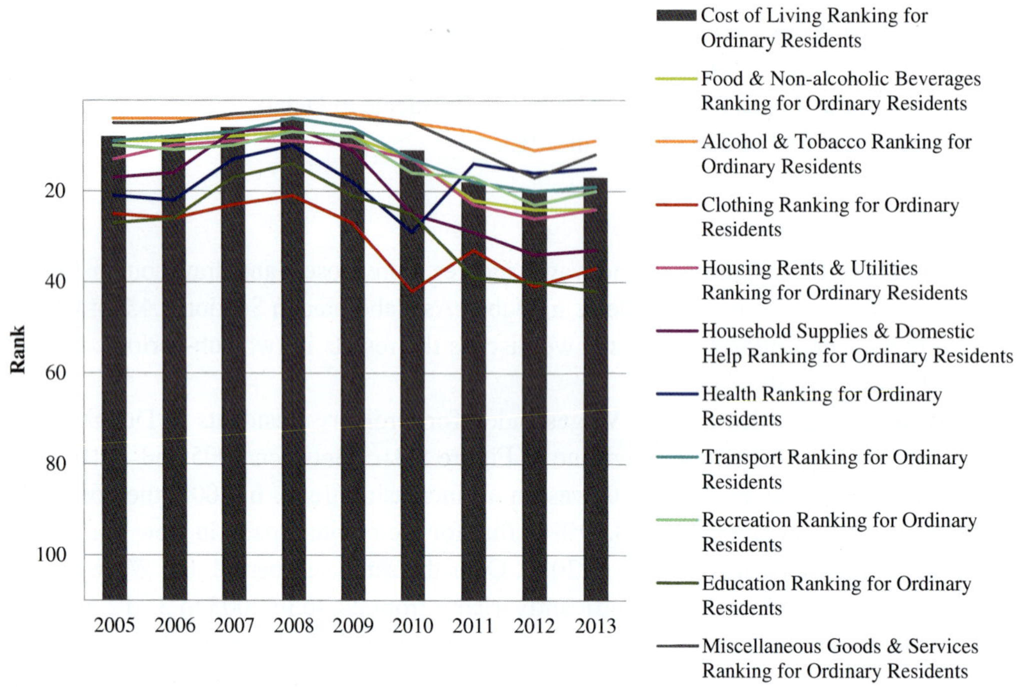

Source: Asia Competitiveness Institute

Figure 5.32b: Gross Hourly Wages in USD and Wages Ranking for Ordinary Residents in Dublin, Ireland

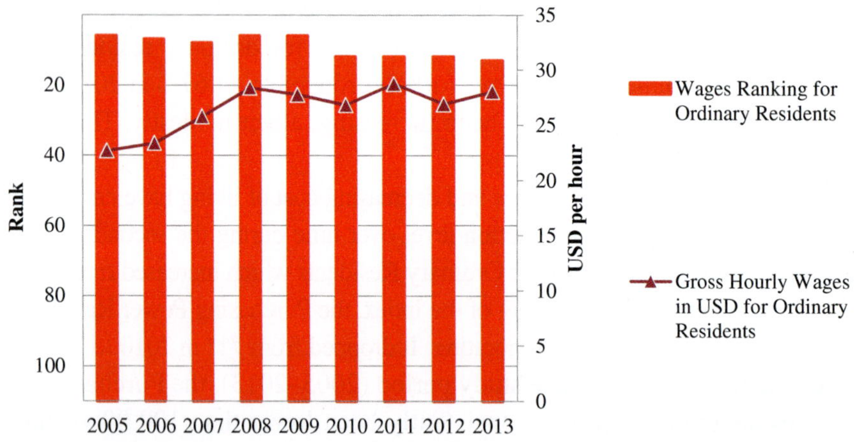

Source: Asia Competitiveness Institute

DUBLIN
Ireland

Figure 5.32c: Cost of Living, Wages and Purchasing Power Indices and Purchasing Power Ranking for Ordinary Residents in Dublin, Ireland

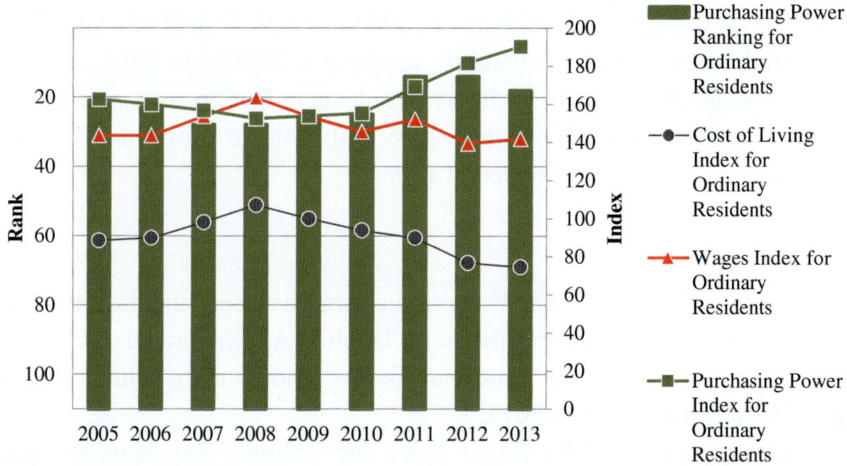

Source: Asia Competitiveness Institute

Figure 5.32a

Dublin is the capital and largest city of Ireland with an estimated population of 1.1 million. The city's Cost of Living Ranking for Ordinary Residents, as shown in the grey bars, fell from eighth to 11th between 2005 and 2010, but rose from 18th to 17th between 2011 and 2013 (see Figure 5.32a). As elaborated in Section 3.4.2 of Chapter 3, for a more rigorous comparison of rankings, we have split the analysis into two sub-periods.

From 2005 to 2010, Education was the only category that rose in ranking from 27th to 25th. Health Ranking slipped eight places from 21st in 2005 to 29th in 2010. Food & Non-alcoholic Beverages and Transport Rankings both moved down four spots from ninth to 13th over the first sub-period. Housing Rents & Utilities Ranking rose from 13th in 2005 to ninth in 2007 and 2008 before falling back to 13th in 2010.

The rankings of all 10 categories declined over the second sub-period between 2011 and 2013. In particular, Education Ranking fell three places from 39th in 2011 to 42nd in 2013, making it the lowest ranked category in 2013. Food & Non-alcoholic Beverages Ranking slipped two spots from 22nd in 2011 to 24th in 2013. Likewise, Alcohol & Tobacco Ranking went down from seventh to ninth from 2011 to 2013. Nonetheless, it remained as the highest ranked category throughout the second sub-period. Housing Rents & Utilities Ranking dropped one place from 23rd in 2011 to 24th in 2013. Likewise, Health and Transport Rankings declined from 14th to 15th and 18th to 19th, respectively, over the same sub-period.

DUBLIN
Ireland

Figure 5.32b

The Gross Hourly Wages in USD for Ordinary Residents in Dublin, as depicted by the red line in Figure 5.32b, initially rose from US$22.68 in 2005 to US$28.37 in 2008. After 2008, Dublin's wage level has exhibited moderate fluctuations, reaching US$28.02 in 2013.

Meanwhile, the Wages Ranking for Ordinary Residents in Dublin, as denoted by the red bars, was initially stable at around sixth between 2005 and 2009. It dropped to 12th in 2010 and remained there until 2013, when it dropped to 13th.

Figure 5.32c

Let us now analyse the cost of living and wages indices more closely and draw conclusions about the purchasing power of ordinary residents in Dublin. As elaborated in Section 3.4.2 of Chapter 3, for a more precise and rigorous analysis, we discuss the results in two sub-periods: from 2005 to 2010 and from 2011 to 2013.

The Cost of Living Index and the Wages Index for Ordinary Residents in Dublin are represented respectively by the grey and red line in Figure 5.32c. Between 2005 and 2010, the Cost of Living Index for Ordinary Residents fluctuated substantially. In 2005, the cost of living for ordinary residents in Dublin was 88.37% of that for their counterparts in New York (the base city). It increased steadily to its peak at 107.12% in 2008 and then began to decrease until it reached 93.81% in 2010. Over the same sub-period, the Wages Index for Ordinary Residents fluctuated in a similar pattern but at different rates. Overall, from 143.64 in 2005, the index reached 145.51 in 2010.

The net result of the fluctuations in wages and cost of living was that in 2010, the amount of goods and services ordinary residents in Dublin could afford was lower than that in 2005. The Purchasing Power Index for Ordinary Residents in Dublin, as represented by the green line in Figure 5.32c, dropped from 162.53 in 2005 to 155.11 in 2010. Meanwhile, the Purchasing Power Ranking for Ordinary Residents in Dublin, as represented by the green bars, dropped from 21st in 2005 to its lowest point at 28th in 2007 and 2008 before improving to reach 25th in 2010.

Over the second sub-period (2011–2013), the Cost of Living Index for Ordinary Residents has been on a steady decreasing trend. In 2011, the cost of living for ordinary residents in Dublin was 89.87% of that for their counterparts in New York It dropped to 74.49% in 2013. Over the same sub-period, the Wages Index for Ordinary Residents has also been on a decreasing trend, declining from 151.98 in 2011 to 141.73 in 2013.

Wages have decreased at a slower rate than cost of living. Thus, throughout the second sub-period, ordinary residents in Dublin have actually been able to afford more goods and services over time. This is evident in the steady increase of the Purchasing Power Index for Ordinary Residents from 169.10 in 2011 to 190.27 in 2013. Despite this good showing of the index, the

DUBLIN
Ireland

Purchasing Power Ranking for Ordinary Residents in Dublin has actually deteriorated, dropping from 14th in 2011 to 18th in 2013.

Finally, we note that over the entire study period (2005–2013), the Purchasing Power Index for Ordinary Residents in Dublin has always been higher than 100.00 — the base index value. This means that ordinary residents in Dublin have been able to consume more goods and services than their counterparts in New York, given the same number of working hours.

FRANKFURT
Germany

Figure 5.33a: Cost of Living and 10 Consumption Categories Rankings for Ordinary Residents in Frankfurt, Germany

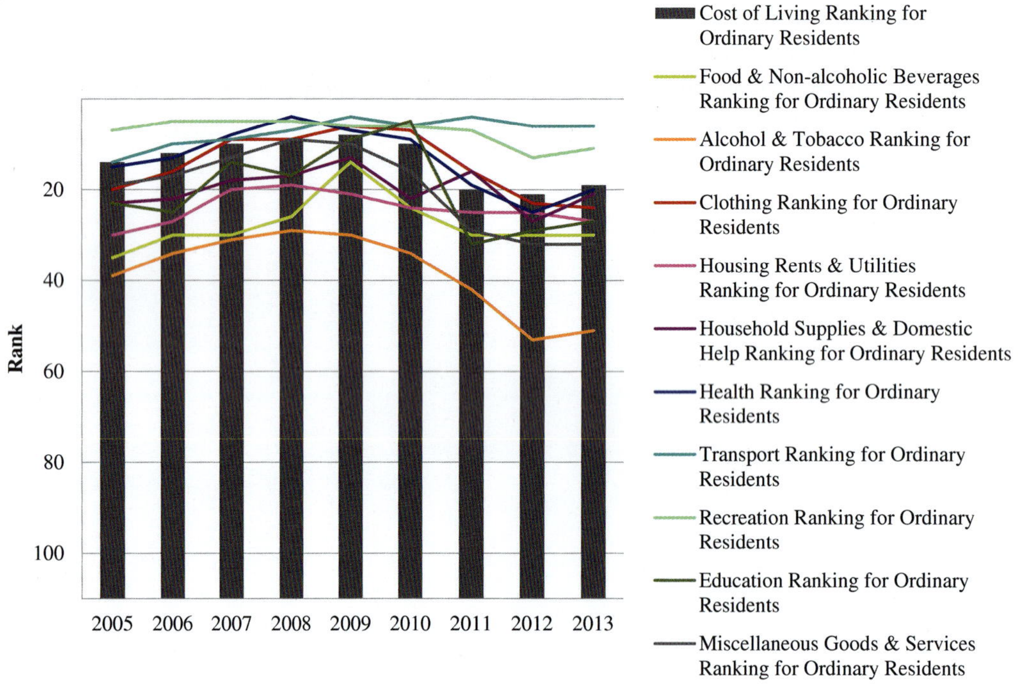

Source: Asia Competitiveness Institute

Figure 5.33b: Gross Hourly Wages in USD and Wages Ranking for Ordinary Residents in Frankfurt, Germany

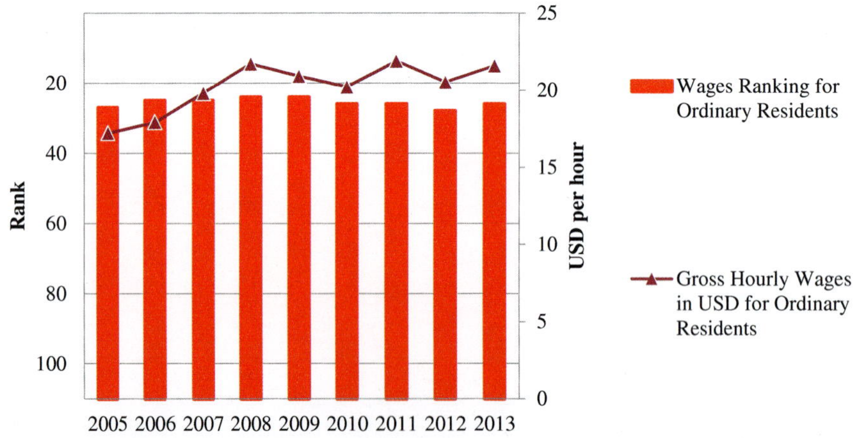

Source: Asia Competitiveness Institute

FRANKFURT
Germany

Figure 5.33c: Cost of Living, Wages and Purchasing Power Indices and Purchasing Power Ranking for Ordinary Residents in Frankfurt, Germany

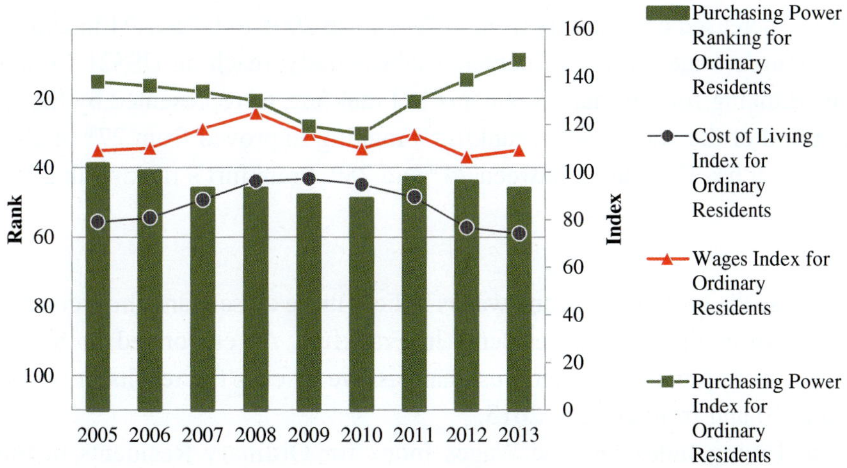

Source: Asia Competitiveness Institute

Figure 5.33a

Although Frankfurt is the fifth largest city in Germany with an estimated population of 700,000, it is home to one of the busiest international airports by passenger traffic. The city's Cost of Living Ranking for Ordinary Residents, as shown in the grey bars, rose from 14th to 10th between 2005 and 2010, and from 20th to 19th between 2011 and 2013 (see Figure 5.33a). As explained in Section 3.4.2 of Chapter 3, for a more precise comparison of rankings, we have split the analysis into two sub-periods.

The rankings of all 10 categories went up over the first sub-period from 2005 to 2010. In particular, Education Ranking climbed 18 places from 23rd in 2005 to fifth in 2010. Food & Non-alcoholic Beverages Ranking jumped 11 spots from 35th to 24th over the second sub-period. Transport Ranking moved up eight places from 14th in 2005 to sixth in 2010. Housing Rents & Utilities and Health Rankings both jumped six spots from 30th to 24th and 15th to ninth, respectively, over the same sub-period.

In contrast, Education was the only category that rose in ranking in the second sub-period from 32nd in 2011 to 27th in 2013. Housing Rents & Utilities and Transport Rankings both slipped two places from 25th to 27th and fourth to sixth, respectively, over the same sub-period. Nonetheless, Transport remained as the highest ranked category for the entire second sub-period. Health Ranking declined slightly from 19th in 2011 to 20th in 2013. Food & Non-alcoholic Beverages Ranking remained unchanged at 30th between 2011 and 2013. Alcohol & Tobacco was consistently the lowest ranked category throughout both sub-periods as its ranking rose from 39th in 2005 to 34th in 2010, and declined from 42nd in 2011 to 51st in 2013.

FRANKFURT
Germany

Figure 5.33b

The Gross Hourly Wages in USD for Ordinary Residents in Frankfurt, as denoted by the red line in Figure 5.33b, increased consistently from US$17.21 in 2005 to US$21.71 in 2008. From 2008 onwards, Frankfurt's wage level has fluctuated substantially, reaching US$21.59 in 2013.

The Wages Ranking for Ordinary Residents in Frankfurt, as represented by the red bars, has mirrored the trend of the wage level. Frankfurt's ranking improved from 27th in 2005 to 24th in 2008. Since then, it has fluctuated between 24th and 28th. Frankfurt's ranking in 2013 was 26th.

Figure 5.33c

Let us now analyse the cost of living and wages indices more closely and draw conclusions about the purchasing power of ordinary residents in Frankfurt. As elaborated in Section 3.4.2 of Chapter 3, for a more precise and rigorous analysis, we discuss the results in two sub-periods: from 2005 to 2010 and from 2011 to 2013.

The Cost of Living Index and the Wages Index for Ordinary Residents in Frankfurt are represented respectively by the grey and red line in Figure 5.33c. Between 2005 and 2010, the Cost of Living Index for Ordinary Residents was generally on an increasing trend. In 2005, the cost of living for ordinary residents in Frankfurt was 79.06% of that for their counterparts in New York (the base city). It rose to 94.64% in 2010. In contrast, the Wages Index for Ordinary Residents exhibited more substantial fluctuations. From 109.01 in 2005, this index rose to peak at 124.85 in 2008 before dropping over the remaining years to eventually reach 109.68 in 2010, which was almost the same as its initial value.

Between 2005 and 2008 when both wages and cost of living were increasing, wages rose more slowly than the latter. Later on in the first sub-period, wages were decreasing while cost of living remained relatively unchanged over time. As a result, throughout the first sub-period, ordinary residents in Frankfurt could not maintain the same consumption level over time. This is reflected in the Purchasing Power Index for Ordinary Residents in Frankfurt, which is represented by the green line in Figure 5.33c. Between 2005 and 2010, this index decreased from 137.88 to 115.89. Ranking-wise, the Purchasing Power Ranking for Ordinary Residents in Frankfurt, as represented by the green bars, also deteriorated significantly over the first sub-period, dropping from 39th in 2005 to 49th in 2010.

Over the second sub-period (2011–2013), the Cost of Living Index for Ordinary Residents has been on a decreasing trend. In 2011, the cost of living for ordinary residents in Frankfurt was 89.44% of that for ordinary residents in New York. It dropped over the years to reach 74.24% in 2013. The Wages Index for Ordinary Residents has also been on a downward trend, falling from 115.75 in 2011 to 109.22 in 2013.

Wages have in fact decreased more slowly than cost of living. Thus, throughout the second sub-period, ordinary residents in Frankfurt have actually been able to afford a higher consumption level over time. This is reflected in the Purchasing Power Index for Ordinary Residents which rose steadily from 129.41 in 2011 to 147.11 in 2013. Despite the positive showing of the index, the Purchasing Power Ranking for Ordinary Residents has deteriorated over the second sub-period, slipping from 43rd in 2011 to 46th in 2013.

Finally, we note that over the entire study period (2005–2013), the Purchasing Power Index for Ordinary Residents in Frankfurt has always been higher than 100.00 — the base index value. This means that ordinary residents in Frankfurt have consistently been able to afford a higher consumption level than their counterparts in New York, given the same number of working hours.

GENEVA
Switzerland

Figure 5.34a: Cost of Living and 10 Consumption Categories Rankings for Ordinary Residents in Geneva, Switzerland

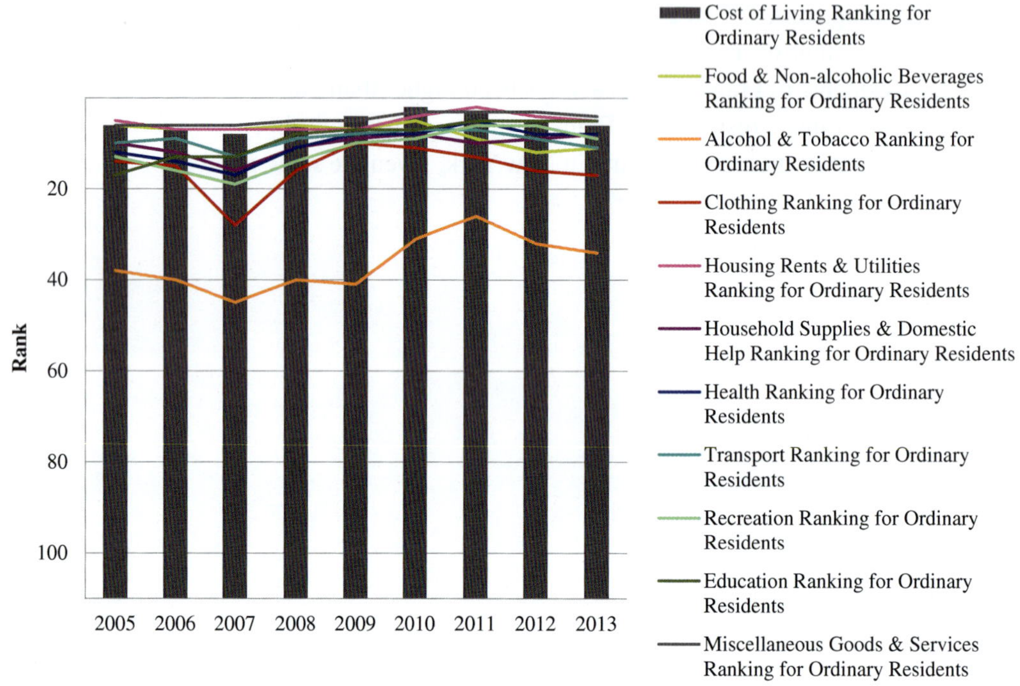

Source: Asia Competitiveness Institute

Figure 5.34b: Gross Hourly Wages in USD and Wages Ranking for Ordinary Residents in Geneva, Switzerland

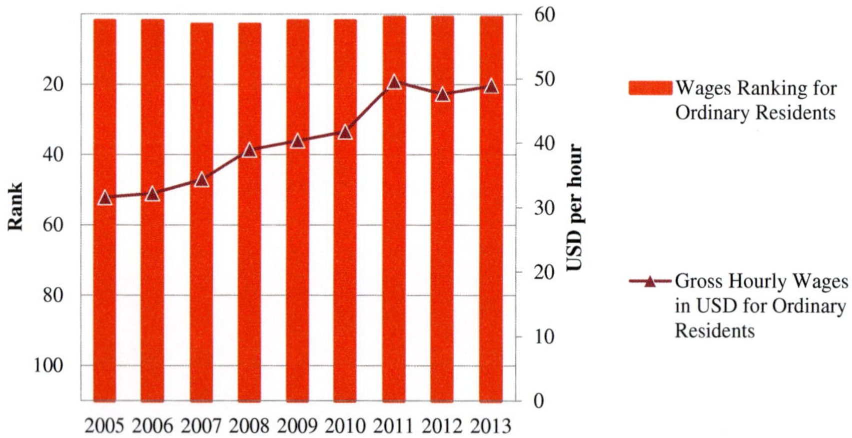

Source: Asia Competitiveness Institute

GENEVA
Switzerland

Figure 5.34c: Cost of Living, Wages and Purchasing Power Indices and Purchasing Power Ranking for Ordinary Residents in Geneva, Switzerland

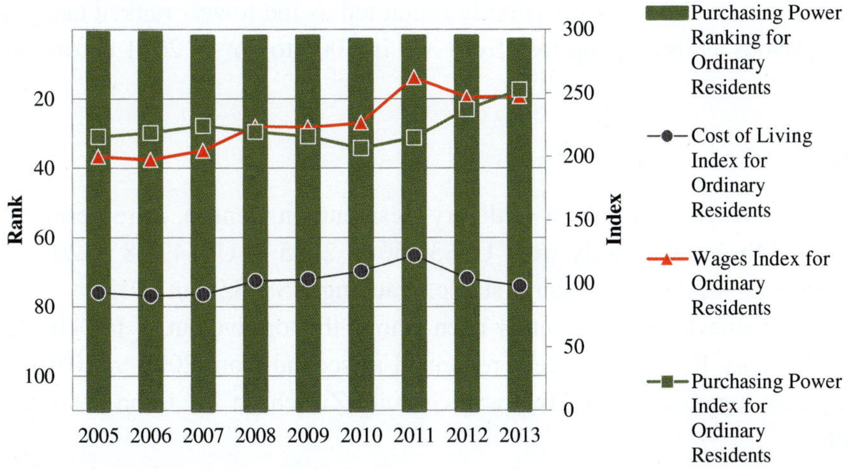

Source: Asia Competitiveness Institute

Figure 5.34a

Renowned for its sizeable private banking sector, Geneva is the second most populous city in Switzerland with a population of approximately 196,000. The city's Cost of Living Ranking for Ordinary Residents, as denoted by the grey bars, rose from sixth to second between 2005 and 2010, but declined from third to sixth between 2011 and 2013 (see Figure 5.34a). As elaborated in Section 3.4.2 of Chapter 3, for a more precise comparison of rankings, we have split the analysis into two sub-periods.

The rankings of all 10 categories went up over the first sub-period from 2005 to 2010. In particular, Education Ranking climbed 10 places from 17th in 2005 to seventh in 2010. Health Ranking jumped four spots from 12th to eighth over the first sub-period. Transport Ranking went up three places from 10th to seventh between 2005 and 2010. Food & Non-alcoholic Beverages and Housing Rents & Utilities Rankings both moved up one spot from sixth to fifth and fifth to fourth, respectively, over the same sub-period.

In the second sub-period between 2011 and 2013, nine out of 10 categories declined in rankings. Household Supplies & Domestic Help was the only category that rose in ranking from 10th in 2011 to eighth in 2013. Transport Ranking slipped four places from seventh to 11th over the second sub-period. Housing Rents & Utilities and Health Rankings both moved down three spots from second to fifth and fifth to eighth, respectively, between 2011 and 2013. Food & Non-alcoholic Beverages Ranking declined from ninth to 11th over the same sub-period. Miscellaneous Goods & Services became the highest ranked category in 2013 although its ranking went down

GENEVA
Switzerland

from third in 2011 to fourth in 2013. Education Ranking remained unchanged at fifth in the second sub-period, making it the second highest ranked category together with Housing Rents & Utilities. Alcohol & Tobacco consistently remained as the lowest ranked category throughout both sub-periods as its ranking rose from 38th in 2005 to 26th in 2011 before falling to 34th in 2013.

Figure 5.34b

The Gross Hourly Wages in USD for Ordinary Residents in Geneva, as represented by the red line in Figure 5.34b, grew steadily from US$31.56 in 2005 to US$49.58 in 2011. Since then, Geneva's wage level has remained fairly stable, reaching US$48.92 in 2013.

Ranking-wise, Geneva has consistently been among the top five out of 103 cities. The Wages Ranking for Ordinary Residents largely remained at second from 2005 to 2010. Geneva then rose to first place, together with its fellow Swiss city Zurich, in 2011 and has retained the top spot ever since.

Figure 5.34c

Let us now analyse the cost of living and wages indices more closely and draw conclusions about the purchasing power of ordinary residents in Geneva. As elaborated in Section 3.4.2 of Chapter 3, for a more precise and rigorous analysis, we discuss the results in two sub-periods: from 2005 to 2010 and from 2011 to 2013.

The Cost of Living Index and the Wages Index for Ordinary Residents in Geneva are represented respectively by the grey and red line in Figure 5.34c. Between 2005 and 2010, the Cost of Living Index for Ordinary Residents was generally on an increasing trend. In 2005, the cost of living for ordinary residents in Geneva was 92.80% of that for their counterparts in New York (the base city). It increased over the years to reach 109.72% in 2010. Meanwhile, the Wages Index for Ordinary Residents was also on an increasing trend, rising from 199.89 in 2005 to 226.47 in 2010.

Between 2005 and 2007, wages increased faster than cost of living. However, during the remaining years of the first sub-period, wages could not keep up with the latter. As a result, ordinary residents in Geneva were only able to afford more goods and services over time between 2005 and 2007 but could not do so thereafter. These trends are reflected in the Purchasing Power Index for Ordinary Residents in Geneva, which is represented by the green line in Figure 5.34c. This index initially rose from 215.39 in 2005 to 224.13 in 2007 and then declined over the rest of the first sub-period. Overall, the purchasing power index was lower in 2010 (206.40) than it was in 2005. Ranking-wise, the Purchasing Power Ranking for Ordinary Residents in Geneva, as represented by the green bars, declined slightly over the first sub-period. It dropped from first to third between 2005 and 2010.

GENEVA
Switzerland

Over the second sub-period (2011–2013), the Cost of Living Index for Ordinary Residents has been on a decreasing trend. In 2011, the cost of living for ordinary residents in Geneva was 1.22 times that for ordinary residents in New York. It dropped over the years to 98.02% in 2013. The Wages Index for Ordinary Residents has also been decreasing, dropping from 262.30 in 2011 to 247.47 in 2013.

Wages have in fact decreased more slowly than cost of living, so throughout the second sub-period, ordinary residents in Geneva have actually been able to afford more goods and services over time. This is reflected in the Purchasing Index for Ordinary Residents, which rose from 214.72 in 2011 to 252.46 in 2013. Meanwhile, the Purchasing Power Ranking for Ordinary Residents has been relatively stable. It was second in both 2011 and 2012 and only decreased marginally to third in 2013.

Finally, we note that over the entire study period (2005–2013), the Purchasing Power Index for Ordinary Residents in Geneva has always been much higher than 100.00 — the base index value. This means that ordinary residents in Geneva have consistently been able to afford a much higher consumption level than their counterparts in New York, given the same number of working hours.

GUANGZHOU
China

Figure 5.35a: Cost of Living and 10 Consumption Categories Rankings for Ordinary Residents in Guangzhou, China

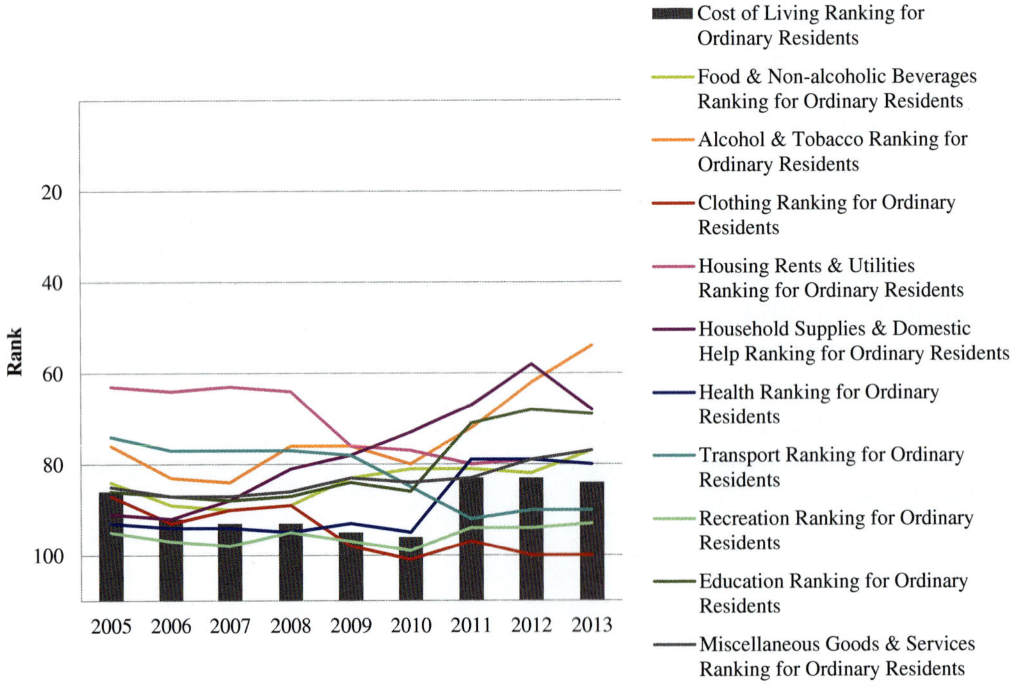

Source: Asia Competitiveness Institute

Figure 5.35b: Gross Hourly Wages in USD and Wages Ranking for Ordinary Residents in Guangzhou, China

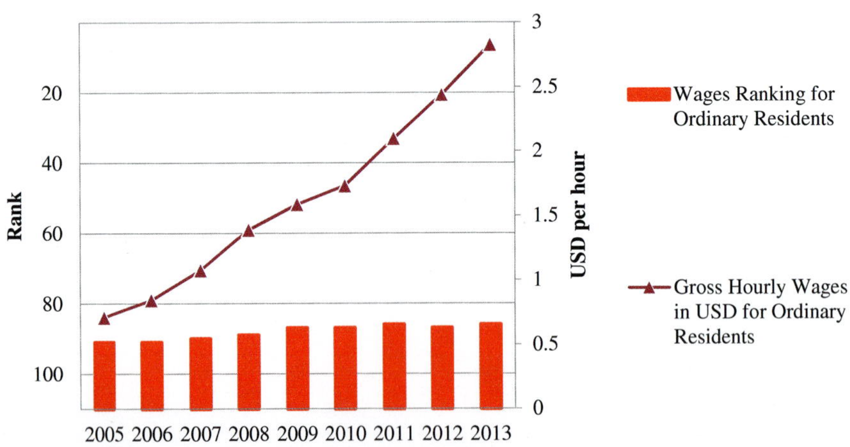

Source: Asia Competitiveness Institute

GUANGZHOU
China

Figure 5.35c: Cost of Living, Wages and Purchasing Power Indices and Purchasing Power Ranking for Ordinary Residents in Guangzhou, China

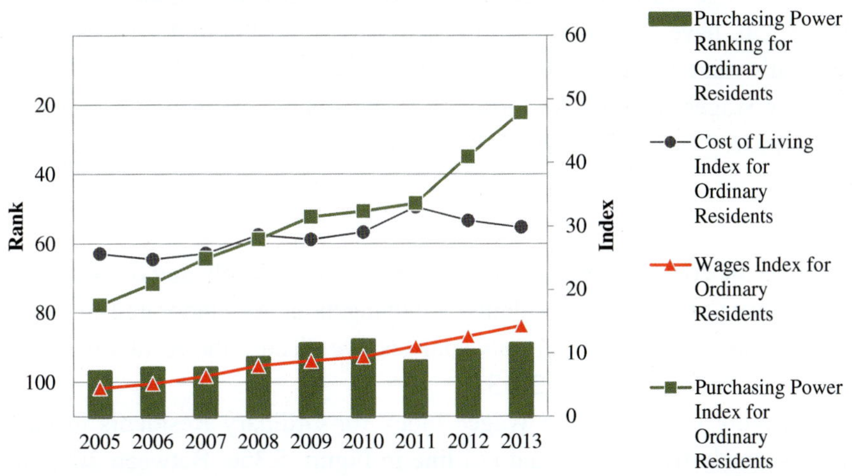

Source: Asia Competitiveness Institute

Figure 5.35a

Located about 120 kilometres northwest of Hong Kong and 145 kilometres north of Macau, Guangzhou, the capital city of Guangdong province, serves as an important national transportation hub and trading port. The city's Cost of Living Ranking for Ordinary Residents, as represented by the grey bars, declined from 86th to 96th between 2005 and 2010, and from 83rd to 84th between 2011 and 2013 (see Figure 5.35a). As explained in Section 3.4.2 of Chapter 3, for a more precise comparison of rankings, we have split the analysis into two sub-periods.

From 2005 to 2010, Food & Non-alcoholic Beverages Ranking jumped three places from 84th to 81st. In contrast, Housing Rents & Utilities Ranking fell 14 spots from 63rd in 2005 to 77th in 2010. Transport Ranking slipped 11 places from 74th to 85th over the first sub-period. Health Ranking declined more modestly from 93rd in 2005 to 95th in 2010. Education Ranking went down from 86th in 2005 to 88th in 2007 before rising back to 86th in 2010.

Between 2011 and 2013, Alcohol & Tobacco became the highest ranked category in 2013 as its ranking climbed 18 places from 72nd to 54th. Food & Non-alcoholic Beverages Ranking jumped four spots from 81st in 2011 to 77th in 2013. Housing Rents & Utilities Ranking rose from 80th to 77th over the second sub-period. Education and Transport Rankings both moved up two places from 71st to 69th and 92nd to 90th, respectively, between 2011 and 2013. In contrast, Clothing Ranking slipped three spots from 97th in 2011 to 100th in 2013, making it the lowest ranked category throughout the second sub-period. Health Ranking fell one place from 79th to 80th over the same sub-period.

GUANGZHOU
China

Figure 5.35b

The Gross Hourly Wages in USD for Ordinary Residents in Guangzhou, as denoted by the red line in Figure 5.35b, have increased significantly between 2005 and 2013. From US$0.71 in 2005, Guangzhou's wage level rose almost fourfold to US$2.83 in 2013.

Meanwhile, the Wages Ranking for Ordinary Residents in Guangzhou, as represented by the red bars, also improved from 91st in 2005 to 86th in 2013.

Figure 5.35c

Let us now analyse the cost of living and wages indices more closely and draw conclusions about the purchasing power of ordinary residents in Guangzhou. As elaborated in Section 3.4.2 of Chapter 3, for a more precise and rigorous analysis, we discuss the results in two sub-periods: from 2005 to 2010 and from 2011 to 2013.

The Cost of Living Index and the Wages Index for Ordinary Residents in Guangzhou are represented respectively by the grey and red line in Figure 5.35c. Between 2005 and 2010, the Cost of Living Index for Ordinary Residents was on an increasing trend. In 2005, the cost of living for ordinary residents in Guangzhou was 25.66% of that for their counterparts in New York (the base city). It rose steadily to 29.05% in 2010. Over the same sub-period, the Wages Index for Ordinary Residents also increased, rising from 4.50 in 2005 to 9.40 in 2010.

Wages rose faster than cost of living throughout the first sub-period. Thus, ordinary residents in Guangzhou were able to afford more goods and services over time during these years. This is reflected in the Purchasing Power Index for Ordinary Residents, which is represented by the green line in Figure 5.35c. From 17.55 in 2005, the index rose to reach 32.36 in 2010. The Purchasing Power Ranking for Ordinary Residents in Guangzhou, which is represented by the green bars, also improved significantly, rising from 97th in 2005 to 88th in 2010.

Over the second sub-period (2011–2013), the Cost of Living Index for Ordinary Residents has been on a decreasing trend. In 2011, the cost of living for ordinary residents in Guangzhou was 33.02% of that for their counterparts in New York. It dropped to 29.85% in 2013. In contrast, the Wages Index for Ordinary Residents has been increasing. The index rose from 11.10 in 2011 to 14.30 in 2013.

The combined trends of increasing wages and decreasing cost of living have enabled ordinary residents in Guangzhou to afford a higher consumption level over time during the second sub-period. This is reflected in the Purchasing Power Index for Ordinary Residents, which increased from 33.61 in 2011 to 47.91 in 2013. The Purchasing Power Ranking for Ordinary Residents in Guangzhou has also been improving. Between 2011 and 2013, this ranking rose from 94th to 89th.

Finally, we note that over the entire study period (2005–2013), the Purchasing Power Index for Ordinary Residents in Guangzhou has consistently been lower than 100.00 — the base index value. This means that ordinary residents in Guangzhou have only been able to afford a lower consumption level than their counterparts in New York, given the same number of working hours.

HELSINKI
Finland

Figure 5.36a: Cost of Living and 10 Consumption Categories Rankings for Ordinary Residents in Helsinki, Finland

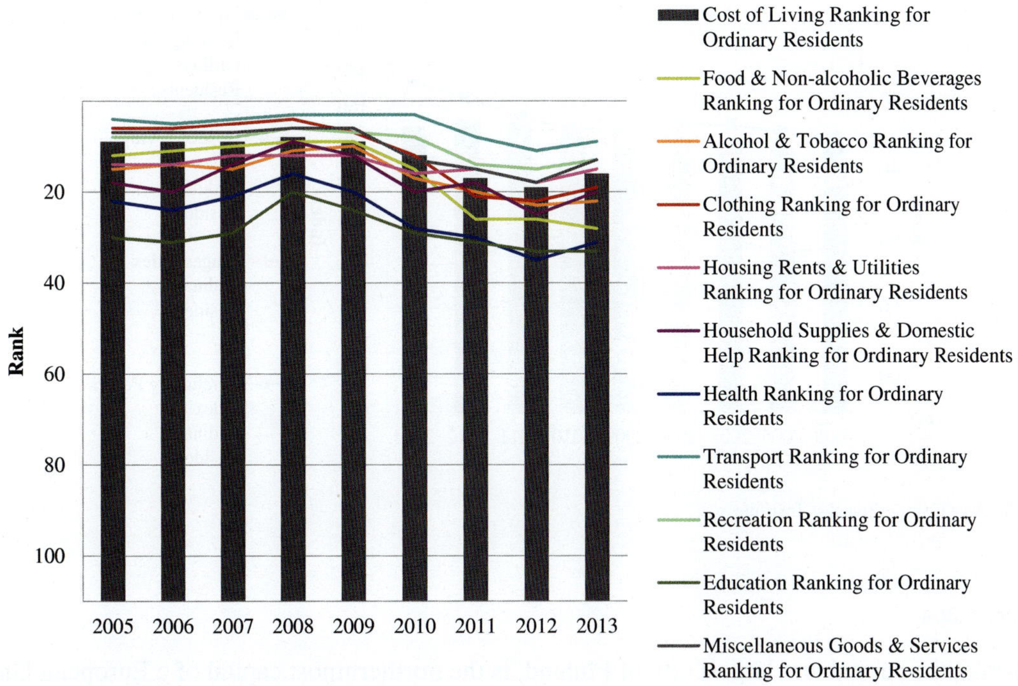

Source: Asia Competitiveness Institute

Figure 5.36b: Gross Hourly Wages in USD and Wages Ranking for Ordinary Residents in Helsinki, Finland

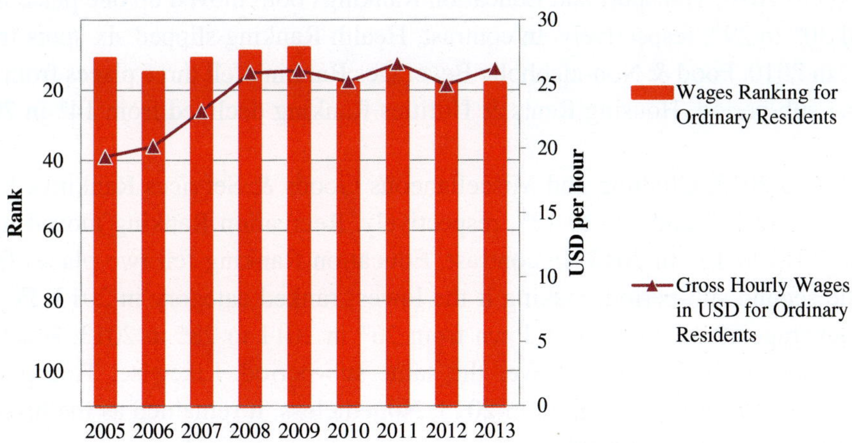

Source: Asia Competitiveness Institute

HELSINKI
Finland

Figure 5.36c: Cost of living, Wages and Purchasing Power Indices and Purchasing Power Ranking for Ordinary Residents in Helsinki, Finland

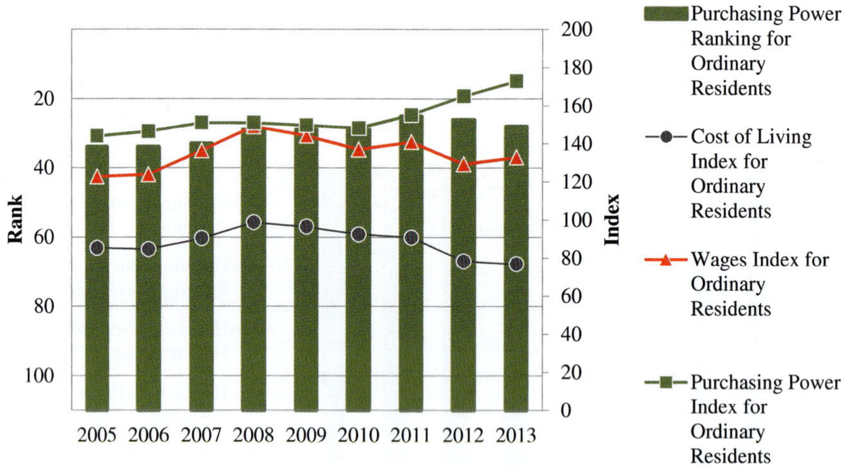

Source: Asia Competitiveness Institute

Figure 5.36a

Helsinki, the capital and largest city of Finland, is the northernmost capital of a European Union member state. The city's Cost of Living Ranking for Ordinary Residents, as shown in grey bars, declined from ninth to 12th between 2005 and 2010, but rose from 17th to 16th between 2011 and 2013 (see Figure 5.36a). As elaborated in Section 3.4.2 of Chapter 3, for a more precise comparison of rankings, we have split the analysis into two sub-periods.

From 2005 to 2010, Transport and Education Rankings both moved up one place from fourth to third and 30th to 29th, respectively. In contrast, Health Ranking slipped six spots from 22nd in 2005 to 28th in 2010. Food & Non-alcoholic Beverages Ranking fell three places from 12th to 15th over the first sub-period. Housing Rents & Utilities Ranking declined from 14th in 2005 to 16th in 2010.

From 2011 to 2013, Clothing and Miscellaneous Goods & Services Rankings jumped two places from 21st to 19th and 15th to 13th, respectively. Recreation Ranking moved up one spot from 14th in 2011 to 13th in 2013. In contrast, Education Ranking fell two places from 31st to 33rd over the second sub-period, making it the lowest ranked category in 2013. Food & Non-alcoholic Beverages Ranking moved down from 26th in 2011 to 28th in 2013. Health Ranking dropped one spot from 30th to 31st over the same sub-period. Likewise, Transport Ranking declined from eighth in 2011 to ninth in 2013. Nonetheless, it remained as the highest ranked category throughout the second sub-period.

HELSINKI
Finland

Figure 5.36b

The Gross Hourly Wages in USD for Ordinary Residents in Helsinki, as depicted by the red line in Figure 5.36b, initially followed a steady increasing trend from US$19.37 in 2005 to US$26.06 in 2009. From 2009 onwards, Helsinki's wage level has exhibited moderate fluctuations. In 2013, it reached US$26.23.

Ranking-wise, the Wages Ranking for Ordinary Residents in Helsinki, as shown by the red bars, has generally deteriorated over the study period. It dropped from 11th in 2005 to 18th in 2013.

Figure 5.36c

Let us now analyse the cost of living and wages indices more closely and draw conclusions about the purchasing power of ordinary residents in Helsinki. As elaborated in Section 3.4.2 of Chapter 3, for a more precise and rigorous analysis, we discuss the results in two sub-periods: from 2005 to 2010 and from 2011 to 2013.

The Cost of Living Index and the Wages Index for Ordinary Residents in Helsinki are represented respectively by the grey and red line in Figure 5.36c. Between 2005 and 2010, the Cost of Living Index for Ordinary Residents exhibited substantial fluctuations. In 2005, the cost of living for ordinary residents in Helsinki was 85.20% of that for their counterparts in New York (the base city). It rose steadily to peak at 98.65% in 2008 and then started to decline until it reached 92.41% in 2010. Over the same sub-period, the Wages Index for Ordinary Residents also tracked a similar pattern, rising from 122.66 in 2005 to peak at 148.94 in 2008 before dropping to 136.87 in 2010.

Not only did wages track a similar pattern to cost of living but wages also rose and fell at the same pace as the latter throughout the first sub-period. Thus, during these years, ordinary residents in Helsinki were able to afford the same consumption level over time. This is reflected in the Purchasing Power Index for Ordinary Residents in Helsinki, which is represented by the green line in Figure 5.36c. This index was relatively stable over the first sub-period, fluctuating around 148.33. Ranking-wise, the Purchasing Power Ranking for Ordinary Residents in Helsinki, as represented by the green bars, improved over the first sub-period, rising from 34th in 2005 to 29th in 2010.

Over the second sub-period (2011–2013), the Cost of Living Index for Ordinary Residents has been on a decreasing trend. In 2011, the cost of living for ordinary residents in Helsinki was 90.74% of that for their counterparts in New York. It dropped to 76.77% in 2013. The Wages Index for Ordinary Residents has also been decreasing. This index dropped from 140.84 in 2011 to 132.72 in 2013.

Wages have dropped more slowly than cost of living. Thus, ordinary residents in Helsinki were able to afford a higher consumption level over time during the second sub-period. This is reflected in the Purchasing Power Index for Ordinary Residents which increased from 155.20 in 2011 to 172.88 in 2013. Despite the positive showing of the index, the Purchasing Power

HELSINKI
Finland

Ranking for Ordinary Residents in Helsinki has been deteriorating. Between 2011 and 2013, this ranking dropped from 25th to 28th.

Finally, we note that over the entire study period (2005–2013), the Purchasing Power Index for Ordinary Residents in Helsinki has always been higher than 100.00 — the base index value. This means that ordinary residents in Helsinki have consistently been able to afford a higher consumption level than their counterparts in New York, given the same number of working hours.

HONG KONG
Hong Kong, China

Figure 5.37a: Cost of Living and 10 Consumption Categories Rankings for Ordinary Residents in Hong Kong, Hong Kong, China

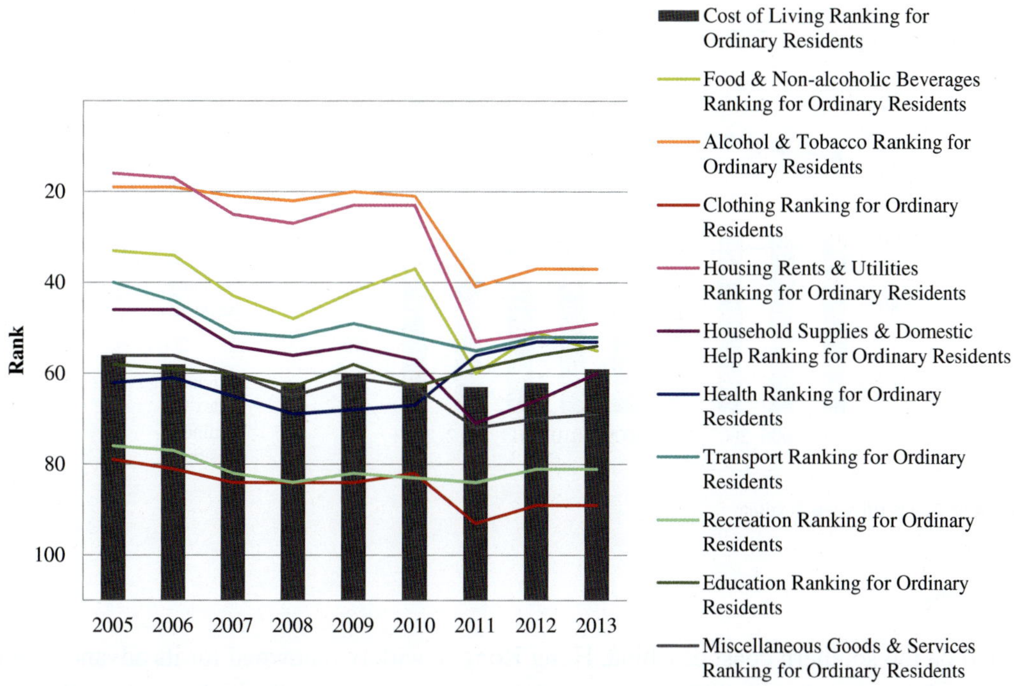

Source: Asia Competitiveness Institute

Figure 5.37b: Gross Hourly Wages in USD and Wages Ranking for Ordinary Residents in Hong Kong, Hong Kong, China

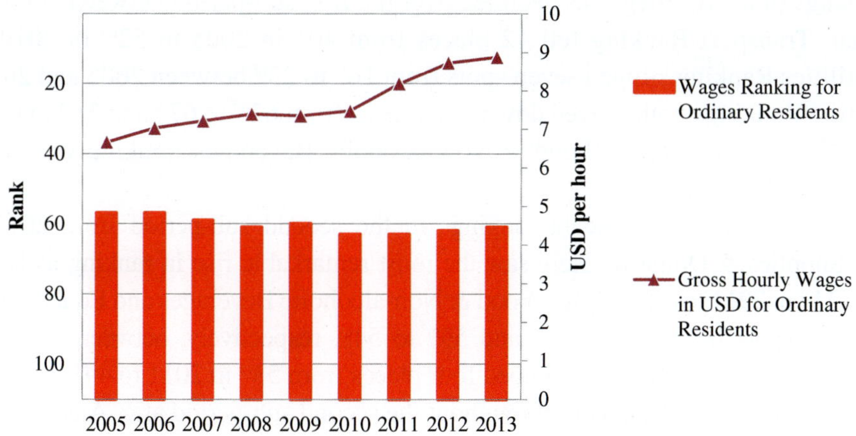

Source: Asia Competitiveness Institute

HONG KONG
Hong Kong, China

Figure 5.37c: Cost of Living, Wages and Purchasing Power Indices and Purchasing Power Ranking for Ordinary Residents in Hong Kong, Hong Kong, China

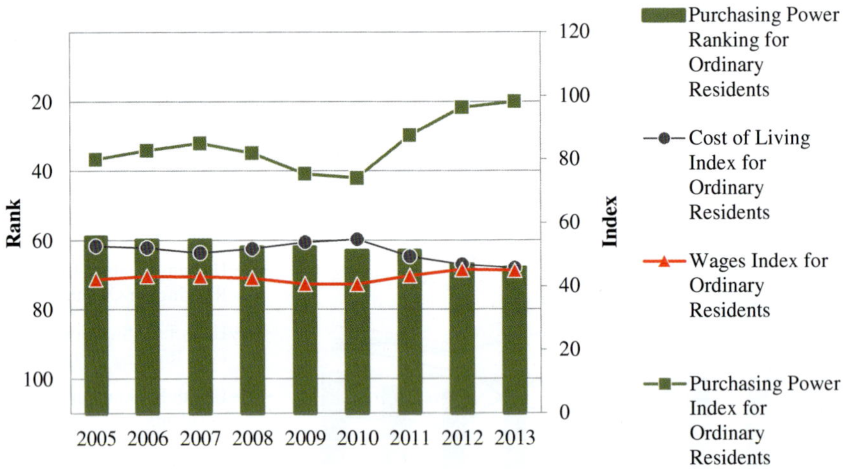

Source: Asia Competitiveness Institute

Figure 5.37a

Situated on the southern coast of China, Hong Kong is widely renowned for its advanced public transportation network with 90% of the population relying on it — the highest rate in the world. The city's Cost of Living Ranking for Ordinary Residents, as denoted by the grey bars, declined from 56th to 62nd between 2005 and 2010, but rose from 63rd to 59th between 2011 and 2013 (see Figure 5.37a). As explained in Section 3.4.2 of Chapter 3, for a more rigorous comparison of rankings, we have split the analysis into two sub-periods.

The rankings of all 10 categories declined over the first sub-period between 2005 and 2010. In particular, Transport Ranking fell 12 places from 40th in 2005 to 52nd in 2010. Housing Rents & Utilities Ranking slipped seven spots from 16th to 23rd between 2005 and 2010. Health and Education Rankings both moved down five places from 62nd to 67th and 58th to 63rd, respectively, over the first sub-period. Food & Non-alcoholic Beverages Ranking went down from 33rd in 2005 to 37th in 2010.

In contrast, all categories rose in rankings in the second sub-period from 2011 to 2013. Household Supplies & Domestic Help saw the most remarkable rise in ranking as it jumped 11 places from 71st in 2011 to 60th in 2013. Food & Non-alcoholic Beverages and Education Rankings moved up five spots from 60th to 55th and 59th to 54th, respectively, between 2011 and 2013. Housing Rents & Utilities Ranking climbed four places from 53rd in 2011 to 49th in 2013, making it the second highest ranked category throughout the second sub-period after Alcohol & Tobacco. Health and Transport Rankings both went up three spots from 56th to 53rd and 55th to 52nd,

HONG KONG
Hong Kong, China

respectively, over the second sub-period. Clothing was consistently the lowest ranked category between 2011 and 2013 although its ranking rose from 93rd to 89th over the same sub-period.

Figure 5.37b

The Gross Hourly Wages in USD for Ordinary Residents in Hong Kong, as denoted by the red line in Figure 5.37b, have consistently been on an upward trend over the study period. From US$6.66 in 2005, Hong Kong's wage level rose to US$8.88 in 2013.

The Wages Ranking for Ordinary Residents in Hong Kong, as shown by the red bars, initially deteriorated from 57th in 2005 to 63rd in 2010 and 2011. Thereafter, it has been recovering, reaching 61st in 2013.

Figure 5.37c

Let us now analyse the cost of living and wages indices more closely and draw conclusions about the purchasing power of ordinary residents in Hong Kong. As elaborated in Section 3.4.2 of Chapter 3, for a more precise and rigorous analysis, we discuss the results in two sub-periods: from 2005 to 2010 and from 2011 to 2013.

The Cost of Living Index and the Wages Index for Ordinary Residents in Hong Kong are represented respectively by the grey and red line in Figure 5.37c. Between 2005 and 2010, the Cost of Living Index for Ordinary Residents exhibited mild fluctuations. In 2005, the cost of living for ordinary residents in Hong Kong was 52.75% of that for their counterparts in New York (the base city). It first dropped to 50.58% in 2007 before rising steadily over the remaining years to 54.78% in 2010. Interestingly, over the first sub-period, the Wages Index for Ordinary Residents followed an opposite pattern to the cost of living index. Between 2005 and 2007, the wages index rose marginally from 42.20 to 43.01. It then steadily declined until it reached 40.58 in 2010.

Since wages rose while cost of living fell between 2005 and 2007, ordinary residents in Hong Kong could afford more goods and services over time during these years. After 2007, however, their consumption level decreased over time as wages fell while cost of living rose. These trends are fully reflected in the Purchasing Power Index for Ordinary Residents in Hong Kong, which is represented by the green line in Figure 5.37c. From its initial value at 80.01 in 2005, this index rose to peak at 85.04 in 2007 and then declined until it reached 74.07 in 2010. Meanwhile, the Purchasing Power Ranking for Ordinary Residents in Hong Kong, which is represented by the green bars, also deteriorated. It dropped steadily from 59th in 2005 to 63rd in 2010.

Over the second sub-period (2011–2013), the Cost of Living Index for Ordinary Residents has been on a decreasing trend. In 2011, the cost of living for ordinary residents in Hong Kong was 49.44% of that for their counterparts in New York. It dropped over the years to reach 45.75% in 2013. In contrast, the Wages Index for Ordinary Residents has been on an increasing trend, rising from 43.26 in 2011 to 44.90 in 2013.

HONG KONG
Hong Kong, China

The combined trends of increasing wages and decreasing cost of living have enabled ordinary residents in Hong Kong to afford more goods and services over time during the second sub-period. This is reflected in the Purchasing Power Index for Ordinary Residents, which rose steadily from 87.50 in 2011 to 98.14 in 2013. Despite the positive showing of the index, the Purchasing Power Ranking for Ordinary Residents has actually deteriorated. It dropped from 63rd in 2011 to 68th by 2013.

Finally, we note that over the entire study period (2005–2013), the Purchasing Power Index for Ordinary Residents in Hong Kong had consistently been lower than 100.00 — the base index value — though it came very close in 2013. This means it was not until recently that ordinary residents in Hong Kong were able to afford the same amount of goods and services as their counterparts in New York, given the same number of working hours.

HONOLULU
United States

Figure 5.38a: Cost of Living and 10 Consumption Categories Rankings for Ordinary Residents in Honolulu, United States

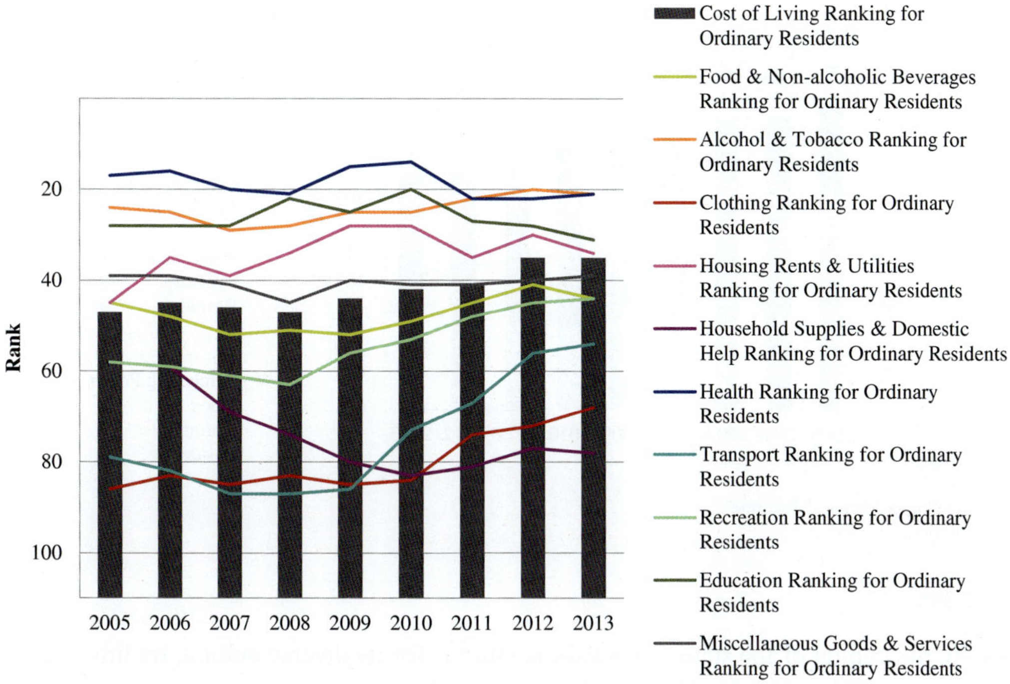

Source: Asia Competitiveness Institute

Figure 5.38b: Gross Hourly Wages in USD and Wages Ranking for Ordinary Residents in Honolulu, United States

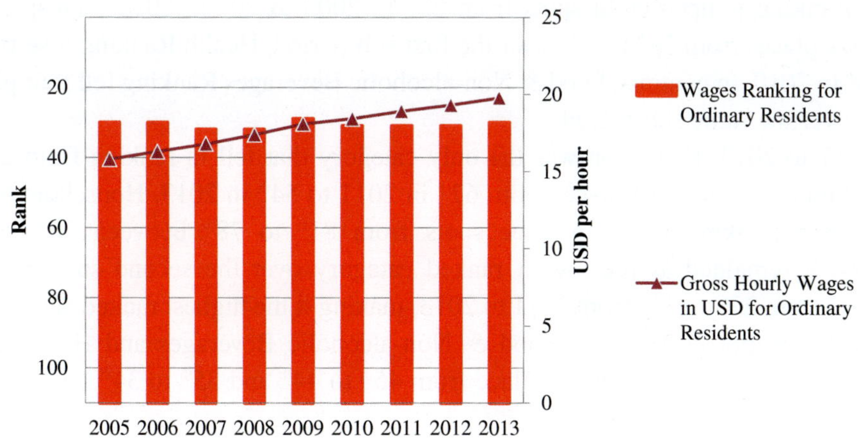

Source: Asia Competitiveness Institute

HONOLULU
United States

Figure 5.38c: Cost of Living, Wages and Purchasing Power Indices and Purchasing Power Ranking for Ordinary Residents in Honolulu, United States

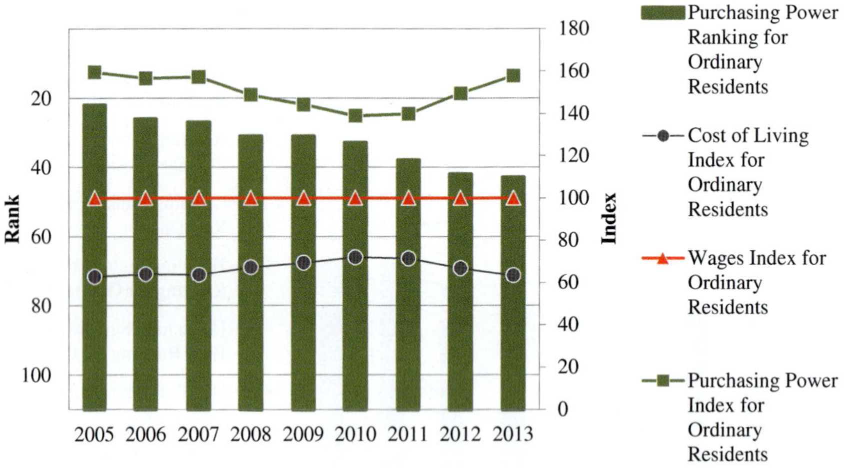

Source: Asia Competitiveness Institute

Figure 5.38a

Honolulu, the capital of the state of Hawaii, is famous for its diverse culture, traditions and cuisine. The city's Cost of Living Ranking for Ordinary Residents, as represented by the grey bar, rose from 47th to 42nd between 2005 and 2010, and from 41st to 35th between 2011 and 2013 (see Figure 5.38a). As elaborated in Section 3.4.2 of Chapter 3, for a more precise comparison of rankings, we have split the analysis into two sub-periods.

From 2005 to 2010, Housing Rents & Utilities Ranking climbed 17 places from 45th to 28th. Education Ranking jumped eight spots from 28th in 2005 to 20th in 2010. Transport Ranking moved up six places from 79th to 73rd over the first sub-period. Health Ranking rose from 17th in 2005 to 14th in 2010. In contrast, Food & Non-alcoholic Beverages Ranking fell four places from 45th to 49th over the same sub-period.

From 2011 to 2013, Education was the only category that fell in ranking from 27th to 31st. Transport Ranking jumped 13 places from 67th in 2011 to 54th in 2013. Household Supplies & Domestic Help Ranking went up three spots from 81st to 78th between 2011 and 2013. Nonetheless, it remained as the lowest ranked category over the second sub-period. Health Ranking rose from 22nd to 21st from 2011 to 2013, making it the highest ranked category in 2013 together with Alcohol & Tobacco. Food & Non-alcoholic Beverages and Housing Rents & Utilities Rankings also moved up one place from 45th to 44th and 35th to 34th, respectively, over the second sub-period.

HONOLULU
United States

Figure 5.38b

The Gross Hourly Wages in USD for Ordinary Residents in Honolulu, as represented by the red line in Figure 5.38b, increased gradually from US$15.79 in 2005 to US$19.77 in 2013.

Despite the consistent increase in the wage level, the Wages Ranking for Ordinary Residents in Honolulu, as depicted by the red bars, has remained rather stable. From 30th in 2005, it rose slightly to 29th in 2009 before dropping to 31st in 2010. The ranking remained at 31st until 2013, when it rose back to 30th.

Figure 5.38c

Let us now analyse the cost of living and wages indices more closely and draw conclusions about the purchasing power of ordinary residents in Honolulu. As elaborated in Section 3.4.2 of Chapter 3, for a more precise and rigorous analysis, we discuss the results in two sub-periods: from 2005 to 2010 and from 2011 to 2013.

The Cost of Living Index and the Wages Index for Ordinary Residents in Honolulu are represented respectively by the grey and red line in Figure 5.38c. As mentioned in Section 3.3 of Chapter 3, wage data are only available at the national level and not by cities. Therefore, wages in all cities in the United States are assumed to be the same. As a result, Honolulu, being a city in the United States, shares a common Wages Index for Ordinary Residents with the base city New York (whose index value is 100.00) over the entire study period (2005–2013).

Between 2005 and 2010, the Cost of Living Index for Ordinary Residents in Honolulu was generally on an increasing trend. Over the first three years (2005–2007), the cost of living for ordinary residents in Honolulu was almost constant at around 63.39% of that for their counterparts in New York. It then increased steadily to eventually reach 71.98% in 2010. Since the Wages Index for Ordinary Residents is constant across the years, the Purchasing Power Index for Ordinary Residents in Honolulu (or any other cities in the United States) depends only on variations in the Cost of Living Index for Ordinary Residents. Thus, the upward trend of the latter caused the Purchasing Power Index for Ordinary Residents to be on a decreasing trend throughout the first sub-period. Between 2005 and 2010, the index, which is represented by the green line in Figure 5.38c, decreased from 159.46 to 138.94. Ranking-wise, the Purchasing Power Ranking for Ordinary Residents in Honolulu, which is represented by the green bars, deteriorated from 22nd to 33rd over the first sub-period.

Over the second sub-period (2011–2013), the Cost of Living Index for Ordinary Residents has steadily declined. In 2011, the cost of living for ordinary residents in Honolulu was 71.50% of that for their counterparts in New York while in 2013, it dropped to 63.38%. As a result, the Purchasing Power Index for Ordinary Residents has steadily increased, rising from 139.87 in 2011 to 157.78

HONOLULU
United States

in 2013. Despite this positive showing of the index, the Purchasing Power Ranking for Ordinary Residents has been deteriorating. Between 2011 and 2013, it dropped from 38th to 43rd.

Finally, we note that over the entire study period (2005–2013), the Purchasing Power Index for Ordinary Residents in Honolulu has always been above 100.00 — the base index value. Thus, ordinary residents in Honolulu have consistently been able to consume more goods and services than their counterparts in New York, given the same number of working hours.

HOUSTON
United States

Figure 5.39a: Cost of Living and 10 Consumption Categories Rankings for Ordinary Residents in Houston, United States

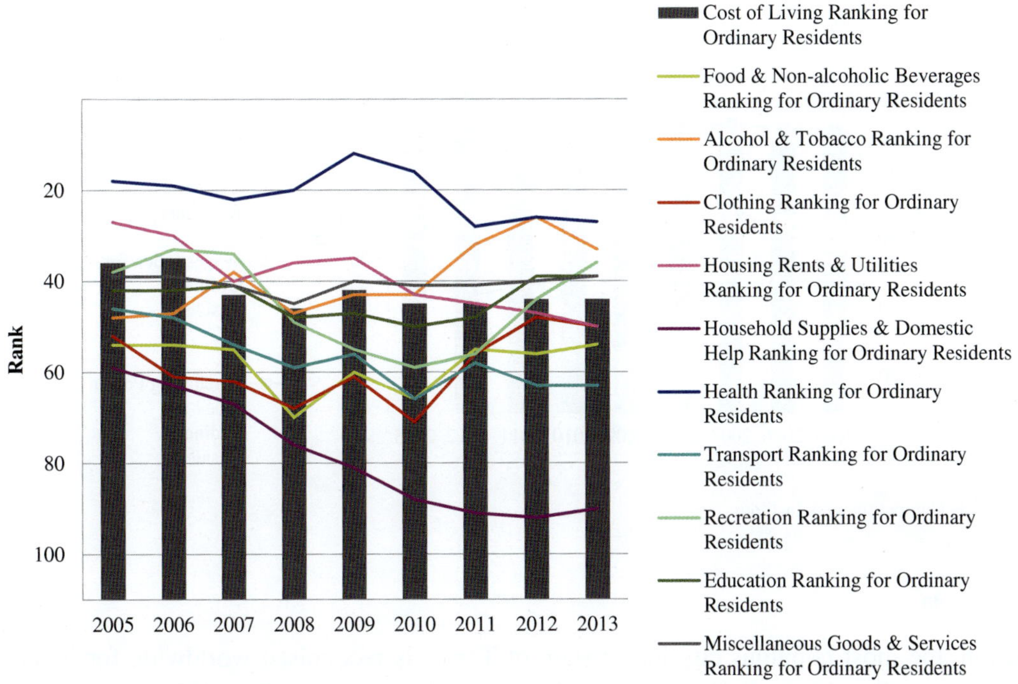

Source: Asia Competitiveness Institute

Figure 5.39b: Gross Hourly Wages in USD and Wages Ranking for Ordinary Residents in Houston, United States

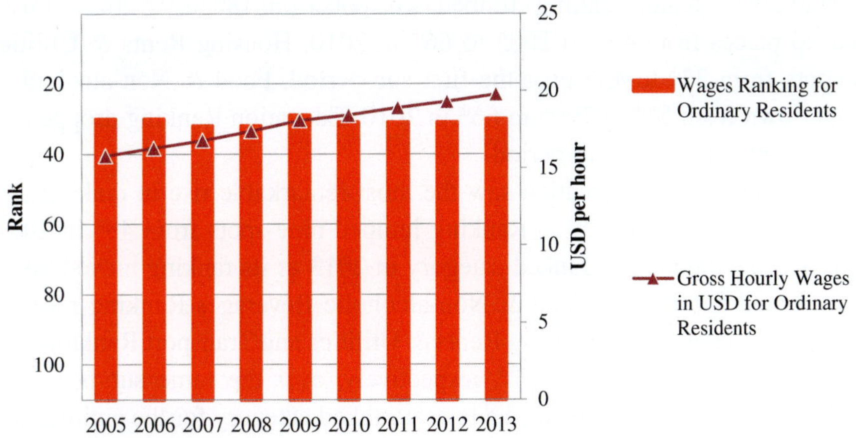

Source: Asia Competitiveness Institute

HOUSTON
United States

Figure 5.39c: Cost of Living, Wages and Purchasing Power Indices and Purchasing Power Ranking for Ordinary Residents in Houston, United States

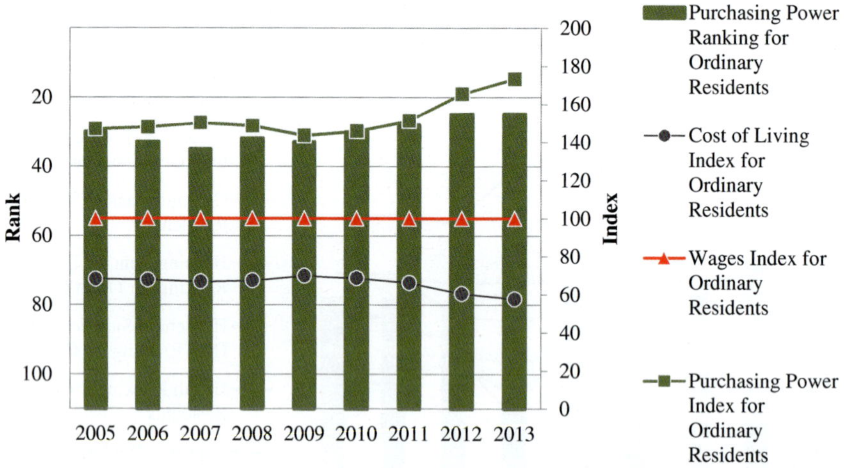

Source: Asia Competitiveness Institute

Figure 5.39a

Houston, the most populous city in the state of Texas, is recognised worldwide for its energy industry as well as biomedical research and aeronautics. The city's Cost of Living Ranking for Ordinary Residents, as shown in the grey bars, declined from 36th to 45th between 2005 and 2010, but rose from 45th to 44th between 2011 and 2013 (see Figure 5.39a). As explained in Section 3.4.2 of Chapter 3, for a more rigorous comparison of rankings, we have split the analysis into two sub-periods.

From 2005 to 2010, Health Ranking climbed two spots from 18th to 16th. In contrast, Transport Ranking fell 20 places from 46th in 2005 to 66th in 2010. Housing Rents & Utilities Ranking slipped 16 spots from 27th to 43rd over the first sub-period. Food & Non-alcoholic Beverages Ranking went down from 54th in 2005 to 66th in 2010. Education Ranking dropped eight places from 42nd to 50th over the same sub-period.

Between 2011 and 2013, Recreation saw the most remarkable rise in ranking as it climbed 20 places from 56th to 36th. Education Ranking jumped nine spots from 48th in 2011 to 39th in 2013. Health became the highest ranked category in 2013 as its ranking moved up from 28th to 27th over the second sub-period. Food & Non-alcoholic Beverages Ranking rose from 55th in 2011 to 54th in 2013. In contrast, Housing Rents & Utilities and Transport Rankings both fell five places from 45th to 50th and 58th to 63rd, respectively, over the same sub-period. Household Supplies & Domestic Help remained as the lowest ranked category for the entire study period as its ranking fell from 59th in 2005 to 88th in 2010 and to 90th in 2013.

HOUSTON
United States

Figure 5.39b

The Gross Hourly Wages in USD for Ordinary Residents in Houston, as represented by the red line in Figure 5.39b, increased gradually from US$15.79 in 2005 to US$19.77 in 2013.

Despite the consistent increase in the wage level, the Wages Ranking for Ordinary Residents in Houston, as depicted by the red bars, has remained rather stable. From 30th in 2005, it rose slightly to 29th in 2009 before dropping to 31st in 2010. The ranking remained at 31st until 2013, when it rose back to 30th.

Figure 5.39c

Let us now analyse the cost of living and wages indices more closely and draw conclusions about the purchasing power of ordinary residents in Houston. As elaborated in Section 3.4.2 of Chapter 3, for a more precise and rigorous analysis, we discuss the results in two sub-periods: from 2005 to 2010 and from 2011 to 2013.

The Cost of Living Index and the Wages Index for Ordinary Residents in Houston are represented respectively by the grey and red line in Figure 5.39c. As mentioned in Section 3.3 of Chapter 3, wage data are only available at the national level and not by cities. Therefore, wages in all cities in the United States are assumed to be the same. As a result, Houston, being a city in the United States, shares a common Wages Index for Ordinary Residents with the base city New York (whose index value is 100.00) over the entire study period (2005–2013).

Between 2005 and 2010, the Cost of Living Index for Ordinary Residents in Houston was rather stable. The cost of living for ordinary residents in Houston generally fluctuated around 67.98% of that for their counterparts in New York. Since the Wages Index for Ordinary Residents is constant across the years, the Purchasing Power Index for Ordinary Residents in Houston (or any other cities in the United States) depends only on variations in the Cost of Living Index for Ordinary Residents. Thus, the relative stability of the latter caused the Purchasing Power Index for Ordinary Residents to be also stable throughout the first sub-period. Between 2005 and 2010, this index, which is represented by the green line in Figure 5.39c, only fluctuated around 147.13. Ranking-wise, the Purchasing Power Ranking for Ordinary Residents in Houston, which is represented by the green bars, was also stable, only fluctuating around the 30th mark over the first sub-period.

Over the second sub-period (2011–2013), the Cost of Living Index for Ordinary Residents has steadily declined. In 2011, the cost of living for ordinary residents in Houston was 66.12% of that for their counterparts in New York while in 2013, it dropped to 57.68%. As a result, the Purchasing Power Index for Ordinary Residents has steadily increased, rising from 151.24 in 2011 to 173.37 in 2013. The Purchasing Power Ranking for Ordinary Residents has also been improving. Between 2011 and 2013, it rose from 28th to 25th.

Finally, we note that over the entire study period (2005–2013), the Purchasing Power Index for Ordinary Residents in Houston has always been above 100.00 — the base index value. Thus, ordinary residents in Houston have consistently been able to consume more goods and services than their counterparts in New York, given the same number of working hours.

ISTANBUL
Turkey

Figure 5.40a: Cost of Living and 10 Consumption Categories Rankings for Ordinary Residents in Istanbul, Turkey

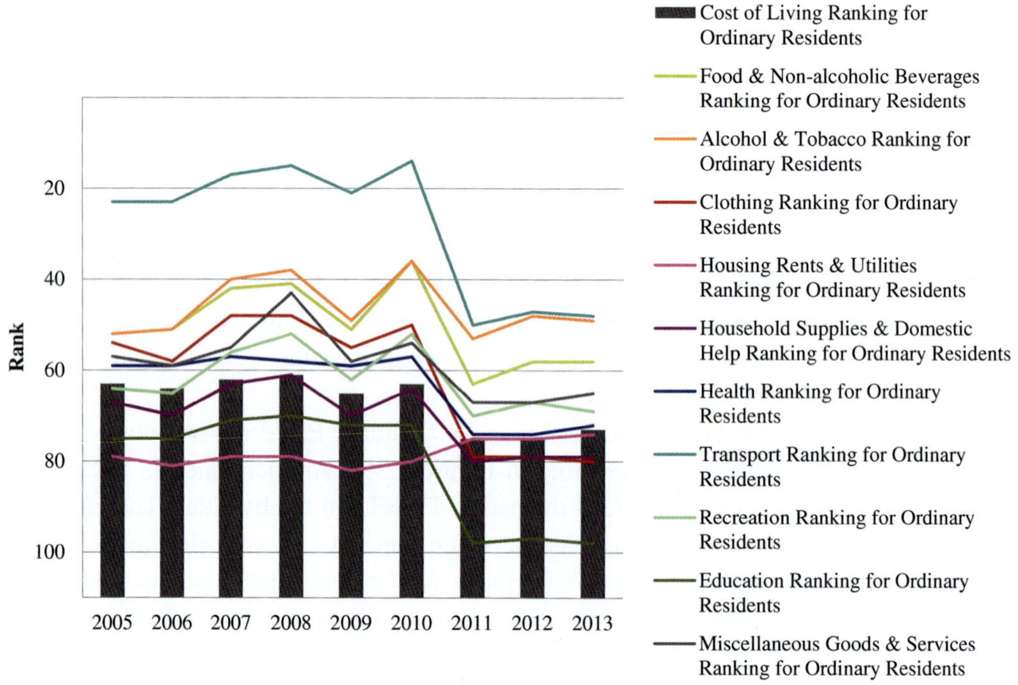

Source: Asia Competitiveness Institute

Figure 5.40b: Gross Hourly Wages in USD and Wages Ranking for Ordinary Residents in Istanbul, Turkey

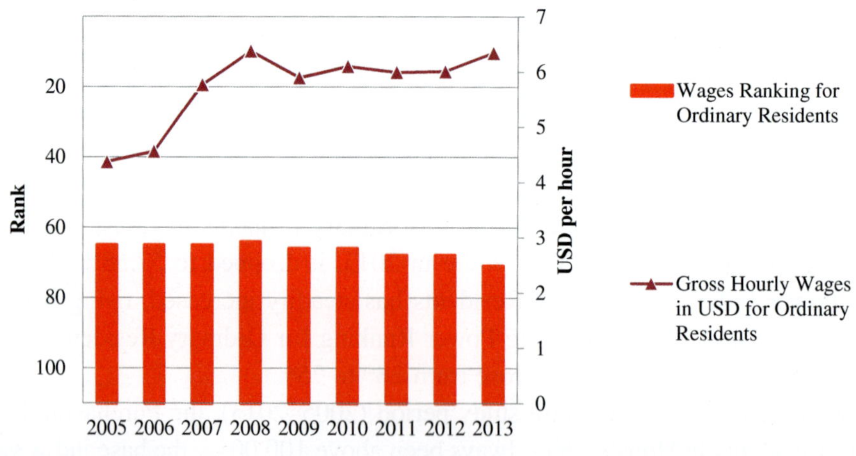

Source: Asia Competitiveness Institute

ISTANBUL
Turkey

Figure 5.40c: Cost of Living, Wages and Purchasing Power Indices and Purchasing Power Ranking for Ordinary Residents in Istanbul, Turkey

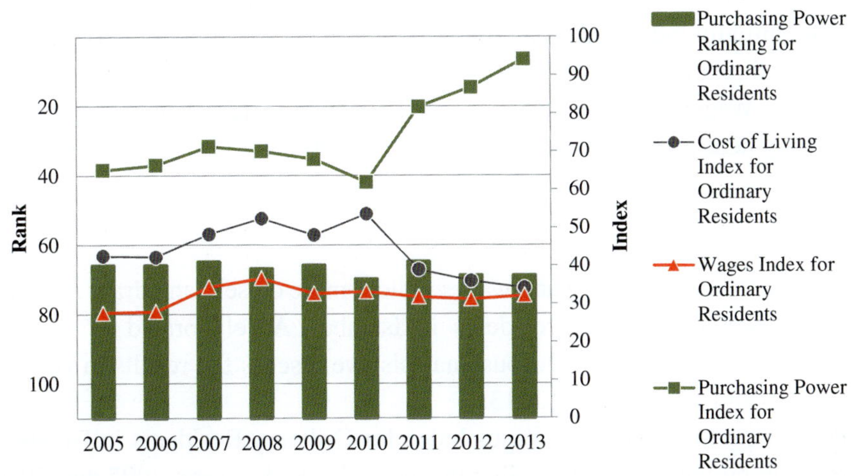

Source: Asia Competitiveness Institute

Figure 5.40a

With a population of approximately 14 million, Istanbul forms the largest urban agglomeration in Europe as well as the largest in the Middle East. The city's Cost of Living Ranking for Ordinary Residents, as denoted by the grey bars, rose from 63rd in 2005 to 61st in 2008 before falling back 63rd in 2010, and rose from 75th to 73rd between 2011 and 2013 (see Figure 5.40a). As elaborated in Section 3.4.2 of Chapter 3, for a more precise comparison of rankings, we have split the analysis into two sub-periods: from 2005 to 2010 and from 2011 to 2013.

Between 2005 and 2010, Housing Rents & Utilities was the only category that declined in ranking from 79th to 80th. Food & Non-alcoholic Beverages Ranking climbed 16 places from 52nd in 2005 to 36th in 2010. Transport Ranking jumped nine spots from 23rd to 14th over the first sub-period. Education Ranking moved up three places from 75th in 2005 to 72nd in 2010. Health Ranking rose from 59th to 57th over the same sub-period.

From 2011 to 2013, Clothing was the only category that saw a dip in ranking from 79th to 80th. Education remained as the lowest ranked category throughout the second sub-period as its ranking primarily stayed at 98th between 2011 and 2013. In contrast, Food & Non-alcoholic Beverages Ranking jumped five places from 63rd in 2011 to 58th in 2013. Health and Transport Rankings both moved up two places from 74th to 72nd and 50th to 48th, respectively, over the same sub-period. Transport was thus consistently the highest ranked category for the entire study period. Housing Rents & Utilities Ranking went up from 75th in 2011 to 74th in 2013.

ISTANBUL
Turkey

Figure 5.40b

The Gross Hourly Wages in USD for Ordinary Residents in Istanbul, as denoted by the red line in Figure 5.40b, initially increased from US$4.37 in 2005 to US$6.38 in 2008. Istanbul's wage level then remained relatively stable from 2009 to 2012 before increasing to US$6.34 in 2013.

Meanwhile, the Wages Ranking for Ordinary Residents in Istanbul, as depicted by the red bars, has generally deteriorated. It dropped from 65th in 2005 to 71st in 2013.

Figure 5.40c

Let us now analyse the cost of living and wages indices more closely and draw conclusions about the purchasing power of ordinary residents in Istanbul. As elaborated in Section 3.4.2 of Chapter 3, for a more precise and rigorous analysis, we discuss the results in two sub-periods: from 2005 to 2010 and from 2011 to 2013.

The Cost of Living Index and the Wages Index for Ordinary Residents in Istanbul are represented respectively by the grey and red line in Figure 5.40c. Between 2005 and 2010, the Cost of Living Index for Ordinary Residents was generally on an increasing trend. In 2005, the cost of living for ordinary residents in Istanbul was 42.51% of that for their counterparts in New York (the base city). It rose to 53.56% in 2010, exhibiting considerable fluctuations in between. Meanwhile, the Wages Index for Ordinary Residents first rose from 27.67 in 2005 to peak at 36.68 in 2008 and then steadily declined until it reached 33.12 in 2010.

Between 2005 and 2007, wages generally rose faster than cost of living. After 2007, however, wages could not keep up with the latter. Thus, ordinary residents in Istanbul were able to afford more goods and services over time until 2007 but could not do so thereafter. These trends are fully reflected in the Purchasing Power Index for Ordinary Residents in Istanbul, which is represented by the green line in Figure 5.40c. This index rose from 65.09 in 2005 to 71.23 in 2007 and then began to decline until it reached 61.84 in 2010. Ranking-wise, the Purchasing Power Ranking for Ordinary Residents in Istanbul, as represented by the green bars, dropped from 66th to 70th between 2005 and 2010.

Over the second sub-period (2011–2013), the Cost of Living Index for Ordinary Residents has been on a decreasing trend. In 2011, the cost of living for ordinary residents in Istanbul was 38.88% of that for their counterparts in New York. It dropped over the years to reach 34.10% in 2013. In contrast, the Wages Index for Ordinary Residents has been on an increasing trend, albeit marginally. This index rose from 31.73 in 2011 to 32.10 in 2013.

The combined trends of increasing wages and decreasing cost of living have enabled ordinary residents in Istanbul to afford more goods and services over time during the second sub-period. This is reflected in the Purchasing Power Index for Ordinary Residents, which rose steadily from 81.59 in 2011 to 94.12 in 2013. Despite the positive showing of the index, the Purchasing

ISTANBUL
Turkey

Power Ranking for Ordinary Residents has actually deteriorated. It dropped from 65th in 2011 to 69th in 2013.

Finally, we note that over the entire study period (2005–2013), the Purchasing Power Index for Ordinary Residents in Istanbul has consistently been lower than 100.00 — the base index value. This means that ordinary residents in Istanbul have only been able to afford a lower consumption level than their counterparts in New York, given the same number of working hours.

JAKARTA
Indonesia

Figure 5.41a: Cost of Living and 10 Consumption Categories Rankings for Ordinary Residents in Jakarta, Indonesia

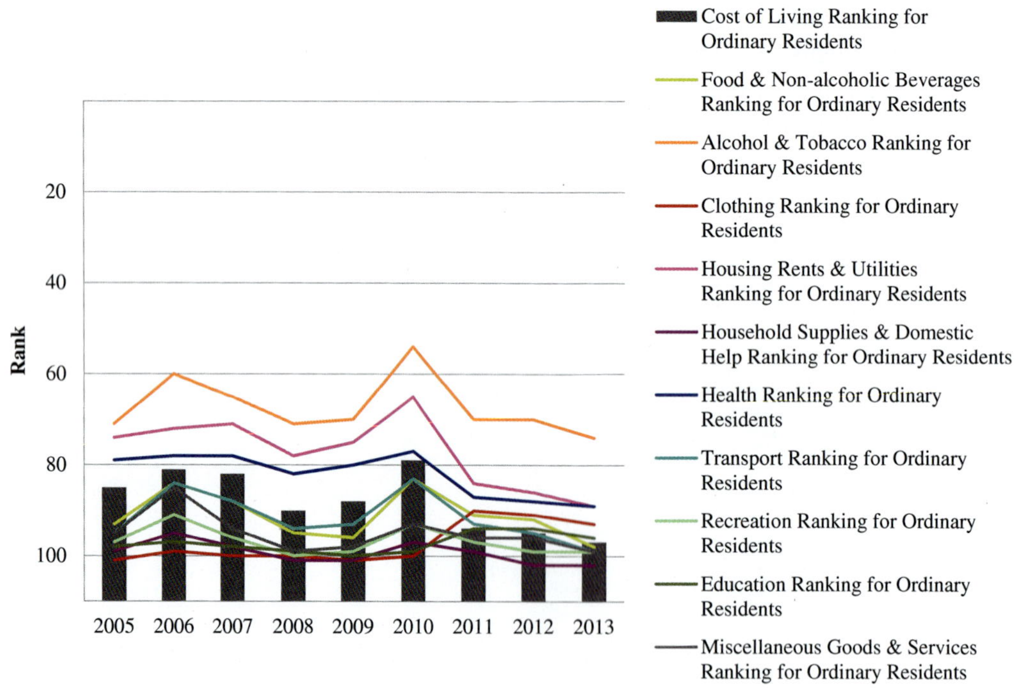

Source: Asia Competitiveness Institute

Figure 5.41b: Gross Hourly Wages in USD and Wages Ranking for Ordinary Residents in Jakarta, Indonesia

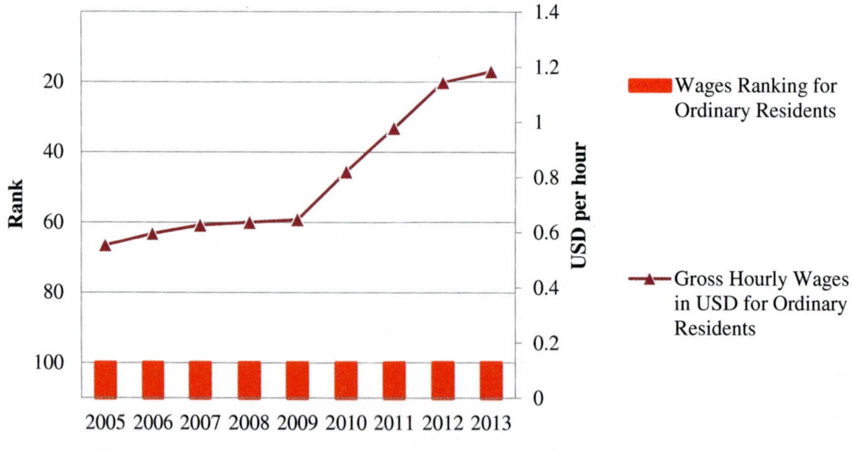

Source: Asia Competitiveness Institute

JAKARTA
Indonesia

Figure 5.41c: Cost of Living, Wages and Purchasing Power Indices and Purchasing Power Ranking for Ordinary Residents in Jakarta, Indonesia

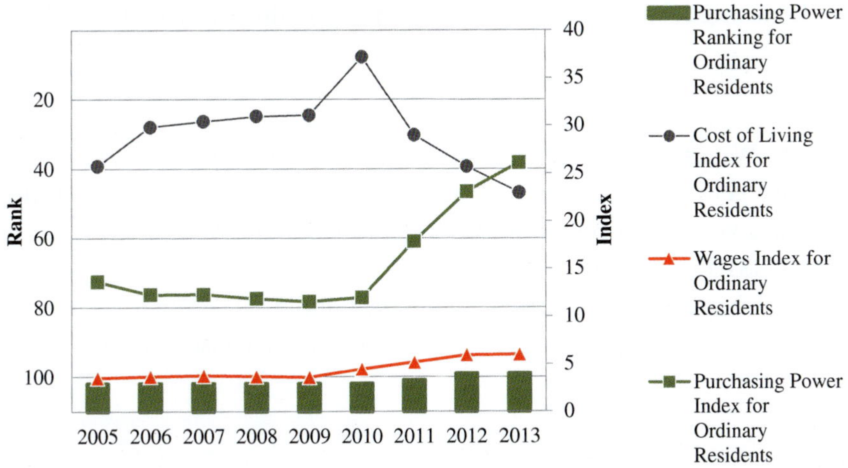

Source: Asia Competitiveness Institute

Figure 5.41a

Jakarta, the capital and most populous city of Indonesia, is the country's economic, cultural and political centre as well as the seat of the Association of Southeast Asian Nations (ASEAN) Secretariat. The city's Cost of Living Ranking for Ordinary Residents, as shown in the grey bars, rose from 85th to 79th between 2005 and 2010, and declined from 94th to 97th between 2011 and 2013 (see Figure 5.41a). As a result, Jakarta was among the top 10 most affordable cities in 2013. As explained in Section 3.4.2 of Chapter 3, for a more rigorous comparison of rankings, we have split the analysis into two sub-periods.

From 2005 to 2010, Alcohol & Tobacco saw the most significant rise in ranking as it climbed 17 places from 71st to 54th. Transport Ranking moved up 12 spots from 95th in 2005 to 83rd in 2010. Food & Non-alcoholic Beverages Ranking jumped 10 places from 93rd to 83rd over the first sub-period. Housing Rents & Utilities Ranking went up nine spots from 74th in 2005 to 65th in 2010. Health Ranking rose more modestly from 79th to 77th between 2005 and 2010. Education Ranking, in contrast, slipped one spot from 98th in 2005 to 99th in 2010.

The rankings of all 10 categories declined between 2011 and 2013. In particular, Food & Non-alcoholic Beverages Ranking fell seven places from 91st in 2011 to 98th in 2013. Transport Ranking dropped six spots from 93rd to 99th over the second sub-period. Housing Rents & Utilities Ranking slipped five places from 84th to 89th between 2011 and 2013. Health Ranking declined slightly from 87th in 2011 to 89th in 2013. Nonetheless, Housing Rents & Utilities and Health were both the second highest ranked categories in 2013 after Alcohol & Tobacco which was at 74th. Household Supplies & Domestic Help Ranking became the lowest ranked category for the entire second sub-period as its ranking slipped three places from 99th to 102nd between 2011 and 2013, making Jakarta the second cheapest city in this category in 2013.

Figure 5.41b

The Gross Hourly Wages in USD for Ordinary Residents in Jakarta, as shown by the red line in Figure 5.41b, have generally been on an increasing trend over the study period. Between 2005 and 2009, Jakarta's wage level rose from US$0.55 to US$0.65. Thereafter, it has grown much faster, reaching US$1.18 in 2013.

Ranking-wise, Jakarta has always been among the bottom. The Wages Ranking for Ordinary Residents in Jakarta, as depicted by the red bars, has remained constant at 100th out of 103 cities over the study period.

Figure 5.41c

Let us now analyse the cost of living and wages indices more closely and draw conclusions about the purchasing power of ordinary residents in Jakarta. As elaborated in Section 3.4.2 of Chapter 3, for a more precise and rigorous analysis, we discuss the results in two sub-periods: from 2005 to 2010 and from 2011 to 2013.

The Cost of Living Index and the Wages Index for Ordinary Residents in Jakarta are represented respectively by the grey and red line in Figure 5.41c. Between 2005 and 2010, the Cost of Living Index for Ordinary Residents was generally on an increasing trend. In 2005, the cost of living for ordinary residents in Jakarta was 25.74% of that for their counterparts in New York (the base city). It rose steadily over time to reach 37.20% in 2010. Over the same sub-period, the Wages Index for Ordinary Residents was rather stable. Between 2005 and 2009, this index only fluctuated around 3.63 before increasing slightly to reach 4.45 in 2010.

The combined trends of stagnant wages and rising cost of living mean that ordinary residents in Jakarta could not afford the same consumption level over time during the first sub-period. This is reflected in the Purchasing Power Index for Ordinary Residents in Jakarta, which is represented by the green line in Figure 5.41c. Between 2005 and 2010, this index dropped from 13.63 to 11.96. Ranking-wise, the Purchasing Power Ranking for Ordinary Residents in Jakarta, as represented by the green bars, remained at 102nd throughout the first sub-period.

Over the second sub-period (2011–2013), the Cost of Living Index for Ordinary Residents has been on a decreasing trend. In 2011, the cost of living for ordinary residents in Jakarta was 28.97% of that for ordinary residents in New York while by 2013, it has dropped to 22.96%. In contrast, the Wages Index for Ordinary Residents has increased, albeit marginally. This index rose from 5.17 in 2011 to 5.99 in 2013.

JAKARTA
Indonesia

The combined trends of increasing wages and decreasing cost of living have enabled ordinary residents in Jakarta to afford more goods and services over time during the second sub-period. This is reflected in the Purchasing Power Index for Ordinary Residents, which increased from 17.86 in 2011 to 26.09 by 2013. The Purchasing Power Ranking for Ordinary Residents has also improved over the second sub-period, rising from 101st in 2011 to 99th in 2013.

Finally, we note that over the entire study period (2005–2013), the Purchasing Power Index for Ordinary Residents in Jakarta has consistently been lower than 100.00 — the base index value. This means that ordinary residents in Jakarta have only been able to afford a lower consumption level than their counterparts in New York, given the same number of working hours.

JOHANNESBURG
South Africa

Figure 5.42a: Cost of Living and 10 Consumption Categories Rankings for Ordinary Residents in Johannesburg, South Africa

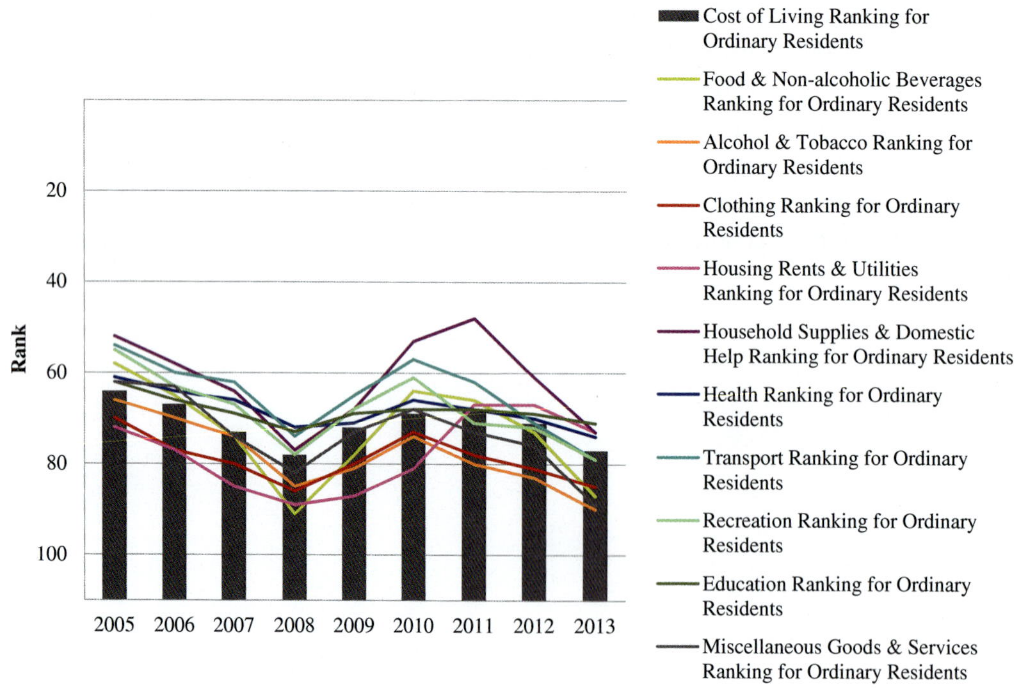

Source: Asia Competitiveness Institute

Figure 5.42b: Gross Hourly Wages in USD and Wages Ranking for Ordinary Residents in Johannesburg, South Africa

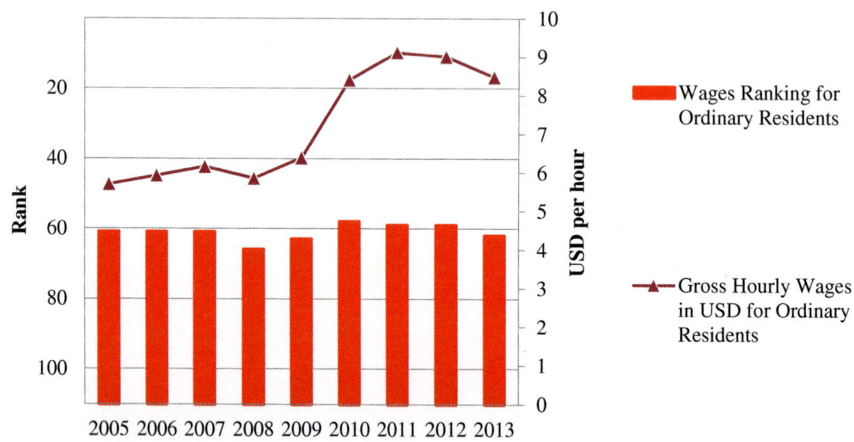

Source: Asia Competitiveness Institute

JOHANNESBURG
South Africa

Figure 5.42c: Cost of Living, Wages and Purchasing Power Indices and Purchasing Power Ranking for Ordinary Residents in Johannesburg, South Africa

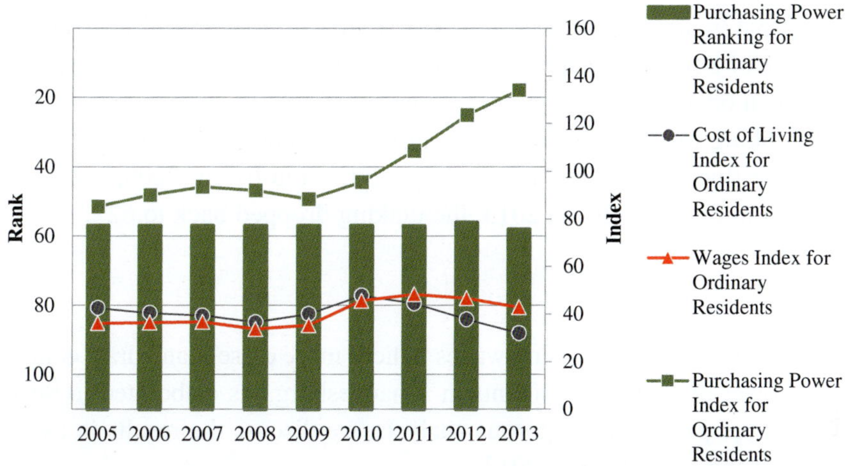

Source: Asia Competitiveness Institute

Figure 5.42a

Johannesburg, the largest city in South Africa, is also the world's largest city not situated on a river, lake or coastline. The city's Cost of Living for Ordinary Residents, as denoted by the grey bars, fell from 64th to 69th between 2005 and 2010, but rose from 68th to 77th between 2011 and 2013 (see Figure 5.42a). As elaborated in Section 3.4.2 of Chapter 3, for a more precise comparison of rankings, we have split the analysis into two sub-periods.

From 2005 to 2010, Housing Rents & Utilities Ranking slipped nine places from 72nd to 81st. Education and Food & Non-alcoholic Beverages Rankings both moved down six spots from 62nd to 68th and 58th to 64th, respectively, over the first sub-period. Health Ranking fell five places from 61st in 2005 to 66th in 2010. Transport Ranking went down from 54th to 57th over the same sub-period.

Between 2011 and 2013, Household Supplies & Domestic Help registered the most significant dip in ranking as it slipped 25 places from 48th to 73rd. Food & Non-alcoholic Beverages Ranking fell 21 spots from 66th in 2011 to 87th in 2013. Transport Ranking moved down 17 places from 62nd to 79th over the second sub-period. Alcohol & Tobacco remained as the lowest ranked category from 2011 to 2013 as its ranking went down from 80th to 90th over the same sub-period. Housing Rents & Utilities and Health Rankings both slipped six spots from 67th to 73rd and 68th to 74th, respectively, between 2011 and 2013. Education Ranking declined from 68th in 2011 to 71st in 2013, making it the highest ranked category throughout the second sub-period.

JOHANNESBURG
South Africa

Figure 5.42b

The Gross Hourly Wages in USD for Ordinary Residents in Johannesburg, as represented by the red line in Figure 5.42b, initially grew from US$5.70 in 2005 to US$9.12 in 2011. However, due to the depreciation of South African rand against US dollar from 2011 onwards, Johannesburg's wage level has been on a decreasing trend, reaching US$8.47 in 2013.

The Wages Ranking for Ordinary Residents in Johannesburg, as denoted by the red bars, has exhibited moderate fluctuations over the study period. From 61st in 2005, it dropped to 66th in 2008 before rising to 58th in 2010. In 2013, the ranking dropped back to 62nd.

Figure 5.42c

Let us now analyse the cost of living and wages indices more closely and draw conclusions about the purchasing power of ordinary residents in Johannesburg. As elaborated in Section 3.4.2 of Chapter 3, for a more precise and rigorous analysis, we discuss the results in two sub-periods: from 2005 to 2010 and from 2011 to 2013.

The Cost of Living Index and the Wages Index for Ordinary Residents in Johannesburg are represented respectively by the grey and red line in Figure 5.42c. Over the first sub-period (2005–2010), the Cost of Living Index for Ordinary Residents fluctuated moderately. In 2005, the cost of living for ordinary residents in Johannesburg was 42.49% of that for their counterparts in New York (the base city). It first decreased over the next three years to reach 36.63% in 2008 and then increased steadily over the remaining years of the first sub-period to reach 47.76% in 2010. Meanwhile, the Wages Index for Ordinary Residents also followed a relatively similar pattern. From 36.13 in 2005, it dropped to 33.68 in 2008 before embarking on an increasing trend over the remaining years to eventually reach 45.58 in 2010.

Between 2005 and 2007, wages were stable while cost of living was decreasing. Thus, during these years, ordinary residents in Johannesburg were able to afford more goods and services over time. Between 2007 and 2009, wages either dropped at a faster rate than cost of living (2007–2008) or rose more slowly than the latter (2008–2009). Thus, the purchasing power of ordinary residents in Johannesburg decreased over time during these years. Finally, over the last leg of the first sub-period (2009–2010), wages rose faster than cost of living so purchasing power of the ordinary residents was once again increasing. These trends are fully reflected in the Purchasing Power Index for Ordinary Residents in Johannesburg, which is represented by the green line in Figure 5.42c. Overall, this index was higher in 2010 (95.44) than it was in 2005 (85.03). Despite the fluctuations of the purchasing power index, the Purchasing Power Ranking for Ordinary Residents in Johannesburg, which is represented by the green bars, was very stable. In fact, it consistently stagnated at 57th over the first sub-period.

Over the second sub-period (2011–2013), the Cost of Living Index for Ordinary Residents has been on a decreasing trend. In 2011, the cost of living for ordinary residents in Johannesburg was 44.45% of that for their counterparts in New York. It dropped to 31.97% in 2013. The Wages Index for Ordinary Residents has also been decreasing, dropping from 48.24 in 2011 to 42.86 in 2013.

Wages have decreased more slowly than cost of living over the second sub-period. Thus, ordinary residents in Johannesburg have been able to afford a higher consumption level over time during these years. This is reflected in the Purchasing Power Index for Ordinary Residents, which rose from 108.53 to 134.05 between 2011 and 2013. Meanwhile, the Purchasing Power Ranking for Ordinary Residents first rose from 57th in 2011 to 56th in 2012 before dropping to 58th in 2013.

Finally, we note that the Purchasing Power Index for Ordinary Residents in Johannesburg was lower than 100.00 — the base index value — over the first sub-period. However, throughout the second sub-period, the index has been consistently above this level. This means that between 2005 and 2010, ordinary residents in Johannesburg could only afford a lower consumption level than their counterparts in New York. However, since 2011, they have been able to afford a higher consumption level than the latter.

KIEV
Ukraine

Figure 5.43a: Cost of Living and 10 Consumption Categories Rankings for Ordinary Residents in Kiev, Ukraine

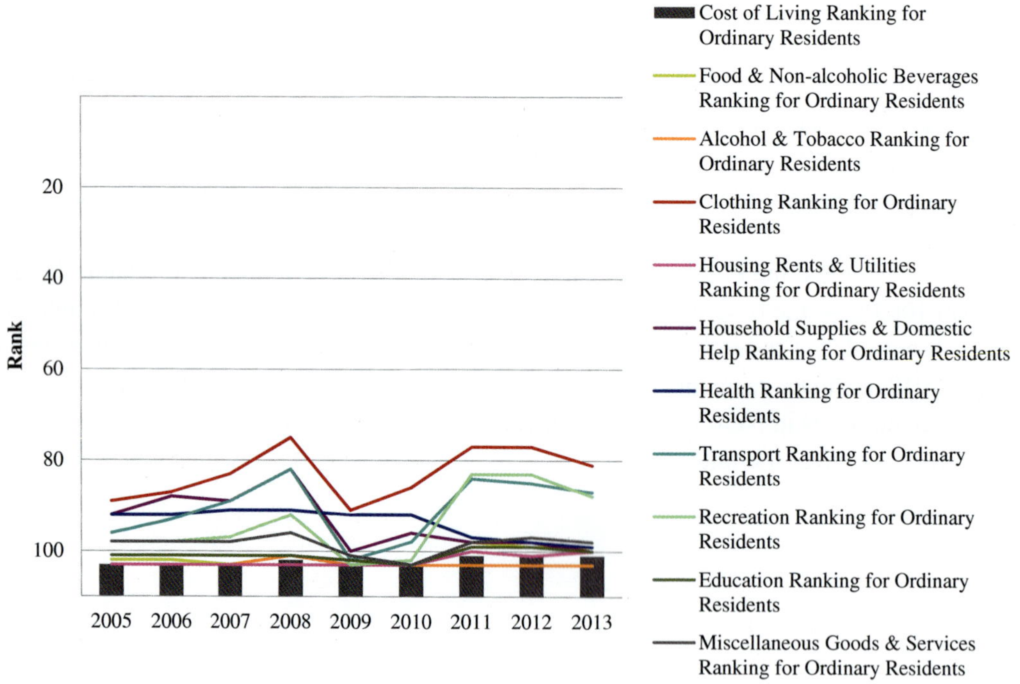

Source: Asia Competitiveness Institute

Figure 5.43b: Gross Hourly Wages in USD and Wages Ranking for Ordinary Residents in Kiev, Ukraine

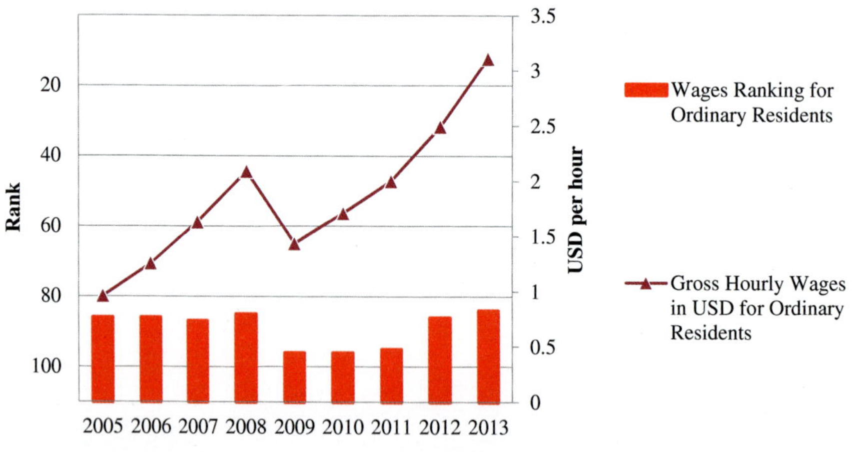

Source: Asia Competitiveness Institute

KIEV
Ukraine

Figure 5.43c: Cost of Living, Wages and Purchasing Power Indices and Purchasing Power Ranking for Ordinary Residents in Kiev, Ukraine

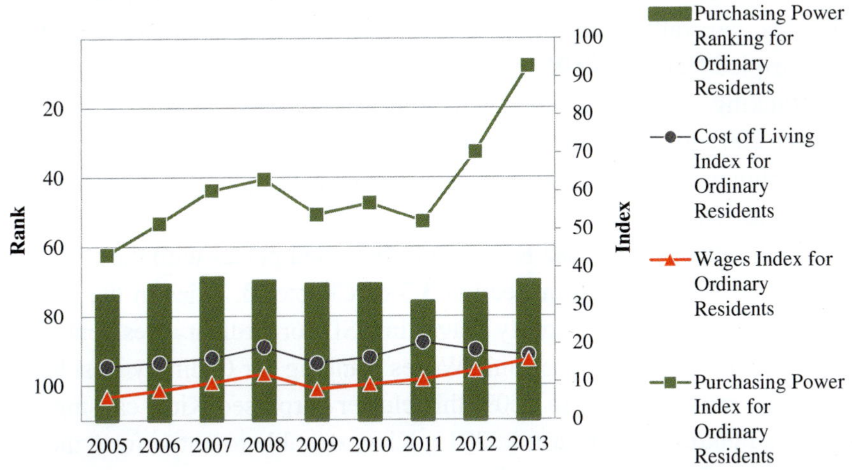

Source: Asia Competitiveness Institute

Figure 5.43a

Kiev, the capital and largest city of Ukraine, is one of the oldest cities in Eastern Europe. The city's Cost of Living Ranking for Ordinary Residents, as represented by the grey bars, largely remained at 103rd between 2005 and 2010, and stayed at 101st between 2011 and 2013 (see Figure 5.43a). As explained in Section 3.4.2 of Chapter 3, for a more rigorous comparison of rankings, we have split the analysis into two sub-periods.

From 2005 to 2010, Housing Rents & Utilities Ranking stayed unchanged at 103rd. Health Ranking also remained stable at 92nd over the first sub-period. Education and Transport Rankings both fell two places from 101st to 103rd and 96th to 98th, respectively, between 2005 and 2010. Food & Non-alcoholic Beverages Ranking moved down one spot from 102nd to 103rd over the same sub-period.

Between 2011 and 2013, Recreation saw the most remarkable dip in ranking from 83rd to 88th. Clothing was consistently the highest ranked category throughout the study period although its ranking slipped four places from 77th in 2011 to 81st in 2013. Transport Ranking fell three spots from 84th to 87th over the second sub-period. Health Ranking dropped two places from 97th in 2011 to 99th in 2013. Food & Non-alcoholic Beverages and Education Rankings both moved down one place from 98th to 99th and 99th to 100th, respectively, between 2011 and 2013. Housing Rents & Utilities Ranking primarily stayed unchanged at 100th over the same sub-period. Alcohol & Tobacco was the lowest ranked category from 2011 to 2013 as its ranking remained at 103rd throughout.

KIEV
Ukraine

Figure 5.43b

The Gross Hourly Wages in USD for Ordinary Residents in Kiev, as denoted by the red line in Figure 5.43b, have generally been on an increasing trend over the study period. Kiev's wage level more than tripled from US$0.96 in 2005 to US$3.11 in 2013.

The Wages Ranking for Ordinary Residents in Kiev, as shown by the red bars, has fluctuated significantly over 2005 to 2013. For example, after four years of remaining at around 85th and 86th, the ranking plunged to 96th in 2009. Another instance was in 2012, when it rose back to 86th in 2012 from 95th in 2011.

The fluctuations happened because Kiev regularly traded places with the eight Chinese cities on the ranking table. As explained in Section 3.3 of Chapter 3, cities in the same country are assumed to share a common Gross Hourly Wages in USD for Ordinary Residents. Consequently, the eight Chinese cities also share the same Wages Ranking for Ordinary Residents and form a cluster on the wage ranking table. In 2009, this cluster surpassed Kiev, causing the significant drop in the latter's ranking. In contrast, in 2011, Kiev was able to outperform the Chinese cities and so moved up significantly on the ranking table.

Figure 5.43c

Let us now analyse the cost of living and wages indices more closely and draw conclusions about the purchasing power of ordinary residents in Kiev. As elaborated in Section 3.4.2 of Chapter 3, for a more precise and rigorous analysis, we discuss the results in two sub-periods: from 2005 to 2010 and from 2011 to 2013.

The Cost of Living Index and the Wages Index for Ordinary Residents in Kiev are represented respectively by the grey and red line in Figure 5.43c. Between 2005 and 2010, the Cost of Living Index for Ordinary Residents fluctuated quite substantially. In 2005, the cost of living for ordinary residents in Kiev was 14.02% of that for their counterparts in New York (the base city). It rose steadily over the years to peak at 19.03% in 2008 before experiencing a sharp plunge to 14.76% in 2009. It then rose again over 2009–2010 to eventually reach 16.32%. Meanwhile, the Wages Index for Ordinary Residents followed a similar pattern. Overall, the wages index was higher in 2010 (9.28) than it was in 2005 (6.08).

The Purchasing Power Index for Ordinary Residents in Kiev, as represented by the green line in Figure 5.43c, generally rose and fell in the same manner as the cost of living and wages indices. Overall, the index value was higher in 2010 (56.90) than it was in 2005 (43.35). This indicates that the amount of goods and services ordinary residents in Kiev could afford in 2010 was higher than what they could in 2005. Ranking-wise, the Purchasing Power Ranking for Ordinary Residents in Kiev, which is represented by the green bars, improved over the first sub-period, rising from 74th in 2005 to 71st in 2010.

KIEV
Ukraine

Over the second sub-period (2011–2013), the Cost of Living Index for Ordinary Residents has been on a decreasing trend. In 2011, the cost of living for ordinary residents in Kiev was 20.36% of that for ordinary residents in New York. It decreased over the years to reach 16.97% in 2013. In contrast, the Wages Index for Ordinary Residents has been on an upward trend, increasing from 10.59 in 2011 to 15.74 in 2013.

The combined trends of increasing wages and decreasing cost of living have enabled ordinary residents in Kiev to afford a higher consumption level over time throughout the second sub-period. This is reflected in the Purchasing Power Index for Ordinary Residents, which rose from 52.04 to 92.71 between 2011 and 2013. The Purchasing Power Ranking for Ordinary Residents has also improved remarkably, rising from 76th in 2011 to 70th in 2013.

Finally, we note that over the entire study period (2005–2013), the Purchasing Power Index for Ordinary Residents in Kiev has consistently been below 100.00 — the base index value. This means that ordinary residents in Kiev have only been able to afford a lower consumption level than their counterparts in New York, given the same number of working hours.

KUALA LUMPUR
Malaysia

Figure 5.44a: Cost of Living and 10 Consumption Categories Rankings for Ordinary Residents in Kuala Lumpur, Malaysia

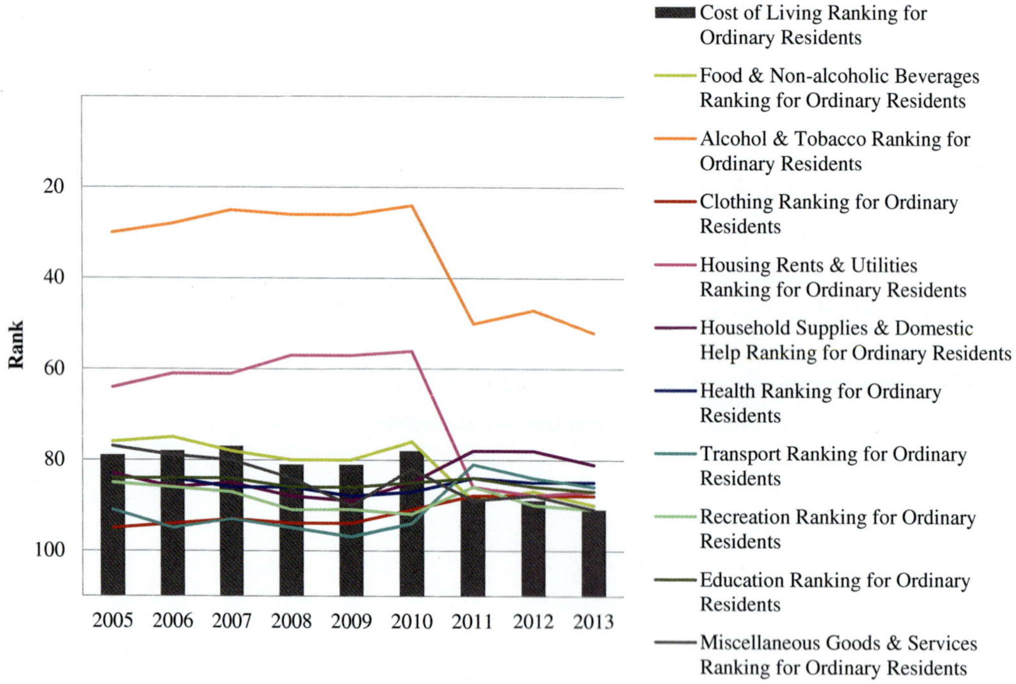

Source: Asia Competitiveness Institute

Figure 5.44b: Gross Hourly Wages in USD and Wages Ranking for Ordinary Residents in Kuala Lumpur, Malaysia

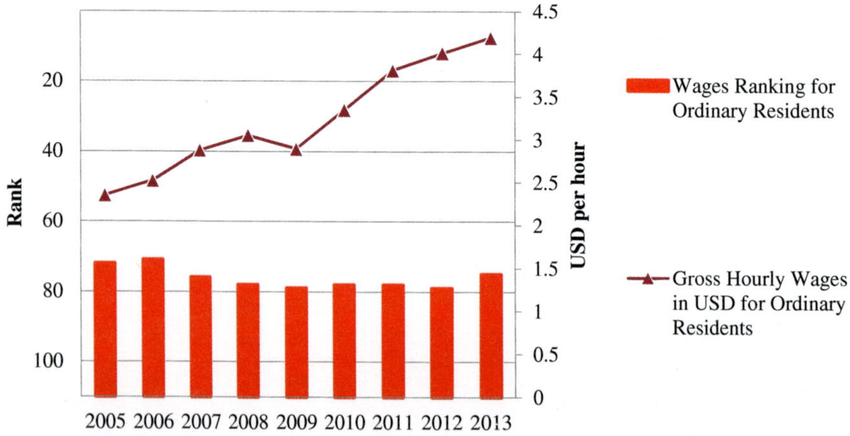

Source: Asia Competitiveness Institute

KUALA LUMPUR
Malaysia

Figure 5.44c: Cost of Living, Wages and Purchasing Power Indices and Purchasing Power Ranking for Ordinary Residents in Kuala Lumpur, Malaysia

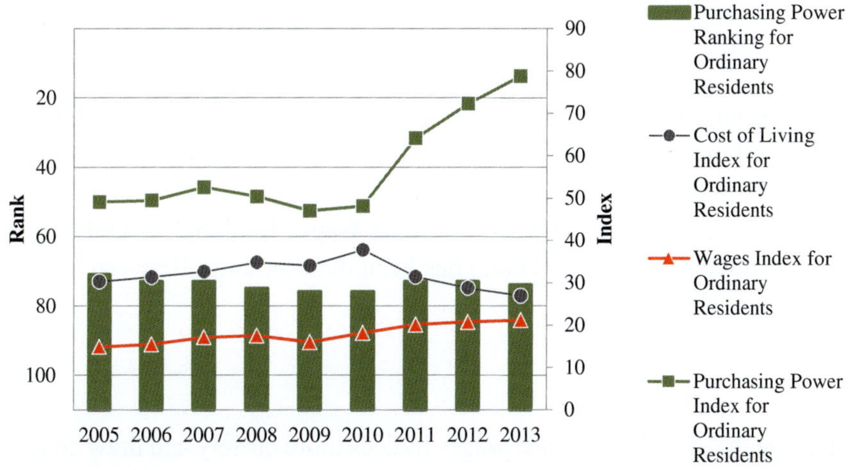

Source: Asia Competitiveness Institute

Figure 5.44a

Kuala Lumpur, the capital and most populous city of Malaysia, is home to the tallest twin buildings in the world, the Petronas Twin Towers. The city's Cost of Living Ranking for Ordinary Residents, as shown in the grey bars, rose from 79th to 78th between 2005 and 2010, but declined from 88th to 91st between 2011 and 2013 (see Figure 5.44a). As elaborated in Section 3.4.2 of Chapter 3, for a more precise comparison of rankings, we have split the analysis into two sub-periods.

Between 2005 and 2010, Housing Rents & Utilities recorded the most remarkable rise in ranking as it jumped eight places from 64th to 56th. Alcohol & Tobacco and Clothing Rankings rose from 30th to 24th and 95th to 91st, respectively, over the first sub-period. In contrast, Health and Transport Rankings both fell three spots from 84th to 87th and 91st to 94th, respectively, between 2005 and 2010. Education Ranking dropped slightly from 84th in 2005 to 85th in 2010. Food & Non-alcoholic Beverages Ranking slipped from 76th in 2005 to 80th in 2008 and 2009 before rising back to 76th in 2010.

From 2011 to 2013, the rankings of all 10 categories declined. In particular, Transport Ranking fell five places from 81st in 2011 to 86th in 2013. Education Ranking moved down three spots from 84th to 87th over the second sub-period. Housing Rents & Utilities and Health Rankings both slipped one place from 86th to 87th and 84th to 85th, respectively, between 2011 and 2013. Likewise, Food & Non-alcoholic Beverages Ranking dropped from 89th in 2011 to 90th in

KUALA LUMPUR
Malaysia

2013, making it the second lowest ranked category in 2013 after Recreation and Miscellaneous Goods & Services which were both at 91st.

Figure 5.44b

Notwithstanding a slight decline in 2009, the Gross Hourly Wages in USD for Ordinary Residents in Kuala Lumpur, as shown by the red line in Figure 5.44b, rose fairly consistently from US$2.35 in 2005 to US$4.19 in 2013.

Despite the steady increase in the wage level, the Wages Ranking for Ordinary Residents in Kuala Lumpur, as depicted by the red bars, has been deteriorating. Between 2005 and 2013, it dropped from 72nd to 75th.

Figure 5.44c

Let us now analyse the cost of living and wages indices more closely and draw conclusions about the purchasing power of ordinary residents in Kuala Lumpur. As elaborated in Section 3.4.2 of Chapter 3, for a more precise and rigorous analysis, we discuss the results in two sub-periods: from 2005 to 2010 and from 2011 to 2013.

The Cost of Living Index and the Wages Index for Ordinary Residents in Kuala Lumpur are represented respectively by the grey and red line in Figure 5.44c. Between 2005 and 2010, the Cost of Living Index for Ordinary Residents was generally on an increasing trend. In 2005, the cost of living for ordinary residents in Kuala Lumpur was 30.30% of that for their counterparts in New York (the base city). It rose steadily over time to reach 37.73% in 2010. Over the same sub-period, the Wages Index for Ordinary Residents also increased, rising from 14.88 in 2005 to 18.17 in 2010.

During the first sub-period, wages kept up with the pace of increase of cost of living. Thus, ordinary residents in Kuala Lumpur could afford the same amount of goods and services over time during these years. This is reflected in the Purchasing Power Index for Ordinary Residents in Kuala Lumpur, which is represented by the green line in Figure 5.44c. This index generally fluctuated around 49.45 between 2005 and 2010: it rose from 49.12 in 2005 to its peak at 52.58 in 2007 and eventually reached 48.15 in 2010. Meanwhile, the Purchasing Power Ranking for Ordinary Residents in Kuala Lumpur, as represented by the green bars, actually deteriorated over the first sub-period, dropping from 71st in 2005 to 76th in 2010.

Over the second sub-period (2011–2013), the Cost of Living Index for Ordinary Residents has been on a decreasing trend. In 2011, the cost of living for ordinary residents in Kuala Lumpur was 31.42% of that for ordinary residents in New York. It dropped over the years to reach 26.91% in 2013. In contrast, the Wages Index for Ordinary Residents has been rather stable. It only improved marginally from 20.15 to 21.20 between 2011 and 2013.

KUALA LUMPUR
Malaysia

The combined trends of stable wages and decreasing cost of living have enabled ordinary residents in Kuala Lumpur to afford more goods and services over time throughout the second sub-period. This is evident in the Purchasing Power Index for Ordinary Residents which increased from 64.12 in 2011 to 78.78 in 2013. Despite this positive showing of the index, the Purchasing Power Ranking for Ordinary Residents has actually been rather stable. It remained at 73rd in 2011 and 2012 before dropping to 74th in 2013.

Finally, we note that over the entire study period (2005–2013), the Purchasing Power Index for Ordinary Residents in Kuala Lumpur has consistently been lower than 100.00 — the base index value. This means that ordinary residents in Kuala Lumpur have only been able to afford a lower consumption level than their counterparts in New York, given the same number of working hours.

KUWAIT
Kuwait

Figure 5.45a: Cost of Living and 10 Consumption Categories Rankings for Ordinary Residents in Kuwait, Kuwait

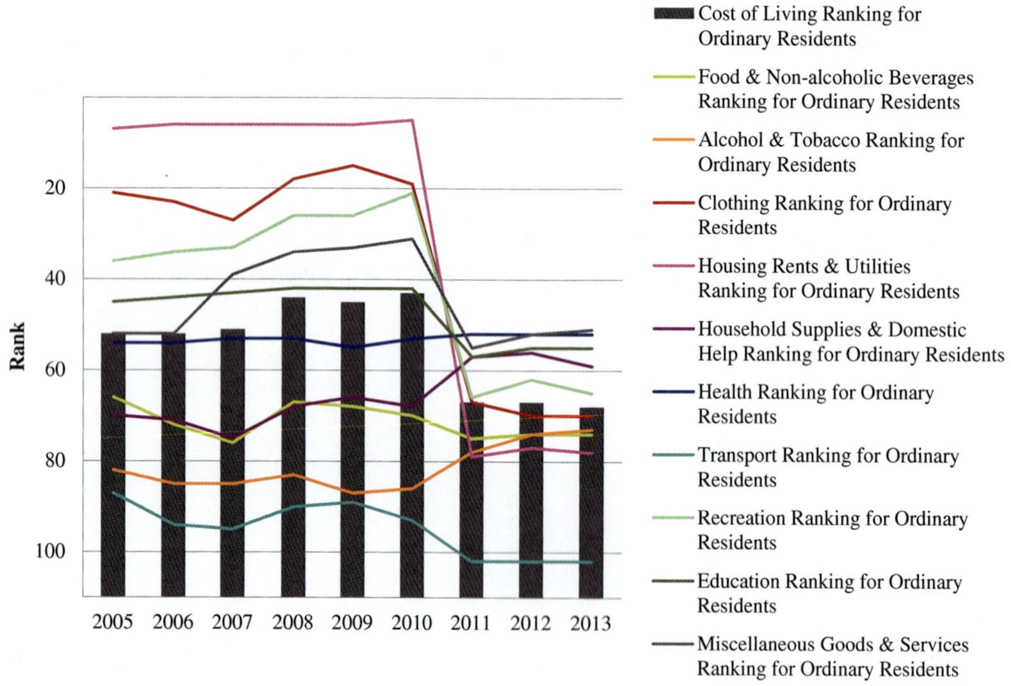

Source: Asia Competitiveness Institute

Figure 5.45b: Gross Hourly Wages in USD and Wages Ranking for Ordinary Residents in Kuwait, Kuwait

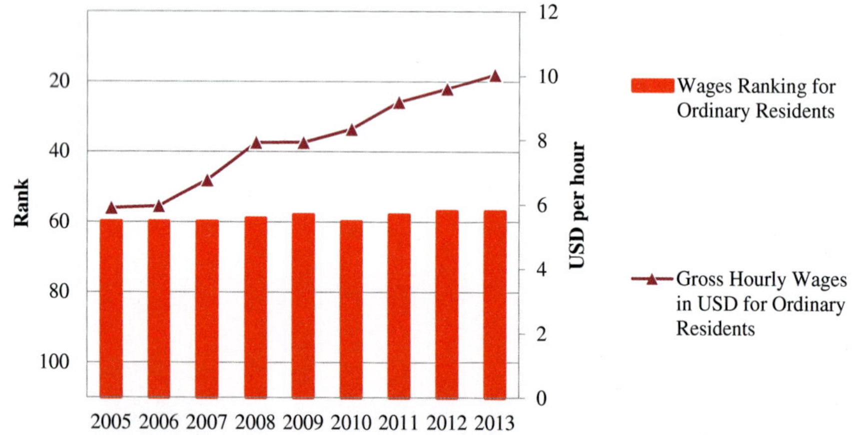

Source: Asia Competitiveness Institute

KUWAIT
Kuwait

Figure 5.45c: Cost of Living, Wages and Purchasing Power Indices and Purchasing Power Ranking for Ordinary Residents in Kuwait, Kuwait

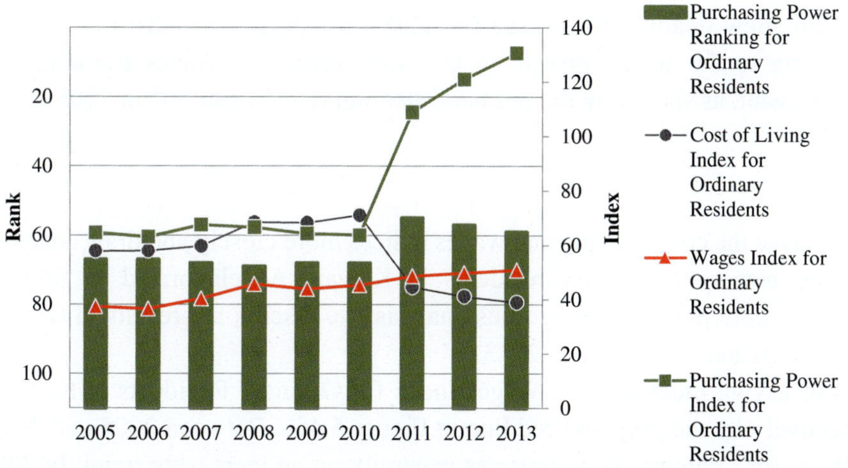

Source: Asia Competitiveness Institute

Figure 5.45a

Kuwait City is the capital and largest city of Kuwait with a population of approximately 2.1 million in the metropolitan area. The city's Cost of Living Ranking for Ordinary Residents, as denoted by the grey bars, rose from 52nd to 43rd between 2005 and 2010, but fell from 67th to 68th between 2011 and 2013 (see Figure 5.45a). As explained in Section 3.4.2 of Chapter 3, for a more rigorous comparison of rankings, we have split the analysis into two sub-periods.

From 2005 to 2010, Education Ranking moved up three spots from 45th to 42nd. Housing Rents & Utilities Ranking jumped two places from seventh in 2005 to fifth in 2010. Health Ranking went up from 54th to 53rd over the first sub-period. In contrast, Transport Ranking slipped six spots from 87th in 2005 to 93rd in 2010. Food & Non-alcoholic Beverages Ranking fell four places from 66th in 2005 to 70th in 2010.

From 2011 to 2013, Miscellaneous Goods & Services Ranking moved up four spots from 55th to 51st, making it the highest ranked category in 2013. Education Ranking jumped two places from 57th in 2011 to 55th in 2013. Housing Rents & Utilities and Food & Non-alcoholic Beverages Rankings both rose one spot from 79th to 78th and 75th to 74th, respectively, over the same sub-period. Health and Transport Rankings remained unchanged at 52nd and 102nd, respectively, between 2011 and 2013. Consequently, Kuwait became the second cheapest city in terms of Transport over the second sub-period.

KUWAIT
Kuwait

Figure 5.45b

The Gross Hourly Wages in USD for Ordinary Residents in Kuwait, as denoted by the red line in Figure 5.45b, grew steadily from US$5.89 in 2005 to US$10.03 in 2013.

Corresponding to the steady growth in the wage level, the Wages Ranking for Ordinary Residents in Kuwait, as shown by the red bars, also improved from 60th in 2005 to 57th in 2013.

Figure 5.45c

Let us now analyse the cost of living and wages indices more closely and draw conclusions about the purchasing power of ordinary residents in Kuwait. As elaborated in Section 3.4.2 of Chapter 3, for a more precise and rigorous analysis, we discuss the results in two sub-periods: from 2005 to 2010 and from 2011 to 2013.

The Cost of Living Index and the Wages Index for Ordinary Residents in Kuwait are represented respectively by the grey and red line in Figure 5.45c. Between 2005 and 2010, the Cost of Living Index for Ordinary Residents was generally on an increasing trend. In 2005, the cost of living for ordinary residents in Kuwait was 57.80% of that for their counterparts in New York (the base city). It rose steadily over time to reach 71.00% in 2010. Over the same sub-period, the Wages Index for Ordinary Residents also increased, rising from 37.33 in 2005 to 45.25 in 2010.

Over the first sub-period, wages kept up with the pace of increase of cost of living. Thus, ordinary residents in Kuwait could afford the same amount of goods and services over time during these years. This is reflected in the Purchasing Power Index for Ordinary Residents in Kuwait, which is represented by the green line in Figure 5.45c. This index generally fluctuated around 64.93 between 2005 and 2010: it rose from 64.58 in 2005 to its peak at 67.50 in 2007 and eventually reached 63.73 in 2010. Meanwhile, the Purchasing Power Ranking for Ordinary Residents in Kuwait, as represented by the green bars, was also relatively stable, fluctuating between 67th and 69th over 2005–2010.

Over the second sub-period (2011–2013), the Cost of Living Index for Ordinary Residents has been on a decreasing trend. In 2011, the cost of living for ordinary residents in Kuwait was 44.54% of that for ordinary residents in New York. It dropped over the years to reach 38.88% in 2013. In contrast, the Wages Index for Ordinary Residents has been increasing. It rose from 48.53 to 50.77 between 2011 and 2013.

The combined trends of increasing wages and decreasing cost of living have enabled ordinary residents in Kuwait to afford more goods and services over time throughout the second sub-period. This is evident in the Purchasing Power Index for Ordinary Residents, which increased from 108.96 in 2011 to 130.56 in 2013. Despite this positive showing of the index, the Purchasing Power Ranking for Ordinary Residents has actually deteriorated. It dropped from 55th in 2011 to 59th in 2013.

KUWAIT
Kuwait

Finally, we note that the Purchasing Power Index for Ordinary Residents in Kuwait was lower than 100.00, the base index value, over the first sub-period. However, throughout the second sub-period, the index has been consistently above this level. This means that between 2005 and 2010, ordinary residents in Kuwait could only afford a lower consumption level than their counterparts in New York. However, since 2011, they have been able to afford a higher consumption level than the latter.

LEXINGTON
United States

Figure 5.46a: Cost of Living and 10 Consumption Categories Rankings for Ordinary Residents in Lexington, United States

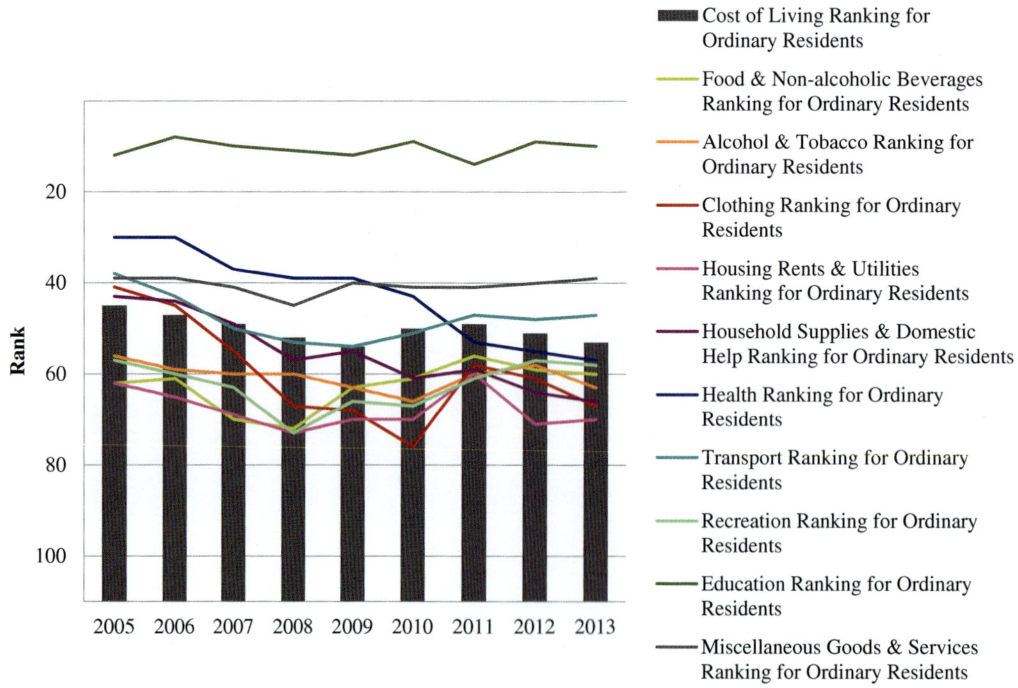

Source: Asia Competitiveness Institute

Figure 5.46b: Gross Hourly Wages in USD and Wages Ranking for Ordinary Residents in Lexington, United States

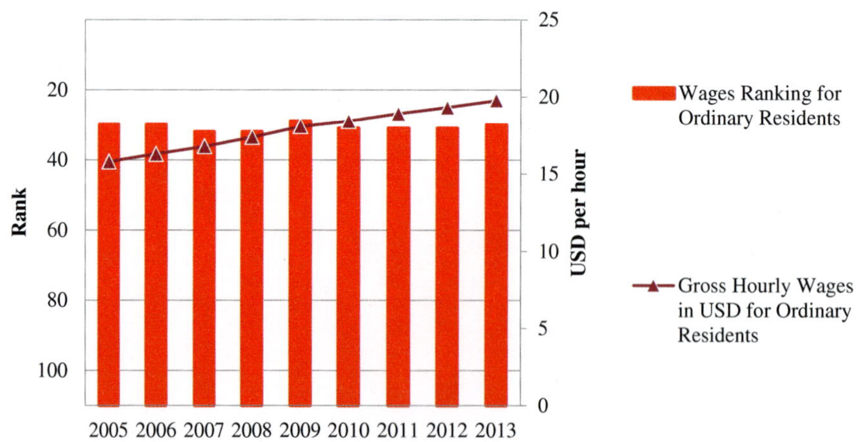

Source: Asia Competitiveness Institute

LEXINGTON
United States

Figure 5.46c: Cost of Living, Wages and Purchasing Power Indices and Purchasing Power Ranking for Ordinary Residents in Lexington, United States

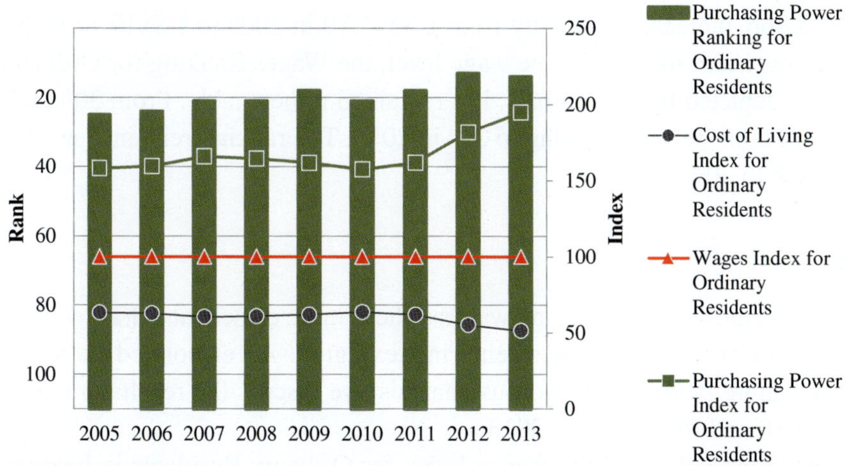

Source: Asia Competitiveness Institute

Figure 5.46a

Lexington is the second largest city in the state of Kentucky and the 61st largest in the United States. The city's Cost of Living Ranking for Ordinary Residents, as represented by the grey bars, declined from 45th to 50th between 2005 and 2010, and from 49th to 53rd between 2011 and 2013 (see Figure 5.46a). As elaborated in Section 3.4.2 of Chapter 3, for a more precise comparison of rankings, we have split the analysis into two sub-periods.

From 2005 to 2010, Health and Transport Rankings both fell 13 places from 30th to 43rd and 38th to 51st, respectively. Housing Rents & Utilities Ranking slipped eight spots from 62nd in 2005 to 70th in 2010. In contrast, Education Ranking jumped three places from 12th to ninth over the first sub-period. Food & Non-alcoholic Beverages Ranking moved up one spot from 62nd in 2005 to 61st in 2010 while also exhibiting substantial fluctuations in between.

Between 2011 and 2013, Housing Rents & Utilities Ranking slipped 10 places from 60th to 70th, making it the lowest ranked category in 2012 and 2013. Clothing Ranking moved down nine spots from 58th in 2011 to 67th in 2013. Health and Food & Non-alcoholic Beverages Rankings both dropped four spots from 53rd to 57th and 56th to 60th, respectively over the second sub-period. Transport Ranking largely remained at 47th from 2011 to 2013. In contrast, Education was consistently the highest ranked category over the study period as its ranking rose from 14th to 10th between 2011 and 2013. Recreation Ranking jumped three places from 61st in 2011 to 58th in 2013. Miscellaneous Goods & Services Ranking moved up two spots from 41st to 39th over the same sub-period.

LEXINGTON
United States

Figure 5.46b

The Gross Hourly Wages in USD for Ordinary Residents in Lexington, as represented by the red line in Figure 5.46b, increased gradually from US$15.79 in 2005 to US$19.77 in 2013.

Despite the consistent increase in the wage level, the Wages Ranking for Ordinary Residents in Lexington, as depicted by the red bars, has remained rather stable. From 30th in 2005, it rose slightly to 29th in 2009 before dropping to 31st in 2010. The ranking remained at 31st until 2013, when it rose back to 30th.

Figure 5.46c

Let us now analyse the cost of living and wages indices more closely and draw conclusions about the purchasing power of ordinary residents in Lexington. As elaborated in Section 3.4.2 of Chapter 3, for a more precise and rigorous analysis, we discuss the results in two sub-periods: from 2005 to 2010 and from 2011 to 2013.

The Cost of Living Index and the Wages Index for Ordinary Residents in Lexington are represented respectively by the grey and red line in Figure 5.46c. As mentioned in Section 3.3 of Chapter 3, wage data are only available at the national level and not by cities. Therefore, wages in all cities in the United States are assumed to be the same. As a result, Lexington, being a city in the United States, shares a common Wages Index for Ordinary Residents with the base city New York (whose index value is 100.00) over the entire study period (2005–2013).

Between 2005 and 2010, the Cost of Living Index for Ordinary Residents in Lexington was rather stable. The cost of living for ordinary residents in Lexington generally fluctuated around 62.12% of that for their counterparts in New York. Since the Wages Index for Ordinary Residents is constant across the years, the Purchasing Power Index for Ordinary Residents in Lexington (or any other cities in the United States) depends only on variations in the Cost of Living Index for Ordinary Residents. Thus, the relative stability of the latter caused the Purchasing Power Index for Ordinary Residents to be also stable throughout the first sub-period. Between 2005 and 2010, this index, which is represented by the green line in Figure 5.45c, only fluctuated around 161.00, notwithstanding a sharp rise to 165.77 in 2007. Ranking-wise, the Purchasing Power Ranking for Ordinary Residents in Lexington, which is represented by the green bars, improved over the first sub-period, rising from 25th in 2005 to 21st in 2010.

Over the second sub-period (2011–2013), the Cost of Living Index for Ordinary Residents has steadily declined. In 2011, the cost of living for ordinary residents in Lexington was 61.86% of that for their counterparts in New York. It dropped over the years to 51.33% in 2013. As a result, the Purchasing Power Index for Ordinary Residents has steadily increased, rising from 161.67 in 2011 to 194.83 in 2013. The Purchasing Power Ranking for Ordinary Residents has also been improving. Between 2011 and 2013, it rose from 18th to 14th.

LEXINGTON
United States

Finally, we note that over the entire study period (2005–2013), the Purchasing Power Index for Ordinary Residents in Lexington has always been above 100.00 — the base index value. Thus, ordinary residents in Lexington have consistently been able to consume more goods and services than their counterparts in New York, given the same number of working hours.

LIMA
Peru

Figure 5.47a: Cost of Living and 10 Consumption Categories Rankings for Ordinary Residents in Lima, Peru

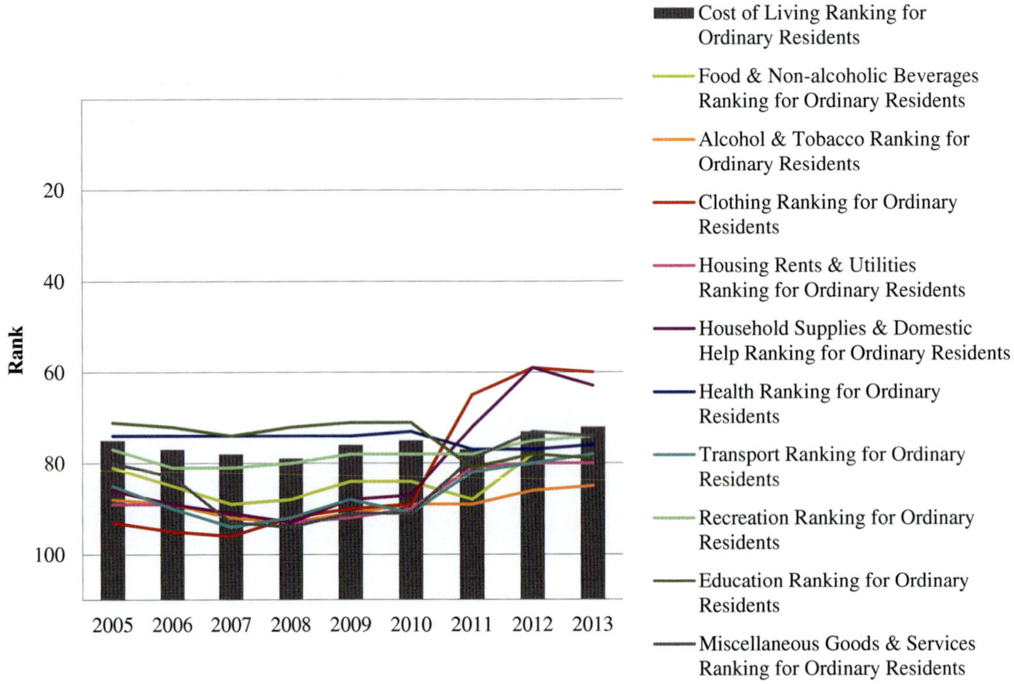

Source: Asia Competitiveness Institute

Figure 5.47b: Gross Hourly Wages in USD and Wages Ranking for Ordinary Residents in Lima, Peru

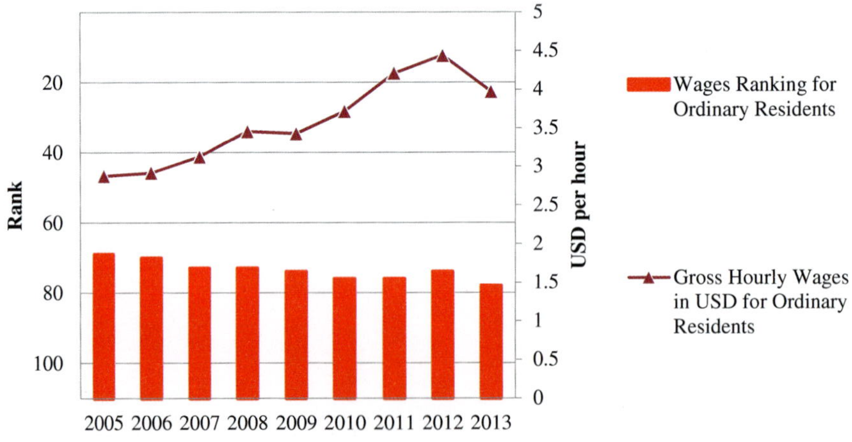

Source: Asia Competitiveness Institute

LIMA
Peru

Figure 5.47c: Cost of Living, Wages and Purchasing Power Indices and Purchasing Power Ranking for Ordinary Residents in Lima, Peru

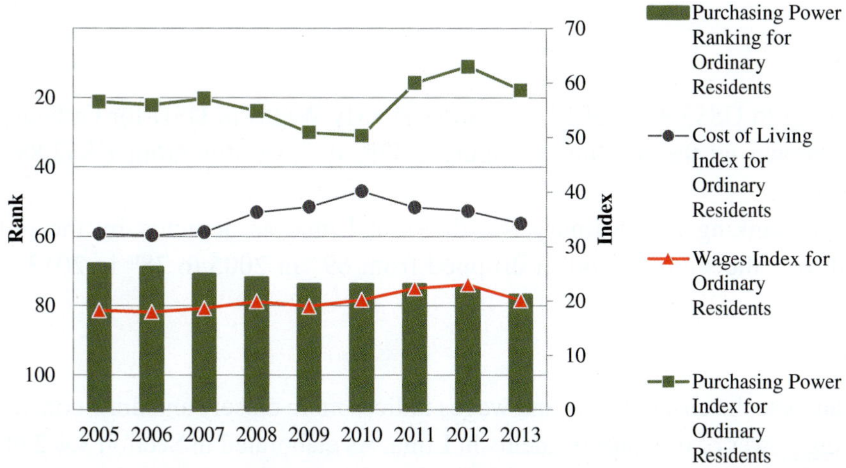

Source: Asia Competitiveness Institute

Figure 5.47a

Lima, the capital and largest city of Peru, accounts for more than two-thirds of the country's industrial production. The city's Cost of Living Ranking for Ordinary Residents, as shown in the grey bars, fell from 75th in 2005 to 79th in 2009 before rising back to 75th in 2010, and rose from 77th to 72nd between 2011 and 2013 (see Figure 5.47a). As explained in Section 3.4.2 of Chapter 3, for a more rigorous comparison of rankings, we have split the analysis into two sub-periods: from 2005 to 2010 and from 2011 to 2013.

Between 2005 and 2010, Health Ranking climbed one place from 74th to 73rd. In contrast, Transport Ranking fell six spots from 85th in 2005 to 91st in 2010. Food & Non-alcoholic Beverages Ranking slipped three places from 81st to 84th over the first sub-period. Housing Rents & Utilities Ranking dropped one spot from 89th to 90th between 2005 and 2010. Education Ranking primarily stayed at 71st over the same sub-period.

The rankings of all 10 categories went up over the second sub-period between 2011 and 2013. In particular, Food & Non-alcoholic Beverages and Household Supplies & Domestic Help Rankings both climbed nine places from 88th to 79th and 72nd to 63rd, respectively, from 2011 to 2013. Clothing overtook Household Supplies & Domestic Help to become the highest ranked category in 2013 as its ranking moved up five spots from 65th in 2011 to 60th in 2013. Alcohol & Tobacco remained as the lowest ranked category throughout the second sub-period although its ranking rose from 89th to 85th over the same sub-period. Transport Ranking jumped four places from 82nd to 78th between 2011 and 2013. Education Ranking rose from 81st in 2011 to 79th in

LIMA
Peru

2013. Housing Rents & Utilities Ranking moved up one spot from 81st to 80th over the second sub-period.

Figure 5.47b

Before dropping to US$3.97 in 2013, the Gross Hourly Wages in USD for Ordinary Residents in Lima, as shown by the red line in Figure 5.47b, rose steadily from US$2.88 in 2005 to US$4.44 in 2012.

The Wages Ranking for Ordinary Residents in Lima, as depicted by the red bars, has deteriorated over the study period. It dropped from 69th in 2005 to 78th in 2013.

Figure 5.47c

Let us now analyse the cost of living and wages indices more closely and draw conclusions about the purchasing power of ordinary residents in Lima. As elaborated in Section 3.4.2 of Chapter 3, for a more precise and rigorous analysis, we discuss the results in two sub-periods: from 2005 to 2010 and from 2011 to 2013.

The Cost of Living Index and the Wages Index for Ordinary Residents in Lima are represented respectively by the grey and red line in Figure 5.47c. Between 2005 and 2010, the Cost of Living Index for Ordinary Residents was generally on an increasing trend. In 2005, the cost of living for ordinary residents in Lima was 32.25% of that for their counterparts in New York (the base city). It rose steadily over time to reach 40.11% in 2010. Over the same sub-period, the Wages Index for Ordinary Residents also increased, rising from 18.24 in 2005 to 20.16 in 2010.

Wages rose more slowly than cost of living so throughout the first sub-period, ordinary residents in Lima could not afford the same consumption level over time. This is reflected in the Purchasing Power Index for Ordinary Residents in Lima, which is represented by the green line in Figure 5.47c. This index dropped from 56.54 in 2005 to 50.28 in 2010. Ranking-wise, the Purchasing Power Ranking for Ordinary Residents in Lima, as represented by the green bars, deteriorated over the first sub-period, dropping from 68th in 2005 to 74th in 2010.

Over the second sub-period (2011–2013), the Cost of Living Index for Ordinary Residents has been on a decreasing trend. In 2011, the cost of living for ordinary residents in Lima was 37.13% of that for ordinary residents in New York. It dropped over the years to reach 34.23% in 2013. Meanwhile, the Wages Index for Ordinary Residents has also decreased over the second sub-period. It was stable at around 22.63 between 2011 and 2012 before dropping to 20.09 in 2013.

Since wages were stable and cost of living was decreasing between 2011 and 2012, ordinary residents in Lima were able to afford more goods and services over time during these years. However, between 2012 and 2013 when both cost of living and wages were dropping, wages decreased faster than cost of living. Thus, the purchasing power of ordinary residents in Lima was eroded and they could not maintain their consumption level over time. These trends are reflected in the Purchasing Power Index for Ordinary Residents. The index increased from 59.98 in 2011 to 62.98 in 2012 before dropping to 58.69 in 2013. In contrast, the Purchasing Power Ranking for Ordinary Residents has been steadily deteriorating, dropping from 74th in 2011 to 77th in 2013.

Finally, we note that the Purchasing Power Index for Ordinary Residents in Lima has consistently been lower than 100.00 — the base index value — over the entire study period (2005–2013). This means that ordinary residents in Lima have only been able to afford a lower consumption level than their counterparts in New York, given the same number of working hours.

LISBON
Portugal

Figure 5.48a: Cost of Living and 10 Consumption Categories Rankings for Ordinary Residents in Lisbon, Portugal

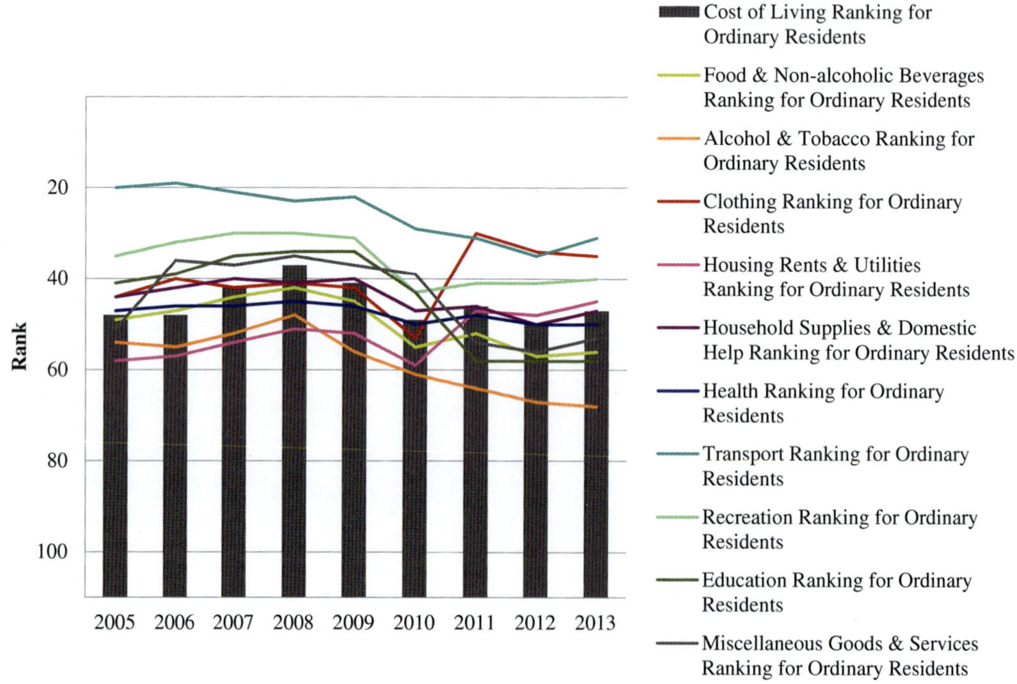

Source: Asia Competitiveness Institute

Figure 5.48b: Gross Hourly Wages in USD and Wages Ranking for Ordinary Residents in Lisbon, Portugal

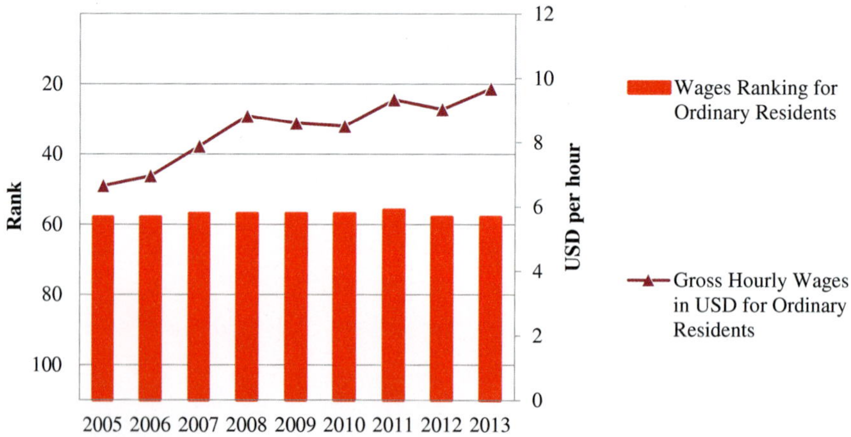

Source: Asia Competitiveness Institute

LISBON
Portugal

Figure 5.48c: Cost of Living, Wages and Purchasing Power Indices and Purchasing Power Ranking for Ordinary Residents in Lisbon, Portugal

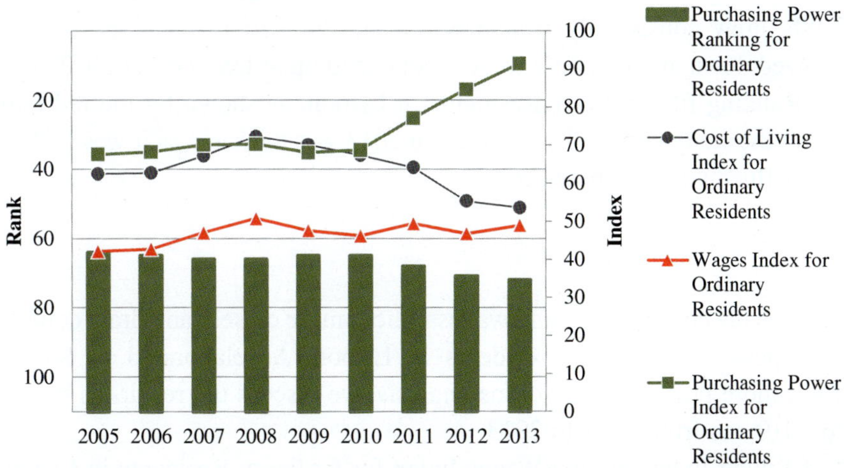

Source: Asia Competitiveness Institute

Figure 5.48a

Lisbon, the capital and largest city of Portugal, is the oldest city in Western Europe. The city's Cost of Living Ranking for Ordinary Residents, as shown in the grey bars, fell from 48th to 49th between 2005 and 2010, and from 46th to 47th between 2011 and 2013 (see Figure 5.48a). As elaborated in Section 3.4.2 of Chapter 3, for a more precise comparison of rankings, we have split the analysis into two sub-periods.

Miscellaneous Goods & Services was the only category that rose in ranking from 51st to 39th in the first sub-period from 2005 to 2010. Transport Ranking slipped nine places from 20th in 2005 to 29th in 2010. Food & Non-alcoholic Beverages moved down six spots from 49th to 55th between 2005 and 2010. Health Ranking fell three places from 47th to 50th over the same sub-period. Education Ranking declined from 41st in 2005 to 43rd in 2010.

In the second sub-period from 2011 to 2013, Housing Rents & Utilities Ranking jumped two places from 47th to 45th. Education Ranking remained at 58th throughout the same sub-period. Transport overtook Clothing to become the highest ranked category in 2013 as its ranking largely remained at 31st while Clothing Ranking slipped five places from 30th in 2011 to 35th in 2013. Food & Non-alcoholic Beverages Ranking fell four spots from 52nd to 56th between 2011 and 2013. Meanwhile, Alcohol & Tobacco remained as the lowest ranked category throughout the second sub-period as its ranking went down from 64th in 2011 to 68th in 2013. Health Ranking dropped two places from 48th to 50th over the same sub-period.

LISBON
Portugal

Figure 5.48b

The Gross Hourly Wages in USD for Ordinary Residents in Lisbon, as denoted by the red line in Figure 5.48b, grew consistently from US$6.65 in 2005 to US$8.82 in 2008. Since then, growth has slowed down and Lisbon's wage level ended up at US$9.67 in 2013.

The Wages Ranking for Ordinary Residents in Lisbon, as shown by the red bars, has been fairly stable over the study period. The ranking in 2013 was the same as it was in 2005 and there were very minor fluctuations in between.

Figure 5.48c

Let us now analyse the cost of living and wages indices more closely and draw conclusions about the purchasing power of ordinary residents in Lisbon. As elaborated in Section 3.4.2 of Chapter 3, for a more precise and rigorous analysis, we discuss the results in two sub-periods: from 2005 to 2010 and from 2011 to 2013.

The Cost of Living Index and the Wages Index for Ordinary Residents in Lisbon are represented respectively by the grey and red line in Figure 5.48c. Between 2005 and 2010, the Cost of Living Index for Ordinary Residents exhibited moderate fluctuations. In 2005, the cost of living for ordinary residents in Lisbon was 62.42% of that for their counterparts in New York (the base city). It first rose steadily over time to peak at 72.29% in 2008 and then decreased until it reached 67.28% in 2010. Over the same sub-period, the Wages Index for Ordinary Residents also followed a similar pattern, first rising from 42.14 in 2005 to 50.72 in 2008 and then dropping until it reached 46.16 in 2010.

Regardless of whether they were both rising or falling, wages generally changed at similar rates as cost of living throughout the first sub-period. Thus, during these years, ordinary residents in Lisbon could afford the same consumption level over time. This is reflected in the Purchasing Power Index for Ordinary Residents in Lisbon, which is represented by the green line in Figure 5.48c. This index only fluctuated around 68.73 between 2005 and 2010. Ranking-wise, the Purchasing Power Ranking for Ordinary Residents in Lisbon, as represented by the green bars, was also generally stable. It only fluctuated between 64th and 66th over the first sub-period.

Over the second sub-period (2011–2013), the Cost of Living Index for Ordinary Residents has been on a decreasing trend. In 2011, the cost of living for ordinary residents in Lisbon was 64.08% of that for ordinary residents in New York. It dropped over the years to reach 53.55% in 2013. In contrast, the Wages Index for Ordinary Residents has been relatively stable. From 49.37 in 2011, it dropped slightly to 46.78 in 2012 and then recovered to 48.94 in 2013.

Since wages were stable and cost of living was decreasing, ordinary residents in Lisbon was able to afford more goods and services over time throughout the second sub-period. This is reflected in the Purchasing Power Index for Ordinary Residents, which increased from 77.05 in

2011 to 91.38 in 2013. Despite this positive showing of the index, the Purchasing Power Ranking for Ordinary Residents has been deteriorating, dropping from 68th in 2011 to 72nd in 2013.

Finally, we note that the Purchasing Power Index for Ordinary Residents in Lisbon has consistently been lower than 100.00 — the base index value — over the entire study period (2005–2013). This means that ordinary residents in Lisbon have only been able to afford a lower consumption level than their counterparts in New York, given the same number of working hours.

LONDON
Great Britain

Figure 5.49a: Cost of Living and 10 Consumption Categories Rankings for Ordinary Residents in London, Great Britain

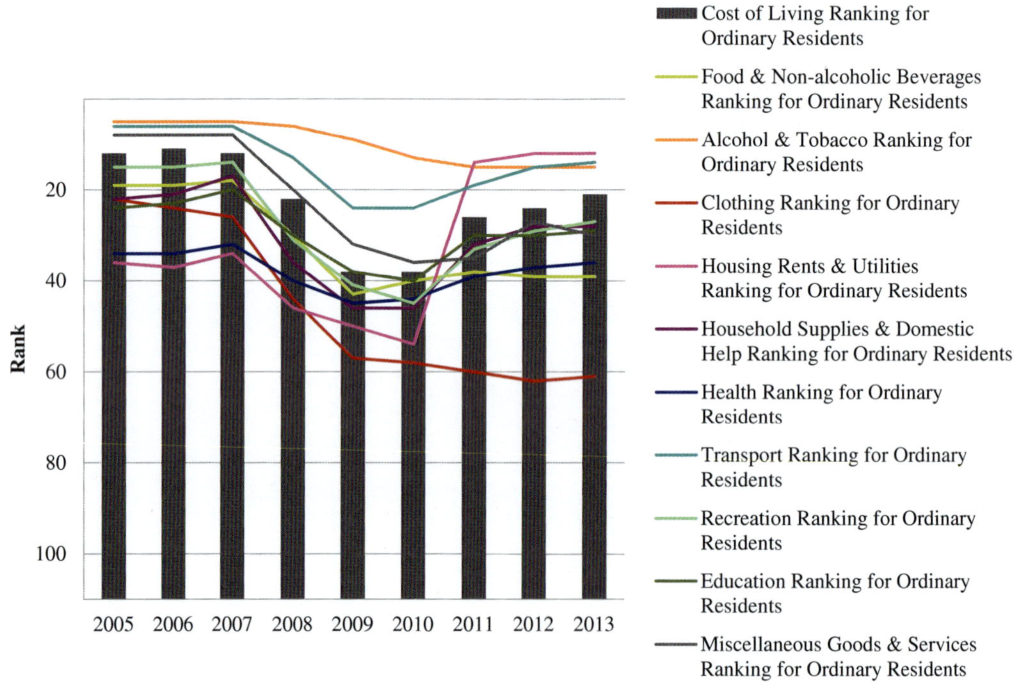

Source: Asia Competitiveness Institute

Figure 5.49b: Gross Hourly Wages in USD and Wages Ranking for Ordinary Residents in London, Great Britain

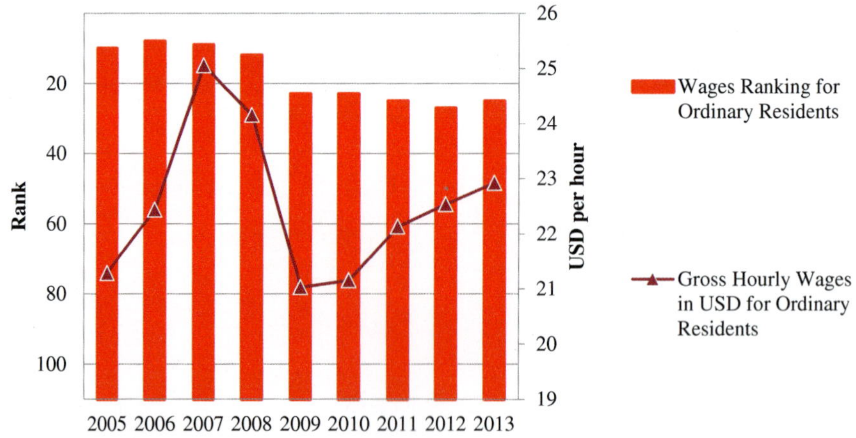

Source: Asia Competitiveness Institute

LONDON
Great Britain

Figure 5.49c: Cost of Living, Wages and Purchasing Power Indices and Purchasing Power Ranking for Ordinary Residents in London, Great Britain

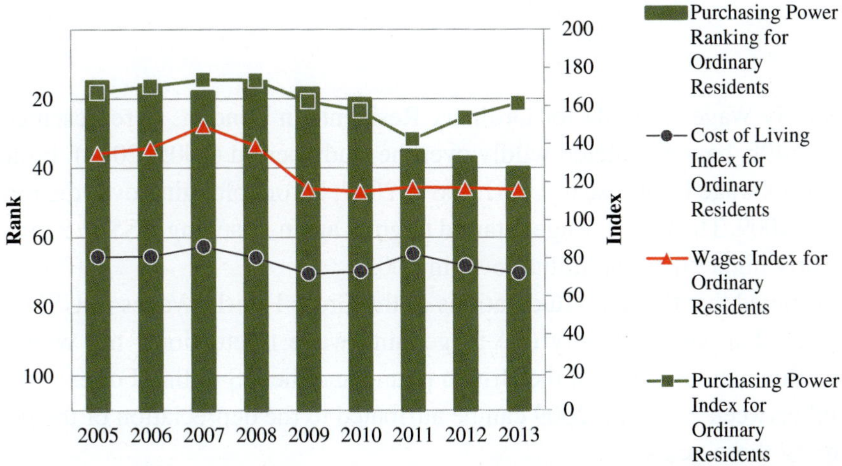

Source: Asia Competitiveness Institute

Figure 5.49a

London, the capital city of the United Kingdom, is renowned for its ethnic and cultural diversity with more than 300 languages spoken within the city. The city's Cost of Living Ranking for Ordinary Residents, as denoted by the grey bars, declined sharply from 12th to 38th between 2005 and 2010, but rose from 26th to 21st between 2011 and 2013 (see Figure 5.49a). As explained in Section 3.4.2 of Chapter 3, for a more rigorous comparison of rankings, we have split the analysis into two sub-periods.

The rankings of all categories went down over the first sub-period from 2005 to 2010. In particular, Clothing Ranking fell 36 places from 22nd in 2005 to 58th in 2010. Household Supplies & Domestic Help Ranking slipped 24 spots from 22nd to 46th between 2005 and 2010. Food & Non-alcoholic Beverages Ranking moved down 21 places from 19th to 40th over the first sub-period. Housing Rents & Utilities and Transport Rankings both dropped 18 spots from 36th to 54th and sixth to 24th, respectively, between 2005 and 2010. Health and Education Rankings declined from 34th to 44th and 24th to 40th, respectively, over the same sub-period.

In the second sub-period between 2011 and 2013, Transport Ranking jumped five places from 19th to 14th. Household Supplies & Domestic Help Ranking went up four spots from 32nd in 2011 to 28th in 2013. Health Ranking moved up three places from 39th to 36th over the same sub-period. Housing Rents & Utilities was the highest ranked category for the entire second sub-period as its ranking rose from 14th in 2011 to 12th in 2013. Education Ranking went up slightly from 30th to 29th between 2011 and 2013. In contrast, Clothing and Food & Non-alcoholic Beverages

LONDON
Great Britain

Rankings both slipped one spot from 60th to 61st and 38th to 39th, respectively, over the same sub-period, making them the lowest and second lowest ranked category in 2013.

Figure 5.49b

The Gross Hourly Wages in USD for Ordinary Residents in London, as represented by the red line in Figure 5.49b, have fluctuated wildly over the study period (2005–2013). From US$21.29 in 2005, London's wage level rose to US$25.06 in 2007, before plunging over the next two years to US$21.03 in 2009. Thereafter, wages started to grow again, reaching US$22.92 in 2013 which was only slightly higher than the initial level in 2005.

It should be noted that the large fluctuations of the Gross Hourly Wages in USD for Ordinary Residents in London were not only due to genuine wage fluctuations, but were also due to exchange rate fluctuations between the British pound and the US dollar. For example, the sharp drop observed between 2007 and 2009 can be attributed to the depreciation of the pound against the dollar during those years.

Ranking-wise, over the study period, the Wages Ranking for Ordinary Residents in London, which is represented by the red bars, has deteriorated consistently, dropping from 10th in 2005 to 25th in 2013.

Figure 5.49c

Let us now analyse the cost of living and wages indices more closely and draw conclusions about the purchasing power of ordinary residents in London. As elaborated in Section 3.4.2 of Chapter 3, for a more precise and rigorous analysis, we discuss the results in two sub-periods: from 2005 to 2010 and from 2011 to 2013.

The Cost of Living Index and the Wages Index for Ordinary Residents in London are represented respectively by the grey and red line in Figure 5.49c. Between 2005 and 2010, the Cost of Living Index for Ordinary Residents was generally on a decreasing trend. In 2005, the cost of living for ordinary residents in London was 80.74% of that for their counterparts in New York (the base city). It rose to 86.01% in 2007 but decreased steadily thereafter to reach 72.90% in 2010. Meanwhile, the Wages Index for Ordinary Residents exhibited substantial fluctuations over the first sub-period, but eventually reached a lower value in 2010 (114.80) as compared to its initial value in 2005 (134.83).

Between 2005 and 2007, wages rose while cost of living either stagnated or increased more slowly than wages. However, between 2008 and 2010 when both wages and cost of living were decreasing, wages fell faster than the latter. Thus, ordinary residents in London were able to afford more goods and services over time during 2005–2007 but could not do so over the remaining years of the first sub-period. These trends are fully reflected in the Purchasing Power Index for Ordinary Residents in London, which is represented by the green line in Figure 5.49c. From its initial level at 166.99 in 2005, this index rose to peak at around 173.50 in 2007 and 2008 and then started to decline until it reached 157.48 in 2010. Ranking-wise, the Purchasing Power Ranking for Ordinary Residents in London, as represented by the green bars, deteriorated over the first sub-period. It dropped from 15th in 2005 to 20th in 2010.

Over the second sub-period (2011–2013), the Cost of Living Index for Ordinary Residents has been on a decreasing trend. In 2011, the cost of living for ordinary residents in London was 82.26% of that for their counterparts in New York. It dropped over the years to reach 71.90% in 2013. The Wages Index for Ordinary Residents has also been on a decreasing trend, albeit more marginally. This index dropped from 117.09 in 2011 to 115.97 in 2013.

Wages has decreased more slowly than cost of living, so during the second sub-period, ordinary residents in London have actually been able to afford more goods and services over time. This is reflected in the Purchasing Power Index for Ordinary Residents, which rose from 142.35 in 2011 to 161.31 in 2013. Despite the good showing of the index, the Purchasing Power Ranking for Ordinary Residents has deteriorated over the second sub-period, dropping from 35th in 2011 to 40th in 2013.

Finally, we note that over the entire study period (2005–2013), the Purchasing Power Index for Ordinary Residents in London has always been higher than 100.00 — the base index value. This means that ordinary residents in London have consistently been able to afford a higher consumption level than their counterparts in New York, given the same number of working hours.

LOS ANGELES
United States

Figure 5.50a: Cost of Living and 10 Consumption Categories Rankings for Ordinary Residents in Los Angeles, United States

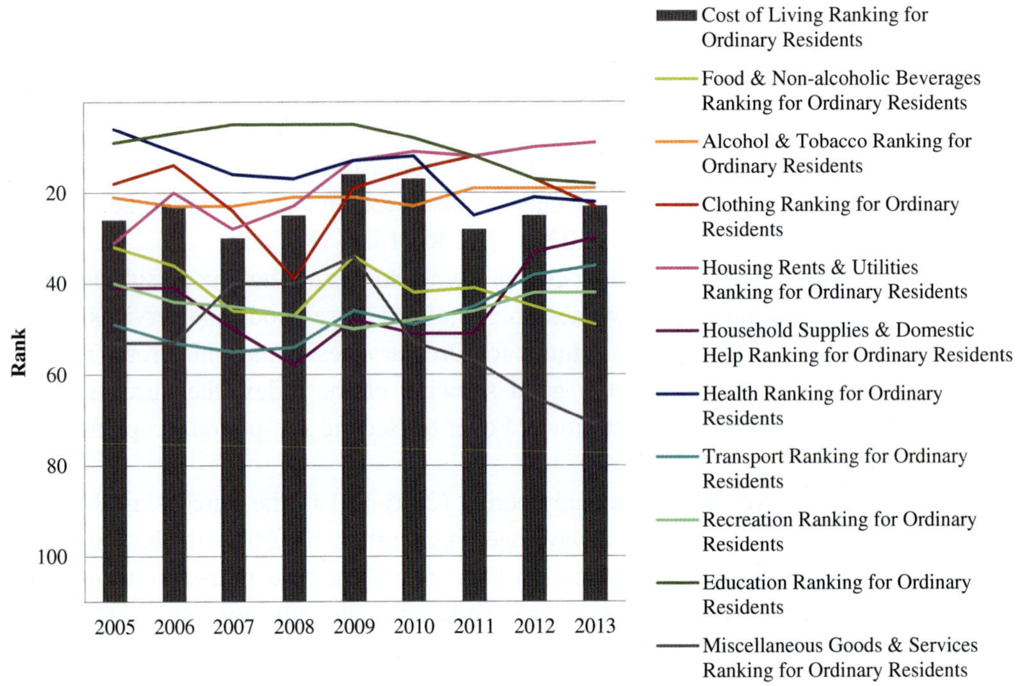

Source: Asia Competitiveness Institute

Figure 5.50b: Gross Hourly Wages in USD and Wages Ranking for Ordinary Residents in Los Angeles, United States

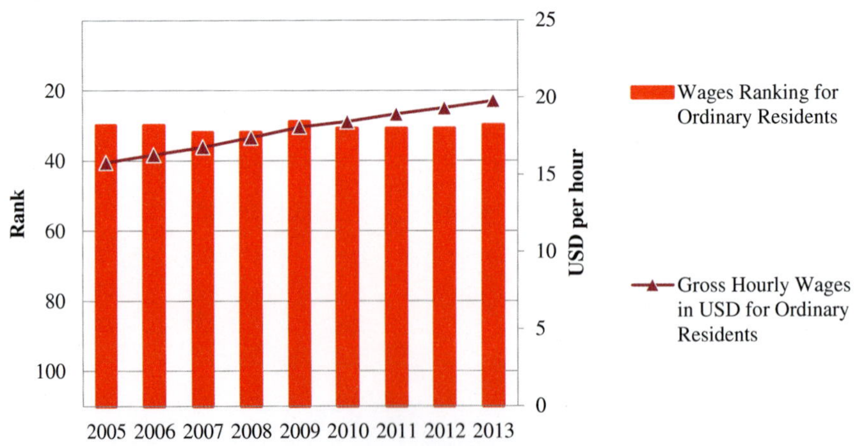

Source: Asia Competitiveness Institute

LOS ANGELES
United States

Figure 5.50c: Cost of Living, Wages and Purchasing Power Indices and Purchasing Power Ranking for Ordinary Residents in Los Angeles, United States

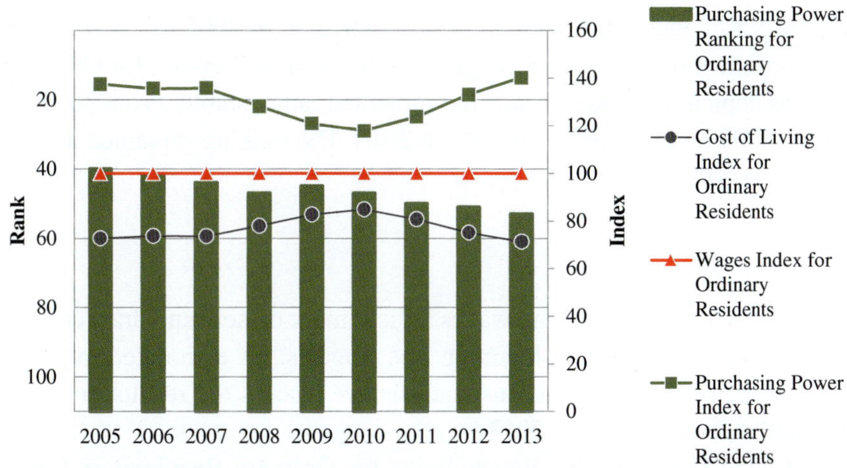

Source: Asia Competitiveness Institute

Figure 5.50a

Home to Hollywood, the world renowned film and entertainment district, Los Angeles is the largest city in the state of California and the second largest city in the United States. The city's Cost of Living Ranking for Ordinary Residents, as represented by the grey bars, rose from 26th to 17th between 2005 and 2010, and from 28th to 23rd between 2011 and 2013 (see Figure 5.50a). As elaborated in Section 3.4.2 of Chapter 3, for a more precise comparison of rankings, we have split the analysis into two sub-periods.

From 2005 to 2010, Housing Rents & Utilities registered the most significant rise in ranking as it climbed 20 places from 31st to 11th. Education Ranking rose more modestly from ninth in 2005 to eighth in 2010. In contrast, Food & Non-alcoholic Beverages Ranking fell 10 places from 32nd to 42nd over the first sub-period. Health Ranking slipped six spots from sixth in 2005 to 12th in 2010. Transport Ranking declined from 49th in 2005 to 55th in 2007 before rising back to 49th in 2010.

From 2011 to 2013, Household Supplies & Domestic Help Ranking jumped 21 places from 51st to 30th. Transport Ranking moved up nine spots from 45th in 2011 to 36th in 2013. Housing Rents & Utilities became the highest ranked category in 2012 and 2013 as its ranking rose from 12th to ninth over the second sub-period. In contrast, Miscellaneous Goods & Services remained as the lowest ranked category from 2011 to 2013 as its ranking fell 14 places from 57th to 71st over the same sub-period. Food & Non-alcoholic Beverages Ranking slipped eight spots from 41st in 2011 to 49th in 2013. Education Ranking declined from 12th to 18th over the second sub-period.

LOS ANGELES
United States

Figure 5.50b

The Gross Hourly Wages in USD for Ordinary Residents in Los Angeles, as represented by the red line in Figure 5.50b, increased gradually from US$15.79 in 2005 to US$19.77 in 2013.

Despite the consistent increase in the wage level, the Wages Ranking for Ordinary Residents in Los Angeles, as depicted by the red bars, has remained rather stable. From 30th in 2005, it rose slightly to 29th in 2009 before dropping to 31st in 2010. The ranking remained at 31st until 2013, when it rose back to 30th.

Figure 5.50c

Let us now analyse the cost of living and wages indices more closely and draw conclusions about the purchasing power of ordinary residents in Los Angeles. As elaborated in Section 3.4.2 of Chapter 3, for a more precise and rigorous analysis, we discuss the results in two sub-periods: from 2005 to 2010 and from 2011 to 2013.

The Cost of Living Index and the Wages Index for Ordinary Residents in Los Angeles are represented respectively by the grey and red line in Figure 5.50c. As mentioned in Section 3.3 of Chapter 3, wage data are only available at the national level and not by cities. Therefore, wages in all cities in the United States are assumed to be the same. As a result, Los Angeles, being a city in the United States, shares a common Wages Index for Ordinary Residents with the base city New York (whose index value is 100.00) over the entire study period (2005–2013).

Between 2005 and 2010, the Cost of Living Index for Ordinary Residents in Los Angeles was generally on an increasing trend. It was stable between 2005 and 2007 at around 73.38 and then started to increase steadily until it reached 84.91 in 2010. Since the Wages Index for Ordinary Residents is constant across the years, how the Purchasing Power Index for Ordinary Residents in Los Angeles (or any other cities in the United States) changes depends only on variations in the Cost of Living Index for Ordinary Residents. Thus, the upward trend of the latter caused the Purchasing Power Index for Ordinary Residents to decrease throughout the first sub-period. Between 2005 and 2010, this index, which is represented by the green line in Figure 5.50c, dropped from 137.46 to 117.78. Ranking-wise, the Purchasing Power Ranking for Ordinary Residents in Los Angeles, which is represented by the green bars, deteriorated over the first sub-period, dropping from 40th in 2005 to 47th in 2010.

Over the second sub-period (2011–2013), the Cost of Living Index for Ordinary Residents has steadily declined. In 2011, the cost of living for ordinary residents in Los Angeles was 80.78% of that for their counterparts in New York. It dropped to 71.34% in 2013. As a result, the Purchasing Power Index for Ordinary Residents has steadily increased, rising from 123.80 in 2011 to 140.17 in 2013. Despite this positive showing of the index, the Purchasing Power Ranking for Ordinary Residents has been deteriorating. Between 2011 and 2013, it dropped from 50th to 53rd.

LOS ANGELES
United States

Finally, we note that over the entire study period (2005–2013), the Purchasing Power Index for Ordinary Residents in Los Angeles has always been above 100.00 — the base index value. Thus, ordinary residents in Los Angeles have consistently been able to consume more goods and services than their counterparts in New York, given the same number of working hours.

LUXEMBOURG
Luxembourg

Figure 5.51a: Cost of Living and 10 Consumption Categories Rankings for Ordinary Residents in Luxembourg, Luxembourg

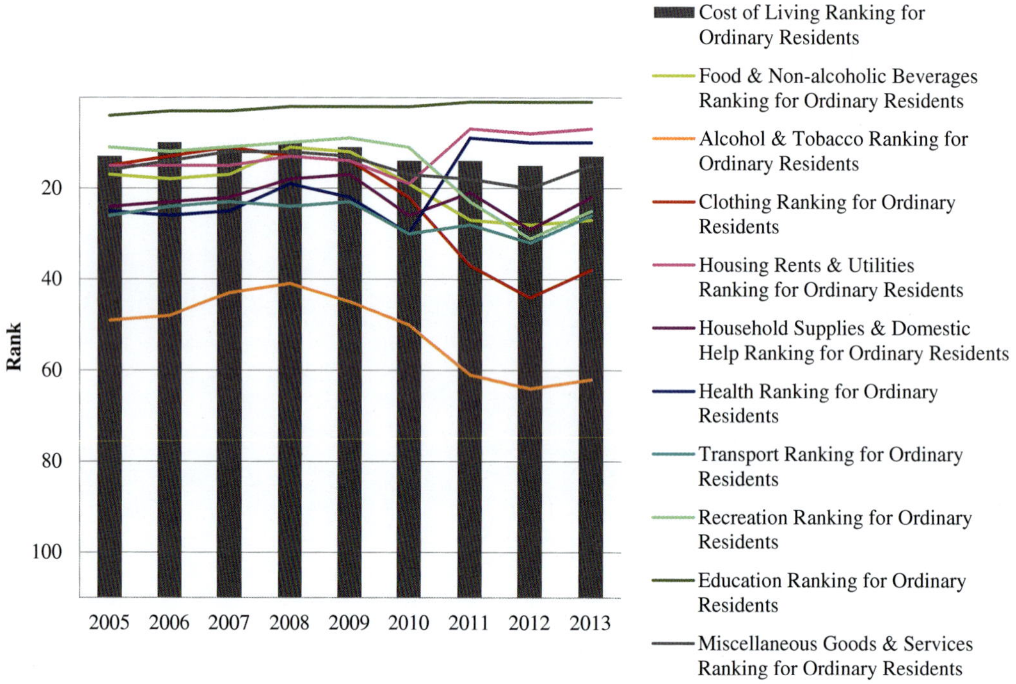

Source: Asia Competitiveness Institute

Figure 5.51b: Gross Hourly Wages in USD and Wages Ranking for Ordinary Residents in Luxembourg, Luxembourg

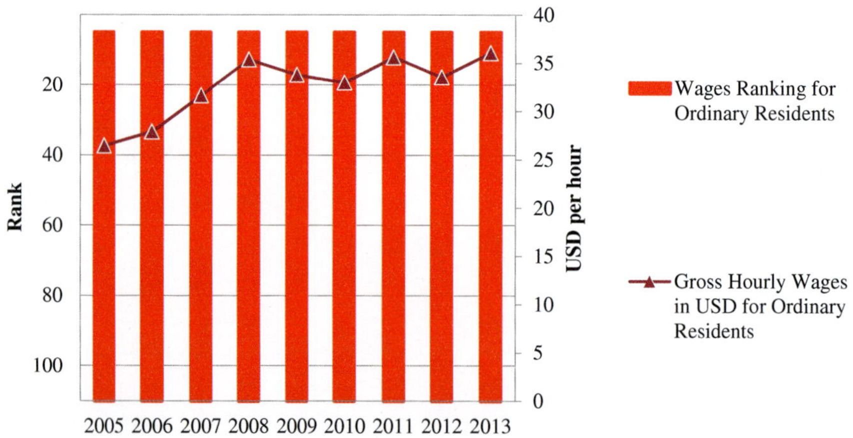

Source: Asia Competitiveness Institute

LUXEMBOURG
Luxembourg

Figure 5.51c: Cost of Living, Wages and Purchasing Power Indices and Purchasing Power Ranking for Ordinary Residents in Luxembourg, Luxembourg

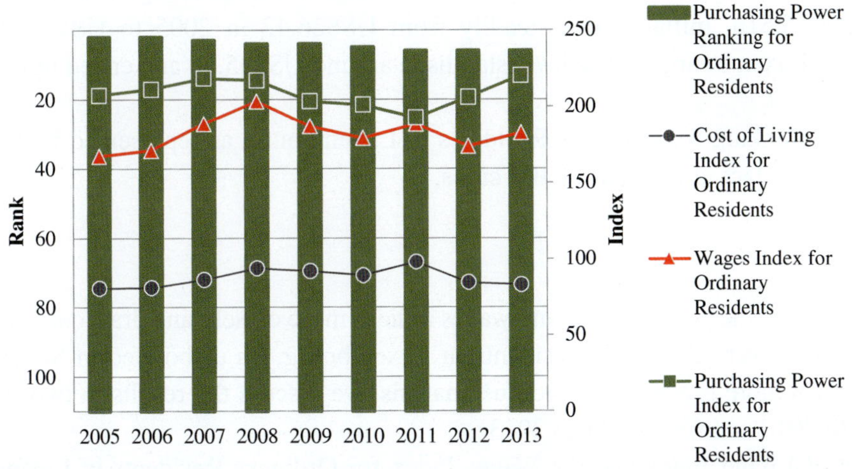

Source: Asia Competitiveness Institute

Figure 5.51a

Luxembourg, the capital of Luxembourg, is known for hosting many institutions of the European Union, including the European Court of Justice, the Secretariat of the European Parliament and the European Investment Bank. The city's Cost of Living Ranking for Ordinary Residents, as shown in the grey bars, fell from 13th to 14th between 2005 and 2010, but rose from 14th to 13th between 2011 and 2013 (see Figure 5.51a). As explained in Section 3.4.2 of Chapter 3, for a more rigorous comparison of rankings, we have split the analysis into two sub-periods.

From 2005 to 2010, Education was the only category that rose in ranking as it moved up from fourth to second. Health Ranking slipped five places from 25th in 2005 to 30th in 2010. Housing Rents & Utilities and Transport Rankings both fell four spots from 15th to 19th and from 26th to 30th, respectively, over the first sub-period. Food & Non-alcoholic Beverages Ranking moved down two places from 17th to 19th between 2005 and 2010.

Between 2011 and 2013, Education Ranking was unchanged at the top, making Luxembourg the most expensive city in this category in the second sub-period. Housing Rents & Utilities and Food & Non-alcoholic Beverages Rankings largely stayed at seventh and 27th, respectively, from 2011 to 2013. Transport Ranking moved up two spots from 28th in 2011 to 26th in 2013. In contrast, Health Ranking slipped one place from ninth to tenth between 2011 and 2013. Likewise, Clothing Ranking declined from 37th in 2011 to 38th in 2013, making it the second lowest ranked category throughout the second sub-period after Alcohol & Tobacco.

LUXEMBOURG
Luxembourg

Figure 5.51b

The Gross Hourly Wages in USD for Ordinary Residents in Luxembourg, as denoted by the red line in Figure 5.51b, initially rose steadily from US$26.42 in 2005 to US$35.36 in 2008. Subsequently, Luxembourg's wage level stabilised around US$35.00 and ended up at US$36.06 in 2013.

The Wages Ranking for Ordinary Residents in Luxembourg, as represented by the red bars, has remained constant at fifth out of 103 cities.

Figure 5.51c

Let us now analyse the cost of living and wages indices more closely and draw conclusions about the purchasing power of ordinary residents in Luxembourg. As elaborated in Section 3.4.2 of Chapter 3, for a more precise and rigorous analysis, we discuss the results in two sub-periods: from 2005 to 2010 and from 2011 to 2013.

The Cost of Living Index and the Wages Index for Ordinary Residents in Luxembourg are represented respectively by the grey and red line in Figure 5.51c. Between 2005 and 2010, the Cost of Living Index for Ordinary Residents was generally on an increasing trend. In 2005, the cost of living for ordinary residents in Luxembourg was 80.70% of that for their counterparts in New York (the base city). It increased steadily to peak at 93.66% in 2008 before falling slightly to 88.99% in 2010. Meanwhile, the Wages Index for Ordinary Residents exhibited more substantial fluctuations over the first sub-period. It rose from 167.37 in 2005 to peak at 203.31 in 2008 before dropping steadily over the remaining years to reach 178.88 in 2010.

Between 2005 and 2008 when both wages and cost of living were rising, wages increased faster than cost of living. However, during the remaining years of the first sub-period when both were decreasing, wages dropped faster than the latter. Thus, ordinary residents in Luxembourg were able to afford more goods and services over time during 2005–2008 but could not do so thereafter. These trends are fully reflected in the Purchasing Power Index for Ordinary Residents in Luxembourg, which is represented by the green line in Figure 5.51c. From its initial level at 207.40 in 2005, this index rose to peak at around 217.75 in 2007 and 2008 and then started to decline until it reached 201.01 in 2010. Ranking-wise, the Purchasing Power Ranking for Ordinary Residents in Luxembourg, as represented by the green bars, deteriorated over the first sub-period. It dropped from second in 2005 to fifth in 2010.

Over the second sub-period (2011–2013), the Cost of Living Index for Ordinary Residents has been on a decreasing trend. In 2011, the cost of living for ordinary residents in Luxembourg was 97.81% of that for their counterparts in New York. It dropped over the years to reach 82.85% in 2013. The Wages Index for Ordinary Residents has fluctuated more substantially. This index dropped from 188.23 in 2011 to 173.60 in 2012 before rising again to 182.45 in 2013.

LUXEMBOURG
Luxembourg

When both wages and cost of living were decreasing between 2011 and 2012, wages dropped more slowly than the latter. In addition, between 2012 and 2013, wages rose while cost of living was decreasing. Thus, over the second sub-period, ordinary residents in Luxembourg have been able to afford more goods and services over time. This is reflected in the Purchasing Power Index for Ordinary Residents which rose from 192.43 in 2011 to 220.22 in 2013. Despite the good showing of the index, the Purchasing Power Ranking for Ordinary Residents has been stable over the second sub-period, remaining at sixth throughout.

Finally, we note that over the entire study period (2005–2013), the Purchasing Power Index for Ordinary Residents in Luxembourg has always been above 100.00 — the base index value. This means that ordinary residents in Luxembourg have consistently been able to afford a higher consumption level than their counterparts in New York, given the same number of working hours.

LYON
France

Figure 5.52a: Cost of Living and 10 Consumption Categories Rankings for Ordinary Residents in Lyon, France

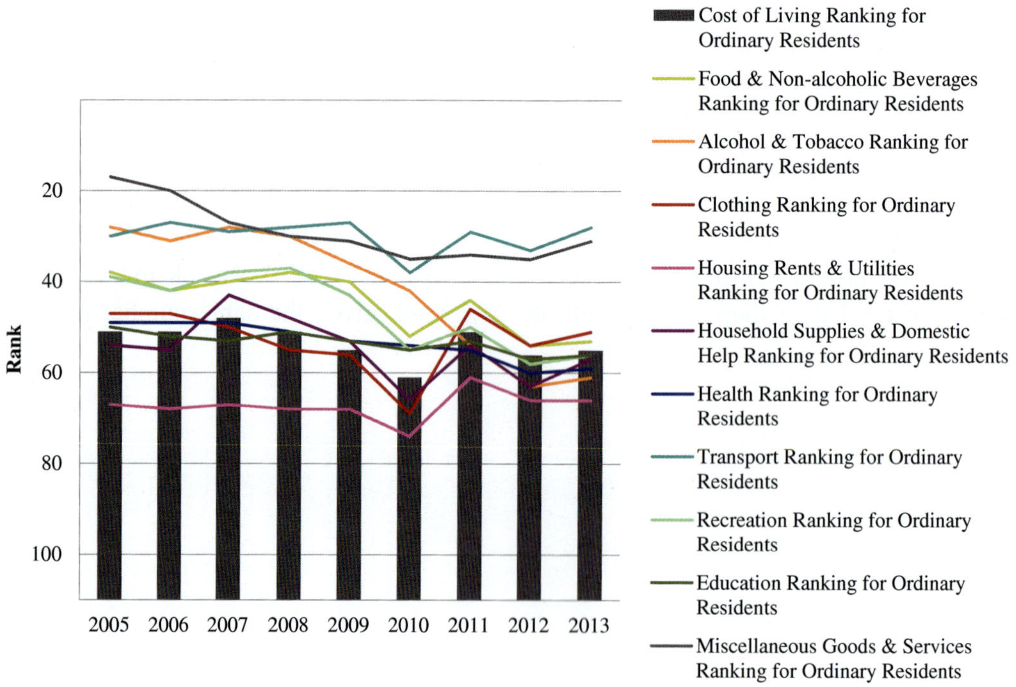

Source: Asia Competitiveness Institute

Figure 5.52b: Gross Hourly Wages in USD and Wages Ranking for Ordinary Residents in Lyon, France

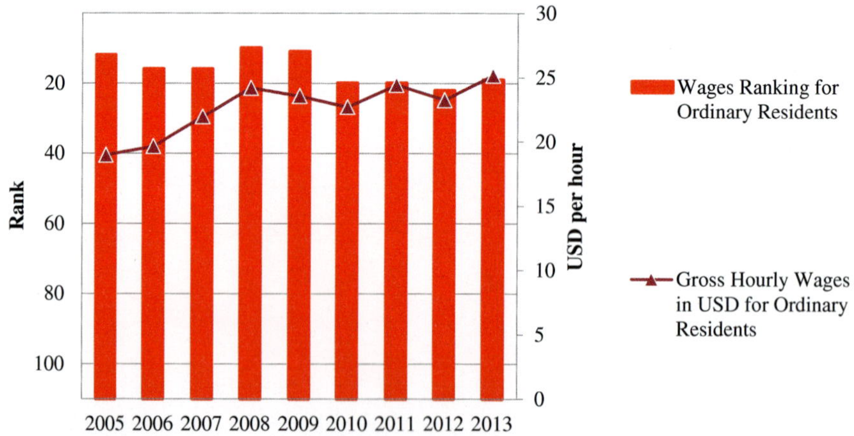

Source: Asia Competitiveness Institute

LYON
France

Figure 5.52c: Cost of Living, Wages and Purchasing Power Indices and Purchasing Power Ranking for Ordinary Residents in Lyon, France

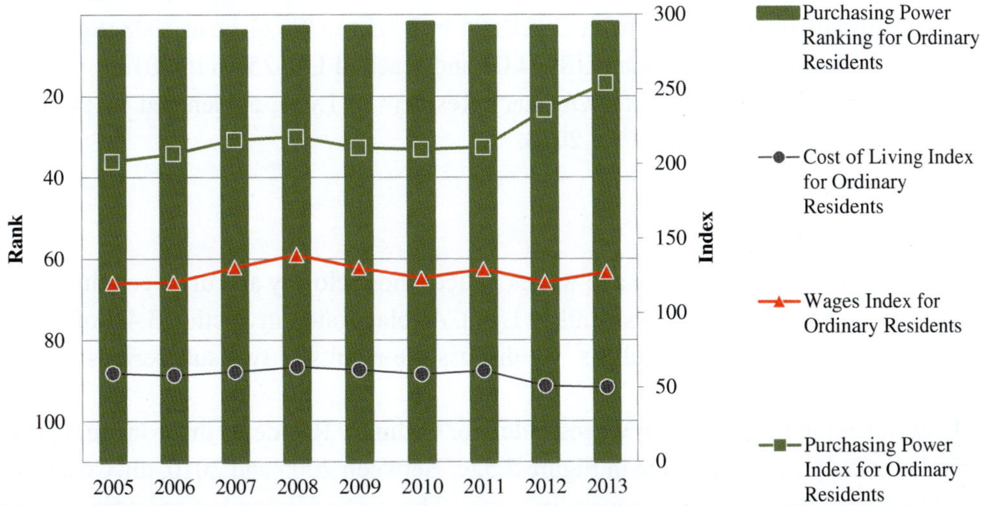

Source: Asia Competitiveness Institute

Figure 5.52a

Known for its historical and architectural landmarks, Lyon, a city in east-central France, is a UNESCO World Heritage Site. The city's Cost of Living Ranking for Ordinary Residents, as denoted by the grey bars, fell from 51st to 61st between 2005 and 2010, and from 51st to 55th between 2011 and 2013 (see Figure 5.52a). As elaborated in Section 3.4.2 of Chapter 3, for a more precise comparison of rankings, we have split the analysis into two sub-periods.

The rankings of all 10 categories went down over the first sub-period from 2005 to 2010. In particular, Food & Non-alcoholic Beverages slipped 14 places from 38th in 2005 to 52nd in 2010. Transport Ranking went down from 30th to 38th over the first sub-period. Housing Rents & Utilities Ranking fell seven spots from 67th in 2005 to 74th in 2010. Health and Education Rankings both dropped five places from 49th to 54th and 50th to 55th, respectively, over the same sub-period.

Between 2011 and 2013, Transport Ranking moved up one spot from 29th to 28th, making it the highest ranked category throughout the second sub-period. Miscellaneous Goods & Services Ranking jumped three places from 34th in 2011 to 31st in 2013. In contrast, Food & Non-alcoholic Beverages Ranking slipped nine spots from 44th to 53rd from 2011 to 2013. Housing Rents & Utilities remained as the lowest ranked category in the second sub-period as its ranking declined from 61st in 2011 to 66th in 2013. Health Ranking fell four places from 55th to 59th between 2011 and 2013. Education Ranking dropped three spots from 53rd to 56th over the same sub-period.

LYON
France

Figure 5.52b

The Gross Hourly Wages in USD for Ordinary Residents in Lyon, as depicted by the red line in Figure 5.52b, initially rose steadily from US$18.94 in 2005 to US$24.18 in 2008. Subsequently, Lyon's wage level stabilised at around US$24.00 and reached US$25.16 in 2013.

Meanwhile, the Wages Ranking for Ordinary Resident in Lyon, as denoted by the red bars, deteriorated from 12th in 2005 to 19th in 2013.

Figure 5.52c

Let us now analyse the cost of living and wages indices more closely and draw conclusions about the purchasing power of ordinary residents in Lyon. As elaborated in Section 3.4.2 of Chapter 3, for a more precise and rigorous analysis, we discuss the results in two sub-periods: from 2005 to 2010 and from 2011 to 2013.

The Cost of Living Index and the Wages Index for Ordinary Residents in Lyon are represented respectively by the grey and red line in Figure 5.52c. Between 2005 and 2010, the Cost of Living Index for Ordinary Residents was generally stable. The cost of living for ordinary residents in Lyon only fluctuated around 60.46% of that for their counterparts in New York (the base city) during these years. In contrast, the Wages Index for Ordinary Residents exhibited more substantial fluctuations. It rose from 119.98 in 2005 to peak at 139.07 in 2008 before dropping steadily over the remaining years to reach 123.16 in 2010.

Since the Cost of Living Index for Ordinary Residents was stable, how the Purchasing Power Index for Ordinary Residents in Lyon changed over the first sub-period only depends on the variations in the Wages Index for Ordinary Residents during those years. The Purchasing Power Index for Ordinary Residents in Lyon is represented by the green line in Figure 5.52c. Between 2005 and 2010, this index tracked the wages index quite closely. Overall, the purchasing power index was higher in 2010 (209.56) than it was in 2005 (201.45). This indicates that ordinary residents in Lyon were able to afford a higher consumption level in 2010 than they could in 2005. Ranking-wise, the Purchasing Power Ranking for Ordinary Residents in Lyon, as represented by the green bars, improved steadily over the first sub-period. It rose from fourth in 2005 to a very respectable second in 2010.

Over the second sub-period (2011–2013), the Cost of Living Index for Ordinary Residents has been on a decreasing trend. In 2011, the cost of living for ordinary residents in Lyon was 61.24% of that for their counterparts in New York. It dropped over the years to reach 50.08% in 2013. In contrast, the Wages Index for Ordinary Residents has fluctuated more substantially. This index dropped from 129.19 in 2011 to 120.40 in 2012 before rising again to 127.28 in 2013.

When both wages and cost of living were decreasing between 2011 and 2012, wages dropped more slowly than the latter. In addition, between 2012 and 2013, wages rose while cost of living decreased. Thus, over the second sub-period, ordinary residents in Lyon have actually been able to afford more goods and services over time. This is reflected in the Purchasing Power Index for Ordinary Residents, which rose from 210.97 in 2011 to 254.14 in 2013. The Purchasing Power Ranking for Ordinary Residents has improved slightly over the second sub-period, rising from third in 2011 and 2012 to second in 2013.

Finally, we note that over the entire study period (2005–2013), the Purchasing Power Index for Ordinary Residents in Lyon has always been above 100.00 — the base index value. This means that ordinary residents in Lyon have consistently been able to afford a higher consumption level than their counterparts in New York, given the same number of working hours.

MADRID
Spain

Figure 5.53a: Cost of Living and 10 Consumption Categories Rankings for Ordinary Residents in Madrid, Spain

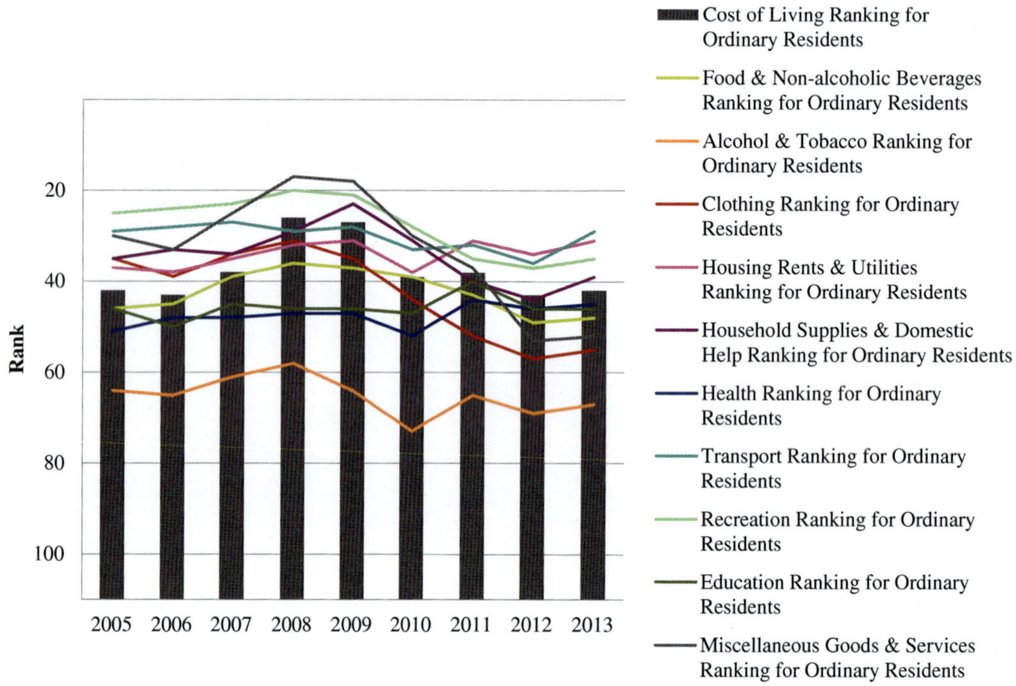

Source: Asia Competitiveness Institute

Figure 5.53b: Gross Hourly Wages in USD and Wages Ranking for Ordinary Residents in Madrid, Spain

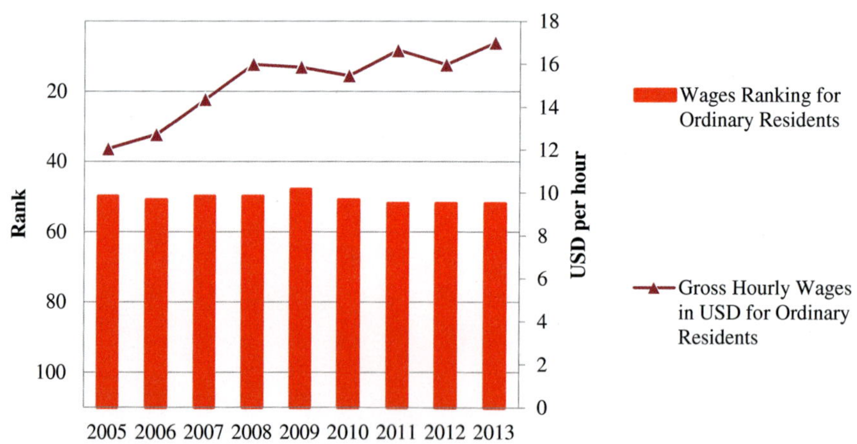

Source: Asia Competitiveness Institute

MADRID
Spain

Figure 5.53c: Cost of Living, Wages and Purchasing Power Indices and Purchasing Power Ranking for Ordinary Residents in Madrid, Spain

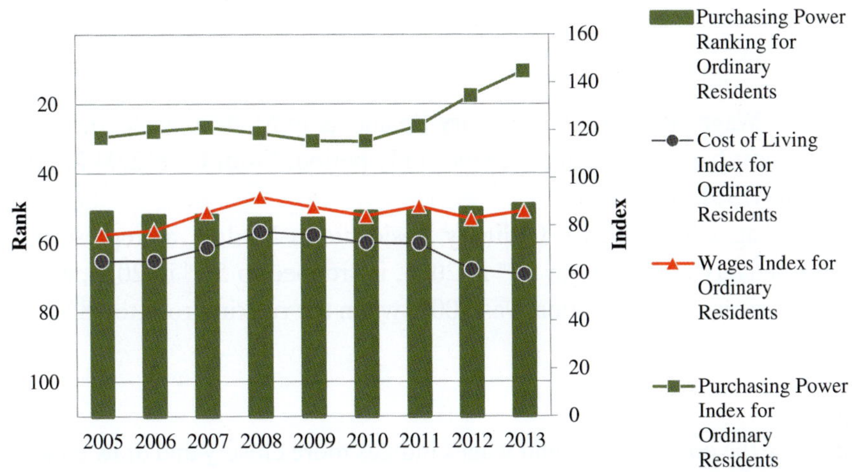

Source: Asia Competitiveness Institute

Figure 5.53a

Madrid, the capital and largest city of Spain with an estimated population of 3.2 million, is the third largest city in the European Union after London and Berlin. The city's Cost of Living Ranking for Ordinary Residents, as represented by the grey bars, declined from 42nd to 39th between 2005 and 2010, and from 38th to 42nd between 2011 and 2013 (see Figure 5.53a). As explained in Section 3.4.2 of Chapter 3, for a more rigorous comparison of rankings, we have split the analysis into two sub-periods.

From 2005 to 2010, Food & Non-alcoholic Beverages Ranking jumped seven places from 46th to 39th. Household Supplies & Domestic Help Ranking moved up four spots from 35th in 2005 to 31st in 2010. In contrast, Transport Ranking slipped four places from 29th to 33rd over the first sub-period. Housing Rents & Utilities Ranking dropped one spot from 37th to 38th between 2005 and 2010. Likewise, Health and Education Rankings declined from 51st to 52nd and 46th to 47th, respectively, over the same sub-period.

From 2011 to 2013, Transport Ranking moved up three places from 32nd to 29th, making it the highest ranked category in 2013. Household Supplies & Domestic Help Ranking jumped one place from 40th in 2011 to 39th in 2013. In contrast, Education Ranking fell six spots from 40th to 46th over the second sub-period. Food & Non-alcoholic Beverages Ranking slipped five places from 43rd to 48th between 2011 and 2013. Clothing Ranking moved down three spots from 52nd in 2011 to 55th in 2013. Consequently, it became the second lowest ranked category throughout the second sub-period after Alcohol & Tobacco. Health Ranking declined from 44th to 45th from

MADRID
Spain

2011 to 2013. Housing Rents & Utilities Ranking declined from 31st in 2011 to 34th in 2012 before rising back to 31st in 2013.

Figure 5.53b

The Gross Hourly Wages in USD for Ordinary Residents in Madrid, as denoted by the red line in Figure 5.53b, have been increasing over the study period. From US$12.04 in 2005, Madrid's wage level rose to US$17.00 in 2013.

However, the Wages Ranking for Ordinary Residents in Madrid, as represented by the red bars, has been relatively stable. From 50th in 2005, it dropped to 52nd in 2013, exhibiting minor fluctuations in between. The exception was 2009, when the ranking rose to 48th.

Figure 5.53c

Let us now analyse the cost of living and wages indices more closely and draw conclusions about the purchasing power of ordinary residents in Madrid. As elaborated in Section 3.4.2 of Chapter 3, for a more precise and rigorous analysis, we discuss the results in two sub-periods: from 2005 to 2010 and from 2011 to 2013.

The Cost of Living Index and the Wages Index for Ordinary Residents in Madrid are represented respectively by the grey and red line in Figure 5.53c. Between 2005 and 2010, the Cost of Living Index for Ordinary Residents exhibited moderate fluctuations. In 2005, the cost of living for ordinary residents in Madrid in 2005 was 65.16% of that for their counterparts in New York (the base city). It first rose steadily until it reached 77.43% in 2008 and then decreased over the remaining years to reach 72.70% in 2010. The Wages Index for Ordinary Residents generally tracked a similar pattern. It first rose from 76.26 in 2005 to peak at 91.91 in 2008 before dropping steadily over the remaining years to reach 83.87 in 2010.

Wages generally changed at similar rates as cost of living, both when they were rising together and when they were falling together. Thus, throughout the first sub-period, ordinary residents in Madrid were able to maintain their consumption level over time. This is reflected in the Purchasing Power Index for Ordinary Residents in Madrid, which is represented by the green line in Figure 5.53c. This index only fluctuated around 117.88 between 2005 and 2010. Ranking-wise, the Purchasing Power Ranking for Ordinary Residents in Madrid, which is represented by the green bars, was also rather stable. It was the same in 2010 as it was in 2005 at 51st and only fluctuated modestly in between.

Over the second sub-period (2011–2013), the Cost of Living Index for Ordinary Residents has been on a decreasing trend. In 2011, the cost of living for ordinary residents in Madrid was 72.34% of that for their counterparts in New York. It dropped over the years to reach 59.43% in 2013. In contrast, the Wages Index for Ordinary Residents has fluctuated more substantially. This index dropped from 88.03 in 2011 to 82.70 in 2012 before rising again to 86.00 in 2013.

MADRID
Spain

When both wages and cost of living were decreasing between 2011 and 2012, wages dropped more slowly than the latter. In addition, between 2012 and 2013, wages rose while cost of living was decreasing. Thus, over the second sub-period, ordinary residents in Madrid have been able to afford more goods and services over time. This is reflected in the Purchasing Power Index for Ordinary Residents, which rose from 121.69 in 2011 to 144.73 in 2013. Ranking-wise, the Purchasing Power Ranking for Ordinary Residents has also improved, rising from 51st in 2011 to 49th in 2013.

Finally, we note that over the entire study period (2005–2013), the Purchasing Power Index for Ordinary Residents in Madrid has always been above 100.00 — the base index value. This means that ordinary residents in Madrid have consistently been able to afford a higher consumption level than their counterparts in New York, given the same number of working hours.

MANILA
Philippines

Figure 5.54a: Cost of Living and 10 Consumption Categories Rankings for Ordinary Residents in Manila, Philippines

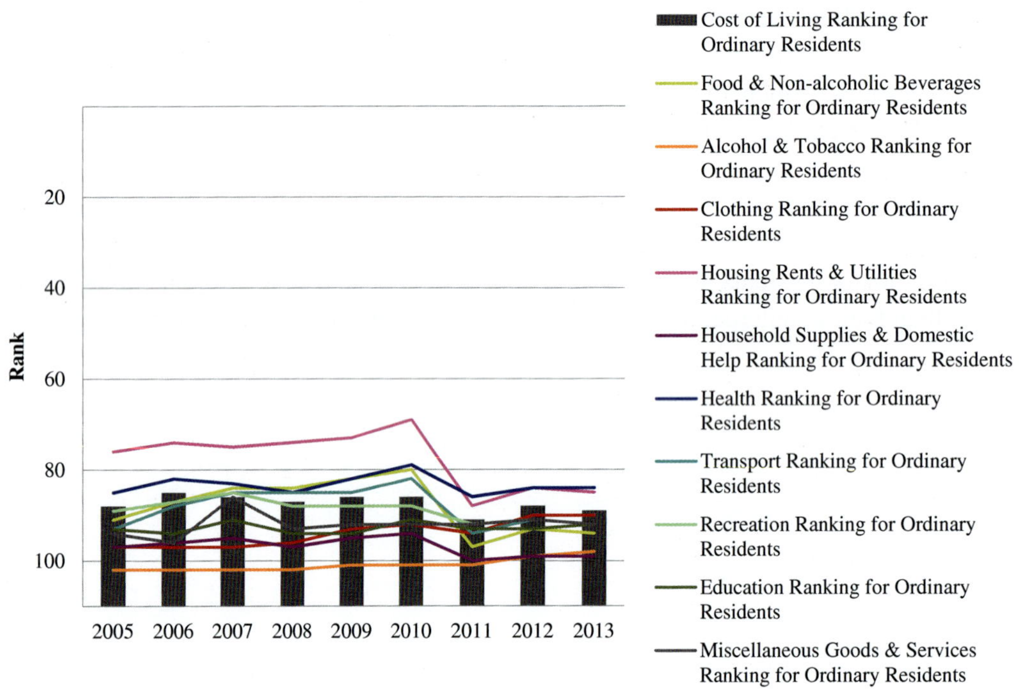

Source: Asia Competitiveness Institute

Figure 5.54b: Gross Hourly Wages in USD and Wages Ranking for Ordinary Residents in Manila, Philippines

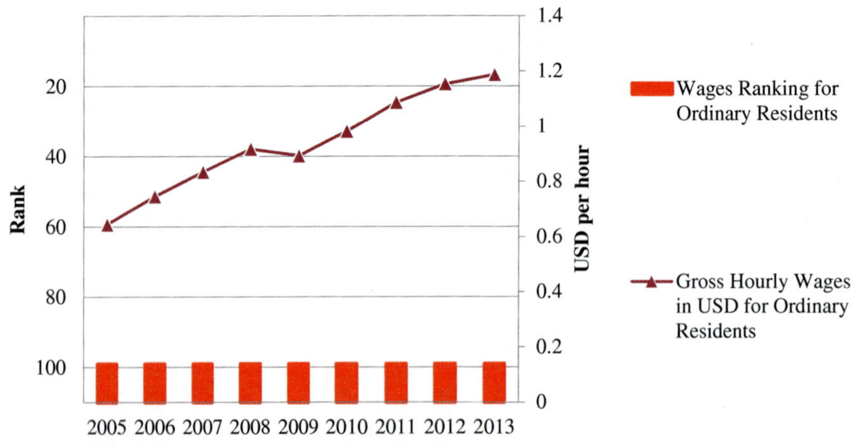

Source: Asia Competitiveness Institute

MANILA
Philippines

Figure 5.54c: Cost of Living, Wages and Purchasing Power Indices and Purchasing Power Ranking for Ordinary Residents in Manila, Philippines

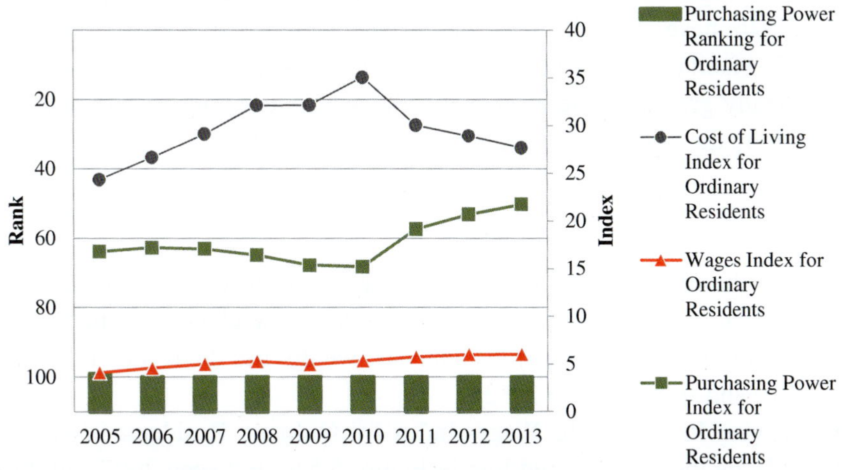

Source: Asia Competitiveness Institute

Figure 5.54a

Manila is the political and economic capital of the Philippines and the country's centre of commerce. The city's Cost of Living Ranking for Ordinary Residents, as shown in the grey bars, rose from 88th to 86th between 2005 and 2010, and from 91st to 89th between 2011 and 2013 (see Figure 5.54a). As elaborated in Section 3.4.2 of Chapter 3, for a more precise comparison of rankings, we have split the analysis into two sub-periods.

The rankings of all 10 categories went up over the first sub-period from 2005 to 2010. In particular Food & Non-alcoholic Beverages and Transport Rankings climbed 11 places from 91st to 80th and 93rd to 82nd, respectively, between 2005 and 2010. Housing Rents & Utilities Ranking jumped seven spots from 76th in 2005 to 69th in 2010. Health Ranking moved up six places from 85th to 79th over the same sub-period. Education Ranking rose from 93rd in 2005 to 91st in 2010.

Between 2011 and 2013, Recreation and Miscellaneous Goods & Services Rankings largely remained at 92nd. In contrast, Housing Rents & Utilities and Food & Non-alcoholic Beverages Rankings both jumped three places from 88th to 85th and 97th to 94th, respectively, from 2011 to 2013. Health and Transport Rankings moved up two spots from 86th to 84th and 94th to 92nd, respectively, over the same sub-period. Health thus overtook Housing Rents & Utilities to become the highest ranked category in 2013. Education Ranking rose from 93rd in 2011 to 92nd in 2013. Likewise, Household Supplies & Domestic Help Ranking jumped one spot from 100th to 99th between 2011 and 2013. Nonetheless, it was the lowest ranked category in 2013.

MANILA
Philippines

Figure 5.54b

The Gross Hourly Wages in USD for Ordinary Residents in Manila, as represented by the red line in Figure 5.54b, have generally been on an increasing trend over the study period. From US$0.64 in 2005, Manila's wage level rose steadily to US$1.19 in 2013.

Despite the steady growth in the wage level, the Wages Ranking for Ordinary Residents in Manila, as shown by the red bars, has remained constant at 99th.

Figure 5.54c

Let us now analyse the cost of living and wages indices more closely and draw conclusions about the purchasing power of ordinary residents in Manila. As elaborated in Section 3.4.2 of Chapter 3, for a more precise and rigorous analysis, we discuss the results in two sub-periods: from 2005 to 2010 and from 2011 to 2013.

The Cost of Living Index and the Wages Index for Ordinary Residents in Manila are represented respectively by the grey and red line in Figure 5.54c. Between 2005 and 2010, the Cost of Living Index for Ordinary Residents was generally on an increasing trend. In 2005, the cost of living for ordinary residents in Manila in 2005 was 24.32% of that for their counterparts in New York (the base city). It rose steadily until it reached 35.05% in 2010. Over the same sub-period, the Wages Index for Ordinary Residents also followed an increasing trend, rising from 4.08 in 2005 to 5.33 in 2010.

Wages could not keep up with cost of living throughout the first sub-period so during these years, ordinary residents in Manila could not afford the same amount of goods and services over time. This is reflected in the Purchasing Power Index for Ordinary Residents in Manila, which is represented by the green line in Figure 5.54c. This index dropped from 16.80 to 15.20 between 2005 and 2010. Ranking-wise, the Purchasing Power Ranking for Ordinary Residents in Manila, which is represented by the green bars, was stable at a very low position. It dropped from 99th in 2005 to 100th in 2006 and stagnated at that level thereafter.

Over the second sub-period (2011–2013), the Cost of Living Index for Ordinary Residents has been on a decreasing trend. In 2011, the cost of living for ordinary residents in Manila was 30.04% of that for their counterparts in New York. It dropped over the years to reach 27.64% in 2013. In contrast, the Wages Index for Ordinary Residents has been increasing, albeit marginally. This index rose from 5.75 in 2011 to 6.01 in 2013.

The combined trends of increasing wages and decreasing cost of living have enabled ordinary residents in Manila to afford more goods and services over time throughout the second sub-period. This is reflected in the Purchasing Power Index for Ordinary Residents, which rose from 19.14 in 2011 to 21.73 in 2013. Meanwhile, the Purchasing Power Ranking for Ordinary Residents has stagnated at 100th throughout the second sub-period.

MANILA
Philippines

Finally, we note that over the entire study period (2005–2013), the Purchasing Power Index for Ordinary Residents in Manila has consistently been lower than 100.00 — the base index value. This means that ordinary residents in Manila have only been able to afford a lower consumption level than their counterparts in New York, given the same number of working hours.

MELBOURNE
Australia

Figure 5.55a: Cost of Living and 10 Consumption Categories Rankings for Ordinary Residents in Melbourne, Australia

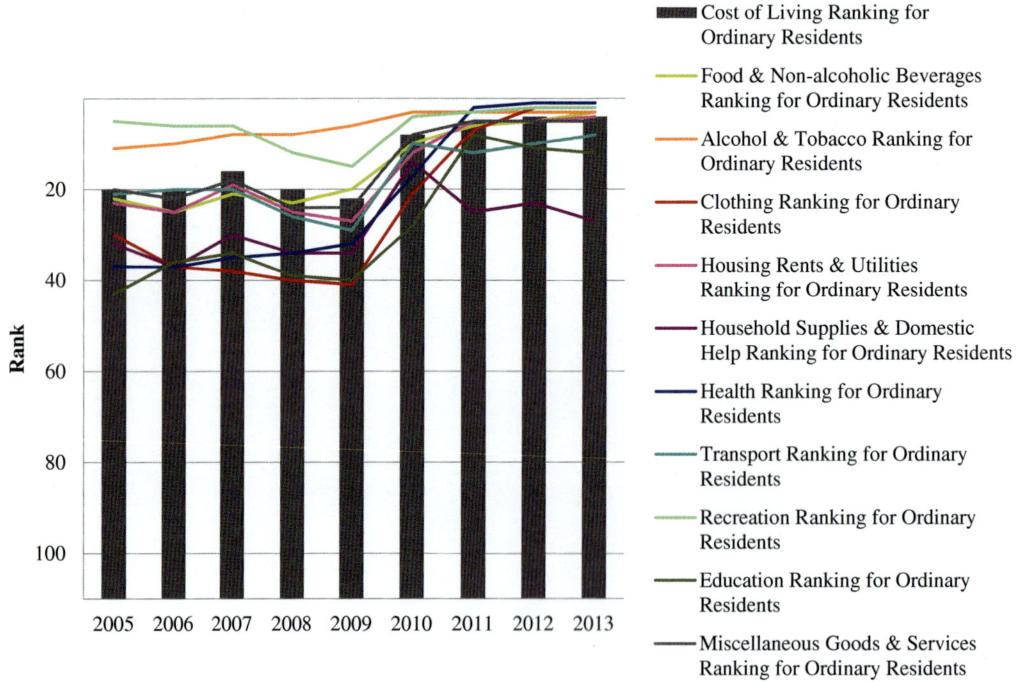

Source: Asia Competitiveness Institute

Figure 5.55b: Gross Hourly Wages in USD and Wages Ranking for Ordinary Residents in Melbourne, Australia

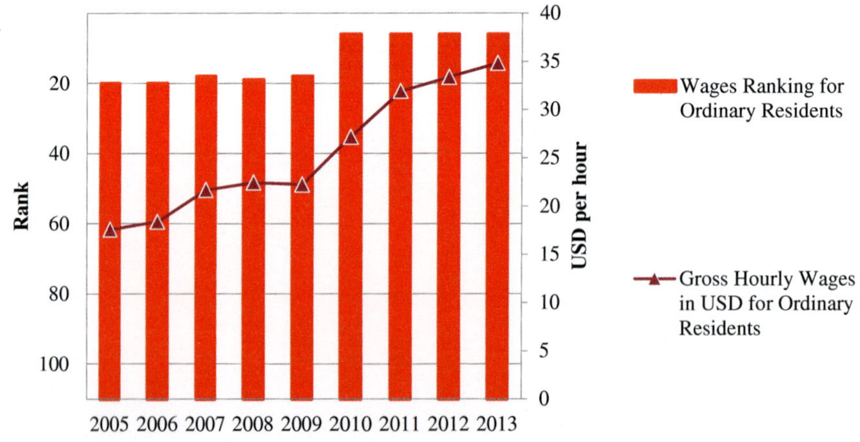

Source: Asia Competitiveness Institute

MELBOURNE
Australia

Figure 5.55c: Cost of Living, Wages and Purchasing Power Indices and Purchasing Power Ranking for Ordinary Residents in Melbourne, Australia

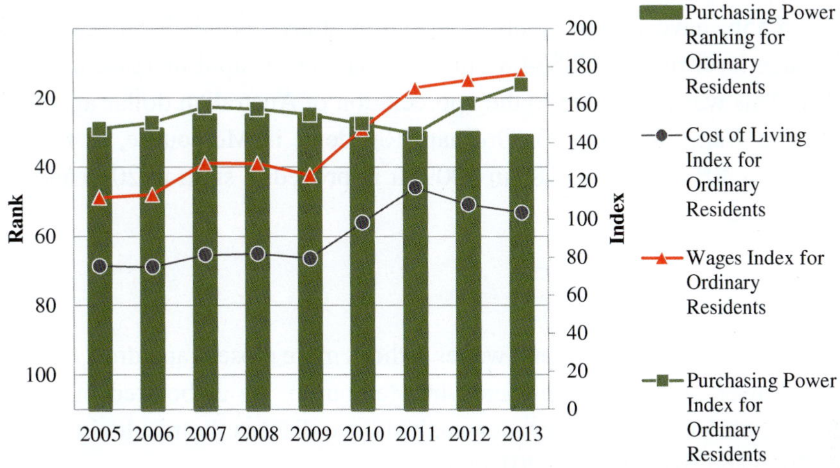

Source: Asia Competitiveness Institute

Figure 5.55a

Melbourne is the second most populous city in Australia with a population of approximately 4.4 million. The city's Cost of Living Ranking for Ordinary Residents, as denoted by the grey bars, rose from 20th to eighth between 2005 and 2010, and from fifth to fourth between 2011 and 2013 (see Figure 5.55a). As explained in Section 3.4.2 of Chapter 3, for a more rigorous comparison of rankings, we have split the analysis into two sub-periods.

The rankings of all 10 categories went up over the first sub-period from 2005 to 2010. In particular, Health Ranking climbed 20 places from 37th in 2005 to 17th in 2010. Education Ranking moved up 15 spots from 43rd to 28th between 2005 and 2010. Food & Non-alcoholic Beverages Ranking rose from 22nd in 2005 to 10th in 2010. Housing Rents & Utilities and Transport Rankings both went up 11 places from 23rd to 12th and 21st to 10th, respectively, over the first sub-period.

In the second sub-period between 2011 and 2013, Clothing Ranking jumped five places from seventh to second. Transport Ranking moved up four spots from 12th in 2011 to eighth in 2013. Food & Non-alcoholic Beverages Ranking rose from sixth to third over the same sub-period. Housing Rents & Utilities and Health Rankings both went up one spot from fifth to fourth and second to first, respectively, between 2011 and 2013. Melbourne therefore became the most expensive city in terms of Health in 2013. In contrast, Education Ranking fell four places from eighth in 2011 to 12th in 2013. Household Supplies & Domestic Help Ranking slipped two spots from 25th to 27th between 2011 and 2013, making it the lowest ranked category throughout the second sub-period.

MELBOURNE
Australia

Figure 5.55b

The Gross Hourly Wages in USD for Ordinary Residents in Melbourne, as denoted by the red line in Figure 5.55b, have almost doubled over the study period. From US$17.56 in 2005, Melbourne's wage level rose to US$34.83 in 2013. The most rapid increase happened between 2009 and 2011. This was partly due to the appreciation of Australian dollar against US dollar.

Meanwhile, the Wages Ranking for Ordinary Residents in Melbourne, as shown by the red bars, first rose from 20th in 2005 to 18th in 2009. It improved to sixth in 2010 and has remained at that level thereafter.

Figure 5.55c

Let us now analyse the cost of living and wages indices more closely and draw conclusions about the purchasing power of ordinary residents in Melbourne. As elaborated in Section 3.4.2 of Chapter 3, for a more precise and rigorous analysis, we discuss the results in two sub-periods: from 2005 to 2010 and from 2011 to 2013.

The Cost of Living Index and the Wages Index for Ordinary Residents in Melbourne are represented respectively by the grey and red line in Figure 5.55c. Between 2005 and 2010, the Cost of Living Index for Ordinary Residents was generally on an increasing trend. In 2005, the cost of living for ordinary residents in Melbourne was 75.38% of that for their counterparts in New York (the base city). It rose steadily until it reached 98.14% in 2010. Over the same sub-period, the Wages Index for Ordinary Residents also followed an increasing trend, rising from 111.21 in 2005 to 147.34 in 2010.

Between 2005 and 2007, wages rose faster than cost of living but over the remaining years of the first sub-period, wages could not keep up with the latter. Hence, ordinary residents in Melbourne could only afford a higher consumption level over time during 2005–2007 but could not do so after 2007. These trends are reflected in the Purchasing Power Index for Ordinary Residents in Melbourne, which is represented by the green line in Figure 5.55c. This index initially rose from 147.52 in 2005 to 158.90 in 2007, before dropping steadily until it reached 150.14 in 2010. Ranking-wise, the Purchasing Power Ranking for Ordinary Residents in Melbourne, which is represented by the green bars, improved over the first sub-period, rising from 29th in 2005 to 26th in 2010.

Over the second sub-period (2011–2013), the Cost of Living Index for Ordinary Residents has been on a decreasing trend. In 2011, the cost of living for ordinary residents in Melbourne was 1.17 times that for their counterparts in New York. It dropped over the years to reach 1.03 times in 2013. In contrast, the Wages Index for Ordinary Residents has been increasing, rising from 168.86 in 2011 to 176.22 in 2013.

The combined trends of increasing wages and decreasing cost of living have enabled ordinary residents in Melbourne to afford more goods and services over time throughout the second sub-period. This is reflected in the Purchasing Power Index for Ordinary Residents, which rose from 144.89 in 2011 to 170.59 in 2013. Despite this positive showing of the index, the Purchasing Power Ranking for Ordinary Residents has been relatively stable. It remained at 30th in 2011 and 2012 before dropping slightly to 31st in 2013.

Finally, we note that over the entire study period (2005–2013), the Purchasing Power Index for Ordinary Residents in Melbourne has always been above 100.00 — the base index value. This means that ordinary residents in Melbourne have consistently been able to afford a higher consumption level than their counterparts in New York, given the same number of working hours.

MEXICO CITY
Mexico

Figure 5.56a: Cost of Living and 10 Consumption Categories Rankings for Ordinary Residents in Mexico City, Mexico

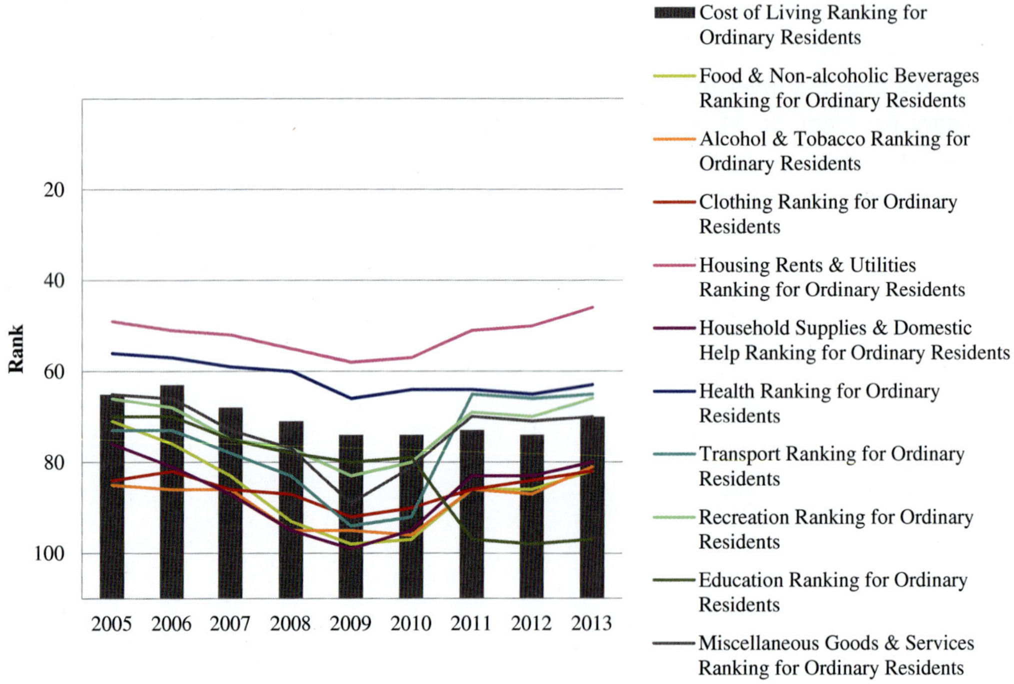

Source: Asia Competitiveness Institute

Figure 5.56b: Gross Hourly Wages in USD and Wages Ranking for Ordinary Residents in Mexico City, Mexico

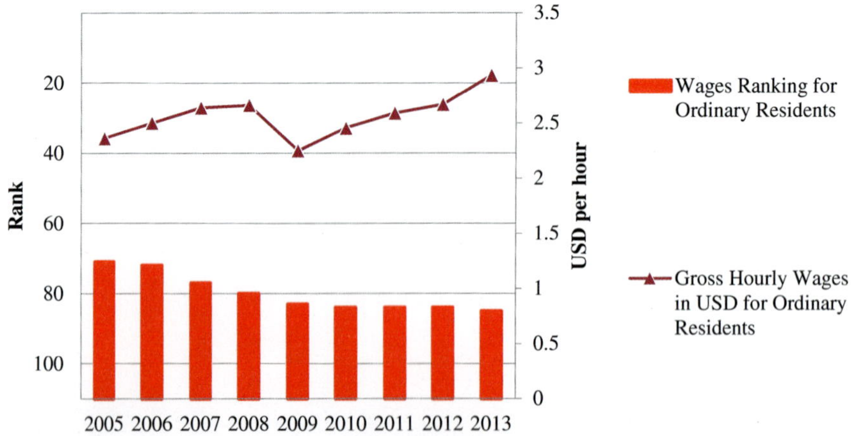

Source: Asia Competitiveness Institute

MEXICO CITY
Mexico

Figure 5.56c: Cost of Living, Wages and Purchasing Power Indices and Purchasing Power Ranking for Ordinary Residents in Mexico City, Mexico

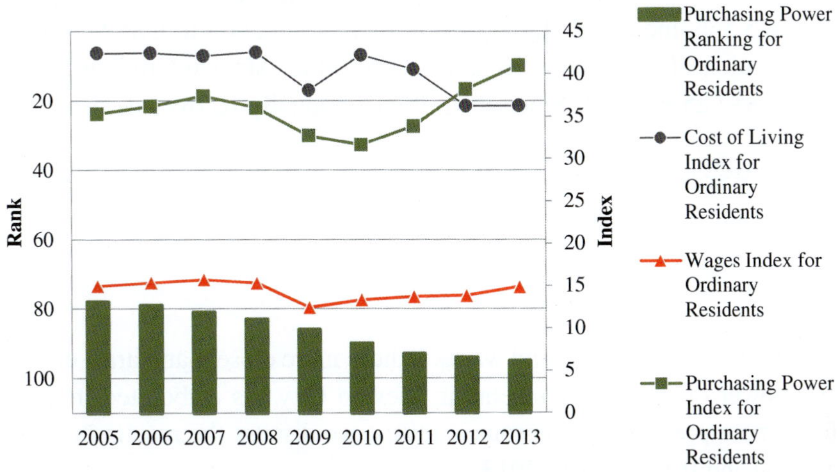

Source: Asia Competitiveness Institute

Figure 5.56a

Mexico City is the capital and largest city of Mexico with a population of approximately 8.8 million. The city's Cost of Living Ranking for Ordinary Residents, as represented by the grey bars, fell from 65th to 74th between 2005 and 2010, but rose from 73rd to 70th between 2011 and 2013 (see Figure 5.56a). As elaborated in Section 3.4.2 of Chapter 3, for a more precise comparison of rankings, we have split the analysis into two sub-periods.

The rankings of all 10 categories went down over the first sub-period from 2005 to 2010. In particular, Food & Non-alcoholic Beverages Ranking slipped 26 places from 71st in 2005 to 97th in 2010. Transport Ranking moved down 19 spots from 73rd to 92nd over the same sub-period. Education Ranking fell nine places from 70th to 79th between 2005 and 2010. Housing Rents & Utilities and Health Rankings both slipped eight spots from 49th to 57th and 56th to 64th, respectively, over the first sub-period.

In the second sub-period between 2011 and 2013, Transport and Education Rankings largely remained at 65th and 97th, respectively. Education was thus the lowest ranked category throughout the second sub-period. In contrast, Housing Rents & Utilities consistently remained as the highest ranked category in both sub-periods as its ranking jumped five places from 51st in 2011 to 46th in 2013. Food & Non-alcoholic Beverages Ranking moved up four spots from 86th to 82nd between 2011 and 2013. Health Ranking rose from 64th to 63rd over the same sub-period.

MEXICO CITY
Mexico

Figure 5.56b

The Gross Hourly Wages in USD for Ordinary Residents in Mexico City, as represented by the red line in Figure 5.56b, increased slightly from US$2.36 in 2005 to US$2.66 in 2008. Mainly due to the depreciation of Mexican peso against US dollar, Mexico City's wage level dropped considerably to US$2.25 in 2009. Since then, it has gradually recovered, rising to US$2.94 in 2013.

Meanwhile, the Wages Ranking for Ordinary Residents in Mexico City, as denoted by the red bars, deteriorated from 71st in 2005 to 85th in 2013.

Figure 5.56c

Let us now analyse the cost of living and wages indices more closely and draw conclusions about the purchasing power of ordinary residents in Mexico City. As elaborated in Section 3.4.2 of Chapter 3, for a more precise and rigorous analysis, we discuss the results in two sub-periods: from 2005 to 2010 and from 2011 to 2013.

The Cost of Living Index and the Wages Index for Ordinary Residents in Mexico City are represented respectively by the grey and red line in Figure 5.56c. Between 2005 and 2008, the Cost of Living Index for Ordinary Residents was relatively stable at around 42.37. In 2009, the cost of living index plunged to 38.04 before recovering to 42.18 in 2010. The drop in 2009 was caused mainly by a significant depreciation of the peso against the US dollar in that year. Over the first sub-period, the Wages Index for Ordinary Residents generally followed a similar pattern. Like the cost of living index, the wages index was stable between 2005 and 2008, fluctuating around 15.34. It also experienced a sharp drop in 2009 because of exchange rate fluctuations. However, unlike the cost of living index, the wages index only recovered partially to 13.33 in 2010, which was lower than the index value for 2005 (14.96).

Since both wages and cost of living were relatively stable between 2005 and 2008, ordinary residents in Mexico City were generally able to maintain the same consumption level over time during these years. However, between 2008 and 2009 when both wages and cost of living plunged, wages dropped faster than cost of living. In addition, the subsequent recovery of wages was also much slower than that of the latter. Thus, during 2008–2010, the purchasing power of ordinary residents in Mexico City was eroded. These trends are fully reflected in the Purchasing Power Index for Ordinary Residents in Mexico City, which is represented by the green line in Figure 5.56c. Between 2005 and 2008, this index only fluctuated modestly around 36.20. However, it steadily decreased over 2008–2010 to eventually reach 31.60 in 2010. Ranking-wise, the Purchasing Power Ranking for Ordinary Residents in Mexico City deteriorated throughout the first sub-period, dropping from 78th in 2005 to 90th in 2010.

Over the second sub-period (2011–2013), the Cost of Living Index for Ordinary Residents has been on a decreasing trend. In 2011, the cost of living for ordinary residents in Mexico City was

40.51% of that for their counterparts in New York (the base city). It dropped over the years to reach 36.25% in 2013. In contrast, the Wages Index for Ordinary Residents has been increasing, albeit marginally. It rose from 13.71 in 2011 to 14.85 in 2013.

The combined trends of increasing wages and decreasing cost of living have enabled ordinary residents in Mexico City to afford more goods and services over time throughout the second sub-period. This is reflected in the Purchasing Power Index for Ordinary Residents, which rose from 33.84 in 2011 to 40.98 in 2013. Despite this positive showing of the index, the Purchasing Power Ranking for Ordinary Residents has deteriorated over the second sub-period, dropping from 93rd in 2011 to 95th in 2013.

Finally, we note that over the entire study period (2005–2013), the Purchasing Power Index for Ordinary Residents in Mexico City has consistently been lower than 100.00 — the base index value. This means that ordinary residents in Mexico City have only been able to afford a lower consumption level than their counterparts in New York, given the same number of working hours.

MIAMI
United States

Figure 5.57a: Cost of Living and 10 Consumption Categories Rankings for Ordinary Residents in Miami, United States

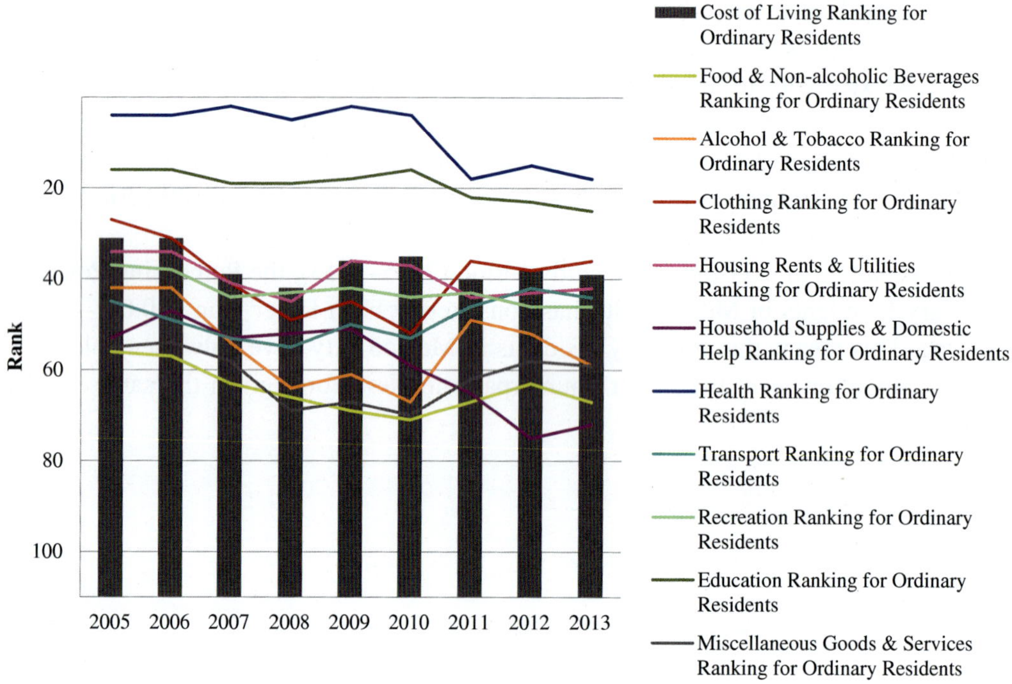

Source: Asia Competitiveness Institute

Figure 5.57b: Gross Hourly Wages in USD and Wages Ranking for Ordinary Residents in Miami, United States

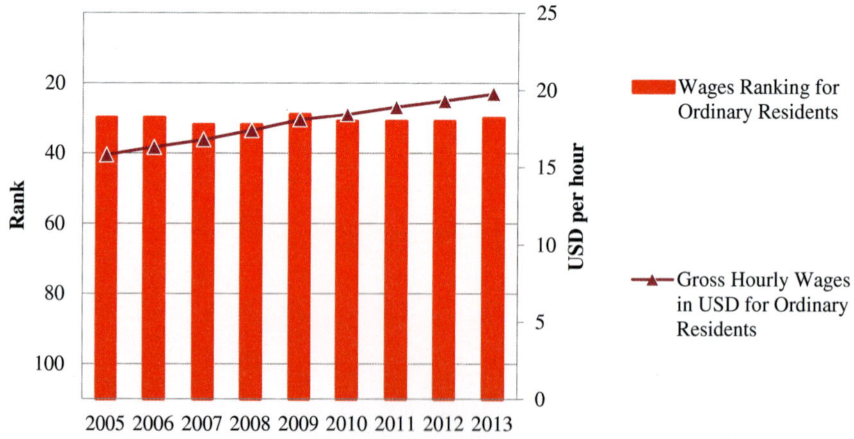

Source: Asia Competitiveness Institute

MIAMI
United States

Figure 5.57c: Cost of Living, Wages and Purchasing Power Indices and Purchasing Power Ranking for Ordinary Residents in Miami, United States

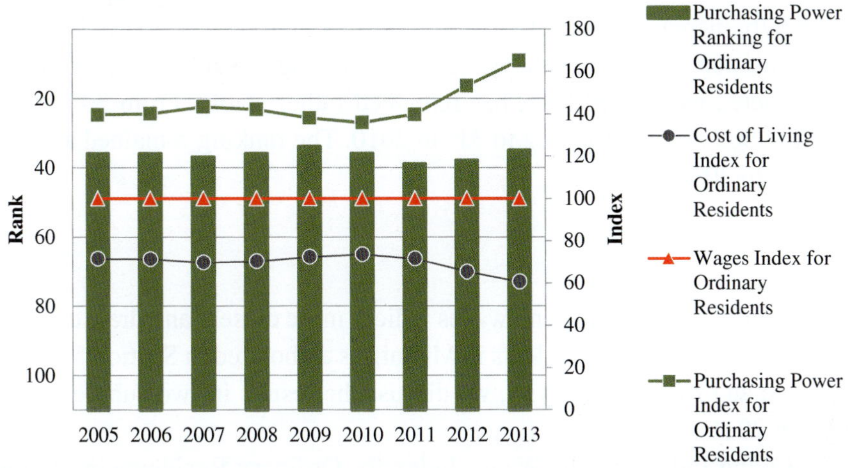

Source: Asia Competitiveness Institute

Figure 5.57a

Located on the Atlantic coast in south-eastern Florida, Miami is the 44th most populous city in the United States. The city's Cost of Living Ranking for Ordinary Residents, as shown in the grey bars, fell from 31st to 35th between 2005 and 2010, but rose from 40th to 39th between 2011 and 2013 (see Figure 5.57a). As explained in Section 3.4.2 of Chapter 3, for a more rigorous comparison of rankings, we have split the analysis into two sub-periods.

From 2005 to 2010, Food & Non-alcoholic Beverages Ranking slipped 15 places from 56th to 71st. Transport Ranking moved down eight spots from 45th in 2005 to 53rd in 2010. Housing Rents & Utilities Ranking declined from 34th to 37th over the first sub-period. Education Ranking fell from 16th in 2005 to 19th in 2007 and 2008 before rising back to 16th in 2010. Likewise, Health Ranking slipped from fourth in 2005 to fifth in 2008 before jumping back to fourth in 2010.

Between 2011 and 2013, Housing Rents & Utilities and Transport Rankings both jumped two places from 44th to 42nd and 46th to 44th. In contrast, Household Supplies & Domestic Help Ranking fell seven spots from 65th in 2011 to 72nd in 2013, making it the lowest ranked category in 2013. Education Ranking slipped three places from 22nd to 25th over the second sub-period. Food & Non-alcoholic Beverages Ranking rose from 67th in 2011 to 63rd in 2012 before falling back to 67th in 2013. Likewise, Health Ranking jumped from 18th in 2011 to 15th in 2012 before slipping back to 18th in 2013. Consequently, Health remained as the highest ranked category in both sub-periods.

MIAMI
United States

Figure 5.57b

The Gross Hourly Wages in USD for Ordinary Residents in Miami, as represented by the red line in Figure 5.57b, increased gradually from US$15.79 in 2005 to US$19.77 in 2013.

Despite the consistent increase in the wage level, the Wages Ranking for Ordinary Residents in Miami, as depicted by the red bars, has remained rather stable. From 30th in 2005, it rose slightly to 29th in 2009 before dropping to 31st in 2010. The ranking remained at 31st until 2013, when it rose back to 30th.

Figure 5.57c

Let us now analyse the cost of living and wages indices more closely and draw conclusions about the purchasing power of ordinary residents in Miami. As elaborated in Section 3.4.2 of Chapter 3, for a more precise and rigorous analysis, we discuss the results in two sub-periods: from 2005 to 2010 and from 2011 to 2013.

The Cost of Living Index and the Wages Index for Ordinary Residents in Miami are represented respectively by the grey and red line in Figure 5.57c. As mentioned in Section 3.3 of Chapter 3, wage data are only available at the national level and not by cities. Therefore, wages in all cities in the United States are assumed to be the same. As a result, Miami, being a city in the United States, shares a common Wages Index for Ordinary Residents with the base city New York (whose index value is 100.00) over the entire study period (2005–2013).

Between 2005 and 2010, the Cost of Living Index for Ordinary Residents in Miami was generally stable. The cost of living for ordinary residents in Miami only fluctuated around 71.49% of that for ordinary residents in New York over this first sub-period. Since the Wages Index for Ordinary Residents is constant across the years, how the Purchasing Power Index for Ordinary Residents in Miami (or any other cities in the United States) changes depends only on variations in the Cost of Living Index for Ordinary Residents. Thus, the relative stability of the latter caused the Purchasing Power Index for Ordinary Residents to also be stable throughout the first sub-period. Between 2005 and 2010, this index, which is represented by the green line in Figure 5.57c, only fluctuated around 139.92. Ranking-wise, the Purchasing Power Ranking for Ordinary Residents in Miami, which is represented by the green bars, was also stable. Miami's ranking in 2005 was the same as that in 2010 at 36th and notwithstanding a brief improvement to 34th in 2009, it only fluctuated among 36th and 37th in between.

Over the second sub-period (2011–2013), the Cost of Living Index for Ordinary Residents has steadily declined. In 2011, the cost of living for ordinary residents in Miami was 71.51% of that for their counterparts in New York. It dropped over the years to 60.58% in 2013. As a result, the Purchasing Power Index for Ordinary Residents has steadily increased, rising from 139.84 in 2011 to 165.08 in 2013. Meanwhile, the Purchasing Power Ranking for Ordinary Residents has also been improving. Between 2011 and 2013, it rose from 39th to 35th.

MIAMI
United States

Finally, we note that over the entire study period (2005–2013), the Purchasing Power Index for Ordinary Residents in Miami has always been above 100.00 — the base index value. This indicates that ordinary residents in Miami have consistently been able to consume more goods and services than their counterparts in New York, given the same number of working hours.

MILAN
Italy

Figure 5.58a: Cost of Living and 10 Consumption Categories Rankings for Ordinary Residents in Milan, Italy

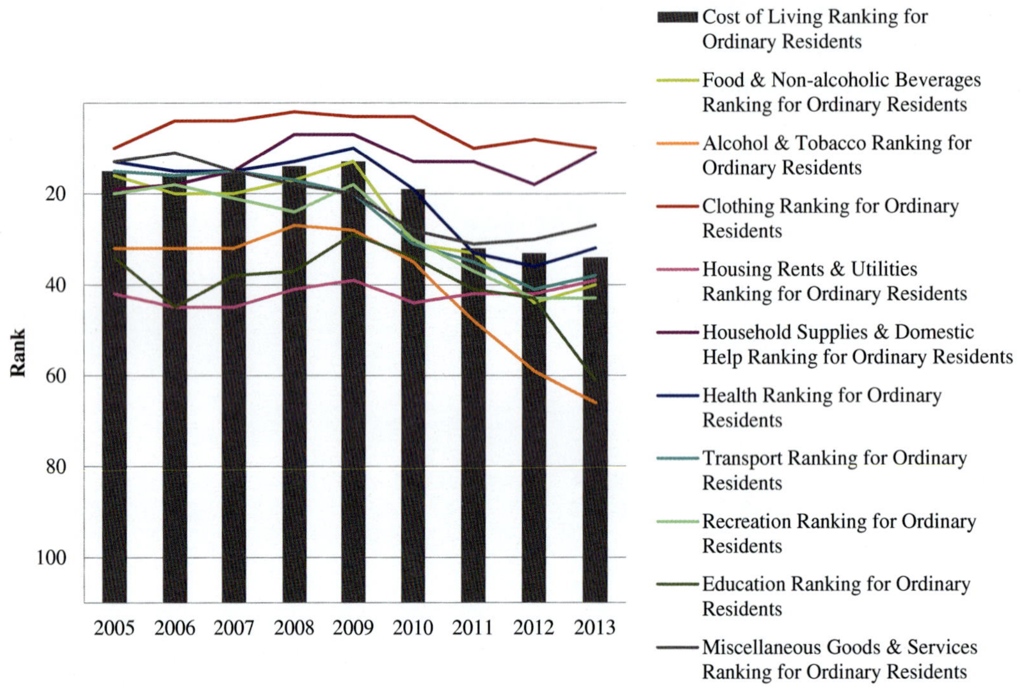

Source: Asia Competitiveness Institute

Figure 5.58b: Gross Hourly Wages in USD and Wages Ranking for Ordinary Residents in Milan, Italy

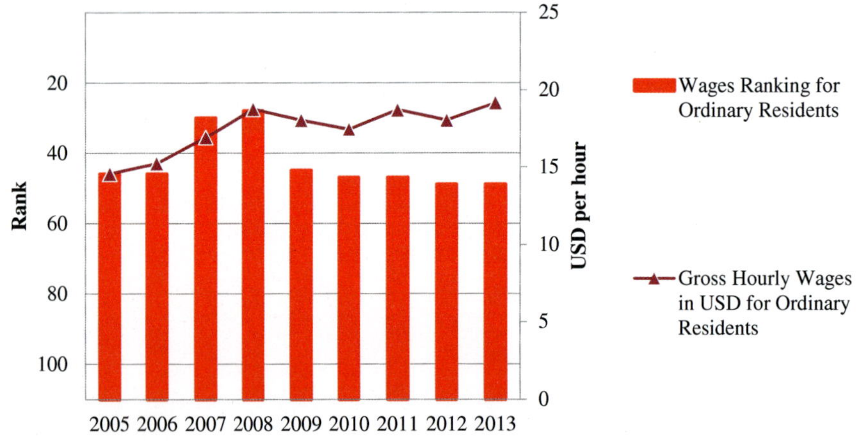

Source: Asia Competitiveness Institute

MILAN
Italy

Figure 5.58c: Cost of Living, Wages and Purchasing Power Indices and Purchasing Power Ranking for Ordinary Residents in Milan, Italy

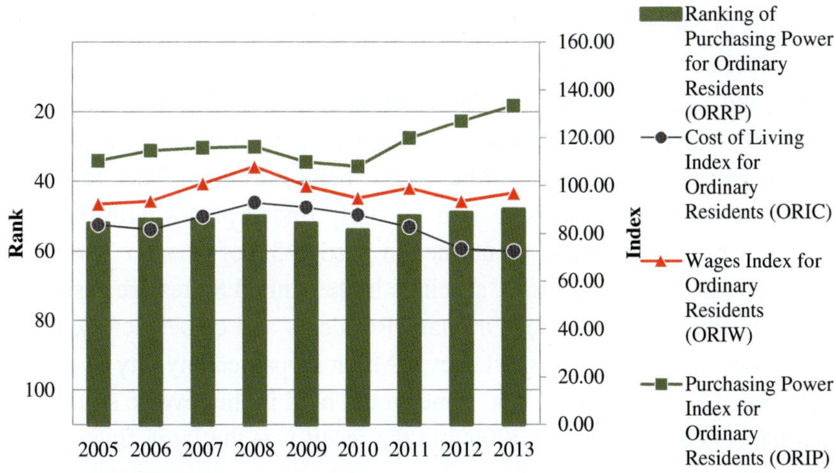

Source: Asia Competitiveness Institute

Figure 5.58a

Widely known for fashion and football, Milan is the second most populous city in Italy with an estimated population of 1.3 million. The city's Cost of Living Ranking for Ordinary Residents, as denoted by the grey bars, declined from 15th to 19th between 2005 and 2010, and from 32nd to 34th between 2011 and 2013 (see Figure 5.58a). As elaborated in Section 3.4.2 of Chapter 3, for a more precise comparison of rankings, we have split the analysis into two sub-periods.

From 2005 to 2010, Transport Ranking slipped 16 places from 15th to 31st. Food & Non-alcoholic Beverages Ranking fell 15 spots from 16th in 2005 to 31st in 2010. Health Ranking moved down six places from 13th to 19th over the first sub-period. In contrast, Clothing Ranking jumped seven places from 10th to third between 2005 and 2010. Household Supplies & Domestic Help Ranking moved up six spots from 19th to 13th over the same sub-period. Education Ranking fell from 34th in 2005 to 45th in 2006 before rising back to 34th in 2010.

From 2011 to 2013, Housing Rents & Utilities Ranking jumped three places from 42nd to 39th. Health Ranking moved up one spot from 33rd to 32nd over the second sub-period. Clothing Ranking rose from 10th in 2011 to eighth in 2012 before falling back to 10th in 2013, making it the highest ranked category in the second sub-period. In contrast, Education Ranking slipped 20 places from 41st in 2011 to 61st in 2013. Alcohol & Tobacco Ranking fell 18 spots from 48th to 66th between 2011 and 2013. Consequently, it became the lowest ranked category throughout the second sub-period. Food & Non-alcoholic Beverages Ranking went down from 33rd in 2011 to 40th in 2013. Transport Ranking slipped three places from 35th to 38th over the same sub-period.

MILAN
Italy

Figure 5.58b

After experiencing steady growth from 2005 to 2008, the Gross Hourly Wages in USD for Ordinary Residents in Milan, as denoted by the red line in Figure 5.58b, started to fluctuate and ended up at US$19.15 in 2013.

Ranking-wise, the Wages Ranking for Ordinary Residents in Milan, as depicted by the red bars, has exhibited considerable fluctuations. For example, from 46th in 2005, the ranking jumped to 30th in 2007. It rose slightly further to 28th before dropping back to 45th in 2009.

Such fluctuations happened because Milan regularly traded places with the 16 cities in the United States on the ranking table. As mentioned in Section 3.3 of Chapter 3, wage data are only available at the national level. Therefore, all cities in the United States are assumed to have the same Gross Hourly Wages in USD for Ordinary Residents and consequently, the same Wages Ranking for Ordinary Residents. Thus, whenever Milan surpassed any city in the United States, it overtook the other 15 cities as well. The same would hold in the reverse situation. These were precisely what happened in 2007 and 2009 and the result was the large fluctuations in Milan's ranking as observed.

Figure 5.58c

Let us now analyse the cost of living and wages indices more closely and draw conclusions about the purchasing power of ordinary residents in Milan. As elaborated in Section 3.4.2 of Chapter 3, for a more precise and rigorous analysis, we discuss the results in two sub-periods: from 2005 to 2010 and from 2011 to 2013.

The Cost of Living Index and the Wages Index for Ordinary Residents in Milan are represented respectively by the grey and red line in Figure 5.58c. Between 2005 and 2010, the Cost of Living Index for Ordinary Residents exhibited moderate fluctuations. In 2005, the cost of living for ordinary residents in Milan was 79.02% of that for their counterparts in New York (the base city). It rose between 2005 and 2008 and after peaking at 87.20% in 2008, the index started to decrease until it reached 84.02% in 2010. Over the first sub-period, the Wages Index for Ordinary Residents also followed a similar pattern, rising from its initial level at 92.29 in 2005 to peak at 107.86 in 2008 before reversing to a decreasing trend. In 2010, the value for the wages index was 94.67, only slightly higher than its value in 2005.

Between 2005 and 2008 when both wages and cost of living were rising, wages increased faster than cost of living. Thus, during these initial years of the first sub-period, ordinary residents in Milan were able to afford more goods and services over time. However, between 2008 and 2010 when both cost of living and wages were decreasing, wages dropped faster than the former. Thus, during these years, ordinary residents in Milan could only afford a lower consumption level over time. These trends are fully reflected in the Purchasing Power Index for Ordinary Residents in Milan, which is represented by the green line in Figure 5.58c. Between 2005 and

2007, this index rose from 116.80 to 123.78. It then steadily decreased thereafter until it reached 112.68 in 2010. Ranking-wise, the Purchasing Power Ranking for Ordinary Residents in Milan, as represented by the green bars, also fluctuated in the same manner as the purchasing power index. It improved from 52nd in 2005 to 50th in 2008 before deteriorating to 54th in 2010.

Over the second sub-period (2011–2013), the Cost of Living Index for Ordinary Residents has been on a decreasing trend. In 2011, the cost of living for ordinary residents in Milan was 78.68% of that for their counterparts in New York. It dropped over the years to reach 63.92% in 2013. The Wages Index for Ordinary Residents has also been decreasing, dropping from 98.96 in 2011 to 96.87 in 2013, with a deeper plunge to 93.44 in 2012.

Though both have been decreasing, wages have dropped more slowly than cost of living. Thus, throughout the second sub-period, ordinary residents in Milan were able to afford more goods and services over time. This is reflected in the Purchasing Power Index for Ordinary Residents, which rose from 125.77 in 2011 to 151.54 in 2013. Meanwhile, the Purchasing Power Ranking for Ordinary Residents has also improved over the second sub-period, rising from 47th in 2011 to 44th in 2013.

Finally, we note that over the entire study period (2005–2013), the Purchasing Power Index for Ordinary Residents in Milan has always been above 100.00 — the base index value. This means that ordinary residents in Milan have consistently been able to afford more goods and services than their counterparts in New York, given the same number of working hours.

MINNEAPOLIS
United States

Figure 5.59a: Cost of Living and 10 Consumption Categories Rankings for Ordinary Residents in Minneapolis, United States

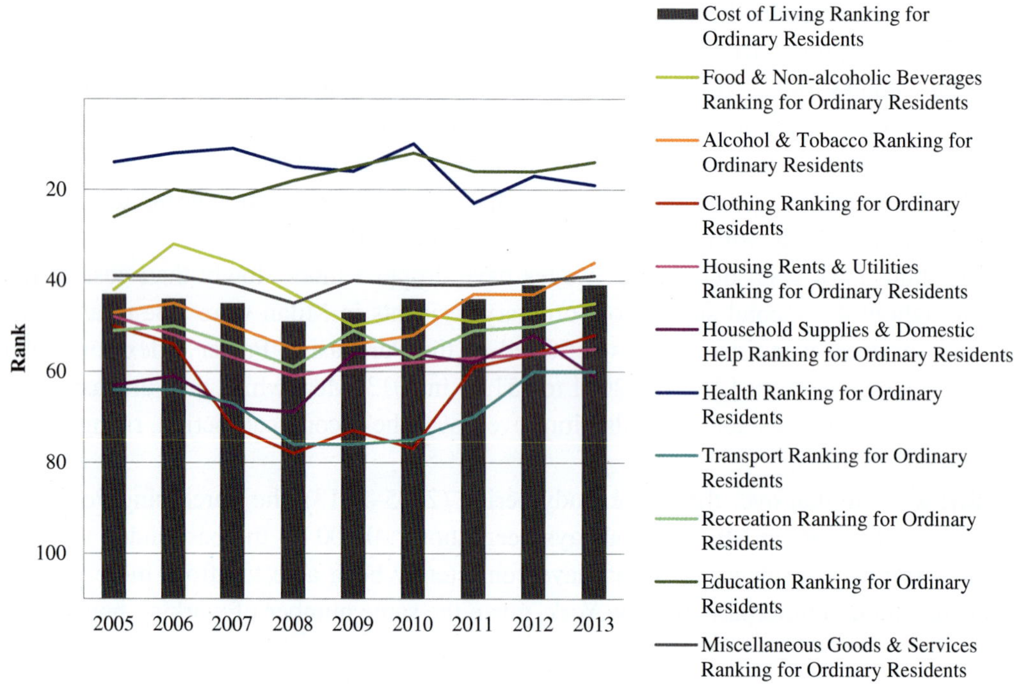

Source: Asia Competitiveness Institute

Figure 5.59b: Gross Hourly Wages in USD and Wages Ranking for Ordinary Residents in Minneapolis, United States

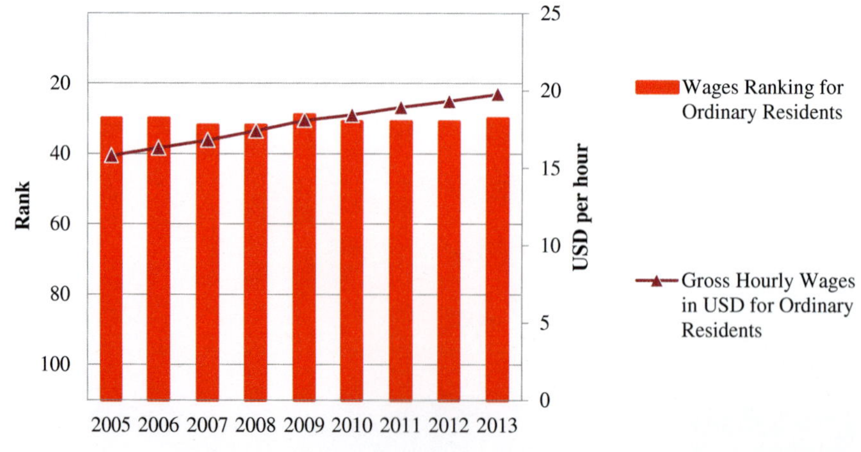

Source: Asia Competitiveness Institute

MINNEAPOLIS
United States

Figure 5.59c: Cost of Living, Wages and Purchasing Power Indices and Purchasing Power Ranking for Ordinary Residents in Minneapolis, United States

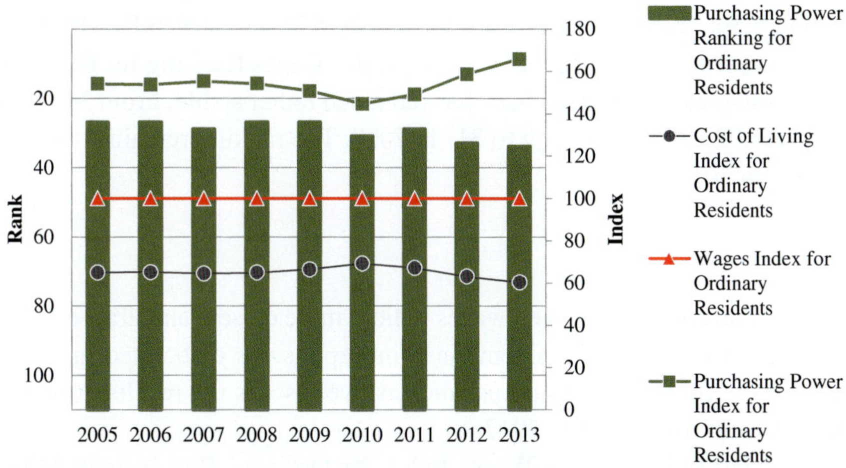

Source: Asia Competitiveness Institute

Figure 5.59a

Straddling on both banks of the Mississippi River, Minneapolis, the largest city in the state of Minnesota, is known for its abundance in water with over 20 lakes and wetland areas. The city's Cost of Living Ranking for Ordinary Residents, as represented by the grey bars, fell from 43rd to 44th between 2005 and 2010, but rose from 44th to 41st between 2011 and 2013 (see Figure 5.59a). As explained in Section 3.4.2 of Chapter 3, for a more rigorous comparison of rankings, we have split the analysis into two sub-periods.

From 2005 to 2010, Education Ranking jumped 14 places from 26th to 12th. Health Ranking moved up four spots from 14th in 2005 to 10th in 2010. In contrast, Transport Ranking slipped 11 places from 64th to 75th over the first sub-period. Housing Rents & Utilities Ranking fell 10 spots from 48th to 58th between 2005 and 2010. Food & Non-alcoholic Beverages Ranking declined from 42nd in 2005 to 47th in 2010.

From 2011 to 2013, Household Supplies & Domestic Help was the only category that fell in ranking from 58th to 61st and consequently became the lowest ranked category in 2013. Transport Ranking jumped 10 places from 70th in 2011 to 60th in 2013. Food & Non-alcoholic Beverages and Health Rankings both moved up four spots from 49th to 45th and 23rd to 19th over the second sub-period. Housing Rents & Utilities Ranking went up from 57th in 2011 to 55th in 2013. Likewise, Education Ranking jumped two places from 16th to 14th over the same sub-period, making it the highest ranked category in the second sub-period.

MINNEAPOLIS
United States

Figure 5.59b

The Gross Hourly Wages in USD for Ordinary Residents in Minneapolis, as represented by the red line in Figure 5.59b, increased gradually from US$15.79 in 2005 to US$19.77 in 2013.

Despite the consistent increase in the wage level, the Wages Ranking for Ordinary Residents in Minneapolis, as depicted by the red bars, has remained rather stable. From 30th in 2005, it rose slightly to 29th in 2009 before dropping to 31st in 2010. The ranking remained at 31st until 2013, when it rose back to 30th.

Figure 5.59c

Let us now analyse the cost of living and wages indices more closely and draw conclusions about the purchasing power of ordinary residents in Minneapolis. As elaborated in Section 3.4.2 of Chapter 3, for a more precise and rigorous analysis, we discuss the results in two sub-periods: from 2005 to 2010 and from 2011 to 2013.

The Cost of Living Index and the Wages Index for Ordinary Residents in Minneapolis are represented respectively by the grey and red line in Figure 5.59c. As mentioned in Section 3.3 of Chapter 3, wage data are only available at the national level and not by cities. Therefore, wages in all cities in the United States are assumed to be the same. As a result, Minneapolis, being a city in the United States, shares a common Wages Index for Ordinary Residents with the base city New York (whose index value is 100.00) over the entire study period (2005–2013).

Over the first sub-period (2005–2010), the Cost of Living Index for Ordinary Residents in Minneapolis was initially stable but it followed an upward trend in the later years. Between 2005 and 2008, the cost of living for ordinary residents in Minneapolis only fluctuated modestly around 64.79% of that for ordinary residents in New York. Thereafter, however, it rose steadily until it reached 69.10% in 2010.

Since the Wages Index for Ordinary Residents is constant across the years, how the Purchasing Power Index for Ordinary Residents in Minneapolis (or any other cities in the United States) changes depends only on variations in the Cost of Living Index for Ordinary Residents. Thus, between 2005 and 2008 when the latter index was generally stable, the purchasing power index was also stable, only fluctuating around 154.36. However, it switched to a decreasing trend between 2008 and 2010 when the cost of living index was increasing. Overall, the purchasing power index was lower in 2010 (144.72) than it was in 2005 (154.13), indicating an erosion in ordinary residents' purchasing power over the first sub-period. Ranking-wise, the Purchasing Power Ranking for Ordinary Residents in Minneapolis, which is represented by the green bars, largely remained at 27th over the first sub-period. However, in 2010, the ranking dropped to 31st.

Over the second sub-period (2011–2013), the Cost of Living Index for Ordinary Residents has steadily declined. In 2011, the cost of living for ordinary residents in Minneapolis was 67.07%

of that for their counterparts in New York. It dropped over the years to 60.29% in 2013. As a result, the Purchasing Power Index for Ordinary Residents has steadily increased, rising from 149.10 in 2011 to 165.86 in 2013. Despite this positive showing of the index, the Purchasing Power Ranking for Ordinary Residents has been deteriorating. Between 2011 and 2013, it dropped from 29th to 34th.

Finally, we note that over the entire study period (2005–2013), the Purchasing Power Index for Ordinary Residents in Minneapolis has always been above 100.00 — the base index value. This indicates that ordinary residents in Minneapolis have consistently been able to consume more goods and services than their counterparts in New York, given the same number of working hours.

MONTEVIDEO
Uruguay

Figure 5.60a: Cost of Living and 10 Consumption Categories Rankings for Ordinary Residents in Montevideo, Uruguay

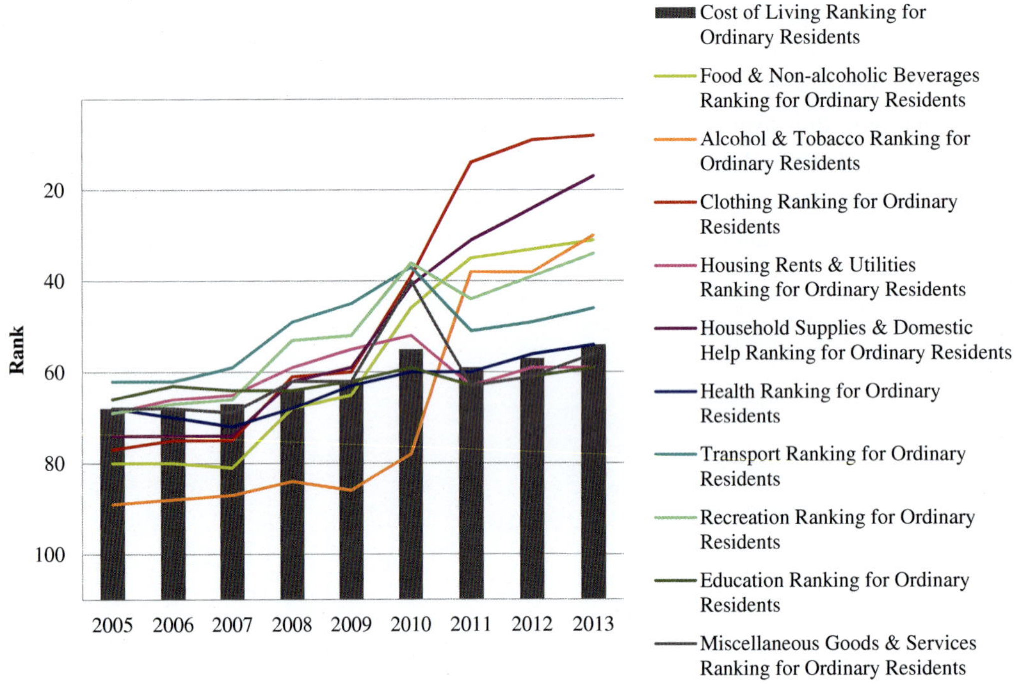

Source: Asia Competitiveness Institute

Figure 5.60b: Gross Hourly Wages in USD and Wages Ranking for Ordinary Residents in Montevideo, Uruguay

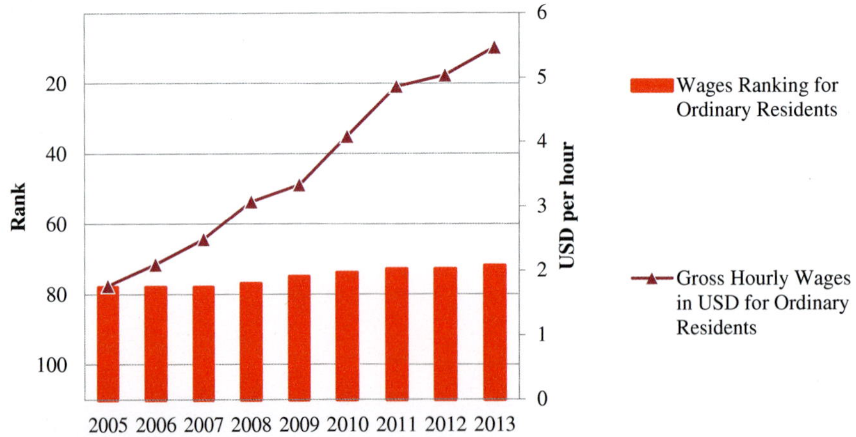

Source: Asia Competitiveness Institute

MONTEVIDEO
Uruguay

Figure 5.60c: Cost of Living, Wages and Purchasing Power Indices and Purchasing Power Ranking for Ordinary Residents in Montevideo, Uruguay

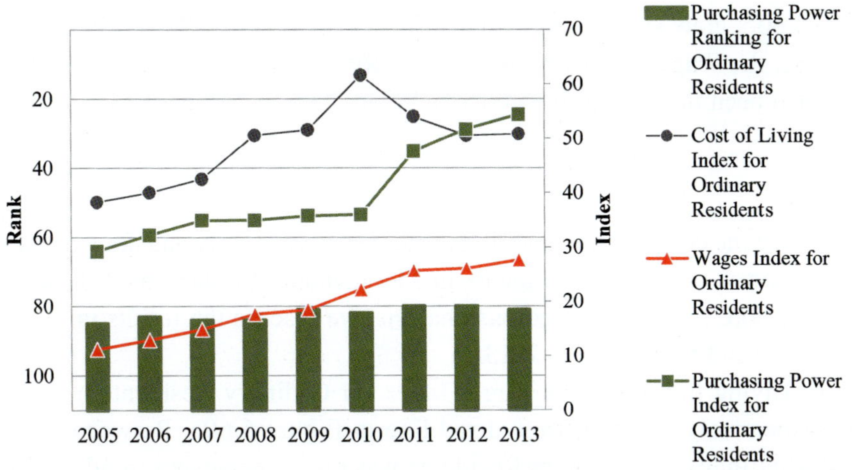

Source: Asia Competitiveness Institute

Figure 5.60a

Montevideo, the capital and largest city of Uruguay, is the southernmost capital city in the Americas. The city's Cost of Living Ranking for Ordinary Residents, as shown in the grey bars, rose from 68th to 55th between 2005 and 2010, and from 59th to 54th between 2011 and 2013 (see Figure 5.60a). As elaborated in Section 3.4.2 of Chapter 3, for a more precise comparison of rankings, we have split the analysis into two sub-periods.

The rankings of all 10 categories went up over the first sub-period from 2005 to 2010. In particular, Food & Non-alcoholic Beverages Ranking climbed 34 places from 80th in 2005 to 46th in 2010. Transport Ranking jumped 25 spots from 62nd to 37th between 2005 and 2010. Housing Rents & Utilities Ranking moved up 17 places from 69th to 52nd over the same sub-period. Health and Education Rankings rose from 68th to 60th and 66th to 59th, respectively, over the first sub-period.

Between 2011 and 2013, Clothing Ranking jumped six places from 14th to eighth, making it the highest ranked category throughout the second sub-period. Health Ranking also climbed six spots from 60th in 2011 to 54th in 2013. Transport Ranking moved up five places from 51st to 46th over the same sub-period. Education Ranking rose from 63rd in 2011 to 59th in 2013. Nonetheless, Education was the lowest ranked category in 2013. Housing Rents & Utilities and Food & Non-alcoholic Beverages Rankings both jumped four places from 63rd to 59th and 35th to 31st, respectively, over the second sub-period.

MONTEVIDEO
Uruguay

Figure 5.60b

The Gross Hourly Wages in USD for Ordinary Residents in Montevideo, as shown by the red line in Figure 5.60b, grew significantly from US$1.77 in 2005 to US$5.47 in 2013.

Ranking-wise, the Wages Ranking for Ordinary Residents in Montevideo, as denoted by the red bars, has also been improving. It rose from 78th in 2005 to 72nd in 2013.

Figure 5.60c

Let us now analyse the cost of living and wages indices more closely and draw conclusions about the purchasing power of ordinary residents in Montevideo. As elaborated in Section 3.4.2 of Chapter 3, for a more precise and rigorous analysis, we discuss the results in two sub-periods: from 2005 to 2010 and from 2011 to 2013.

The Cost of Living Index and the Wages Index for Ordinary Residents in Montevideo are represented respectively by the grey and red line in Figure 5.60c. Between 2005 and 2010, the Cost of Living Index for Ordinary Residents was on an increasing trend. In 2005, the cost of living for ordinary residents in Montevideo was 38.29% of that for their counterparts in New York (the base city). It rose over the years to reach 61.63% in 2010. Over the first sub-period, the Wages Index for Ordinary Residents also followed an increasing trend, rising from 11.20 in 2005 to 22.17 in 2010.

Wages rose faster than cost of living, so throughout the first sub-period, ordinary residents in Montevideo could afford more goods and services over time. This is reflected in the Purchasing Power Index for Ordinary Residents in Montevideo, which is represented by the green line in Figure 5.60c. Between 2005 and 2010, this index rose from 29.25 to 35.98. Ranking-wise, the Purchasing Power Ranking for Ordinary Residents in Montevideo, as represented by the green bars, generally improved over the first sub-period, rising from 85th in 2005 to 82nd in 2010 while also exhibiting moderate fluctuations in between.

Over the second sub-period (2011–2013), the Cost of Living Index for Ordinary Residents has been on a decreasing trend. In 2011, the cost of living for ordinary residents in Montevideo was 54.03% of that for their counterparts in New York. It dropped over the years to reach 50.80% in 2013. In contrast, the Wages Index for Ordinary Residents has been increasing. Between 2011 and 2013, this index rose from 25.72 to 27.65.

The combined trends of increasing wages and decreasing cost of living have enabled ordinary residents in Montevideo to afford more goods and services over time throughout the second sub-period. This is reflected in the Purchasing Power Index for Ordinary Residents, which rose from 47.60 in 2011 to 54.43 in 2013. Despite this positive showing of the index, the Purchasing Power Ranking for Ordinary Residents has deteriorated over the second sub-period. It stagnated at 80th in 2011 and 2012 before dropping to 81st in 2013.

MONTEVIDEO
Uruguay

Finally, we note that over the entire study period (2005–2013), the Purchasing Power Index for Ordinary Residents in Montevideo has consistently been lower than 100.00 — the base index value. This means that ordinary residents in Montevideo have only been able to afford a lower consumption level than their counterparts in New York, given the same number of working hours.

MONTREAL
Canada

Figure 5.61a: Cost of Living and 10 Consumption Categories Rankings for Ordinary Residents in Montreal, Canada

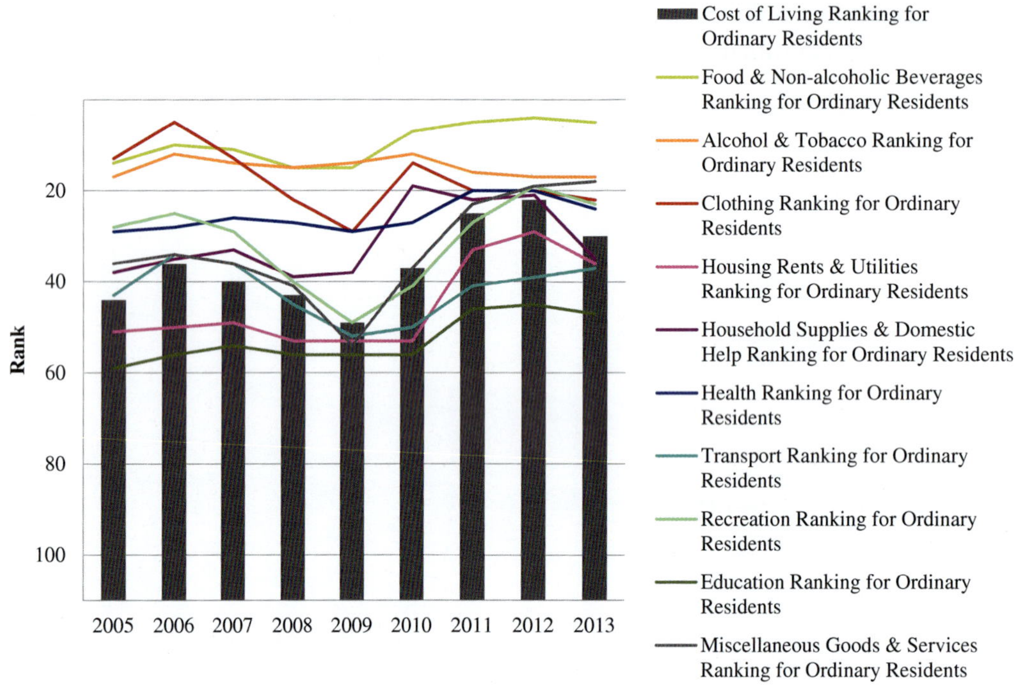

Source: Asia Competitiveness Institute

Figure 5.61b: Gross Hourly Wages in USD and Wages Ranking for Ordinary Residents in Montreal, Canada

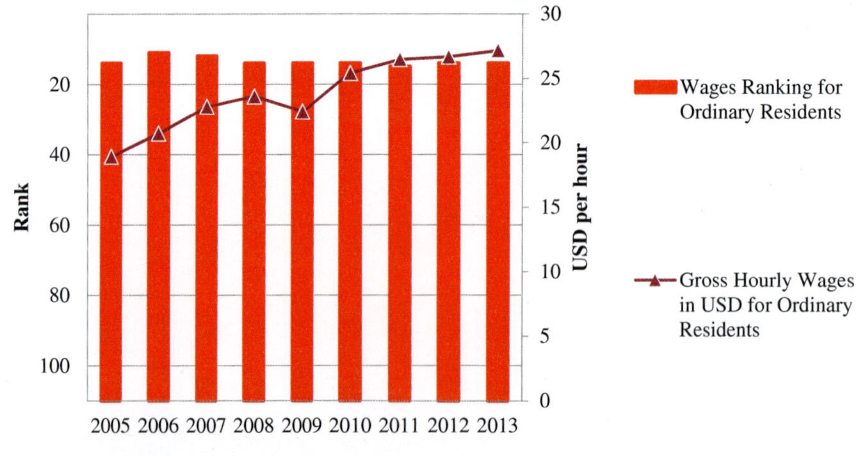

Source: Asia Competitiveness Institute

MONTREAL
Canada

Figure 5.61c: Cost of Living, Wages and Purchasing Power Indices and Purchasing Power Ranking for Ordinary Residents in Montreal, Canada

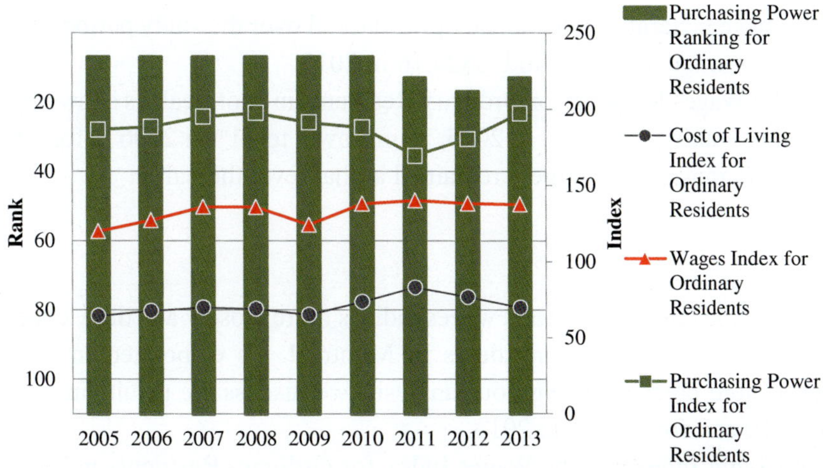

Source: Asia Competitiveness Institute

Figure 5.61a

Montreal, the second largest city in Canada, is the country's centre of commerce, aerospace and pharmaceuticals. The city's Cost of Living Ranking for Ordinary Residents, as denoted by the grey bars, rose from 44th to 37th between 2005 and 2010, but declined from 25th to 30th between 2011 and 2013 (see Figure 5.61a). As explained in Section 3.4.2 of Chapter 3, for a more rigorous comparison of rankings, we have split the analysis into two sub-periods.

From 2005 to 2010, Food & Non-alcoholic Beverages Ranking jumped seven places from 14th to seventh. Education Ranking moved up three places from 59th in 2005 to 56th in 2010. Health Ranking rose from 29th to 27th over the first sub-period. In contrast, Transport Ranking slipped seven places from 43rd in 2005 to 50th in 2010. Housing Rents & Utilities Ranking fell two spots from 51st to 53rd over the same sub-period.

From 2011 to 2013, Food & Non-alcoholic Beverages Ranking went up from fifth in 2011 to fourth in 2013 before falling back to fifth in 2013, making it the highest ranked category throughout the second sub-period. Transport Ranking jumped four places from 41st in 2011 to 37th in 2013. In contrast, Household Supplies & Domestic Help Ranking fell 13 spots from 22nd to 35th between 2011 and 2013. Health Ranking slipped four places from 20th to 24th over the second sub-period. Housing Rents & Utilities Ranking declined from 33rd in 2011 to 36th in 2013. Education Ranking slipped one spot from 46th to 47th over the same sub-period. Consequently, Education remained as the lowest ranked category for the entire study period.

MONTREAL
Canada

Figure 5.61b

The Gross Hourly Wages in USD for Ordinary Residents in Montreal, as denoted by the red line in Figure 5.61b, have generally followed an upward trend over the study period. From US$18.91 in 2005, Montreal's wage level rose to US$27.16 in 2013.

Meanwhile, the Wages Ranking for Ordinary Residents in Montreal, as shown by the red bars, has been relatively stable. From 14th in 2005, it improved to 11th in 2006 before dropping back to 14th in 2008. The ranking has largely remained at that level thereafter.

Figure 5.61c

Let us now analyse the cost of living and wages indices more closely and draw conclusions about the purchasing power of ordinary residents in Montreal. As elaborated in Section 3.4.2 of Chapter 3, for a more precise and rigorous analysis, we discuss the results in two sub-periods: from 2005 to 2010 and from 2011 to 2013.

The Cost of Living Index and the Wages Index for Ordinary Residents in Montreal are represented respectively by the grey and red line in Figure 5.61c. Over the first sub-period (2005–2010), the Cost of Living Index for Ordinary Residents was generally on an increasing trend. In 2005, the cost of living for ordinary residents in Montreal was 64.17% of that for their counterparts in New York (the base city). It rose over the years to 68.73% in 2008, dropping to 64.85% in 2009 before picking up again until it reached 73.33% in 2010. Meanwhile, the Wages Index for Ordinary Residents also followed a similar pattern. Like the cost of living index, this index was also on an increasing trend that was temporarily interrupted by a plunge in 2009. Overall, the wages index was higher in 2010 (137.89) than it was in 2005 (119.76).

Not only did wages and cost of living change in the same manner but they also changed at almost the same rates. Thus, throughout the first sub-period, ordinary residents in Montreal were able to generally maintain their consumption level over time. This is reflected in the Purchasing Power Index for Ordinary Residents in Montreal, which is represented by the green line in Figure 5.61c. This index was rather stable, only fluctuating around 191.14 between 2005 and 2010. Ranking-wise, the Purchasing Power Ranking for Ordinary Residents in Montreal, as represented by the green bars, consistently remained at seventh over the first sub-period.

Over the second sub-period (2011–2013), the Cost of Living Index for Ordinary Residents has been on a decreasing trend. In 2011, the cost of living for ordinary residents in Montreal was 82.83% of that for their counterparts in New York. It dropped to 69.64% in 2013. The Wages Index for Ordinary Residents has also been decreasing, albeit more marginally. From 140.07 in 2011, the index dropped to 137.38 in 2013.

That wages have decreased much more slowly than cost of living means that ordinary residents in Montreal have been able to afford more goods and services over time throughout the second sub-period. This is reflected in the Purchasing Power Index for Ordinary Residents, which rose from 169.12 in 2011 to 197.28 in 2013. Despite this positive showing of the index, the Purchasing Power Ranking for Ordinary Residents has not improved over the second sub-period. From 13th in 2005, it dropped to 17th in 2012 before climbing back to 13th in 2013.

Finally, we note that over the entire study period (2005–2013), the Purchasing Power Index for Ordinary Residents in Montreal has always been above 100.00 — the base index value. This means that ordinary residents in Montreal have consistently been able to afford a higher consumption level than their counterparts in New York, given the same number of working hours.

MOSCOW
Russia

Figure 5.62a: Cost of Living and 10 Consumption Categories Rankings for Ordinary Residents in Moscow, Russia

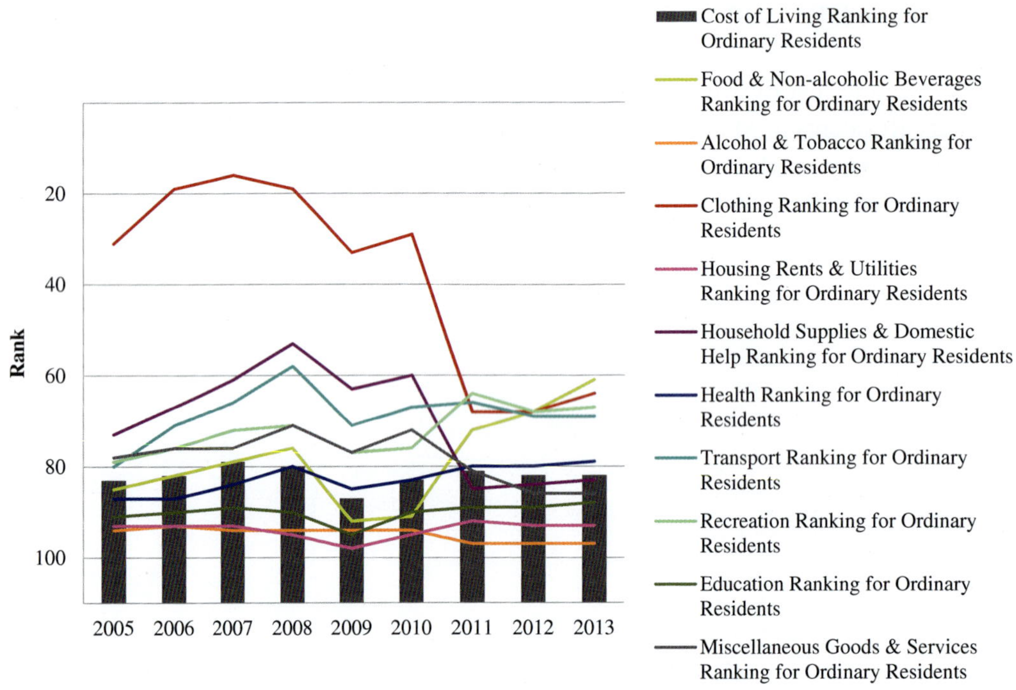

Source: Asia Competitiveness Institute

Figure 5.62b: Gross Hourly Wages in USD and Wages Ranking for Ordinary Residents in Moscow, Russia

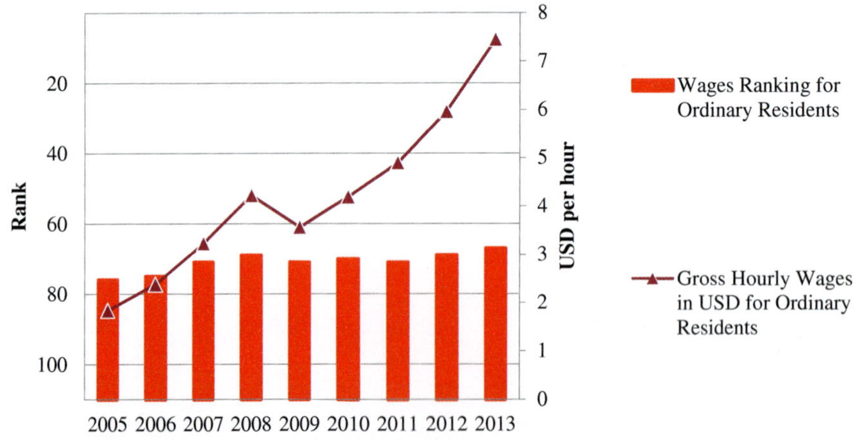

Source: Asia Competitiveness Institute

MOSCOW
Russia

Figure 5.62c: Cost of Living, Wages and Purchasing Power Indices and Purchasing Power Ranking for Ordinary Residents in Moscow, Russia

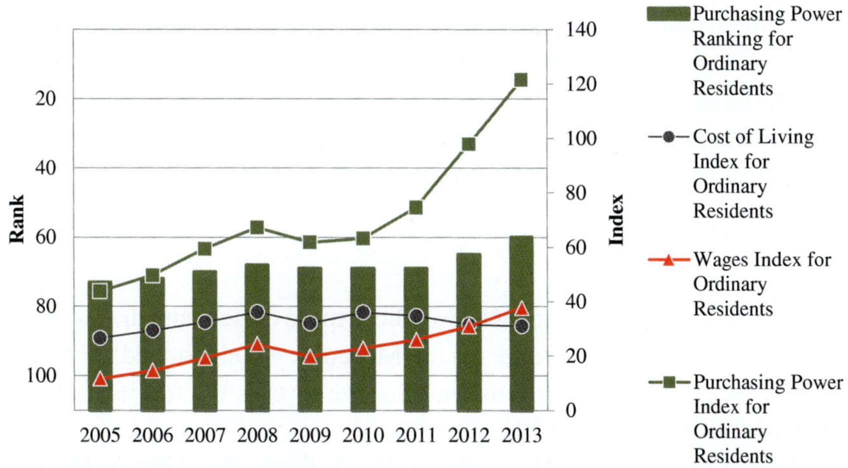

Source: Asia Competitiveness Institute

Figure 5.62a

Moscow, the capital city of Russia, is the world's northernmost and coldest megacity as well as the most populous city in Europe. The city's Cost of Living Ranking for Ordinary Residents, as represented by the grey bars, rose from 83rd in 2005 to 79th in 2007 before falling back to 83rd in 2010, and declined from 81st to 82nd between 2011 and 2013 (see Figure 5.62a). As elaborated in Section 3.4.2 of Chapter 3, for a more precise comparison of rankings, we have split the analysis into two sub-periods.

From 2005 to 2010, Transport Ranking climbed 13 places from 80th to 67th. Health Ranking jumped four spots from 87th in 2005 to 83rd in 2010. Education Ranking moved up one place from 91st to 90th over the first sub-period. In contrast, Food & Non-alcoholic Beverages Ranking fell six places from 85th to 91st between 2005 and 2010. Housing Rents & Utilities Ranking slipped two spots from 93rd to 95th over the same sub-period.

Between 2011 and 2013, Food & Non-alcoholic Beverages Ranking jumped 11 places from 72nd to 61st, making it the highest ranked category in 2013. Health and Education Rankings both moved up one place from 80th to 79th and 89th to 88th, respectively, over the second sub-period. In contrast, Transport Ranking fell three places from 66th in 2011 to 69th in 2013. Housing Rents & Utilities Ranking slipped one spot from 92nd to 93rd over the same sub-period. Alcohol & Tobacco remained as the lowest ranked category throughout the second sub-period as its ranking stayed unchanged at 97th from 2011 to 2013.

MOSCOW
Russia

Figure 5.62b

The Gross Hourly Wages in USD for Ordinary Residents in Moscow, as denoted by the red line in Figure 5.62b, increased more than fourfold from US$1.84 in 2005 to US$7.45 in 2013. However, there was a plunge in 2009, which happened because of the depreciation of Russian rouble against US dollar in that year.

Meanwhile, the Wages Ranking for Ordinary Residents in Moscow, as shown by the red bars, has also improved, rising from 76th to 67th over the study period.

Figure 5.62c

Let us now analyse the cost of living and wages indices more closely and draw conclusions about the purchasing power of ordinary residents in Moscow. As elaborated in Section 3.4.2 of Chapter 3, for a more precise and rigorous analysis, we discuss the results in two sub-periods: from 2005 to 2010 and from 2011 to 2013.

The Cost of Living Index and the Wages Index for Ordinary Residents in Moscow are represented respectively by the grey and red line in Figure 5.62c. Between 2005 and 2010, the Cost of Living Index for Ordinary Residents was generally on an increasing trend. In 2005, the cost of living for ordinary residents in Moscow was 26.53% of that for their counterparts in New York (the base city). It rose over the years to peak at 36.10% in 2008 and then dropped to 31.94% in 2009 before resuming its increasing trend to reach 35.95% in 2010. Over the first sub-period, the Wages Index for Ordinary Residents also followed a similar pattern. Like the cost of living index, this index was also on an increasing trend that was temporarily interrupted by a decline in 2009. Overall, the wages index was higher in 2010 (22.74) than it was in 2005 (11.63).

Wages generally rose faster than cost of living so throughout the first sub-period, ordinary residents in Moscow were able to afford more goods and services over time. This is reflected in the Purchasing Power Index for Ordinary Residents in Moscow, which is represented by the green line in Figure 5.62c. This index rose from 43.83 in 2005 to 63.24 in 2010. Meanwhile, the Purchasing Power Ranking for Ordinary Residents, as represented by the green bars, also improved over the first sub-period, rising from 73rd in 2005 to 69th in 2010.

Over the second sub-period (2011–2013), the Cost of Living Index for Ordinary Residents has been on a decreasing trend. In 2011, the cost of living for ordinary residents in Moscow was 34.70% of that for their counterparts in New York. It dropped over the years to reach 31.01% in 2013. In contrast, the Wages Index for Ordinary Residents has been increasing. From 25.89 in 2011, the index increased to 37.69 in 2013.

The combined trends of increasing wages and decreasing cost of living have enabled ordinary residents in Moscow to afford more goods and services over time throughout the second sub-period. This is reflected in the Purchasing Power Index for Ordinary Residents, which rose from 74.60 in 2011 to 121.56 in 2013. Ranking-wise, the Purchasing Power Ranking for Ordinary

Residents also improved substantially over the second sub-period, rising from 69th in 2011 to 60th in 2013.

Finally, we note that over the entire study period (2005–2013), the Purchasing Power Index for Ordinary Residents in Moscow had consistently been lower than 100.00 — the base index value — until 2013. This means it was not until recently that ordinary residents in Moscow were able to afford more goods and services than ordinary residents in New York, given the same number of working hours. Before 2013, ordinary residents in Moscow had only been able to afford a lower consumption level.

MUMBAI
India

Figure 5.63a: Cost of Living and 10 Consumption Categories Rankings for Ordinary Residents in Mumbai, India

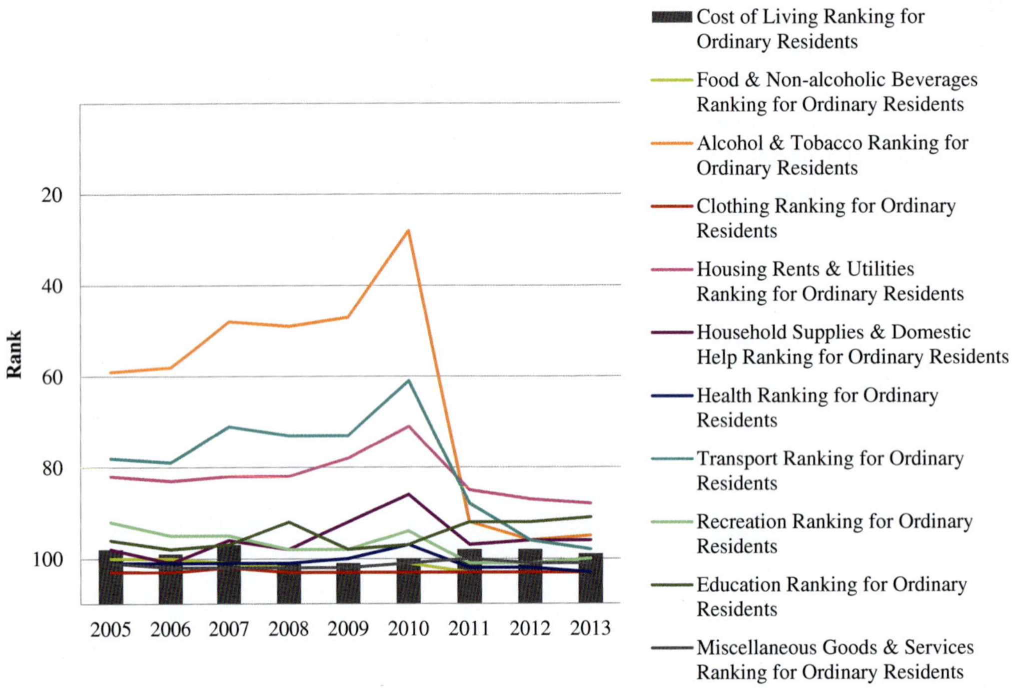

Source: Asia Competitiveness Institute

Figure 5.63b: Gross Hourly Wages in USD and Wages Ranking for Ordinary Residents in Mumbai, India

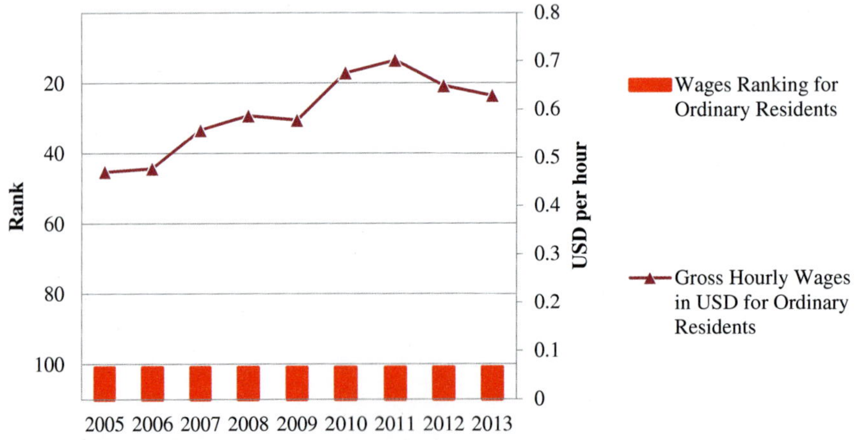

Source: Asia Competitiveness Institute

MUMBAI
India

Figure 5.63c: Cost of Living, Wages and Purchasing Power Indices and Purchasing Power Ranking for Ordinary Residents in Mumbai, India

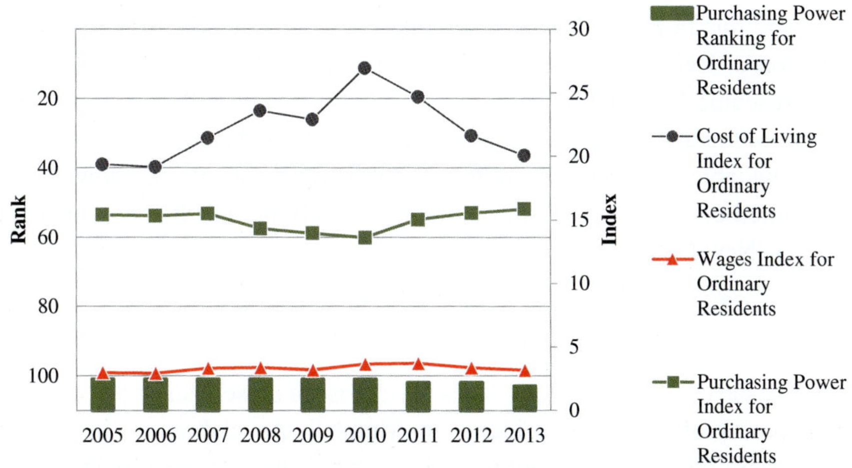

Source: Asia Competitiveness Institute

Figure 5.63a

With an estimated population of 18.4 million, Mumbai is the most populous city in India and the eighth most populous city in the world. The city's Cost of Living Ranking for Ordinary Residents, as shown in the grey bars, fell from 98th to 100th between 2005 and 2010, and from 98th to 99th between 2011 and 2013 (see Figure 5.63a). As explained in Section 3.4.2 of Chapter 3, for a more rigorous comparison of rankings, we have split the analysis into two sub-periods.

From 2005 to 2010, Transport Ranking climbed 17 places from 78th to 61st. Housing Rents & Utilities Ranking jumped 11 spots from 82nd in 2005 to 71st in 2010. Health Ranking moved up four places from 101st to 97th over the first sub-period. In contrast, Education and Food & Non-alcoholic Beverages Rankings slipped one spot from 96th to 97th and 100th to 101st, respectively, between 2005 and 2010.

From 2011 to 2013, Education Ranking jumped one place from 92nd to 91st. Food & Non-alcoholic Beverages and Clothing Rankings both remained unchanged at 103rd between 2011 and 2013, making Mumbai the cheapest city in these categories in the second sub-period. Housing Rents & Utilities Ranking fell three spots from 85th in 2011 to 88th in 2013. Nonetheless, it was consistently the highest ranked category throughout the second sub-period. Health Ranking slipped one place from 102nd to 103rd from 2011 to 2013. Mumbai thus became the most affordable city in terms of Health in 2013.

MUMBAI
India

Figure 5.63b

From 2005 to 2011, the Gross Hourly Wages in USD for Ordinary Residents in Mumbai, as depicted by the red line in Figure 5.63b, rose from US$0.47 to US$0.70. However, mainly due to the depreciation of Indian rupee against US dollar from 2011 onwards, the wage level has been declining, reaching US$0.63 in 2013.

Ranking-wise, Mumbai has been consistently ranked among the bottom three out of 103 cities in the wage ranking table. The Wages Ranking for Ordinary Residents, as shown by the red bars, has always remained constant at 101st throughout the study period. It shares this spot with the capital of India — New Delhi.

Figure 5.63c

Let us now analyse the cost of living and wages indices more closely and draw conclusions about the purchasing power of ordinary residents in Mumbai. As elaborated in Section 3.4.2 of Chapter 3, for a more precise and rigorous analysis, we discuss the results in two sub-periods: from 2005 to 2010 and from 2011 to 2013.

The Cost of Living Index and the Wages Index for Ordinary Residents in Mumbai are represented respectively by the grey and red line in Figure 5.63c. Over the first sub-period (2005–2010), the Cost of Living Index for Ordinary Residents was generally on an increasing trend. In 2005, the cost of living for ordinary residents in Mumbai was 19.35% of that for their counterparts in New York (the base city). It rose over the years to reach 26.93% in 2010. Over the first sub-period, the Wages Index for Ordinary Residents was also on an upward trend, rising from 2.98 in 2005 to 3.66 in 2010.

Between 2005 and 2007, wages rose at similar rates as cost of living. Thus, ordinary residents in Mumbai were able to afford the same consumption level over time during these years. However, they were unable to do so during remaining years of the first sub-period because throughout these years, wages could not keep up with the pace of increase of cost of living. These trends are reflected in the Purchasing Power Index for Ordinary Residents in Mumbai, which is represented by the green line in Figure 5.63c. This index was stable between 2005 and 2007, only fluctuating slightly around 15.40. After 2007, however, it steadily decreased until it reached 13.60 in 2010. Meanwhile, the Purchasing Power Ranking for Ordinary Residents, as represented by the green bars, stagnated at 101st over the first sub-period.

Over the second sub-period (2011–2013), the Cost of Living Index for Ordinary Residents has been on a decreasing trend. In 2011, the cost of living for ordinary residents in Mumbai was 24.68% of that for their counterparts in New York. It dropped over the years to reach 20.05% in 2013. The Wages Index for Ordinary Residents has also been decreasing, albeit very marginally. From 3.71 in 2011, the index dropped to 3.18 in 2013.

MUMBAI
India

Wages have decreased more slowly than cost of living so the purchasing power of ordinary residents in Mumbai has increased over the second sub-period. This is reflected in the increase of the Purchasing Power Index for Ordinary Residents which rose from 15.04 in 2011 to 15.85 in 2013. However, it is worth noting that the increase in the index value was very small. This indicates that although ordinary residents in Mumbai have indeed gained more purchasing power over the second sub-period, this gain has been at best marginal. Over the same sub-period, ordinary residents in other cities have gained much more. As such, it is unsurprising that the Purchasing Power Ranking for Ordinary Residents in Mumbai has deteriorated over the second sub-period, dropping from 102nd in 2011 and 2012 to 103rd in 2013 out of 103 cities studied.

Finally, we note that over the entire study period (2005–2013), the Purchasing Power Index for Ordinary Residents in Mumbai has consistently been lower than 100.00 — the base index value — by almost a factor of nine. This means that ordinary residents in Mumbai have only been able to afford a much lower consumption level than their counterparts in New York, given the same number of working hours.

MUNICH
Germany

Figure 5.64a: Cost of Living and 10 Consumption Categories Rankings for Ordinary Residents in Munich, Germany

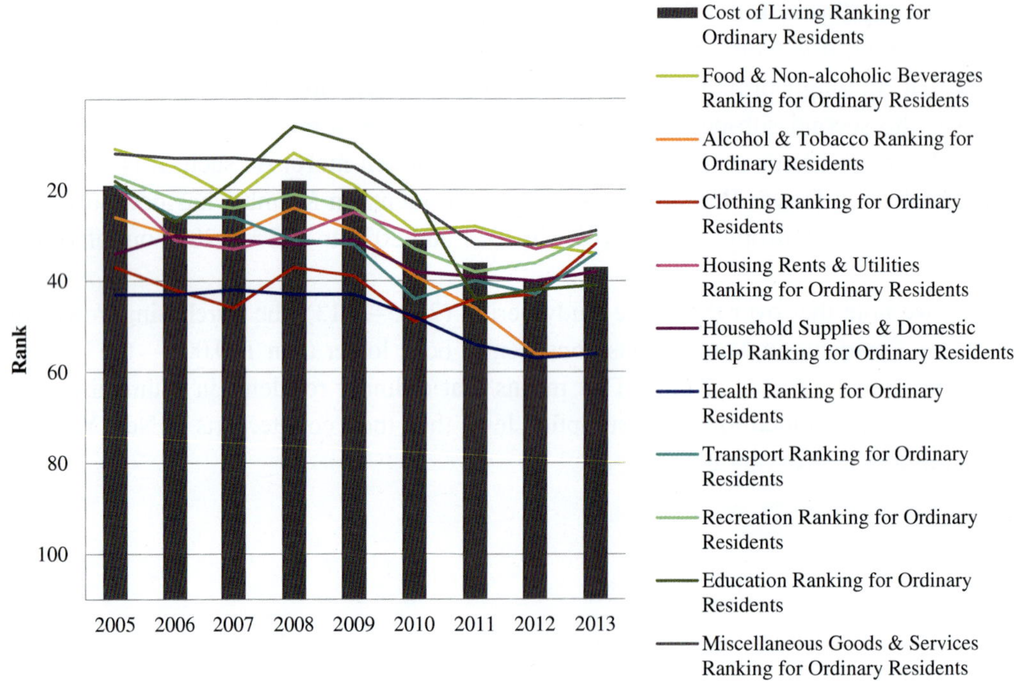

Source: Asia Competitiveness Institute

Figure 5.64b: Gross Hourly Wages in USD and Wages Ranking for Ordinary Residents in Munich, Germany

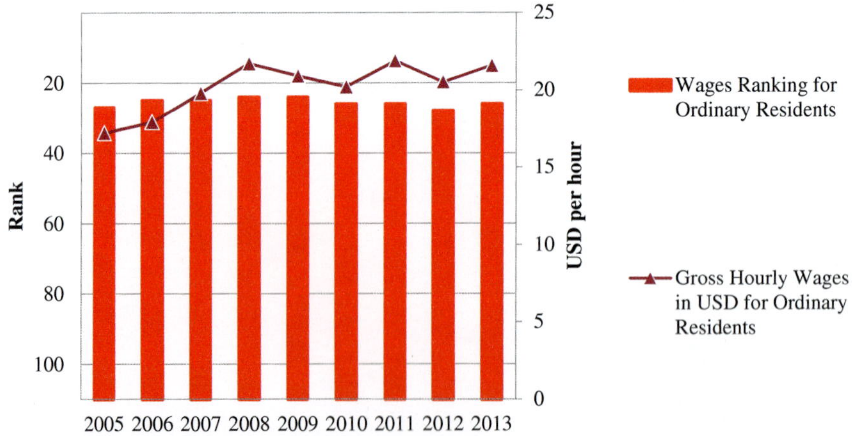

Source: Asia Competitiveness Institute

MUNICH
Germany

Figure 5.64c: Cost of Living, Wages and Purchasing Power Indices and Purchasing Power Ranking for Ordinary Residents in Munich, Germany

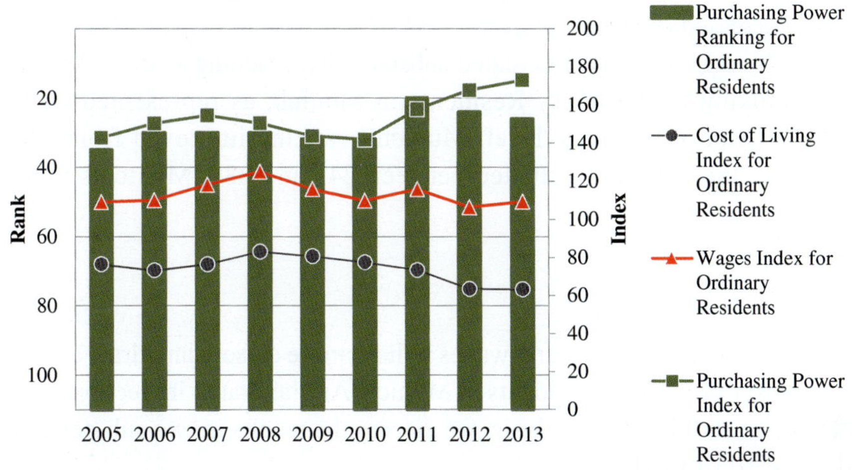

Source: Asia Competitiveness Institute

Figure 5.64a

Munich, the third largest city of Germany, is the economic centre of southern Germany. The city's Cost of Living Ranking for Ordinary Residents, as denoted by the grey bars, fell from 19th to 31st between 2005 and 2010, and from 36th to 37th between 2011 and 2013 (see Figure 5.64a). As elaborated in Section 3.4.2 of Chapter 3, for a more precise comparison of rankings, we have split the analysis into two sub-periods.

The rankings of all 10 categories went down over the first sub-period from 2005 to 2010. Transport registered the most significant dip in ranking as it slipped 25 places from 19th in 2005 to 44th in 2010. Food & Non-alcoholic Beverages Ranking declined from 11th to 29th between 2005 and 2010. Housing Rents & Utilities Ranking fell 11 spots from 19th to 30th over the same sub-period. Health and Education Rankings went down from 43rd to 48th and 18th to 21st, respectively, over the first sub-period.

Between 2011 and 2013, Transport Ranking jumped six places from 40th to 34th. Education and Miscellaneous Goods & Services Rankings both moved up three spots from 44th to 41st and 32nd to 29th, respectively, over the second sub-period. Consequently, Miscellaneous Goods & Services became the highest ranked category in 2013. In contrast, Food & Non-alcoholic Beverages Ranking slipped six places from 28th in 2011 to 34th in 2013. Health Ranking fell two spots from 54th to 56th between 2011 and 2013, making it the lowest ranked category in 2013 together with Alcohol & Tobacco. Housing Rents & Utilities Ranking declined slightly from 29th in 2011 to 30th in 2013.

MUNICH
Germany

Figure 5.64b

The Gross Hourly Wages in USD for Ordinary Residents in Munich, as denoted by the red line in Figure 5.64b, increased consistently from US$17.21 in 2005 to US$21.71 in 2008. From 2008 onwards, Munich's wage level has fluctuated substantially, reaching US$21.59 in 2013.

The Wages Ranking for Ordinary Residents in Munich, as represented by the red bars, has mirrored the trend of the wage level. Munich's ranking improved from 27th in 2005 to 24th in 2008. Since then, it has fluctuated between 24th and 28th. Munich's ranking in 2013 was 26th.

Figure 5.64c

Let us now analyse the cost of living and wages indices more closely and draw conclusions about the purchasing power of ordinary residents in Munich. As elaborated in Section 3.4.2 of Chapter 3, for a more precise and rigorous analysis, we discuss the results in two sub-periods: from 2005 to 2010 and from 2011 to 2013.

The Cost of Living Index and the Wages Index for Ordinary Residents in Munich are represented respectively by the grey and red line in Figure 5.64c. Between 2005 and 2010, the Cost of Living Index for Ordinary Residents exhibited moderate fluctuations. In 2005, the cost of living for ordinary residents in Munich was 76.35% of that for their counterparts in New York (the base city). It rose between 2005 and 2008 and after peaking at 83.00% in 2008, the index started to decrease until it reached 77.39% in 2010. Over the first sub-period, the Wages Index for Ordinary Residents also followed a similar pattern, rising from its initial level at 109.01 in 2005 to peak at 124.85 in 2008 before reversing to a decreasing trend. In 2010, the value for the wages index was 109.68, only slightly higher than its value in 2005.

Between 2005 and 2007 when both wages and cost of living were rising, wages increased at a faster pace than cost of living. Thus, during these initial years of the first sub-period, ordinary residents in Munich were able to afford more goods and services over time. After 2007, wages could no longer keep up with cost of living and during 2008–2010 when both wages and cost of living were decreasing, wages fell faster than the latter. Thus, between 2007 and 2010, ordinary residents in Munich had to reduce their consumption level over time. These trends are fully reflected in the Purchasing Power Index for Ordinary Residents in Munich, which is represented by the green line in Figure 5.64c. Between 2005 and 2007, this index rose from 142.78 to 154.53. It then steadily decreased after 2007 until it reached 141.73 in 2010. Surprisingly, the Purchasing Power Ranking for Ordinary Residents in Munich, as represented by the green bars, generally improved over the first sub-period. From 35th in 2005, Munich's ranking rose to remain at 30th from 2006 to 2008. It then dropped slightly to 32nd in 2009 and 2010, a level which was still higher than its initial level.

MUNICH
Germany

Over the second sub-period (2011–2013), the Cost of Living Index for Ordinary Residents has been on a decreasing trend. In 2011, the cost of living for ordinary residents in Munich was 73.35% of that for their counterparts in New York. It dropped to 63.10% in 2013. The Wages Index for Ordinary Residents has also been decreasing, dropping from 115.75 in 2011 to 109.22 in 2013.

Wages have dropped more slowly than cost of living. Thus, throughout the second sub-period, ordinary residents in Munich were able to afford more goods and services over time. This is reflected in the Purchasing Power Index for Ordinary Residents, which rose from 157.79 in 2011 to 173.09 in 2013. Despite this positive showing of the index, the Purchasing Power Ranking for Ordinary Residents has actually deteriorated over the second sub-period, dropping from 20th in 2011 to 26th in 2013.

Finally, we note that over the entire study period (2005–2013), the Purchasing Power Index for Ordinary Residents in Munich has always been above 100.00 — the base index value. This means that ordinary residents in Munich have consistently been able to afford more goods and services than their counterparts in New York, given the same number of working hours.

NAIROBI
Kenya

Figure 5.65a: Cost of Living and 10 Consumption Categories Rankings for Ordinary Residents in Nairobi, Kenya

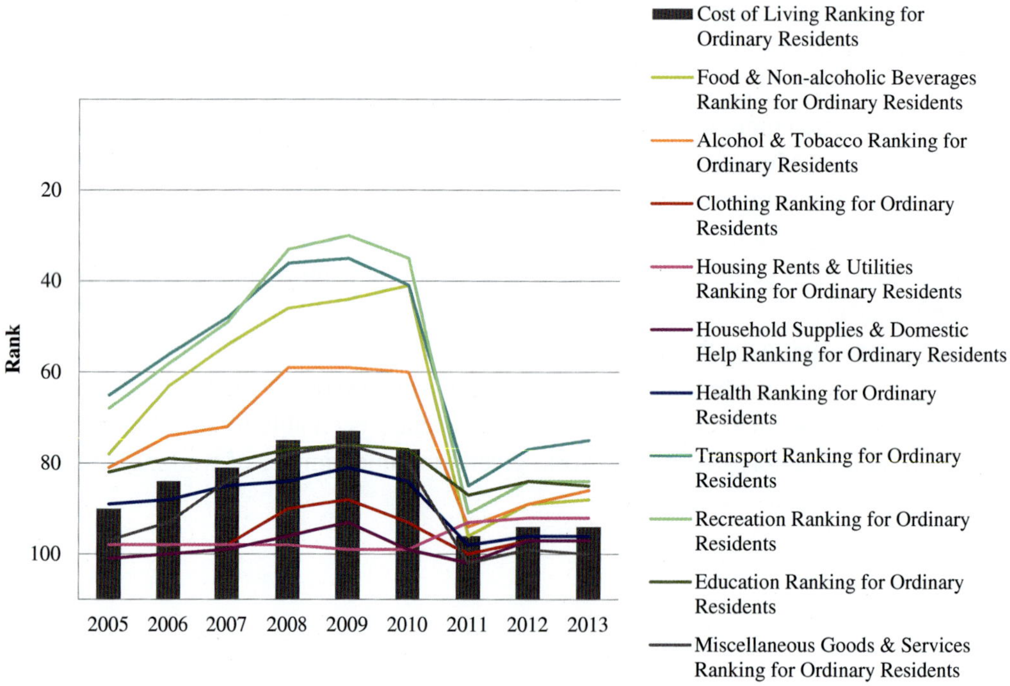

Source: Asia Competitiveness Institute

Figure 5.65b: Gross Hourly Wages in USD and Wages Ranking for Ordinary Residents in Nairobi, Kenya

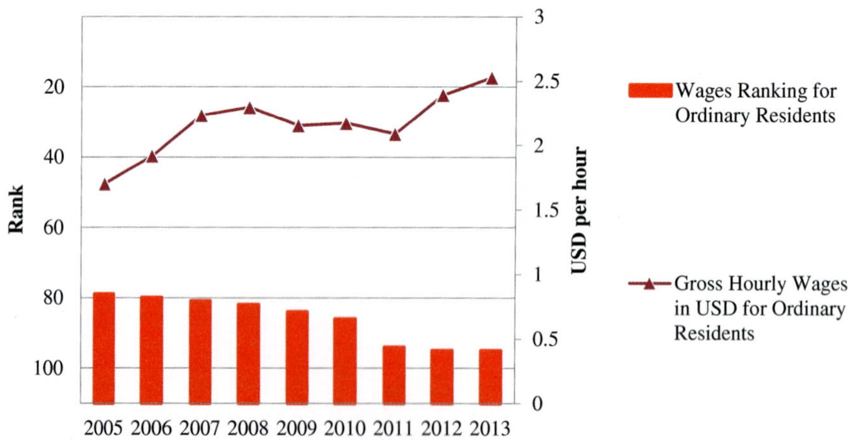

Source: Asia Competitiveness Institute

NAIROBI
Kenya

Figure 5.65c: Cost of Living, Wages and Purchasing Power Indices and Purchasing Power Ranking for Ordinary Residents in Nairobi, Kenya

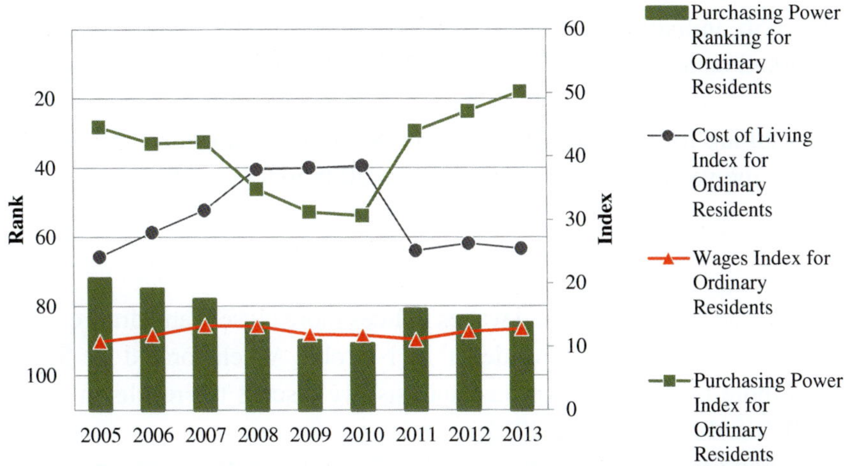

Source: Asia Competitiveness Institute

Figure 5.65a

Nairobi, the capital and largest city of Kenya, is home to major local businesses and over 100 international companies and organisations. The city's Cost of Living Ranking for Ordinary Residents, as represented by the grey bars, rose from 90th to 77th between 2005 and 2010, and from 96th to 94th between 2011 and 2013 (see Figure 5.65a). As explained in Section 3.4.2 of Chapter 3, for a more rigorous comparison of rankings, we have split the analysis into two sub-periods.

From 2005 to 2010, Housing Rents & Utilities was the only category that declined in ranking from 98th to 99th. Food & Non-alcoholic Beverages Ranking climbed 37 places from 78th in 2005 to 41st in 2010. Transport Ranking jumped 24 spots from 65th to 41st between 2005 and 2010. Health and Education Rankings rose more modestly from 89th to 84th and 82nd to 77th, respectively, over the first sub-period.

The rankings of all 10 categories went up over the second sub-period between 2011 and 2013. In particular, Transport Ranking jumped 10 places from 85th to 75th from 2011 to 2013, making it the highest ranked category throughout the second sub-period. Food & Non-alcoholic Beverages Ranking moved up eight spots from 96th in 2011 to 88th in 2013. Health and Education Rankings both rose two places from 98th to 96th and 87th to 85th, respectively, over the second sub-period. Likewise, Miscellaneous Goods & Services Ranking went up from 102nd in 2011 to 100th in 2013. Consequently, it remained as the lowest ranked category over the same sub-period. Housing Rents & Utilities Ranking climbed one spot from 93rd in 2011 to 92nd in 2013.

NAIROBI
Kenya

Figure 5.65b

The Gross Hourly Wages in USD for Ordinary Residents in Nairobi, as represented by the red line in Figure 5.65b, initially rose from US$1.70 in 2005 to US$2.30 in 2008. Nairobi's wage level then embarked on a decreasing trend until 2011 when it started to pick up again, reaching US$2.53 in 2013.

The Wages Ranking for Ordinary Residents in Nairobi, as shown by the red bars, has been deteriorating over the years. It declined from 79th in 2005 to 95th in 2013.

Figure 5.65c

Let us now analyse the cost of living and wages indices more closely and draw conclusions about the purchasing power of ordinary residents in Nairobi. As elaborated in Section 3.4.2 of Chapter 3, for a more precise and rigorous analysis, we discuss the results in two sub-periods: from 2005 to 2010 and from 2011 to 2013.

The Cost of Living Index and the Wages Index for Ordinary Residents in Nairobi are represented respectively by the grey and red line in Figure 5.64c. Between 2005 and 2010, the Cost of Living Index for Ordinary Residents followed two distinct trends. In 2005, the cost of living for ordinary residents in Nairobi was 24.15% of that for their counterparts in New York (the base city). It rose over the years to reach 37.94% in 2008 and thereafter, the index stabilised at around that level. In contrast, the Wages Index for Ordinary Residents followed a different pattern. It was also increasing between 2005 and 2008 but after 2008, this index reversed to a decreasing trend instead of stabilising. Overall, the wages index was only slightly higher in 2010 (11.79) than it was in 2005 (10.77).

Between 2005 and 2008 when both wages and cost of living were rising, wages could not keep up with the latter. In addition, during the remaining years of the first sub-period, wages were decreasing while cost of living remained stable. Thus, throughout the entire first sub-period, ordinary residents in Nairobi were unable to afford the same consumption level over time. This is reflected in the Purchasing Power Index for Ordinary Residents in Nairobi, which is represented by the green line in Figure 5.65c. Between 2005 and 2010, this index dropped from 44.61 to 30.62. Ranking-wise, the Purchasing Power Ranking for Ordinary Residents in Nairobi, as represented by the green bars, also deteriorated over the first sub-period. From 72nd in 2005, it dropped over the years to 91st in 2010.

Over the second sub-period (2011–2013), the Cost of Living Index for Ordinary Residents has been rather stable. It only fluctuated around 25.62 between 2011 and 2013. In contrast, the Wages Index for Ordinary Residents in Nairobi has been on an upward trend. From 11.05 in 2011, this index rose to 12.78 in 2013.

The combined trends of increasing wages and stable cost of living have enabled ordinary residents in Nairobi to afford more goods and services over time. This is reflected in the

NAIROBI
Kenya

Purchasing Power Index for Ordinary Residents, which rose from 43.99 in 2011 to 50.21 in 2013. Despite this positive showing of the index, the Purchasing Power Ranking for Ordinary Residents has actually deteriorated over the second sub-period, dropping from 81st in 2011 to 85th in 2013.

Finally, we note that over the entire study period (2005–2013), the Purchasing Power Index for Ordinary Residents in Nairobi has consistently been lower than 100.00 — the base index value. This means that ordinary residents in Nairobi have only been able to afford a lower consumption level than their counterparts in New York, given the same number of working hours.

NEW DELHI
India

Figure 5.66a: Cost of Living and 10 Consumption Categories Rankings for Ordinary Residents in New Delhi, India

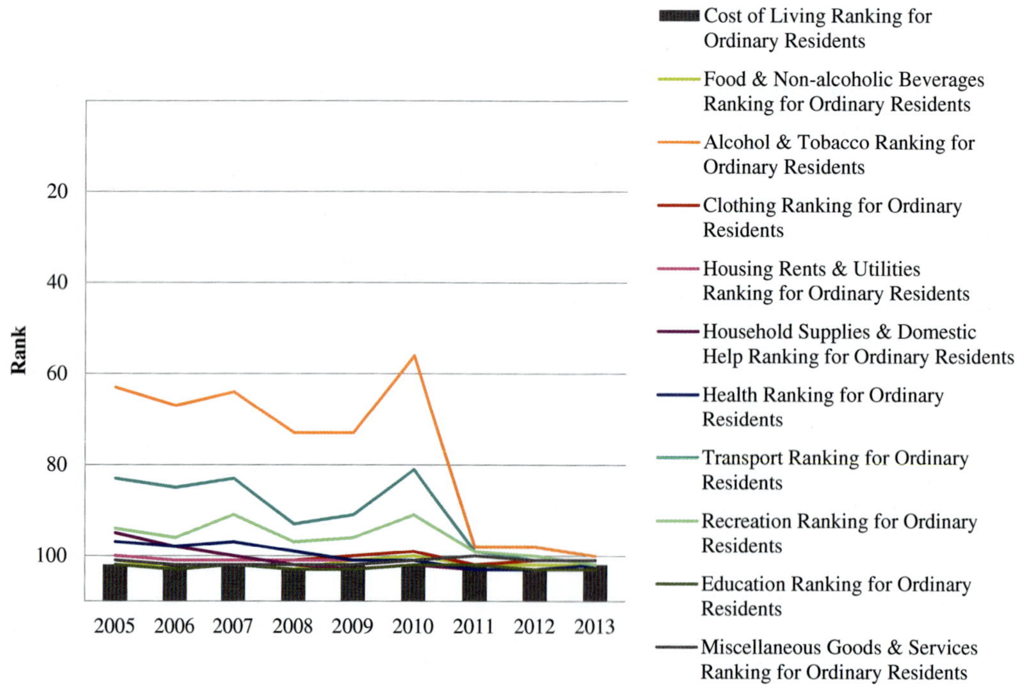

Source: Asia Competitiveness Institute

Figure 5.66b: Gross Hourly Wages in USD and Wages Ranking for Ordinary Residents in New Delhi, India

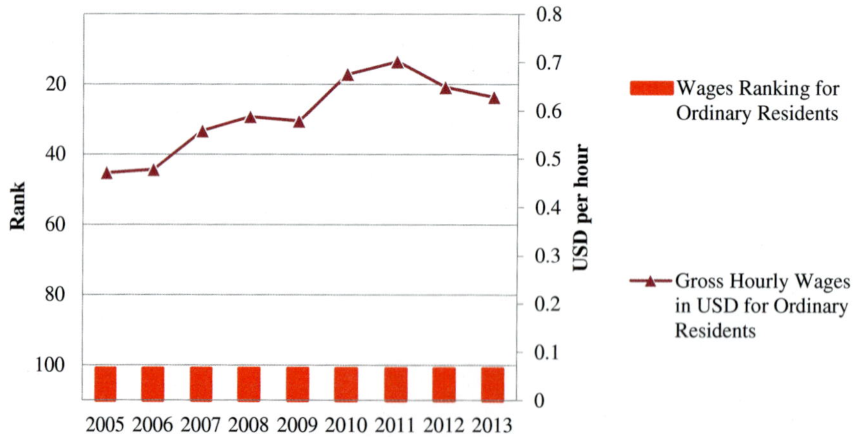

Source: Asia Competitiveness Institute

NEW DELHI
India

Figure 5.66c: Cost of Living, Wages and Purchasing Power Indices and Purchasing Power Ranking for Ordinary Residents in New Delhi, India

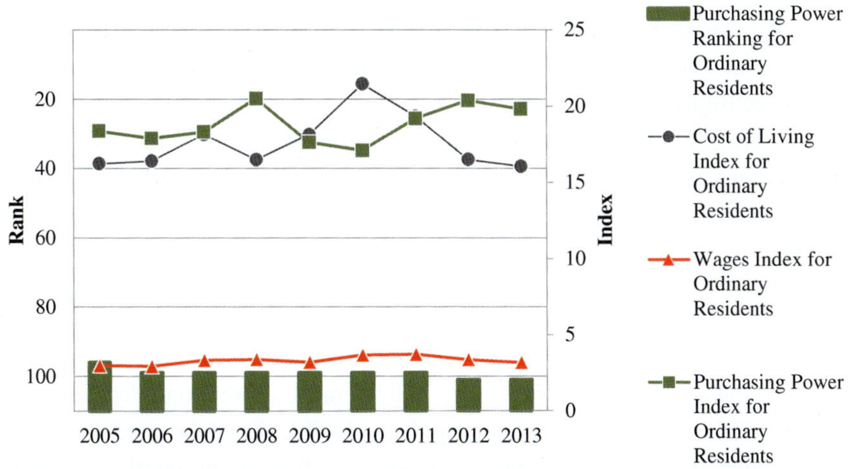

Source: Asia Competitiveness Institute

Figure 5.66a

New Delhi, the capital of India, is one of the country's primary commercial and financial centres with an expanding service sector that includes information technology, telecommunications, banking, media and tourism. The city's Cost of Living Ranking for Ordinary Residents, as shown in the grey bars, largely remained at 102nd between 2005 and 2010 and between 2011 and 2013, making it the second cheapest among the 103 cities studied (see Figure 5.66a). As elaborated in Section 3.4.2 of Chapter 3, for a more precise comparison of rankings, we have split the analysis into two sub-periods.

From 2005 to 2010, Transport Ranking climbed two places from 83rd to 81st. Food & Non-alcoholic Beverages Ranking moved up one spot from 101st in 2005 to 100th in 2010. In contrast, Health Ranking slipped four places from 97th to 101st over the first sub-period. Housing Rents & Utilities Ranking fell one spot from 100th to 101st between 2005 and 2010. Education Ranking primarily remained at 102nd over the same sub-period.

Between 2011 and 2013, Health Ranking moved up one place from 103rd to 102nd. Food & Non-alcoholic Beverages and Housing Rents & Utilities Rankings stayed unchanged at 102nd and 103rd, respectively, over the second sub-period. Transport Ranking slipped two spots from 99th in 2011 to 101st in 2013. Education Ranking fell from 102nd to 103rd between 2011 and 2013. New Delhi therefore became the most affordable city in terms of Housing Rent & Utilities and Education in 2013.

NEW DELHI
India

Figure 5.66b

From 2005 to 2011, the Gross Hourly Wages in USD for Ordinary Residents in New Delhi, as depicted by the red line in Figure 5.66b, rose from US$0.47 to US$0.70. However, mainly due to the depreciation of Indian rupee against US dollar from 2011 onwards, the wage level has been declining, reaching US$0.63 in 2013.

Ranking-wise, New Delhi has been consistently ranked among the bottom three out of 103 cities. The Wages Ranking for Ordinary Residents, as shown by the red bars, has always remained constant at 101st throughout the study period. It shares this spot with another city from India — Mumbai.

Figure 5.66c

Let us now analyse the cost of living and wages indices more closely and draw conclusions about the purchasing power of ordinary residents in New Delhi. As elaborated in Section 3.4.2 of Chapter 3, for a more precise and rigorous analysis, we discuss the results in two sub-periods: from 2005 to 2010 and from 2011 to 2013.

The Cost of Living Index and the Wages Index for Ordinary Residents in New Delhi are represented respectively by the grey and red line in Figure 5.66c. Over the first sub-period (2005–2010), the Cost of Living Index for Ordinary Residents was generally on an increasing trend. In 2005, the cost of living for ordinary residents in New Delhi was 16.22% of that for their counterparts in New York (the base city). It rose to 21.45% in 2010, exhibiting considerable fluctuations in between. Over the first sub-period, the Wages Index for Ordinary Residents was also on an upward trend, rising from 2.98 in 2005 to 3.66 in 2010.

Between 2005 and 2007, wages rose faster than cost of living. In addition, between 2007 and 2008, wages continued on its upward trajectory while cost of living abruptly decreased. Thus, during 2005–2008, ordinary residents in New Delhi were able to afford more goods and services over time. However, they could not do so for the rest of the first sub-period, as wages could not keep up with the pace of increase of cost of living during these years. These trends are fully reflected in the Purchasing Power Index for Ordinary Residents in New Delhi, which is represented by the green line in Figure 5.66c. This index was on the rise between 2005 and 2008, increasing from 18.38 to 20.50. After 2008, however, it steadily decreased until it reached 17.08 in 2010. Meanwhile, the Purchasing Power Ranking for Ordinary Residents, as represented by the green bars, deteriorated from 96th in 2005 to 99th in 2006 and remained there thereafter.

Over the second sub-period (2011–2013), the Cost of Living Index for Ordinary Residents has been on a decreasing trend. In 2011, the cost of living for ordinary residents in New Delhi was 19.34% of that for their counterparts in New York. It dropped over the years to reach 16.04% in 2013. The Wages Index for Ordinary Residents has also been decreasing, albeit very marginally. From 3.71 in 2011, the index dropped to 3.18 in 2013.

NEW DELHI
India

Wages decreased more slowly than cost of living so the purchasing power of ordinary residents in New Delhi has increased over the second sub-period. This is reflected in the increase of the Purchasing Power Index for Ordinary Residents which rose from 19.19 in 2011 to 19.82 in 2013. However, it is worth noting that the increase in the index value was very small. This indicates that though ordinary residents in New Delhi have indeed gained more purchasing power over the second sub-period, this gain has been at best marginal. Over the same sub-period, ordinary residents in other cities have gained much more. As such it is unsurprising that the Purchasing Power Ranking for Ordinary Residents in New Delhi has deteriorated over the second sub-period, dropping from 99th in 2011 to 101st in 2012 and 2013.

Finally, we note that over the entire study period (2005–2013), the Purchasing Power Index for Ordinary Residents in New Delhi has consistently been lower than 100.00 — the base index value — by almost a factor of five. This means that ordinary residents in New Delhi have only been able to afford a much lower consumption level than their counterparts in New York, given the same number of working hours.

NEW YORK
United States

Figure 5.67a: Cost of Living and 10 Consumption Categories Rankings for Ordinary Residents in New York, United States

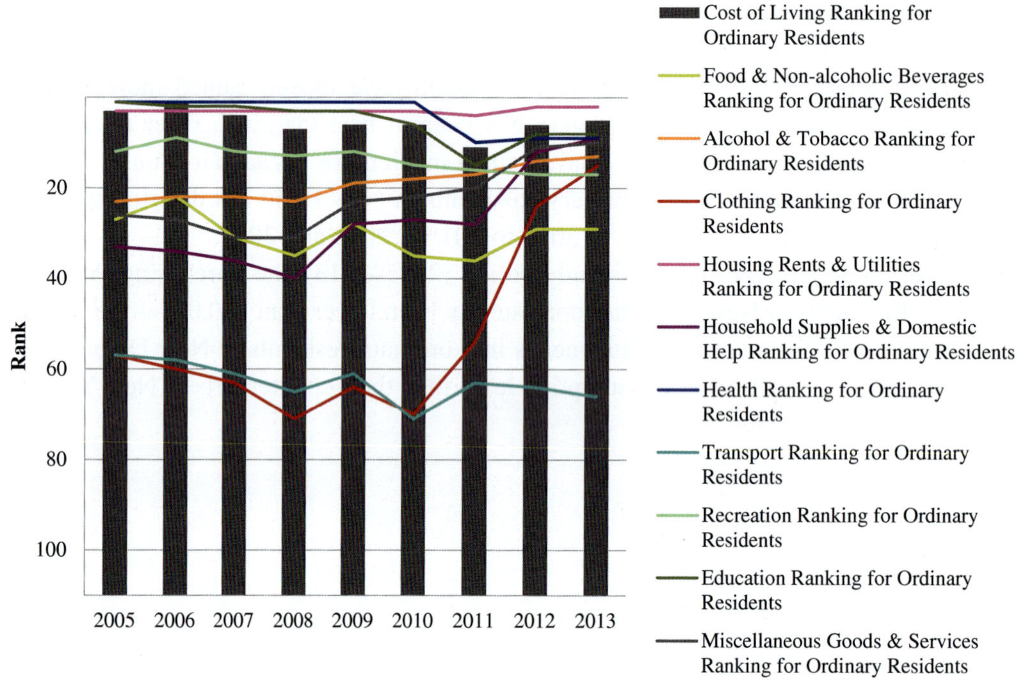

Source: Asia Competitiveness Institute

Figure 5.67b: Gross Hourly Wages in USD and Wages Ranking for Ordinary Residents in New York, United States

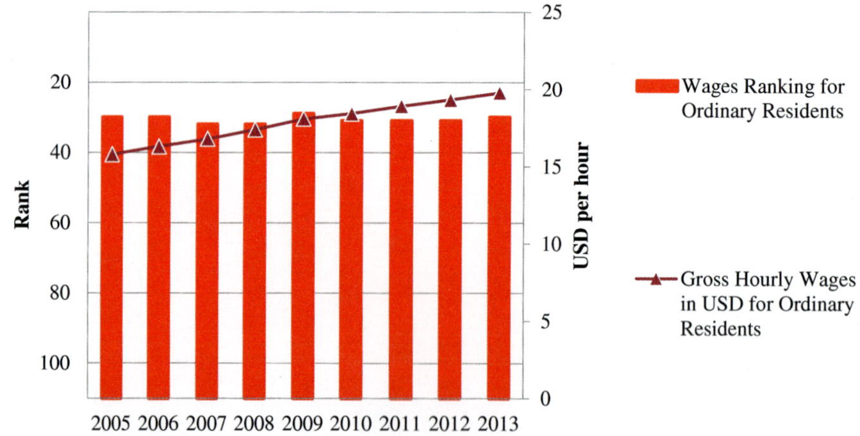

Source: Asia Competitiveness Institute

NEW YORK
United States

Figure 5.67c: Cost of Living, Wages and Purchasing Power Indices and Purchasing Power Ranking for Ordinary Residents in New York, United States

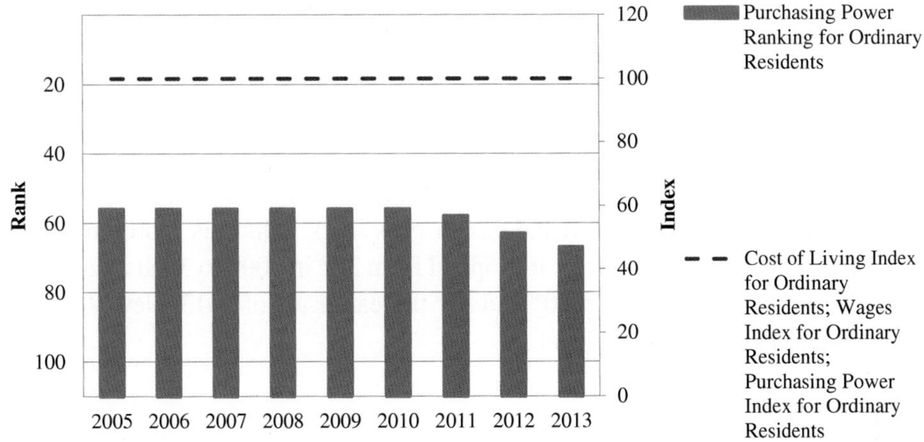

Source: Asia Competitiveness Institute

Figure 5.67a

Widely known as the headquarter of the American financial industry and home to the renowned Wall Street, New York is the most populous city in the United States with a population of approximately 8.4 million. The city's Cost of Living Ranking for Ordinary Residents, as denoted by the grey bars, declined from third to sixth between 2005 and 2010, but rose from 11th to fifth between 2011 and 2013 (see Figure 5.67a). As explained in Section 3.4.2 of Chapter 3, for a more rigorous comparison of rankings, we have split the analysis into two sub-periods.

Between 2005 and 2010, Transport saw the most remarkable dip in ranking as it fell 14 places from 57th to 71st. Food & Non-alcoholic Beverages Ranking slipped eight spots from 27th in 2005 to 35th in 2010. Education Ranking moved down five places from first to sixth over the first sub-period. Housing Rents & Utilities and Health Rankings remained unchanged at third and first, respectively, between 2005 and 2010. In contrast, Household Supplies & Domestic Help Ranking jumped six places from 33rd in 2005 to 27th in 2010.

From 2011 to 2013, Clothing registered the sharpest rise in ranking as it climbed 39 places from 54th to 15th. Household Supplies & Domestic Help Ranking jumped 19 spots from 28th in 2011 to ninth in 2013. Food & Non-alcoholic Beverages and Education Rankings both moved up seven places from 36th to 29th and 15th to eighth, respectively, over the second sub-period. Nonetheless, these upward trends appear to be levelling off as good news. Housing Rents & Utilities consistently remained as the highest ranked category for the entire second sub-period as its ranking rose from fourth in 2011 to second in 2013, making New York the second most expensive city in this category in 2013. Health Ranking went up from 10th to ninth between 2011

NEW YORK
United States

and 2013. In contrast, Transport Ranking slipped three places from 63rd in 2011 to 66th in 2013. Consequently, Transport was the lowest ranked category throughout the second sub-period.

Figure 5.67b

The Gross Hourly Wages in USD for Ordinary Resident in New York, as represented by the red line in Figure 5.67b, have been on an increasing trend throughout the study period. From US$15.79 in 2005, New York's wage level rose to US$19.77 in 2013.

The Wages Ranking for Ordinary Residents in New York, which is represented by the red bars, has however remained fairly stable. It dropped from 30th in 2005 to 32nd in 2008, recovered to 29th in 2009 and fluctuated between 30th and 31st thereafter. As of 2013, New York ranked 30th in terms of ordinary residents' wage level.

Figure 5.67c

New York is the base city for the study, with other cities being benchmarked against it. Therefore, the Cost of Living Index for Ordinary Residents, the Wages Index for Ordinary Residents and the Purchasing Power Index for Ordinary Residents all shares the same value of 100.00 throughout the study period (2005–2013). As a result, unlike other cities, all three indices are represented by a common purple dashed line in Figure 5.67c.

The Purchasing Power Ranking for Ordinary Residents in New York, however, is still represented by the green bars. Between 2005 and 2010, New York consistently ranked 56th in terms of ordinary residents' purchasing power. Over the rest of the study period, however, it has dropped steadily over the years. In 2013, the ranking reached 67th.

OSAKA–KOBE
Japan

Figure 5.68a: Cost of Living and 10 Consumption Categories Rankings for Ordinary Residents in Osaka–Kobe, Japan

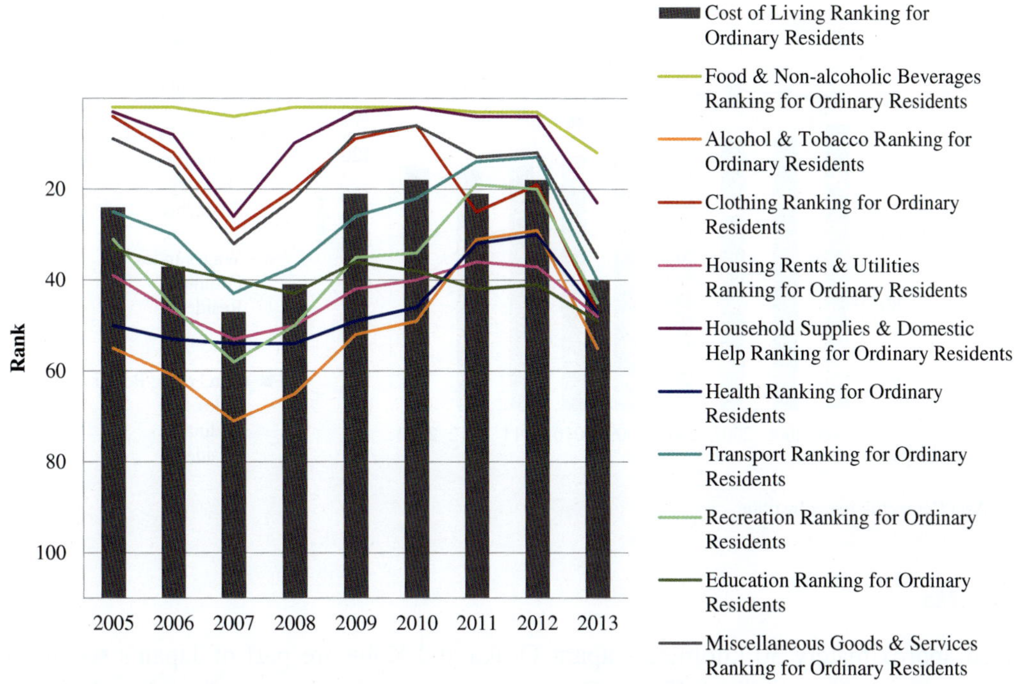

Source: Asia Competitiveness Institute

Figure 5.68b: Gross Hourly Wages in USD and Wages Ranking for Ordinary Residents in Osaka–Kobe, Japan

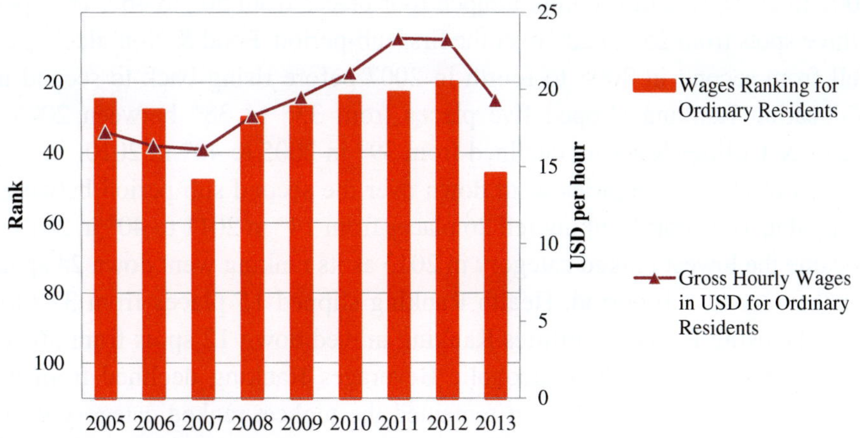

Source: Asia Competitiveness Institute

OSAKA–KOBE
Japan

Figure 5.68c: Cost of Living, Wages and Purchasing Power Indices and Purchasing Power Ranking for Ordinary Residents in Osaka–Kobe, Japan

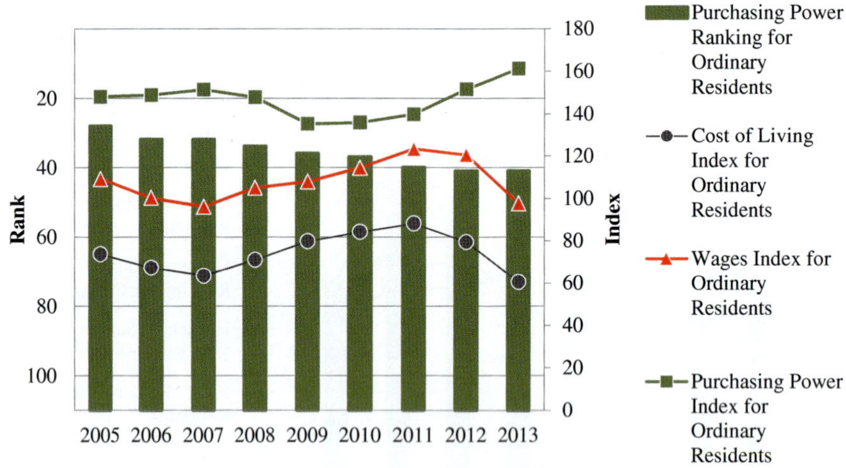

Source: Asia Competitiveness Institute

Figure 5.68a

Located approximately 30 kilometres apart, Osaka and Kobe are part of Japan's second most populous metropolitan area of Kyoto–Osaka–Kobe. The cities' Cost of Living Ranking for Ordinary Residents, as represented by the grey bars, rose from 24th to 18th between 2005 and 2010, but fell from 21st to 40th between 2011 and 2013 (see Figure 5.68a). As elaborated in Section 3.4.2 of Chapter 3, for a more precise comparison of rankings, we have split the analysis into two sub-periods.

From 2005 to 2010, Health Ranking jumped four places from 50th to 46th. Transport Ranking moved up three spots from 25th to 22nd over the first sub-period. Food & Non-alcoholic Beverages Ranking fell from second in 2005 to fourth in 2007 before rising back to second in 2010. In contrast, Education Ranking slipped five places from 33rd to 38th between 2005 and 2010. Housing Rents & Utilities Ranking declined from 39th in 2005 to 40th in 2010.

The rankings of all 10 categories went down over the second sub-period between 2011 and 2013. In particular, Transport Ranking fell 26 places from 14th in 2011 to 40th in 2013. Alcohol & Tobacco became the lowest ranked category in 2013 as its ranking went down 24 spots from 31st to 55th over the second sub-period. Health Ranking slipped 15 places from 32nd to 47th from 2011 to 2013. Housing Rents & Utilities Ranking moved down 12 spots from 36th to 48th over the same sub-period. Food & Non-alcoholic Beverages Ranking declined from third to 12th between 2011 and 2013. Nonetheless, it remained the highest ranked category throughout the second sub-period. Education Ranking fell seven places from 42nd in 2011 to 49th in 2013.

OSAKA–KOBE
Japan

Figure 5.68b

The Gross Hourly Wages in USD for Ordinary Residents in Osaka–Kobe, as represented by the red line in Figure 5.68b, have fluctuated substantially over the study period. Between 2005 and 2007, Osaka–Kobe's wage level dropped from US$17.24 to US$16.11. It then grew steadily to peak at US$23.25 in 2012 before declining to reach US$19.29 in 2013.

The fluctuations were due in part to genuine wage fluctuations in Japan during those years. However, they also happened because of exchange rate volatility. The first downward trend between 2005 and 2007 corresponded to a period when the Japanese yen depreciated against the US dollar. The upward trend observed next corresponded to a prolonged appreciation of the yen. Finally, the considerable decline of the Gross Hourly Wages in USD for Ordinary Residents in Osaka–Kobe between 2012 and 2013 corresponded to another episode of depreciation.

Ranking-wise, the Wages Ranking for Ordinary Residents in Osaka–Kobe, as represented by the red bars, has also fluctuated significantly over the study period. In 2013, Osaka–Kobe ranked 46th in terms of ordinary residents' wages among 103 cities.

Figure 5.68c

Let us now analyse the cost of living and wages indices more closely and draw conclusions about the purchasing power of ordinary residents in Osaka–Kobe. As elaborated in Section 3.4.2 of Chapter 3, for a more precise and rigorous analysis, we discuss the results in two sub-periods: from 2005 to 2010 and from 2011 to 2013.

The Cost of Living Index and the Wages Index for Ordinary Residents in Osaka–Kobe are represented respectively by the grey and red line in Figure 5.68c. Between 2005 and 2010, the Cost of Living Index for Ordinary Residents fluctuated substantially. In 2005, the cost of living for ordinary residents in Osaka–Kobe was 73.72% of that for their counterparts in New York (the base city). It dropped over the next two years to 63.44% in 2007 and then started to increase until it reached 84.20% in 2010. The Wages Index for Ordinary Residents followed a similar pattern as the cost of living index. It was also on a decreasing trend between 2005 and 2007 before reversing to an increasing trend subsequently. Overall, the wages index was higher in 2010 (114.42) than it was in 2005 (109.17).

Between 2005 and 2007, wages and cost of living generally fell at similar rates. As such, during these years, ordinary residents in Osaka–Kobe were able to afford the same consumption level over time. However, they could no longer do so after 2007. This is because between 2007 and 2010, wages and cost of living were both increasing and cost of living rose faster than wages. These trends are fully reflected in the Purchasing Power Index for Ordinary Residents in Osaka–Kobe, which is represented by the green line in Figure 5.68c. This index only fluctuated around 149.43 between 2005 and 2007 but steadily decreased thereafter and reached 135.89 in 2010. Meanwhile, the Purchasing Power Ranking for Ordinary Residents in Osaka–Kobe, as

OSAKA–KOBE
Japan

represented by the green bars, also fluctuated significantly over the first sub-period. Overall, however, it dropped from 28th in 2005 to 37th in 2010.

Over the second sub-period (2011–2013), the Cost of Living Index for Ordinary Residents has been on a decreasing trend. In 2011, the cost of living for ordinary residents in Osaka–Kobe was 88.18% of that for ordinary residents in New York. It dropped over the years to reach 60.55% in 2013. The Wages Index for Ordinary Residents has also been on a decreasing trend, dropping from 123.29 in 2011 to 97.61 in 2013.

Wages have decreased more slowly than cost of living. Thus, throughout the second sub-period, ordinary residents in Osaka–Kobe have actually been able to afford a higher consumption level over time. This is reflected in the Purchasing Power Index for Ordinary Residents, which rose steadily from 139.82 in 2011 to 161.22 in 2013. Despite the positive showing of the index, the Purchasing Power Ranking for Ordinary Residents in Osaka–Kobe has deteriorated over the second sub-period, albeit marginally. It dropped from 40th in 2011 to 41st in 2012 and 2013.

Finally, we note that over the entire study period (2005–2013), the Purchasing Power Index for Ordinary Residents in Osaka–Kobe has always been above 100.00 — the base index value. This means that ordinary residents in Osaka–Kobe have consistently been able to afford a higher consumption level than their counterparts in New York, given the same number of working hours.

OSLO
Norway

Figure 5.69a: Cost of Living and 10 Consumption Categories Rankings for Ordinary Residents in Oslo, Norway

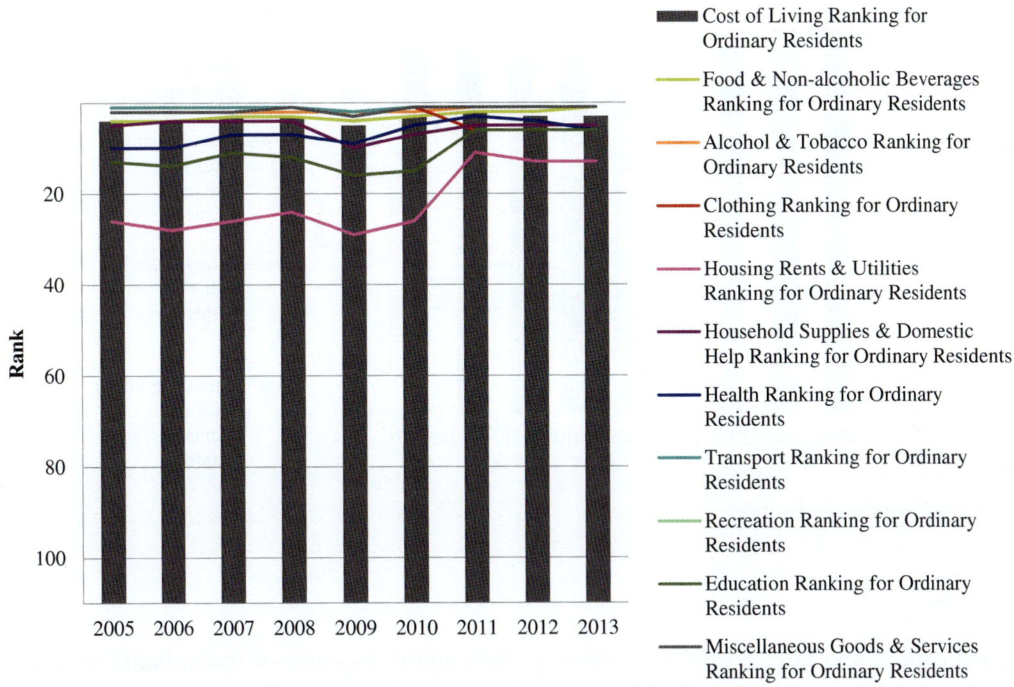

Source: Asia Competitiveness Institute

Figure 5.69b: Gross Hourly Wages in USD and Wages Ranking for Ordinary Residents in Oslo, Norway

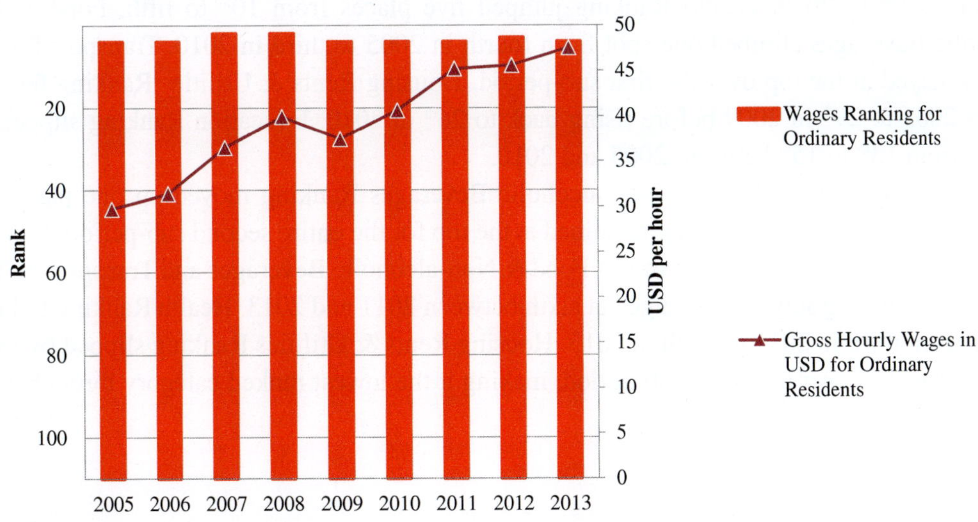

Source: Asia Competitiveness Institute

OSLO
Norway

Figure 5.69c: Cost of Living, Wages and Purchasing Power Indices and Purchasing Power Ranking for Ordinary Residents in Oslo, Norway

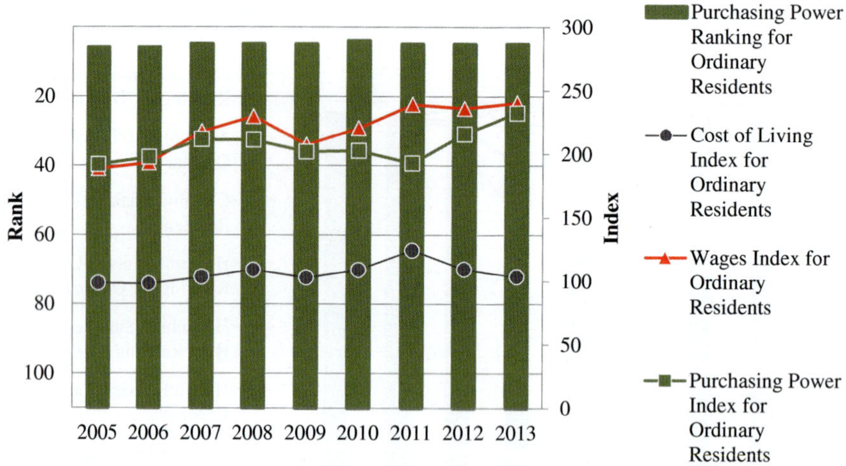

Source: Asia Competitiveness Institute

Figure 5.69a

Oslo, the capital and largest city of Norway, is the country's centre of trade, banking and shipping. The city's Cost of Living Ranking for Ordinary Residents, as shown in the grey bars, rose from fourth to third between 2005 and 2010, and fell from second to third between 2011 and 2013 (see Figure 5.69a). As explained in Section 3.4.2 of Chapter 3, for a more rigorous comparison of rankings, we have split the analysis into two sub-periods.

From 2005 to 2010, Health Ranking jumped five places from 10th to fifth. Food & Non-alcoholic Beverages climbed one spot from fourth in 2005 to third in 2010. Transport Ranking largely stayed at the top over the first sub-period. Housing Rents & Utilities Ranking fell from 26th in 2005 to 29th in 2009 before rising back to 26th in 2010. Education Ranking slipped two places from 13th to 15th between 2005 and 2010.

From 2011 to 2013, Food & Non-alcoholic Beverages Ranking moved up one place from second to first. Transport Ranking remained at the top for the entire second sub-period. Oslo was thus the most expensive city in terms of Food & Non-alcoholic Beverages and Transport in 2013. Education Ranking stayed unchanged at sixth between 2011 and 2013. Health Ranking fell three places from third in 2011 to sixth in 2013. Housing Rents & Utilities Ranking slipped two spots from 11th to 13th over the same sub-period, making it the lowest ranked category throughout the study period.

OSLO
Norway

Figure 5.69b

The Gross Hourly Wages in USD for Ordinary Residents in Oslo, as shown by the red line in Figure 5.69b, have generally been on an increasing trend. From US$29.74 in 2005, Oslo's wage level rose to US$47.51 in 2013.

Ranking-wise, Oslo has been ranked consistently among the top five out of 103 cities. The Wages Ranking for Ordinary Residents, as denoted by the red bars, has remained largely at fourth though there were also years when it rose to third (2012) or second (2007 and 2008).

Figure 5.69c

Let us now analyse the cost of living and wages indices more closely and draw conclusions about the purchasing power of ordinary residents in Oslo. As elaborated in Section 3.4.2 of Chapter 3, for a more precise and rigorous analysis, we discuss the results in two sub-periods: from 2005 to 2010 and from 2011 to 2013.

The Cost of Living Index and the Wages Index for Ordinary Residents in Oslo are represented respectively by the grey and red line in Figure 5.69c. Between 2005 and 2010, the Cost of Living Index for Ordinary Residents was generally on an increasing trend. In 2005, the cost of living for ordinary residents in Oslo was 98.26% of that for their counterparts in New York (the base city). It rose to 108.79% in 2008 and dropped abruptly to 102.63% in 2009 before recovering to 108.80% in 2010. Over the same sub-period, the Wages Index for Ordinary Residents was also on a general upward trend interrupted by an abrupt decline in 2009. Overall, the wages index was higher in 2010 (220.39) than it was in 2005 (188.40).

Between 2005 and 2007, wages generally rose faster than cost of living. However, after 2007, wages could no longer keep up with the latter. As such, ordinary residents in Oslo were able to afford more goods and services over time up until 2007 but could not do so thereafter. These trends are fully reflected in the Purchasing Power Index for Ordinary Residents in Oslo, which is represented by the green line in Figure 5.69c. This index rose from 191.74 to 211.43 between 2005 and 2007 and then started to decrease until it reached 202.56 in 2010. Meanwhile, the Purchasing Power Ranking for Ordinary Residents in Oslo, as represented by the green bars, improved over the first sub-period. It rose from sixth in 2005 and 2006 to fifth between 2007 and 2009 before rising further to fourth in 2010.

Over the second sub-period (2011–2013), the Cost of Living Index for Ordinary Residents has been on a decreasing trend. In 2011, the cost of living for ordinary residents in Oslo was 1.24 times that for ordinary residents in New York. It dropped to 1.03 times in 2013. In contrast, the Wages Index for Ordinary Residents has been rather stable, fluctuating around 238.53.

The combined trends of stable wages and decreasing cost of living have enabled ordinary residents in Oslo to afford a higher consumption level over time. This is reflected in the Purchasing Power Index for Ordinary Residents, which rose steadily from 192.61 in 2011 to 232.40 in 2013.

OSLO
Norway

Despite the positive showing of the index, the Purchasing Power Ranking for Ordinary Residents in Oslo has not improved, but consistently remained at fifth throughout the second sub-period.

Finally, we note that over the entire study period (2005–2013), the Purchasing Power Index for Ordinary Residents in Oslo has always been above 100.00 — the base index value. This means that ordinary residents in Oslo have consistently been able to afford a higher consumption level than their counterparts in New York, given the same number of working hours.

PARIS
France

Figure 5.70a: Cost of Living and 10 Consumption Categories Rankings for Ordinary Residents in Paris, France

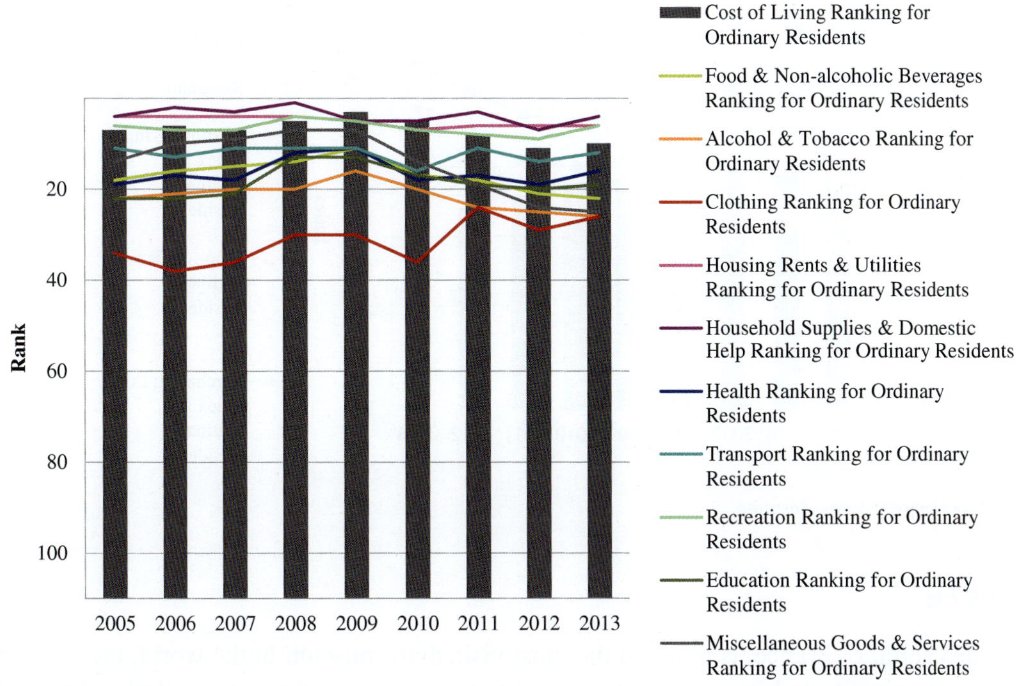

Source: Asia Competitiveness Institute

Figure 5.70b: Gross Hourly Wages in USD and Wages Ranking for Ordinary Residents in Paris, France

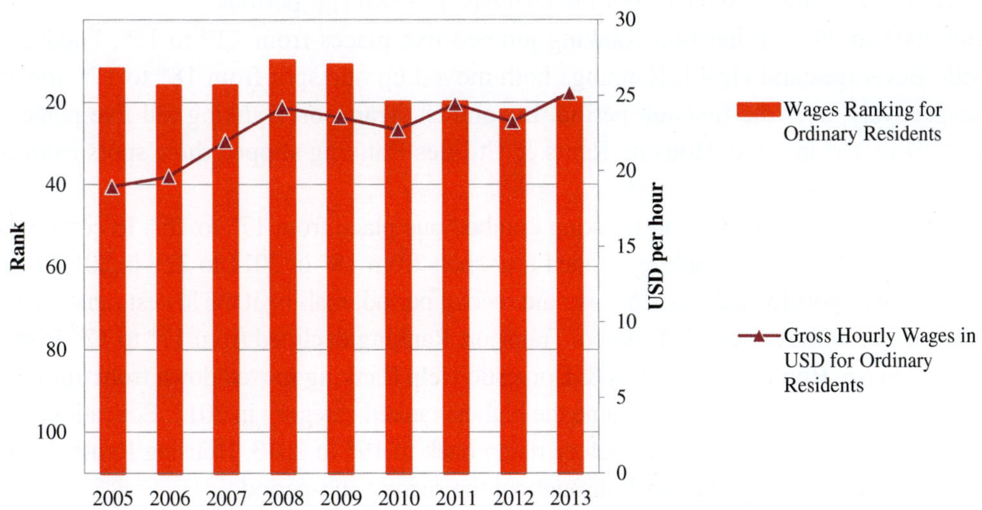

Source: Asia Competitiveness Institute

PARIS
France

Figure 5.70c: Cost of Living, Wages and Purchasing Power Indices and Purchasing Power Ranking for Ordinary Residents in Paris, France

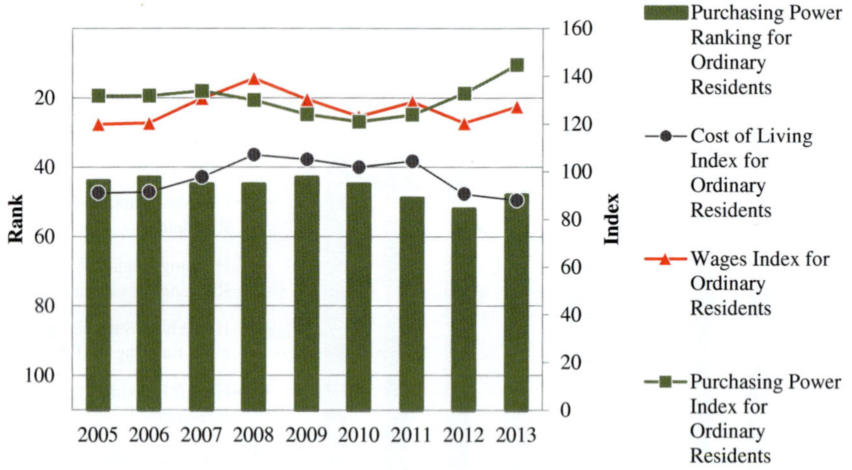

Source: Asia Competitiveness Institute

Figure 5.70a

Paris, the capital of France, is home to the most visited art museum in the world, the Louvre as well as many notable architectural landmarks including the Notre Dame Cathedral and the Eiffel Tower. The city's Cost of Living Ranking for Ordinary Residents, as denoted by the grey bars, rose from seventh to fifth between 2005 and 2010, but declined from eighth to 10th between 2011 and 2013 (see Figure 5.70a). As elaborated in Section 3.4.2 of Chapter 3, for a more precise comparison of rankings, we have split the analysis into two sub-periods.

From 2005 to 2010, Education Ranking jumped five places from 22nd to 17th. Food & Non-alcoholic Beverages and Health Rankings both moved up one spot from 18th to 17th and 19th to 18th, respectively, over the first sub-period. In contrast, Transport Ranking fell five places from 11th in 2005 to 16th in 2010. Housing Rents & Utilities Ranking slipped three spots from fourth to seventh over the same sub-period.

Between 2011 and 2013, Health Ranking climbed one place from 17th to 16th. In contrast, Food & Non-alcoholic Beverages Ranking slipped four spots from 18th in 2011 to 22nd in 2013. Clothing Ranking fell two spots from 24th to 26th over the second period, making it the lowest ranked category in 2013 together with Alcohol & Tobacco. Transport Ranking declined from 11th to 12th from 2011 to 2013. Likewise, Household Supplies & Domestic Help Ranking moved down from third in 2011 to fourth in 2013. Consequently, it became the highest ranked category in 2013. Education Ranking fell from 19th in 2011 to 20th in 2012 before rising back to 19th in 2013. Housing Rents & Utilities Ranking remained unchanged at sixth throughout the second sub-period.

PARIS
France

Figure 5.70b

The Gross Hourly Wages in USD for Ordinary Residents in Paris, as depicted by the red line in Figure 5.70b, initially rose steadily from US$18.94 in 2005 to US$24.18 in 2008. Subsequently, Paris's wage level stabilised at around US$24.00 and reached US$25.16 in 2013.

Meanwhile, the Wages Ranking for Ordinary Resident in Paris, as denoted by the red bars, deteriorated from 12th in 2005 to 19th in 2013.

Figure 5.70c

Let us now analyse the cost of living and wages indices more closely and draw conclusions about the purchasing power of ordinary residents in Paris. As elaborated in Section 3.4.2 of Chapter 3, for a more precise and rigorous analysis, we discuss the results in two sub-periods: from 2005 to 2010 and from 2011 to 2013.

The Cost of Living Index and the Wages Index for Ordinary Residents in Paris are represented respectively by the grey and red line in Figure 5.70c. Between 2005 and 2010, the Cost of Living Index for Ordinary Residents exhibited moderate fluctuations. In 2005, the cost of living for ordinary residents in Paris was 91.04% of that for their counterparts in New York (the base city). It rose between 2005 and 2008 and after peaking at 106.96% in 2008, the index started to decrease until it reached 101.83% in 2010. Over the first sub-period, the Wages Index for Ordinary Residents also followed a similar pattern, rising from its initial level at 119.98 in 2005 to peak at 139.07 in 2008 before reversing to a decreasing trend. In 2010, the value for the wages index was 123.16, higher than its value in 2005.

Between 2005 and 2007, both wages and cost of living were rising at about the same rates. Thus, during these years, ordinary residents in Paris were able to maintain their consumption level over time. However, between 2007 and 2008, wages could no longer keep up with cost of living and when both were decreasing between 2008 and 2010, wages decreased faster than the latter. Thus, after 2007, the consumption level of ordinary residents in Paris decreased over time. These trends are fully reflected in the Purchasing Power Index for Ordinary Residents in Paris, which is represented by the green line in Figure 5.70c. Between 2005 and 2007, this index was generally stable, only fluctuating around 132.48. After 2007, it steadily decreased until it reached 120.95 in 2010. Ranking-wise, the Purchasing Power Ranking for Ordinary Residents in Paris, as represented by the green bars, was quite stable. It only fluctuated between 43rd and 45th over the first sub-period.

Over the second sub-period (2011–2013), the Cost of Living Index for Ordinary Residents has been on a decreasing trend. In 2011, the cost of living for ordinary residents in Paris was 1.04 times that for their counterparts in New York. It dropped over the years to reach 87.94% in 2013. The Wages Index for Ordinary Residents has also been decreasing, dropping from 129.19 in 2011 to 127.28 in 2013, with a deeper plunge to 120.40 in 2012.

PARIS
France

Wages have dropped more slowly than cost of living. Thus, throughout the second sub-period, ordinary residents in Paris were able to afford more goods and services over time. This is reflected in the Purchasing Power Index for Ordinary Residents, which rose from 123.91 in 2011 to 144.74 in 2013. Despite the consistently positive showing of the index, the Purchasing Power Ranking for Ordinary Residents has not been steadily improving over the second sub-period. From 49th in 2011, it dropped to 52nd in 2012 before rising slightly to 48th in 2013.

Finally, we note that over the entire study period (2005–2013), the Purchasing Power Index for Ordinary Residents in Paris has always been above 100.00 — the base index value. This means that ordinary residents in Paris have consistently been able to afford more goods and services than their counterparts in New York, given the same number of working hours.

PERTH
Australia

Figure 5.71a: Cost of Living and 10 Consumption Categories Rankings for Ordinary Residents in Perth, Australia

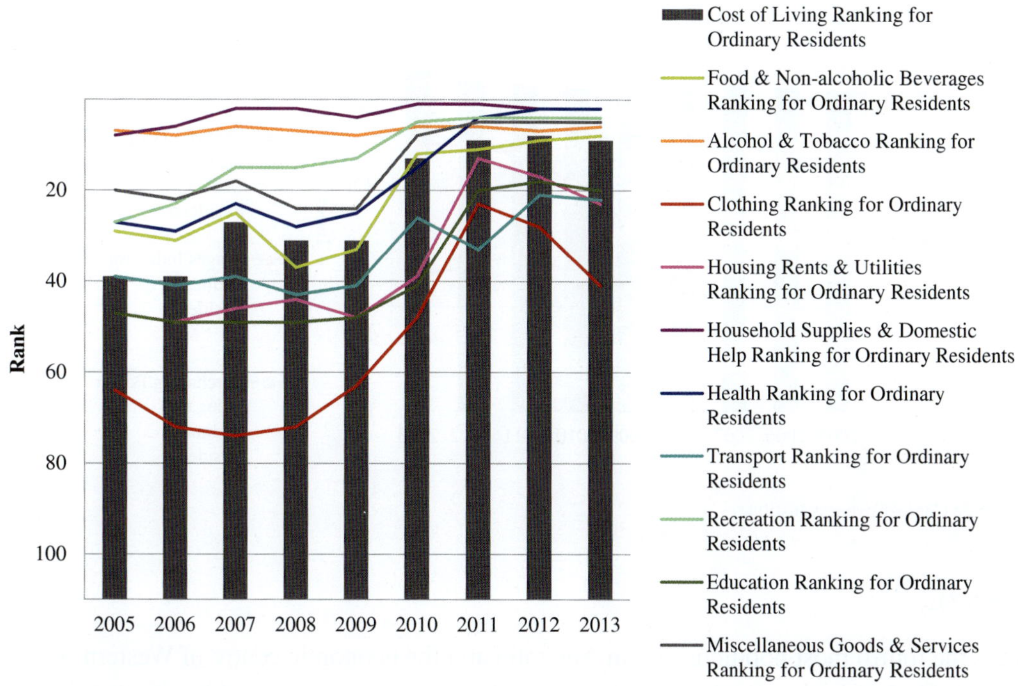

Source: Asia Competitiveness Institute

Figure 5.71b: Gross Hourly Wages in USD and Wages Ranking for Ordinary Residents in Perth, Australia

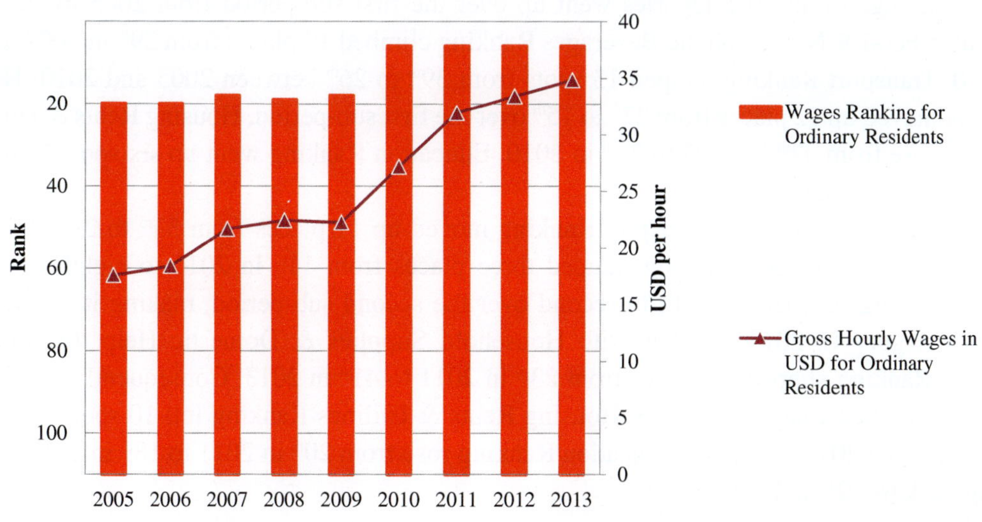

Source: Asia Competitiveness Institute

PERTH
Australia

Figure 5.71c: Cost of Living, Wages and Purchasing Power Indices and Purchasing Power Ranking for Ordinary Residents in Perth, Australia

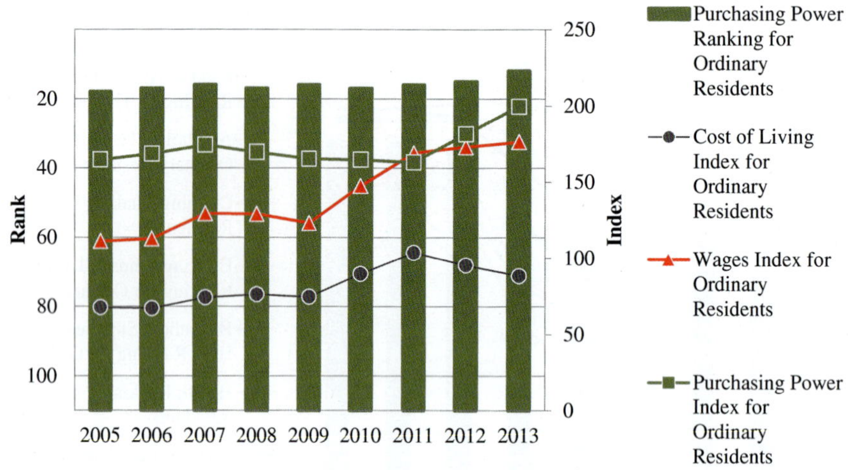

Source: Asia Competitiveness Institute

Figure 5.71a

Perth is the fourth most populous city in Australia and the economic centre of Western Australia. The city's Cost of Living Ranking for Ordinary Residents, as represented by the grey bars, rose from 39th to 13th between 2005 and 2010, and largely remained at ninth between 2011 and 2013 (see Figure 5.71a). As explained in Section 3.4.2 of Chapter 3, for a more rigorous comparison of rankings, we have split the analysis into two sub-periods.

The rankings of all 10 categories went up over the first sub-period from 2005 to 2010. In particular, Food & Non-alcoholic Beverages Ranking climbed 17 places from 29th in 2005 to 12th in 2010. Transport Ranking jumped 13 spots from 39th to 26th between 2005 and 2010. Health Ranking moved up 12 places from 27th to 15th over the first sub-period. Housing Rents & Utilities Ranking rose from 47th in 2005 to 39th in 2010. Education Ranking went up six spots from 47th to 41st over the same sub-period.

Between 2011 and 2013, Transport Ranking moved up 11 places from 33rd to 22nd. Food & Non-alcoholic Beverages Ranking jumped three places from 11th in 2011 to eighth in 2013. Health Ranking rose from fourth to second over the second sub-period, making it the highest ranked category in 2013 together with Household Supplies & Domestic Help. In contrast, Clothing Ranking slipped 18 places from 23rd in 2011 to 41st in 2013. Consequently, it became the lowest ranked category in 2013. Housing Rents & Utilities Ranking fell 10 spots from 13th to 23rd between 2011 and 2013. Education Ranking rose from 20th in 2011 to 18th in 2012 before falling back to 20th in 2013.

PERTH
Australia

Figure 5.71b

The Gross Hourly Wages in USD for Ordinary Residents in Perth, as denoted by the red line in Figure 5.71b, have almost doubled over the study period. From US$17.56 in 2005, Perth's wage level rose to US$34.83 in 2013. The most rapid increase happened between 2009 and 2011. This was partly due to the appreciation of Australian dollar against US dollar.

Meanwhile, the Wages Ranking for Ordinary Residents in Perth, as shown by the red bars, first rose from 20th in 2005 to 18th in 2009. It improved to sixth in 2010 and has remained at that level thereafter.

Figure 5.71c

Let us now analyse the cost of living and wages indices more closely and draw conclusions about the purchasing power of ordinary residents in Perth. As elaborated in Section 3.4.2 of Chapter 3, for a more precise and rigorous analysis, we discuss the results in two sub-periods: from 2005 to 2010 and from 2011 to 2013.

The Cost of Living Index and the Wages Index for Ordinary Residents in Perth are represented respectively by the grey and red line in Figure 5.71c. Between 2005 and 2010, the Cost of Living Index for Ordinary Residents was generally on an increasing trend. In 2005, the cost of living for ordinary residents in Perth was 67.58% of that for their counterparts in New York (the base city). It rose steadily until it reached 89.53% in 2010. Over the same sub-period, the Wages Index for Ordinary Residents also followed an increasing trend, rising from 111.21 in 2005 to 147.34 in 2010.

Between 2005 and 2007, wages rose faster than cost of living but during the remaining years of the first sub-period, wages could not keep up with the latter. Hence, ordinary residents in Perth could only afford a higher consumption level over time up until 2007 but could not do so thereafter. These trends are reflected in the Purchasing Power index for Ordinary Residents in Perth, which is represented by the green line in Figure 5.71c. Between 2005 and 2007, this index rose from 164.55 to 174.22. It then started to decrease until it reached 164.58 in 2010. Ranking-wise, the Purchasing Power Ranking for Ordinary Residents in Perth, which is represented by the green bars, improved slightly over the first sub-period, rising from 18th in 2005 to 17th in 2010.

Over the second sub-period (2011–2013), the Cost of Living Index for Ordinary Residents has been on a decreasing trend. In 2011, the cost of living for ordinary residents in Perth was 1.03 times that for their counterparts in New York. It dropped to 88.29% in 2013. In contrast, the Wages Index for Ordinary Residents has been increasing, rising from 168.86 in 2011 to 176.22 in 2013.

The combined trends of increasing wages and decreasing cost of living have enabled ordinary residents in Perth to afford more goods and services over time throughout the second

PERTH
Australia

sub-period. This is reflected in the Purchasing Power Index for Ordinary Residents, which rose from 162.89 in 2011 to 199.59 in 2013. Meanwhile, the Purchasing Power Ranking for Ordinary Residents has also improved over the second sub-period. Between 2011 and 2013, it improved from 16th to 12th.

Finally, we note that over the entire study period (2005–2013), the Purchasing Power Index for Ordinary Residents in Perth has always been above 100.00 — the base index value. This means that ordinary residents in Perth have consistently been able to afford a higher consumption level than their counterparts in New York, given the same number of working hours.

PITTSBURGH
United States

Figure 5.72a: Cost of Living and 10 Consumption Categories Rankings for Ordinary Residents in Pittsburgh, United States

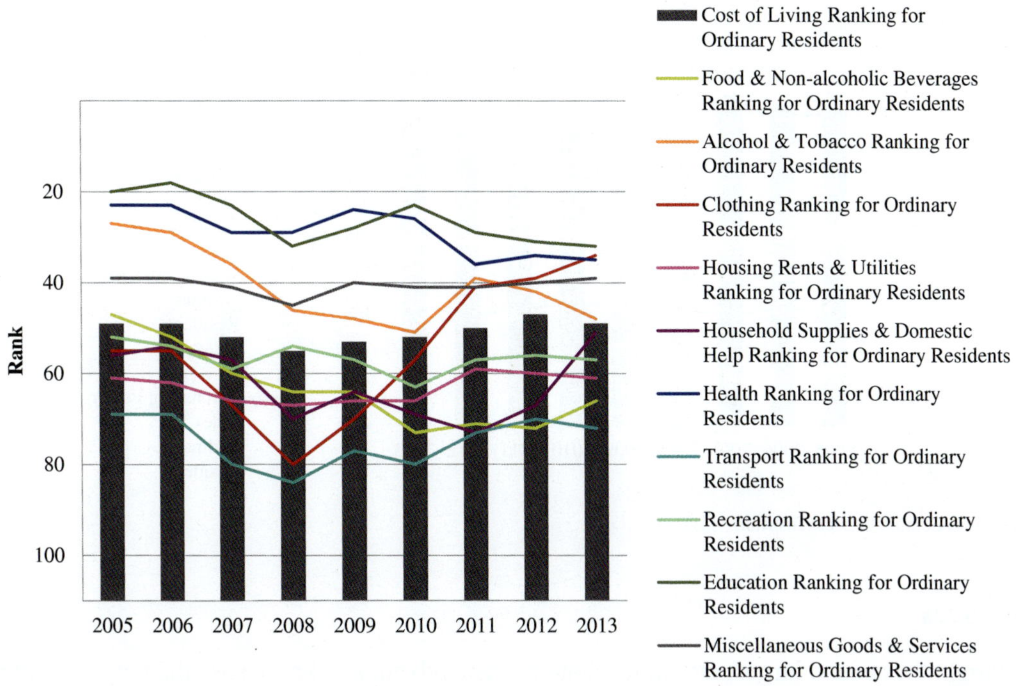

Source: Asia Competitiveness Institute

Figure 5.72b: Gross Hourly Wages in USD and Wages Ranking for Ordinary Residents in Pittsburgh, United States

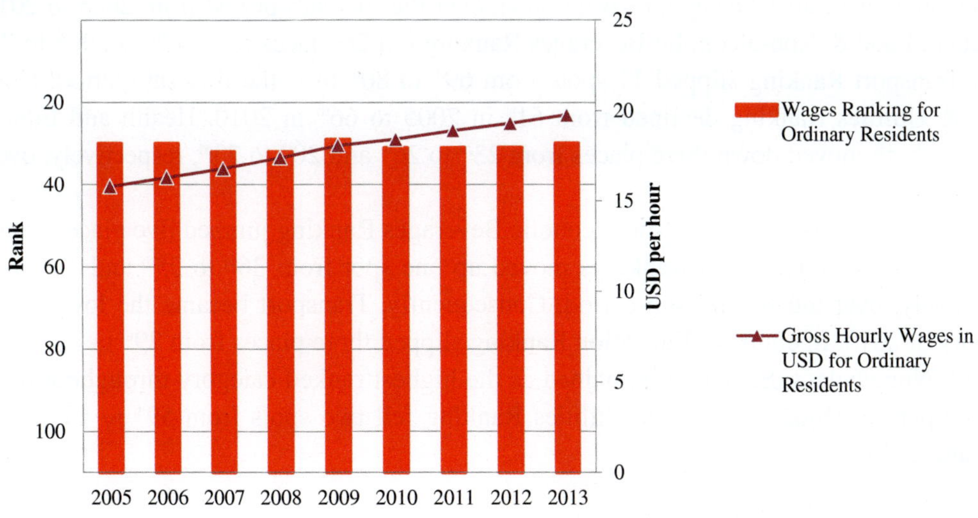

Source: Asia Competitiveness Institute

PITTSBURGH
United States

Figure 5.72c: Cost of Living, Wages and Purchasing Power Indices and Purchasing Power Ranking for Ordinary Residents in Pittsburgh, United States

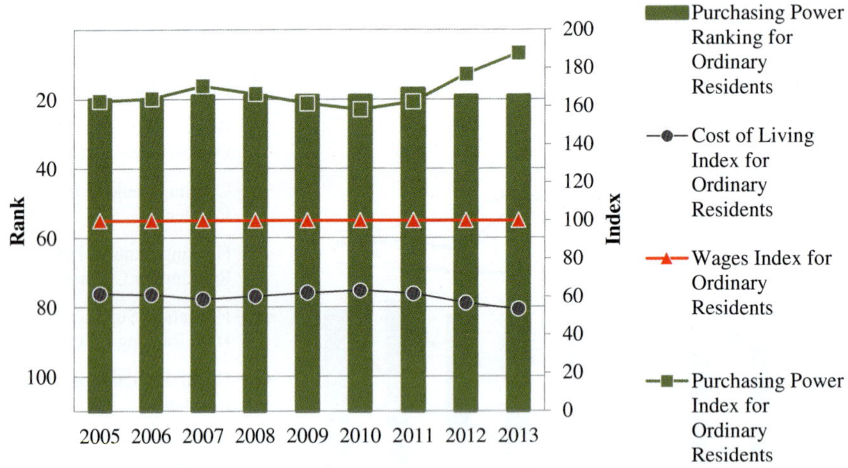

Source: Asia Competitiveness Institute

Figure 5.72a

Pittsburgh, the second largest city in the state of Pennsylvania, is known as "the City of Bridges" for its 446 bridges. The city's Cost of Living Ranking for Ordinary Residents, as shown in the grey bars, declined from 49th to 52nd between 2005 and 2010, and rose from 50th to 49th between 2011 and 2013 (see Figure 5.72a). As elaborated in Section 3.4.2 of Chapter 3, for a more precise comparison of rankings, we have split the analysis into two sub-periods.

The rankings of all 10 categories went down over the first sub-period from 2005 to 2010. In particular, Food & Non-alcoholic Beverages Ranking fell 26 places from 47th in 2005 to 73rd in 2010. Transport Ranking slipped 11 spots from 69th to 80th over the first sub-period. Housing Rents & Utilities Ranking declined from 61st in 2005 to 66th in 2010. Health and Education Rankings both moved down three places from 23rd to 26th and 20th to 23rd, respectively, over the same sub-period.

From 2011 to 2013, Food & Non-alcoholic Beverages Ranking jumped five places from 71st to 66th. Health and Transport Rankings moved up one spot from 36th to 35th and 73rd to 72nd, respectively, over the second sub-period. Consequently, Transport became the lowest ranked category in 2013. In contrast, Education Ranking slipped three places from 29th in 2011 to 32nd in 2013. Nonetheless, Education remained as the highest ranked category throughout the second sub-period. Housing Rents & Utilities Ranking fell two spots from 59th to 61st between 2011 and 2013.

PITTSBURGH
United States

Figure 5.72b

The Gross Hourly Wages in USD for Ordinary Residents in Pittsburgh, as represented by the red line in Figure 5.72b, increased gradually from US$15.79 in 2005 to US$19.77 in 2013.

Despite the consistent increase in the average wage, the Wages Ranking for Ordinary Residents in Pittsburgh, as depicted by the red bars, has remained rather stable. From 30th in 2005, it rose slightly to 29th in 2009 before dropping to 31st in 2010. The ranking remained at 31st until 2013, when it rose back to 30th.

Figure 5.72c

Let us now analyse the cost of living and wages indices more closely and draw conclusions about the purchasing power of ordinary residents in Pittsburgh. As elaborated in Section 3.4.2 of Chapter 3, for a more precise and rigorous analysis, we discuss the results in two sub-periods: from 2005 to 2010 and from 2011 to 2013.

The Cost of Living Index and the Wages Index for Ordinary Residents in Pittsburgh are represented respectively by the grey and red line in Figure 5.72c. As mentioned in Section 3.3 of Chapter 3, wage data are only available at the national level and not by cities. Therefore, wages in all cities in the United States are assumed to be the same. As a result, Pittsburgh, being a city in the United States, shares a common Wages Index for Ordinary Residents with the base city New York (whose index value is 100.00) over the entire study period (2005–2013).

Over the first sub-period (2005–2010), the Cost of Living Index for Ordinary Residents in Pittsburgh was initially on a decreasing trend but it reversed to an upward trend during the later years. Specifically, between 2005 and 2007, the index decreased from 61.44 to 58.62. Thereafter, it rose steadily until it reached 63.20 in 2010.

Since the Wages Index for Ordinary Residents is constant across the years, how the Purchasing Power Index for Ordinary Residents in Pittsburgh (or any other cities in the United States) changes depends only on variations in the Cost of Living Index for Ordinary Residents. Thus, between 2005 and 2007 when the latter index was decreasing, the purchasing power index also followed an upward trend, rising from 162.76 to 170.58. It then switched to a decreasing trend between 2008 and 2010 when the cost of living index was increasing. Overall, the purchasing power index was lower in 2010 (158.24) than it was in 2005. This indicates an erosion in ordinary residents' purchasing power over the first sub-period. Ranking-wise, the Purchasing Power Ranking for Ordinary Residents in Pittsburgh, which is represented by the green bars, improved from 20th in 2005 and 2006 to 19th in 2007 and remained there thereafter.

Over the second sub-period (2011–2013), the Cost of Living Index for Ordinary Residents has steadily declined. In 2011, the cost of living for ordinary residents in Pittsburgh was 61.59% of that for their counterparts in New York. It dropped to 53.25% in 2013. As a result, the Purchasing Power Index for Ordinary Residents has steadily increased, rising from 162.35 in 2011 to 187.78

PITTSBURGH
United States

in 2013. Despite this positive showing of the index, the Purchasing Power Ranking for Ordinary Residents has been deteriorating. From 17th in 2011, it dropped to 19th in 2013.

Finally, we note that over the entire study period (2005–2013), the Purchasing Power Index for Ordinary Residents in Pittsburgh has always been above 100.00 — the base index value. This indicates that ordinary residents in Pittsburgh have consistently been able to consume more goods and services than their counterparts in New York, given the same number of working hours.

PRAGUE
Czech Republic

Figure 5.73a: Cost of Living and 10 Consumption Categories Rankings for Ordinary Residents in Prague, Czech Republic

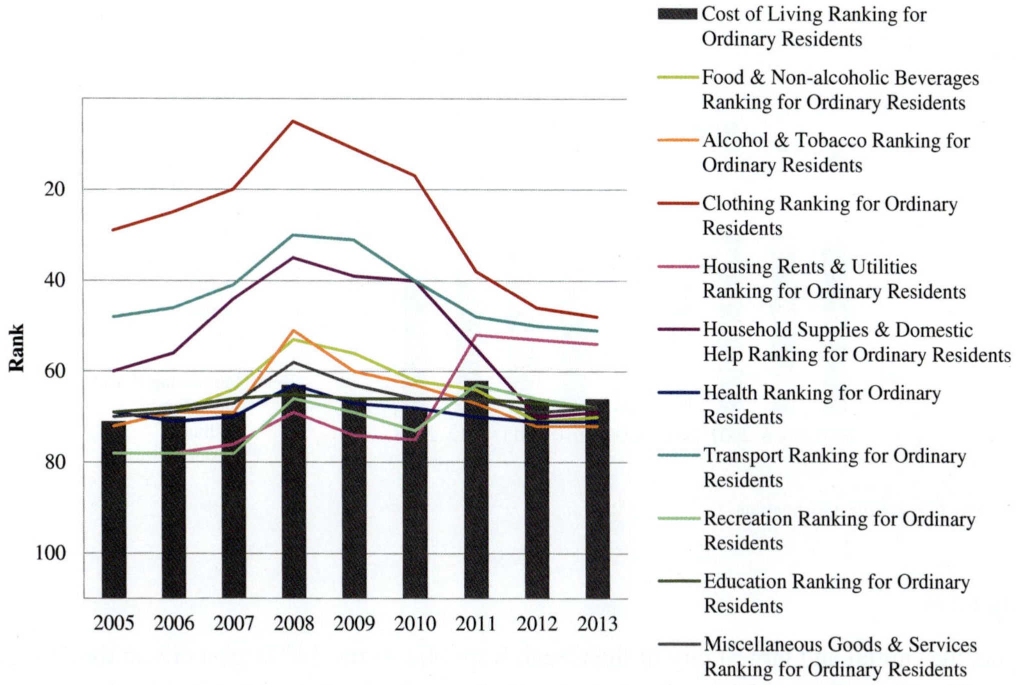

Source: Asia Competitiveness Institute

Figure 5.73b: Gross Hourly Wages in USD and Wages Ranking for Ordinary Residents in Prague, Czech Republic

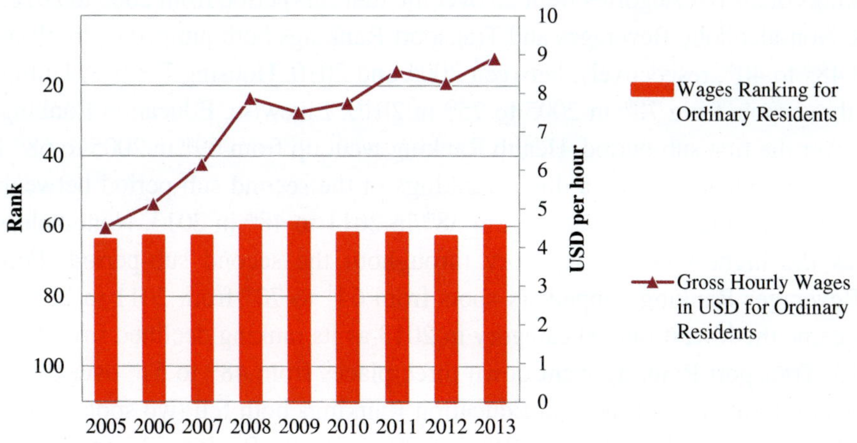

Source: Asia Competitiveness Institute

PRAGUE
Czech Republic

Figure 5.73c: Cost of Living, Wages and Purchasing Power Indices and Purchasing Power Ranking for Ordinary Residents in Prague, Czech Republic

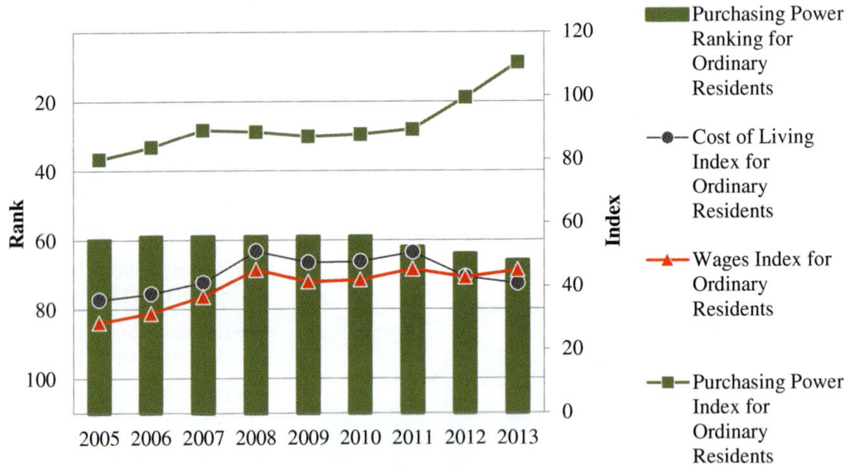

Source: Asia Competitiveness Institute

Figure 5.73a

Prague, the capital and largest city of the Czech Republic, is the 14th largest city in the European Union. The city's Cost of Living Ranking for Ordinary Residents, as denoted by the grey bars, rose from 71st to 68th between 2005 and 2010, and fell from 62nd to 66th between 2011 and 2013 (see Figure 5.73a). As explained in Section 3.4.2 of Chapter 3, for a more rigorous comparison of rankings, we have split the analysis into two sub-periods.

The rankings of all 10 categories went up over the first sub-period from 2005 to 2010. In particular, Food & Non-alcoholic Beverages and Transport Rankings both jumped eight places from 70th to 62nd and 48th to 40th, respectively, between 2005 and 2010. Housing Rents & Utilities Ranking moved up three spots from 78th in 2005 to 75th in 2010. Likewise, Education Ranking rose from 69th to 66th over the first sub-period. Health Ranking went up from 69th in 2005 to 68th in 2010.

In contrast, all categories saw a dip in rankings in the second sub-period between 2011 and 2013. Clothing Ranking fell 10 places from 38th in 2011 to 48th in 2013. Nonetheless, Clothing remained as the highest ranked category throughout the second sub-period. Food & Non-alcoholic Beverages Ranking slipped six spots from 64th to 70th from 2011 to 2013. Alcohol & Tobacco became the lowest ranked category in 2013 as its ranking declined from 67th in 2011 to 72nd in 2013. Transport Ranking went down three places from 48th to 51st over the second sub-period. Housing Rents & Utilities and Education Rankings both fell two spots from 52nd to 54th and 66th to 68th, respectively, between 2011 and 2013. Health Ranking dropped one place from 70th to 71st over the same sub-period.

PRAGUE
Czech Republic

Figure 5.73b

The Gross Hourly Wages in USD for Ordinary Residents in Prague, as depicted by the red line in Figure 5.73b, have generally been on an increasing trend over the study period. From US$4.50 in 2005, Prague's wage level rose to US$8.90 in 2013.

Meanwhile, the Wages Ranking for Ordinary Residents in Prague, as denoted by the red bars, has also generally improved. It rose from 64th in 2005 to 60th in 2013.

Figure 5.73c

Let us now analyse the cost of living and wages indices more closely and draw conclusions about the purchasing power of ordinary residents in Prague. As elaborated in Section 3.4.2 of Chapter 3, for a more precise and rigorous analysis, we discuss the results in two sub-periods: from 2005 to 2010 and from 2011 to 2013.

The Cost of Living Index and the Wages Index for Ordinary Residents in Prague are represented respectively by the grey and red line in Figure 5.73c. Between 2005 and 2010, the Cost of Living Index for Ordinary Residents was generally on an increasing trend. In 2005, the cost of living for ordinary residents in Prague was 35.67% of that for their counterparts in New York (the base city). It rose over the years to 47.78% in 2010. Over the first sub-period, the Wages Index for Ordinary Residents also increased, rising from 28.53 in 2005 to 42.00 in 2010.

Wages generally rose faster than cost of living so throughout the first sub-period, ordinary residents in Prague were able to afford more goods and services over time. This is reflected in the Purchasing Power Index for Ordinary Residents in Prague, which is represented by the green line in Figure 5.73c. Between 2005 and 2010, this index rose from 79.98 to 87.89. Ranking-wise, the Purchasing Power Ranking for Ordinary Residents in Prague, as represented by the green bars, did not fluctuate much over the first sub-period. From 60th in 2005, Prague's ranking rose to 59th in 2006 and remained there thereafter.

Over the second sub-period (2011–2013), the Cost of Living Index for Ordinary Residents has been on a decreasing trend. In 2011, the cost of living for ordinary residents in Prague was 50.69% of that for their counterparts in New York. It dropped to 40.78% in 2013. In contrast, the Wages Index for Ordinary Residents has been relatively stable. It only fluctuated around 44.36 between 2011 and 2013.

The combined trends of stable wages and decreasing cost of living have enabled ordinary residents in Prague to afford more goods and services over time. This is reflected in the Purchasing Power Index for Ordinary Residents, which rose from 89.41 in 2011 to 110.36 in 2013. Despite this positive showing of the index, the Purchasing Power Ranking for Ordinary Residents has actually deteriorated over the second sub-period, dropping from 62nd in 2011 to 66th in 2013.

Finally, we note that the Purchasing Power Index for Ordinary Residents in Prague had consistently been lower than 100.00 — the base index value — until 2013. This means it was not until 2013 that ordinary residents in Prague were able to afford more goods and services than their counterparts in New York, given the same number of working hours. Before 2013, they had only been able to afford a lower consumption level.

PRETORIA
South Africa

Figure 5.74a: Cost of Living and 10 Consumption Categories Rankings for Ordinary Residents in Pretoria, South Africa

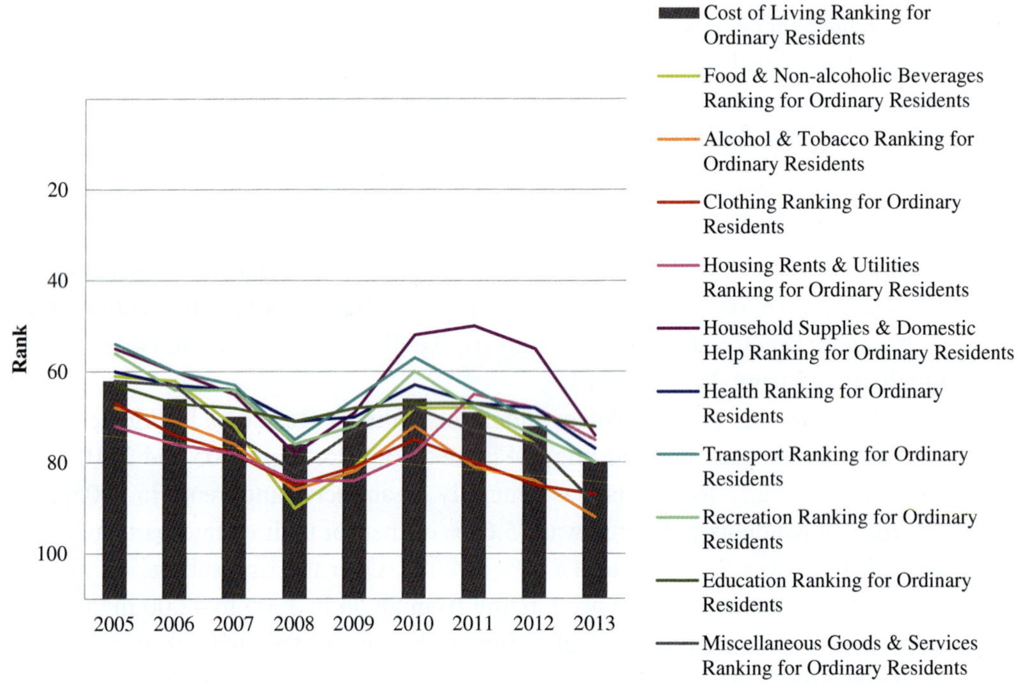

Source: Asia Competitiveness Institute

Figure 5.74b: Gross Hourly Wages in USD and Wages Ranking for Ordinary Residents in Pretoria, South Africa

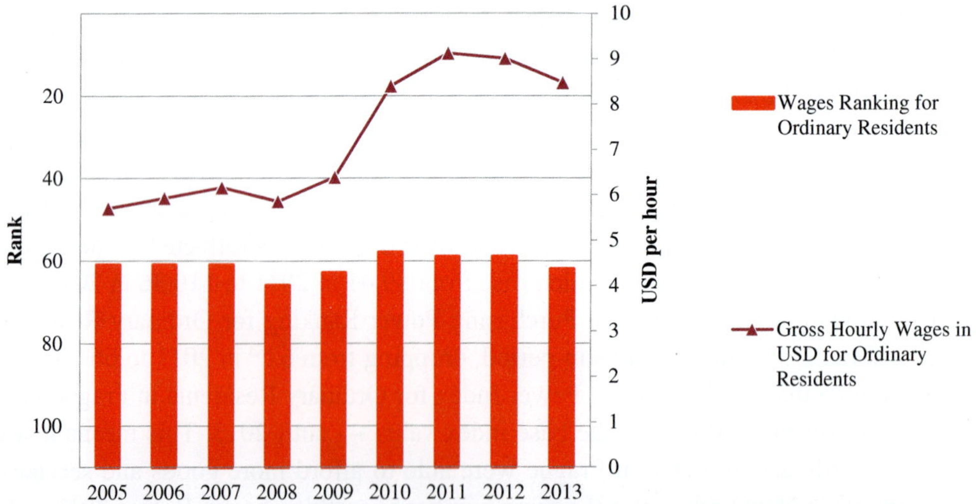

Source: Asia Competitiveness Institute

PRETORIA
South Africa

Figure 5.74c: Cost of Living, Wages and Purchasing Power Indices and Purchasing Power Ranking for Ordinary Residents in Pretoria, South Africa

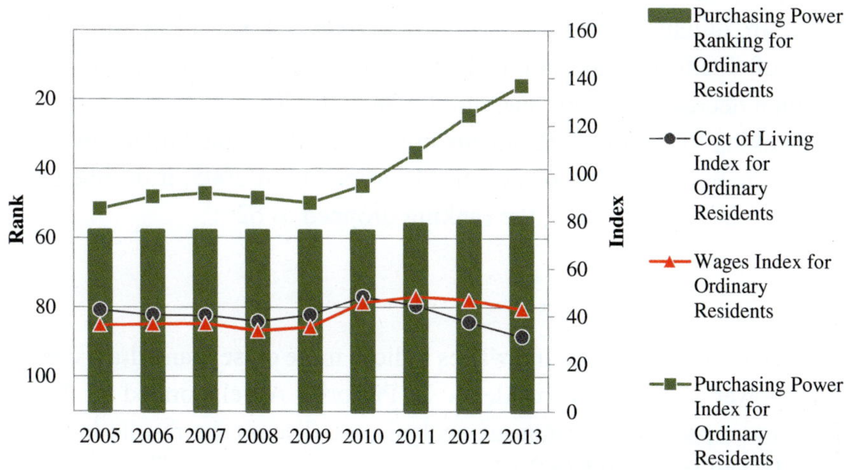

Source: Asia Competitiveness Institute

Figure 5.74a

Pretoria is one of South Africa's three capital cities, serving as the administrative and *de facto* national capital. The city's Cost of Living Ranking for Ordinary Residents, as represented by the grey bars, declined from 62nd to 66th between 2005 and 2010, and from 69th to 80th between 2011 and 2013 (see Figure 5.74a). As elaborated in Section 3.4.2 of Chapter 3, for a more precise comparison of rankings, we have split the analysis into two sub-periods.

From 2005 to 2010, Household Supplies & Domestic Help was the only category that rose in ranking from 55th to 52nd. Food & Non-alcoholic Beverages Ranking fell seven places from 61st in 2005 to 68th in 2010. Housing Rents & Utilities Ranking slipped six spots from 72nd to 78th over the first sub-period. Education Ranking declined from 63rd to 67th between 2005 and 2010. Health and Transport Rankings both moved down three places from 60th to 63rd and 54th to 57th, respectively, over the same sub-period.

The rankings of all 10 categories went down over the second sub-period between 2011 and 2013. In particular, Food & Non-alcoholic Beverages Ranking slipped 21 places from 68th in 2011 to 89th in 2013. Transport Ranking fell 16 spots from 64th to 80th over the second sub-period. Alcohol & Tobacco became the lowest ranked category in 2013 as its ranking declined from 81st to 92nd between 2011 and 2013. Housing Rents & Utilities and Health Rankings went down from 65th to 75th and 67th to 77th, respectively, over the same sub-period. Education Ranking slipped five places from 67th in 2011 to 72nd in 2013. Nonetheless, Education was the highest ranked category in 2013.

PRETORIA
South Africa

Figure 5.74b

The Gross Hourly Wages in USD for Ordinary Residents in Pretoria, as represented by the red line in Figure 5.74b, initially grew from US$5.70 in 2005 to US$9.12 in 2011. However, due to the depreciation of South African rand against US dollar from 2011 onwards, Pretoria's wage level has been on a decreasing trend, reaching US$8.47 in 2013.

The Wages Ranking for Ordinary Residents in Pretoria, as denoted by the red bars, has exhibited moderate fluctuations over the study period. From 61st in 2005, it dropped to 66th in 2008 before rising to 58th in 2010. In 2013, the ranking dropped to 62nd.

Figure 5.74c

Let us now analyse the cost of living and wages indices more closely and draw conclusions about the purchasing power of ordinary residents in Pretoria. As elaborated in Section 3.4.2 of Chapter 3, for a more precise and rigorous analysis, we discuss the results in two sub-periods: from 2005 to 2010 and from 2011 to 2013.

The Cost of Living Index and the Wages Index for Ordinary Residents in Pretoria are represented respectively by the grey and red line in Figure 5.74c. Over the first sub-period (2005–2010), the Cost of Living Index for Ordinary Residents exhibited moderate fluctuations. In 2005, the cost of living for ordinary residents in Pretoria was initially 42.55% of that for their counterparts in New York. It first decreased over the next three years to reach 37.60% in 2008 and then increased steadily over the remaining years of the first sub-period to 48.15% in 2010. Over the first sub-period, the Wages Index for Ordinary Residents also followed a relatively similar pattern. The wages index was stable between 2005 at 2007 at around 36.42. It dropped to 33.68 in 2008 before increasing over the years to eventually reach 45.58 in 2010.

Between 2005 and 2007, wages were stable while cost of living was decreasing. Thus, during these years, ordinary residents in Pretoria were able to afford more goods and services over time. Between 2007 and 2009, wages either dropped at a faster rate than cost of living or rose more slowly than the latter. Thus, the purchasing power of ordinary residents in Pretoria was eroded over time during these years. Finally, over the last leg of the first sub-period (2009–2010), wages rose faster than cost of living so purchasing power of the ordinary residents was once again increasing. These trends are fully reflected in the Purchasing Power Index for Ordinary Residents in Pretoria, which is represented by the green line in Figure 5.74c. Overall, this index was higher in 2010 (94.68) than it was in 2005 (84.90). Despite the fluctuations of the purchasing power index, the Purchasing Power Ranking for Ordinary Residents in Pretoria, which is represented by the green bars, consistently stagnated at 58th over the first sub-period.

Over the second sub-period (2011–2013), the Cost of Living Index for Ordinary Residents has been on a decreasing trend. In 2011, the cost of living for ordinary residents in Pretoria was 44.40% of that for their counterparts in New York. It dropped over the years to 31.33% in 2013.

PRETORIA
South Africa

The Wages Index for Ordinary Residents has also been decreasing, dropping from 48.24 in 2011 to 42.86 in 2013.

Wages have decreased more slowly than cost of living over the second sub-period, so ordinary residents in Pretoria have been able to afford a higher consumption level over time during these years. This is reflected in the Purchasing Power Index for Ordinary Residents, which rose from 108.67 to 136.78 between 2011 and 2013. Meanwhile, the Purchasing Power Ranking for Ordinary Residents has also been improving. Between 2011 and 2013, it rose from 56th to 54th.

Finally, we note that the Purchasing Power Index for Ordinary Residents in Pretoria was lower than 100.00 — the base index value — over the first sub-period. However, throughout the second sub-period, the index has been consistently above this base level. This means that between 2005 and 2010, ordinary residents in Pretoria could only afford a lower consumption level than their counterparts in New York. However, since 2011, they have been able to afford a higher level than the latter.

QINGDAO
China

Figure 5.75a: Cost of Living and 10 Consumption Categories Rankings for Ordinary Residents in Qingdao, China

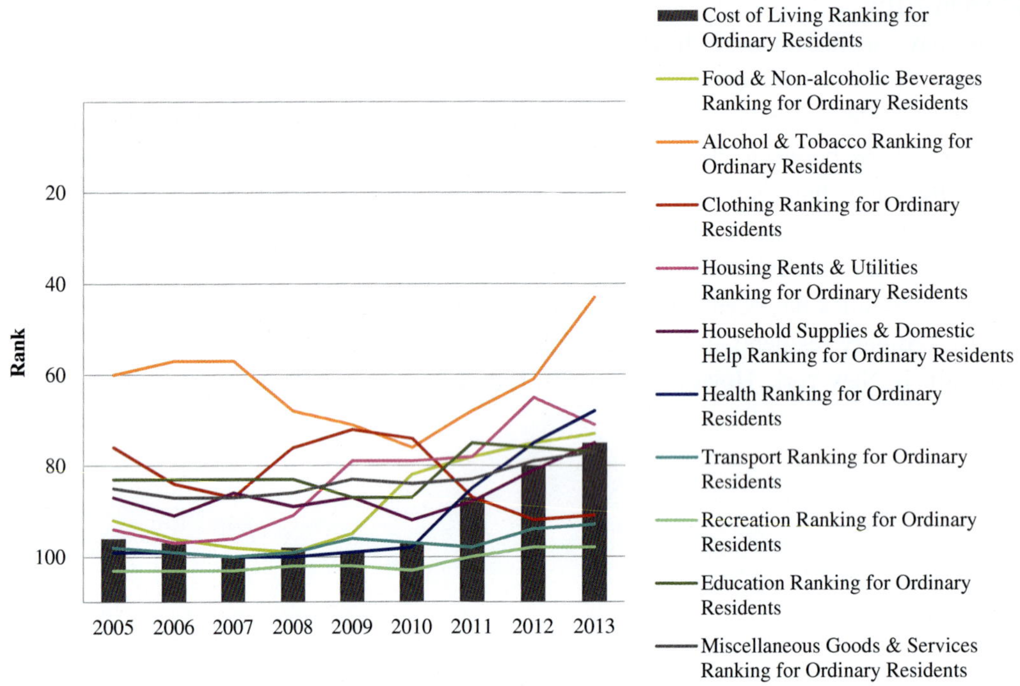

Source: Asia Competitiveness Institute

Figure 5.75b: Gross Hourly Wages in USD and Wages Ranking for Ordinary Residents in Qingdao, China

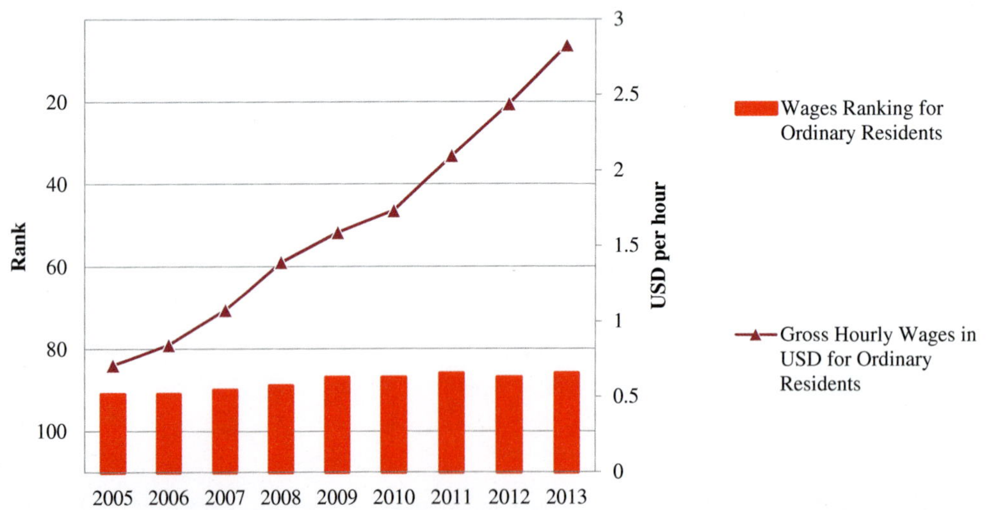

Source: Asia Competitiveness Institute

QINGDAO
China

Figure 5.75c: Cost of Living, Wages and Purchasing Power Indices and Purchasing Power Ranking for Ordinary Residents in Qingdao, China

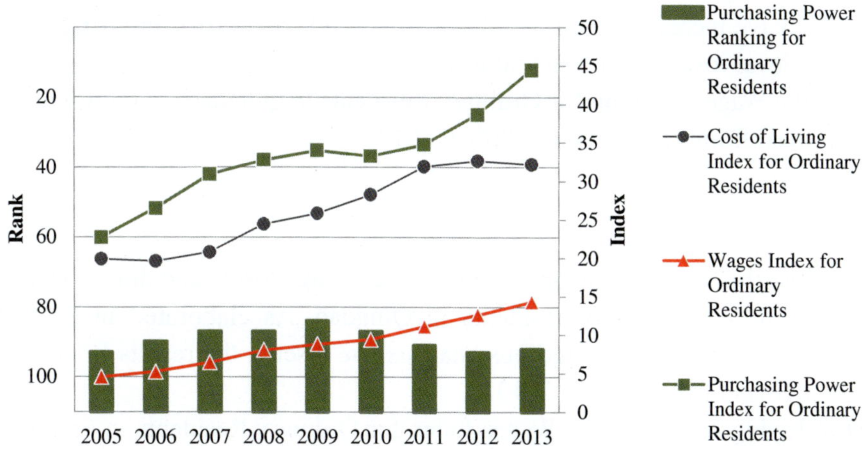

Source: Asia Competitiveness Institute

Figure 5.75a

Qingdao is an important seaport, naval base and industrial centre in eastern China's Shandong province. The city's Cost of Living Ranking for Ordinary Residents, as shown in the grey bars, fell from 96th to 97th between 2005 and 2010, and rose from 87th to 75th between 2011 and 2013 (see Figure 5.75a). As explained in Section 3.4.2 of Chapter 3, for a more rigorous comparison of rankings, we have split the analysis into two sub-periods.

From 2005 to 2010, Education Ranking slipped four spots from 83rd to 87th. In contrast, Housing Rents & Utilities Ranking climbed 15 places from 94th in 2005 to 79th in 2010. Food & Non-alcoholic Beverages Ranking moved up 10 places from 92nd to 82nd over the first sub-period. Health and Transport Rankings both moved up one spot from 99th to 98th and 98th to 97th, respectively, between 2005 and 2010.

From 2011 to 2013, Alcohol & Tobacco Ranking climbed 25 places from 68th to 43rd, making it the highest ranked category throughout the second sub-period. Health Ranking jumped 17 spots from 85th in 2011 to 68th in 2013. Housing Rents & Utilities Ranking moved up seven places from 78th to 71st between 2011 and 2013. Food & Non-alcoholic Beverages and Transport Rankings rose from 78th to 73rd and 98th to 93rd, respectively, over the second sub-period. Recreation Ranking climbed two spots from 100th in 2011 to 98th in 2013. Nonetheless, Recreation remained as the lowest ranked category in both sub-periods.

QINGDAO
China

Figure 5.75b

The Gross Hourly Wages in USD for Ordinary Residents in Qingdao, as denoted by the red line in Figure 5.75b, have increased significantly between 2005 and 2013. From US$0.71 in 2005, Qingdao's wage level rose almost fourfold to US$2.83 in 2013.

Meanwhile, the Wages Ranking for Ordinary Residents in Qingdao, as represented by the red bars, also improved from 91st in 2005 to 86th in 2013.

Figure 5.75c

Let us now analyse the cost of living and wages indices more closely and draw conclusions about the purchasing power of ordinary residents in Qingdao. As elaborated in Section 3.4.2 of Chapter 3, for a more precise and rigorous analysis, we discuss the results in two sub-periods: from 2005 to 2010 and from 2011 to 2013.

The Cost of Living Index and the Wages Index for Ordinary Residents in Pretoria are represented respectively by the grey and red line in Figure 5.75c. Between 2005 and 2010, the Cost of Living Index for Ordinary Residents was on an increasing trend. In 2005, the cost of living for ordinary residents in Qingdao was initially 19.87% of that for their counterparts in New York (the base city). It rose over the years to reach 28.26% in 2010. Over the first sub-period, the Wages Index for Ordinary Residents also followed an upward trend, rising from 4.50 to 9.40 in 2010.

Wages generally rose faster than cost of living, so throughout the first sub-period, ordinary residents in Qingdao were able to afford more goods and services over time. This is reflected in the Purchasing Power Index for Ordinary Residents in Qingdao, which is represented by the green line in Figure 5.75c. Between 2005 and 2010, this index rose from 22.66 to 33.27. Meanwhile, the Purchasing Power Ranking for Ordinary Residents in Qingdao, which is represented by the green bars, also improved steadily over the first sub-period. Qingdao's ranking rose from 93rd in 2005 to 87th in 2010.

Over the second sub-period (2011–2013), the Cost of Living Index for Ordinary Residents has been on an increasing trend. In 2011, the cost of living for ordinary residents in Qingdao was 31.90% of that for their counterparts in New York. It rose to 32.17% in 2013. The Wages Index for Ordinary Residents has also been increasing, rising from 11.10 in 2011 to 14.30 in 2013.

Wages have grown faster than cost of living over the second sub-period. Thus, ordinary residents in Qingdao have been able to afford a consumption level over time during these years. This is reflected in the Purchasing Power Index for Ordinary Residents, which rose from 34.79 to 44.46 between 2011 and 2013. Meanwhile, the Purchasing Power Ranking for Ordinary Residents has also been improving. Between 2011 and 2013, it rose from 91st to 92nd.

Finally, we note that the Purchasing Power Index for Ordinary Residents in Qingdao has consistently been lower than 100.00 — the base index value. Thus, ordinary residents in Qingdao have only been able to afford a lower consumption level than their counterparts in New York, given the same number of working hours.

QUITO
Ecuador

Figure 5.76a: Cost of Living and 10 Consumption Categories Rankings for Ordinary Residents in Quito, Ecuador

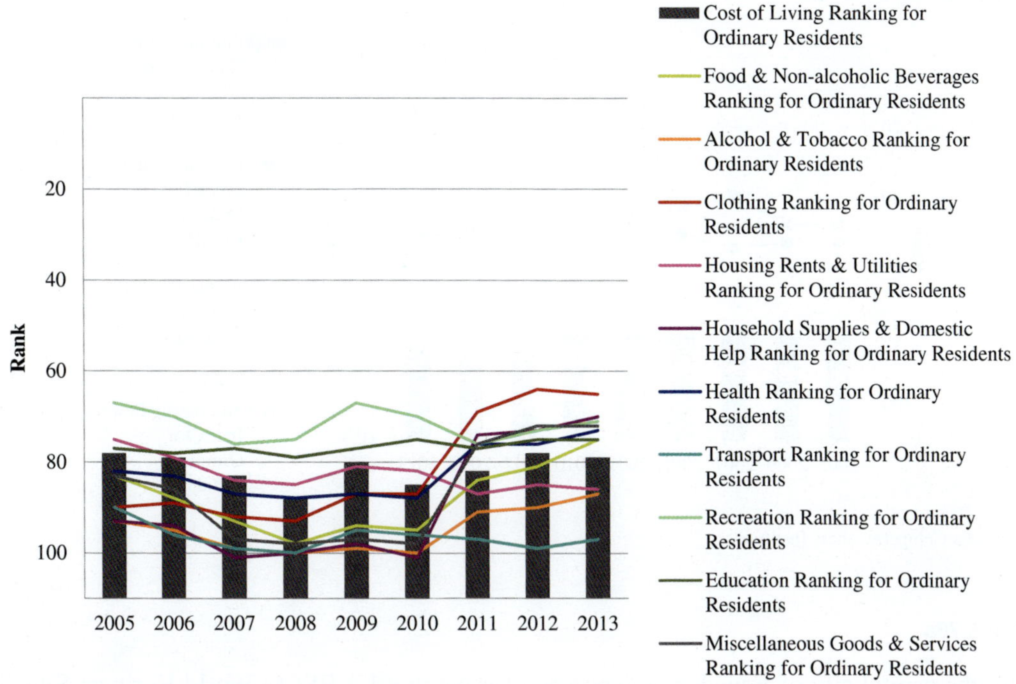

Source: Asia Competitiveness Institute

Figure 5.76b: Gross Hourly Wages in USD and Wages Ranking for Ordinary Residents in Quito, Ecuador

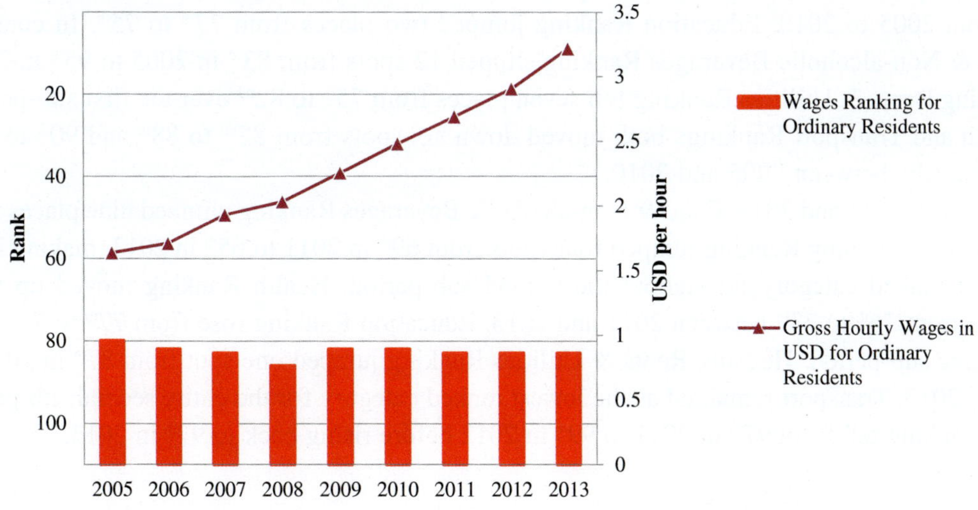

Source: Asia Competitiveness Institute

QUITO
Ecuador

Figure 5.76c: Cost of Living, Wages and Purchasing Power Indices and Purchasing Power Ranking for Ordinary Residents in Quito, Ecuador

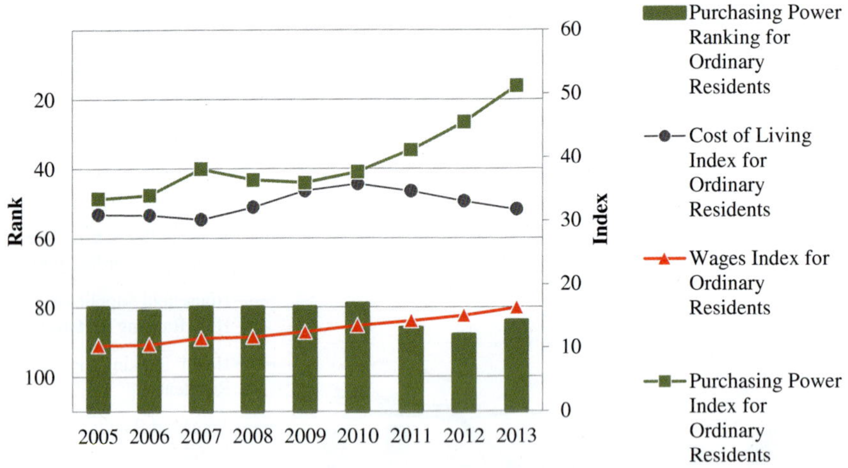

Source: Asia Competitiveness Institute

Figure 5.76a

Quito, the capital city of Ecuador, is renowned for being a UNESCO World Heritage Site. The city's Cost of Living Ranking for Ordinary Residents, as denoted by the grey bars, fell from 78th to 85th between 2005 and 2010, but rose from 82nd to 79th between 2011 and 2013 (see Figure 5.76a). As elaborated in Section 3.4.2 of Chapter 3, for a more precise comparison of rankings, we have split the analysis into two sub-periods.

From 2005 to 2010, Education Ranking jumped two places from 77th to 75th. In contrast, Food & Non-alcoholic Beverages Ranking slipped 12 spots from 83rd in 2005 to 95th in 2010. Housing Rents & Utilities Ranking fell seven places from 75th to 82nd over the first sub-period. Health and Transport Rankings both moved down six spots from 82nd to 88th and 90th to 96th, respectively, between 2005 and 2010.

Between 2011 and 2013, Food & Non-alcoholic Beverages Ranking climbed nine places from 84th to 75th. Clothing Ranking jumped four spots from 69th in 2011 to 65th in 2013, making it the highest ranked category throughout the second sub-period. Health Ranking moved up three places from 76th to 73rd between 2011 and 2013. Education Ranking rose from 77th to 75th over the same sub-period. Housing Rents & Utilities Ranking jumped one spot from 87th in 2011 to 86th in 2013. Transport remained as the lowest ranked category for the entire second sub-period as its ranking fell from 97th in 2011 to 99th in 2012 before rising back to 97th in 2013.

QUITO
Ecuador

Figure 5.76b

The Gross Hourly Wages in USD for Ordinary Residents in Quito, as shown by the red line in Figure 5.76b, have consistently been on an increasing trend over the study period. From US$1.64 in 2005, Quito's wage level rose to US$3.22 in 2013.

Despite the consistent growth in the wage level, the Wages Ranking for Ordinary Residents in Quito, as depicted by the red bars, has been deteriorating. The ranking dropped from 80th in 2005 to 83rd in 2013.

Figure 5.76c

Let us now analyse the cost of living and wages indices more closely and draw conclusions about the purchasing power of ordinary residents in Quito. As elaborated in Section 3.4.2 of Chapter 3, for a more precise and rigorous analysis, we discuss the results in two sub-periods: from 2005 to 2010 and from 2011 to 2013.

The Cost of Living Index and the Wages Index for Ordinary Residents in Quito are represented respectively by the grey and red line in Figure 5.76c. Between 2005 and 2010, the Cost of Living Index for Ordinary Residents was on an increasing trend. In 2005, the cost of living for ordinary residents in Quito was 30.98% of that for their counterparts in New York (the base city). It rose over the years to reach 35.77% in 2010. Over the first sub-period, the Wages Index for Ordinary Residents also followed an upward trend, rising from 10.36 to 13.47 in 2010.

Wages generally rose faster than cost of living, so throughout the first sub-period, ordinary residents in Quito were able to afford more goods and services over time. This is reflected in the Purchasing Power Index for Ordinary Residents in Quito, which is represented by the green line in Figure 5.76c. Between 2005 and 2010, this index rose from 33.45 to 37.65, while also exhibiting substantial fluctuations in between. Meanwhile, the Purchasing Power Ranking for Ordinary Residents in Quito, which is represented by the green bars, was stable over the first sub-period. Aside from a one-off deterioration to 81st in 2006 and an improvement to 79th in 2010, Quito's ranking remained at 80th for the remaining years of the first sub-period.

Over the second sub-period (2011–2013), the Cost of Living Index for Ordinary Residents has been on a decreasing trend. In 2011, the cost of living for ordinary residents in Quito was 34.62% of that for their counterparts in New York. It decreased to 31.75% in 2013. In contrast, the Wages Index for Ordinary Residents has been increasing, rising from 14.23 in 2011 to 16.27 in 2013.

The combined trends of increasing wages and decreasing cost of living have enabled ordinary residents in Quito to be able to afford more goods and services over time throughout the first sub-period. This is reflected in the Purchasing Power Index for Ordinary Residents, which rose from 41.11 to 51.24 between 2011 and 2013. Meanwhile, the Purchasing Power Ranking for

QUITO
Ecuador

Ordinary Residents has fluctuated quite substantially over the second sub-period. From 86th in 2011, it dropped to 88th in 2012 before climbing back to 84th in 2013.

Finally, we note that the Purchasing Power Index for Ordinary Residents in Quito has consistently been lower than 100.00 — the base index value. Thus, ordinary residents in Quito have only been able to afford a lower consumption level than their counterparts in New York, given the same number of working hours.

REYKJAVIK
Iceland

Figure 5.77a: Cost of Living and 10 Consumption Categories Rankings for Ordinary Residents in Reykjavik, Iceland

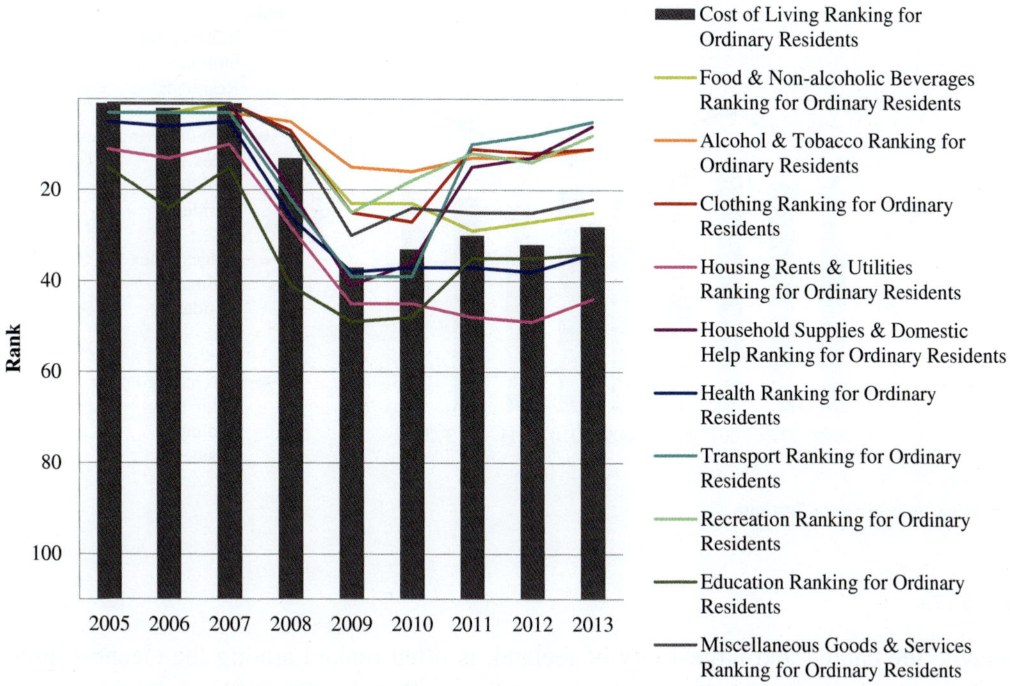

Source: Asia Competitiveness Institute

Figure 5.77b: Gross Hourly Wages in USD and Wages Ranking for Ordinary Residents in Reykjavik, Iceland

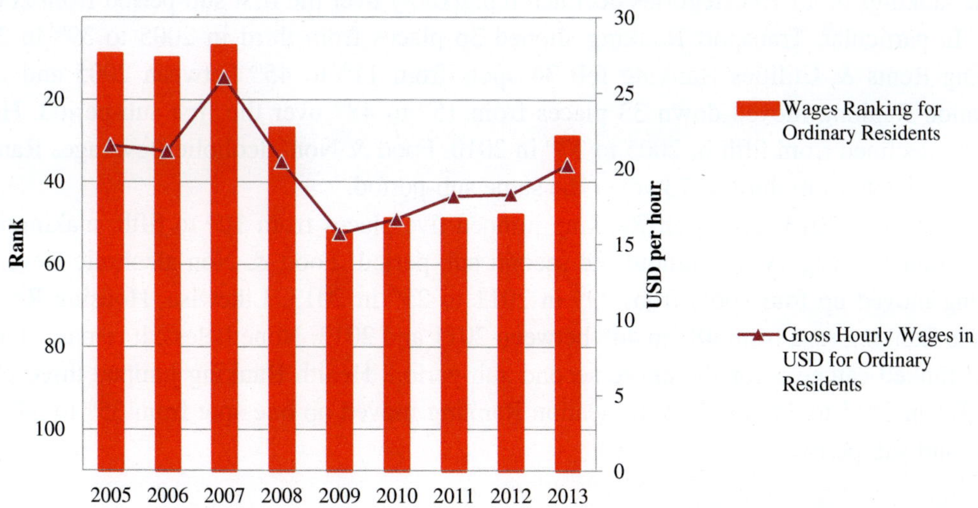

Source: Asia Competitiveness Institute

REYKJAVIK
Iceland

Figure 5.77c: Cost of Living, Wages and Purchasing Power Indices and Purchasing Power Ranking for Ordinary Residents in Reykjavik, Iceland

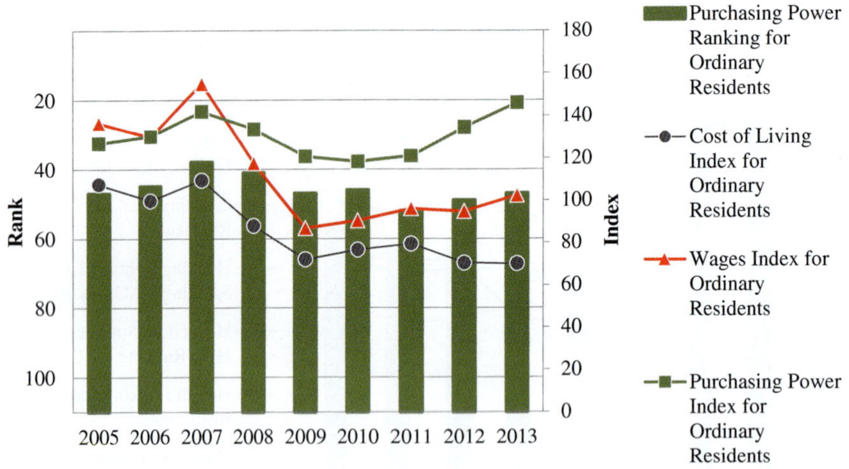

Source: Asia Competitiveness Institute

Figure 5.77a

Reykjavik, the capital and largest city of Iceland, is often ranked among the cleanest, greenest and safest cities in the world. The city's Cost of Living Ranking for Ordinary Residents, as represented by the grey bars, fell from first to 33rd between 2005 and 2010, but rose from 30th to 28th between 2011 and 2013 (see Figure 5.77a). As explained in Section 3.4.2 of Chapter 3, for a more rigorous comparison of rankings, we have split the analysis into two sub-periods.

The rankings of all 10 categories declined remarkably over the first sub-period from 2005 to 2010. In particular, Transport Ranking slipped 36 places from third in 2005 to 39th in 2010. Housing Rents & Utilities Ranking fell 34 spots from 11th to 45th between 2005 and 2010. Education Ranking moved down 33 places from 15th to 48th over the first sub-period. Health Ranking declined from fifth in 2005 to 37th in 2010. Food & Non-alcoholic Beverages Ranking slipped 20 spots from third to 23rd over the same sub-period.

From 2011 to 2013, Transport Ranking jumped five places from 10th to fifth, making it the highest ranked category throughout the second sub-period. Food & Non-alcoholic Beverages Ranking moved up four spots from 29th in 2011 to 25th in 2013. Likewise, Housing Rents & Utilities Ranking rose from 48th to 44th between 2011 and 2013. Nonetheless, it remained as the lowest ranked category for the entire second sub-period. Health Ranking jumped three places from 37th in 2011 to 34th in 2013. Education Ranking moved up one spot from 35th to 34th over the second sub-period.

REYKJAVIK
Iceland

Figure 5.77b

The Gross Hourly Wages in USD for Ordinary Residents in Reykjavik, as denoted by the red line in Figure 5.77b, have fluctuated substantially over the study period. This was due both to genuine changes in wages in Iceland but also to exchange rate fluctuations. For example, the sharp drop between 2007 and 2009 corresponded to an episode of substantial depreciation of the Icelandic krona against the US dollar. As the exchange rate stabilised after 2009, the Gross Hourly Wages in USD for Ordinary Residents started to recover and reached US$20.21 in 2013.

Ranking-wise, the Wages Ranking for Ordinary Residents in Reykjavik, as depicted by the red bars, has also fluctuated greatly. From ninth in 2005, it has deteriorated over the next few years and hit a low of 52nd in 2009. The ranking then started to improve and it reached 29th in 2013.

Figure 5.77c

Let us now analyse the cost of living and wages indices more closely and draw conclusions about the purchasing power of ordinary residents in Reykjavik. As elaborated in Section 3.4.2 of Chapter 3, for a more precise and rigorous analysis, we discuss the results in two sub-periods: from 2005 to 2010 and from 2011 to 2013.

The Cost of Living Index and the Wages Index for Ordinary Residents in Reykjavik are represented respectively by the grey and red line in Figure 5.77c. Between 2005 and 2010, both indices exhibited large fluctuations. Among other causes, these large variations in the indices are the results of exchange rate fluctuations. In general, however, the Cost of Living Index for Ordinary Residents was on a decreasing trend. In 2005, the cost of living for ordinary residents in Reykjavik was 1.07 times that for their counterparts in New York (the base city). This dropped over the years to reach 76.55%. The Wages Index for Ordinary Residents followed a similar pattern. Overall, this index was lower in 2010 (90.35) than it was in 2005 (136.28).

The Purchasing Power Index for Ordinary Residents in Reykjavik tracked the cost of living and wages indices quite closely. Between 2005 and 2007, the index rose from 126.84 to 141.84, signifying an improvement in the purchasing power of ordinary residents in Reykjavik. This gain happened because during 2005–2007, wages either fell more slowly than cost of living or they rose faster than the latter. However, after 2007, the purchasing power of ordinary residents in Reykjavik was gradually eroded over time. This is reflected in the steady decline of the Purchasing Power Index for Ordinary Residents between 2007 and 2010. It happened because both wages and cost of living were decreasing during those years and wages decreased at a faster rate than the latter. Ranking-wise, the Purchasing Power Ranking for Ordinary Residents in Reykjavik, as represented by the green bars, also fluctuated quite wildly. Overall, however, Reykjavik's ranking in 2010 was 46th, up from 45th in 2005.

REYKJAVIK
Iceland

Over the second sub-period (2011–2013), the Cost of Living Index for Ordinary Residents has been on a decreasing trend. In 2011, the cost of living for ordinary residents in Reykjavik was 79.40% of that for their counterparts in New York. It decreased to 70.02% in 2013. In contrast, the Wages Index for Ordinary Residents has been increasing, rising from 95.97 in 2011 to 102.24 in 2013.

The combined trends of increasing wages and decreasing cost of living have enabled ordinary residents in Reykjavik to be able to afford more goods and services over time throughout the first sub-period. This is reflected in the Purchasing Power Index for Ordinary Residents, which rose from 120.87 to 146.01 between 2011 and 2013. Meanwhile, the Purchasing Power Ranking for Ordinary Residents has also improved over the second sub-period. It rose from 52nd in 2011 to 47th in 2013.

Finally, we note that over the study period (2005–2010), the Purchasing Power Index for Ordinary Residents in Reykjavik has always been higher than 100.00 — the base index value. Thus, ordinary residents in Reykjavik have consistently been able to afford a higher consumption level than their counterparts in New York, given the same number of working hours.

RIO DE JANEIRO
Brazil

Figure 5.78a: Cost of Living and 10 Consumption Categories Rankings for Ordinary Residents in Rio de Janeiro, Brazil

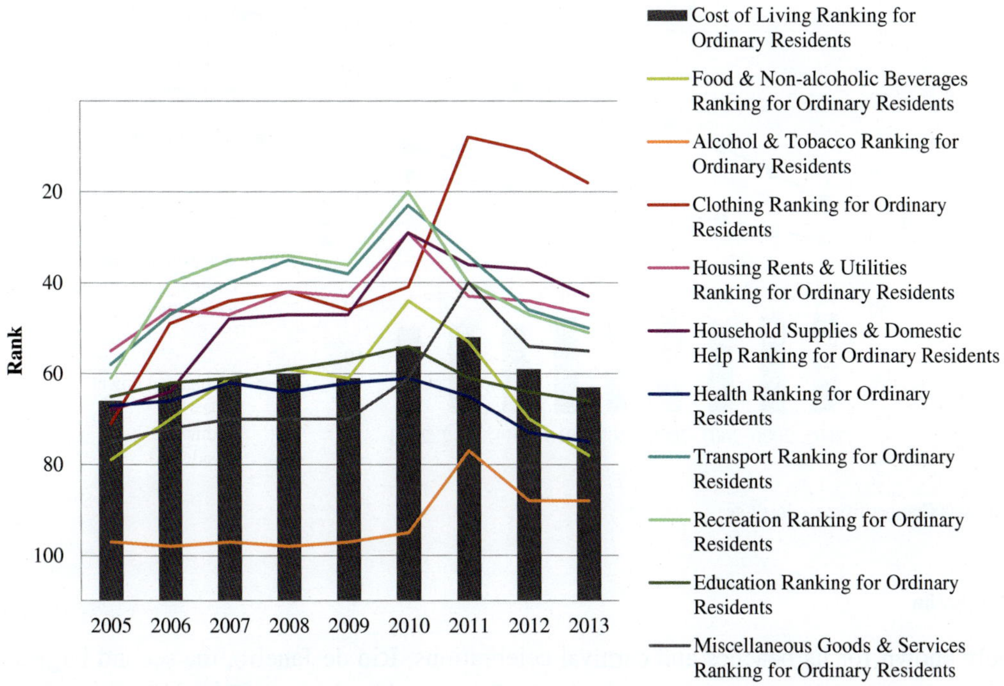

Source: Asia Competitiveness Institute

Figure 5.78b: Gross Hourly Wages in USD and Wages Ranking for Ordinary Residents in Rio de Janeiro, Brazil

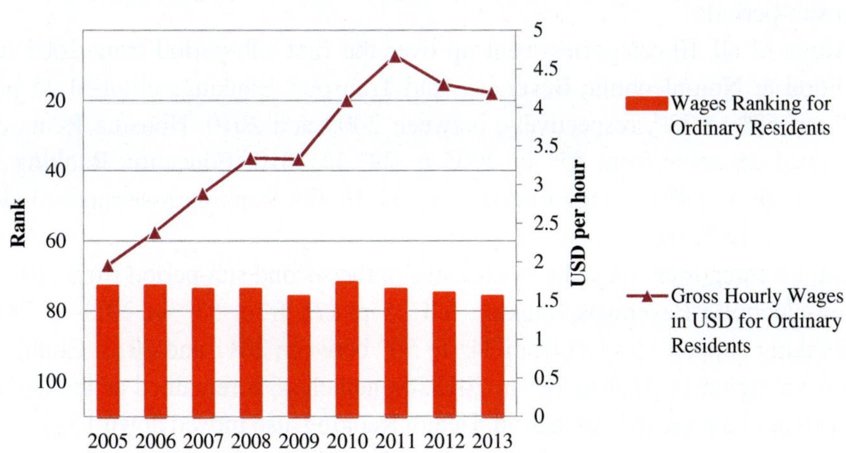

Source: Asia Competitiveness Institute

RIO DE JANEIRO
Brazil

Figure 5.78c: Cost of Living, Wages and Purchasing Power Indices and Purchasing Power Ranking for Ordinary Residents in Rio de Janeiro, Brazil

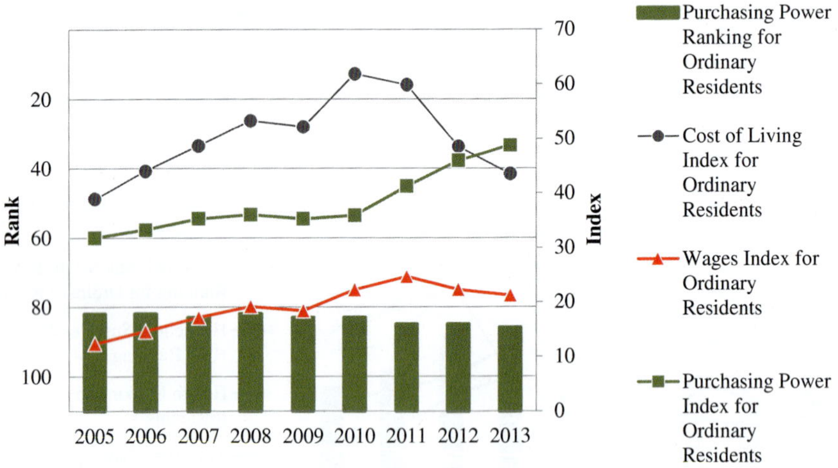

Source: Asia Competitiveness Institute

Figure 5.78a

Widely known for its beaches and carnival celebrations, Rio de Janeiro, the second largest city in Brazil, is one of the most visited cities in the Southern Hemisphere. The city's Cost of Living Ranking for Ordinary Residents, as shown in the grey bars, rose from 66th to 54th between 2005 and 2010, but slipped from 52nd to 63rd between 2011 and 2013 (see Figure 5.78a). As elaborated in Section 3.4.2 of Chapter 3, for a more precise comparison of rankings, we have split the analysis into two sub-periods.

The rankings of all 10 categories went up over the first sub-period from 2005 to 2010. In particular, Food & Non-alcoholic Beverages and Transport Rankings climbed 35 places from 79th to 44th and 58th to 23rd, respectively, between 2005 and 2010. Housing Rents & Utilities Ranking jumped 26 spots from 55th in 2005 to 29th in 2010. Education Ranking moved up 11 places from 65th to 54th over the first sub-period. Health Ranking rose more modestly from 67th in 2005 to 61st in 2010.

In contrast, all categories saw a dip in rankings in the second sub-period from 2011 and 2013. Food & Non-alcoholic Beverages Ranking fell 25 places from 53rd in 2011 to 78th in 2013. Transport Ranking slipped 16 spots from 34th to 50th between 2011 and 2013. Clothing Ranking went down from eighth in 2011 to 18th in 2013. Nonetheless, it remained as the highest ranked category throughout the second sub-period. Health Ranking also moved down 10 places from 65th to 75th over the second sub-period. Education Ranking fell five spots from 61st in 2011 to 66th in 2013. Housing Rents & Utilities Ranking declined from 43rd to 47th over the same sub-period.

RIO DE JANEIRO
Brazil

Figure 5.78b

The Gross Hourly Wages in USD for Ordinary Residents in Rio de Janeiro, as represented by the red line in Figure 5.78b, grew rather consistently from US$1.96 in 2005 to US$4.67 in 2011. Thereafter, Rio de Janeiro's wage level has been on a decreasing trend, reaching US$4.19 in 2013.

Meanwhile, the Wages Ranking for Ordinary Residents in Rio de Janeiro, as shown by the red bars, has generally deteriorated. It dropped from 73rd in 2005 to 76th in 2013.

Figure 5.78c

Let us now analyse the cost of living and wages indices more closely and draw conclusions about the purchasing power of ordinary residents in Rio de Janeiro. As elaborated in Section 3.4.2 of Chapter 3, for a more precise and rigorous analysis, we discuss the results in two sub-periods: from 2005 to 2010 and from 2011 to 2013.

The Cost of Living Index and the Wages Index for Ordinary Residents in Rio de Janeiro are represented respectively by the grey and red line in Figure 5.78c. Between 2005 and 2010, the Cost of Living Index for Ordinary Residents was on an increasing trend. In 2005, the cost of living for ordinary residents in Rio de Janeiro was 38.94% of that for their counterparts in New York (the base city). It rose over the years to reach 61.85% in 2010. Over the first sub-period, the Wages Index for Ordinary Residents also followed an upward trend, rising from 12.40 to 22.23 in 2010.

Wages generally rose faster than cost of living, so throughout the first sub-period, ordinary residents in Rio de Janeiro were able to afford more goods and services over time. This is reflected in the Purchasing Power Index for Ordinary Residents in Rio de Janeiro, which is represented by the green line in Figure 5.78c. Between 2005 and 2010, this index rose from 31.85 to 35.94. Meanwhile, the Purchasing Power Ranking for Ordinary Residents in Rio de Janeiro, which is represented by the green bars, was stable over the first sub-period. It only fluctuated between 82nd and 83rd during these years.

Over the second sub-period (2011–2013), the Cost of Living Index for Ordinary Residents has been on a decreasing trend. In 2011, the cost of living for ordinary residents in Rio de Janeiro was 59.85% of that for their counterparts in New York. It decreased over the years to 43.47% in 2013. The Wages Index for Ordinary Residents has also been decreasing. This index dropped from 24.68 in 2011 to 21.19 in 2013.

Wages have decreased more slowly than cost of living over the second sub-period. Thus, ordinary residents in Rio de Janeiro have actually been able to afford a higher consumption level over time during these years. This is reflected in the Purchasing Power Index for Ordinary Residents which rose from 41.24 to 48.74 between 2011 and 2013. Ranking-wise, the Purchasing Power Ranking for Ordinary Residents has been deteriorating, dropping from 85th in 2011 and 2012 to 86th in 2013.

Finally, we note that the Purchasing Power Index for Ordinary Residents in Rio de Janeiro has consistently been lower than 100.00 — the base index value. Thus, ordinary residents in Rio de Janeiro have only been able to afford a lower consumption level than their counterparts in New York, given the same number of working hours.

ROME
Italy

Figure 5.79a: Cost of Living and 10 Consumption Categories Rankings for Ordinary Residents in Rome, Italy

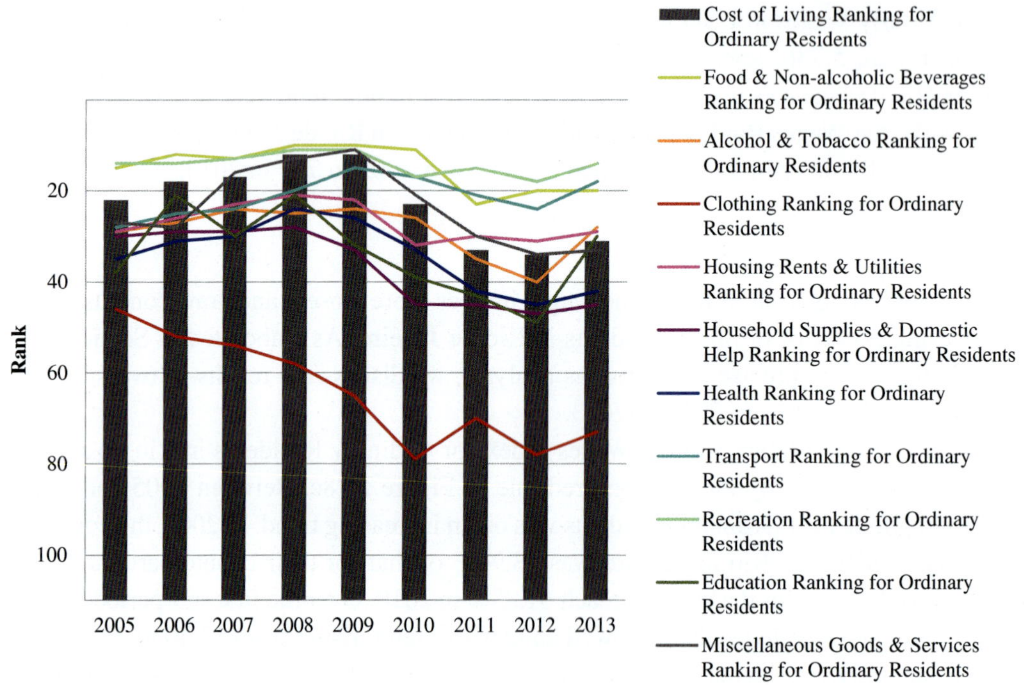

Source: Asia Competitiveness Institute

Figure 5.79b: Gross Hourly Wages in USD and Wages Ranking for Ordinary Residents in Rome, Italy

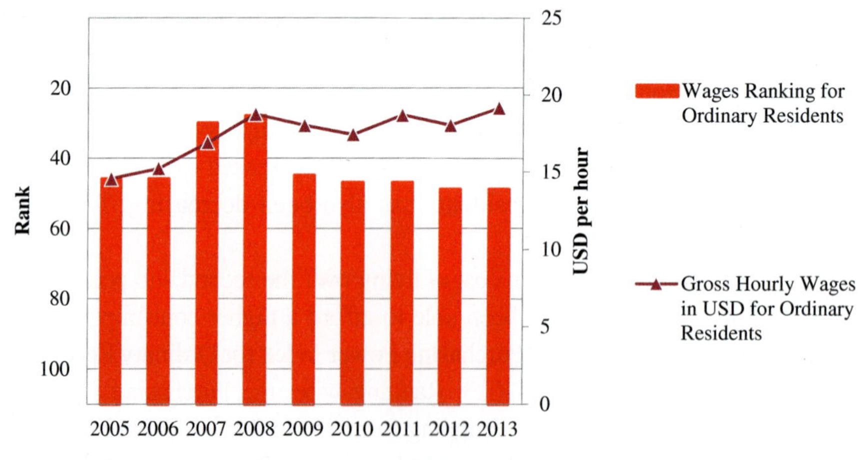

Source: Asia Competitiveness Institute

ROME
Italy

Figure 5.79c: Cost of Living, Wages and Purchasing Power Indices and Purchasing Power Ranking for Ordinary Residents in Rome, Italy

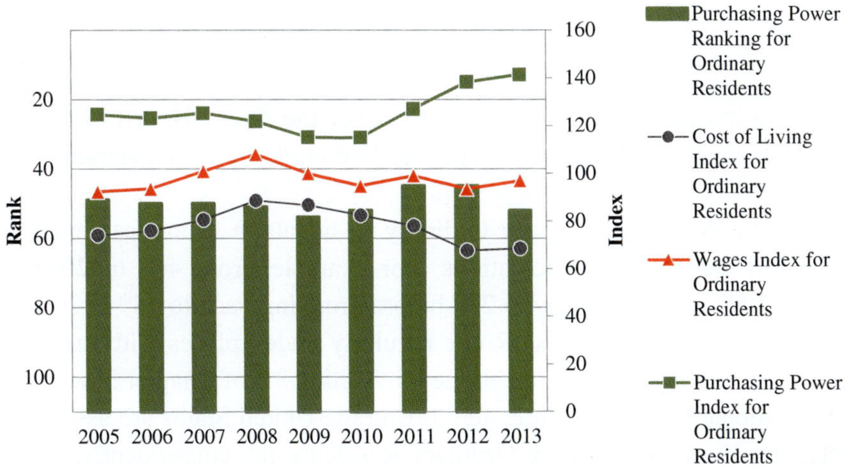

Source: Asia Competitiveness Institute

Figure 5.79a

With an estimated population of 2.9 million, Rome is the largest city in Italy and the fourth largest city in the European Union by population within city limits. The city's Cost of Living Ranking for Ordinary Residents, as denoted by the grey bars, declined from 22nd to 23rd between 2005 and 2010, but rose from 33rd to 31st between 2011 and 2013 (see Figure 5.79a). As explained in Section 3.4.2 of Chapter 3, for a more rigorous comparison of rankings, we have split the analysis into two sub-periods.

From 2005 to 2010, Transport Ranking jumped 11 places from 28th to 17th. Food & Non-alcoholic Beverages Ranking moved up four spots from 15th to 11th over the first sub-period. Health Ranking rose from 35th in 2005 to 33rd in 2010. In contrast, Clothing Ranking fell 33 places from 46th to 79th between 2005 and 2010. Housing Rents & Utilities Ranking slipped three spots from 29th to 32nd over the same sub-period. Education Ranking declined from 38th in 2005 to 39th in 2010.

Between 2011 and 2013, Education Ranking climbed 13 places from 43rd to 30th. Food & Non-alcoholic Beverages and Transport Rankings jumped three spots from 23rd to 20th and 21st to 18th, respectively, over the second sub-period. Housing Rents & Utilities Ranking moved up one place from 30th in 2011 to 29th in 2013. Recreation remained as the highest ranked category from 2011 and 2013 as its ranking rose from 15th to 14th over the same sub-period. Health Ranking fell from 42nd in 2011 to 45th in 2012 before jumping back to 42nd in 2013. Clothing was consistently the lowest ranked category in both sub-periods as its ranking slipped three places from 70th to 73rd between 2011 and 2013.

Figure 5.79b

After experiencing steady growth from 2005 to 2008, the Gross Hourly Wages in USD for Ordinary Residents in Rome, as denoted by the red line in Figure 5.79b, started to fluctuate and ended up at US$19.15 in 2013.

Ranking-wise, the Wages Ranking for Ordinary Residents in Rome, as depicted by the red bars, has exhibited considerable fluctuations. For example, from 46th in 2005, the ranking jumped to 30th in 2007. It rose slightly to 28th before dropping back to 45th in 2009.

Such fluctuations happened because Rome regularly traded places with the 16 cities in the United States on the ranking table. As mentioned in Section 3.3 of Chapter 3, wage data are only available at the national level. Therefore, all cities in the United States are assumed to have the same Gross Hourly Wages in USD for Ordinary Residents and consequently, the same Wages Ranking for Ordinary Residents. Thus, whenever Rome surpassed any city in the United States, it overtook the other 15 cities as well. The same would hold in the reverse situation. These were precisely what happened in 2007 and 2009 and the result was the large fluctuations in Rome's ranking as observed.

Figure 5.79c

Let us now analyse the cost of living and wages indices more closely and draw conclusions about the purchasing power of ordinary residents in Rome. As elaborated in Section 3.4.2 of Chapter 3, for a more precise and rigorous analysis, we discuss the results in two sub-periods: from 2005 to 2010 and from 2011 to 2013.

The Cost of Living Index and the Wages Index for Ordinary Residents in Rome are represented respectively by the grey and red line in Figure 5.79c. Over the first sub-period (2005–2010), the Cost of Living Index for Ordinary Residents exhibited moderate fluctuations. In 2005, the cost of living for ordinary residents in Rome was 74.01% of that for their counterparts in New York (the base city). It rose to peak at 88.49% in 2008 before dropping to 82.34% in 2010. Over the first sub-period, the Wages Index for Ordinary Residents also followed a similar pattern. This index was also on an upward trend from 2005 to 2008 before embarking on a decreasing trend. The index value in 2010 was 94.67.

When both wages and cost of living were rising, wages rose more slowly than the latter. In addition, when both were falling, wages dropped faster than cost of living. As a result, ordinary residents in Rome could not afford the same consumption level over time throughout the first sub-period. This is reflected in the Purchasing Power Index for Ordinary Residents in Rome, which is represented by the green line in Figure 5.79c. Between 2005 and 2010, this index

ROME
Italy

dropped from 124.69 to 114.98. Meanwhile, the Purchasing Power Ranking for Ordinary Residents in Rome, as represented by the green bars, deteriorated over the first sub-period. It dropped from 49th in 2005 to 54th in 2009 before recovering slightly to 52nd in 2010.

Over the second sub-period (2011–2013), the Cost of Living Index for Ordinary Residents has been on a decreasing trend. In 2011, the cost of living for ordinary residents in Rome was 77.91% of that for their counterparts in New York. It decreased over the years to 68.53% in 2013. The Wages Index for Ordinary Residents has also been decreasing, dropping from 98.96 in 2011 to 96.87 in 2013.

Wages have decreased more slowly than cost of living over the second sub-period. Thus, ordinary residents in Rome have actually been able to afford more goods and services over time during these years. This is reflected in the Purchasing Power Index for Ordinary Residents, which rose from 127.01 to 141.37 between 2011 and 2013. Ranking-wise, the Purchasing Power Ranking for Ordinary Residents has been improving, rising from 45th in 2011 and 2012 to 42nd in 2013.

Finally, we note that the Purchasing Power Index for Ordinary Residents in Rome has always been higher than 100.00 — the base index value. Thus, ordinary residents in Rome have consistently been able to afford a higher consumption level than their counterparts in New York, given the same number of working hours.

SAN FRANCISCO
United States

Figure 5.80a: Cost of Living and 10 Consumption Categories Rankings for Ordinary Residents in San Francisco, United States

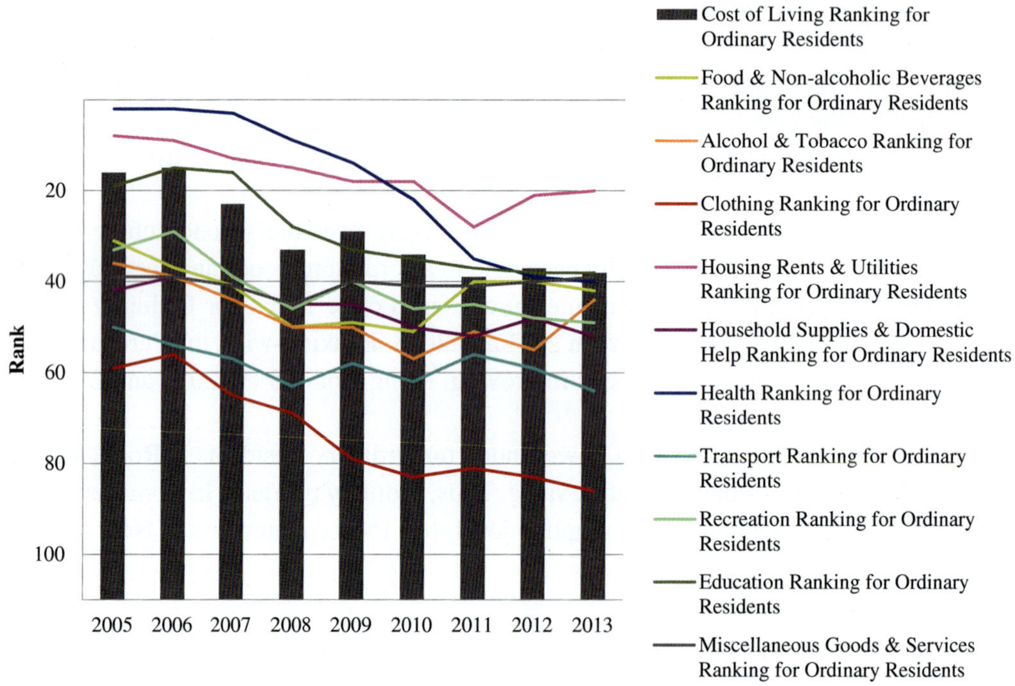

Source: Asia Competitiveness Institute

Figure 5.80b: Gross Hourly Wages in USD and Wages Ranking for Ordinary Residents in San Francisco, United States

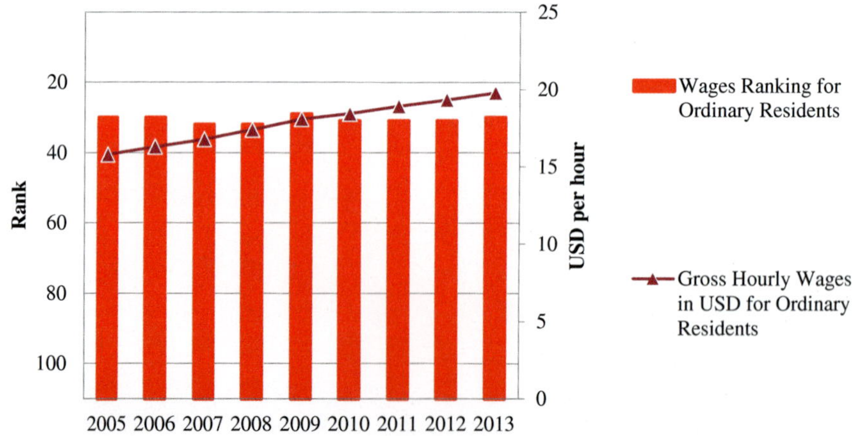

Source: Asia Competitiveness Institute

SAN FRANCISCO
United States

Figure 5.80c: Cost of Living, Wages and Purchasing Power Indices and Purchasing Power Ranking for Ordinary Residents in San Francisco, United States

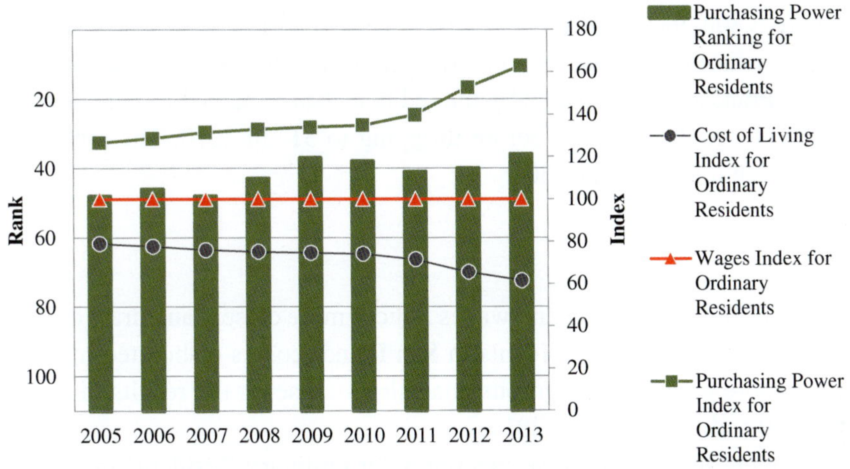

Source: Asia Competitiveness Institute

Figure 5.80a

Renowned for its cool summers and diverse mix of architecture, particularly the iconic Golden Gate Bridge, San Francisco is the fourth most populous city in the state of California. The city's Cost of Living Ranking for Ordinary Residents, as represented by the grey bars, fell from 16th to 34th between 2005 and 2010, and rose from 39th to 38th between 2011 and 2013 (see Figure 5.80a). As elaborated in Section 3.4.2 of Chapter 3, for a more precise comparison of rankings, we have split the analysis into two sub-periods.

The rankings of all 10 categories declined over the first sub-period from 2005 and 2010. In particular, Food & Non-alcoholic Beverages and Health Rankings both slipped 20 places from 31st to 51st and second to 22nd, respectively, between 2005 and 2010. Education Ranking moved down 16 spots from 19th in 2005 to 35th in 2010. Transport Ranking fell 12 places from 50th to 62nd over the first sub-period. Housing Rents & Utilities Ranking went down 10 spots from eighth in 2005 to 18th in 2010.

From 2011 to 2013, Housing Rents & Utilities Ranking jumped eight places from 28th to 20th, making it the highest ranked category throughout the second sub-period. In contrast, Transport Ranking slipped eight spots from 56th in 2011 to 64th in 2013. Clothing and Health Rankings both fell five places from 81st to 86th and 35th to 40th, respectively, over the second sub-period. Clothing thus remained as the lowest ranked category in both sub-periods. Food & Non-alcoholic Beverages Ranking moved down two spots from 40th in 2011 to 42nd in 2013. Education Ranking declined from 37th to 38th over the same sub-period.

SAN FRANCISCO
United States

Figure 5.80b

The Gross Hourly Wages in USD for Ordinary Residents in San Francisco, as represented by the red line in Figure 5.80b, increased gradually from US$15.79 in 2005 to US$19.77 in 2013.

Despite the consistent increase in the average wage, the Wages Ranking for Ordinary Residents in San Francisco, as depicted by the red bars, has remained rather stable. From 30th in 2005, it rose slightly to 29th in 2009 before dropping to 31st in 2010. The ranking remained at 31st until 2013, when it rose back to 30th.

Figure 5.80c

Let us now analyse the cost of living and wages indices more closely and draw conclusions about the purchasing power of ordinary residents in San Francisco. As elaborated in Section 3.4.2 of Chapter 3, for a more precise and rigorous analysis, we discuss the results in two sub-periods: from 2005 to 2010 and from 2011 to 2013.

The Cost of Living Index and the Wages Index for Ordinary Residents in San Francisco are represented respectively by the grey and red line in Figure 5.80c. As mentioned in Section 3.3 of Chapter 3, wage data are only available at the national level and not by cities. Therefore, wages in all cities in the United States are assumed to be the same. As a result, San Francisco, being a city in the United States, shares a common Wages Index for Ordinary Residents with the base city New York (whose index value is 100.00) over the entire study period (2005–2013).

Between 2005 and 2010, the Cost of Living Index for Ordinary Residents was on a decreasing trend. In 2005, the cost of living for ordinary residents in San Francisco was 78.94% of that for their counterparts in New York. It dropped steadily over the years to reach 74.12% in 2010. Since the Wages Index for Ordinary Residents is constant across the years, how the Purchasing Power Index for Ordinary Residents in San Francisco (or any other cities in the United States) changes depends only on variations in the Cost of Living Index for Ordinary Residents. Thus, the steady decline of the latter index resulted in the purchasing power index following an upward trend over the first sub-period. As represented by the green line in Figure 5.80c, this index rose from 126.29 in 2005 to 134.92 in 2010. Ranking-wise, the Purchasing Power Ranking for Ordinary Residents in San Francisco, which is represented by the green bars, improved from 48th in 2005 to 38th in 2010.

Over the second sub-period (2011–2013), the Cost of Living Index for Ordinary Residents has steadily declined. In 2011, the cost of living for ordinary residents in San Francisco was 71.52% of that for their counterparts in New York. It dropped to 61.39% in 2013. As a result, the Purchasing Power Index for Ordinary Residents has increased, rising from 139.82 in 2011 to 162.89 in 2013. Meanwhile, the Purchasing Power Ranking for Ordinary Residents has also been improving, climbing from 41st in 2011 to 36th in 2013.

SAN FRANCISCO
United States

Finally, we note that over the entire study period (2005–2013), the Purchasing Power Index for Ordinary Residents in San Francisco has always been above 100.00 — the base index value. This indicates that ordinary residents in San Francisco have consistently been able to consume more goods and services than their counterparts in New York, given the same number of working hours.

SANTIAGO
Chile

Figure 5.81a: Cost of Living and 10 Consumption Categories Rankings for Ordinary Residents in Santiago, Chile

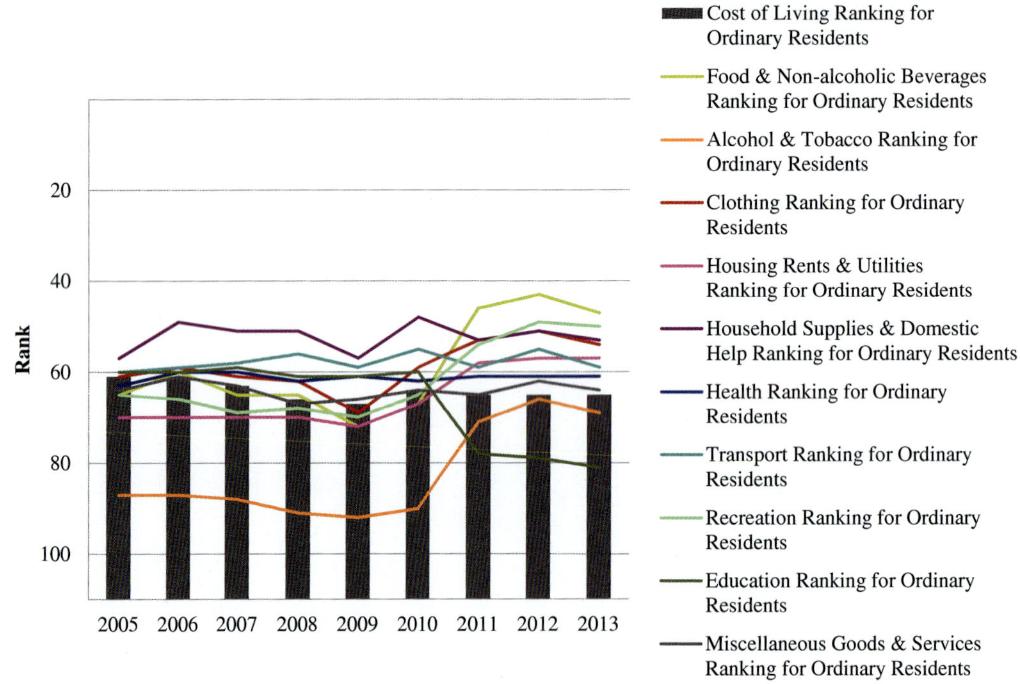

Source: Asia Competitiveness Institute

Figure 5.81b: Gross Hourly Wages in USD and Wages Ranking for Ordinary Residents in Santiago, Chile

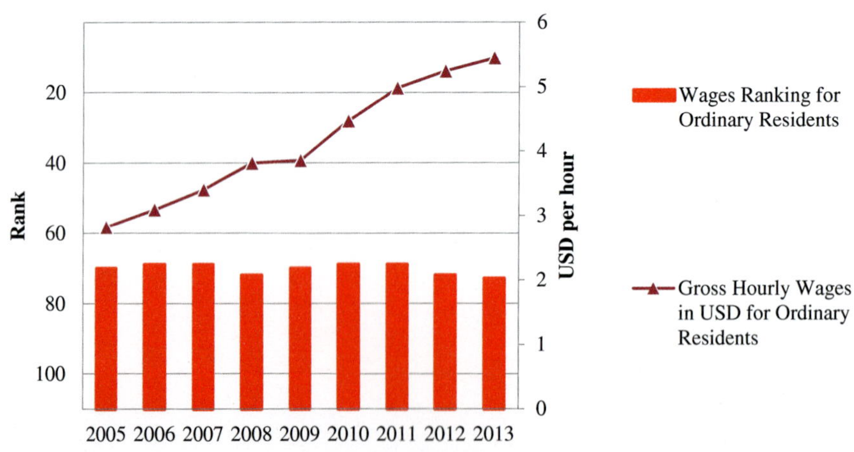

Source: Asia Competitiveness Institute

SANTIAGO
Chile

Figure 5.81c: Cost of Living, Wages and Purchasing Power Indices and Purchasing Power Ranking for Ordinary Residents in Santiago, Chile

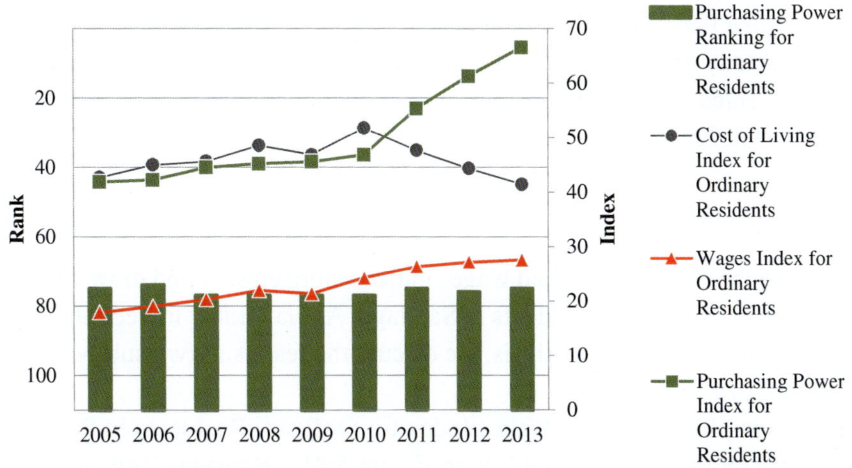

Source: Asia Competitiveness Institute

Figure 5.81a

Known for its 19th century neoclassical architecture, Santiago is the capital and largest city of Chile with a population of approximately 5 million. The city's Cost of Living Ranking for Ordinary Residents, as shown in the grey bars, fell from 61st to 64th between 2005 and 2010, and remained at 65th between 2011 and 2013 (see Figure 5.81a). As explained in Section 3.4.2 of Chapter 3, for a more rigorous comparison of rankings, we have split the analysis into two sub-periods.

From 2005 to 2010, Transport Ranking climbed five places from 60th to 55th. Housing Rents & Utilities Ranking jumped three spots from 70th in 2005 to 67th in 2010. Health Ranking rose from 63rd to 62nd over the first sub-period. In contrast, Food & Non-alcoholic Beverages Ranking slipped two places from 65th to 67th between 2005 and 2010. Education Ranking went up from 60th in 2005 to 61st in 2008 and 2009 before falling back to 60th in 2010.

From 2011 to 2013, Housing Rents & Utilities Ranking moved up one spot from 58th to 57th. Health Ranking stayed unchanged at 61st throughout the second sub-period. Transport Ranking rose from 59th in 2011 to 55th in 2012 before dropping back to 59th in 2013. Education Ranking slipped three places from 78th to 81st between 2011 and 2013, making it the lowest ranked category for the entire second sub-period. Food & Non-alcoholic Beverages Ranking moved down from 46th in 2011 to 47th in 2013. Nonetheless, it remained as the highest ranked category throughout the second sub-period.

SANTIAGO
Chile

Figure 5.81b

The Gross Hourly Wages in USD for Ordinary Residents in Santiago, as shown by the red line in Figure 5.81b, grew fairly steadily from US$2.82 in 2005 to US$5.45 in 2013.

In spite of the steady growth in the wage level, the Wages Ranking for Ordinary Residents in Santiago, as represented by the red bars, has deteriorated over the study period. It dropped from 70th in 2005 to 73rd in 2013.

Figure 5.81c

Let us now analyse the cost of living and wages indices more closely and draw conclusions about the purchasing power of ordinary residents in Santiago. As elaborated in Section 3.4.2 of Chapter 3, for a more precise and rigorous analysis, we discuss the results in two sub-periods: from 2005 to 2010 and from 2011 to 2013.

The Cost of Living Index and the Wages Index for Ordinary Residents in Santiago are represented respectively by the grey and red line in Figure 5.81c. Between 2005 and 2010, the Cost of Living Index for Ordinary Residents was on an increasing trend. In 2005, the cost of living for ordinary residents in Santiago was 42.68% of that for their counterparts in New York (the base city). It rose over the years to reach 51.76% in 2010. Over the first sub-period, the Wages Index for Ordinary Residents was also on an increasing trend, rising from 17.87 in 2005 to 24.24 in 2010.

Wages generally rose faster than cost of living, so throughout the first sub-period, ordinary residents in Santiago could afford more goods and services over time. This is reflected in the Purchasing Power Index for Ordinary Residents in Santiago, which is represented by the green line in Figure 5.81c. Between 2005 and 2010, this index rose from 41.88 to 46.84. Meanwhile, the Purchasing Power Ranking for Ordinary Residents in Santiago, as represented by the green bars, deteriorated over the first sub-period. It dropped from 75th in 2005 to 77th in 2007 and stagnated there for the rest of the first sub-period.

Over the second sub-period (2011–2013), the Cost of Living Index for Ordinary Residents has been on a decreasing trend. In 2011, the cost of living for ordinary residents in Santiago was 47.63% of that for their counterparts in New York. It decreased to 41.42% in 2013. In contrast, the Wages Index for Ordinary Residents has been on an upward trend, albeit rather modestly. The index rose from 26.36 in 2011 to 27.56 in 2013.

The combined trends of increasing wages and decreasing cost of living have enabled ordinary residents in Santiago to afford a higher consumption level over time throughout the second sub-period. This is reflected in the Purchasing Power Index for Ordinary Residents, which rose from 55.34 to 66.54 between 2011 and 2013. Despite this positive showing of the index, the Purchasing Power Ranking for Ordinary Residents has been relatively stable. It dropped from 75th in 2011 to 76th in 2012 before recovering to 75th in 2013.

SANTIAGO
Chile

Finally, we note that over the entire study period (2005–2013), the Purchasing Power Index for Ordinary Residents in Santiago has consistently been lower than 100.00 — the base index value. Thus, ordinary residents in Santiago have only been able to afford a lower consumption level than their counterparts in New York, given the same number of working hours.

SAO PAULO
Brazil

Figure 5.82a: Cost of Living and 10 Consumption Categories Rankings for Ordinary Residents in Sao Paulo, Brazil

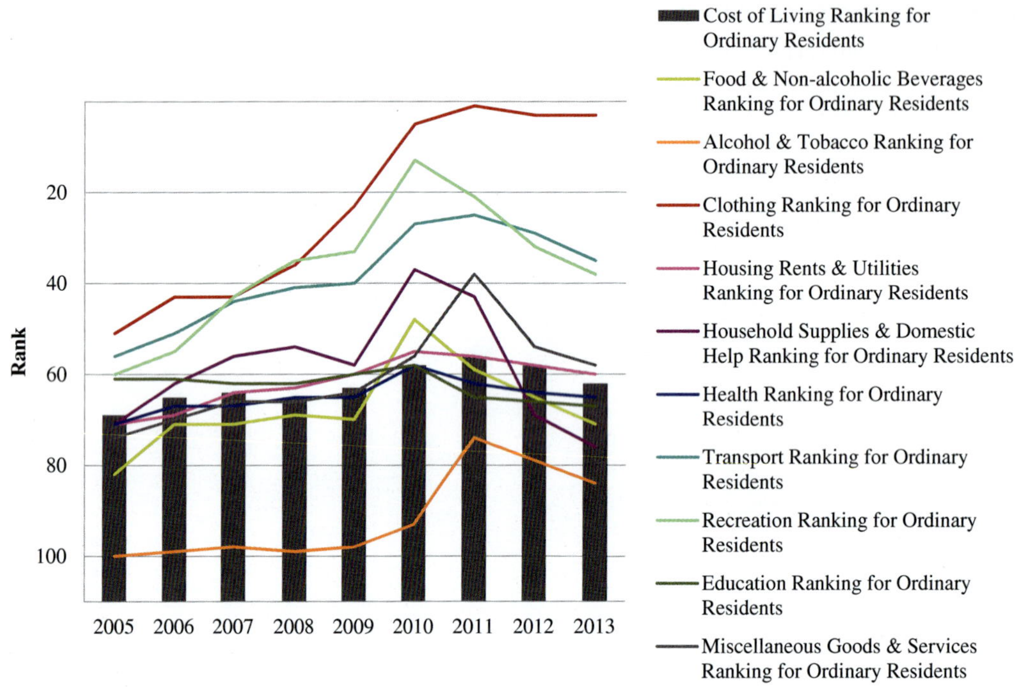

Source: Asia Competitiveness Institute

Figure 5.82b: Gross Hourly Wages in USD and Wages Ranking for Ordinary Residents in Sao Paulo, Brazil

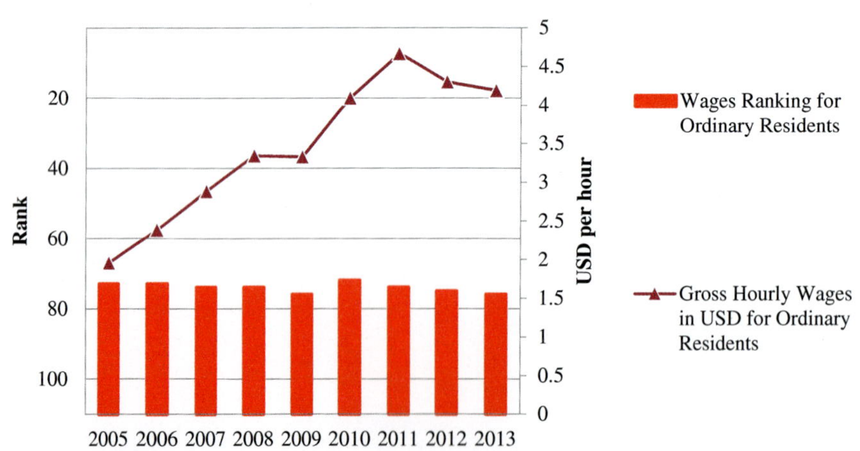

Source: Asia Competitiveness Institute

SAO PAULO
Brazil

Figure 5.82c: Cost of Living, Wages and Purchasing Power Indices and Purchasing Power Ranking for Ordinary Residents in Sao Paulo, Brazil

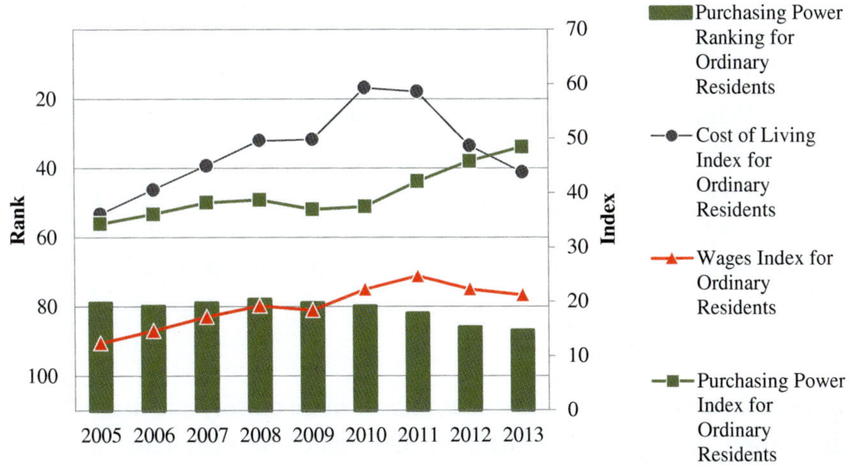

Source: Asia Competitiveness Institute

Figure 5.82a

With an estimated population of 11.9 million, Sao Paulo is the most populous city in Brazil, in the Americas and in the Western Hemisphere. The city's Cost of Living Ranking for Ordinary Residents, as denoted by the grey bars, rose from 69th to 58th between 2005 and 2010, and declined from 56th to 62nd between 2011 and 2013 (see Figure 5.82a). As elaborated in Section 3.4.2 of Chapter 3, for a more precise comparison of rankings, we have split the analysis into two sub-periods.

The rankings of all 10 categories went up over the first sub-period from 2005 to 2010. In particular, Food & Non-alcoholic Beverages Ranking climbed 34 places from 82nd in 2005 to 48th in 2010. Transport Ranking jumped 29 spots from 56th to 27th between 2005 and 2010. Housing Rents & Utilities Ranking moved up 16 places from 71st to 55th over the first sub-period. Health Ranking rose from 71st in 2005 to 58th in 2010. Education Ranking went up more modestly from 61st to 58th over the same sub-period.

In contrast, all categories saw a dip in rankings in the second sub-period between 2011 and 2013. Household Supplies & Domestic Help registered the most significant decline in ranking as it fell 33 places from 43rd in 2011 to 76th in 2013, making it the second lowest ranked category in 2013 after Alcohol & Tobacco at 84th. Food & Non-alcoholic Beverages Ranking slipped 12 spots from 59th to 71st over the second sub-period. Housing Rents & Utilities Ranking went down four places from 56th to 60th between 2011 and 2013. Health Ranking fell three places from 62nd in 2011 to 65th in 2013. Education Ranking moved down two spots from 65th to 67th over the

SAO PAULO
Brazil

same sub-period. Likewise, Clothing Ranking declined from first in 2011 to third in 2013, making Sao Paulo the third most expensive city in this category in 2013.

Figure 5.82b

The Gross Hourly Wages in USD for Ordinary Residents in Sao Paulo, as represented by the red line in Figure 5.82b, grew rather consistently from US$1.96 in 2005 to US$4.67 in 2011. Thereafter, Sao Paulo's wage level has been on a decreasing trend, reaching US$4.19 in 2013.

Meanwhile, the Wages Ranking for Ordinary Residents in Sao Paulo, as shown by the red bars, has generally deteriorated. It dropped from 73rd in 2005 to 76th in 2013.

Figure 5.82c

Let us now analyse the cost of living and wages indices more closely and draw conclusions about the purchasing power of ordinary residents in Sao Paulo. As elaborated in Section 3.4.2 of Chapter 3, for a more precise and rigorous analysis, we discuss the results in two sub-periods: from 2005 to 2010 and from 2011 to 2013.

The Cost of Living Index and the Wages Index for Ordinary Residents in Sao Paulo are represented respectively by the grey and red line in Figure 5.82c. Over the first sub-period (2005–2010), the Cost of Living Index for Ordinary Residents was on an increasing trend. In 2005, the cost of living for ordinary residents in Sao Paulo was 36.11% of that for their counterparts in New York (the base city). It rose over the years to reach 59.31% in 2010. Over the first sub-period, the Wages Index for Ordinary Residents also followed an upward trend, rising from 12.40 to 22.23 in 2010.

Wages generally rose faster than cost of living, so throughout the first sub-period, ordinary residents in Sao Paulo were able to afford more goods and services over time. This is reflected in the Purchasing Power Index for Ordinary Residents in Sao Paulo, which is represented by the green line in Figure 5.82c. Between 2005 and 2010, this index rose from 34.34 to 37.48. Meanwhile, the Purchasing Power Ranking for Ordinary Residents in Sao Paulo, which is represented by the green bars, was stable over the first sub-period. It only fluctuated among 78th, 79th and 80th during these years. Sao Paulo's ranking in 2010 was 80th, down from 79th in 2005.

Over the second sub-period (2011–2013), the Cost of Living Index for Ordinary Residents has been on a decreasing trend. In 2011, the cost of living for ordinary residents in Sao Paulo was 58.62% of that for their counterparts in New York. It decreased to 43.77% in 2013. The Wages Index for Ordinary Residents has also been decreasing. It dropped from 24.68 in 2011 to 21.19 in 2013.

Wages have decreased more slowly than cost of living over the second sub-period. Thus, ordinary residents in Sao Paulo have actually been able to afford more goods and services over time during these years. This is reflected in the Purchasing Power Index for Ordinary

Residents, which rose from 42.11 to 48.42 between 2011 and 2013. Ranking-wise, the Purchasing Power Ranking for Ordinary Residents has been deteriorating, dropping from 82nd in 2011 to 87th in 2013.

Finally, we note that the Purchasing Power Index for Ordinary Residents in Sao Paulo has consistently been lower than 100.00 — the base index value. Thus, ordinary residents in Sao Paulo have only been able to afford a lower consumption level than their counterparts in New York, given the same number of working hours.

SEATTLE
United States

Figure 5.83a: Cost of Living and 10 Consumption Categories Rankings for Ordinary Residents in Seattle, United States

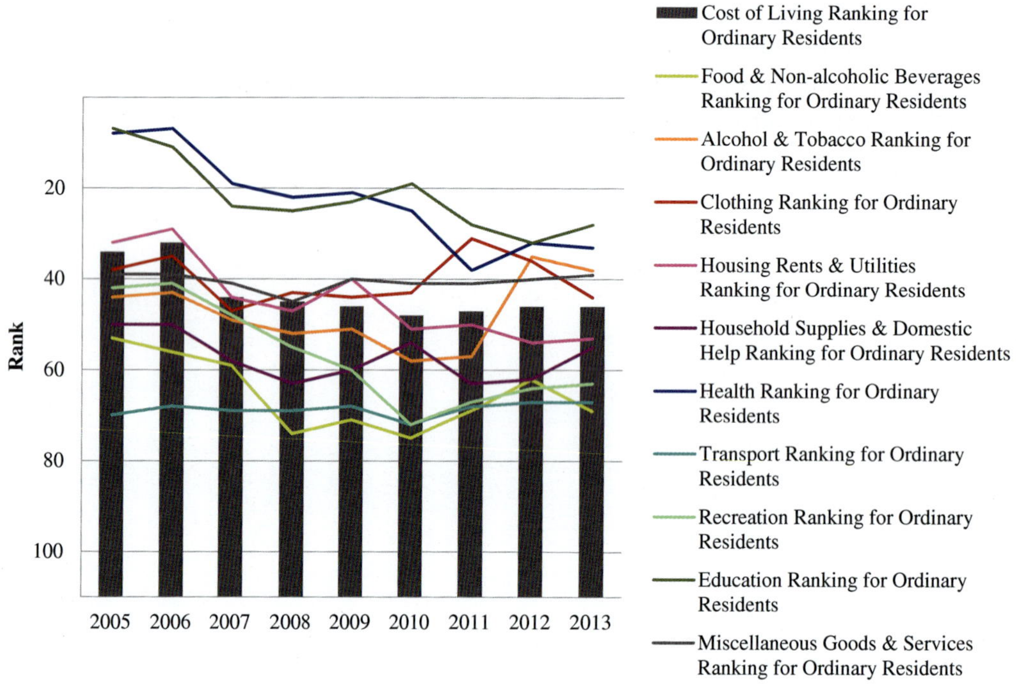

Source: Asia Competitiveness Institute

Figure 5.83b: Gross Hourly Wages in USD and Wages Ranking for Ordinary Residents in Seattle, United States

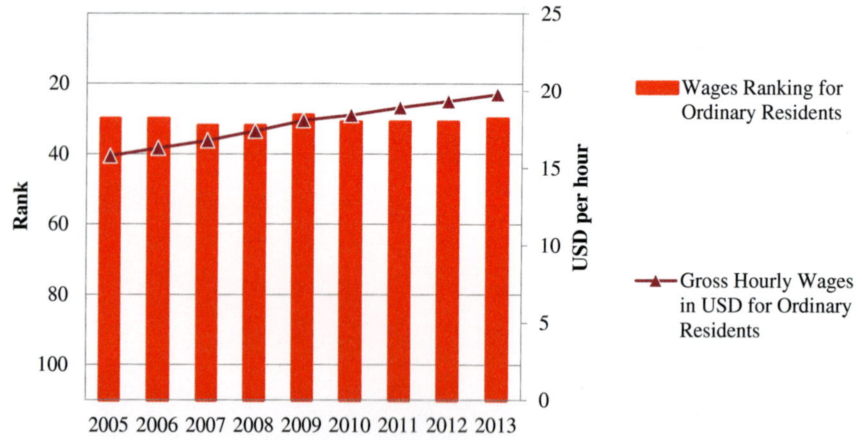

Source: Asia Competitiveness Institute

SEATTLE
United States

Figure 5.83c: Cost of Living, Wages and Purchasing Power Indices and Purchasing Power Ranking for Ordinary Residents in Seattle, United States

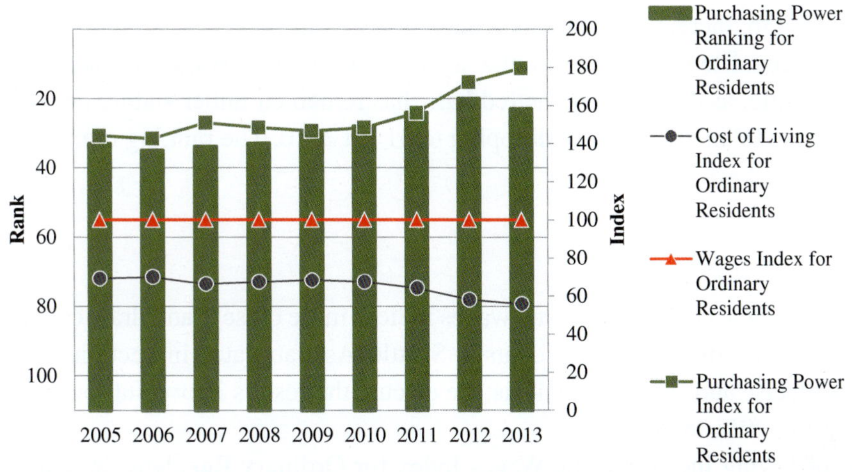

Source: Asia Competitiveness Institute

Figure 5.83a

Seattle is the largest city in the state of Washington and one of America's hotbeds for start-up businesses, particularly in clean technologies. The city's Cost of Living Ranking for Ordinary Residents, as represented by the grey bars, fell from 34th to 48th between 2005 and 2010, and rose from 47th to 46th between 2011 and 2013 (see Figure 5.83a). As explained in Section 3.4.2 of Chapter 3, for a more rigorous comparison of rankings, we have split the analysis into two sub-periods.

The rankings of all 10 categories declined over the first sub-period from 2005 to 2010. In particular, Food & Non-alcoholic Beverages Ranking slipped 22 places from 53rd in 2005 to 75th in 2010. Housing Rents & Utilities Ranking fell 19 spots from 32nd to 51st between 2005 and 2010. Health Ranking went down 17 places from eighth to 25th over the first sub-period. Education Ranking fell 12 spots from seventh in 2005 to 19th in 2010. Transport Ranking declined more modestly from 70th to 72nd over the same sub-period.

Between 2011 and 2013, Health Ranking moved up five places from 38th to 33rd. Transport Ranking jumped one spot from 68th in 2011 to 67th in 2013. In contrast, Housing Rents & Utilities Ranking slipped three places from 50th to 53rd over the second sub-period. Food & Non-alcoholic Beverages Ranking rose from 69th in 2011 to 62nd in 2012 before falling back to 69th in 2013, making it the lowest ranked category in 2013. Education Ranking fell from 28th in 2011 to 32nd in 2012 but jumped back to 28th in 2013. Consequently, Education was the highest ranked category in 2013.

SEATTLE
United States

Figure 5.83b

The Gross Hourly Wages in USD for Ordinary Residents in Seattle, as represented by the red line in Figure 5.83b, increased gradually from US$15.79 in 2005 to US$19.77 in 2013.

Despite the consistent increase in the average wage, the Wages Ranking for Ordinary Residents in Seattle, as depicted by the red bars, has remained rather stable. From 30th in 2005, it rose slightly to 29th in 2009 before dropping to 31st in 2010. The ranking remained at 31st until 2013, when it rose back to 30th.

Figure 5.83c

Let us now analyse the cost of living and wages indices more closely and draw conclusions about the purchasing power of ordinary residents in Seattle. As elaborated in Section 3.4.2 of Chapter 3, for a more precise and rigorous analysis, we discuss the results in two sub-periods: from 2005 to 2010 and from 2011 to 2013.

The Cost of Living Index and the Wages Index for Ordinary Residents in Seattle are represented respectively by the grey and red line in Figure 5.83c. As mentioned in Section 3.3 of Chapter 3, wage data are only available at the national level and not by cities. Therefore, wages in all cities in the United States are assumed to be the same. As a result, Seattle, being a city in the United States, shares a common Wages Index for Ordinary Residents with the base city New York (whose index value is 100.00) over the entire study period (2005–2013).

Between 2005 and 2010, the Cost of Living Index for Ordinary Residents was on a decreasing trend. In 2005, the cost of living for ordinary residents in Seattle was 69.29% of that for their counterparts in New York. It dropped steadily over the years to reach 67.38% in 2010. Since the Wages Index for Ordinary Residents is constant across the years, how the Purchasing Power Index for Ordinary Residents in Seattle (or any other cities in the United States) changes depends only on variations in the Cost of Living Index for Ordinary Residents. Thus, the steady decline of the latter index resulted in the purchasing power index following an upward trend over the first sub-period. As represented by the green line in Figure 5.83c, this index rose from 144.31 in 2005 to 148.41 in 2010. The upward trend of the purchasing power index signifies the ability of ordinary residents in Seattle to afford more goods and services over time. Ranking-wise, the Purchasing Power Ranking for Ordinary Residents in Seattle, which is represented by the green bars, improved from 33rd in 2005 to 28th in 2010.

Over the second sub-period (2011–2013), the Cost of Living Index for Ordinary Residents has steadily declined. In 2011, the cost of living for ordinary residents in Seattle was 64.04% of that for their counterparts in New York. It dropped to 55.68% in 2013. As a result, the Purchasing Power Index for Ordinary Residents has steadily increased, rising from 156.15 in 2011 to 179.59 in 2013. Meanwhile, the Purchasing Power Ranking for Ordinary Residents has also been improving, albeit much more marginally. From 24th in 2011, it climbed to 23rd in 2013.

SEATTLE
United States

Finally, we note that over the entire study period (2005–2013), the Purchasing Power Index for Ordinary Residents in Seattle has always been above 100.00 — the base index value. This indicates that ordinary residents in Seattle have consistently been able to consume more goods and services than their counterparts in New York, given the same number of working hours.

SEOUL
South Korea

Figure 5.84a: Cost of Living and 10 Consumption Categories Rankings for Ordinary Residents in Seoul, South Korea

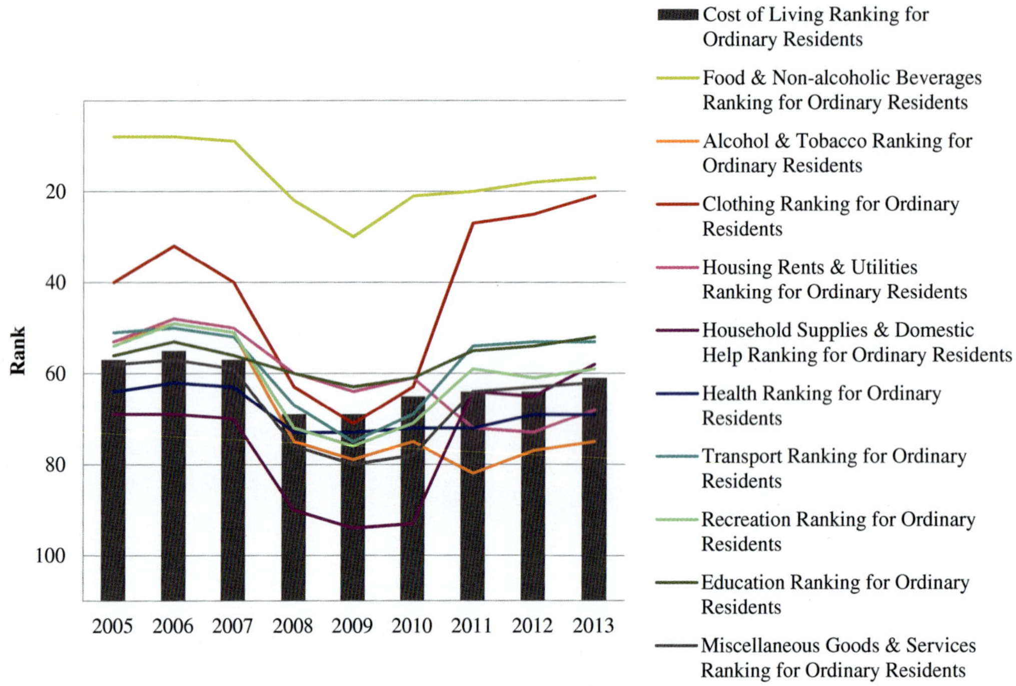

Source: Asia Competitiveness Institute

Figure 5.84b: Gross Hourly Wages in USD and Wages Ranking for Ordinary Residents in Seoul, South Korea

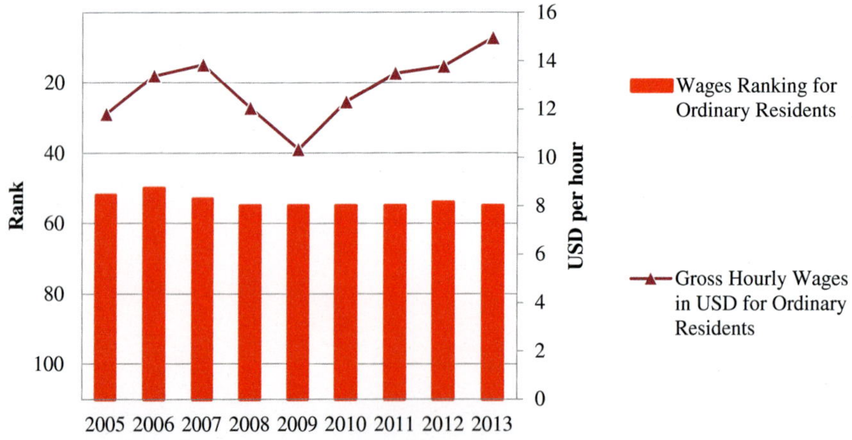

Source: Asia Competitiveness Institute

SEOUL
South Korea

Figure 5.84c: Cost of Living, Wages and Purchasing Power Indices and Purchasing Power Ranking for Ordinary Residents in Seoul, South Korea

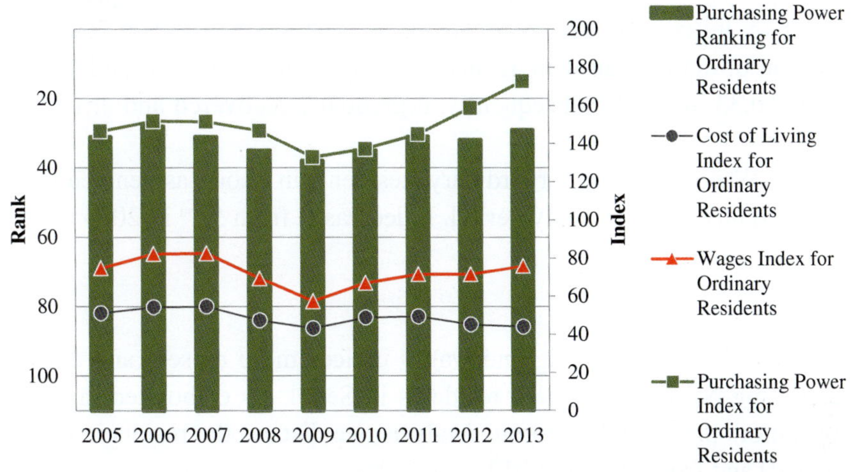

Source: Asia Competitiveness Institute

Figure 5.84a

With a history spanning more than 2,000 years, Seoul, the capital and largest metropolis of South Korea, is one of the world's most visited cities. The city's Cost of Living Ranking for Ordinary Residents, as shown in the grey bars, fell from 57th to 65th between 2005 and 2010, and rose from 64th to 61st between 2011 and 2013 (see Figure 5.84a). As elaborated in Section 3.4.2 of Chapter 3, for a more precise comparison of rankings, we have split the analysis into two sub-periods.

The rankings of all 10 categories went down over the first sub-period from 2005 to 2010. In particular, Transport Ranking fell 18 places from 51st in 2005 to 69th in 2010. Food & Non-alcoholic Beverages Ranking slipped 13 spots from eighth to 21st between 2005 and 2010. Housing Rents & Utilities and Health Rankings both moved down eight places from 53rd to 61st and 64th to 72nd, respectively, over the first sub-period. Education Ranking fell five spots from 56th in 2005 to 61st in 2010.

From 2011 to 2013, Alcohol & Tobacco Ranking jumped seven places from 82nd to 75th. Nonetheless, it remained as the lowest ranked category throughout the second sub-period. Housing Rents & Utilities Ranking moved up four spots from 72nd in 2011 to 68th in 2013. Health and Education Rankings rose from 72nd to 69th and 55th to 52nd, respectively, over the same sub-period. Food & Non-alcoholic Beverages Ranking jumped three places from 20th in 2011 to 17th in 2013, making it the highest ranked category in both sub-periods. Transport Ranking went up from 54th to 53rd between 2011 and 2013.

SEOUL
South Korea

Figure 5.84b

The Gross Hourly Wages in USD for Ordinary Residents in Seoul, as represented by the red line in Figure 5.84b, initially rose from US$11.80 in 2005 to US$13.85 in 2007. However, due to the depreciation of the Korean won against the US dollar, Seoul's wage level dropped considerably to US$10.33 in 2009. Subsequently, it gradually recovered and arrived at US$14.96 in 2013.

Meanwhile, the Wages Ranking for Ordinary Residents in Seoul, as denoted by the red bars, has deteriorated slightly over the study period. It decreased from 52nd in 2005 to 55th in 2013.

Figure 5.84c

Let us now analyse the cost of living and wages indices more closely and draw conclusions about the purchasing power of ordinary residents in Seoul. As elaborated in Section 3.4.2 of Chapter 3, for a more precise and rigorous analysis, we discuss the results in two sub-periods: from 2005 to 2010 and from 2011 to 2013.

The Cost of Living Index and the Wages Index for Ordinary Residents in Seoul are represented respectively by the grey and red line in Figure 5.84c. Over the first sub-period (2005–2010), the Cost of Living Index for Ordinary Residents exhibited considerable fluctuations. In 2005, the cost of living for ordinary residents in Seoul was 51.02% of that for their counterparts in New York (the base city). It first rose to 54.45% in 2007 and then steadily declined to 43.06% in 2009. Finally, between 2009 and 2010, the index recovered slightly to 48.69% which was lower than its initial value in 2005. Over the first sub-period, the Wages Index for Ordinary Residents also tracked a similar pattern. Overall, the wages index value in 2010 (66.77) was lower than it was in 2005 (74.74).

The Purchasing Power Index for Ordinary Residents in Seoul, as represented by the green line in Figure 5.84c, fluctuated in the same manner as the wages and cost of living indices. It first increased over 2005–2007, decreased between 2007 and 2009 and then recovered slightly between 2009 and 2010. All in all, the index value in 2010 (137.14) was lower than it was in 2005 (146.51). This signifies that the purchasing power of ordinary residents in Seoul was eroded over the first sub-period and they could not afford the same consumption level in 2010 as that in 2005. Ranking-wise, the Purchasing Power Ranking for Ordinary Residents in Seoul, as represented by the green bars, also fluctuated quite substantially. Seoul's ranking in 2010 (35th) was lower than its ranking in 2005 (31st).

Over the second sub-period (2011–2013), the Cost of Living Index for Ordinary Residents has been on a decreasing trend. In 2011, the cost of living for ordinary residents in Seoul was 49.27% of that for their counterparts in New York. It decreased to 43.84% in 2013. In contrast, the Wages Index for Ordinary Residents has been improving. Between 2011 and 2013, it rose from 71.38 in 2011 to 75.69 in 2013.

SEOUL
South Korea

The combined trends of increasing wages and decreasing cost of living have enabled ordinary residents in Seoul to afford more goods and services over time throughout the second sub-period. This is reflected in the Purchasing Power Index for Ordinary Residents, which rose from 144.88 in 2011 to 172.64 in 2013. Ranking-wise, the Purchasing Power Ranking for Ordinary Residents has also been improving, rising from 31st in 2011 to 29th in 2013.

Finally, we note that the Purchasing Power Index for Ordinary Residents in Seoul has always been higher than 100.00 — the base index value. This indicates that ordinary residents in Seoul have been able to afford a higher consumption level than their counterparts in New York, given the same number of working hours.

SHANGHAI
China

Figure 5.85a: Cost of Living and 10 Consumption Categories Rankings for Ordinary Residents in Shanghai, China

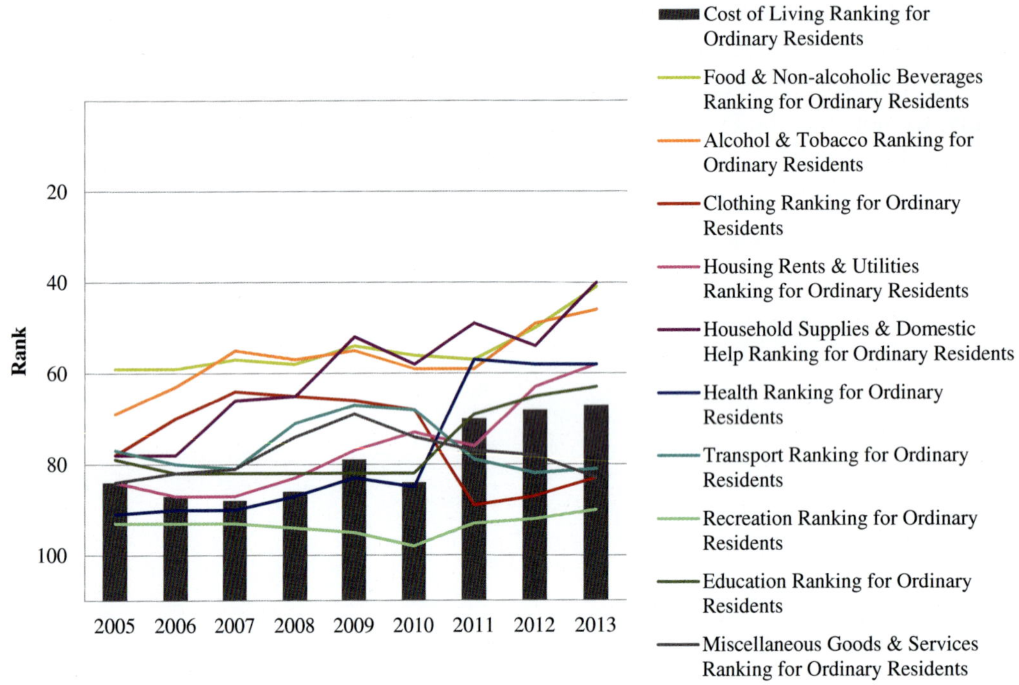

Source: Asia Competitiveness Institute

Figure 5.85b: Gross Hourly Wages in USD and Wages Ranking for Ordinary Residents in Shanghai, China

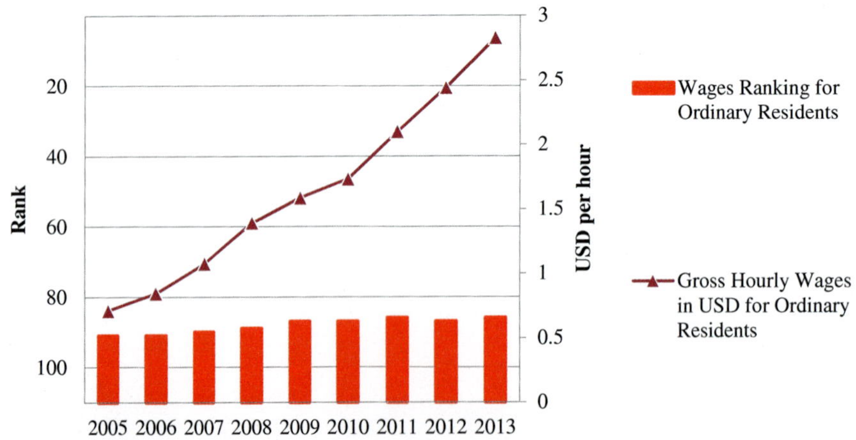

Source: Asia Competitiveness Institute

SHANGHAI
China

Figure 5.85c: Cost of Living, Wages and Purchasing Power Indices and Purchasing Power Ranking for Ordinary Residents in Shanghai, China

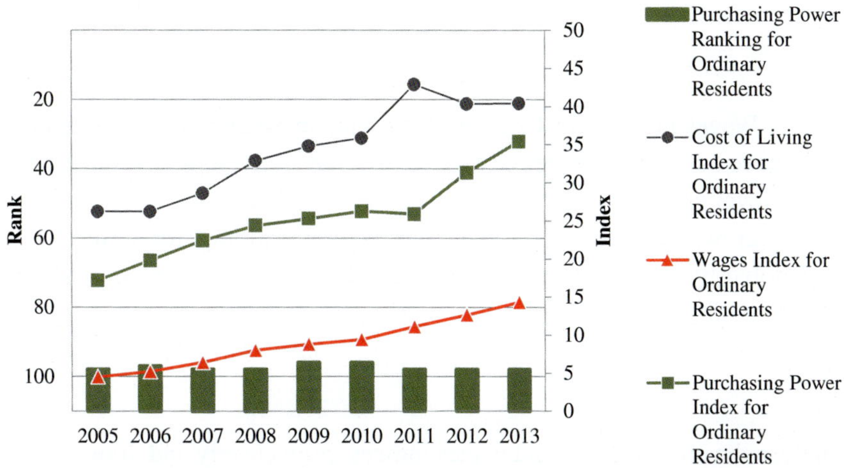

Source: Asia Competitiveness Institute

Figure 5.85a

Located at the heart of the Yangtze River Delta, Shanghai, the most populous city in China, has the busiest container port in the world and is also home to the country's heavy industries including steel and shipbuilding. The city's Cost of Living Ranking for Ordinary Residents, as denoted by the grey bars, fell from 84th in 2005 to 88th in 2007 before rising back to 84th in 2010, and rose from 70th to 67th between 2011 and 2013 (see Figure 5.85a). As explained in Section 3.4.2 of Chapter 3, for a more rigorous comparison of rankings, we have split the analysis into two sub-periods: from 2005 to 2010 and from 2011 to 2013.

Between 2005 and 2010, Household Supplies & Domestic Help Ranking climbed 20 places from 78th to 58th. Housing Rents & Utilities Ranking jumped 11 spots from 84th in 2005 to 73rd in 2010. Transport and Health Rankings moved up from 77th to 68th and 91st to 85th, respectively, over the first sub-period. Education Ranking, in contrast, fell three places from 79th in 2005 to 82nd in 2010.

From 2011 to 2013, Housing Rents & Utilities registered the most significant rise in ranking as it climbed 18 places from 76th to 58th. Food & Non-alcoholic Beverages Ranking also rose sharply from 57th in 2011 to 41st in 2013. Household Supplies & Domestic Help became the highest ranked category in 2013 as its ranking jumped nine spots from 49th to 40th over the second sub-period. Education Ranking moved up six places from 69th to 63rd between 2011 and 2013. In contrast, Transport and Health Rankings declined from 79th to 81st and 57th to 58th, respectively, over the same sub-period. Recreation consistently remained as the lowest ranked

SHANGHAI
China

category in both sub-periods as its ranking dropped from 93rd in 2005 to 98th in 2010, and went up from 93rd in 2011 to 90th in 2013.

Figure 5.85b

The Gross Hourly Wages in USD for Ordinary Residents in Shanghai, as denoted by the red line in Figure 5.85b, have been on an increasing trend over the study period. From US$0.71 in 2005, Shanghai's wage level grew almost fourfold to US$2.83 in 2013.

Reflecting the growth of the wage level, the Wages Ranking for Ordinary Residents in Shanghai, as denoted by the red bars, has also steadily improved over the study period, rising from 91st in 2005 to 86th in 2013.

Figure 5.85c

Let us now analyse the cost of living and wages indices more closely and draw conclusions about the purchasing power of ordinary residents in Shanghai. As elaborated in Section 3.4.2 of Chapter 3, for a more precise and rigorous analysis, we discuss the results in two sub-periods: from 2005 to 2010 and from 2011 to 2013.

The Cost of Living Index and the Wages Index for Ordinary Residents in Shanghai are represented respectively by the grey and red line in Figure 5.85c. Between 2005 and 2010, the Cost of Living Index for Ordinary Residents was generally on an increasing trend. In 2005, the cost of living for ordinary residents in Shanghai was 26.20% of that for their counterparts in New York (the base city). It rose steadily over time to reach 35.83% in 2010. Over the same sub-period, the Wages Index for Ordinary Residents also increased significantly, rising from 4.50 in 2005 to 9.40 in 2010.

Wages increased faster than cost of living so throughout the first sub-period, ordinary residents in Shanghai were able to afford more goods and services over time. This is reflected in the Purchasing Power Index for Ordinary Residents in Shanghai, which is represented by the green line in Figure 5.85c. Between 2005 and 2010, this index increased steadily from 17.19 to 26.24. The Purchasing Power Ranking for Ordinary Residents in Shanghai, as represented by the green bars, also improved modestly over the first sub-period, rising from 98th in 2005 to 96th in 2010.

Over the second sub-period (2011–2013), the Cost of Living Index for Ordinary Residents has been on a moderately decreasing trend. In 2011, the cost of living for ordinary residents in Shanghai was 42.89% of that for ordinary residents in New York. It dropped to 40.41% in 2013. In contrast, the Wages Index for Ordinary Residents has been increasing. This index rose from 11.10 in 2011 to 14.30 in 2013.

SHANGHAI
China

The combined trends of increasing wages and decreasing cost of living have enabled ordinary residents in Shanghai to afford more goods and services over time during the second sub-period. This is reflected in the Purchasing Power Index for Ordinary Residents, which increased rather significantly from 25.87 in 2011 to 35.39 in 2013. Despite this positive showing of the index, the Purchasing Power Ranking for Ordinary Residents has stagnated at 98th throughout the second sub-period.

Finally, we note that over the entire study period (2005–2013), the Purchasing Power Index for Ordinary Residents in Shanghai has consistently been lower than 100.00 — the base index value. This means that ordinary residents in Shanghai have only been able to afford a lower consumption level than their counterparts in New York, given the same number of working hours.

SHENZHEN
China

Figure 5.86a: Cost of Living and 10 Consumption Categories Rankings for Ordinary Residents in Shenzhen, China

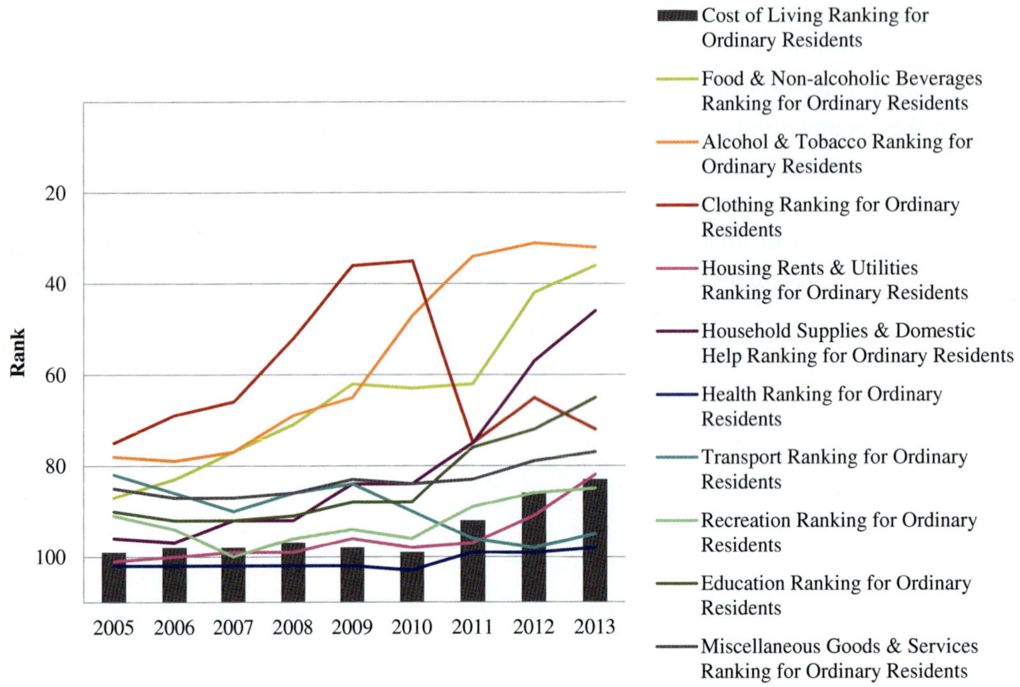

Source: Asia Competitiveness Institute

Figure 5.86b: Gross Hourly Wages in USD and Wages Ranking for Ordinary Residents in Shenzhen, China

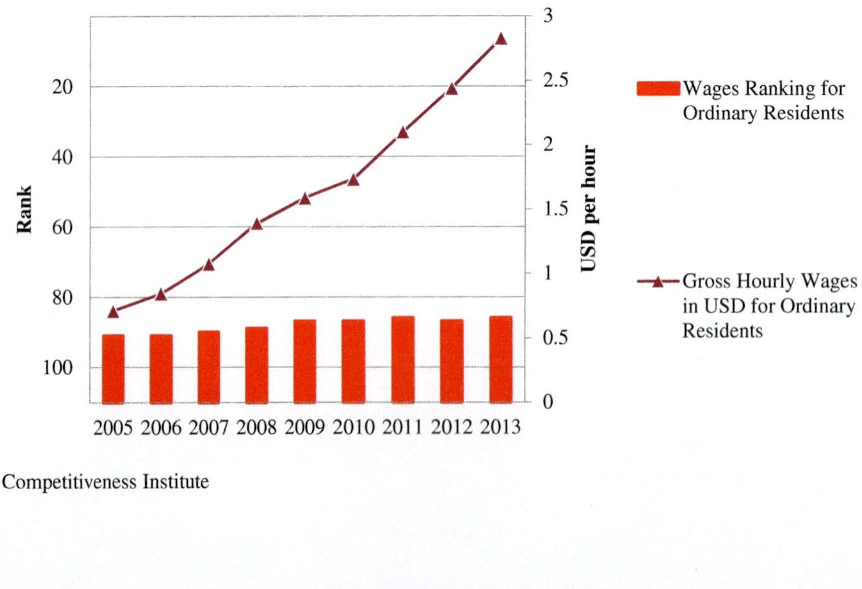

Source: Asia Competitiveness Institute

SHENZHEN
China

Figure 5.86c: Cost of Living, Wages and Purchasing Power Indices and Purchasing Power Ranking for Ordinary Residents in Shenzhen, China

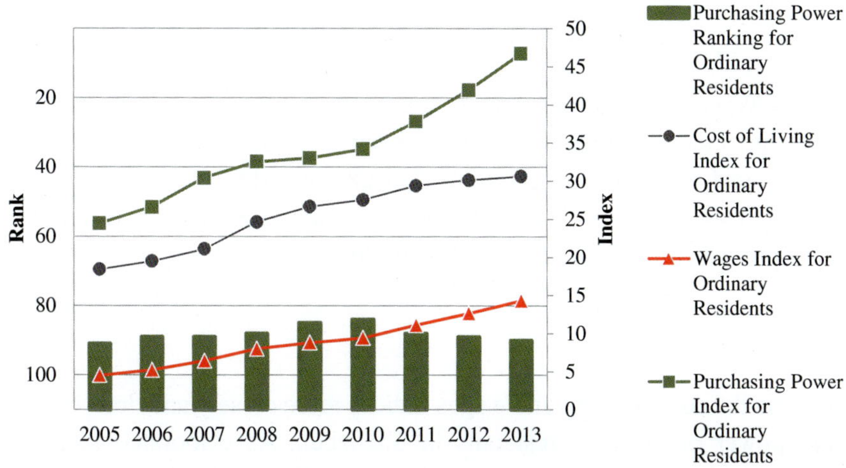

Source: Asia Competitiveness Institute

Figure 5.86a

Located in the south of southern China's Guangdong province, Shenzhen is home to some of the country's most successful technology companies including Huawei, BYD and Tencent. The city's Cost of Living Ranking for Ordinary Residents, as represented by the grey bars, rose from 99th in 2005 to 97th in 2008 before falling back to 99th in 2010, and moved up from 92nd to 83rd between 2011 and 2013 (see Figure 5.86a). As elaborated in Section 3.4.2 of Chapter 3, for a more precise comparison of rankings, we have split the analysis into two sub-periods: from 2005 to 2010 and from 2011 and 2013.

Between 2005 and 2010, Food & Non-alcoholic Beverages Ranking climbed 24 places from 87th to 63rd. Housing Rents & Utilities Ranking jumped three spots from 101st in 2005 to 98th in 2010. Education Ranking moved up two places 90th to 88th over the first sub-period. In contrast, Transport Ranking slipped eight spots from 82nd in 2005 to 90th in 2010. Health Ranking declined from 102nd to 103rd over the same sub-period.

The rankings of all 10 categories went up over the second sub-period from 2011 to 2013. Household Supplies & Domestic Help saw the most remarkable rise in ranking as it climbed 29 places from 75th in 2011 to 46th in 2013. Food & Non-alcoholic Beverages Ranking jumped 26 spots from 62nd to 36th between 2011 and 2013. Housing Rents & Utilities Ranking moved up 15 places from 97th to 82nd over the same sub-period. Alcohol & Tobacco Ranking rose more modestly from 34th in 2011 to 32nd in 2013. Nonetheless, it remained as the highest ranked category throughout the second sub-period. Health and Transport Rankings both went up one spot

SHENZHEN
China

from 99th to 98th and 96th to 95th, respectively, between 2011 and 2013. Nonetheless, Health was consistently the lowest ranked category for the entire second sub-period.

Figure 5.86b

The Gross Hourly Wages in USD for Ordinary Residents in Shenzhen, as denoted by the red line in Figure 5.86b, have increased significantly between 2005 and 2013. From US$0.71 in 2005, Shenzhen's wage level rose almost fourfold to US$2.83 in 2013.

Meanwhile, the Wages Ranking for Ordinary Residents in Shenzhen, as represented by the red bars, also improved from 91st in 2005 to 86th in 2013.

Figure 5.86c

Let us now analyse the cost of living and wages indices more closely and draw conclusions about the purchasing power of ordinary residents in Shenzhen. As elaborated in Section 3.4.2 of Chapter 3, for a more precise and rigorous analysis, we discuss the results in two sub-periods: from 2005 to 2010 and from 2011 to 2013.

The Cost of Living Index and the Wages Index for Ordinary Residents in Shenzhen are represented respectively by the grey and red line in Figure 5.86c. Between 2005 and 2010, the Cost of Living Index for Ordinary Residents was generally on an increasing trend. In 2005, the cost of living for ordinary residents in Shenzhen was 18.43% of that for their counterparts in New York (the base city). It rose steadily over time to reach 27.52% in 2010. Over the same sub-period, the Wages Index for Ordinary Residents also increased significantly, rising from 4.50 in 2005 to 9.40 in 2010.

Wages increased faster than cost of living so throughout the first sub-period, ordinary residents in Shenzhen were able to afford more goods and services over time. This is reflected in the Purchasing Power Index for Ordinary Residents in Shenzhen, which is represented by the green line in Figure 5.86c. Between 2005 and 2010, this index increased steadily from 24.43 to 34.16. The Purchasing Power Ranking for Ordinary Residents in Shenzhen, as represented by the green bars, also improved over the first sub-period, rising from 91st in 2005 to 84th in 2010.

Over the second sub-period (2011–2013), the Cost of Living Index for Ordinary Residents has been on a marginally increasing trend. In 2011, the cost of living for ordinary residents in Shenzhen was 29.37% of that for ordinary residents in New York. It increased to 30.61% in 2013. The Wages Index for Ordinary Residents has also been increasing. This index has risen from 11.10 in 2011 to 14.30 by 2013.

Wages have generally risen faster than cost of living, so ordinary residents in Shenzhen have been able to afford more goods and services over time during the second sub-period. This is reflected in the Purchasing Power Index for Ordinary Residents, which increased rather significantly from 37.78 in 2011 to 46.72 in 2013. Despite this positive showing of the index, the

SHENZHEN
China

Purchasing Power Ranking for Ordinary Residents has deteriorated over the second sub-period, dropping from 88th to 90th between 2011 and 2013.

Finally, we note that over the entire study period (2005–2013), the Purchasing Power Index for Ordinary Residents in Shenzhen has consistently been lower than 100.00 — the base index value. This means that ordinary residents in Shenzhen have only been able to afford a lower consumption level than their counterparts in New York, given the same number of working hours.

SINGAPORE
Singapore

Figure 5.87a: Cost of Living and 10 Consumption Categories Rankings for Ordinary Residents in Singapore, Singapore

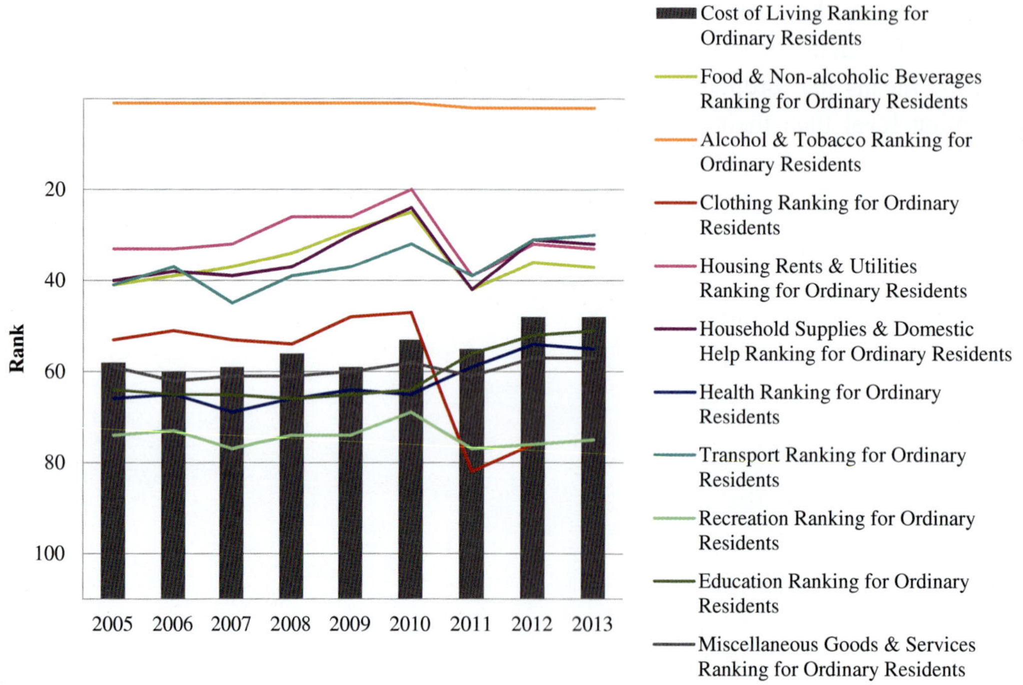

Source: Asia Competitiveness Institute

Figure 5.87b: Gross Hourly Wages in USD and Wages Ranking for Ordinary Residents in Singapore, Singapore

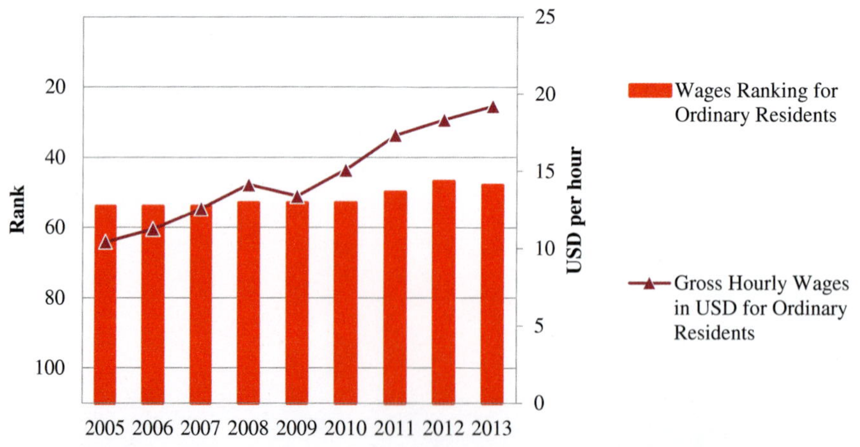

Source: Asia Competitiveness Institute

SINGAPORE
Singapore

Figure 5.87c: Cost of Living, Wages and Purchasing Power Indices and Purchasing Power Ranking for Ordinary Residents in Singapore, Singapore

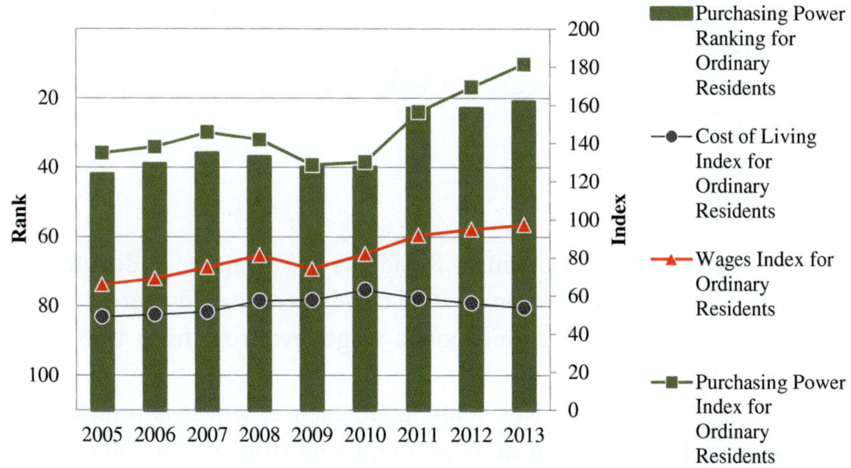

Source: Asia Competitiveness Institute

Figure 5.87a

Widely renowned as one of the four Asian Tigers, Singapore has developed rapidly into one of the world's major commercial and financial hubs since its independence in 1965. The city-state's Cost of Living Ranking for Ordinary Residents, as denoted by the grey bars, moved up five places from 58th to 53rd between 2005 and 2010, and jumped seven places from 55th to 48th between 2011 and 2013 (see Figure 5.87a). As explained in Section 3.4.2 of Chapter 3, for a more precise comparison of rankings, we have split the analysis into two sub-periods.

In the first sub-period from 2005 to 2010, Food & Non-alcoholic Beverages and Household Supplies & Domestic Help registered the most significant rise in ranking as they both climbed 16 spots from 41st to 25th and 40th to 24th, respectively. Housing Rents & Utilities Ranking jumped 13 places from 33rd in 2005 to 20th in 2010. Transport Ranking went up nine spots from 41st to 32nd over the first sub-period. Health Ranking rose more modestly from 66th in 2005 to 65th in 2010. Education Ranking fell from 64th in 2005 to 66th in 2008 before rising back to 64th in 2010.

In the second sub-period between 2011 and 2013, Household Supplies & Domestic Help saw the sharpest increase in ranking from 42nd to 32nd. Transport Ranking climbed nine places from 39th in 2011 to 30th in 2013, making it the second highest ranked category in 2013. Housing Rents & Utilities Ranking moved up six spots from 39th to 33rd over the second sub-period. Food & Non-alcoholic Beverages and Education Rankings both jumped five spots from 42nd to 37th and 56th to 51st, respectively, between 2011 and 2013. Health Ranking went

SINGAPORE
Singapore

up four places from 59th in 2011 to 55th in 2013. Nonetheless, these upward trends appear to be levelling off as good news. Alcohol & Tobacco consistently remained as the highest ranked category for the entire study period as its ranking dropped from first in the first sub-period to second in the second sub-period. Consequently, Singapore was the second most expensive city in terms of Alcohol & Tobacco in 2013. Clothing and Recreation were the lowest ranked categories in 2013 at 75th.

Figure 5.87b

The Gross Hourly Wages in USD for Ordinary Residents in Singapore, as denoted by the red line in Figure 5.87b, have generally been on an upward trend over the study period. Notwithstanding a slowdown between 2008 and 2009, Singapore's wage level rose from US$10.40 in 2005 to US$19.21 in 2013.

The Wages Ranking for Ordinary Residents in Singapore, which is represented by the red bars, has also improved throughout the study period, rising from 54th in 2005 to 48th in 2013.

Figure 5.87c

Let us now analyse the cost of living and wages indices more closely and draw conclusions about the purchasing power of ordinary residents in Singapore. As elaborated in Section 3.4.2 of Chapter 3, for a more precise and rigorous analysis, we discuss the results in two sub-periods: from 2005 to 2010 and from 2011 to 2013.

The Cost of Living Index and the Wages Index for Ordinary Residents in Singapore are represented respectively by the grey and red line in Figure 5.87c. Between 2005 and 2010, the Cost of Living Index for Ordinary Residents was generally on an increasing trend. In 2005, the cost of living for ordinary residents in Singapore was 48.87% of that for their counterparts in New York (the base city). It rose steadily over time to reach 62.96% in 2010. Over the same sub-period, the Wages Index for Ordinary Residents also increased, rising from 65.89 in 2005 to 81.88 in 2010.

Between 2005 and 2007, wages increased faster than cost of living. In contrast, throughout the remaining years of the first sub-period, wages could not keep up with the latter. Thus, ordinary residents in Singapore were only able to afford more goods and services over time initially but could not do so later on in the first sub-period. These trends are reflected in the Purchasing Power Index for Ordinary Residents in Singapore, which is represented by the green line in Figure 5.87c. From 134.83 in 2005, this index rose steadily to peak at 145.87 in 2007 and then began to decline until it reached 130.07 in 2010. Meanwhile, the Purchasing Power Ranking for Ordinary Residents in Singapore, as represented by the green bars, fluctuated quite substantially. In 2005, Singapore ranked 42nd in terms of ordinary residents' purchasing power. The ranking improved to 36th in 2007 but then deteriorated steadily until it reached 40th in 2010.

SINGAPORE
Singapore

Over the second sub-period (2011–2013), the Cost of Living Index for Ordinary Residents has been on a decreasing trend. In 2011, the cost of living for ordinary residents in Singapore was 58.63% of that for ordinary residents in New York. It dropped to 53.54% in 2013. In contrast, the Wages Index for Ordinary Residents improved steadily over the second sub-period, rising from 91.69 in 2011 to 97.16 in 2013.

The combined trends of increasing wages and decreasing cost of living have enabled ordinary residents in Singapore to afford more goods and services over time throughout the second sub-period. This is evident in the Purchasing Power Index for Ordinary Residents which increased significantly from 156.40 in 2011 to 181.47 by 2013. The Purchasing Power Ranking for Ordinary Residents has also improved, albeit marginally. Between 2011 and 2013, Singapore climbed two places from 23rd to 21st.

Finally, we note that over the entire study period (2005–2013), the Purchasing Power Index for Ordinary Residents in Singapore has always been above 100.00 — the base index value. This means that ordinary residents in Singapore have consistently been able to afford a higher consumption level than their counterparts in New York, given the same number of working hours.

SOFIA
Bulgaria

Figure 5.88a: Cost of Living and 10 Consumption Categories Rankings for Ordinary Residents in Sofia, Bulgaria

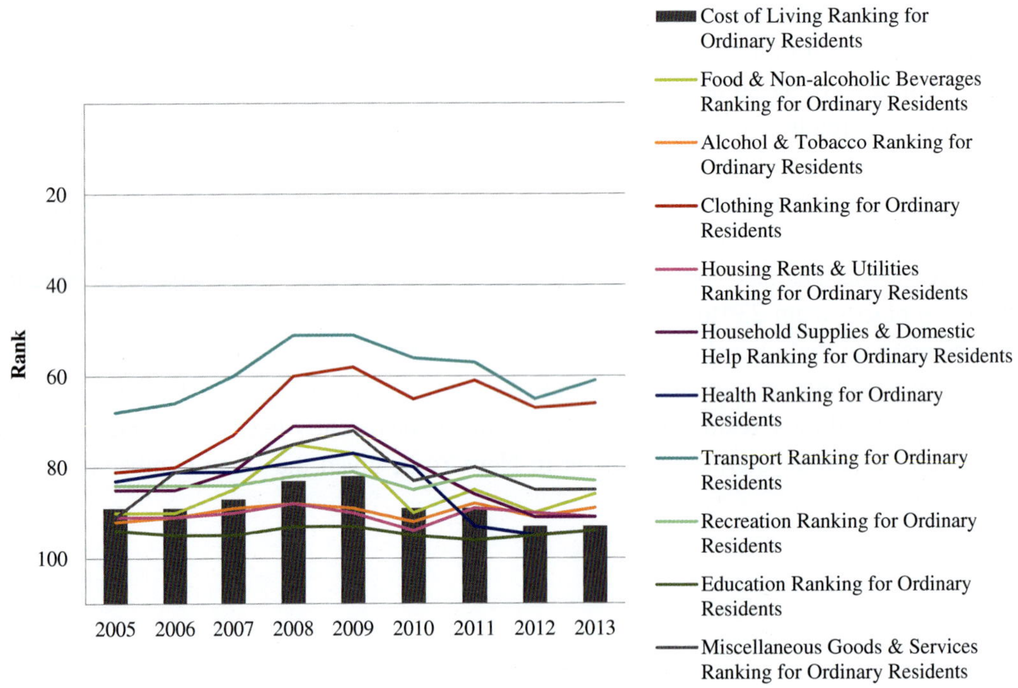

Source: Asia Competitiveness Institute

Figure 5.88b: Gross Hourly Wages in USD and Wages Ranking for Ordinary Residents in Sofia, Bulgaria

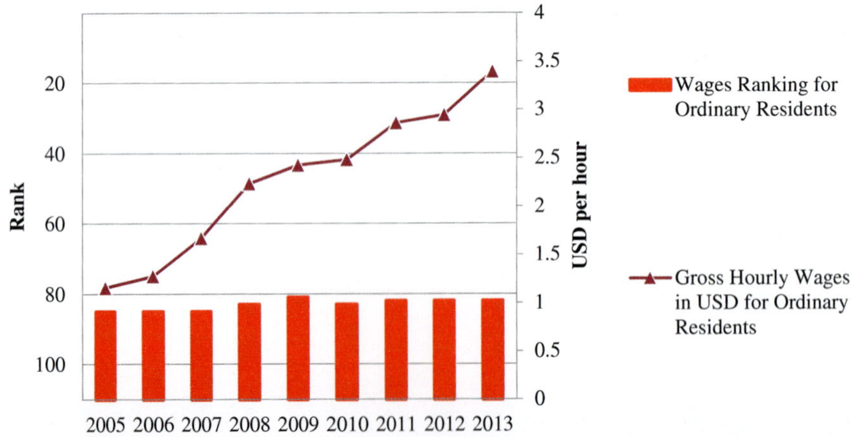

Source: Asia Competitiveness Institute

SOFIA
Bulgaria

Figure 5.88c: Cost of Living, Wages and Purchasing Power Indices and Purchasing Power Ranking for Ordinary Residents in Sofia, Bulgaria

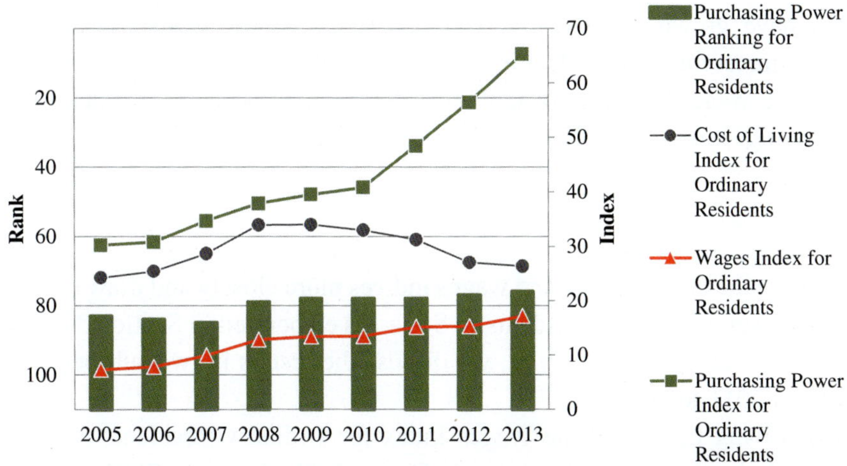

Source: Asia Competitiveness Institute

Figure 5.88a

Sofia, the capital and largest city of Bulgaria, is the 14th largest city in the European Union with a population of approximately 1.3 million. The city's Cost of Living Ranking for Ordinary Residents, as represented by the grey bars, rose from 89th in 2005 to 82nd in 2009 before falling back to 89th in 2010, and declined from 89th to 93rd between 2011 and 2013 (see Figure 5.88a). As elaborated in Section 3.4.2 of Chapter 3, for a more precise comparison of rankings, we have split the analysis into two sub-periods: from 2005 to 2010 and from 2011 and 2013.

From 2005 to 2010, Transport Ranking jumped 12 places from 68th to 56th. Health Ranking moved up three spots from 83rd in 2005 to 80th in 2010. Food & Non-alcoholic Beverages Ranking rose from 90th in 2005 to 75th in 2008 before slipping back to 90th in 2010. Education Ranking fell one spot from 94th to 95th over the first sub-period. Housing Rents & Utilities Ranking dropped three places from 91st to 94th between 2005 and 2010.

From 2011 to 2013, Education was the only category that rose in ranking from 96th to 94th. Transport Ranking fell four places from 57th in 2011 to 61st in 2013. Nonetheless, it remained as the highest ranked category throughout the second sub-period. Housing Rents & Utilities Ranking slipped two spots from 89th to 91st between 2011 and 2013. Food & Non-alcoholic Beverages Ranking moved down one place from 85th to 86th over the same sub-period. Likewise, Health Ranking declined from 93rd in 2011 to 94th in 2013, making it the lowest ranked category in 2013 together with Education.

SOFIA
Bulgaria

Figure 5.88b

The Gross Hourly Wages in USD for Ordinary Residents in Sofia, as depicted by the red line in Figure 5.88b, have grown consistently over the study period. Sofia's wage level in 2013 (US$3.40) was almost three times its initial value in 2005 (US$1.16).

Meanwhile, the Wages Ranking for Ordinary Residents in Sofia, as denoted by the red bars, has been improving. It rose from 85th in 2005 to 82nd in 2013.

Figure 5.88c

Let us now analyse the cost of living and wages indices more closely and draw conclusions about the purchasing power of ordinary residents in Sofia. As elaborated in Section 3.4.2 of Chapter 3, for a more precise and rigorous analysis, we discuss the results in two sub-periods: from 2005 to 2010 and from 2011 to 2013.

The Cost of Living Index and the Wages Index for Ordinary Residents in Sofia are represented respectively by the grey and red line in Figure 5.88c. Between 2005 and 2010, the Cost of Living Index for Ordinary Residents was generally on an increasing trend. In 2005, the cost of living for ordinary residents in Sofia was 24.23% of that for their counterparts in New York (the base city). It rose steadily over time to reach 32.98% in 2010. Over the same sub-period, the Wages Index for Ordinary Residents also increased significantly, rising from 7.32 in 2005 to 13.47 in 2010.

Wages increased faster than cost of living so throughout the first sub-period, ordinary residents in Sofia were able to afford more goods and services over time. This is reflected in the Purchasing Power Index for Ordinary Residents in Sofia, which is represented by the green line in Figure 5.88c. Between 2005 and 2010, this index increased steadily from 30.22 to 40.83. The Purchasing Power Ranking for Ordinary Residents in Sofia, as represented by the green bars, also improved over the first sub-period, rising from 83rd in 2005 to 78th in 2010.

Over the second sub-period (2011–2013), the Cost of Living Index for Ordinary Residents has been on a decreasing trend. In 2011, the cost of living for ordinary residents in Sofia was 31.25% of that for ordinary residents in New York. It dropped to 26.32% in 2013. In contrast, the Wages Index for Ordinary Residents has been increasing. This index rose from 15.13 in 2011 to 17.18 in 2013.

The combined trends of increasing wages and falling cost of living have enabled ordinary residents in Sofia to afford more goods and services over time during the second sub-period. This is reflected in the Purchasing Power Index for Ordinary Residents, which increased rather significantly from 48.42 in 2011 to 65.27 in 2013. Meanwhile, the Purchasing Power Ranking for Ordinary Residents has also improved over the second sub-period, rising from 78th to 76th between 2011 and 2013.

SOFIA
Bulgaria

Finally, we note that over the entire study period (2005–2013), the Purchasing Power Index for Ordinary Residents in Sofia has consistently been lower than 100.00 — the base index value. This means that ordinary residents in Sofia have only been able to afford a lower consumption level than their counterparts in New York, given the same number of working hours.

ST PETERSBURG
Russia

Figure 5.89a: Cost of Living and 10 Consumption Categories Rankings for Ordinary Residents in St Petersburg, Russia

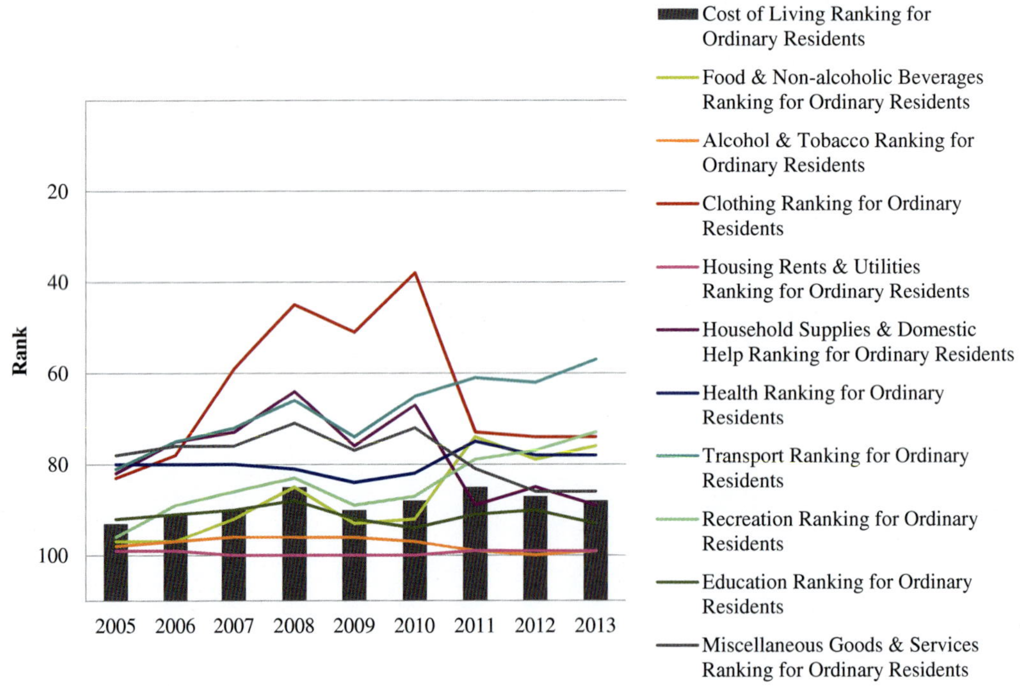

Source: Asia Competitiveness Institute

Figure 5.89b: Gross Hourly Wages in USD and Wages Ranking for Ordinary Residents in St Petersburg, Russia

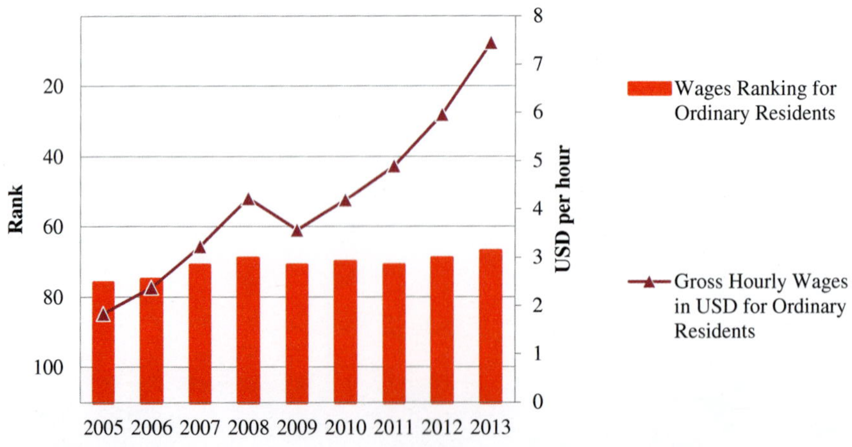

Source: Asia Competitiveness Institute

ST PETERSBURG
Russia

Figure 5.89c: Cost of Living, Wages and Purchasing Power Indices and Purchasing Power Ranking for Ordinary Residents in St Petersburg, Russia

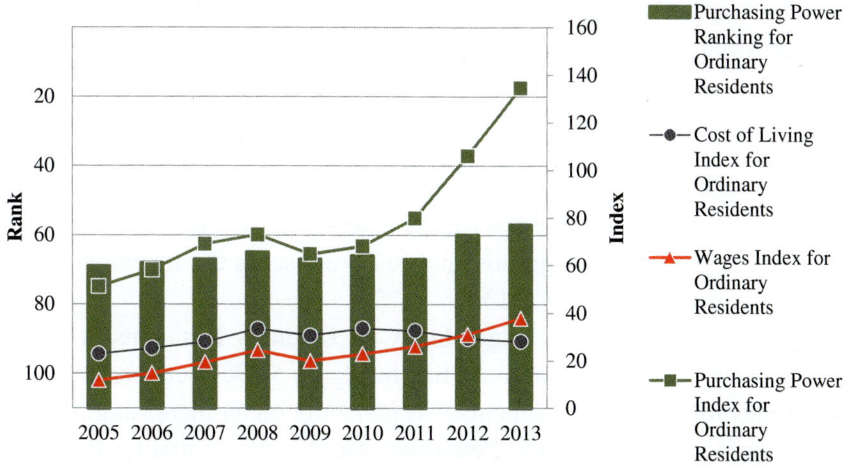

Source: Asia Competitiveness Institute

Figure 5.89a

St Petersburg is the second largest city in Russia and widely regarded as the country's cultural capital. The city's Cost of Living Ranking for Ordinary Residents, as shown in the grey bars, rose from 93rd to 88th between 2005 and 2010, but fell from 85th to 88th between 2011 and 2013 (see Figure 5.89a). As explained in Section 3.4.2 of Chapter 3, for a more precise comparison of rankings, we have split the analysis into two sub-periods.

From 2005 to 2010, Transport Ranking jumped 16 places from 81st to 65th. Food & Non-alcoholic Beverages Ranking moved up five spots from 97th in 2005 to 92nd in 2010. In contrast, Health and Education Rankings slipped two places from 80th to 82nd and 92nd to 94th, respectively, over the first sub-period. Housing Rents & Utilities Ranking fell one spot from 99th in 2005 to 100th in 2010.

Between 2011 and 2013, Transport Ranking moved up four places from 61st to 57th, making it the highest ranked category throughout the second sub-period. Health Ranking fell three spots from 75th in 2011 to 78th in 2013. Food & Non-alcoholic Beverages and Education Rankings both slipped two places from 74th to 76th and 91st to 93rd, respectively, over the second sub-period. Housing Rents & Utilities became the lowest ranked category in 2013 together with Alcohol & Tobacco as its ranking remained at 99th from 2011 and 2013.

Figure 5.89b

The Gross Hourly Wages in USD for Ordinary Residents in St Petersburg, as denoted by the red line in Figure 5.89b, increased more than fourfold from US$1.84 in 2005 to US$7.45 in 2013.

ST PETERSBURG
Russia

However, there was a plunge in 2009, which happened because of the depreciation of Russian rouble against US dollar in that year.

Meanwhile, the Wages Ranking for Ordinary Residents in St Petersburg, as shown by the red bars, has also improved, rising from 76th to 67th over the study period.

Figure 5.89c

Let us now analyse the cost of living and wages indices more closely and draw conclusions about the purchasing power of ordinary residents in St Petersburg. As elaborated in Section 3.4.2 of Chapter 3, for a more precise and rigorous analysis, we discuss the results in two sub-periods: from 2005 to 2010 and from 2011 to 2013.

The Cost of Living Index and the Wages Index for Ordinary Residents in St Petersburg are represented respectively by the grey and red line in Figure 5.89c. Between 2005 and 2010, the Cost of Living Index for Ordinary Residents was generally on an increasing trend. In 2005, the cost of living for ordinary residents in St Petersburg was 22.75% of that for their counterparts in New York (the base city). It rose steadily over time to reach 33.41% in 2010. Over the same sub-period, the Wages Index for Ordinary Residents also increased significantly, rising from 11.63 in 2005 to 22.74 in 2010.

Wages increased faster than cost of living, so throughout the first sub-period, ordinary residents in St Petersburg were able to afford more goods and services over time. This is reflected in the Purchasing Power Index for Ordinary Residents in St Petersburg, which is represented by the green line in Figure 5.89c. Between 2005 and 2010, this index increased steadily from 51.12 to 68.05. The Purchasing Power Ranking for Ordinary Residents in St Petersburg, as represented by the green bars, also improved over the first sub-period, rising from 69th in 2005 to 66th in 2010.

Over the second sub-period (2011–2013), the Cost of Living Index for Ordinary Residents has been on a decreasing trend. In 2011, the cost of living for ordinary residents in St Petersburg was 32.43% of that for ordinary residents in New York. It dropped to 28.01% in 2013. In contrast, the Wages Index for Ordinary Residents has been increasing. This index rose from 25.89 in 2011 to 37.69 in 2013.

The combined trends of increasing wages and falling cost of living have enabled ordinary residents in St Petersburg to afford more goods and services over time during the second sub-period. This is reflected in the Purchasing Power Index for Ordinary Residents which increased steadily from 79.84 in 2011 to 134.58 in 2013. Meanwhile, the Purchasing Power Ranking for Ordinary Residents has improved significantly over the second sub-period, rising from 67th to 57th between 2011 and 2013.

ST PETERSBURG
Russia

Finally, we note that over the entire study period (2005–2013), the Purchasing Power Index for Ordinary Residents in St Petersburg had consistently been lower than 100.00 — the base index value — until 2012. This means it was not until 2012 that ordinary residents in St Petersburg could afford more goods and services than their counterparts in New York, given the same number of working hours. Before 2012, they had only been able to afford a lower consumption level.

STOCKHOLM
Sweden

Figure 5.90a: Cost of Living and 10 Consumption Categories Rankings for Ordinary Residents in Stockholm, Sweden

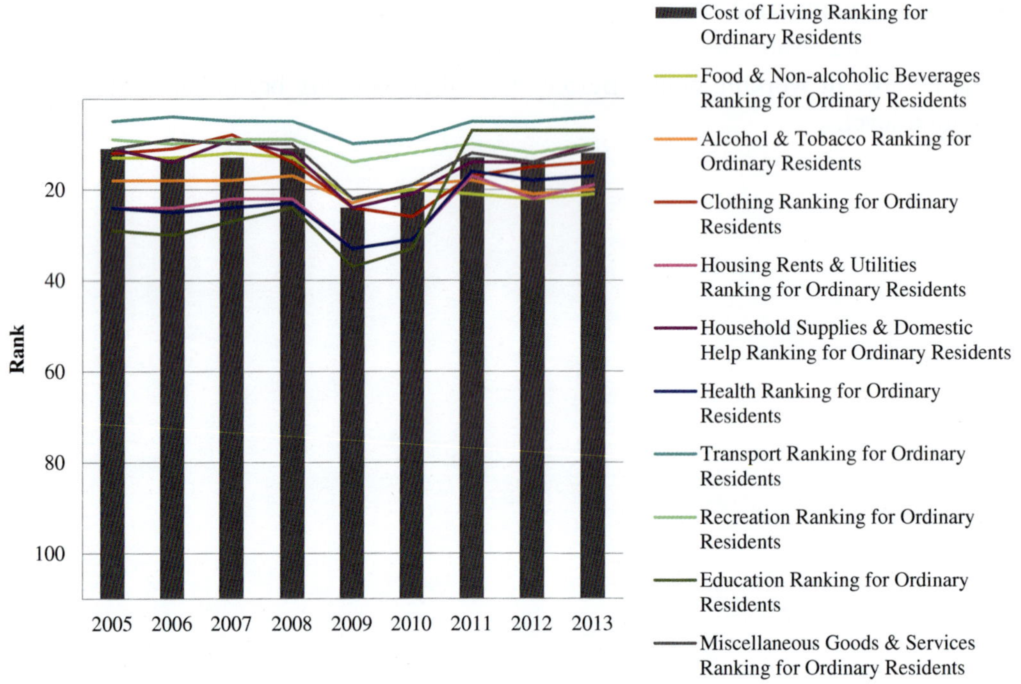

Source: Asia Competitiveness Institute

Figure 5.90a: Cost of Living and 10 Consumption Categories Rankings for Ordinary Residents in Stockholm, Sweden

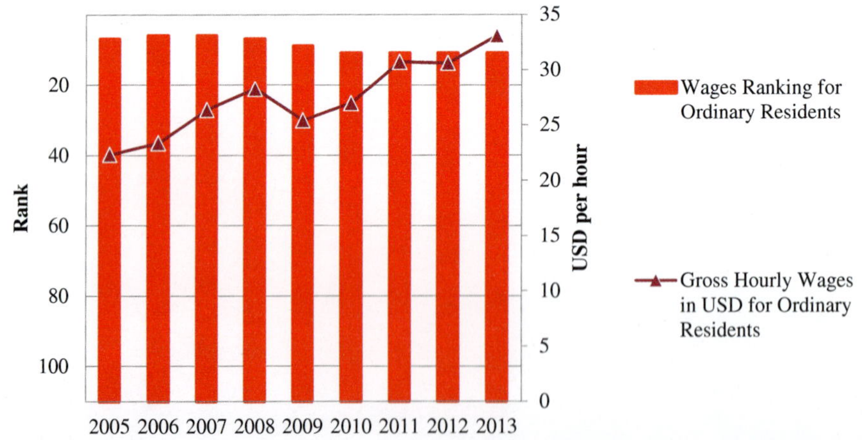

Source: Asia Competitiveness Institute

STOCKHOLM
Sweden

Figure 5.90a: Cost of Living and 10 Consumption Categories Rankings for Ordinary Residents in Stockholm, Sweden

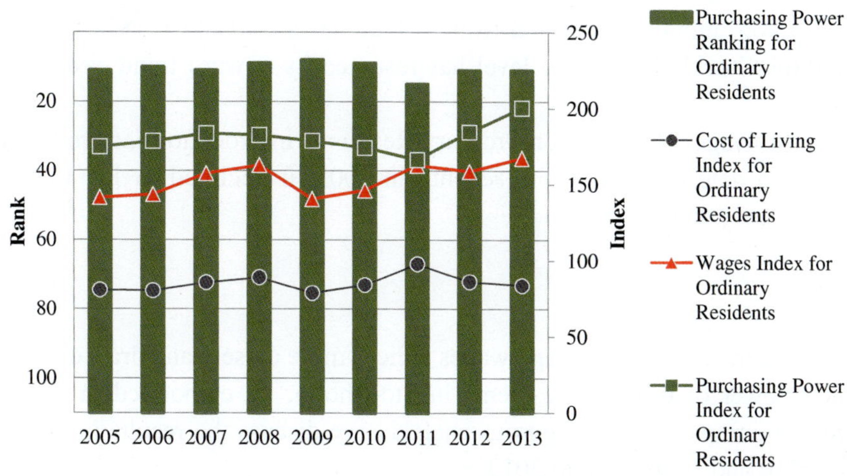

Source: Asia Competitiveness Institute

Figure 5.90a

With a population of approximately 2.2 million in the metropolitan area, Stockholm, the capital of Sweden, is the most populous city in the Nordic region. The city's Cost of Living Ranking for Ordinary Residents, as denoted by the grey bars, fell from 11th to 20th between 2005 and 2010, and rose from 13th to 12th between 2011 and 2013 (see Figure 5.90a). As elaborated in Section 3.4.2 of Chapter 3, for a more precise comparison of rankings, we have split the analysis into two sub-periods.

The rankings of all 10 categories went down over the first sub-period from 2005 to 2010. In particular, Food & Non-alcoholic Beverages Ranking slipped seven places from 13th in 2005 to 20th in 2010. Likewise, Housing Rents & Utilities and Health Rankings declined from 24th to 31st between 2005 and 2010. Transport and Education Rankings both fell four places from fifth to ninth and 29th to 33rd, respectively, over the first sub-period.

In the second sub-period from 2011 to 2013, Transport Ranking moved up one place from fifth to fourth, making it the highest ranked category in both sub-periods. In contrast, Housing Rents & Utilities Ranking slipped two spots from 17th in 2011 to 19th in 2013. Health Ranking declined from 16th to 17th over the same sub-period. Education Ranking remained at seventh throughout the second sub-period. Food & Non-alcoholic Beverages Ranking dropped from 21st in 2011 to 22nd in 2012 before rising back to 21st in 2013. Consequently, Food & Non-alcoholic Beverages became the lowest ranked category in 2013.

STOCKHOLM
Sweden

Figure 5.90b

The Gross Hourly Wages in USD for Ordinary Residents in Stockholm, as depicted by the red line in Figure 5.90b, initially increased from US$22.32 in 2005 to US$28.27 in 2008. After a decline in 2009, Stockholm's wage level has resumed its upward trend, reaching US$33.09 in 2013.

Meanwhile, the Wages Ranking for Ordinary Residents in Stockholm, as represented by the red bars, has been deteriorating. From seventh in 2005, it declined to 11th in 2010 and has stagnated at that level thereafter.

Figure 5.90c

Let us now analyse the cost of living and wages indices more closely and draw conclusions about the purchasing power of ordinary residents in Stockholm. As elaborated in Section 3.4.2 of Chapter 3, for a more precise and rigorous analysis, we discuss the results in two sub-periods: from 2005 to 2010 and from 2011 to 2013.

The Cost of Living Index and the Wages Index for Ordinary Residents in Stockholm are represented respectively by the grey and red line in Figure 5.90c. Between 2005 and 2010, the Cost of Living Index for Ordinary Residents exhibited considerable fluctuations. In 2005, the cost of living for ordinary residents in Stockholm was 80.81% of that for their counterparts in New York (the base city). It first rose steadily until it peaked at 89.06 in 2008. The index then dropped to 78.59% in 2009 before recovering modestly to 84.00% in 2010. Over the same sub-period, the Wages Index for Ordinary Residents also followed a similar pattern as the cost of living index. It also first rose to peak in 2008, then abruptly plunged in 2009 before recovering over 2009–2010. Overall, the wages index in 2010 (146.23) was slightly higher than it was in 2005 (141.40).

Not only did wages fluctuate in the same manner as cost of living but wages also changed at generally similar rates as the latter. As a result, ordinary residents in Stockholm were able to mostly afford the same consumption level over time throughout the first sub-period. This is reflected in the relative stability of Purchasing Power Index for Ordinary Residents in Stockholm, which is represented by the green line in Figure 5.90c. Between 2005 and 2010, this index only fluctuated around 178.75. Ranking-wise, the Purchasing Power Ranking for Ordinary Residents in Stockholm, as represented by the green bars, moderately improved over the first sub-period, rising from 11th in 2005 to ninth in 2010.

Over the second sub-period (2011–2013), the Cost of Living Index for Ordinary Residents has been on a decreasing trend. In 2011, the cost of living for ordinary residents in Stockholm was 97.83% of that for ordinary residents in New York. It dropped to 83.52% in 2013. In contrast, the Wages Index for Ordinary Residents has been increasing. This index rose from 162.49 in 2011 to 167.39 in 2013.

STOCKHOLM
Sweden

The combined trends of increasing wages and falling cost of living have enabled ordinary residents in Stockholm to afford more goods and services over time during the second sub-period. This is reflected in the Purchasing Power Index for Ordinary Residents which increased steadily from 166.08 in 2011 to 200.43 in 2013. Meanwhile, the Purchasing Power Ranking for Ordinary Residents has also improved over the second sub-period, rising from 15th to 11th between 2011 and 2013.

Finally, we note that over the entire study period (2005–2013), the Purchasing Power Index for Ordinary Residents in Stockholm has always been higher than 100.00 — the base index value. This means that ordinary residents in Stockholm have consistently been able to afford more goods and services than their counterparts in New York, given the same number of working hours.

SUZHOU
China

Figure 5.91a: Cost of Living and 10 Consumption Categories Rankings for Ordinary Residents in Suzhou, China

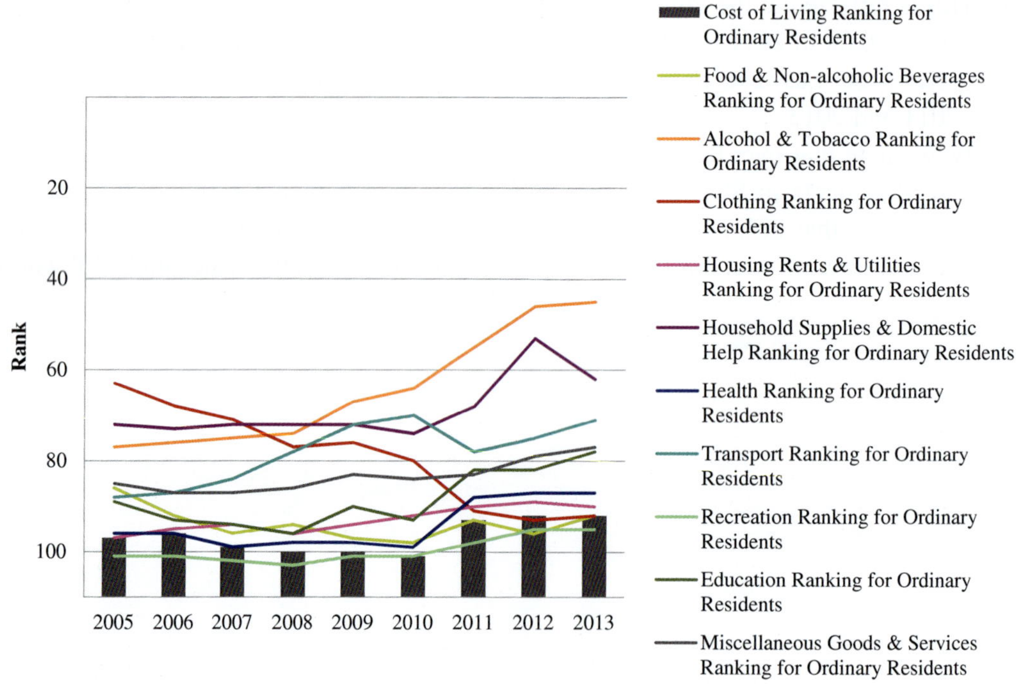

Source: Asia Competitiveness Institute

Figure 5.91b: Gross Hourly Wages in USD and Wages Ranking for Ordinary Residents in Suzhou, China

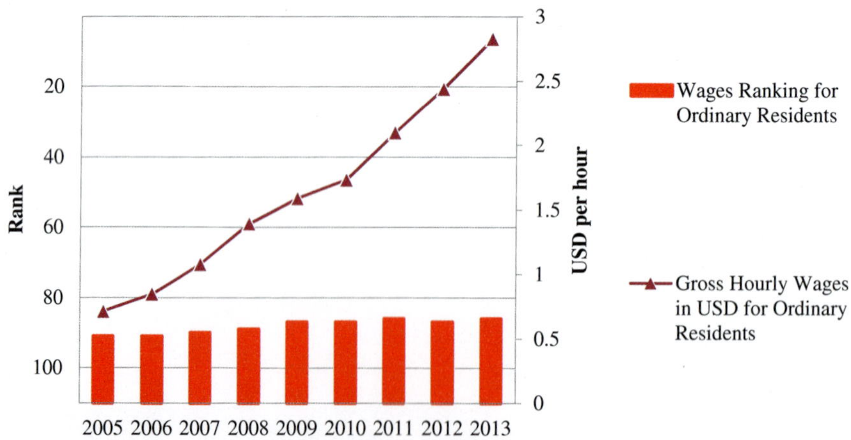

Source: Asia Competitiveness Institute

SUZHOU
China

Figure 5.91c: Cost of Living, Wages and Purchasing Power Indices and Purchasing Power Ranking for Ordinary Residents in Suzhou, China

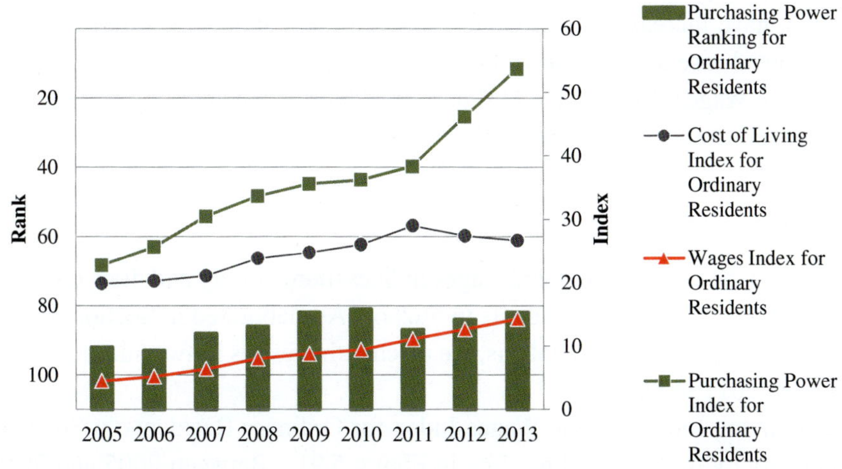

Source: Asia Competitiveness Institute

Figure 5.91a

Often dubbed the "Venice of China", Suzhou is a major economic centre in eastern China's Jiangsu province. The city's Cost of Living Ranking for Ordinary Residents, as represented by the grey bars, declined from 97th to 101st between 2005 and 2010, and rose from 93rd to 92nd between 2011 and 2013 (see Figure 5.91a). As explained in Section 3.4.2 of Chapter 3, for a more precise comparison of rankings, we have split the analysis into two sub-periods.

From 2005 to 2010, Transport saw the most significant rise in ranking as it climbed 18 places from 88th to 70th. Housing Rents & Utilities Ranking jumped five spots from 97th in 2005 to 92nd in 2010. In contrast, Food & Non-alcoholic Beverages Ranking slipped 12 places from 86th to 98th over the first sub-period. Education Ranking fell four spots from 89th to 93rd between 2005 and 2010. Health Ranking moved down three places from 96th to 99th over the same sub-period.

From 2011 to 2013, Alcohol & Tobacco Ranking jumped 10 places from 55th to 45th, making it the highest ranked category throughout the second sub-period. Transport Ranking moved up seven spots from 78th in 2011 to 71st in 2013. Education Ranking rose from 82nd to 78th between 2011 and 2013. Recreation Ranking went up from 98th in 2011 to 95th in 2013. Nonetheless, it was the lowest ranked category in 2013. Food & Non-alcoholic Beverages and Health Rankings both climbed one spot from 93rd to 92nd and 88th to 87th, respectively, over the same sub-period. Housing Rents & Utilities Ranking rose from 90th in 2011 to 89th in 2012 before slipping back to 90th in 2013.

SUZHOU
China

Figure 5.91b

The Gross Hourly Wages in USD for Ordinary Residents in Suzhou, as denoted by the red line in Figure 5.91b, have increased significantly between 2005 and 2013. From US$0.71 in 2005, Suzhou's wage level rose almost fourfold to US$2.83 in 2013.

Meanwhile, the Wages Ranking for Ordinary Residents in Suzhou, as represented by the red bars, also improved from 91st in 2005 to 86th in 2013.

Figure 5.91c

Let us now analyse the cost of living and wages indices more closely and draw conclusions about the purchasing power of ordinary residents in Suzhou. As elaborated in Section 3.4.2 of Chapter 3, for a more precise and rigorous analysis, we discuss the results in two sub-periods: from 2005 to 2010 and from 2011 to 2013.

The Cost of Living Index and the Wages Index for Ordinary Residents in Suzhou are represented respectively by the grey and red line in Figure 5.91c. Between 2005 and 2010, the Cost of Living Index for Ordinary Residents was generally on an increasing trend. In 2005, the cost of living for ordinary residents in Suzhou was 19.82% of that for their counterparts in New York (the base city). It rose steadily over time to reach 25.99% in 2010. Over the same sub-period, the Wages Index for Ordinary Residents also increased significantly, rising from 4.50 in 2005 to 9.40 in 2010.

Wages increased faster than cost of living, so throughout the first sub-period, ordinary residents in Suzhou were able to afford more goods and services over time. This is reflected in the Purchasing Power Index for Ordinary Residents in Suzhou, which is represented by the green line in Figure 5.91c. Between 2005 and 2010, this index increased steadily from 22.72 to 36.17. The Purchasing Power Ranking for Ordinary Residents in Suzhou, as represented by the green bars, also improved significantly over the first sub-period, rising from 92nd in 2005 to 81st in 2010.

Over the second sub-period (2011–2013), the Cost of Living Index for Ordinary Residents has been on a decreasing trend. In 2011, the cost of living for ordinary residents in Suzhou was 28.98% of that for ordinary residents in New York. It decreased to 26.66% in 2013. In contrast, the Wages Index for Ordinary Residents has been increasing, rising from 11.10 in 2011 to 14.30 in 2013.

The combined trends of increasing wages and decreasing cost of living have enabled ordinary residents in Suzhou to afford more goods and services over time throughout the second sub-period. This is reflected in the Purchasing Power Index for Ordinary Residents, which increased rather significantly from 38.29 in 2011 to 53.64 in 2013. Meanwhile, the Purchasing Power Ranking for Ordinary Residents has improved steadily over the second sub-period, rising from 87th in 2011 to 82nd in 2013.

SUZHOU
China

Finally, we note that over the entire study period (2005–2013), the Purchasing Power Index for Ordinary Residents in Suzhou has consistently been lower than 100.00 — the base index value. This means that ordinary residents in Suzhou have only been able to afford a lower consumption level than their counterparts in New York, given the same number of working hours.

SYDNEY
Australia

Figure 5.92a: Cost of Living and 10 Consumption Categories Rankings for Ordinary Residents in Sydney, Australia

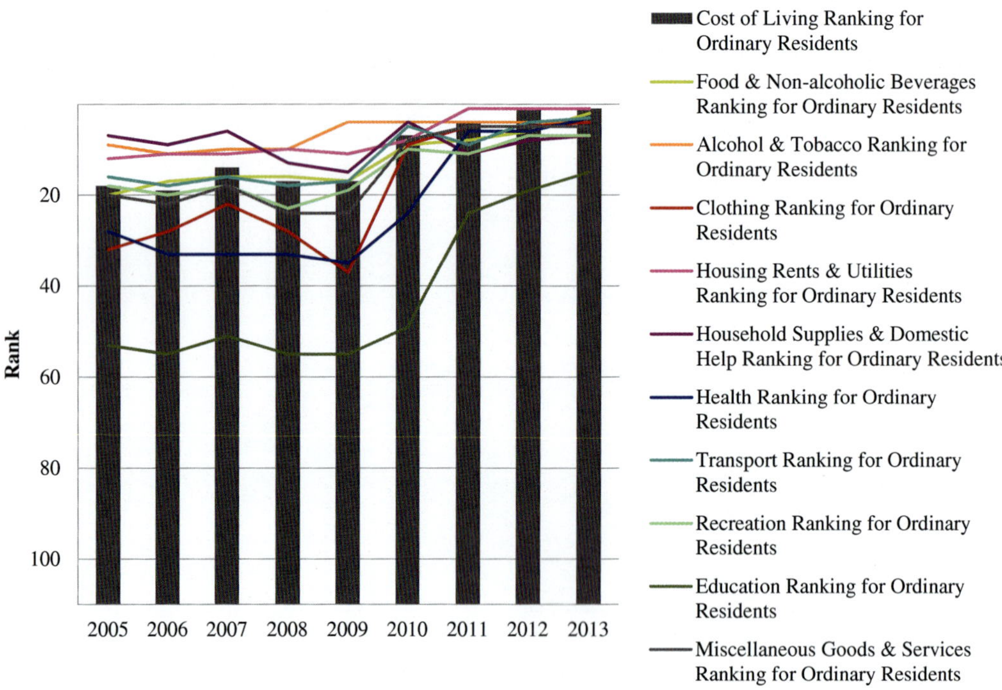

Source: Asia Competitiveness Institute

Figure 5.92b: Gross Hourly Wages in USD and Wages Ranking for Ordinary Residents in Sydney, Australia

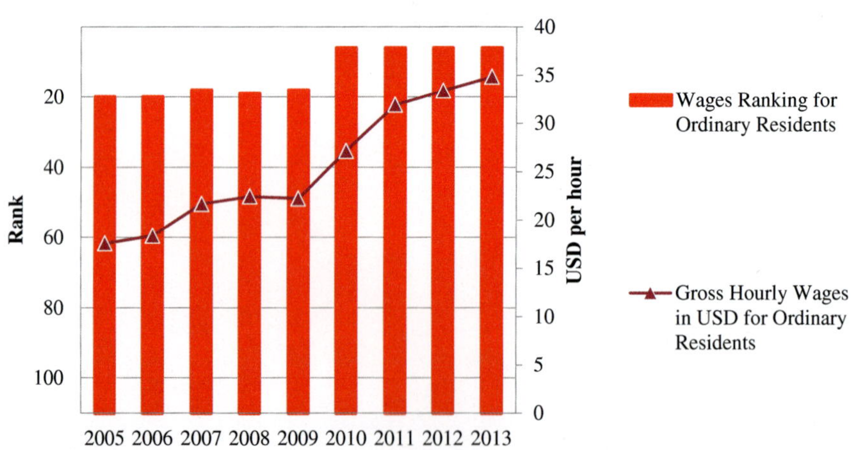

Source: Asia Competitiveness Institute

SYDNEY
Australia

Figure 5.92c: Cost of Living, Wages and Purchasing Power Indices and Purchasing Power Ranking for Ordinary Residents in Sydney, Australia

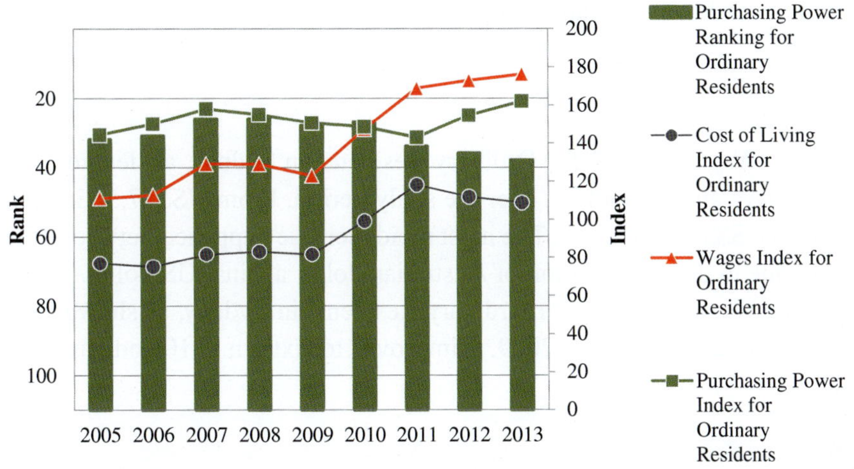

Source: Asia Competitiveness Institute

Figure 5.92a

Located on Australia's east coast, Sydney is the most populous city in the country as well as Oceania with an estimated population of 4.8 million. The city's Cost of Living Ranking for Ordinary Residents, as shown in the grey bars, rose from 18th to seventh between 2005 and 2010, and from fourth to first between 2011 and 2013, making it the most expensive among the 103 cities studied in 2013 (see Figure 5.92a). As elaborated in Section 3.4.2 of Chapter 3, for a more precise comparison of rankings, we have split the analysis into two sub-periods.

The rankings of all 10 categories went up over the first sub-period from 2005 to 2010. In particular, Clothing registered the most remarkable rise in ranking as it climbed 23 places from 32nd in 2005 to ninth in 2010. Food & Non-alcoholic Beverages and Transport Rankings jumped 11 places from 20th to ninth and 16th to fifth, respectively, between 2005 and 2010. Housing Rents & Utilities Ranking moved up four spots from 12th in 2005 to eighth in 2010. Likewise, Health and Education Rankings rose from 28th to 24th and 53rd to 49th, respectively, over the same sub-period.

Between 2011 and 2013, Housing Rents & Utilities Ranking remained at the top, making it the highest ranked category throughout the second sub-period. Sydney was thus the most expensive city in terms of Housing Rents & Utilities in three consecutive years from 2011 to 2013. Alcohol & Tobacco and Miscellaneous Goods & Services Rankings stayed unchanged at fourth and fifth, respectively, over the second sub-period. Education Ranking jumped nine places from 24th in 2011 to 15th in 2013. Nonetheless, Education was the lowest ranked category in the second

SYDNEY
Australia

sub-period. Food & Non-alcoholic Beverages and Transport Rankings both moved up six spots from eighth to second and ninth to third, respectively, between 2011 and 2013. Health Ranking rose from sixth to third over the same sub-period.

Figure 5.92b

The Gross Hourly Wages in USD for Ordinary Residents in Sydney, as denoted by the red line in Figure 5.92b, have almost doubled over the study period. From US$17.56 in 2005, Sydney's wage level rose to US$34.83 in 2013. The most rapid increase happened between 2009 and 2011. This was partly due to the appreciation of Australian dollar against US dollar.

Meanwhile, the Wages Ranking for Ordinary Residents in Sydney, as shown by the red bars, first rose from 20th in 2005 to 18th in 2009. It improved to sixth in 2010 and has remained at that level thereafter.

Figure 5.92c

Let us now analyse the cost of living and wages indices more closely and draw conclusions about the purchasing power of ordinary residents in Sydney. As elaborated in Section 3.4.2 of Chapter 3, for a more precise and rigorous analysis, we discuss the results in two sub-periods: from 2005 to 2010 and from 2011 to 2013.

The Cost of Living Index and the Wages Index for Ordinary Residents in Sydney are represented respectively by the grey and red line in Figure 5.92c. Between 2005 and 2010, the Cost of Living Index for Ordinary Residents was generally on an increasing trend. In 2005, the cost of living for ordinary residents in Sydney was 76.99% of that for their counterparts in New York (the base city). It rose over the years to reach 99.14% in 2010. Over the same sub-period, the Wages Index for Ordinary Residents also followed an increasing trend, rising from 111.21 in 2005 to 147.34 in 2010.

Between 2005 and 2007, wages rose faster than cost of living but during the remaining years of the first sub-period, it could not keep up with the latter. Hence, ordinary residents in Sydney could only afford higher consumption level over time during 2005–2007 but could not do so after 2007. These trends are reflected in the Purchasing Power Index for Ordinary Residents in Sydney, which is represented by the green line in Figure 5.92c. This index initially rose from 144.44 in 2005 to 158.10 in 2007, before dropping steadily until it reached 148.62 in 2010. Ranking-wise, the Purchasing Power Ranking for Ordinary Residents in Sydney, which is represented by the green bars, improved over the first sub-period, rising from 32nd in 2005 to 27th in 2010.

Over the second sub-period (2011–2013), the Cost of Living Index for Ordinary Residents has been on a decreasing trend. In 2011, the cost of living for ordinary residents in Sydney was 1.18 times that for their counterparts in New York. It dropped to 1.09 times in 2013. In contrast, the

SYDNEY
Australia

Wages Index for Ordinary Residents has been increasing, rising from 168.86 in 2011 to 176.22 in 2013.

The combined trends of increasing wages and decreasing cost of living have enabled ordinary residents in Sydney to afford more goods and services over time throughout the second sub-period. This is reflected in the Purchasing Power Index for Ordinary Residents, which rose from 143.02 in 2011 to 162.03 in 2013. Despite this positive showing of the index, the Purchasing Power Ranking for Ordinary Residents has actually deteriorated over the second sub-period. It dropped from 34th in 2011 to 38th in 2013.

Finally, we note that over the entire study period (2005–2013), the Purchasing Power Index for Ordinary Residents in Sydney has always been above 100.00 — the base index value. This means that ordinary residents in Sydney have consistently been able to afford a higher consumption level than their counterparts in New York, given the same number of working hours.

TAIPEI
Taiwan, China

Figure 5.93a: Cost of Living and 10 Consumption Categories Rankings for Ordinary Residents in Taipei, Taiwan, China

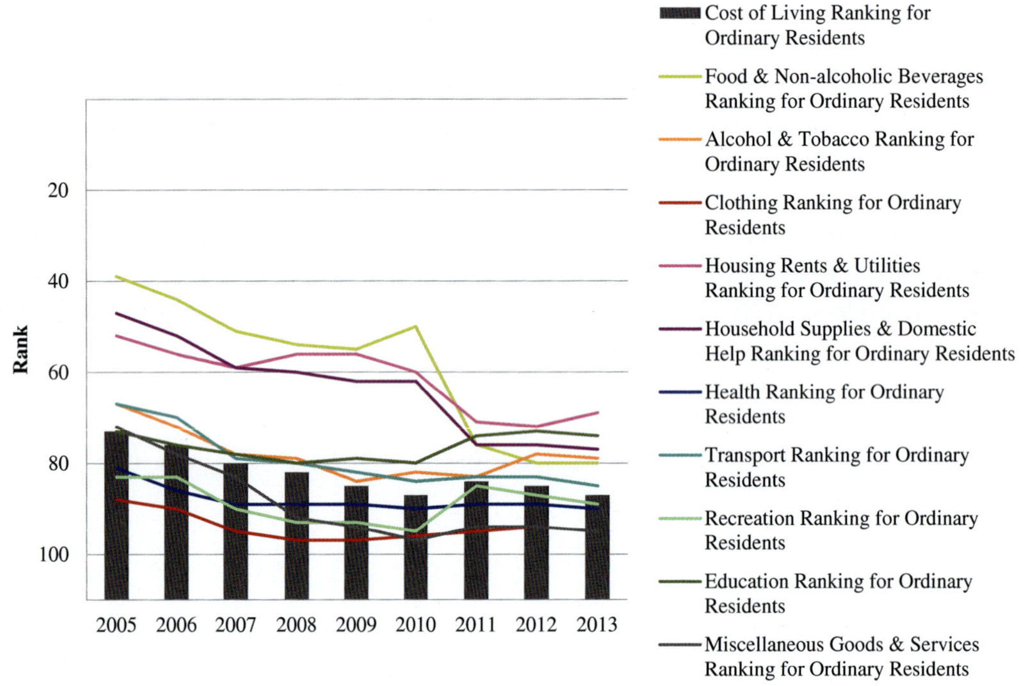

Source: Asia Competitiveness Institute

Figure 5.93b: Gross Hourly Wages in USD and Wages Ranking for Ordinary Residents in Taipei, Taiwan, China

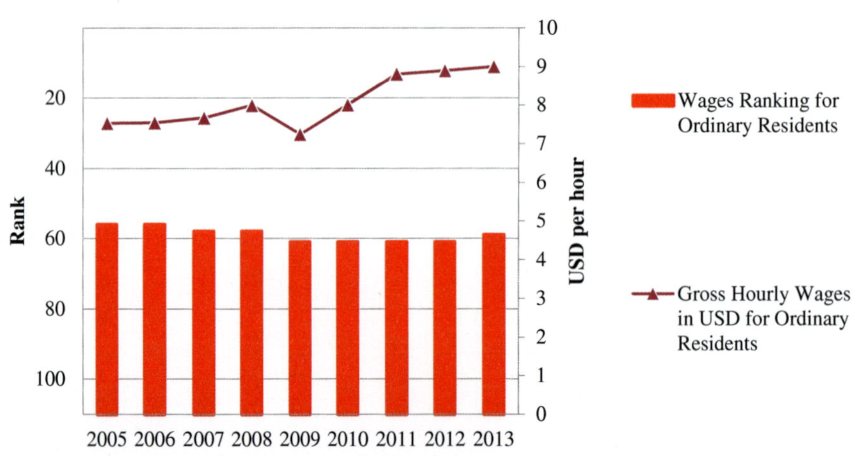

Source: Asia Competitiveness Institute

TAIPEI
Taiwan, China

Figure 5.93c: Cost of Living, Wages and Purchasing Power Indices and Purchasing Power Ranking for Ordinary Residents in Taipei, Taiwan, China

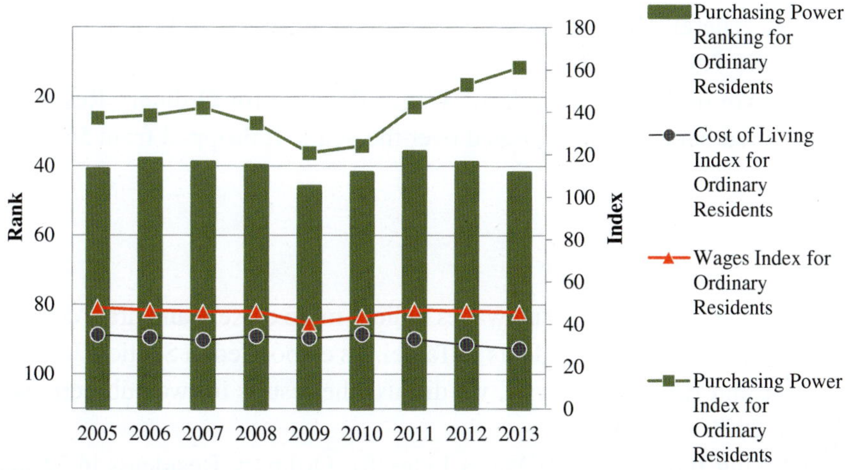

Source: Asia Competitiveness Institute

Figure 5.93a

Situated at the northern tip of Taiwan, Taipei is the country's capital and one of the most visited cities in Asia. The city's Cost of Living Ranking for Ordinary Residents, as denoted by the grey bars, fell from 73rd to 87th between 2005 and 2010, and from 84th to 87th between 2011 and 2013 (see Figure 5.93a). As explained in Section 3.4.2 of Chapter 3, for a more precise comparison of rankings, we have split the analysis into two sub-periods.

The rankings of all 10 categories declined over the first sub-period from 2005 to 2010. In particular, Transport Ranking slipped 17 places from 67th in 2005 to 84th in 2010. Food & Non-alcoholic Beverages Ranking fell 11 spots from 39th to 50th between 2005 and 2010. Health Ranking moved down nine places from 81st to 90th over the first sub-period. Housing Rents & Utilities Ranking dropped eight spots from 52nd in 2005 to 60th in 2010. Education Ranking declined from 73rd to 80th over the same sub-period.

From 2011 to 2013, Housing Rents & Utilities Ranking jumped four places from 71st to 69th, making it the highest ranked category throughout the second sub-period. In contrast, Food & Non-alcoholic Beverages Ranking fell four spots from 76th to 80th between 2011 and 2013. Transport Ranking slipped two places from 83rd in 2011 to 85th in 2013. Health Ranking dropped from 89th to 90th over the same sub-period. Education Ranking rose from 74th in 2011 to 73rd in 2012 before slipping back to 74th in 2013. Likewise, Clothing Ranking went up from 95th in 2011 to 94th in 2012 before falling back to 95th in 2013. Clothing was therefore the lowest ranked category in 2013 together with Miscellaneous Goods & Services.

TAIPEI
Taiwan, China

Figure 5.93b

The Gross Hourly Wages in USD for Ordinary Residents in Taipei, as denoted by the red line in Figure 5.93b, have generally been on an increasing trend. Between 2005 and 2013, Taipei's wage level grew from US$ 7.53 to US$9.00.

Despite the growth in the wage level, the Wages Ranking for Ordinary Residents in Taipei, as depicted by the red bars, has deteriorated over the years. It dropped from 56th in 2005 to 59th in 2013.

Figure 5.93c

Let us now analyse the cost of living and wages indices more closely and draw conclusions about the purchasing power of ordinary residents in Taipei. As elaborated in Section 3.4.2 of Chapter 3, for a more precise and rigorous analysis, we discuss the results in two sub-periods: from 2005 to 2010 and from 2011 to 2013.

The Cost of Living Index and the Wages Index for Ordinary Residents in Taipei are represented respectively by the grey and red line in Figure 5.93c. Although not apparent from Figure 5.93c, the Cost of Living Index for Ordinary Residents actually followed two distinct trends between 2005 and 2010. In 2005, the cost of living for ordinary residents in Taipei was 34.81% of that for their counterparts in New York (the base city). It first decreased to 32.25% in 2007 before embarking on an upward trend until 2010, when it reached 35.03%. Over the same sub-period, the Wages Index for Ordinary Residents was generally on a decreasing trend, dropping from 47.69 in 2005 to 43.43 in 2010.

Between 2005 and 2007, wages decreased more slowly than cost of living, so during these years, ordinary residents in Taipei were able to afford more goods and services over time. However, for the remaining years of the first sub-period, they could no longer do so as wages fell while cost of living rose. These trends are fully reflected in the Purchasing Power Index for Ordinary Residents in Taipei, which is represented by the green line in Figure 5.93c. This index initially rose from 136.99 in 2005 to 141.72 in 2007, before dropping steadily until it reached 124.00 in 2010. Ranking-wise, the Purchasing Power Ranking for Ordinary Residents in Taipei, which is represented by the green bars, fluctuated substantially throughout the first sub-period. From 41st in 2005, the ranking rose to 38th in 2009. It then dropped steadily to 46th in 2009 before climbing back to 42nd in 2010.

Over the second sub-period (2011–2013), the Cost of Living Index for Ordinary Residents has been on a decreasing trend. In 2011, the cost of living for ordinary residents in Taipei was 32.75% of that for their counterparts in New York. It dropped to 28.29% in 2013. The Wages Index for Ordinary Residents has also been decreasing, albeit much more marginally. This index decreased from 46.58 in 2011 to 45.56 in 2013.

TAIPEI
Taiwan, China

Wages have decreased much more slowly than cost of living, so ordinary residents in Taipei were able to afford more goods and services over time throughout the second sub-period. This is reflected in the Purchasing Power Index for Ordinary Residents, which rose from 142.24 in 2011 to 161.05 in 2013. Ranking-wise, the Purchasing Power Ranking for Ordinary Residents has deteriorated over the second sub-period. It dropped from 36th in 2011 to 42nd in 2013.

Finally, we note that over the entire study period (2005–2013), the Purchasing Power Index for Ordinary Residents in Taipei has always been above 100.00 — the base index value. This means that ordinary residents in Taipei have consistently been able to afford a higher consumption level than their counterparts in New York, given the same number of working hours.

TEL AVIV
Israel

Figure 5.94a: Cost of Living and 10 Consumption Categories Rankings for Ordinary Residents in Tel Aviv, Israel

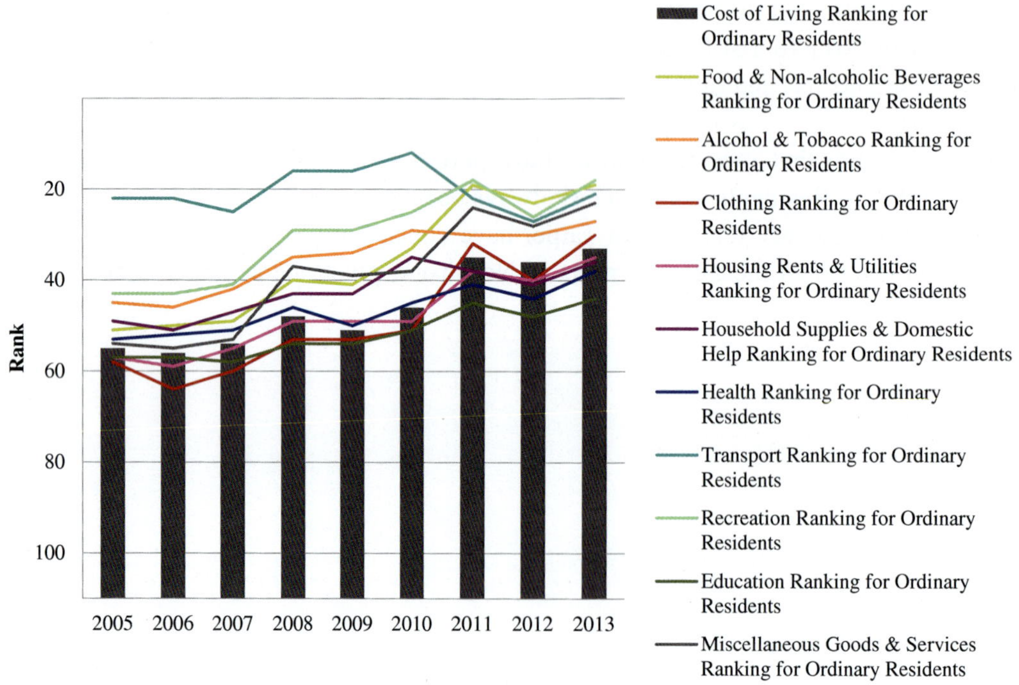

Source: Asia Competitiveness Institute

Figure 5.94b: Gross Hourly Wages in USD and Wages Ranking for Ordinary Residents in Tel Aviv, Israel

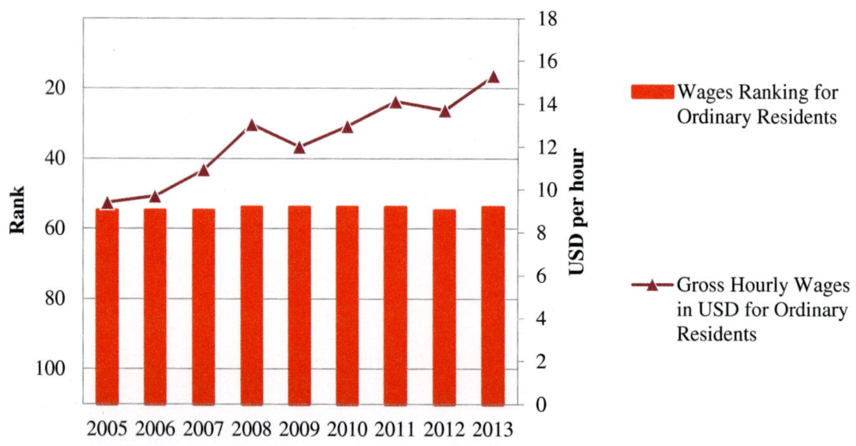

Source: Asia Competitiveness Institute

TEL AVIV
Israel

Figure 5.94c: Cost of Living and 10 Consumption Categories Rankings for Ordinary Residents in Tel Aviv, Israel

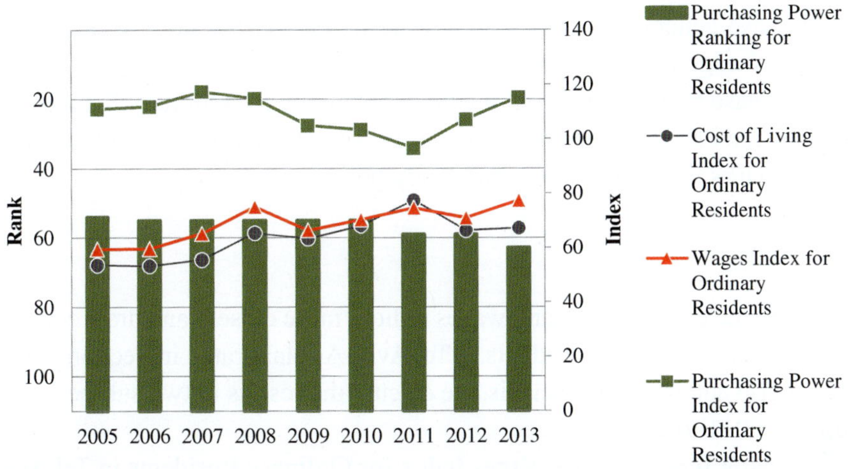

Source: Asia Competitiveness Institute

Figure 5.94a

Situated on the Mediterranean coast in central-west Israel, Tel Aviv is the country's second most populous city and centre for finance, business and performing arts. The city's Cost of Living Ranking for Ordinary Residents, as represented by the grey bars, rose from 55th to 46th between 2005 and 2010, and from 35th to 33rd between 2011 and 2013 (see Figure 5.94a). As elaborated in Section 3.4.2 of Chapter 3, for a more precise comparison of rankings, we have split the analysis into two sub-periods.

The rankings of all 10 categories went up over the first sub-period from 2005 to 2010. In particular, Food & Non-alcoholic Beverages Ranking climbed 18 places from 51st in 2005 to 33rd in 2010. Transport Ranking jumped 10 spots from 22nd to 12th between 2005 and 2010. Housing Rents & Utilities and Health Rankings both moved up eight places from 57th to 49th and 53rd to 45th, respectively, over the first sub-period. Education Ranking rose from 57th in 2005 to 51st in 2010.

Between 2011 and 2013, Housing Rents & Utilities and Health Rankings jumped three places from 38th to 35th and 41st to 38th, respectively. Transport Ranking moved up one spot from 22nd in 2011 to 21st in 2013. Likewise, Education Ranking rose from 45th to 44th between 2011 and 2013. Nonetheless, it remained as the lowest ranked category throughout the second sub-period. Food & Non-alcoholic Beverages Ranking fell from 19th in 2011 to 23rd in 2012 before jumping back to 19th in 2013. Likewise, Recreation Ranking dropped from 18th in 2011 to 26th in 2011 before rising back to 18th in 2013, making it the highest ranked category in 2013.

TEL AVIV
Israel

Figure 5.94b

The Gross Hourly Wages in USD for Ordinary Residents in Tel Aviv, as shown by the red line in Figure 5.94b, have generally followed an upward trend over the study period. From US$9.38 in 2005, Tel Aviv's wage level rose to US$15.30 in 2013.

Despite the increase in the wage level, the Wages Ranking for Ordinary Residents in Tel Aviv, as depicted by the red bars, has been fairly stable. Tel Aviv's ranking has only fluctuated between the 54th and 55th marks throughout the entire study period.

Figure 5.94c

Let us now analyse the cost of living and wages indices more closely and draw conclusions about the purchasing power of ordinary residents in Tel Aviv. As elaborated in Section 3.4.2 of Chapter 3, for a more precise and rigorous analysis, we discuss the results in two sub-periods: from 2005 to 2010 and from 2011 to 2013.

The Cost of Living Index and the Wages Index for Ordinary Residents in Tel Aviv are represented respectively by the grey and red line in Figure 5.94c. Between 2005 and 2010, the Cost of Living Index for Ordinary Residents was generally on an increasing trend. In 2005, the cost of living for ordinary residents in Tel Aviv was 53.58% of that for their counterparts in New York (the base city). It rose steadily to reach 68.12% in 2010. Over the same sub-period, the Wages Index for Ordinary Residents was also increasing. This index rose from 59.44 in 2005 to 70.33 in 2010.

Between 2005 and 2007, wages rose at a slightly faster rate than cost of living but during the subsequent years, wages could no longer keep up with the latter. Thus, for the greater part of the first sub-period, ordinary residents in Tel Aviv could not afford the same consumption level over time. This is evident in the Purchasing Power Index for Ordinary Residents in Tel Aviv, which is represented by the green line in Figure 5.94c. This index increased slightly from 110.95 to 117.34 between 2005 and 2007 but then decreased steadily until it reached 103.25 in 2010. Ranking-wise, the Purchasing Power Ranking for Ordinary Residents was stable throughout the first sub-period. It dropped from 54th in 2005 to 55th in 2006 and remained there thereafter.

Over the second sub-period (2011–2013), the Cost of Living Index for Ordinary Residents has been on a decreasing trend. In 2011, the cost of living for ordinary residents in Tel Aviv was 77.33% of that for their counterparts in New York. It dropped to 67.20% in 2013. In contrast, the Wages Index for Ordinary Residents has been increasing. This index rose from 74.60 in 2011 to 77.40 in 2013.

The combined trends of increasing wages and decreasing cost of living have enabled ordinary residents in Tel Aviv to afford more goods and services over time throughout the second sub-period. This is reflected in the Purchasing Power Index for Ordinary Residents, which rose from 96.47 in 2011 to 115.18 in 2013. Ranking-wise, the Purchasing Power Ranking for

TEL AVIV
Israel

Ordinary Residents has deteriorated over the second sub-period. It dropped from 59th in 2011 to 63rd in 2013.

Finally, we note that except for 2009, the Purchasing Power Index for Ordinary Residents in Tel Aviv has always been above 100.00 — the base index value — over the entire study period (2005–2013). This means that ordinary residents in Tel Aviv have generally been able to afford a higher consumption level as their counterparts in New York, given the same number of working hours.

TIANJIN
China

Figure 5.95a: Cost of Living and 10 Consumption Categories Rankings for Ordinary Residents in Tianjin, China

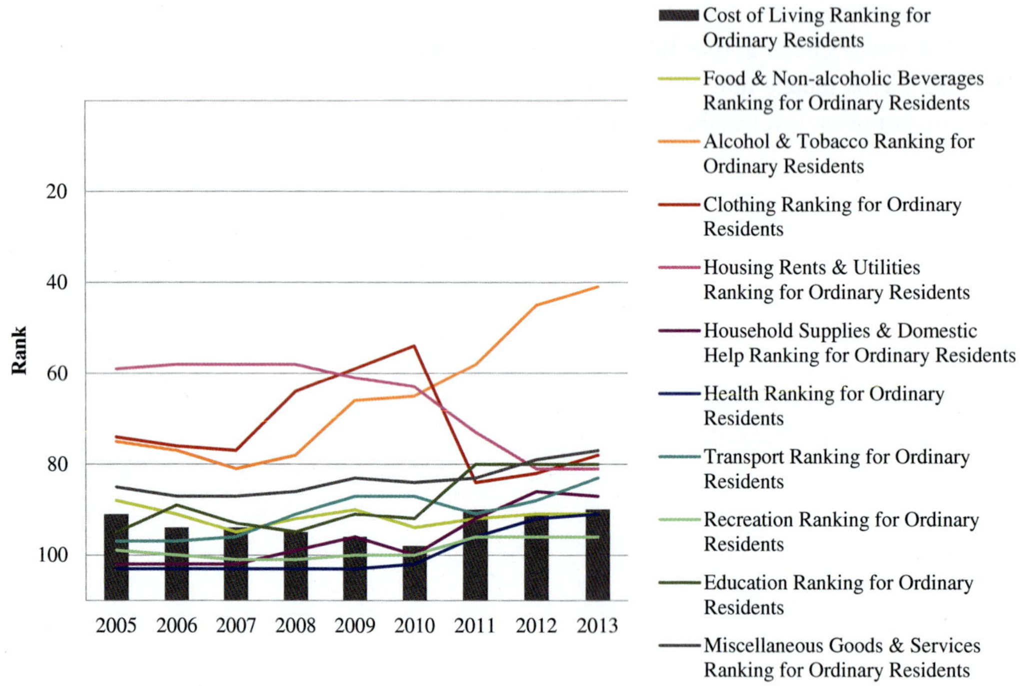

Source: Asia Competitiveness Institute

Figure 5.95b: Gross Hourly Wages in USD and Wages Ranking for Ordinary Residents in Tianjin, China

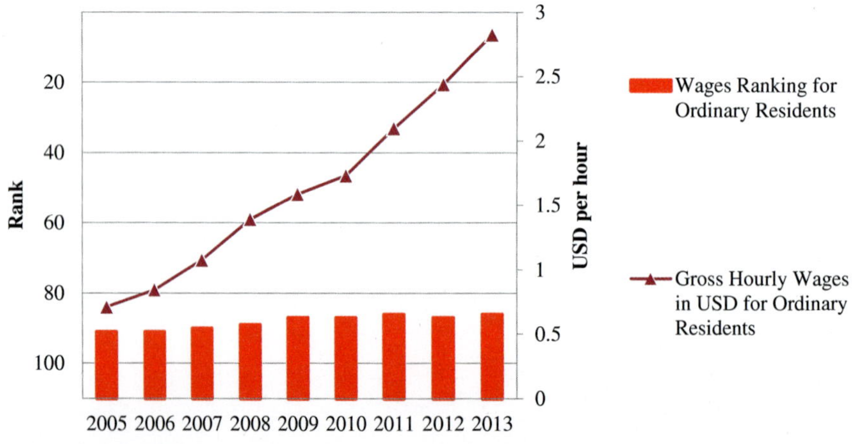

Source: Asia Competitiveness Institute

TIANJIN
China

Figure 5.95c: Cost of Living, Wages and Purchasing Power Indices and Purchasing Power Ranking for Ordinary Residents in Tianjin, China

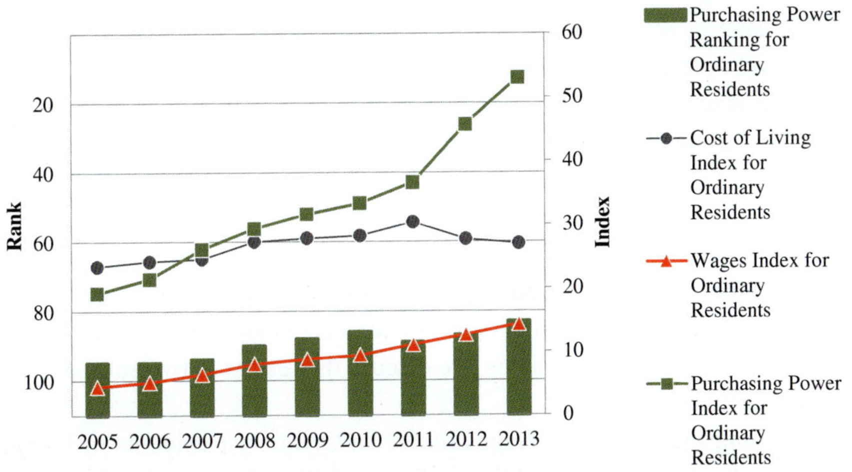

Source: Asia Competitiveness Institute

Figure 5.95a

Tianjin is the largest coastal city in northern China and one of the country's four direct-controlled municipalities besides Beijing, Chongqing, and Shanghai. The city's Cost of Living Ranking for Ordinary Residents, as shown in the grey bars, declined from 91st to 98th between 2005 and 2010, and largely remained at 90th between 2011 and 2013 (see Figure 5.95a). As explained in Section 3.4.2 of Chapter 3, for a more precise comparison of rankings, we have split the analysis into two sub-periods.

From 2005 to 2010, Transport Ranking jumped 10 places from 97th to 87th. Education Ranking moved up three spots from 95th in 2005 to 92nd in 2010. Health Ranking rose from 103rd to 102nd over the first sub-period. In contrast, Food & Non-alcoholic Beverages Ranking fell six places from 88th to 94th between 2005 and 2010. Housing Rents & Utilities Ranking slipped four spots from 59th in 2005 to 63rd in 2010.

From 2011 to 2013, Alcohol & Tobacco Ranking climbed 17 places from 58th to 41st, making it the highest ranked category throughout the second sub-period. Transport Ranking jumped eight spots from 91st in 2011 to 83rd in 2013. Health Ranking moved up five places from 96th to 91st between 2011 and 2013. Food & Non-alcoholic Beverages Ranking rose slightly from 92nd to 91st over the same sub-period. Education and Recreation Rankings remained at 80th and 96th, respectively, from 2011 to 2013. Recreation was thus the lowest ranked category for the entire second sub-period. In contrast, Housing Rents & Utilities Ranking fell eight places from 73rd in 2011 to 81st in 2013.

TIANJIN
China

Figure 5.95b

The Gross Hourly Wages in USD for Ordinary Residents in Tianjin, as denoted by the red line in Figure 5.95b, have increased significantly between 2005 and 2013. From US$0.71 in 2005, Tianjin's wage level rose almost fourfold to US$2.83 in 2013.

Meanwhile, the Wages Ranking for Ordinary Residents in Tianjin, as represented by the red bars, also improved from 91st in 2005 to 86th in 2013.

Figure 5.95c

Let us now analyse the cost of living and wages indices more closely and draw conclusions about the purchasing power of ordinary residents in Tianjin. As elaborated in Section 3.4.2 of Chapter 3, for a more precise and rigorous analysis, we discuss the results in two sub-periods: from 2005 to 2010 and from 2011 to 2013.

The Cost of Living Index and the Wages Index for Ordinary Residents in Tianjin are represented respectively by the grey and red line in Figure 5.95c. Between 2005 and 2010, the Cost of Living Index for Ordinary Residents was generally on an increasing trend. In 2005, the cost of living for ordinary residents in Tianjin was 23.41% of that for their counterparts in New York (the base city). It rose steadily over time to reach 28.20% in 2010. Over the same sub-period, the Wages Index for Ordinary Residents doubled, rising from 4.50 in 2005 to 9.40 in 2010.

Wages increased faster than cost of living so throughout the first sub-period, ordinary residents in Tianjin were able to afford more goods and services over time. This is reflected in the Purchasing Power Index for Ordinary Residents in Tianjin, which is represented by the green line in Figure 5.95c. Between 2005 and 2010, this index increased steadily from 19.23 to 33.33. The Purchasing Power Ranking for Ordinary Residents in Tianjin, as represented by the green bars, also improved over the first sub-period, rising from 95th in 2005 to 86th in 2010.

Over the second sub-period (2011–2013), the Cost of Living Index for Ordinary Residents has been on a decreasing trend. In 2011, the cost of living for ordinary residents in Tianjin was 30.33% of that for ordinary residents in New York. It decreased to 26.96% in 2013. In contrast, the Wages Index for Ordinary Residents has been increasing. This index rose from 11.10 in 2011 to 14.30 in 2013.

The combined trends of increasing wages and decreasing cost of living have enabled ordinary residents in Tianjin to afford more goods and services over time during the second sub-period. This is reflected in the Purchasing Power Index for Ordinary Residents, which increased rather significantly from 36.59 in 2011 to 53.04 in 2013. Ranking-wise, the Purchasing Power Ranking for Ordinary Residents has improved over the second sub-period, rising from 89th to 83rd between 2011 and 2013.

TIANJIN
China

Finally, we note that over the entire study period (2005–2013), the Purchasing Power Index for Ordinary Residents in Tianjin has consistently been lower than 100.00 — the base index value. This means that ordinary residents in Tianjin have only been able to afford a lower consumption level than their counterparts in New York, given the same number of working hours.

TOKYO
Japan

Figure 5.96a: Cost of Living and 10 Consumption Categories Rankings for Ordinary Residents in Tokyo, Japan

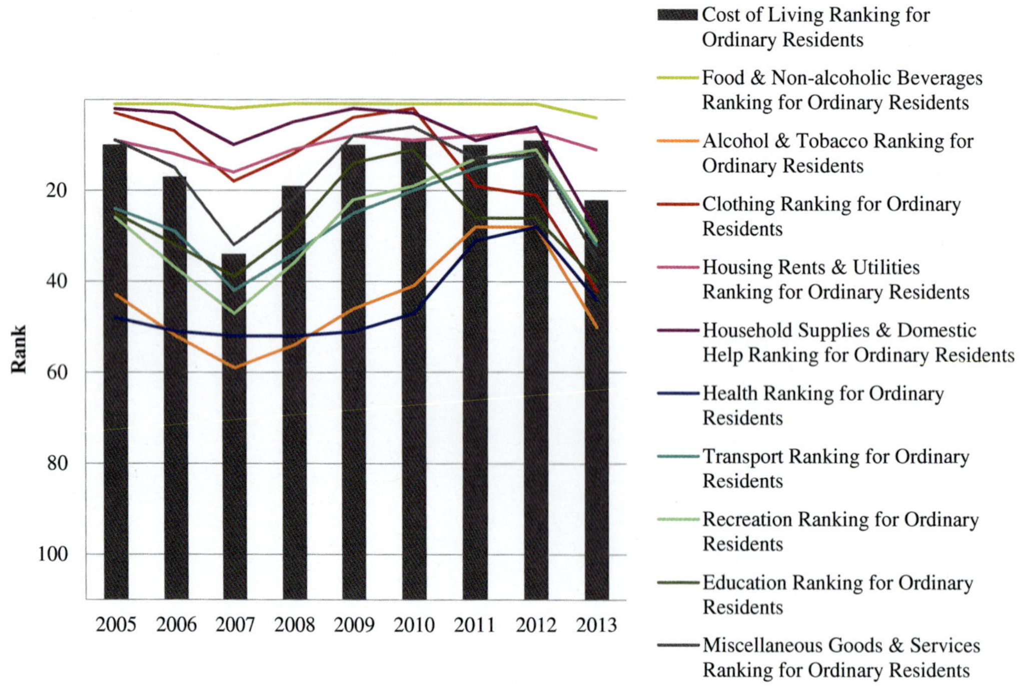

Source: Asia Competitiveness Institute

Figure 5.96b: Gross Hourly Wages in USD and Wages Ranking for Ordinary Residents in Tokyo, Japan

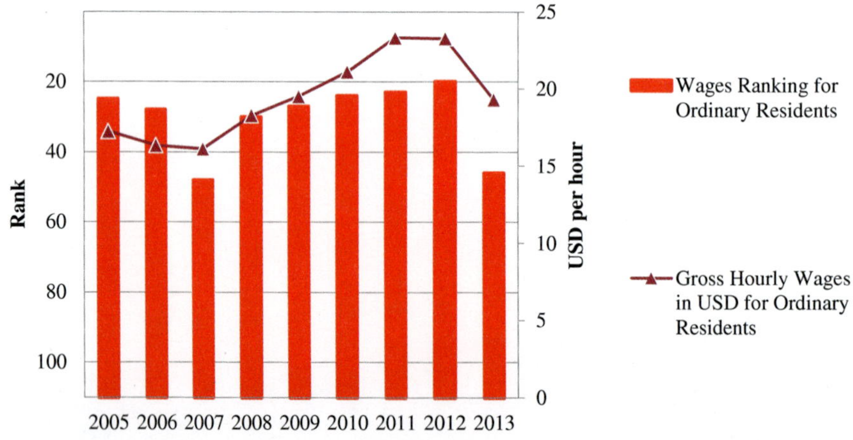

Source: Asia Competitiveness Institute

TOKYO
Japan

Figure 5.96c: Cost of Living, Wages and Purchasing Power Indices and Purchasing Power Ranking for Ordinary Residents in Tokyo, Japan

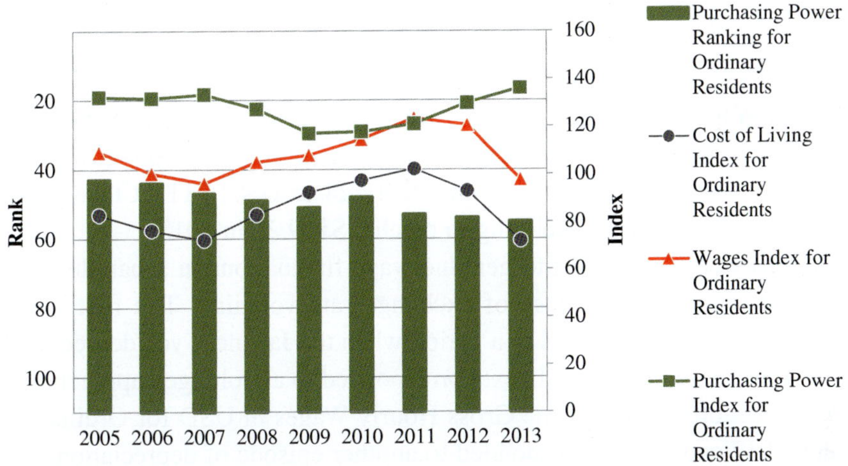

Source: Asia Competitiveness Institute

Figure 5.96a

Tokyo, the capital of Japan, serves as an international financial hub as well as a centre for the country's electronics, publishing and broadcasting industries. The city's Cost of Living Ranking for Ordinary Residents, as shown in the grey bars, rose from 10th to ninth between 2005 and 2010, but declined from 10th to 22nd between 2011 and 2013 (see Figure 5.96a). As elaborated in Section 3.4.2 of Chapter 3, for a more precise comparison of rankings, we have split the analysis into two sub-periods.

From 2005 to 2010, Education registered the most significant rise in ranking as it climbed 14 places from 25th to 11th. Transport Ranking moved up four spots from 24th to 20th between 2005 and 2010. Health Ranking jumped one place from 48th in 2005 to 47th in 2010. Housing Rents & Utilities Ranking fell from ninth in 2005 to 16th in 2007 before rising back to ninth in 2010. Food & Non-alcoholic Beverages Ranking remained largely unchanged at the top throughout the first sub-period.

The rankings of all 10 categories went down between 2011 and 2013. In particular, Alcohol & Tobacco Ranking fell 22 places from 28th in 2011 to 50th in 2013, making it the lowest ranked category in 2013. Household Supplies & Domestic Help Ranking slipped 20 places from ninth to 29th over the second sub-period. Transport Ranking dropped 17 spots from 15th to 32nd between 2011 and 2013. Education Ranking declined from 26th in 2011 to 40th in 2013. Health Ranking went down from 31st to 44th over the same sub-period. Food & Non-alcoholic Beverages and Housing Rents & Utilities Rankings both fell three places from first to fourth and eighth to 11th,

TOKYO
Japan

respectively, over the second sub-period, making them the highest and second highest ranked category in 2013.

Figure 5.96b

The Gross Hourly Wages in USD for Ordinary Residents in Tokyo, as represented by the red line in Figure 5.96b, have fluctuated substantially over the study period (2005–2013). Between 2005 and 2007, Tokyo's wage level dropped from US$17.24 to US$16.11. It then grew steadily to peak at US$23.25 in 2012 before declining to reach US$19.29 in 2013.

The fluctuations were due in part to genuine wage fluctuations in Japan during those years. However, they also happened because of exchange rate volatility. The first downward trend between 2005 and 2007 corresponded to a period when the Japanese yen depreciated against the US dollar. The upward trend observed next corresponded to a prolonged appreciation of the yen. Finally, the considerable decline of the Gross Hourly Wages in USD for Ordinary Residents in Tokyo between 2012 and 2013 corresponded to another episode of depreciation.

Ranking-wise, the Wages Ranking for Ordinary Residents in Tokyo, as represented by the red bars, has also fluctuated significantly over the study period. In 2013, Tokyo ranked 46th in terms of ordinary residents' wages among 103 cities.

Figure 5.96c

Let us now analyse the cost of living and wages indices more closely and draw conclusions about the purchasing power of ordinary residents in Tokyo. As elaborated in Section 3.4.2 of Chapter 3, for a more precise and rigorous analysis, we discuss the results in two sub-periods: from 2005 to 2010 and from 2011 to 2013.

The Cost of Living Index and the Wages Index for Ordinary Residents in Tokyo are represented respectively by the grey and red line in Figure 5.96c. Between 2005 and 2010, the Cost of Living Index for Ordinary Residents fluctuated substantially. In 2005, the cost of living for ordinary residents in Tokyo was 82.59% of that for their counterparts in New York (the base city). It dropped over the next two years to 72.07% in 2007 and then started to increase until it reached 97.25% in 2010. The Wages Index for Ordinary Residents followed a similar pattern as the cost of living index. It was also on a decreasing trend between 2005 and 2007 before reversing to an increasing trend subsequently. Overall, the wages index was higher in 2010 (114.42) than it was in 2005 (109.17).

Between 2005 and 2007, wages and cost of living generally fell at the same rate. Thus, during these years, ordinary residents in Tokyo were able to afford the same amount of goods and services over time. However, they could no longer do so after 2007: between 2007 and 2010 when both wages and cost of living were increasing, cost of living rose faster than the former. These trends are fully reflected in the Purchasing Power Index for Ordinary Residents in Tokyo, which is represented by the green line in Figure 5.96c. This index only fluctuated around 132.38 between 2005 and 2007 but steadily decreased thereafter and reached 117.65 in 2010. Meanwhile, the Purchasing Power Ranking for Ordinary Residents in Tokyo, as represented by the green bars, also fluctuated significantly over the first sub-period. Overall, however, Tokyo's ranking dropped from 43rd in 2005 to 48th in 2010.

Over the second sub-period (2011–2013), the Cost of Living Index for Ordinary Residents has been on a decreasing trend. In 2011, the cost of living for ordinary residents in Tokyo was 1.02 times that for ordinary residents in New York. It dropped to 71.78% in 2013. The Wages Index for Ordinary Residents has also been on a decreasing trend, dropping from 123.29 in 2011 to 97.61 in 2013.

Wages have decreased more slowly than cost of living, so throughout the second sub-period, ordinary residents in Tokyo have been able to afford a higher consumption level over time. This is reflected in the Purchasing Power Index for Ordinary Residents, which rose steadily from 120.86 in 2011 to 135.99 in 2013. Despite the positive showing of the index, the Purchasing Power Ranking for Ordinary Residents in Tokyo has deteriorated over the second sub-period, dropping from 53rd in 2011 to 55th in 2013.

Finally, we note that over the entire study period (2005–2013), the Purchasing Power Index for Ordinary Residents in Tokyo has always been above 100.00 — the base index value. This means that ordinary residents in Tokyo have consistently been able to afford a higher consumption level than their counterparts in New York, given the same number of working hours.

TORONTO
Canada

Figure 5.97a: Cost of Living and 10 Consumption Categories Rankings for Ordinary Residents in Toronto, Canada

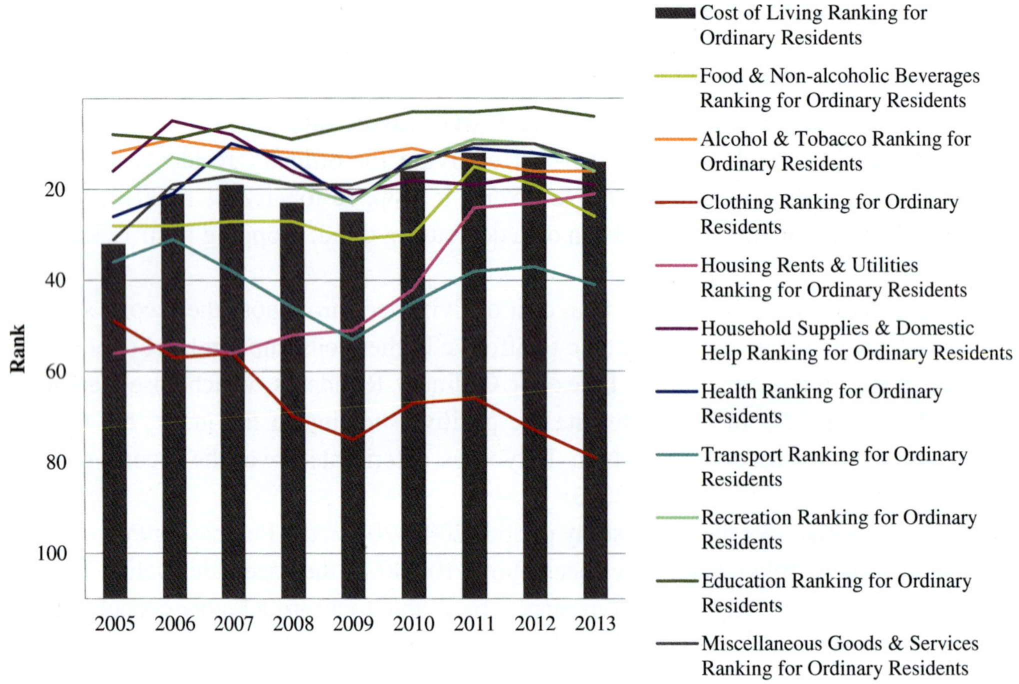

Source: Asia Competitiveness Institute

Figure 5.97b: Gross Hourly Wages in USD and Wages Ranking for Ordinary Residents in Toronto, Canada

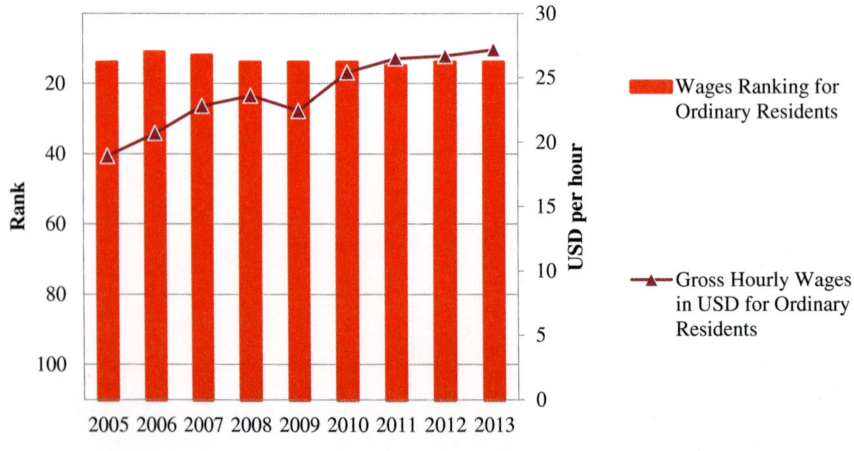

Source: Asia Competitiveness Institute

TORONTO
Canada

Figure 5.97c: Cost of Living, Wages and Purchasing Power Indices and Purchasing Power Ranking for Ordinary Residents in Toronto, Canada

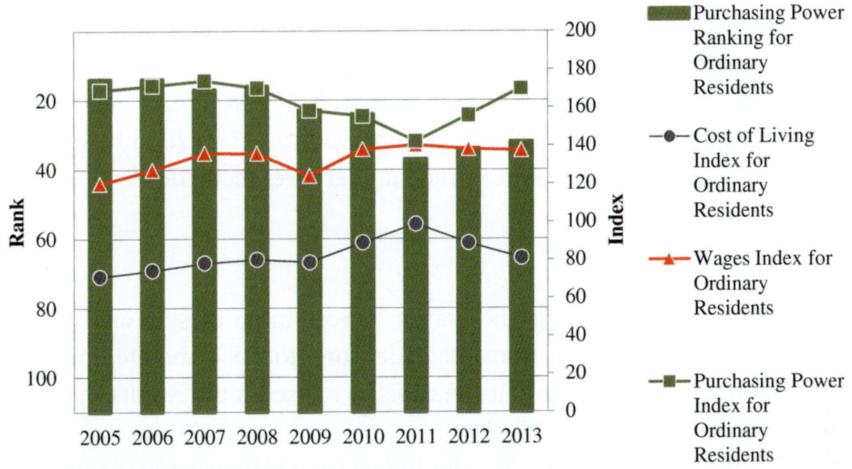

Source: Asia Competitiveness Institute

Figure 5.97a

With a population of approximately 2.6 million, Toronto is the most populous city in Canada and the fourth most populous city in North America after Mexico City, New York and Los Angeles. The city's Cost of Living Ranking for Ordinary Residents, as denoted by the grey bars, rose from 32nd to 16th between 2005 and 2010, and fell from 12th to 14th between 2011 and 2013 (see Figure 5.97a). As explained in Section 3.4.2 of Chapter 3, for a more precise comparison of rankings, we have split the analysis into two sub-periods.

From 2005 to 2010, Housing Rents & Utilities Ranking jumped 14 places from 56th to 42nd. Health Ranking moved up 13 spots from 26th in 2005 to 13th in 2010. Education Ranking rose more modestly from eighth to third over the first sub-period. In contrast, Transport Ranking slipped nine places from 36th to 45th between 2005 and 2010. Food & Non-alcoholic Beverages Ranking went down from 28th in 2005 to 30th in 2010.

From 2011 to 2013, Housing Rents & Utilities was the only category that rose in ranking from 24th to 21st. Clothing registered the most remarkable dip in ranking as it fell 13 places from 66th in 2011 to 79th in 2013, making it the lowest ranked category throughout the second sub-period. Food & Non-alcoholic Beverages Ranking slipped 11 spots from 15th to 26th between 2011 and 2013. Health and Transport Rankings both moved down three places from 11th to 14th and 38th to 41st, respectively, over the same sub-period. Education Ranking declined slightly from third in 2011 to fourth in 2013. Consequently, Education remained as the highest ranked category for the entire second sub-period.

TORONTO
Canada

Figure 5.97b

The Gross Hourly Wages in USD for Ordinary Residents in Toronto, as denoted by the red line in Figure 5.97b, have generally followed an upward trend over the study period. From US$18.91 in 2005, Toronto's wage level rose to US$27.16 in 2013.

Meanwhile, the Wages Ranking for Ordinary Residents in Toronto, as shown by the red bars, has been relatively stable. From 14th in 2005, it improved to 11th in 2006 before dropping back to 14th in 2008. The ranking has largely remained at that level thereafter.

Figure 5.97c

Let us now analyse the cost of living and wages indices more closely and draw conclusions about the purchasing power of ordinary residents in Toronto. As elaborated in Section 3.4.2 of Chapter 3, for a more precise and rigorous analysis, we discuss the results in two sub-periods: from 2005 to 2010 and from 2011 to 2013.

The Cost of Living Index and the Wages Index for Ordinary Residents in Toronto are represented respectively by the grey and red line in Figure 5.97c. Over the first sub-period (2005–2010), the Cost of Living Index for Ordinary Residents was generally on an increasing trend. In 2005, the cost of living for ordinary residents in Toronto was 70.98% of that for their counterparts in New York (the base city). It rose over the years to 79.85% in 2008, then dropped marginally to 78.43% in 2009 before rising to 88.80% in 2010. Meanwhile, the Wages Index for Ordinary Residents also followed a similar pattern. Like the cost of living index, this index was also on an increasing trend that was temporarily interrupted by a plunge in 2009. Overall, the wages index was higher in 2010 (137.89) than it was in 2005 (119.76).

Between 2005 and 2007, wages rose slightly faster than cost of living but thereafter, wages could no longer keep up with the latter. Thus, ordinary residents in Toronto could not afford the same amount of goods and services over time for most of the sub-period. This is reflected in the Purchasing Power Index for Ordinary Residents in Toronto, which is represented by the green line in Figure 5.97c. Aside from a short and mild upward trend between 2005 and 2007, the index generally followed a decreasing trend for most of the first sub-period. Overall, the index was lower in 2010 (155.28) than it was in 2005 (168.72). Ranking-wise, the Purchasing Power Ranking for Ordinary Residents in Toronto, as represented by the green bars, deteriorated significantly over the first sub-period, dropping 10 places from 14th in 2005 to 24th in 2013.

Over the second sub-period (2011–2013), the Cost of Living Index for Ordinary Residents has been on a decreasing trend. In 2011, the cost of living for ordinary residents in Toronto was 98.62% of that for their counterparts in New York. It dropped over the years to reach 80.89% in

2013. The Wages Index for Ordinary Residents has also been decreasing, albeit more marginally. From 140.07 in 2011, the index dropped to 137.38 in 2013.

That wages have decreased more slowly than cost of living means that ordinary residents in Toronto have been able to afford more goods and services over time throughout the second sub-period. This is reflected in the Purchasing Power Index for Ordinary Residents, which rose from 142.04 in 2011 to 169.84 in 2013. Meanwhile, the Purchasing Power Ranking for Ordinary Residents has improved over the second sub-period, rising from 37th in 2011 to 32nd in 2013.

Finally, we note that over the entire study period (2005–2013), the Purchasing Power Index for Ordinary Residents in Toronto has always been above 100.00 — the base index value. This means that ordinary residents in Toronto have consistently been able to afford a higher consumption level than their counterparts in New York, given the same number of working hours.

VANCOUVER
Canada

Figure 5.98a: Cost of Living and 10 Consumption Categories Rankings for Ordinary Residents in Vancouver, Canada

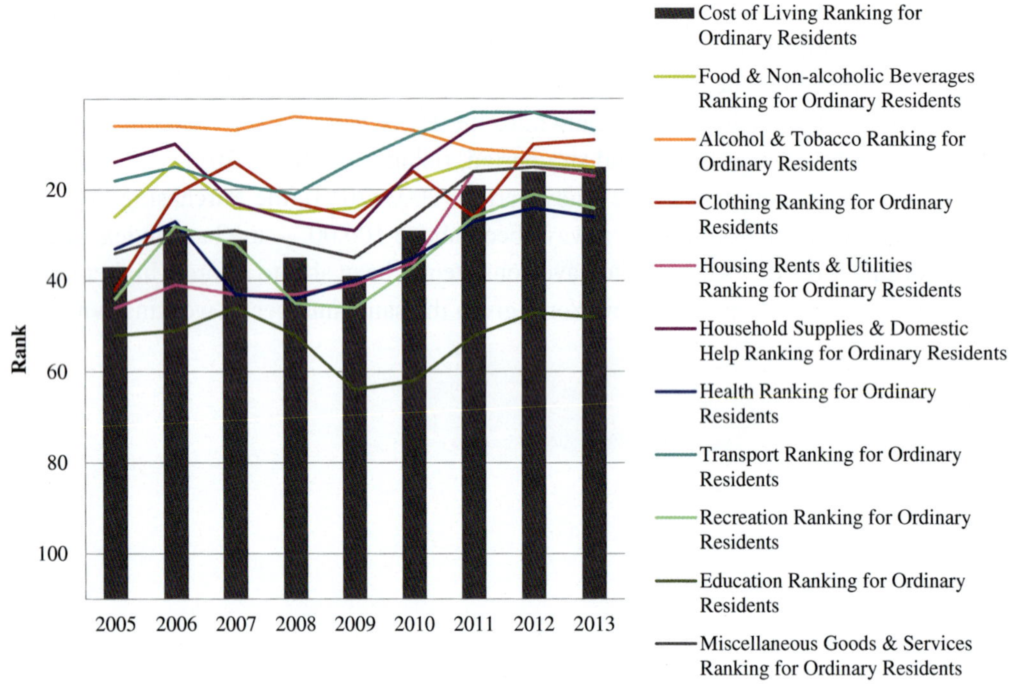

Source: Asia Competitiveness Institute

Figure 5.98b: Gross Hourly Wages in USD and Wages Ranking for Ordinary Residents in Vancouver, Canada

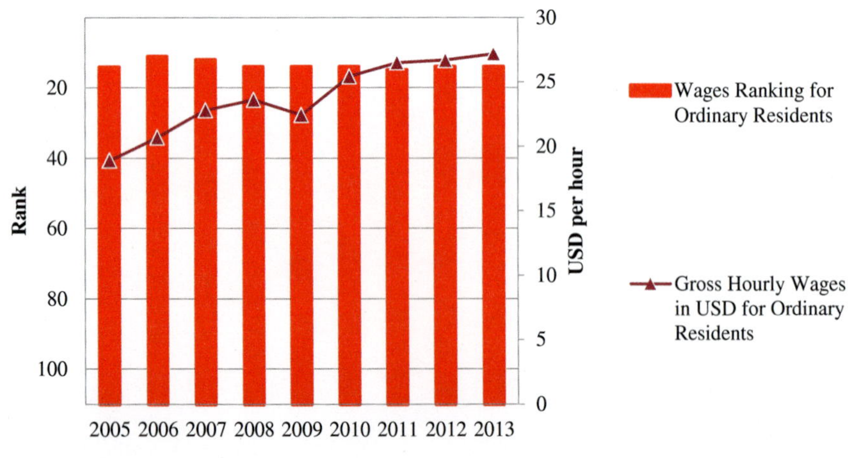

Source: Asia Competitiveness Institute

VANCOUVER
Canada

Figure 5.98c: Cost of Living, Wages and Purchasing Power Indices and Purchasing Power Ranking for Ordinary Residents in Vancouver, Canada

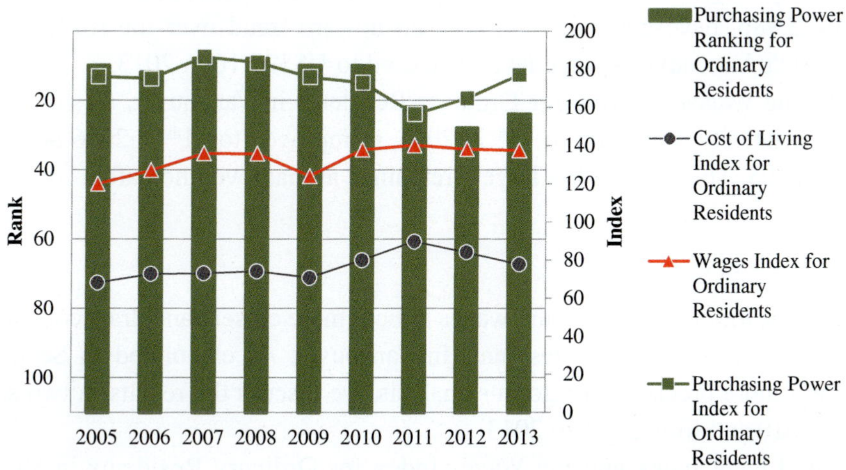

Source: Asia Competitiveness Institute

Figure 5.98a

Vancouver is a coastal seaport city on the mainland of the British Columbia province and home to Canada's major film production studios. The city's Cost of Living Ranking for Ordinary Residents, as represented by the grey bars, rose from 37th to 29th between 2005 and 2010, and from 19th to 15th between 2011 and 2013 (see Figure 5.98a). As elaborated in Section 3.4.2 of Chapter 3, for a more precise comparison of rankings, we have split the analysis into two sub-periods.

From 2005 to 2010, Housing Rents & Utilities and Transport Rankings both climbed 10 places from 46th to 36th and 18th to eighth, respectively. Food & Non-alcoholic Beverages Ranking moved up eight spots from 26th in 2005 to 18th in 2010. In contrast, Education Ranking slipped 10 places from 52nd to 62nd over the first sub-period. Health Ranking fell two spots from 33rd to 35th between 2005 and 2010.

Between 2011 and 2013, Education Ranking jumped four spots from 52nd to 48th. Nonetheless, Education remained as the lowest ranked category in both sub-periods. Household Supplies & Domestic Help overtook Transport to become the highest ranked category in 2013 as its ranking rose from sixth in 2011 to third in 2013. Health Ranking moved up one place from 27th to 26th over the same sub-period. In contrast, Transport Ranking slipped four spots from third in 2011 to seventh in 2013. Housing Rents & Utilities and Food & Non-alcoholic Beverages Rankings both fell one place from 16th to 17th and 14th to 15th, respectively, over the second sub-period.

VANCOUVER
Canada

Figure 5.98b

The Gross Hourly Wages in USD for Ordinary Residents in Vancouver, as denoted by the red line in Figure 5.98b, have generally followed an upward trend over the study period. From US$18.91 in 2005, Vancouver's wage level increased to US$27.16 in 2013.

Meanwhile, the Wages Ranking for Ordinary Residents in Vancouver, as shown by the red bars, has been relatively stable. From 14th in 2005, it improved to 11th in 2006 before dropping back to 14th in 2008. The ranking has largely remained at that level thereafter.

Figure 5.98c

Let us now analyse the cost of living and wages indices more closely and draw conclusions about the purchasing power of ordinary residents in Vancouver. As elaborated in Section 3.4.2 of Chapter 3, for a more precise and rigorous analysis, we discuss the results in two sub-periods: from 2005 to 2010 and from 2011 to 2013.

The Cost of Living Index and the Wages Index for Ordinary Residents in Vancouver are represented respectively by the grey and red line in Figure 5.98c. Over the first sub-period (2005–2010), the Cost of Living Index for Ordinary Residents was generally on an increasing trend. In 2005, the cost of living for ordinary residents in Vancouver was 68.06% of that for their counterparts in New York (the base city). It rose over the years to 74.03% in 2008, then dropped slightly to 70.60% in 2009 before rising to 79.79% in 2010. Meanwhile, the Wages Index for Ordinary Residents also followed a similar pattern. Like the cost of living index, this index was also on an increasing trend that was temporarily interrupted by a plunge in 2009. Overall, the wages index was higher in 2010 (137.89) than it was in 2005 (119.76).

Between 2005 and 2007, wages rose slightly faster than cost of living but thereafter, wages could no longer keep up with the latter. Thus, ordinary residents in Vancouver were able to maintain, and even slightly increase, their consumption level over time until 2007. After 2007, however, they could no longer do so. These trends are reflected in the Purchasing Power Index for Ordinary Residents in Vancouver, which is represented by the green line in Figure 5.98c. The index followed a short and mild upward trend between 2005 and 2007. However, for the remaining of the first sub-period, the index generally followed a decreasing trend. Overall, the index was lower in 2010 (172.82) than it was in 2005 (175.97), indicating an erosion of purchasing power. Ranking-wise, the Purchasing Power Ranking for Ordinary Residents in Vancouver, as represented by the green bars, fluctuated moderately over the first sub-period. From 10th in 2005, it dropped to 12th in 2006. It then improved to eighth for the next two years before dropping again to 10th in 2009 and 2010.

Over the second sub-period (2011–2013), the Cost of Living Index for Ordinary Residents has been on a decreasing trend. In 2011, the cost of living for ordinary residents in Vancouver was 89.55% of that for their counterparts in New York. It dropped over the years to reach 77.66% in

VANCOUVER
Canada

2013. The Wages Index for Ordinary Residents has also been decreasing, albeit more marginally. From 140.07 in 2011, the index dropped to 137.38 in 2013.

That wages have decreased more slowly than cost of living means that ordinary residents in Vancouver have been able to afford more goods and services over time throughout the second sub-period. This is reflected in the Purchasing Power Index for Ordinary Residents, which rose from 156.41 in 2011 to 176.91 in 2013. Despite the positive showing of the index, the Purchasing Power Ranking for Ordinary Residents has deteriorated over the second sub-period, dropping from 22nd in 2011 to 24th in 2013 with even a deeper plunge to 28th in 2012.

Finally, we note that over the entire study period (2005–2013), the Purchasing Power Index for Ordinary Residents in Vancouver has always been above 100.00 — the base index value. This means that ordinary residents in Vancouver have consistently been able to afford a higher consumption level than their counterparts in New York, given the same number of working hours.

VIENNA
Austria

Figure 5.99a: Cost of Living and 10 Consumption Categories Rankings for Ordinary Residents in Vienna, Austria

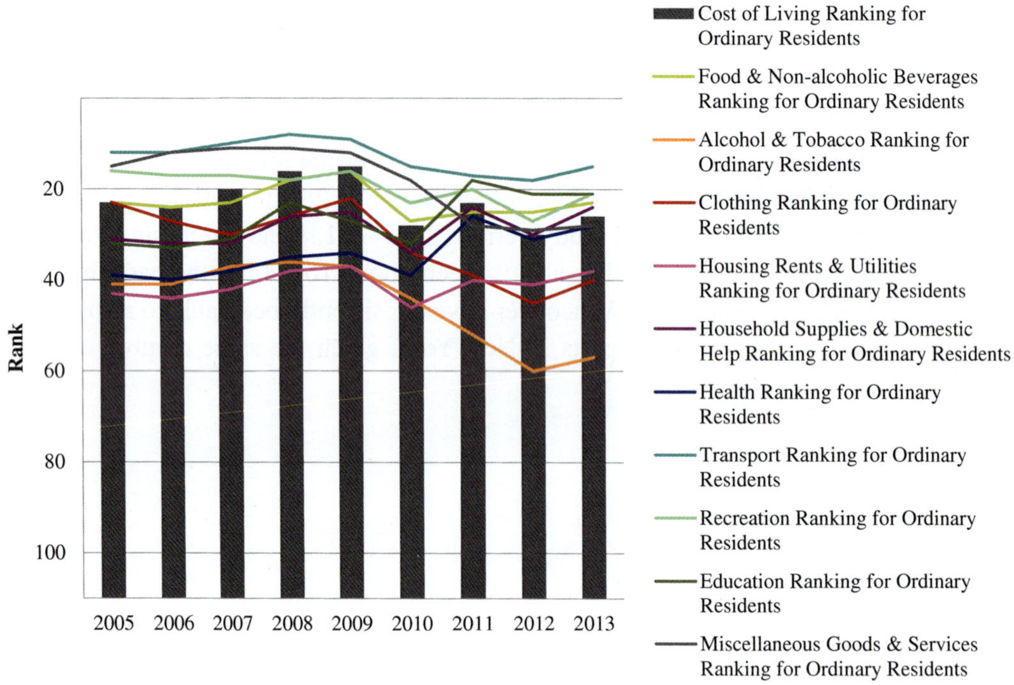

Source: Asia Competitiveness Institute

Figure 5.99b: Gross Hourly Wages in USD and Wages Ranking for Ordinary Residents in Vienna, Austria.

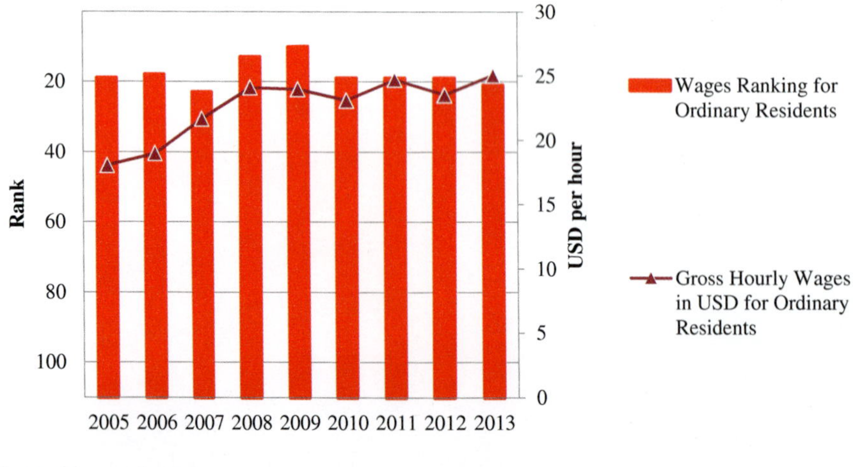

Source: Asia Competitiveness Institute

VIENNA
Austria

Figure 5.99c: Cost of Living, Wages and Purchasing Power Indices and Purchasing Power Ranking for Ordinary Residents in Vienna, Austria

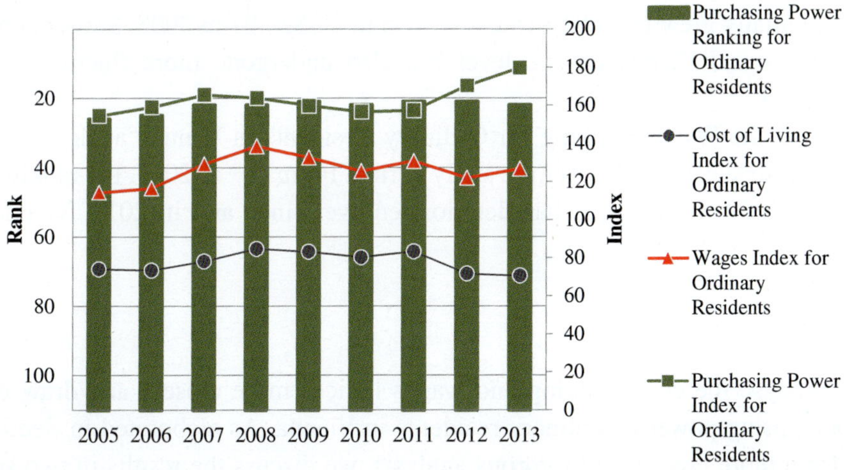

Source: Asia Competitiveness Institute

Figure 5.99a

Vienna is the capital and largest city of Austria and the seventh largest city by population within city limits in the European Union with a population of about 1.8 million. The city's Cost of Living Ranking for Ordinary Residents, as shown in the grey bars, fell from 23rd to 28th between 2005 and 2010, and from 23rd to 26th between 2011 and 2013 (see Figure 5.99a). As explained in Section 3.4.2 of Chapter 3, for a more precise comparison of rankings, we have split the analysis into two sub-periods.

From 2005 to 2010, Food & Non-alcoholic Beverages Ranking slipped four places from 23rd to 27th. Housing Rents & Utilities and Transport Rankings both moved down three spots from 43rd to 46th and 12th to 15th, respectively, over the first sub-period. Health Ranking rose from 39th in 2005 to 34th in 2009 before falling back to 39th in 2010. Likewise, Education Ranking went up from 32nd in 2005 to 23rd in 2008 before slipping back to 32nd in 2010.

From 2011 to 2013, Transport Ranking jumped two places from 17th to 15th, making it the highest ranked category throughout the second sub-period. Likewise, Food & Non-alcoholic Beverages and Housing Rents & Utilities Rankings rose from 25th to 23rd and 40th to 38th, respectively, between 2011 and 2013. In contrast, Alcohol & Tobacco Ranking slipped five places from 52nd in 2011 to 57th in 2013. Consequently, it remained as the lowest ranked category for the entire second sub-period. Education Ranking fell three spots from 18th to 21st between 2011 and 2013. Health Ranking moved down two places from 26th to 28th over the same sub-period.

VIENNA
Austria

Figure 5.99b

The Gross Hourly Wages in USD for Ordinary Residents in Vienna, as shown by the red line in Figure 5.99b, initially grew from US$18.04 in 2005 to US$24.07 in 2008. Subsequently, growth has slowed down and Vienna's wage level has also undergone more fluctuations, reaching US$25.03 in 2013.

Ranking-wise, the Wages Ranking for Ordinary Residents in Vienna, as denoted by the red bars, has fluctuated substantially over the study period. From 19th in 2005, the ranking rose to its peak of 10th in 2009. However, it has deteriorated ever since and in 2013, Vienna's ranking dropped to 21st.

Figure 5.99c

Let us now analyse the cost of living and wages indices more closely and draw conclusions about the purchasing power of ordinary residents in Vienna. As elaborated in Section 3.4.2 of Chapter 3, for a more precise and rigorous analysis, we discuss the results in two sub-periods: from 2005 to 2010 and from 2011 to 2013.

The Cost of Living Index and the Wages Index for Ordinary Residents in Vienna are represented respectively by the grey and red line in Figure 5.99c. Between 2005 and 2010, the Cost of Living Index for Ordinary Residents exhibited moderate fluctuations. In 2005, the cost of living for ordinary residents in Vienna was 73.95% of that for their counterparts in New York (the base city). It first rose to peak at 84.54% in 2008 before starting to decrease until it reached 80.07% in 2010. Over the first sub-period, the Wages Index for Ordinary Residents also followed a similar pattern, rising from its initial level at 114.24 in 2005 to peak at 138.43 in 2008 before reversing to a decreasing trend. In 2010, the value for the wages index was 125.33, which was higher than its value in 2005.

Between 2005 and 2007, wages increased faster than cost of living. However, between 2007 and 2008, wages could no longer keep up with the latter. In addition, over 2008–2010 when both were falling, wages fell faster than cost of living. As a result, ordinary residents in Vienna were only able to afford higher consumption level over time during 2005–2007. After 2007, they could no longer do so. These trends are fully reflected in the Purchasing Power Index for Ordinary Residents in Vienna, which is represented by the green line in Figure 5.99c. Between 2005 and 2007, this index rose from 154.49 to 165.42. After 2007, it steadily decreased until it reached 156.52 in 2010, only slightly higher than its initial level in 2005. Surprisingly, the Purchasing Power Ranking for Ordinary Residents in Vienna, as represented by the green bars, generally improved over the first sub-period. It rose from 26th in 2005 to 22nd in 2010.

Over the second sub-period (2011–2013), the Cost of Living Index for Ordinary Residents has been on a decreasing trend. In 2011, the cost of living for ordinary residents in Vienna was 83.14% of that for their counterparts in New York. It dropped to 70.48% in 2013. The Wages

Index for Ordinary Residents has also been decreasing, dropping from 130.66 in 2011 to 126.61 in 2013.

Although both have been decreasing, wages have dropped more slowly than cost of living. Thus, throughout the second sub-period, ordinary residents in Vienna were able to afford more goods and services over time. This is reflected in the Purchasing Power Index for Ordinary Residents, which rose from 157.16 in 2011 to 179.63 in 2013. Despite this positive showing of the index, the Purchasing Power Ranking for Ordinary Residents has actually deteriorated, albeit marginally, over the second sub-period, dropping from 21st in 2011 to 22nd in 2013.

Finally, we note that over the entire study period (2005–2013), the Purchasing Power Index for Ordinary Residents in Vienna has always been above 100.00 — the base index value. This means that ordinary residents in Vienna have consistently been able to afford more goods and services than their counterparts in New York, given the same number of working hours.

WARSAW
Poland

Figure 5.100a: Cost of Living and 10 Consumption Categories Rankings for Ordinary Residents in Warsaw, Poland

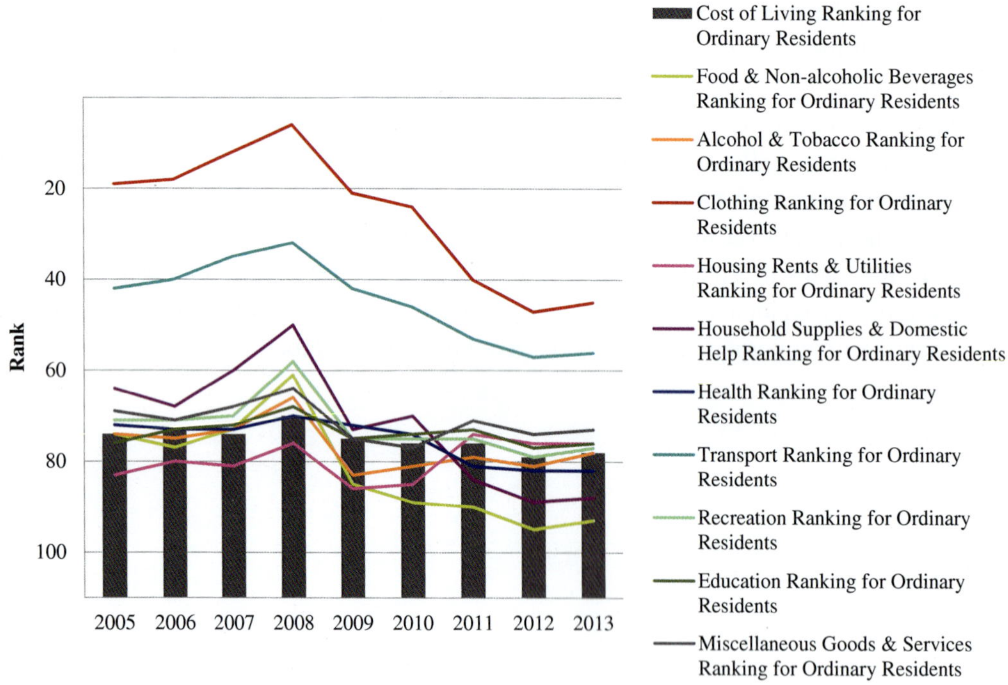

Source: Asia Competitiveness Institute

Figure 5.100b: Gross Hourly Wages in USD and Wages Ranking for Ordinary Residents in Warsaw, Poland

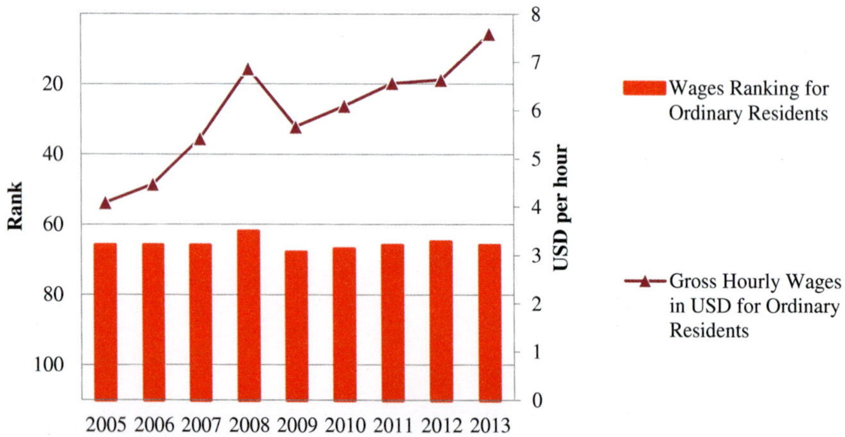

Source: Asia Competitiveness Institute

WARSAW
Poland

Figure 5.100c: Cost of Living, Wages and Purchasing Power Indices and Purchasing Power Ranking for Ordinary Residents in Warsaw, Poland

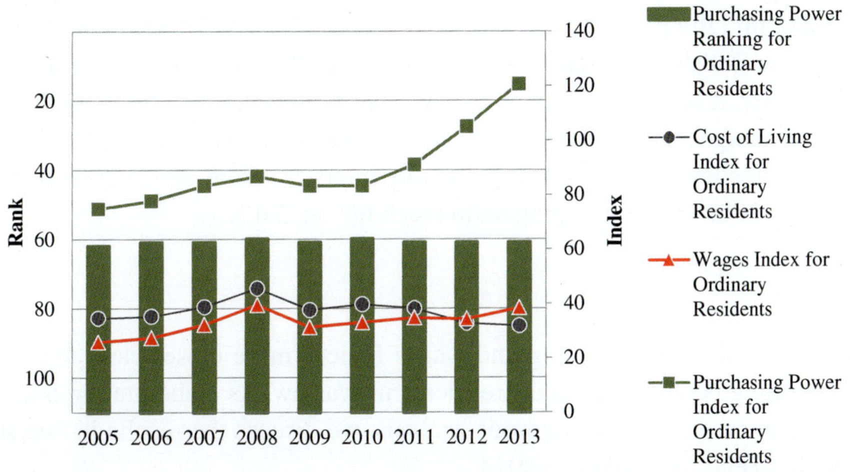

Source: Asia Competitiveness Institute

Figure 5.100a

Widely known for its picturesque architecture, Warsaw is the capital and largest city of Poland with an estimated population of 1.7 million. The city's Cost of Living Ranking for Ordinary Residents, as denoted by the grey bars, fell from 74th to 76th between 2005 and 2010, and from 76th to 78th between 2011 and 2013 (see Figure 5.100a). As elaborated in Section 3.4.2 of Chapter 3, for a more precise comparison of rankings, we have split the analysis into two sub-periods.

In the first sub-period from 2005 to 2010, Education was the only category that rose in ranking from 76th to 74th. Food & Non-alcoholic Beverages saw the most significant dip in ranking as it slipped 15 places from 74th in 2005 to 89th in 2010. Transport Ranking fell four spots from 42nd to 46th between 2005 and 2010. Housing Rents & Utilities and Health Rankings both moved down two places from 83rd to 85th and 72nd to 74th, respectively, over the same sub-period.

Between 2011 and 2013, Clothing Ranking slipped five spots from 40th to 45th. Nonetheless, Clothing remained as the highest ranked category throughout both sub-periods. Household Supplies & Domestic Help Ranking moved down four places from 84th in 2011 to 88th in 2013. Food & Non-alcoholic Beverages Ranking fell three places from 90th to 93rd over the second sub-period, making it the lowest ranked category for the entire second sub-period. Likewise, Education and Transport Rankings declined from 73rd to 76th and 53rd to 56th, respectively, between 2011 and 2013. Housing Rents & Utilities Ranking slipped two spots from 74th in 2011 to 76th in 2013.

WARSAW
Poland

Figure 5.100b

The Gross Hourly Wages in USD for Ordinary Residents in Warsaw, as denoted by the red line in Figure 5.100b, initially grew steadily from US$4.09 in 2005 to US$6.87 in 2008. Due to the depreciation of the Polish zloty against the US dollar in 2009, Warsaw's wage level plunged in that year. Thereafter, it has reversed to an upward trend to reach US$7.59 in 2013.

The Wages Ranking for Ordinary Residents in Warsaw, as shown by the red bars, has mirrored the trend of the wage level quite closely. It initially improved from 66th in 2005 to 62nd in 2008, dropped to 68th in 2009 before rising again to reach 66th in 2013.

Figure 5.100c

Let us now analyse the cost of living and wages indices more closely and draw conclusions about the purchasing power of ordinary residents in Warsaw. As elaborated in Section 3.4.2 of Chapter 3, for a more precise and rigorous analysis, we discuss the results in two sub-periods: from 2005 to 2010 and from 2011 to 2013.

The Cost of Living Index and the Wages Index for Ordinary Residents in Warsaw are represented respectively by the grey and red line in Figure 5.100c. Over the first sub-period (2005–2010), the Cost of Living Index for Ordinary Residents was generally on an increasing trend. In 2005, the cost of living for ordinary residents in Warsaw was 34.61% of that for their counterparts in New York (the base city). It rose over the years to reach 39.69% in 2010, with a sharp spike to 45.55% in 2008. Meanwhile, the Wages Index for Ordinary Residents also followed a similar pattern. From 25.88 in 2005, this index rose to 33.05 in 2010.

Throughout the first sub-period, wages generally rose faster than cost of living. Thus, ordinary residents in Warsaw were able to afford a higher consumption level over time during these years. This is reflected in the Purchasing Power Index for Ordinary Residents in Warsaw, which is represented by the green line in Figure 5.100c. The index increased from 74.79 in 2005 to 83.28 in 2010. Ranking-wise, the Purchasing Power Ranking for Ordinary Residents in Warsaw, as represented by the green bars, was relatively stable. It only fluctuated between 60th and 62nd throughout the first sub-period.

Over the second sub-period (2011–2013), the Cost of Living Index for Ordinary Residents has been on a decreasing trend. In 2011, the cost of living for ordinary residents in Warsaw was 38.18% of that for their counterparts in New York. It dropped over the years to reach 31.84% in 2013. In contrast, the Wages Index for Ordinary Residents has been increasing. It rose from 34.73 in 2011 to 38.41 in 2013.

The combined trends of increasing wages and decreasing cost of living have enabled ordinary residents in Warsaw to afford more goods and services over time throughout the second sub-period. This is reflected in the Purchasing Power Index for Ordinary Residents which rose from

90.97 in 2011 to 120.63 in 2013. Despite the positive showing of the index, the Purchasing Power Ranking for Ordinary Residents has stagnated at 61st over the second sub-period.

Finally, we note that over the entire study period (2005–2013), the Purchasing Power Index for Ordinary Residents in Warsaw had always been below 100.00 — the base index value — until 2012. This means it was not until 2012 that ordinary residents in Warsaw were able to afford more goods and services than their counterparts in New York. Before 2012, they had only been able to afford a lower consumption level.

WASHINGTON DC
United States

Figure 5.101a: Cost of Living and 10 Consumption Categories Rankings for Ordinary Residents in Washington DC, United States

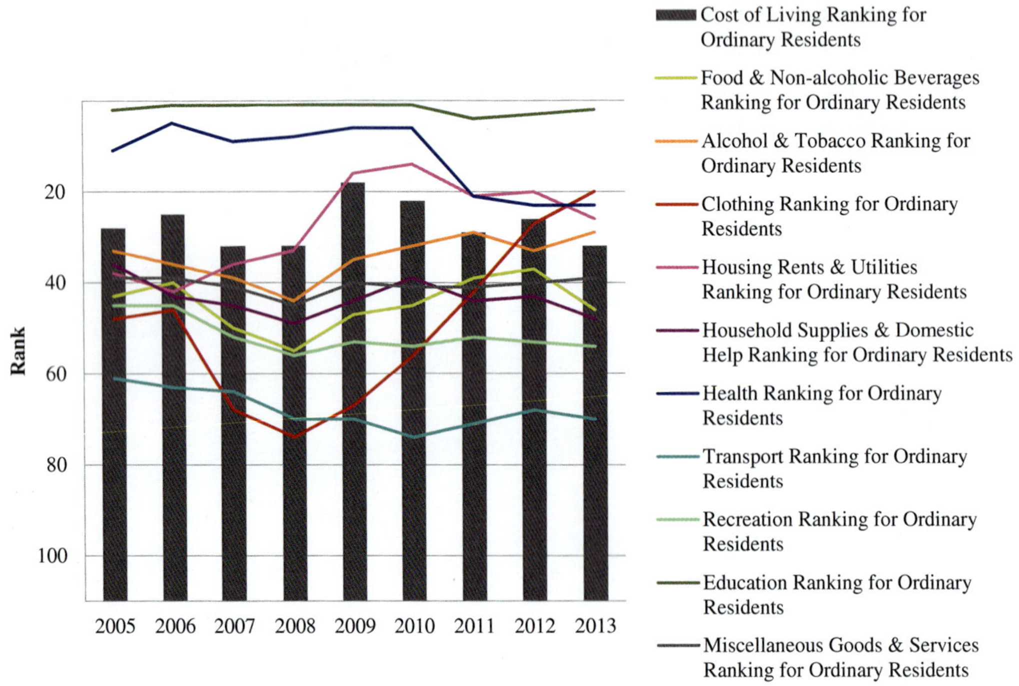

Source: Asia Competitiveness Institute

Figure 5.101b: Gross Hourly Wages in USD and Wages Ranking for Ordinary Residents in Washington DC, United States

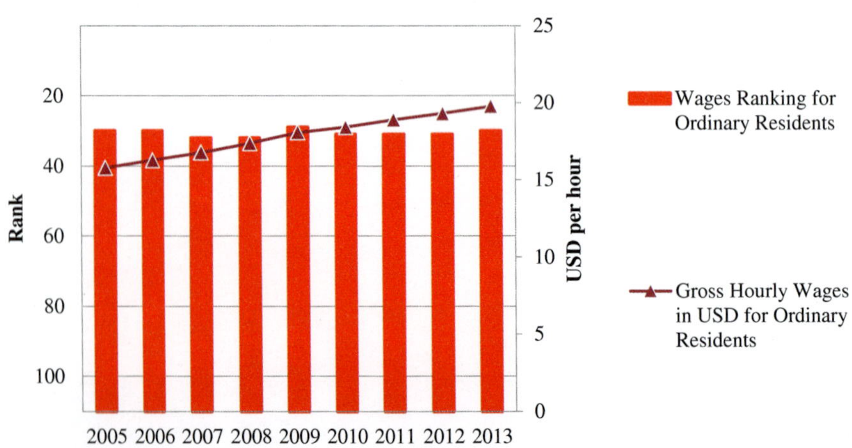

Source: Asia Competitiveness Institute

WASHINGTON DC
United States

Figure 5.101c: Cost of Living, Wages and Purchasing Power Indices and Purchasing Power Ranking for Ordinary Residents in Washington DC, United States

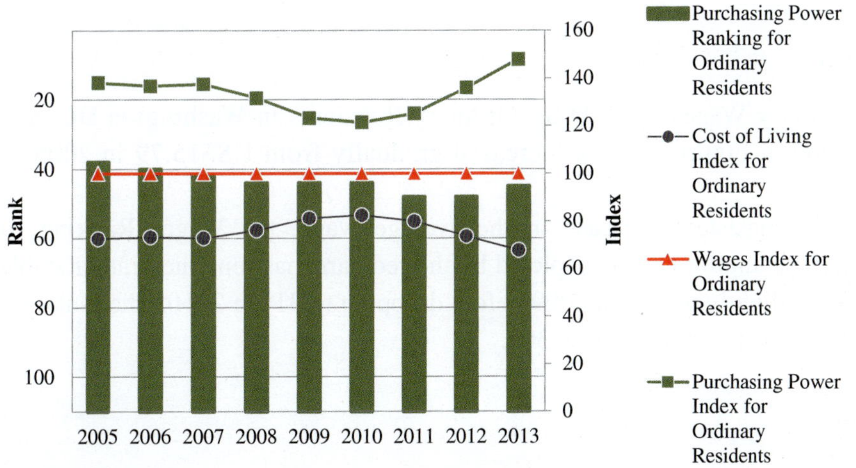

Source: Asia Competitiveness Institute

Figure 5.101a

As the capital of the United States, Washington DC is home to the President, the Congress, the Supreme Court, 176 foreign embassies as well as the headquarters of many international organisations. The city's Cost of Living Ranking for Ordinary Residents, as represented by the grey bars, rose from 28th to 22nd between 2005 and 2010, and declined from 29th to 32nd between 2011 and 2013 (see Figure 5.101a). As explained in Section 3.4.2 of Chapter 3, for a more precise comparison of rankings, we have split the analysis into two sub-periods.

From 2005 to 2010, Housing Rents & Utilities Ranking climbed 24 places from 38th to 14th. Health Ranking moved up five spots from 11th in 2005 to sixth in 2010. Education Ranking rose from second to first over the first sub-period. In contrast, Transport Ranking slipped 13 places from 61st to 74th between 2005 and 2010. Food & Non-alcoholic Beverages Ranking fell two spots from 43rd to 45th over the same sub-period.

From 2011 to 2013, Clothing registered the most significant rise in ranking as it climbed 22 places from 42nd to 20th and became the second highest ranked category in 2013. Education remained as the highest ranked category in both sub-periods as its ranking moved up two places from fourth in 2011 to second in 2013, making Washington DC the second most expensive city in this category in 2013. Transport was consistently the lowest ranked category for the entire second sub-period as its ranking rose from 71st to 70th between 2011 and 2013. In contrast, Food & Non-alcoholic Beverages Ranking slipped seven spots from 39th in 2011 to 46th in 2013.

WASHINGTON DC
United States

Housing Rents & Utilities Ranking fell five places from 21st to 26th over the second sub-period. Health Ranking moved down two spots from 21st in 2011 to 23rd in 2013.

Figure 5.101b

The Gross Hourly Wages in USD for Ordinary Residents in Washington DC, as represented by the red line in Figure 5.101b, increased gradually from US$15.79 in 2005 to US$19.77 in 2013.

Despite the consistent increase in the average wage, the Wages Ranking for Ordinary Residents in Washington DC, as depicted by the red bars, has remained rather stable. From 30th in 2005, it rose slightly to 29th in 2009 before dropping to 31st in 2010. The ranking remained at 31st until 2013, when it rose back to 30th.

Figure 5.101c

Let us now analyse the cost of living and wages indices more closely and draw conclusions about the purchasing power of ordinary residents in Washington DC. As elaborated in Section 3.4.2 of Chapter 3, for a more precise and rigorous analysis, we discuss the results in two sub-periods: from 2005 to 2010 and from 2011 to 2013.

The Cost of Living Index and the Wages Index for Ordinary Residents in Washington DC are represented respectively by the grey and red line in Figure 5.101c. As mentioned in Section 3.3 of Chapter 3, wage data are only available at the national level and not by cities. Therefore, wages in all cities in the United States are assumed to be the same. As a result, Washington DC, being a city in the United States, shares a common Wages Index for Ordinary Residents with the base city New York (whose index value is 100.00) over the entire study period (2005–2013).

Between 2005 and 2010, the Cost of Living Index for Ordinary Residents was first stable before it embarked on an increasing trend. In 2005, the cost of living for ordinary residents in Washington DC was 72.48% of that for their counterparts in New York. It remained at around that level until 2007, after which it rose steadily until it reached 82.44% in 2010. Since the Wages Index for Ordinary Residents is constant across the years, how the Purchasing Power Index for Ordinary Residents in Washington DC (or any other cities in the United States) changes depends only on variations in the Cost of Living Index for Ordinary Residents. Thus, the purchasing power index was initially stable but after 2007, it followed a decreasing trend. As represented by the green line in Figure 5.101c, this index remained at around 137.35 throughout 2005–2007, after which it steadily declined to 121.29 in 2010. Ranking-wise, the Purchasing Power Ranking for Ordinary Residents in Washington DC, which is represented by the green bars, generally deteriorated. It dropped from 38th in 2005 to 44th in 2010.

WASHINGTON DC
United States

Over the second sub-period (2011–2013), the Cost of Living Index for Ordinary Residents has steadily declined. In 2011, the cost of living for ordinary residents in Washington DC was 79.98% of that for their counterparts in New York. It dropped to 67.64% in 2013. As a result, the Purchasing Power Index for Ordinary Residents has steadily increased, rising from 125.03 in 2011 to 147.83 in 2013. Meanwhile, the Purchasing Power Ranking for Ordinary Residents has also been improving. From 48th in 2011, it climbed to 45th in 2013.

Finally, we note that over the entire study period (2005–2013), the Purchasing Power Index for Ordinary Residents in Washington DC has always been above 100.00 — the base index value. This indicates that ordinary residents in Washington DC have consistently been able to consume more goods and services than their counterparts in New York, given the same number of working hours.

WELLINGTON
New Zealand

Figure 5.102a: Cost of Living and 10 Consumption Categories Rankings for Ordinary Residents in Wellington, New Zealand

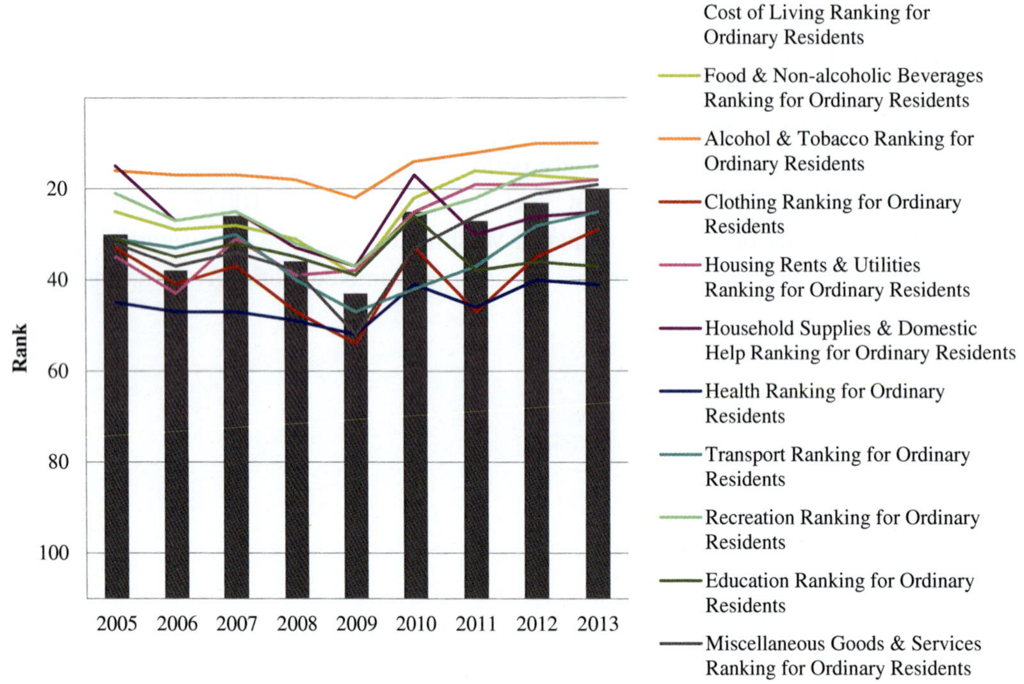

Source: Asia Competitiveness Institute

Figure 5.102b: Gross Hourly Wages in USD and Wages Ranking for Ordinary Residents in Wellington, New Zealand

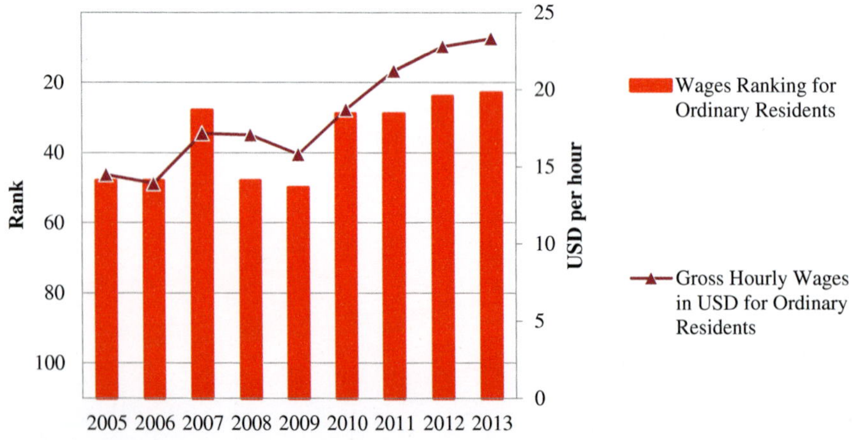

Source: Asia Competitiveness Institute

WELLINGTON
New Zealand

Figure 5.102c: Cost of Living, Wages and Purchasing Power Indices and Purchasing Power Ranking for Ordinary Residents in Wellington, New Zealand

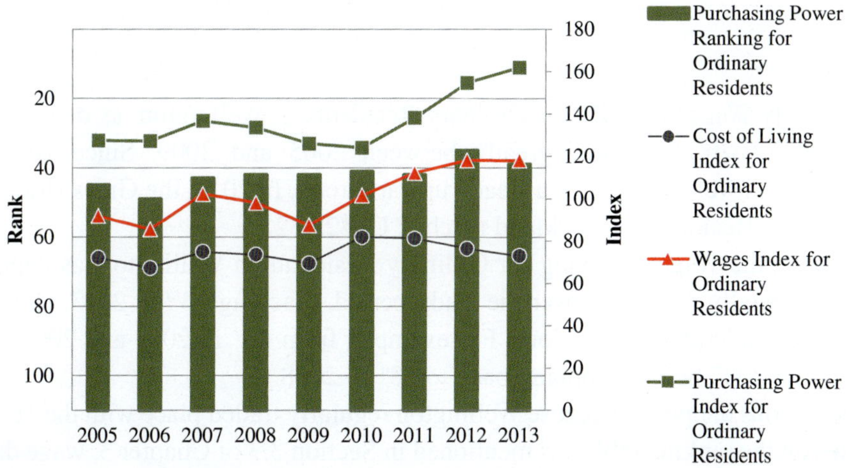

Source: Asia Competitiveness Institute

Figure 5.102a

Renowned for its scenic natural harbour and green hillsides, Wellington, the capital of New Zealand, is a popular conference tourism destination. The city's Cost of Living Ranking for Ordinary Residents, as shown in the grey bars, rose from 30th to 25th between 2005 and 2010, and from 27th to 20th between 2011 and 2013 (see Figure 5.102a). As elaborated in Section 3.4.2 of Chapter 3, for a more precise comparison of rankings, we have split the analysis into two sub-periods.

From 2005 to 2010, Housing Rents & Utilities Ranking jumped 10 places from 35th to 25th. Education Ranking moved up five spots from 31st in 2005 to 26th in 2010. Health Ranking rose from 45th to 41st over the first sub-period. Food & Non-alcoholic Beverages Ranking went up three places from 25th in 2005 to 22nd in 2010. In contrast, Transport Ranking slipped 11 spots from 31st to 42nd over the same sub-period.

Between 2011 and 2013, Food & Non-alcoholic Beverages was the only category that declined in ranking from 16th to 18th. Clothing saw the most remarkable rise in ranking as it climbed 18 places from 47th in 2011 to 29th in 2013. Transport Ranking jumped 12 spots from 37th to 25th over the second sub-period. Health Ranking moved up five places from 46th to 41st between 2011 and 2013. Nonetheless, Health was the lowest ranked category in 2012 and 2013. Alcohol & Tobacco remained as the highest ranked category throughout the second sub-period as its ranking rose from 12th in 2011 to 10th in 2013. Housing Rents & Utilities and Education

WELLINGTON
New Zealand

Rankings both went up one spot from 19th to 18th and 38th to 37th, respectively, over the second sub-period.

Figure 5.102b

The Gross Hourly Wages in USD for Ordinary Residents in Wellington, as denoted by the red line in Figure 5.102b, fluctuated greatly between 2005 and 2009. Since 2009, however, Wellington's wage level has been on a steady upward trend. In 2013, the Gross Hourly Wages in USD for Ordinary Residents in Auckland reached US$23.32.

Ranking-wise, the Wages Ranking for Ordinary Residents in Wellington, as depicted by the red bars, has generally improved over the study period, reaching 23rd in 2013. However, it has also exhibited considerable fluctuations. For example, from 48th in 2005 and 2006, the ranking jumped to 28th in 2007 before dropping back to 48th in 2008.

Such fluctuations happened because Wellington regularly traded place with the 16 cities in the United States on the ranking table. As mentioned in Section 3.3 of Chapter 3, wage data are only available at the national level. Therefore, all cities in the United States are assumed to have the same Gross Hourly Wages in USD for Ordinary Residents and consequently, the same Wages Ranking for Ordinary Residents. Thus, whenever Wellington surpassed any city in the United States, it overtook the other 15 cities as well. The same would hold in the reverse situation. These were precisely what happened between 2006 and 2008 and the result was the large fluctuations in Wellington's ranking as observed.

Figure 5.102c

Let us now analyse the cost of living and wages indices more closely and draw conclusions about the purchasing power of ordinary residents in Wellington. As elaborated in Section 3.4.2 of Chapter 3, for a more precise and rigorous analysis, we discuss the results in two sub-periods: from 2005 to 2010 and from 2011 to 2013.

The Cost of Living Index and the Wages Index for Ordinary Residents in Wellington are represented respectively by the grey and red line in Figure 5.102c. Between 2005 and 2010, the Cost of Living Index for Ordinary Residents exhibited large fluctuations. However, as compared to its value in 2005, the index in 2010 was higher. In 2005, the cost of living for ordinary residents in Wellington was 72.02% of that for ordinary residents in New York (the base city) while in 2010, it was 81.81%. Over the same period, the Wages Index for Ordinary Residents tracked the Cost of Living Index for Ordinary Residents quite closely. As compared to 2005 (91.79), the wages index was higher in 2010 (101.47).

Reflecting the fluctuations in the wages and cost of living indices, the Purchasing Power Index for Ordinary Residents in Wellington, which is represented by the green line in Figure 5.102c, also exhibited considerable fluctuations. Overall, however, the index value in

WELLINGTON
New Zealand

2010 (124.04) was lower than it was in 2005 (127.45). This indicates that ordinary residents in Wellington were unable to afford the same consumption level in 2010 as that in 2005. Surprisingly, the Purchasing Power Ranking for Ordinary Residents in Wellington, as represented by the green bars, improved over the first sub-period, rising from 45th in 2005 to 41st in 2010.

Over the second sub-period (2011–2013), the Cost of Living Index for Ordinary Residents has been on a decreasing trend. In 2011, the cost of living for ordinary residents in Wellington was 81.21% of that for their counterparts in New York while in 2013, it dropped to 72.86%. Meanwhile, the Wages Index for Ordinary Residents has been on a moderately increasing trend, rising from 112.13 in 2011 to 117.97 in 2013.

The combined trends of increasing wages and decreasing cost of living have enabled ordinary residents in Wellington to afford a higher consumption level over time throughout the second sub-period. This is evident in that the Purchasing Power Index for Ordinary Residents steadily increased from 138.07 in 2011 to 161.91 in 2013. The Purchasing Power Ranking for Ordinary Residents has also been improving. It rose from 42nd in 2011 to 39th in 2013.

Finally, we note that over the entire study period (2005–2013), the Purchasing Power Index for Ordinary Residents in Wellington has always been above 100.00 — the base index value. This means that ordinary residents in Wellington have consistently been able to consumer more goods and services than their counterparts in New York, given the same number of working hours.

ZURICH
Switzerland

Figure 5.103a: Cost of Living and 10 Consumption Categories Rankings for Ordinary Residents in Zurich, Switzerland.

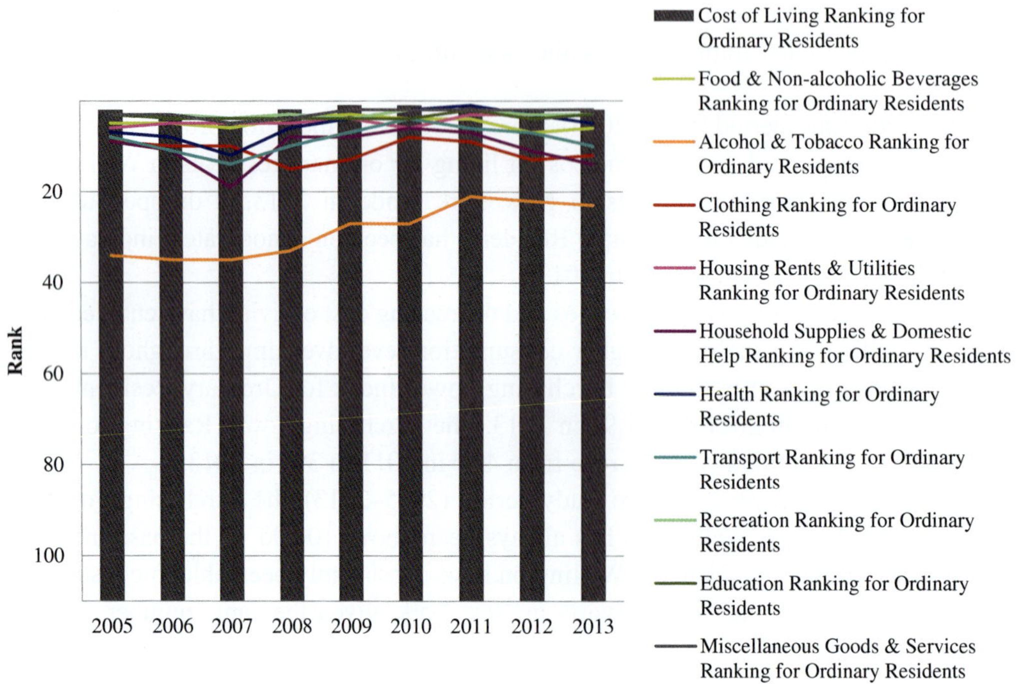

Source: Asia Competitiveness Institute

Figure 5.103b: Gross Hourly Wages in USD and Wages Ranking for Ordinary Residents in Zurich, Switzerland.

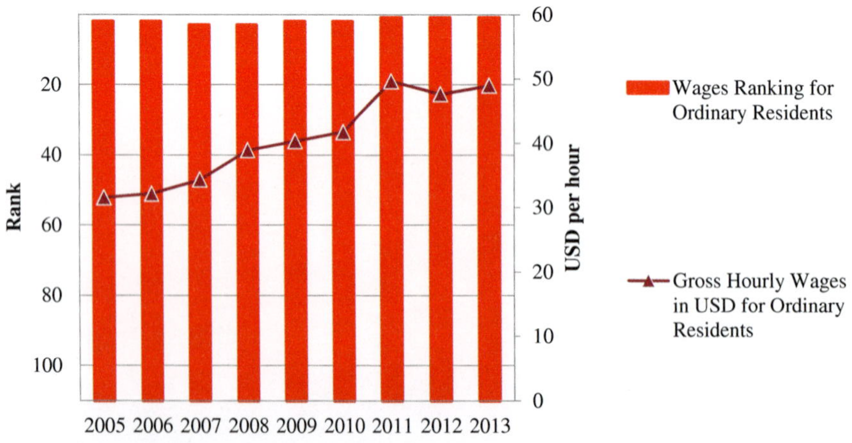

Source: Asia Competitiveness Institute

ZURICH
Switzerland

Figure 5.103c: Cost of Living, Wages and Purchasing Power Indices and Purchasing Power Ranking for Ordinary Residents in Zurich, Switzerland.

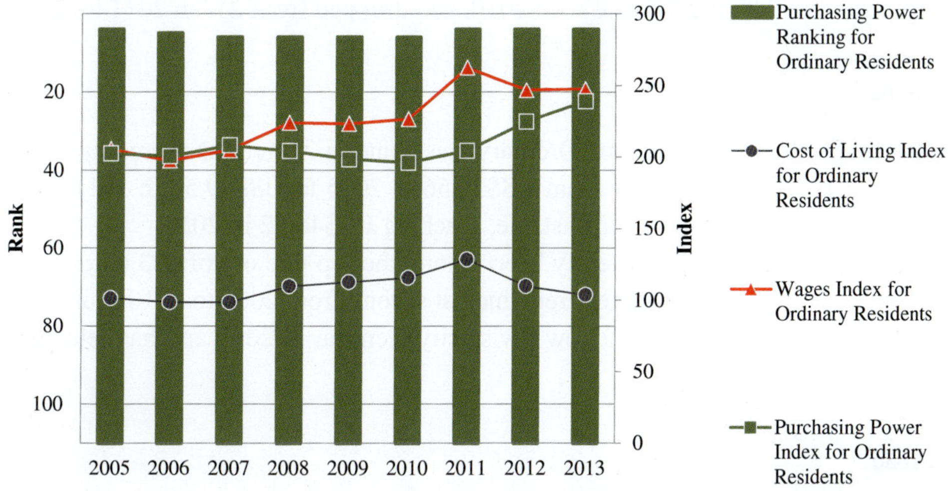

Source: Asia Competitiveness Institute

Figure 5.103a

Often referred to as Switzerland's cultural capital, Zurich is home to some of the country's finest museums, art galleries and theatres. The city's Cost of Living Ranking for Ordinary Residents, as denoted by the grey bars, rose from second to first between 2005 and 2010, and declined from first to second between 2011 and 2013 (see Figure 5.103a). As explained in Section 3.4.2 of Chapter 3, for a more precise comparison of rankings, we have split the analysis into two sub-periods.

In the first sub-period from 2005 to 2010, Health Ranking jumped five places from seventh to second. Transport Ranking moved up four spots from eighth in 2005 to fourth in 2010. Food & Non-alcoholic Beverages Ranking rose from fifth to fourth between 2005 and 2010. In contrast, Education Ranking slipped one spot from third to fourth over the same sub-period. Housing Rents & Utilities Ranking went up from sixth in 2005 to fourth in 2009 before falling back to sixth in 2010.

Between 2011 and 2013, Miscellaneous Goods & Services Ranking remained at second, making it the highest ranked category throughout the second sub-period. Likewise, Housing Rents & Utilities Ranking stayed unchanged at third. In contrast, Household Supplies & Domestic Help Ranking slipped seven places from seventh in 2011 to 14th in 2013. Health and Transport Rankings both fell four spots from first to fifth and sixth to 10th, respectively, over the second sub-period. Food & Non-alcoholic Beverages Ranking moved down two places from fourth in

ZURICH
Switzerland

2011 to sixth in 2013. Education Ranking declined from second to third over the same sub-period. Alcohol & Tobacco was consistently the lowest ranked category in both sub-periods as its ranking rose from 34th in 2005 to 27th in 2010, and dropped from 21st in 2011 to 23rd in 2013.

Figure 5.103b

The Gross Hourly Wages in USD for Ordinary Residents in Zurich, as represented by the red line in Figure 5.103b, grew steadily from US$31.56 in 2005 to US$49.58 in 2011. Since then, Zurich's wage level has remained fairly stable, reaching US$48.92 in 2013.

Ranking-wise, Zurich has consistently been among the top five out of 103 cities. The Wages Ranking for Ordinary Residents largely remained at second from 2005 to 2010. Zurich then rose to the first place, together with its fellow Swiss city Geneva, in 2011 and has retained the top spot ever since.

Figure 5.103c

Let us now analyse the cost of living and wages indices more closely and draw conclusions about the purchasing power of ordinary residents in Zurich. As elaborated in Section 3.4.2 of Chapter 3, for a more precise and rigorous analysis, we discuss the results in two sub-periods: from 2005 to 2010 and from 2011 to 2013.

The Cost of Living Index and the Wages Index for Ordinary Residents in Zurich are represented respectively by the grey and red line in Figure 5.103c. Between 2005 and 2010, the Cost of Living Index for Ordinary Residents was generally on an increasing trend. In 2005, the cost of living for ordinary residents in Zurich was 1.01 times that for their counterparts in New York (the base city). It increased over the years to reach 1.16 times in 2010. Meanwhile, the Wages Index for Ordinary Residents was generally also on an increasing trend. It rose from 199.89 in 2005 to 226.47 in 2010.

Between 2005 and 2007, wages increased faster than cost of living but in the remaining years of the first sub-period, wages could not keep up with the latter. As a result, ordinary residents in Zurich were only able to afford more goods and services over time between 2005 and 2007 but could not do so thereafter. These trends are reflected in the Purchasing Power Index for Ordinary Residents in Zurich, which is represented by the green line in Figure 5.103c. This index initially rose from 197.06 in 2005 to 207.98 in 2007 and then declined over the rest of the first sub-period. Overall, the purchasing power index was lower in 2010 (196.02) than it was in 2005. Ranking-wise, the Purchasing Power Ranking for Ordinary Residents in Zurich, as represented by the green bars, declined slightly over the first sub-period. It dropped from fifth to sixth between 2005 and 2010.

Over the second sub-period (2011–2013), the Cost of Living Index for Ordinary Residents has been on a decreasing trend. In 2011, the cost of living for ordinary residents in Zurich was

ZURICH
Switzerland

1.28 times that for ordinary residents in New York. It dropped to 103.66% in 2013. The Wages Index for Ordinary Residents has also been decreasing, dropping from 262.30 in 2011 to 247.47 in 2013.

Wages have in fact decreased more slowly than cost of living, so throughout the second sub-period, ordinary residents in Zurich have been able to afford more goods and services over time. This is reflected in the Purchasing Power Index for Ordinary Residents, which rose from 204.33 in 2011 to 238.74 in 2013. Meanwhile, the Purchasing Power Ranking for Ordinary Residents has been stable at fourth throughout.

Finally, we note that over the entire study period (2005–2013), the Purchasing Power Index for Ordinary Residents in Zurich has always been much higher than 100.00 — the base index value. This means that ordinary residents in Zurich have consistently been able to afford a much higher consumption level than their counterparts in New York, given the same number of working hours.

Chapter 6

Concluding Remarks: Factors and Attributes on Cities' Cost of Living

In this chapter, we first discuss the effects of exchange rates on the cost of living for both expatriates and ordinary residents. Through a simulation study for Singapore and Hong Kong, we show that exchange rate fluctuations have a great impact on the cost of living rankings for both expatriates and ordinary residents. We next highlight an interesting observation emerging from our study, that cities in the developed Western countries are more expensive for ordinary residents than cities in less developed countries elsewhere, especially in Asia. We attribute this to structural difference in labour cost between these two sets of countries. The chapter also highlights our future research agenda.

6.1 The Effects of Exchange Rates on Cost of Living: A Case Study of Singapore and Hong Kong

In any study which endeavours to rank different cities in the world according to their cost of living, the price data used to compute the cities' cost of living indices must always be converted to a common currency. This is done so that international comparisons can be made. However, the side effect is that exchange rates of various currencies are integrated into the calculation of the cost of living indices. As a result, the ranking of a city, which is based on the value of its index, reflects not only its relative expensiveness with respect to the other cities but also the relative strength of its currency. In other words, the position of a city's ranking is not decided purely by the price levels of the consumption items in this city; it is also affected by exchange rates.

The effect that exchange rates have on cost of living rankings is ever-present, as conversion of local prices into a common currency is imperative for any ranking of cities in different parts of the world to be constructed. Our study is no exception to this general rule. In other words, the Cost of Living Ranking for Expatriates and Cost of Living Ranking for Ordinary Residents that we construct for each of the 103 cities in our study are likely to be affected by exchange rate levels in the different cities.

We consider the case of Singapore. Between 2005 and 2013, the Singapore dollar appreciated by about 24.8%[1] against the US dollar — the common currency used to compare all prices in our analysis. In theory, the strong Singapore dollar, ironically due to strong balance of payments surplus reflected in an equal increase in official foreign reserves backing the Singapore dollar has helped to push Singapore's cost of living rankings for expatriates and ordinary residents upward because any generic increases in local prices over this period would be magnified after

[1]Computed by the Asia Competitiveness Institute based on the yearly average exchange rates of the Singapore dollar against the US dollar. The yearly average exchange rate is calculated based on the daily average exchange rate retrieved from the Bloomberg Terminal (See Section 2.2 of Chapter 2 for more details).

currency conversion. This is confirmed in reality by our investigation through a simulation exercise. The baseline scenario is our original analysis, in which exchange rates of the currencies used in all 103 cities (against the US dollar) followed their actual trends. The simulation scenario is one where the exchange rate of the Singapore dollar is assumed to have remained unchanged between 2005 and 2013 while rates of the other currencies are kept as they are in reality. By comparing Singapore's simulated cost of living rankings for expatriates and ordinary residents with its actual rankings, we can verify the extent of the effect of a strong currency on cost of living for all.

For comparison purpose, a similar exercise is also carried out for Hong Kong. We expect, however, that Hong Kong's simulated rankings will not differ much from its original rankings. Unlike Singapore which adopts a managed floating exchange rates system, Hong Kong pegs its currency to the US dollar. As a result, there is very little variation in the exchange rates between the Hong Kong dollar and the US dollar over the years to begin with and thus the simulated scenario is very similar to the baseline scenario for Hong Kong. The simulation results for Hong Kong and Singapore are discussed together in Section 6.1.3 of this chapter. Before delving into the results, however, we will discuss the simulation methodology at length in Section 6.1.1 and Section 6.1.2 for expatriates and ordinary citizens, respectively.

How exchange rates affect cost of living rankings of the cities is an important technical issue which needs to be addressed. Nonetheless, our interest goes beyond technicalities. We are also interested in the effects of exchange rates in the real world. Specifically, we are keen to analyse how a strong Singapore dollar may impact the lives of expatriates and ordinary residents in the city-state. This is the issue taken up in Section 6.1.4 with policy implications for rumination.

6.1.1 Methodology to Simulate the Cost of Living Rankings for Expatriates in Singapore and Hong Kong

Since the methodologies to obtain the Cost of Living Ranking for Expatriates and Cost of Living Ranking for Ordinary Residents are different from one another, the simulations for expatriates and ordinary residents also proceed differently. This section details the simulation methodology for expatriates.

First, let us recall that in the original analysis, the Cost of Living Index for Expatriates in a city in a particular year is calculated as follows:

$$\textit{Cost of Living Index for Expatriates in city } m = \frac{\sum_{i=1}^{n} P_{C,m,i} \times W_i}{\sum_{i=1}^{n} P_{US,NY,i} \times W_i} \times 100 \qquad (2.6.1)$$

where

m = city;

C = the country where city m is located in;

NY = New York;

US = United States;

i = item;
n = number of items in the consumption basket for expatriates;
$P_{C,m,i}$ = average price of item i in city m of country C;
W_i = weight of item i within Cost of Living Index for Expatriates.

Exchange rates enter the calculation through the term $P_{C,m,i}$. This is the US dollar-denominated average price of consumption item i in city m of country C. To obtain this term, we first gather all local currency prices of item i in city m from the Economist Intelligence Unit (EIU) CityData.[2] We then convert these prices into US dollar, proxy for missing data entries where necessary[3] and take the average of all converted prices to get $P_{C,m,i}$. In doing the conversion, we use the average yearly exchange rate between the local currency of city m and the US dollar[4] in the year for which the index is calculated. For example, if we are computing the cost of living index for expatriates in Tokyo in year 2013, the 2013 exchange rate of the yen will be used. The procedure applies to all consumption items except for Miscellaneous Goods & Services. Price data for Miscellaneous Goods and Services, which are acquired from the UBS Prices and Earnings study, are reported in US dollar to begin with. Thus, no further conversion is needed and the value of $P_{C,m,i}$ for this item is simply the raw data value.

Equation 2.6.1 is used to combine all $P_{C,m,i}$ with their respective weights, W_i, to obtain the Cost of Living Index for Expatriates in each city. The Cost of Living Ranking for Expatriates is then generated by arranging the indices in a descending order. In other words, a city which is ranked higher (lower) is the one which has a larger (smaller) index.

We conduct the simulation for all years in the study period except for 2005. In our simulation, the basic framework to compute the cost of living index for expatriates is preserved. Equation 2.6.1 is still used to calculate the indices for both the city of interest, i.e. Singapore or Hong Kong and the other 102 cities. In fact, no change is made to the index computation process for the latter group, such that the indices for these cities under the simulation scenario are exactly the same as they are originally.

For the city of interest, however, some modifications are made to the calculation of the term $P_{C,m,i}$. For an item i which is not Miscellaneous Goods and Services, we still begin by collecting all of its local currency prices from the EIU CityData. Nonetheless, the conversion of these prices into US dollar is now carried out using the 2005 exchange rate, regardless of the year for which the index is being calculated. Proxies, where necessary, are still made by the same method as in the original analysis. All converted prices of item i are then averaged to give us the simulated average price of item i.

$P_{C,m,i}$ for Miscellaneous Goods and Services in the city of interest is also modified. The raw price data for this item have been pre-converted into US dollar using the actual exchange rate of

[2]As explained in Section 2.4 and Section 2.6 of Chapter 2, there are cases where several prices might be available for a single item in the EIU CityData. This is because the EIU collects prices for from various sale locations, e.g. supermarkets, branded stores, chain store, etc.

[3]See Section 2.4 of Chapter 2 for a detailed description of the proxy method.

[4]The yearly average exchange rates are calculated based on the daily average exchange rates obtained from the Bloomberg Terminal. See Appendix 3 for list of all yearly average exchange rates used in this study.

city m's local currency in the year for which the data are reported. Thus, to reflect our simulation assumption that the city of interest has not experienced any exchange rate fluctuations after 2005, we first work out the price of Miscellaneous Goods and Services in local currency and then re-convert it back to US dollar using the 2005 exchange rate. Specifically, the simulated average price of Miscellaneous Goods and Services in the city of interest in any year which comes after 2005 is given by the following equation:

$$P^{simulated}_{\text{C,m,Miscellaneous,T}} = P_{\text{C,m,Miscellaneous,T}} \times \frac{\text{Exchange Rate}_{\text{C,T}}}{\text{Exchange Rate}_{\text{C,2005}}} \forall \text{T} \in (2006, 2007, 2008, 2009, 2010, 2011, 2012 \text{ and } 2013) \quad (6.1.1)$$

where

m = Singapore or Hong Kong;

C = Singapore or Hong Kong, China;

Miscellaneous = Miscellaneous Goods and Services;

T = year;

$P^{simulated}_{\text{C,m,Miscellaneous,T}}$ = simulated average price of Miscellaneous Goods and Services in city m of country C in year T;

$P_{\text{C,m,Miscellaneous}}$ = actual average price of Miscellaneous Goods and Services in city m of country C in year T;

Exchange $\text{Rate}_{\text{C,T}}$ = yearly average exchange rate between country C and the United States in year T (expressed as local currency unit per US dollar);

Exchange $\text{Rate}_{\text{C,2005}}$ = yearly average exchange rate between country C and the United States in year 2005 (expressed as local currency unit per US dollar).

After obtaining the simulated average prices for all consumption items in the city of interest, we plug them back into Equation 2.6.1 to obtain the Simulated Cost of Living Index for Expatriates in that city. We then re-rank all cities to generate a Simulated Cost of Living Ranking for Expatriates and compare the simulated ranking of the city of interest with its original ranking. Findings from this comparison are discussed in Section 6.1.3.

An important assumption underlying the simulation is that consumption patterns of expatriates are insensitive to exchange rate fluctuations. In other words, exchange rates do not affect the composition of an expatriate's consumption basket — the items in it and the importance of each item to him. This assumption is intuitive considering that consumption patterns are formed mainly from the expatriate's consideration of his wants and needs, his relative preferences between different consumption items as well as the relative quality of the goods and services in the basket. These factors are assumed to be unaffected by exchange rates. As a result, the weight of each item in the cost of living index for expatriates, or the term W_i in Equation 2.6.1, is the same in both the original analysis and the simulation scenario.

6.1.2 Methodology to Simulate the Cost of Living Rankings for Ordinary Residents in Singapore and Hong Kong

Recall that in the original analysis, the Cost of Living Index for Ordinary Residents in a city in a particular year is calculated as follows:

$$\textit{Cost of Living Index for Ordinary Residents in city}\ \mathrm{m} = \frac{\mathrm{CP}^{\mathrm{EIU}}_{\mathrm{C,m}} \times \dfrac{\mathrm{NP}^{\mathrm{ICP}}_{\mathrm{C}}}{\mathrm{NP}^{\mathrm{EIU}}_{\mathrm{C}}}}{\mathrm{CP}^{\mathrm{EIU}}_{\mathrm{US,NY}} \times \dfrac{\mathrm{NP}^{\mathrm{ICP}}_{\mathrm{US}}}{\mathrm{NP}^{\mathrm{EIU}}_{\mathrm{US}}}} \qquad (3.4.1)$$

where

m = city;

C = the country where city m is located in;

NY = New York;

US = United States;

$$\mathrm{CP}^{\mathrm{EIU}}_{\mathrm{C,m}} = \sum_{i=1}^{n} \mathrm{P}_{\mathrm{C,m,i}} \times \mathrm{W}_{\mathrm{C,i}} \qquad (3.4.2);$$

i = item;

n = number of items in the consumption basket;

$\mathrm{P}_{\mathrm{C,m,i}}$ = average price of item i in city m of country C;

$\mathrm{W}_{\mathrm{C,I}}$ = weight of item i within Cost of Living Index for Ordinary Residents in country C;

$$\mathrm{NP}^{\mathrm{ICP}}_{\mathrm{C}} = \frac{\text{index of nominal expenditure per capita for country C}}{\text{index of real expenditure per capita for country C}} \qquad (3.4.3);$$

$$\text{index of nominal expenditure per capita for country C} = \frac{\text{nominal expenditure per capita for country C}}{\text{nominal expenditure per capita of the world}};$$

$$\text{index of real expenditure per capita for country C} = \frac{\text{real expenditure per capita for country C}}{\text{real expenditure per capita of the world}};$$

$\mathrm{NP}^{\mathrm{EIU}}_{\mathrm{C}}$ = mean $\mathrm{CP}^{\mathrm{EIU}}_{\mathrm{C,m}}$ from all cities within country C.

Exchange rates enter the calculation through two channels. The first is the term $\mathrm{CP}^{\mathrm{EIU}}_{\mathrm{C,m}}$ and its mean value, the term $\mathrm{NP}^{\mathrm{EIU}}_{\mathrm{C}} \cdot \mathrm{CP}^{\mathrm{EIU}}_{\mathrm{C,m}}$ is the weighted average of US dollar-denominated average prices of the consumption items in city m, country C. Structure-wise, this term is similar to the numerator of Equation 2.6.1, except that the item weights in Equation 3.4.2, $\mathrm{W}_{\mathrm{C,i}}$, are country-specific and represent the consumption patterns of ordinary residents in city m. Meanwhile, the average prices used to compute $\mathrm{CP}^{\mathrm{EIU}}_{\mathrm{C,m}}$, or $\mathrm{P}_{\mathrm{C,m,i}}$, are precisely the ones used in Equation 2.6.1 to calculate the cost of living for expatriates. The process through which these prices are obtained and the role that exchange rates play in the data treatment are already documented in the previous section and shall not be repeated here.

The second channel is the term NP_C^{ICP}. This term can be understood as the US dollar- denominated price level per unit real consumption for ordinary residents living in country C. NP_C^{ICP} in 2005 and 2011 are calculated based on data on nominal and real expenditure per capita in country C reported in the International Comparison Programme (ICP) surveys for these years. Since the ICP data are available every six years, we construct the NP_C^{ICP} for the 2006-2010 period and the 2012–2013 period by incorporating extra information on exchange rates and inflation rates. In particular, the NP_C^{ICP} for any year T within the 2006–2010 period is calculated as follows:

$$NP_{C,T}^{ICP} = NP_{C,2005}^{ICP} \times \frac{\text{Exchange Rate}_{C,2005}}{\text{Exchange Rate}_{C,T}} \times \prod_{t=2006}^{T} (1 + \text{Inflation rate}_{C,t}) \forall T \in (2006, 2007, 2008, 2009 \text{ and } 2010) \tag{3.4.4}$$

where

C = country;

T = year;

$NP_{C,T}^{ICP} = NP_C^{ICP}$ in year T;

$\text{Inflation rate}_{C,t}$ = yearly average inflation rate for country C in year t;

$\text{Exchange Rate}_{C,T}$ = yearly average exchange rate between country C and the United States in year T (expressed as local currency unit per US dollar).

Likewise, the NP_C^{ICP} for any year T within the 2012–2013 period is given by:

$$NP_{C,T}^{ICP} = NP_{C,2011}^{ICP} \times \frac{\text{Exchange Rate}_{C,2011}}{\text{Exchange Rate}_{C,T}} \times \prod_{t=2012}^{T} (1 + \text{Inflation rate}_{C,t}) \forall T \in (2012 \text{ and } 2013) \tag{3.4.5}$$

where

C = country;

T = year;

$NP_{C,T}^{ICP} = NP_C^{ICP}$ in year T;

$\text{Inflation rate}_{C,t}$ = yearly average inflation rate for country C in year t;

$\text{Exchange Rate}_{C,T}$ = yearly average exchange rate between country C and the United States in year T (expressed as local currency unit per US dollar).

Equation 3.4.1 is used to combine $CP_{C,m}^{EIU}$, NP_C^{EIU} and NP_C^{ICP} to obtain the Cost of Living Index for Ordinary Residents in each city. The Cost of Living Ranking for Ordinary Residents is then generated by arranging the indices in a descending order. In other words, a city which is ranked higher (lower) is the one which has a larger (smaller) index.

We conduct the simulation for all years in the study period except for 2005. In our simulation, the basic framework to compute the Cost of Living Index for Ordinary Residents is preserved. Equation 3.4.1 is still used to calculate the indices for both the city of interest, i.e. Singapore or Hong Kong and the other 102 cities. In fact, no change is made to the index computation process for the latter group, such that the indices for these cities under the simulation scenario are exactly the same as they were originally.

For the city of interest, however, we make the following modifications. Firstly, we adopt the procedure used in the simulation for expatriates to generate the simulated average price of each consumption item. Specifically, for any item i which is not Miscellaneous Goods and Services, we use the 2005 exchange rate of the local currency of the city of interest to convert local prices into US dollar, make proxies where necessary and average the converted prices to obtain the item's simulated average price. Meanwhile, for Miscellaneous Goods and Services, we employ Equation 6.1.1 to calculate $P^{simulated}_{\mathrm{C,m,Miscellaneous,T}}$. The terms $\mathrm{CP}^{\mathrm{EIU}}_{\mathrm{C,m}}$ and $\mathrm{NP}^{\mathrm{EIU}}_{\mathrm{C}}$ for the city of interest are then recalculated with the simulated prices as inputs.

Secondly, the $\mathrm{NP}^{\mathrm{ICP}}_{\mathrm{C}}$ term for the city of interest is also modified. From our earlier descriptions, it is easy to see that $\mathrm{NP}^{\mathrm{ICP}}_{\mathrm{C}}$ for a certain year is essentially a price level pre-converted into US dollar using the actual exchange rate of country C's local currency in that year. To reflect our simulation assumption that the city of interest has not experienced any exchange rate fluctuations after 2005, we first work out the value of this price level in local currency and then re-convert it back to US dollar using the 2005 exchange rate. Specifically, the simulated $\mathrm{NP}^{\mathrm{ICP}}_{\mathrm{C}}$ for the city of interest in any year which comes after 2005 is given by the following equation:

$$\mathrm{NP}^{\mathrm{ICP,simulated}}_{\mathrm{C,T}} = \mathrm{NP}^{\mathrm{ICP}}_{\mathrm{C,T}} \times \frac{\text{Exchange Rate}_{\mathrm{C,T}}}{\text{Exchange Rate}_{\mathrm{C,2005}}} \forall T \in (2006, 2007, 2008, 2009, 2010, 2011, 2012 \text{ and } 2013) \quad (6.1.2)$$

where

C = Singapore or Hong Kong, China;

T = year;

$\mathrm{NP}^{\mathrm{ICP,simulated}}_{\mathrm{C,T}}$ = simulated $\mathrm{NP}^{\mathrm{ICP}}_{\mathrm{C}}$ for the country C in year T;

$\mathrm{NP}^{\mathrm{ICP}}_{\mathrm{C,T}}$ = actual $\mathrm{NP}^{\mathrm{ICP}}_{\mathrm{C}}$ for the country C in year T;

Exchange $\text{Rate}_{\mathrm{C,T}}$ = yearly average exchange rate between country C and the United States in year T (expressed as local currency unit per US dollar);

Exchange $\text{Rate}_{\mathrm{C,2005}}$ = yearly average exchange rate between country C and the United States in year 2005 (expressed as local currency unit per US dollar).

After obtaining the simulated terms $\mathrm{CP}^{\mathrm{EIU}}_{\mathrm{C,m}}$, $\mathrm{NP}^{\mathrm{EIU}}_{\mathrm{C}}$ and $\mathrm{NP}^{\mathrm{ICP}}_{\mathrm{C}}$ for the city of interest, we plug them back to Equation 3.4.1 to calculate the Simulated Cost of Living Index for Ordinary Residents in that city. We then re-rank all cities to generate a Simulated Cost of Living Ranking for Ordinary Residents and compare the simulated ranking of the city of interest with its original ranking. Findings from this comparison are discussed in Section 6.1.3.

Just as before, the underlying assumption is that the consumption patterns of ordinary residents are insensitive to exchange rate fluctuations. The argument again is that consumption patterns are formed mainly based on ordinary residents' wants and needs, their relative preferences between the consumption items and the relative quality of the items. These factors are unlikely to be affected by exchange rates. As a result of this assumption, the set of item weights for ordinary residents in each country, $W_{c,i}$, is the same in both the simulation scenario and the original analysis.

6.1.3 Simulation Results and Further Discussions

Table 6.1 presents the simulation results for expatriates together with the original Cost of Living Rankings for Expatriates in Singapore and Hong Kong. Table 6.2 presents the simulation results for ordinary residents together with the original Cost of Living Rankings for Ordinary Residents in Singapore and Hong Kong. The yearly average exchange rates of the Singapore dollar and the Hong Kong dollar against the US dollar over the study period are also shown in Tables 6.1 and 6.2.

Singapore's simulated rankings for both expatriates and ordinary residents are lower than its original rankings in all years for which the simulations are conducted. For example, the Cost of Living Ranking for Expatriates in Singapore in 2013 was fourth in the original analysis. Had the Singapore dollar not appreciated against the US dollar by almost 25% over the study period, Singapore would have ranked 24th instead. In the other years, the simulated ranking for expatriates is always 15th or below, while the original ranking was consistently 13th or above. Not only so, while the original ranking displayed a generally increasing trend throughout, the simulated ranking generally decreased between 2006 and 2011 and reversed to an increasing trend thereafter. Similarly, the Simulated Cost of Living Ranking for Ordinary Residents in Singapore is also always lower than the original Cost of Living Ranking for Ordinary Residents. The simulated ranking is 60th or below throughout the study period while the original ranking ranged between 60th and 48th. Clearly, just as alluded to previously, the strong Singapore dollar has adversely helped to push Singapore's cost of living rankings upward.

Meanwhile, Hong Kong's simulated rankings for both expatriates and ordinary residents are almost always identical to its original rankings. In fact, there is no difference between the Simulated Cost of Living Ranking for Ordinary Residents in Hong Kong and its original counterpart. For expatriates, the simulated and original rankings are also the same for all years, except for 2006 when the two differ by only one place. These observations do not come as a surprise. As pointed out earlier on, the Hong Kong dollar is pegged against the US dollar. Thus, for Hong Kong, the simulated scenario is not very different from the reality hence Hong Kong's rankings remain almost unaltered after the simulation.

The simulation results serve to highlight the effect that the exchange rates of a city's local currency may have on its cost of living rankings. There is, however, another facet to the exchange rate story which is not captured by the simulation: exchange rate fluctuations in other cities may also influence the rankings of the city of interest. To see this aspect, one can analyse the recent rankings of Singapore.

Table 6.1: Original and Simulated Cost of Living Rankings for Expatriates in Singapore and Hong Kong, 2005–2013

	2005	2006	2007	2008	2009	2010	2011	2012	2013
Cost of Living Ranking for Expatriates in Singapore	15	13	12	12	12	10	8	7	4
Simulated Cost of Living Ranking for Expatriates in Singapore	—	15	21	31	25	24	33	22	24
Cost of Living Ranking for Expatriates in Hong Kong	5	6	10	17	13	12	12	9	11
Simulated Cost of Living Ranking for Expatriates in Hong Kong	—	7	10	17	13	12	12	9	11
Singapore dollar/US dollar yearly average exchange rate	1.66446	1.58869	1.5068	1.41473	1.45378	1.36265	1.25716	1.24941	1.25101
Hong Kong dollar/US dollar yearly average exchange rate	7.77746	7.76844	7.802	7.78626	7.75166	7.76887	7.78436	7.75703	7.75663

Source: Asia Competitiveness Institute

Table 6.2: Original and Simulated Cost of Living Rankings for Ordinary Residents in Singapore and Hong Kong, 2005–2013

	2005	2006	2007	2008	2009	2010	2011	2012	2013
Cost of Living Ranking for Ordinary Residents in Singapore	58	60	59	56	59	53	55	48	48
Simulated Cost of Living Ranking for Ordinary Residents in Singapore	—	60	62	65	62	64	69	66	67
Cost of Living Ranking for Ordinary Residents in Hong Kong	56	58	60	62	60	62	63	62	59
Simulated Cost of Living Ranking for Ordinary Residents in Hong Kong	—	58	60	62	60	62	63	62	59
Singapore dollar/US dollar yearly average exchange rate	1.66446	1.58869	1.5068	1.41473	1.45378	1.36265	1.25716	1.24941	1.25101
Hong Kong dollar/US dollar yearly average exchange rate	7.77746	7.76844	7.802	7.78626	7.75166	7.76887	7.78436	7.75703	7.75663

Source: Asia Competitiveness Institute

Consider, for example, the Cost of Living Ranking for Expatriates. Between 2011 and 2013, Singapore's actual ranking rose from eighth to fourth. The yearly average exchange rate of the Singapore dollar against the US dollar was rather stable during this period. In climbing up the ranking table, Singapore overtook Frankfurt (Germany), Geneva (Switzerland), Oslo (Norway), Osaka/Kobe (Japan), London (United Kingdoms), and Tokyo (Japan), all of which ranked above Singapore in 2011. Interestingly, the countries where these cities are in all experienced exchange rate depreciations over the 2011–2013 period. For example, the British pound depreciated by 2.45% against the US dollar; the Norwegian krone by 4.83% and most severely, the Japanese yen by 22.44%.[5] These depreciation episodes served to mask any price increases which had happened in the cities mentioned when the local prices are converted into US dollar. In contrast, since the exchange rates between the Singapore dollar and the US dollar remained stable, any increases in its local prices were fully articulated in the converted prices. Such unequal levels of currency depreciation among these countries against the US dollar helped to push up Singapore's cost of living index for expatriates vis-à-vis the cities mentioned and thus the city-state's ranking as well. It should be acknowledged that exchange rate fluctuations were not the sole cause for the rise in Singapore's ranking. They were, however, an important contributing factor.

The phenomenon is also observed for Singapore's ranking for ordinary residents. Between 2011 and 2013, the Cost of Living Ranking for Ordinary Residents in Singapore rose from 55th to 48th. Comparing the ranking in 2013 with that in 2011, Singapore overtook Atlanta (United States), Berlin (Germany), Buenos Aires (Argentina), Lexington (United States), Lyon (France), Pittsburgh (United States) and Rio de Janeiro (Brazil). Again, we observe that the exchange rates of the non-US cities in this list depreciated over the period. In particular, the euro, which is used in France and Germany, depreciated by 4.71% against the US dollar; the Argentinian peso depreciated by 32.74% and the Brazilian real by 29.08%.

6.1.4 The Effects of Currency Appreciation on Expatriates and Ordinary Residents

We now discuss the effects that currency appreciation may have on the lives of expatriates and ordinary residents using Singapore as an example. In particular, we highlight how a strong Singapore dollar may affect the prices of the different goods and services which they consume and the income and wealth of each group. The analysis in this section concerns a general scenario where the Singapore dollar appreciates against various currencies and not only against the US dollar. We also assume *ceteris paribus*, or that no other factor changes aside from the exchange rates of the Singapore dollar.

As the Singapore dollar strengthens, local prices of imports in Singapore are lowered as it now requires fewer Singapore dollars to buy one unit of foreign currency worth of imports. Consumption items which are imported thus become less expensive. This is beneficial for both

[5]Computed by staffs from the Asia Competitiveness Institute based on the yearly average exchange rates of the Singapore dollar against the US dollar. The yearly average exchange rate is calculated based on the daily average exchange rate retrieved from the Bloomberg Terminal (See Section 2.2 of Chapter 2 for more details).

expatriates and ordinary residents, but especially so for the former because expatriates gear towards consuming high-end imported products to maintain Western lifestyles. At the same time, prices of locally produced goods, especially common foodstuffs, may also decrease, as these goods face greater competition from cheaper imported close substitutes. Goods which are produced using imported inputs may see a greater drop in prices. In contrast to goods, the local prices of most services consumed by expatriates and ordinary residents, such as the price of haircut, are unlikely to be affected. This is because these services are non-tradable, so there is no foreign substitute to these services to create competitive pressure.

Meanwhile, an appreciating Singapore dollar makes the prices of Singapore's exports in the international market less competitive. As a result, international demands for Singapore's exports are likely to be reduced. The extent of this reduction depends on the price elasticity of demand of oversea consumers for Singapore's exports. If demand is relatively inelastic, the decrease in quantities demanded is marginal. However, if the reverse is true, the slump in exports will be great and this may have repercussions on the employment prospects of ordinary residents working in the export sectors.

The above argument notwithstanding, a strong Singapore dollar does not have much of an impact on the income and wealth of ordinary residents. Ordinary residents are remunerated in local currency so the value of their income in terms of Singapore dollar is unaffected by exchange rate fluctuations. Also, since ordinary residents save and invest mostly in local assets, such as Singapore dollar-denominated time deposits or savings with the Central Provident Fund (CPF), exchange rate fluctuations do not have much effect on the value of their wealth either. This argument of course may not apply to the upper strata of the population, who may also hold foreign assets, but it should generally describe the condition of most ordinary residents. Overall, except for the fact that some imported goods consumed by ordinary residents may experience drop in prices, the total resources available for ordinary residents to support their lifestyles are not affected by a strong Singapore dollar.

In contrast, an appreciating Singapore dollar has an income effect on expatriates. The exact nature of the effect, however, depends on their remuneration arrangements. If an expatriate is paid in his home currency, or in US dollar, the value of his income in terms of Singapore dollar will decrease. He will thus have fewer resources at his disposal to support his lifestyle. On the other hand, if the expatriate is compensated in Singapore dollar, the value of his income is not reduced. In fact, a strong Singapore dollar may help to make more income available for consumption because it lessens the burden of remittances. It is likely that the expatriate has to send a portion of his income back to his home country, either to support dependants back home or to settle outstanding financial commitments such as mortgages. A strong Singapore dollar allows the expatriate to remit this pre-set amount of money with fewer Singapore dollars, thus leaving him with more income for consumption.

These conclusions are important to reinforce, justify existing policies or as options for fine-tuning policies with respect to exchange rates. In turn, exchange rate policies affect trade policies among other matters. Singapore as one of the most open economies (in terms of total trade to Gross Domestic Product) does watch exchange rate policies very conscientiously.

Our analysis in this section is stylised and whether the effects we have described fully manifest in reality depends on a host of other relevant factors. However, the insights highlighted generally hold. A strong Singapore dollar is somewhat beneficial as it helps to mitigate imported inflation. Nonetheless, its appreciation should be carefully managed because of the potential adverse consequences on exporting activities. Income-wise, expatriates are more affected than ordinary residents by exchange rate fluctuations. Whether a strong Singapore dollar is a boon or a bane for expatriates depends on their remuneration arrangements with their firms.

As for future research agenda, a number of caveats or assumptions made may be re-examined to incorporate some rethinking and fine-tuning. One area may be to incorporate some analysis on the net effect of the substitution effect and income effect of price changes, which in our case is indirectly due to the strong Singapore dollar rather than any direct change in prices by the sellers or any tax on goods and services. Thus, the changes in the composition of consumer baskets over time as longitudinal studies may be interesting as reflected in the composition of retained imports for consumption for expatriates and ordinary citizens. For ordinary citizens as being less mobile unlike expatriates in choosing where to live, their concerns cannot be ignored as they are the ultimate stakeholders in any economy.

One may also wonder the possibility of expatriates' choice to relocate, while Singapore residents have less of that choice except to shop across the causeway in Malaysian ringgit. Likewise, it may merit delving more deeply how multinational corporations' choice of location is affected by strong or weak exchange rates or other long-term corporate considerations. All parties face trade-offs in policy options that are both economically and politically sensitive.

6.2 Comparing Cost of Living across Geographical Regions

An interesting observation emerges when we compare the cost of living in different cities across geographical regions. Cities in the Western world tend to have higher cost of living for ordinary residents than cities elsewhere. On the other hand, there is no similar pattern in the geographical distribution of the cities according to their cost of living for expatriates. In other words, an Asian city, such as Shanghai, is likely to have a lower cost of living for ordinary residents as compared to a city in Western Europe, such as Amsterdam. However, it may be ranked higher or lower than the latter in terms of cost of living for expatriates.

Figure 6.1 illustrates the pattern concerning the cost of living for ordinary residents. It graphs the Cost of Living Indices for Ordinary Residents in all cities in our study in 2013. The horizontal axis reflects the index values while the different cities are plotted on the vertical axis. The longer the bar, the higher the index value and hence the more expensive for ordinary residents in the particular city as compared to the other cities in 2013. The different colours of the bars represent the region which each city belongs to.

As apparent from Figure 6.1, cities in Western Europe are among the most expensive cities for ordinary residents. They are followed by cities in Australasia (Australia and New Zealand) and North American cities. On the other hand, African and Asian cities tend to be the cheapest,

Figure 6.1: Cost of Living Indices for Ordinary Residents in 103 World's Major Cities in 2013 by Geographical Regions

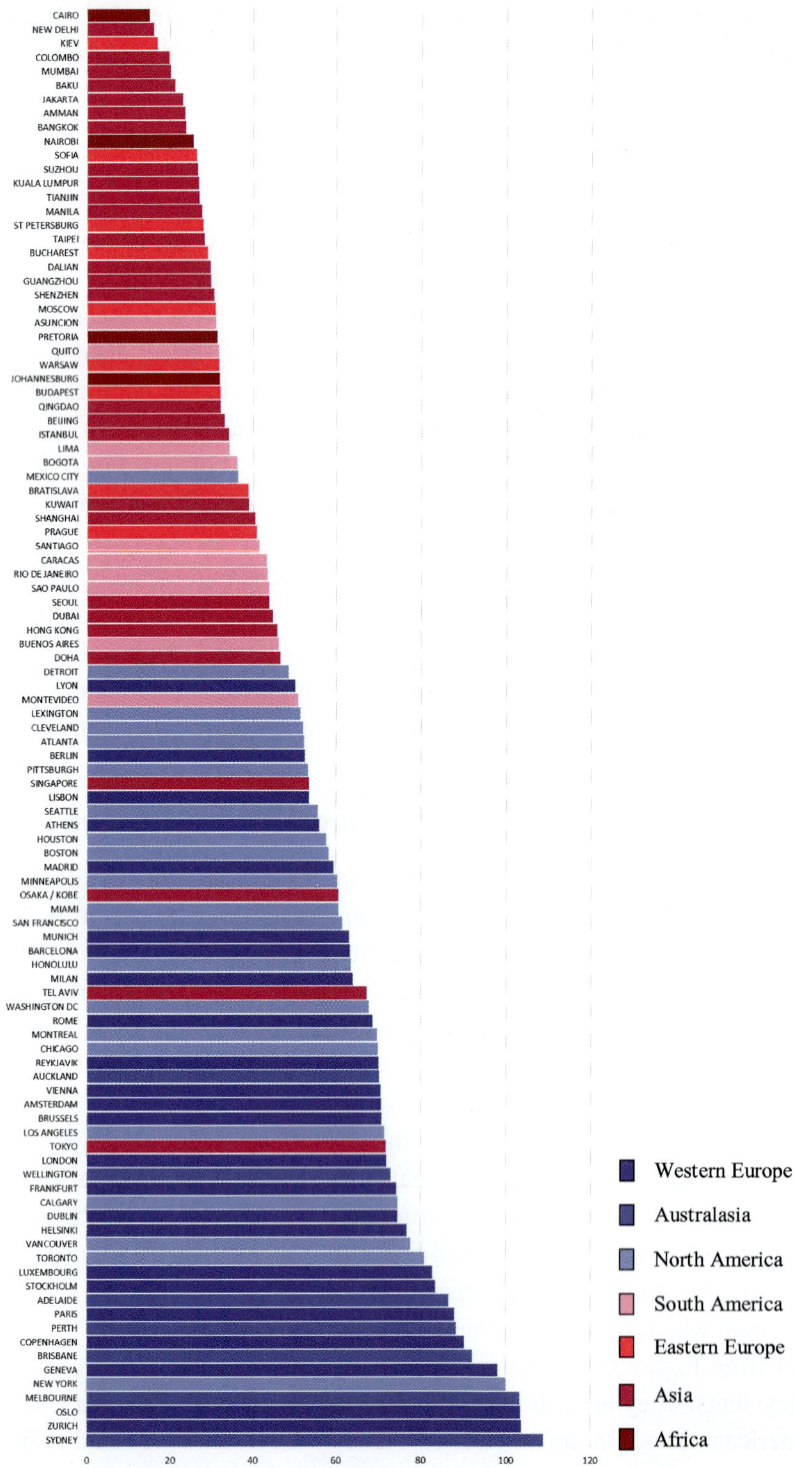

Source: Asia Competitiveness Institute

followed by Eastern European cities and cities in South America. There are of course exceptions. A handful of Asian cities are as expensive as their Western counterparts. The cost of living for ordinary residents in Tokyo, for instance, was more or less similar to that in London and Los Angeles while cost in Singapore was comparable with cost in Lisbon and Pittsburgh. Nevertheless, the general pattern is still that cities in the West have higher cost of living for ordinary residents than cities in the rest of the world, notably in Asia.

This is not so much of the cultural connotations of the Western lifestyles *vis-à-vis* the Eastern ones. It has more to do with the West being relatively more developed in terms of the stage of economic growth and development, while the East comprises more developing economies which neither have attained the take-off stage nor reached the maturity level of developed countries. In turn the cost structure of tradables and non-tradables becomes more relevant. Exceptions for Tokyo and Singapore simply reflect their maturity on par with other Western developed cities and economies.

The explanation for the pattern observed lies in the difference in the cost structure of non-traded goods and especially services between the Western countries and other, less developed countries. Locally provided services which are non-tradable such as haircut constitute an integral part of the ordinary residents' consumption basket and therefore they are important determinants of the cost of living of ordinary residents in a country. By nature, the service industries are labour intensive and the average wages in Western Europe, Australasia and North America are generally significantly higher than those in Africa, Asia, Eastern Europe and South America. For example, the mean of the average gross hourly wages in all Western European cities in our study in 2013 was 27.16 US dollars while that in the Asian cities was only 6.48 US dollars. As a result, the prices of services in the West were more expensive than the prices of services in Asia and elsewhere.

It is of little surprise that our cost of living index for ordinary residents is able to capture the differences in prices of non-tradable goods and services across countries. Such differences are reflected through purchasing power parity (PPP) based exchange rates. Our cost of living index for ordinary residents incorporates data from the International Comparison Programme (ICP) of the World Bank,[6] which is designed to collect data from around the world in order to calculate PPP based exchange rates.

In contrast to the clear pattern observed for ordinary residents, there is no such pattern in the geographic distribution of the cities according to the cost of living for expatriates. This is perhaps because expatriates everywhere gear towards high-end imports to maintain Western lifestyles. As such, their costs of living are mainly affected by exchange rate fluctuations rather than local factors. The lack of pattern in cost of living for expatriates is evident in Figure 6.2, which graphs the Cost of Living Indices for Expatriates in all cities in our study in 2013. Similar to Figure 6.1, the vertical axis plots the cities while the horizontal axis plots the index values. The different colours represent the geographical region each city belongs to.

[6]See Section 3.4.2 in Chapter 3 for a detailed discussion.

Figure 6.2: Cost of Living Indices for Expatriates in 103 World's Major Cities in 2013 by Geographical Regions

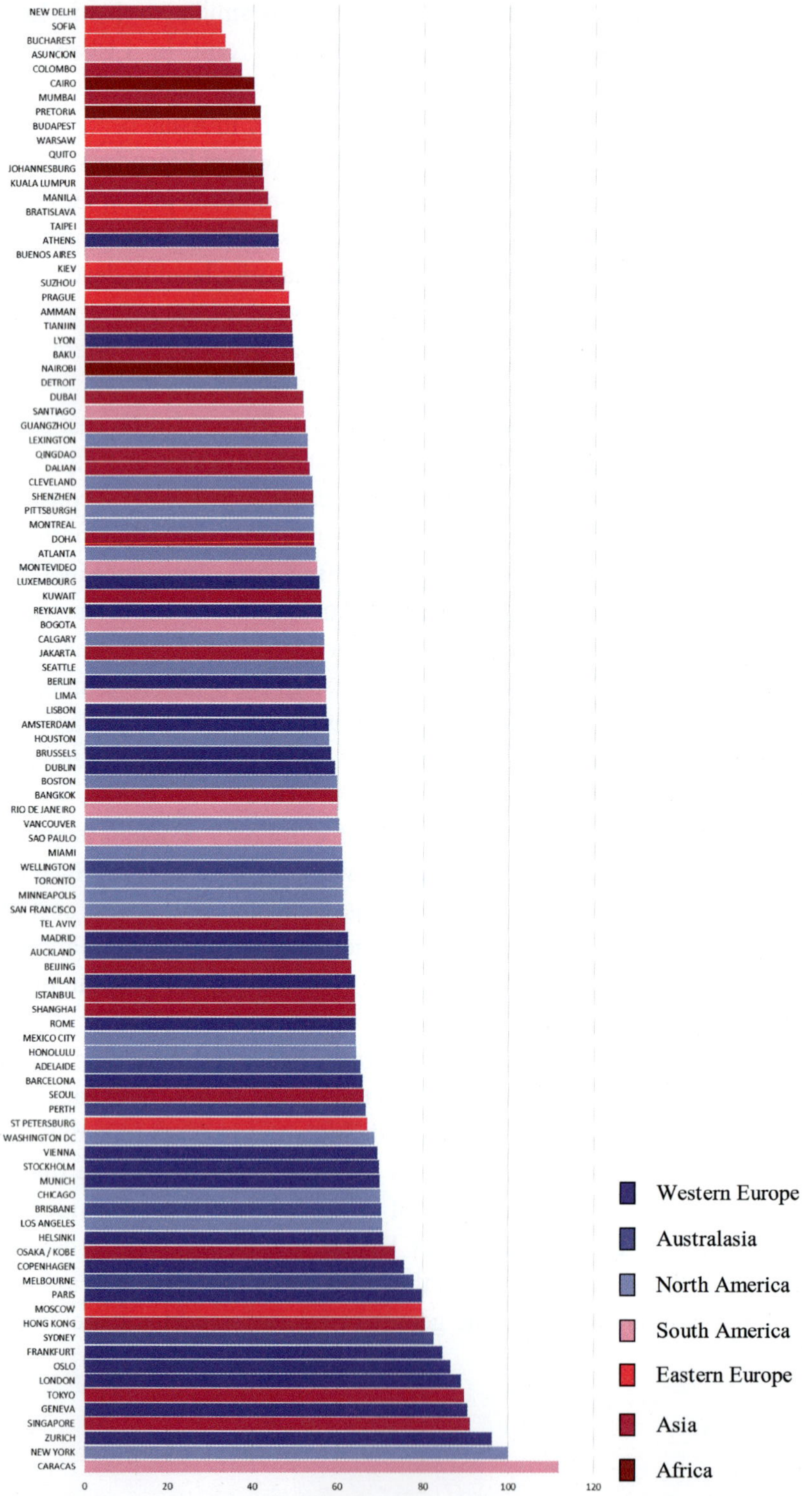

Source: Asia Competitiveness Institute

Discussant Notes 1

Dr Cledan Mandri-Perrott
Head of Infrastructure Finance & Public-Private Partnerships, The World Bank Group

Good morning Ladies and Gentlemen and it is my great pleasure to be with you this morning. I would like to personally thank Dr Tan Khee Giap for inviting me and to acknowledge the relationship the World Bank is building with the ACI. I think that what we have done together over the past year or so shows how practical research can be applied to policy and this is very important.

There is a big gap between reality and perception. What strikes me, fundamentally, about the work that the ACI has done is that it really looks at bridging that gap. Why is this important? It is important because we do live in a globalised world. If you look at professionals who are moving around the world, these are not just people who are very high up in an organisation but they involve all levels. It is actually about industries moving people at all levels of a company's activity, from the IT person to the CEO, the Chairman and all the functions in-between. Industries, companies and institutions are having to make decisions to ensure global mobility and opportunities for their people. For example, the World Bank Group has to decide on whether we should relocate 200 employees to Singapore when the Economist Intelligence Unit claims that Singapore is "the most expensive city in the world". Therefore, one has to demystify this "most expensive city in the world" label.

The piece of work by the ACI is an incredible paradigm shatterer. It breaks the paradigm of misconception. Very often through media reports, misconceptions arise that cost of living for expatriates is the same as that for ordinary residents in a particular city, which in reality are totally different concepts. Furthermore, the ACI's study offers a unique contribution as it is the first ever study which compares cost of living for expatriates and costs for ordinary residents.

By making a distinction between cost of living indices for expatriates and for ordinary residents, the ACI enables multinational corporations to design better compensation packages for their staff working abroad. This is because multinational corporations are now able to draw a more precise comparison between the cost of living borne by expatriates and that borne by ordinary residents in the respective city. Additionally, the ACI's study provides insightful policy implications for mayors or local governments whereby cost of living for ordinary residents must be watched closely over time as it may become a potential source of protest.

For me, there are four key notions which emerge from this research: distinction, relevance, reality and perception. Let me elaborate further on each category. First, there is the notion of distinction in recognising that differences between expatriates and ordinary residents exist. Not only so, the study also recognises that my type of living in Singapore four years ago when I first came and knew nothing about Singapore was slightly different from my type of living today now that I understand Singapore. I now know that I can buy fish at the market at one-twentieth of the price that if I were to buy that same produce in the local Cold Storage which is targeted at the expat market. Hence, the notion of distinction, which is essential in the ACI's methodology, is what I really commend the team for.

Next is the notion of relevance which I have briefly talked about. The study is important because more and more people move. People live in one place and then move to another one. In my own career spanning 22 years, I have lived in seven different countries. It matters for people to understand what it means to be mobile but the decision for mobility needs to be the right decision. The notion of relevance then becomes critical.

The other bit is the notion of reality. I think that there are three sub-topics from the research in terms of reality. First is consumption patterns. The ACI index does what other indices are not doing, which is to recognise social and cultural affiliations. For me, these aspects are absolutely critical in how people live and our expenditure reflects them. Thus, it makes good sense that the ACI index looks to capture social and cultural values. The second point in terms of reality is the exchange rate debate. The discussion about exchange rate is really valuable. It is important to understand and recognise that exchange rate fluctuations may give us the wrong impression about cost of living and the exchange rate simulations for Singapore and Hong Kong demonstrate this point very well. The last point is that the ACI's methodology is insensitive to the choice of base city, which should rightly be so.

I also note with great interest that the ACI's analysis clearly highlights the difference between cost of living for expatriates and ordinary residents in developed economies and less developed economies. As the research team presented earlier, this is due to the cost of non-traded services which tend to be more competitive in less developed economies.

Finally, about the notion of perception, I would like to go back to the point about misconceptions between the cost of living for expatriates and ordinary residents with which I started. Decisions are often made on the basis of incomplete perceptions and it is important that we have the right information. For example, if I am a father looking to send my children to Singapore to be educated and I have the impression that Singapore is a very expensive city, I will probably think that I cannot afford to send my children here. However, such perception is clearly incomplete. A student is not going to buy food at Cold Storage. Rather, he is going to eat chicken rice at $3.50 or even lower at $2.70 if he stays around the Changi area. While Singapore may be expensive for expatriates, it is not so for ordinary residents and foreign students and tourists who do not lead expatriates' lifestyles. Perception, therefore, becomes very important.

With these comments, I would like to congratulate the team and to congratulate Khee Giap for leading this research effort. Thank you very much.

Discussant Notes 2

Dr Vu Minh Khuong
Associate Professor, Lee Kuan Yew School of Public Policy, National University of Singapore

We have listened to the interesting and excellent presentation by the ACI team and thoughtful comments by Dr Mandri-Perrott. I just wanted to add a few additional comments to enhance your understanding of this project along three dimensions: motivation, methodology, and results.

Motivation

Globalisation, urbanisation, and modernisation are the prominent characteristics of the rapid changes the world is experiencing. As a result, cities, especially global cities, play a major role in driving economic growth and creating prosperity. In this rapidly changing and integrated environment, businesses, governments and people need internationally comparable and timely information to be able to make informed decisions. Businesses have to decide on where to make investments and how to deploy their resources across different cities in the world. Governments, including local governments, have to think about how to promote competitiveness of their cities and countries while taking into account the cost of living and purchasing power of the people. Meanwhile, workers and professionals care about their compensation levels and cost of living as well as where they stand in comparison with their peers in other cities in these respects.

The problem is that though information on cost of living, wages and purchasing power are available, they are often not comprehensive enough for stakeholders to make decisions. This point is also mentioned by Dr Mandri-Perrott and it is an important motivation for this project. In particular, the Economist Intelligence Unit (EIU) collects updated data on costs of living but the data is focused on expatriates. On the other hand, the International Comparison Programme (ICP) survey by the World Bank provides comprehensive reliable information on costs of living across nations. However, because it is very time-consuming and costly, the ICP survey is only conducted every six years, with the latest round taking place in 2011.

Extrapolating the valuable information from the EIU and ICP datasets, ACI has systematically constructed an annually updated dataset on the cost of living for ordinary residents in all global major cities. In addition, ACI has combined this estimation results with the wage rates provided by the International Labor Organisation (ILO) to compute the purchasing power of wages for ordinary residents.

Methodology

It should be noted that the method developed by ACI for estimating the cost of living for ordinary residents relies on a fairly strong assumption. The assumption is as follows: among the cities within a given country, the cost of living for expatriates is proportional to that for the ordinary residents. This means that within a country, if a city is more expensive for expatriates to live in, it is also more expensive for ordinary residents. Though strong, the assumption is plausible. Based on this assumption, one can use a mathematical formula to calculate the cost of living index for ordinary residents. It is worth emphasising that ACI's rankings do not depend on the choice of base city. Whether one chooses New York, Singapore or Tokyo as the base city, the ranking results would be the same.

Results

The estimation and rankings results produced by ACI, which are based on an objective, rigorous and comprehensive method, are meaningful. Below is some illustrative evidence.

Let us compare Singapore and Hong Kong. In terms of cost of living for ordinary residents, Singapore ranked 48th while Hong Kong ranked 59th so Hong Kong was less expensive than Singapore. In terms of cost of living for expatriates, Singapore ranked fourth and Hong Kong ranked 11th which was seven places lower than Singapore. This makes sense and Figure 1 gives us a better understanding of this comparison.

The figure shows that compared to an average city in the US, the purchasing power of one US dollar for individual consumption by an ordinary resident, is higher in Singapore by a factor of 1.1 and in Hong Kong by a factor of 1.4.

Figure 1: The Purchasing Power of US$1 in Singapore and Hong Kong by Product Category

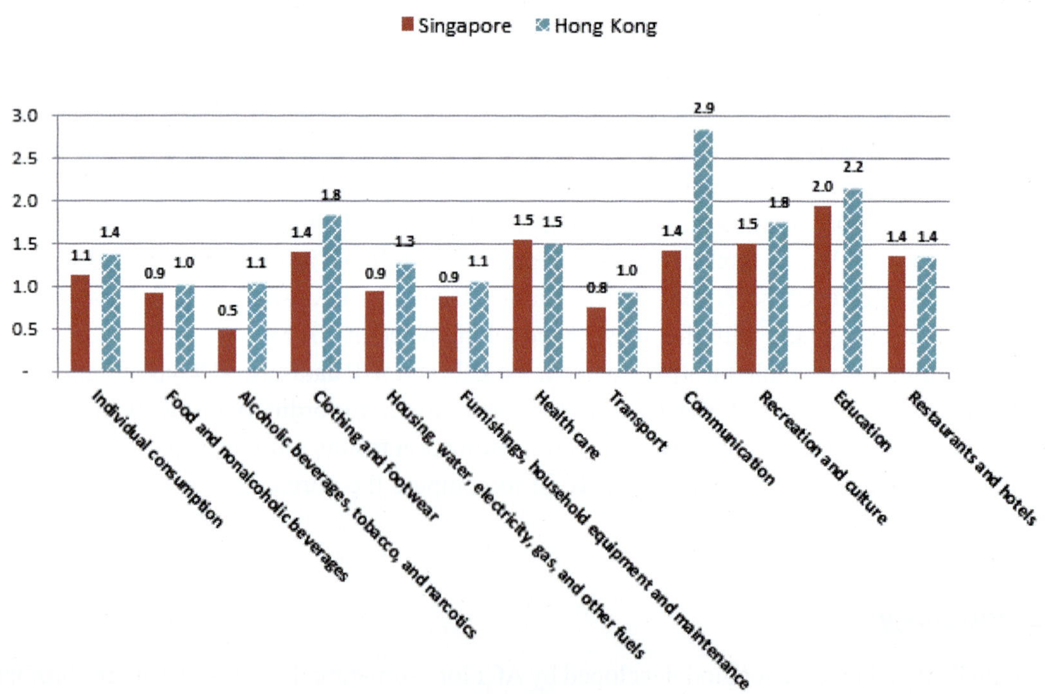

Source: Asia Competitiveness Institute and International Comparison Programme

Cost of living depends on three factors: market (supply and demand), government policy, and exchange rates. Singapore is limited in terms of supply factors such as land, agricultural products, and resources. On the demand side, 7,000 multinational companies headquartered in Singapore and a big pool of foreign workers and tourists substantially increase the country's consumption demand. As a result, Singapore's costs of several consumption categories, including "Food and non-alcoholic beverages", "Alcoholic beverages, tobacco and narcotics", and "Housing, water, electricity" are more expensive than the average US city.

The effect of government policy on cost of living can clearly be seen in several categories such as "Transport", "Education", and "Healthcare". Though Singapore has a good public transport system, in particular the Mass Rapid Transit system, car ownership is very expensive due to the government's strict control of car population. At the same time, however, Singapore is much less expensive than the average US city on "Education" (at a factor of 2.0) and "Healthcare" (1.5) thanks to the government's substantial support and promotion of these sectors.

Regarding the effect of exchange rates on the cost of living, the case of Australian cities provides a good example.

As shown in Figure 2, the Australian dollar was very strong compared to US dollar in 2013–2014. Given the strength of the Australian dollar, one can expect that the costs of living in Australian cities in these years were high as compared to other cities internationally. This is in

Figure 2: Australian Dollar vs. US Dollar during 2007-2015

Source: Bloomberg

fact reflected in the ACI ranking. Five Australian cities — Sydney, Melbourne, Brisbane, Perth and Adelaide — ranked among the top in terms of cost living ranking for ordinary residents. It should be noted, however, that these cities also ranked high in terms of nominal wages because of the high exchange rates. That is, exchange rates have a similar effect on both cost of living and nominal wage rates. As a result, ACI's ranking of purchasing power of wages is not affected by exchange rate fluctuations.

Appendix 1

Cost of Living Rankings for Expatriates and Ordinary Residents in 103 World's Major Cities, 2005–2013

Appendix 1: Cost of Living Rankings for Expatriates and Ordinary Residents in 103 World's Major Cities, 2005–2013

				Year								
No.	City	Country	Rankings	2005	2006	2007	2008	2009	2010	2011	2012	2013
1	Adelaide	Australia	Cost of Living Ranking for Expatriates	64	70	63	67	68	48	36	27	29
			Cost of Living Ranking for Ordinary Residents	40	42	37	38	40	21	15	12	11
2	Amman	Jordan	Cost of Living Ranking for Expatriates	84	83	82	85	82	87	88	81	82
			Cost of Living Ranking for Ordinary Residents	72	72	75	72	70	72	97	97	96
3	Amsterdam	Netherlands	Cost of Living Ranking for Expatriates	30	40	34	35	35	51	51	56	53
			Cost of Living Ranking for Ordinary Residents	27	30	24	21	19	30	24	31	25
4	Asuncion	Paraguay	Cost of Living Ranking for Expatriates	103	102	102	102	102	102	101	100	100
			Cost of Living Ranking for Ordinary Residents	94	90	85	77	83	80	79	81	81
5	Athens	Greece	Cost of Living Ranking for Expatriates	67	69	68	64	61	71	71	88	87
			Cost of Living Ranking for Ordinary Residents	46	46	41	34	33	36	43	45	45
6	Atlanta	United States	Cost of Living Ranking for Expatriates	70	75	78	78	71	70	75	65	65
			Cost of Living Ranking for Ordinary Residents	54	53	55	59	58	57	54	49	51
7	Auckland	New Zealand	Cost of Living Ranking for Expatriates	48	65	62	75	81	68	52	41	37
			Cost of Living Ranking for Ordinary Residents	25	40	28	40	48	32	34	28	27
8	Baku	Azerbaijan	Cost of Living Ranking for Expatriates	77	82	86	88	78	84	84	80	79
			Cost of Living Ranking for Ordinary Residents	101	101	96	96	93	93	100	99	98
9	Bangkok	Thailand	Cost of Living Ranking for Expatriates	79	77	60	63	55	46	42	48	48
			Cost of Living Ranking for Ordinary Residents	92	93	89	92	94	91	95	96	95
10	Barcelona	Spain	Cost of Living Ranking for Expatriates	32	28	20	18	18	25	25	29	28
			Cost of Living Ranking for Ordinary Residents	41	41	36	27	30	40	37	39	36
11	Beijing	China	Cost of Living Ranking for Expatriates	19	21	37	32	30	30	32	31	36
			Cost of Living Ranking for Ordinary Residents	82	86	92	91	89	90	78	76	74

(Continued)

Appendix 1: (*Continued*)

No.	City	Country	Rankings	Year 2005	2006	2007	2008	2009	2010	2011	2012	2013
12	Berlin	Germany	Cost of Living Ranking for Expatriates	33	29	22	24	27	45	47	60	56
			Cost of Living Ranking for Ordinary Residents	35	33	33	30	35	47	48	54	50
13	Bogota	Colombia	Cost of Living Ranking for Expatriates	90	87	80	76	72	60	60	53	60
			Cost of Living Ranking for Ordinary Residents	80	80	76	74	77	73	72	70	71
14	Boston	United States	Cost of Living Ranking for Expatriates	24	24	31	39	32	38	45	43	49
			Cost of Living Ranking for Ordinary Residents	29	29	35	39	34	41	42	42	43
15	Bratislava	Slovakia	Cost of Living Ranking for Expatriates	82	80	77	66	63	79	82	91	89
			Cost of Living Ranking for Ordinary Residents	77	75	71	68	64	70	66	69	69
16	Brisbane	Australia	Cost of Living Ranking for Expatriates	61	63	50	54	53	32	21	19	19
			Cost of Living Ranking for Ordinary Residents	38	34	29	28	26	15	7	7	7
17	Brussels	Belgium	Cost of Living Ranking for Expatriates	45	42	35	31	34	44	43	51	51
			Cost of Living Ranking for Ordinary Residents	21	22	18	15	14	26	22	29	24
18	Bucharest	Romania	Cost of Living Ranking for Expatriates	93	91	88	90	96	100	100	101	101
			Cost of Living Ranking for Ordinary Residents	76	74	72	73	78	81	80	90	86
19	Budapest	Hungary	Cost of Living Ranking for Expatriates	85	88	85	83	88	92	90	96	95
			Cost of Living Ranking for Ordinary Residents	67	71	66	67	68	71	74	77	76
20	Buenos Aires	Argentina	Cost of Living Ranking for Expatriates	101	101	101	95	97	94	92	86	86
			Cost of Living Ranking for Ordinary Residents	81	83	84	89	92	92	53	53	58
21	Cairo	Egypt	Cost of Living Ranking for Expatriates	96	96	98	93	93	93	96	92	98
			Cost of Living Ranking for Ordinary Residents	100	100	101	99	97	95	103	102	103
22	Calgary	Canada	Cost of Living Ranking for Expatriates	55	48	49	57	54	49	50	50	59
			Cost of Living Ranking for Ordinary Residents	33	27	25	29	28	24	16	17	18

(*Continued*)

Appendix 1: (*Continued*)

No.	City	Country	Rankings	Year								
				2005	2006	2007	2008	2009	2010	2011	2012	2013
23	Caracas	Venezuela	Cost of Living Ranking for Expatriates	60	56	42	11	1	13	13	1	1
			Cost of Living Ranking for Ordinary Residents	70	69	65	57	32	67	71	63	64
24	Chicago	United States	Cost of Living Ranking for Expatriates	17	17	24	26	24	22	26	20	20
			Cost of Living Ranking for Ordinary Residents	17	14	21	24	23	27	31	27	29
25	Cleveland	United States	Cost of Living Ranking for Expatriates	68	76	79	80	69	78	78	71	70
			Cost of Living Ranking for Ordinary Residents	53	54	58	58	57	59	57	52	52
26	Colombo	Sri Lanka	Cost of Living Ranking for Expatriates	97	97	97	97	99	98	99	99	99
			Cost of Living Ranking for Ordinary Residents	87	88	91	84	84	82	99	100	100
27	Copenhagen	Denmark	Cost of Living Ranking for Expatriates	7	5	4	7	8	11	11	16	15
			Cost of Living Ranking for Ordinary Residents	5	5	2	1	2	4	6	10	8
28	Dalian	China	Cost of Living Ranking for Expatriates	66	53	57	52	39	53	57	61	71
			Cost of Living Ranking for Ordinary Residents	95	95	95	94	91	94	86	84	85
29	Detroit	United States	Cost of Living Ranking for Expatriates	58	59	66	68	67	77	79	77	77
			Cost of Living Ranking for Ordinary Residents	50	50	50	53	56	60	58	55	56
30	Doha	Qatar	Cost of Living Ranking for Expatriates	74	72	76	69	64	74	72	73	66
			Cost of Living Ranking for Ordinary Residents	59	57	53	50	50	56	60	60	57
31	Dubai	United Arab Emirates	Cost of Living Ranking for Expatriates	72	67	56	29	28	54	64	74	76
			Cost of Living Ranking for Ordinary Residents	59	59	56	54	52	51	61	61	60
32	Dublin	Ireland	Cost of Living Ranking for Expatriates	39	37	27	23	25	43	41	54	50
			Cost of Living Ranking for Ordinary Residents	8	8	6	4	7	11	18	20	17
33	Frankfurt	Germany	Cost of Living Ranking for Expatriates	12	11	5	4	5	5	6	11	9
			Cost of Living Ranking for Ordinary Residents	14	12	10	9	8	10	20	21	19

(*Continued*)

Appendix 1: (*Continued*)

No.	City	Country	Rankings	Year 2005	2006	2007	2008	2009	2010	2011	2012	2013
34	Geneva	Switzerland	Cost of Living Ranking for Expatriates	11	12	11	10	10	6	3	6	5
			Cost of Living Ranking for Ordinary Residents	6	7	8	6	4	2	3	5	6
35	Guangzhou	China	Cost of Living Ranking for Expatriates	22	31	40	43	59	65	66	69	74
			Cost of Living Ranking for Ordinary Residents	86	92	93	93	95	96	83	83	84
36	Helsinki	Finland	Cost of Living Ranking for Expatriates	23	22	18	15	15	17	19	23	17
			Cost of Living Ranking for Ordinary Residents	9	9	9	8	9	12	17	19	16
37	Hong Kong	Hong Kong, China	Cost of Living Ranking for Expatriates	5	6	10	17	13	12	12	9	11
			Cost of Living Ranking for Ordinary Residents	56	58	60	62	60	62	63	62	59
38	Honolulu	United States	Cost of Living Ranking for Expatriates	51	51	59	51	42	42	38	30	30
			Cost of Living Ranking for Ordinary Residents	47	45	46	47	44	42	41	35	35
39	Houston	United States	Cost of Living Ranking for Expatriates	43	45	53	58	44	55	58	52	52
			Cost of Living Ranking for Ordinary Residents	36	35	43	46	42	45	45	44	44
40	Istanbul	Turkey	Cost of Living Ranking for Expatriates	26	23	17	20	26	21	46	33	34
			Cost of Living Ranking for Ordinary Residents	63	64	62	61	65	63	75	75	73
41	Jakarta	Indonesia	Cost of Living Ranking for Expatriates	78	68	71	73	75	64	65	66	58
			Cost of Living Ranking for Ordinary Residents	85	81	82	90	88	79	94	95	97
42	Johannesburg	South Africa	Cost of Living Ranking for Expatriates	89	90	94	99	92	83	83	84	92
			Cost of Living Ranking for Ordinary Residents	64	67	73	78	72	69	68	71	77
43	Kiev	Ukraine	Cost of Living Ranking for Expatriates	42	39	39	37	80	86	89	89	85
			Cost of Living Ranking for Ordinary Residents	103	103	103	102	103	103	101	101	101
44	Kuala Lumpur	Malaysia	Cost of Living Ranking for Expatriates	99	99	96	96	98	96	93	94	91
			Cost of Living Ranking for Ordinary Residents	79	78	77	81	81	78	88	89	91

(*Continued*)

Appendix 1: (*Continued*)

No.	City	Country	Rankings	Year 2005	2006	2007	2008	2009	2010	2011	2012	2013
45	Kuwait	Kuwait	Cost of Living Ranking for Expatriates	31	32	33	50	51	57	54	55	62
			Cost of Living Ranking for Ordinary Residents	52	52	51	44	45	43	67	67	68
46	Lexington	United States	Cost of Living Ranking for Expatriates	54	58	72	71	66	66	68	70	73
			Cost of Living Ranking for Ordinary Residents	45	47	49	52	54	50	49	51	53
47	Lima	Peru	Cost of Living Ranking for Expatriates	83	84	83	82	83	81	81	64	55
			Cost of Living Ranking for Ordinary Residents	75	77	78	79	76	75	77	73	72
48	Lisbon	Portugal	Cost of Living Ranking for Expatriates	52	52	46	38	37	52	49	57	54
			Cost of Living Ranking for Ordinary Residents	48	48	42	37	41	49	46	50	47
49	London	Great Britain	Cost of Living Ranking for Expatriates	2	2	1	2	3	2	4	4	7
			Cost of Living Ranking for Ordinary Residents	12	11	12	22	38	38	26	24	21
50	Los Angeles	United States	Cost of Living Ranking for Expatriates	28	26	29	27	19	16	22	18	18
			Cost of Living Ranking for Ordinary Residents	26	23	30	25	16	17	28	25	23
51	Luxembourg	Luxembourg	Cost of Living Ranking for Expatriates	53	55	48	42	41	58	56	63	63
			Cost of Living Ranking for Ordinary Residents	13	10	11	10	11	14	14	15	13
52	Lyon	France	Cost of Living Ranking for Expatriates	56	60	61	59	56	73	74	82	80
			Cost of Living Ranking for Ordinary Residents	51	51	48	51	55	61	51	56	55
53	Madrid	Spain	Cost of Living Ranking for Expatriates	37	33	25	19	16	24	27	37	38
			Cost of Living Ranking for Ordinary Residents	42	43	38	26	27	39	38	43	42
54	Manila	Philippines	Cost of Living Ranking for Expatriates	100	100	100	100	100	99	98	95	90
			Cost of Living Ranking for Ordinary Residents	88	85	86	87	86	86	91	88	89
55	Melbourne	Australia	Cost of Living Ranking for Expatriates	46	49	38	44	47	19	16	14	14
			Cost of Living Ranking for Ordinary Residents	20	20	16	20	22	8	5	4	4

(*Continued*)

Appendix 1: (*Continued*)

No.	City	Country	Rankings	Year 2005	2006	2007	2008	2009	2010	2011	2012	2013
56	Mexico city	Mexico	Cost of Living Ranking for Expatriates	38	38	51	55	70	59	53	47	31
			Cost of Living Ranking for Ordinary Residents	65	63	68	71	74	74	73	74	70
57	Miami	United States	Cost of Living Ranking for Expatriates	34	36	44	49	36	40	44	40	44
			Cost of Living Ranking for Ordinary Residents	31	31	39	42	36	35	40	38	39
58	Milan	Italy	Cost of Living Ranking for Expatriates	21	19	19	21	21	28	30	32	35
			Cost of Living Ranking for Ordinary Residents	15	16	15	14	13	19	32	33	34
59	Minneapolis	United States	Cost of Living Ranking for Expatriates	47	47	58	62	50	50	55	46	41
			Cost of Living Ranking for Ordinary Residents	43	44	45	49	47	44	44	41	41
60	Montevideo	Uruguay	Cost of Living Ranking for Expatriates	91	93	91	89	85	76	76	72	64
			Cost of Living Ranking for Ordinary Residents	68	68	67	64	62	55	59	57	54
61	Montreal	Canada	Cost of Living Ranking for Expatriates	69	62	67	74	74	62	63	58	67
			Cost of Living Ranking for Ordinary Residents	44	36	40	43	49	37	25	22	30
62	Moscow	Russia	Cost of Living Ranking for Expatriates	14	14	14	13	22	14	15	15	12
			Cost of Living Ranking for Ordinary Residents	83	82	79	80	87	83	81	82	82
63	Mumbai	India	Cost of Living Ranking for Expatriates	95	95	92	92	95	95	94	93	97
			Cost of Living Ranking for Ordinary Residents	98	99	97	101	101	100	98	98	99
64	Munich	Germany	Cost of Living Ranking for Expatriates	13	15	15	16	14	18	18	24	21
			Cost of Living Ranking for Ordinary Residents	19	26	22	18	20	31	36	40	37
65	Nairobi	Kenya	Cost of Living Ranking for Expatriates	92	92	90	91	89	90	95	83	78
			Cost of Living Ranking for Ordinary Residents	90	84	81	75	73	77	96	94	94
66	New Delhi	India	Cost of Living Ranking for Expatriates	102	103	103	103	103	103	103	103	103
			Cost of Living Ranking for Ordinary Residents	102	102	102	103	102	102	102	103	102

(*Continued*)

Appendix 1: (*Continued*)

No.	City	Country	Rankings	2005	2006	2007	2008	2009	2010	2011	2012	2013
67	New York	United States	Cost of Living Ranking for Expatriates	4	3	3	6	9	8	9	5	2
			Cost of Living Ranking for Ordinary Residents	3	1	4	7	6	6	11	6	5
68	Osaka/Kobe	Japan	Cost of Living Ranking for Expatriates	3	4	9	9	7	4	5	8	16
			Cost of Living Ranking for Ordinary Residents	24	37	47	41	21	18	21	18	40
69	Oslo	Norway	Cost of Living Ranking for Expatriates	8	9	7	8	11	7	7	10	8
			Cost of Living Ranking for Ordinary Residents	4	4	3	3	5	3	2	3	3
70	Paris	France	Cost of Living Ranking for Expatriates	9	8	6	3	6	9	10	13	13
			Cost of Living Ranking for Ordinary Residents	7	6	7	5	3	5	8	11	10
71	Perth	Australia	Cost of Living Ranking for Expatriates	63	66	54	61	57	34	29	22	26
			Cost of Living Ranking for Ordinary Residents	39	39	27	31	31	13	9	8	9
72	Pittsburgh	United States	Cost of Living Ranking for Expatriates	57	61	73	72	65	67	70	67	68
			Cost of Living Ranking for Ordinary Residents	49	49	52	55	53	52	50	47	49
73	Prague	Czech Republic	Cost of Living Ranking for Expatriates	65	64	65	46	58	63	62	79	83
			Cost of Living Ranking for Ordinary Residents	71	70	69	63	66	68	62	66	66
74	Pretoria	South Africa	Cost of Living Ranking for Expatriates	88	89	93	94	91	80	80	85	96
			Cost of Living Ranking for Ordinary Residents	62	66	70	76	71	66	69	72	80
75	Qingdao	China	Cost of Living Ranking for Expatriates	76	81	84	77	73	75	73	62	72
			Cost of Living Ranking for Ordinary Residents	96	97	100	98	99	97	87	80	75
76	Quito	Ecuador	Cost of Living Ranking for Expatriates	94	94	95	98	94	97	97	98	93
			Cost of Living Ranking for Ordinary Residents	78	79	83	88	80	85	82	78	79
77	Reykjavik	Iceland	Cost of Living Ranking for Expatriates	20	34	28	70	77	72	69	68	61
			Cost of Living Ranking for Ordinary Residents	1	2	1	13	37	33	30	32	28

(*Continued*)

Appendix 1: (*Continued*)

No.	City	Country	Rankings	Year 2005	2006	2007	2008	2009	2010	2011	2012	2013
78	Rio de Janeiro	Brazil	Cost of Living Ranking for Expatriates	73	54	52	41	40	23	17	35	47
			Cost of Living Ranking for Ordinary Residents	66	62	61	60	61	54	52	59	63
79	Rome	Italy	Cost of Living Ranking for Expatriates	35	30	23	22	23	36	33	38	32
			Cost of Living Ranking for Ordinary Residents	22	18	17	12	12	23	33	34	31
80	San Francisco	United States	Cost of Living Ranking for Expatriates	16	18	26	33	31	37	40	39	40
			Cost of Living Ranking for Ordinary Residents	16	15	23	33	29	34	39	37	38
81	Santiago	Chile	Cost of Living Ranking for Expatriates	81	79	81	86	86	82	77	76	75
			Cost of Living Ranking for Ordinary Residents	61	61	63	66	67	64	65	65	65
82	Sao Paulo	Brazil	Cost of Living Ranking for Expatriates	75	71	64	56	45	26	20	28	45
			Cost of Living Ranking for Ordinary Residents	69	65	64	65	63	58	56	58	62
83	Seattle	United States	Cost of Living Ranking for Expatriates	36	35	47	53	46	56	61	59	57
			Cost of Living Ranking for Ordinary Residents	34	32	44	45	46	48	47	46	46
84	Seoul	South Korea	Cost of Living Ranking for Expatriates	10	10	13	40	62	39	37	26	27
			Cost of Living Ranking for Ordinary Residents	57	55	57	69	69	65	64	64	61
85	Shanghai	China	Cost of Living Ranking for Expatriates	40	43	43	34	29	33	35	34	33
			Cost of Living Ranking for Ordinary Residents	84	87	88	86	79	84	70	68	67
86	Shenzhen	China	Cost of Living Ranking for Expatriates	86	85	87	84	76	85	85	75	69
			Cost of Living Ranking for Ordinary Residents	99	98	98	97	98	99	92	86	83
87	Singapore	Singapore	Cost of Living Ranking for Expatriates	15	13	12	12	12	10	8	7	4
			Cost of Living Ranking for Ordinary Residents	58	60	59	56	59	53	55	48	48

(*Continued*)

Appendix 1: (*Continued*)

No.	City	Country	Rankings	Year								
				2005	2006	2007	2008	2009	2010	2011	2012	2013
88	Sofia	Bulgaria	Cost of Living Ranking for Expatriates	98	98	99	101	101	101	102	102	102
			Cost of Living Ranking for Ordinary Residents	89	89	87	83	82	89	89	93	93
89	St Petersburg	Russia	Cost of Living Ranking for Expatriates	41	41	36	28	33	27	28	25	25
			Cost of Living Ranking for Ordinary Residents	93	91	90	85	90	88	85	87	88
90	Stockholm	Sweden	Cost of Living Ranking for Expatriates	29	25	21	25	43	31	24	21	22
			Cost of Living Ranking for Ordinary Residents	11	13	13	11	24	20	13	14	12
91	Suzhou	China	Cost of Living Ranking for Expatriates	87	86	89	87	79	88	87	87	84
			Cost of Living Ranking for Ordinary Residents	97	96	99	100	100	101	93	92	92
92	Sydney	Australia	Cost of Living Ranking for Expatriates	44	46	32	36	38	15	14	12	10
			Cost of Living Ranking for Ordinary Residents	18	19	14	17	17	7	4	1	1
93	Taipei	Taiwan, China	Cost of Living Ranking for Expatriates	50	57	75	81	87	89	86	90	88
			Cost of Living Ranking for Ordinary Residents	73	76	80	82	85	87	84	85	87
94	Tel Aviv	Israel	Cost of Living Ranking for Expatriates	71	73	69	48	52	41	39	49	39
			Cost of Living Ranking for Ordinary Residents	55	56	54	48	51	46	35	36	33
95	Tianjin	China	Cost of Living Ranking for Expatriates	27	20	41	47	49	61	67	78	81
			Cost of Living Ranking for Ordinary Residents	91	94	94	95	96	98	90	91	90
96	Tokyo	Japan	Cost of Living Ranking for Expatriates	1	1	2	1	2	1	1	2	6
			Cost of Living Ranking for Ordinary Residents	10	17	34	19	10	9	10	9	22
97	Toronto	Canada	Cost of Living Ranking for Expatriates	49	44	45	45	48	35	34	36	42
			Cost of Living Ranking for Ordinary Residents	32	21	19	23	25	16	12	13	14
98	Vancouver	Canada	Cost of Living Ranking for Expatriates	59	50	55	60	60	47	48	42	46
			Cost of Living Ranking for Ordinary Residents	37	28	31	35	39	29	19	16	15

(*Continued*)

Appendix 1: *(Continued)*

No.	City	Country	Rankings	Year								
				2005	**2006**	**2007**	**2008**	**2009**	**2010**	**2011**	**2012**	**2013**
99	Vienna	Austria	Cost of Living Ranking for Expatriates	18	16	16	14	17	29	31	44	23
			Cost of Living Ranking for Ordinary Residents	23	24	20	16	15	28	23	30	26
100	Warsaw	Poland	Cost of Living Ranking for Expatriates	80	78	74	65	90	91	91	97	94
			Cost of Living Ranking for Ordinary Residents	74	73	74	70	75	76	76	79	78
101	Washington DC	United States	Cost of Living Ranking for Expatriates	25	27	30	30	20	20	23	17	24
			Cost of Living Ranking for Ordinary Residents	28	25	32	32	18	22	29	26	32
102	Wellington	New Zealand	Cost of Living Ranking for Expatriates	62	74	70	79	84	69	59	45	43
			Cost of Living Ranking for Ordinary Residents	30	38	26	36	43	25	27	23	20
103	Zurich	Switzerland	Cost of Living Ranking for Expatriates	6	7	8	5	4	3	2	3	3
			Cost of Living Ranking for Ordinary Residents	2	3	5	2	1	1	1	2	2

Appendix 2

Wages and Purchasing Power Rankings for Ordinary Residents in 103 World's Major Cities, 2005–2013

Appendix 2: Wages and Purchasing Power Rankings for Ordinary Residents in 103 World's Major Cities, 2005–2013

No.	City	Country	Rankings	Year								
				2005	2006	2007	2008	2009	2010	2011	2012	2013
1	Adelaide	Australia	Wages Ranking for Ordinary Residents	20	20	18	19	18	6	6	6	6
			Purchasing Power Ranking for Ordinary Residents	17	15	12	11	11	8	11	10	9
2	Amman	Jordan	Wages Ranking for Ordinary Residents	82	83	84	87	86	85	85	85	94
			Purchasing Power Ranking for Ordinary Residents	87	88	91	94	94	94	77	78	78
3	Amsterdam	Netherlands	Wages Ranking for Ordinary Residents	18	19	24	18	13	22	22	26	22
			Purchasing Power Ranking for Ordinary Residents	23	21	23	24	24	23	27	27	27
4	Asuncion	Paraguay	Wages Ranking for Ordinary Residents	87	88	88	88	95	95	96	96	96
			Purchasing Power Ranking for Ordinary Residents	88	91	95	97	97	97	97	97	97
5	Athens	Greece	Wages Ranking for Ordinary Residents	53	53	52	52	47	50	51	51	51
			Purchasing Power Ranking for Ordinary Residents	55	54	53	54	49	53	44	43	37
6	Atlanta	United States	Wages Ranking for Ordinary Residents	30	30	32	32	29	31	31	31	30
			Purchasing Power Ranking for Ordinary Residents	9	11	13	12	12	16	12	18	16
7	Auckland	New Zealand	Wages Ranking for Ordinary Residents	48	48	28	48	50	29	29	24	23
			Purchasing Power Ranking for Ordinary Residents	50	47	41	39	39	39	32	29	33
8	Baku	Azerbaijan	Wages Ranking for Ordinary Residents	89	87	86	84	80	79	81	80	74
			Purchasing Power Ranking for Ordinary Residents	81	78	76	76	75	75	72	68	64
9	Bangkok	Thailand	Wages Ranking for Ordinary Residents	88	89	89	97	98	98	97	98	97
			Purchasing Power Ranking for Ordinary Residents	89	92	92	95	98	98	95	96	96
10	Barcelona	Spain	Wages Ranking for Ordinary Residents	50	51	50	50	48	51	52	52	52
			Purchasing Power Ranking for Ordinary Residents	53	53	54	52	50	50	54	53	56
11	Beijing	China	Wages Ranking for Ordinary Residents	91	91	90	89	87	87	86	87	86
			Purchasing Power Ranking for Ordinary Residents	100	98	97	96	93	92	96	95	93

(Continued)

Appendix 2: (*Continued*)

No.	City	Country	Rankings	Year 2005	2006	2007	2008	2009	2010	2011	2012	2013
12	Berlin	Germany	Wages Ranking for Ordinary Residents	27	25	25	24	24	26	26	28	26
			Purchasing Power Ranking for Ordinary Residents	24	22	24	23	22	18	7	7	7
13	Bogota	Colombia	Wages Ranking for Ordinary Residents	83	84	82	81	85	80	80	81	80
			Purchasing Power Ranking for Ordinary Residents	84	85	82	81	87	85	83	81	79
14	Boston	United States	Wages Ranking for Ordinary Residents	30	30	32	32	29	31	31	31	30
			Purchasing Power Ranking for Ordinary Residents	37	37	40	38	35	34	33	31	30
15	Bratislava	Slovakia	Wages Ranking for Ordinary Residents	68	68	68	65	62	65	64	66	70
			Purchasing Power Ranking for Ordinary Residents	65	64	64	64	63	62	66	70	71
16	Brisbane	Australia	Wages Ranking for Ordinary Residents	20	20	18	19	18	6	6	6	6
			Purchasing Power Ranking for Ordinary Residents	19	19	15	18	20	15	19	16	17
17	Brussels	Belgium	Wages Ranking for Ordinary Residents	8	9	10	8	7	13	13	13	12
			Purchasing Power Ranking for Ordinary Residents	8	8	9	10	9	11	8	9	10
18	Bucharest	Romania	Wages Ranking for Ordinary Residents	75	77	70	71	73	77	70	71	64
			Purchasing Power Ranking for Ordinary Residents	76	76	74	71	72	73	70	62	51
19	Budapest	Hungary	Wages Ranking for Ordinary Residents	63	64	64	63	67	68	67	67	69
			Purchasing Power Ranking for Ordinary Residents	63	62	63	63	64	64	64	66	65
20	Buenos Aires	Argentina	Wages Ranking for Ordinary Residents	81	79	79	79	78	75	77	78	81
			Purchasing Power Ranking for Ordinary Residents	77	77	75	73	70	67	90	92	94
21	Cairo	Egypt	Wages Ranking for Ordinary Residents	90	90	98	98	97	97	98	97	98
			Purchasing Power Ranking for Ordinary Residents	86	87	90	92	95	95	79	79	80
22	Calgary	Canada	Wages Ranking for Ordinary Residents	14	11	12	14	14	14	15	14	14
			Purchasing Power Ranking for Ordinary Residents	13	13	14	13	15	14	26	22	20

(Continued)

Appendix 2: (*Continued*)

No.	City	Country	Rankings	Year								
				2005	2006	2007	2008	2009	2010	2011	2012	2013
23	Caracas	Venezuela	Wages Ranking for Ordinary Residents	84	81	80	76	69	81	79	77	79
			Purchasing Power Ranking for Ordinary Residents	90	86	86	89	92	93	84	82	91
24	Chicago	United States	Wages Ranking for Ordinary Residents	30	30	32	32	29	31	31	31	30
			Purchasing Power Ranking for Ordinary Residents	46	48	49	48	41	43	46	47	50
25	Cleveland	United States	Wages Ranking for Ordinary Residents	30	30	32	32	29	31	31	31	30
			Purchasing Power Ranking for Ordinary Residents	12	9	10	14	13	13	10	12	15
26	Colombo	Sri Lanka	Wages Ranking for Ordinary Residents	103	103	103	103	103	103	103	103	103
			Purchasing Power Ranking for Ordinary Residents	103	103	103	103	103	103	103	103	102
27	Copenhagen	Denmark	Wages Ranking for Ordinary Residents	1	1	1	1	1	1	3	4	3
			Purchasing Power Ranking for Ordinary Residents	3	3	1	1	1	1	1	1	1
28	Dalian	China	Wages Ranking for Ordinary Residents	91	91	90	89	87	87	86	87	86
			Purchasing Power Ranking for Ordinary Residents	94	94	93	91	91	89	92	90	88
29	Detroit	United States	Wages Ranking for Ordinary Residents	30	30	32	32	29	31	31	31	30
			Purchasing Power Ranking for Ordinary Residents	16	18	20	20	14	12	9	8	8
30	Doha	Qatar	Wages Ranking for Ordinary Residents	59	59	56	56	56	56	57	56	56
			Purchasing Power Ranking for Ordinary Residents	61	63	62	61	60	61	60	58	62
31	Dubai	United Arab Emirates	Wages Ranking for Ordinary Residents	67	67	67	68	65	64	65	64	65
			Purchasing Power Ranking for Ordinary Residents	70	70	72	74	73	72	71	72	73
32	Dublin	Ireland	Wages Ranking for Ordinary Residents	6	7	8	6	6	12	12	12	13
			Purchasing Power Ranking for Ordinary Residents	21	23	28	28	26	25	14	14	18
33	Frankfurt	Germany	Wages Ranking for Ordinary Residents	27	25	25	24	24	26	26	28	26
			Purchasing Power Ranking for Ordinary Residents	39	41	46	46	48	49	43	44	46

(*Continued*)

Appendix 2: (*Continued*)

No.	City	Country	Rankings	Year								
				2005	2006	2007	2008	2009	2010	2011	2012	2013
34	Geneva	Switzerland	Wages Ranking for Ordinary Residents	2	2	3	3	2	2	1	1	1
			Purchasing Power Ranking for Ordinary Residents	1	1	2	2	2	3	2	2	3
35	Guangzhou	China	Wages Ranking for Ordinary Residents	91	91	90	89	87	87	86	87	86
			Purchasing Power Ranking for Ordinary Residents	97	96	96	93	89	88	94	91	89
36	Helsinki	Finland	Wages Ranking for Ordinary Residents	11	15	11	9	8	18	14	18	18
			Purchasing Power Ranking for Ordinary Residents	34	34	33	29	29	29	25	26	28
37	Hong Kong	Hong Kong, China	Wages Ranking for Ordinary Residents	57	57	59	61	60	63	63	62	61
			Purchasing Power Ranking for Ordinary Residents	59	60	60	62	62	63	63	67	68
38	Honolulu	United States	Wages Ranking for Ordinary Residents	30	30	32	32	29	31	31	31	30
			Purchasing Power Ranking for Ordinary Residents	22	26	27	31	31	33	38	42	43
39	Houston	United States	Wages Ranking for Ordinary Residents	30	30	32	32	29	31	31	31	30
			Purchasing Power Ranking for Ordinary Residents	30	33	35	32	33	30	28	25	25
40	Istanbul	Turkey	Wages Ranking for Ordinary Residents	65	65	65	64	66	66	68	68	71
			Purchasing Power Ranking for Ordinary Residents	66	66	65	67	66	70	65	69	69
41	Jakarta	Indonesia	Wages Ranking for Ordinary Residents	100	100	100	100	100	100	100	100	100
			Purchasing Power Ranking for Ordinary Residents	102	102	102	102	102	102	101	99	99
42	Johannesburg	South Africa	Wages Ranking for Ordinary Residents	61	61	61	66	63	58	59	59	62
			Purchasing Power Ranking for Ordinary Residents	57	57	57	57	57	57	57	56	58
43	Kiev	Ukraine	Wages Ranking for Ordinary Residents	86	86	87	85	96	96	95	86	84
			Purchasing Power Ranking for Ordinary Residents	74	71	69	70	71	71	76	74	70
44	Kuala Lumpur	Malaysia	Wages Ranking for Ordinary Residents	72	71	76	78	79	78	78	79	75
			Purchasing Power Ranking for Ordinary Residents	71	73	73	75	76	76	73	73	74

(*Continued*)

Appendix 2: (*Continued*)

No.	City	Country	Rankings	Year 2005	2006	2007	2008	2009	2010	2011	2012	2013
45	Kuwait	Kuwait	Wages Ranking for Ordinary Residents	60	60	60	59	58	60	58	57	57
			Purchasing Power Ranking for Ordinary Residents	67	67	68	69	68	68	55	57	59
46	Lexington	United States	Wages Ranking for Ordinary Residents	30	30	32	32	29	31	31	31	30
			Purchasing Power Ranking for Ordinary Residents	25	24	21	21	18	21	18	13	14
47	Lima	Peru	Wages Ranking for Ordinary Residents	69	70	73	73	74	76	76	74	78
			Purchasing Power Ranking for Ordinary Residents	68	69	71	72	74	74	74	75	77
48	Lisbon	Portugal	Wages Ranking for Ordinary Residents	58	58	57	57	57	57	56	58	58
			Purchasing Power Ranking for Ordinary Residents	64	65	66	66	65	65	68	71	72
49	London	Great Britain	Wages Ranking for Ordinary Residents	10	8	9	12	23	23	25	27	25
			Purchasing Power Ranking for Ordinary Residents	15	16	18	15	17	20	35	37	40
50	Los Angeles	United States	Wages Ranking for Ordinary Residents	30	30	32	32	29	31	31	31	30
			Purchasing Power Ranking for Ordinary Residents	40	42	44	47	45	47	50	51	53
51	Luxembourg	Luxembourg	Wages Ranking for Ordinary Residents	5	5	5	5	5	5	5	5	5
			Purchasing Power Ranking for Ordinary Residents	2	2	3	4	4	5	6	6	6
52	Lyon	France	Wages Ranking for Ordinary Residents	12	16	16	10	11	20	20	22	19
			Purchasing Power Ranking for Ordinary Residents	4	4	4	3	3	2	3	3	2
53	Madrid	Spain	Wages Ranking for Ordinary Residents	50	51	50	50	48	51	52	52	52
			Purchasing Power Ranking for Ordinary Residents	51	52	52	53	53	51	51	50	49
54	Manila	Philippines	Wages Ranking for Ordinary Residents	99	99	99	99	99	99	99	99	99
			Purchasing Power Ranking for Ordinary Residents	99	100	100	100	100	100	100	100	100
55	Melbourne	Australia	Wages Ranking for Ordinary Residents	20	20	18	19	18	6	6	6	6
			Purchasing Power Ranking for Ordinary Residents	29	29	25	25	25	26	30	30	31

(*Continued*)

Appendix 2: (*Continued*)

No.	City	Country	Rankings	Year 2005	2006	2007	2008	2009	2010	2011	2012	2013
56	Mexico City	Mexico	Wages Ranking for Ordinary Residents	71	72	77	80	83	84	84	84	85
			Purchasing Power Ranking for Ordinary Residents	78	79	81	83	86	90	93	94	95
57	Miami	United States	Wages Ranking for Ordinary Residents	30	30	32	32	29	31	31	31	30
			Purchasing Power Ranking for Ordinary Residents	36	36	37	36	34	36	39	38	35
58	Milan	Italy	Wages Ranking for Ordinary Residents	46	46	30	28	45	47	47	49	49
			Purchasing Power Ranking for Ordinary Residents	52	51	51	50	52	54	47	46	44
59	Minneapolis	United States	Wages Ranking for Ordinary Residents	30	30	32	32	29	31	31	31	30
			Purchasing Power Ranking for Ordinary Residents	27	27	29	27	27	31	29	33	34
60	Montevideo	Uruguay	Wages Ranking for Ordinary Residents	78	78	78	77	75	74	73	73	72
			Purchasing Power Ranking for Ordinary Residents	85	83	84	84	81	82	80	80	81
61	Montreal	Canada	Wages Ranking for Ordinary Residents	14	11	12	14	14	14	15	14	14
			Purchasing Power Ranking for Ordinary Residents	7	7	7	7	7	7	13	17	13
62	Moscow	Russia	Wages Ranking for Ordinary Residents	76	75	71	69	71	70	71	69	67
			Purchasing Power Ranking for Ordinary Residents	73	72	70	68	69	69	69	65	60
63	Mumbai	India	Wages Ranking for Ordinary Residents	101	101	101	101	101	101	101	101	101
			Purchasing Power Ranking for Ordinary Residents	101	101	101	101	101	101	102	102	103
64	Munich	Germany	Wages Ranking for Ordinary Residents	27	25	25	24	24	26	26	28	26
			Purchasing Power Ranking for Ordinary Residents	35	30	30	30	32	32	20	24	26
65	Nairobi	Kenya	Wages Ranking for Ordinary Residents	79	80	81	82	84	86	94	95	95
			Purchasing Power Ranking for Ordinary Residents	72	75	78	85	90	91	81	83	85
66	New Delhi	India	Wages Ranking for Ordinary Residents	101	101	101	101	101	101	101	101	101
			Purchasing Power Ranking for Ordinary Residents	96	99	99	99	99	99	99	101	101

(*Continued*)

Appendix 2: (*Continued*)

No.	City	Country	Rankings	Year								
				2005	2006	2007	2008	2009	2010	2011	2012	2013
67	New York	United States	Wages Ranking for Ordinary Residents	30	30	32	32	29	31	31	31	30
			Purchasing Power Ranking for Ordinary Residents	56	56	56	56	56	56	58	63	67
68	Osaka/Kobe	Japan	Wages Ranking for Ordinary Residents	25	28	48	30	27	24	23	20	46
			Purchasing Power Ranking for Ordinary Residents	28	32	32	34	36	37	40	41	41
69	Oslo	Norway	Wages Ranking for Ordinary Residents	4	4	2	2	4	4	4	3	4
			Purchasing Power Ranking for Ordinary Residents	6	6	5	5	5	4	5	5	5
70	Paris	France	Wages Ranking for Ordinary Residents	12	16	16	10	11	20	20	22	19
			Purchasing Power Ranking for Ordinary Residents	44	43	45	45	43	45	49	52	48
71	Perth	Australia	Wages Ranking for Ordinary Residents	20	20	18	19	18	6	6	6	6
			Purchasing Power Ranking for Ordinary Residents	18	17	16	17	16	17	16	15	12
72	Pittsburgh	United States	Wages Ranking for Ordinary Residents	30	30	32	32	29	31	31	31	30
			Purchasing Power Ranking for Ordinary Residents	20	20	19	19	19	19	17	19	19
73	Prague	Czech Republic	Wages Ranking for Ordinary Residents	64	63	63	60	59	62	62	63	60
			Purchasing Power Ranking for Ordinary Residents	60	59	59	59	59	59	62	64	66
74	Pretoria	South Africa	Wages Ranking for Ordinary Residents	61	61	61	66	63	58	59	59	62
			Purchasing Power Ranking for Ordinary Residents	58	58	58	58	58	58	56	55	54
75	Qingdao	China	Wages Ranking for Ordinary Residents	91	91	90	89	87	87	86	87	86
			Purchasing Power Ranking for Ordinary Residents	93	90	87	87	84	87	91	93	92
76	Quito	Ecuador	Wages Ranking for Ordinary Residents	80	82	83	86	82	82	83	83	83
			Purchasing Power Ranking for Ordinary Residents	80	81	80	80	80	79	86	88	84
77	Reykjavik	Iceland	Wages Ranking for Ordinary Residents	9	10	7	27	52	49	49	48	29
			Purchasing Power Ranking for Ordinary Residents	47	45	38	41	47	46	52	49	47

(*Continued*)

Appendix 2: (*Continued*)

No.	City	Country	Rankings	Year								
				2005	2006	2007	2008	2009	2010	2011	2012	2013
78	Rio de Janeiro	Brazil	Wages Ranking for Ordinary Residents	73	73	74	74	76	72	74	75	76
			Purchasing Power Ranking for Ordinary Residents	82	82	83	82	83	83	85	85	86
79	Rome	Italy	Wages Ranking for Ordinary Residents	46	46	30	28	45	47	47	49	49
			Purchasing Power Ranking for Ordinary Residents	49	50	50	51	54	52	45	45	52
80	San Francisco	United States	Wages Ranking for Ordinary Residents	30	30	32	32	29	31	31	31	30
			Purchasing Power Ranking for Ordinary Residents	48	46	48	43	37	38	41	40	36
81	Santiago	Chile	Wages Ranking for Ordinary Residents	70	69	69	72	70	69	69	72	73
			Purchasing Power Ranking for Ordinary Residents	75	74	77	77	77	77	75	76	75
82	Sao Paulo	Brazil	Wages Ranking for Ordinary Residents	73	73	74	74	76	72	74	75	76
			Purchasing Power Ranking for Ordinary Residents	79	80	79	78	79	80	82	86	87
83	Seattle	United States	Wages Ranking for Ordinary Residents	30	30	32	32	29	31	31	31	30
			Purchasing Power Ranking for Ordinary Residents	33	35	34	33	30	28	24	20	23
84	Seoul	South Korea	Wages Ranking for Ordinary Residents	52	50	53	55	55	55	55	54	55
			Purchasing Power Ranking for Ordinary Residents	31	28	31	35	38	35	31	32	29
85	Shanghai	China	Wages Ranking for Ordinary Residents	91	91	90	89	87	87	86	87	86
			Purchasing Power Ranking for Ordinary Residents	98	97	98	98	96	96	98	98	98
86	Shenzhen	China	Wages Ranking for Ordinary Residents	91	91	90	89	87	87	86	87	86
			Purchasing Power Ranking for Ordinary Residents	91	89	89	88	85	84	88	89	90
87	Singapore	Singapore	Wages Ranking for Ordinary Residents	54	54	54	53	53	53	50	47	48
			Purchasing Power Ranking for Ordinary Residents	42	39	36	37	40	40	23	23	21
88	Sofia	Bulgaria	Wages Ranking for Ordinary Residents	85	85	85	83	81	83	82	82	82
			Purchasing Power Ranking for Ordinary Residents	83	84	85	79	78	78	78	77	76

(*Continued*)

Appendix 2: (*Continued*)

No.	City	Country	Rankings	Year 2005	2006	2007	2008	2009	2010	2011	2012	2013
89	St Petersburg	Russia	Wages Ranking for Ordinary Residents	76	75	71	69	71	70	71	69	67
			Purchasing Power Ranking for Ordinary Residents	69	68	67	65	67	66	67	60	57
90	Stockholm	Sweden	Wages Ranking for Ordinary Residents	7	6	6	7	9	11	11	11	11
			Purchasing Power Ranking for Ordinary Residents	11	10	11	9	8	9	15	11	11
91	Suzhou	China	Wages Ranking for Ordinary Residents	91	91	90	89	87	87	86	87	86
			Purchasing Power Ranking for Ordinary Residents	92	93	88	86	82	81	87	84	82
92	Sydney	Australia	Wages Ranking for Ordinary Residents	20	20	18	19	18	6	6	6	6
			Purchasing Power Ranking for Ordinary Residents	32	31	26	26	28	27	34	36	38
93	Taipei	Taiwan, China	Wages Ranking for Ordinary Residents	56	56	58	58	61	61	61	61	59
			Purchasing Power Ranking for Ordinary Residents	41	38	39	40	46	42	36	39	42
94	Tel Aviv	Israel	Wages Ranking for Ordinary Residents	55	55	55	54	54	54	54	55	54
			Purchasing Power Ranking for Ordinary Residents	54	55	55	55	55	55	59	59	63
95	Tianjin	China	Wages Ranking for Ordinary Residents	91	91	90	89	87	87	86	87	86
			Purchasing Power Ranking for Ordinary Residents	95	95	94	90	88	86	89	87	83
96	Tokyo	Japan	Wages Ranking for Ordinary Residents	25	28	48	30	27	24	23	20	46
			Purchasing Power Ranking for Ordinary Residents	43	44	47	49	51	48	53	54	55
97	Toronto	Canada	Wages Ranking for Ordinary Residents	14	11	12	14	14	14	15	14	14
			Purchasing Power Ranking for Ordinary Residents	14	14	17	16	23	24	37	34	32
98	Vancouver	Canada	Wages Ranking for Ordinary Residents	14	11	12	14	14	14	15	14	14
			Purchasing Power Ranking for Ordinary Residents	10	12	8	8	10	10	22	28	24
99	Vienna	Austria	Wages Ranking for Ordinary Residents	19	18	23	13	10	19	19	19	21
			Purchasing Power Ranking for Ordinary Residents	26	25	22	22	21	22	21	21	22

(*Continued*)

Appendix 2: (*Continued*)

No.	City	Country	Rankings	Year								
				2005	2006	2007	2008	2009	2010	2011	2012	2013
100	Warsaw	Poland	Wages Ranking for Ordinary Residents	66	66	66	62	68	67	66	65	66
			Purchasing Power Ranking for Ordinary Residents	62	61	61	60	61	60	61	61	61
101	Washington DC	United States	Wages Ranking for Ordinary Residents	30	30	32	32	29	31	31	31	30
			Purchasing Power Ranking for Ordinary Residents	38	40	42	44	44	44	48	48	45
102	Wellington	New Zealand	Wages Ranking for Ordinary Residents	48	48	28	48	50	29	29	24	23
			Purchasing Power Ranking for Ordinary Residents	45	49	43	42	42	41	42	35	39
103	Zurich	Switzerland	Wages Ranking for Ordinary Residents	2	2	3	3	2	2	1	1	1
			Purchasing Power Ranking for Ordinary Residents	5	5	6	6	6	6	4	4	4

Appendix 3

Yearly Average Exchange Rates in 103 World's Major Cities (Local Currency Units per US Dollar), 2005–2013

Appendix 3: Yearly Average Exchange Rates in 103 World's Major Cities (Local Currency Units per US Dollar), 2005–2013

No.	City	Country	Currency	Currency Code	Year 2005	2006	2007	2008	2009	2010	2011	2012	2013
1	Adelaide	Australia	Dollar	AUD	1.31219	1.32774	1.19473	1.19721	1.27908	1.08907	0.96903	0.96592	0.96795
2	Amman	Jordan	Dinar	JOD	0.70889	0.70866	0.70843	0.70822	0.70812	0.70855	0.70879	0.70845	0.70816
3	Amsterdam	Netherlands	Euro	EUR	0.80486	0.79653	0.73053	0.68325	0.71886	0.75533	0.71891	0.77812	0.75278
4	Asuncion	Paraguay	Guarani	PYG	6174.104	5632.565	5029.143	4351.505	4969.731	4747.496	4195.157	4418.37	4310.169
5	Athens	Greece	Euro	EUR	0.80486	0.79653	0.73053	0.68325	0.71886	0.75533	0.71891	0.77812	0.75278
6	Atlanta	United States	Dollar	USD	1	1	1	1	1	1	1	1	1
7	Auckland	New Zealand	Dollar	NZD	1.42039	1.54209	1.36046	1.42546	1.59647	1.387	1.26527	1.23519	1.21878
8	Baku	Azerbaijan	Manat	AZN	0.94582	0.89664	0.8604	0.82343	0.80512	0.8031	0.79004	0.78522	0.78399
9	Bangkok	Thailand	Baht	THB	40.27276	37.92047	32.30588	33.00415	34.32134	31.70351	30.48343	31.06859	30.72327
10	Barcelona	Spain	Euro	EUR	0.80486	0.79653	0.73053	0.68325	0.71886	0.75533	0.71891	0.77812	0.75278
11	Beijing	China	Yuan	CNY	8.19238	7.97309	7.60789	6.95021	6.83151	6.76805	6.46338	6.30932	6.14854
12	Berlin	Germany	Euro	EUR	0.80486	0.79653	0.73053	0.68325	0.71886	0.75533	0.71891	0.77812	0.75278
13	Bogota	Colombia	Peso	COP	2321.552	2360.54	2076.032	1967.682	2153.199	1897.555	1848.124	1797.234	1868.921
14	Boston	United States	Dollar	USD	1	1	1	1	1	1	1	1	1
15	Bratislava	Slovakia	Euro	SKK/EUR	31.06513	29.6483	24.67915	21.35451	0.71886	0.75533	0.71891	0.77812	0.75278
16	Brisbane	Australia	Dollar	AUD	1.31219	1.32774	1.19473	1.19721	1.27908	1.08907	0.96903	0.96592	0.96795
17	Brussels	Belgium	Euro	EUR	0.80486	0.79653	0.73053	0.68325	0.71886	0.75533	0.71891	0.77812	0.75278
18	Bucharest	Romania	Leu	RON	2.91355	2.80829	2.43548	2.51999	3.0459	3.18285	3.04804	3.46924	3.32691
19	Budapest	Hungary	Forint	HUF	199.6884	210.3271	183.5897	172.2992	201.8224	208.0735	201.1138	225.0008	223.5381
20	Buenos Aires	Argentina	Peso	ARS	2.92288	3.07451	3.11534	3.16253	3.72792	3.91183	4.12809	4.55027	5.47967
21	Cairo	Egypt	Pound	EGP	5.79476	5.74261	5.64526	5.43781	5.55254	5.64229	5.94416	6.07065	6.87299
22	Calgary	Canada	Dollar	CAD	1.21128	1.13414	1.07402	1.06702	1.14048	1.03013	0.98913	0.99962	1.0299

(*Continued*)

Appendix 3: (*Continued*)

No.	City	Country	Currency	Currency Code	Year 2005	2006	2007	2008	2009	2010	2011	2012	2013
23	Caracas	Venezuela	Bolivar	VEB/VEF	2108.792	2147.289	2147.3	2.14731	2.14731	4.2542	4.29552	4.29553	6.06345
24	Chicago	United States	Dollar	USD	1	1	1	1	1	1	1	1	1
25	Cleveland	United States	Dollar	USD	1	1	1	1	1	1	1	1	1
26	Colombo	Sri Lanka	Rupee	LKR	100.5102	103.9748	110.649	108.3351	114.9658	113.0177	110.5756	127.7046	129.1382
27	Copenhagen	Denmark	Krone	DKK	5.99823	5.94142	5.4426	5.09405	5.35278	5.62685	5.35613	5.79215	5.61638
28	Dalian	China	Yuan	CNY	8.19238	7.97309	7.60789	6.95021	6.83151	6.76805	6.46338	6.30932	6.14854
29	Detroit	United States	Dollar	USD	1	1	1	1	1	1	1	1	1
30	Doha	Qatar	Riyal	QAR	3.6399	3.64064	3.6395	3.64034	3.64038	3.6405	3.64153	3.64119	3.64094
31	Dubai	United Arab Emirates	Arab Emirate Dirham	AED	3.67327	3.67345	3.67251	3.67277	3.67247	3.67245	3.67256	3.67261	3.67298
32	Dublin	Ireland	Euro	EUR	0.80486	0.79653	0.73053	0.68325	0.71886	0.75533	0.71891	0.77812	0.75278
33	Frankfurt	Germany	Euro	EUR	0.80486	0.79653	0.73053	0.68325	0.71886	0.75533	0.71891	0.77812	0.75278
34	Geneva	Switzerland	Franc	CHF	1.24631	1.25289	1.20004	1.0824	1.08495	1.04236	0.88659	0.93774	0.92673
35	Guangzhou	China	Yuan	CNY	8.19238	7.97309	7.60789	6.95021	6.83151	6.76805	6.46338	6.30932	6.14854
36	Helsinki	Finland	Euro	EUR	0.80486	0.79653	0.73053	0.68325	0.71886	0.75533	0.71891	0.77812	0.75278
37	Hong Kong	Hong Kong, China	Dollar	HKD	7.77746	7.76844	7.802	7.78626	7.75166	7.76887	7.78436	7.75703	7.75663
38	Honolulu	United States	Dollar	USD	1	1	1	1	1	1	1	1	1
39	Houston	United States	Dollar	USD	1	1	1	1	1	1	1	1	1
40	Istanbul	Turkey	Lira	TRY	1.34738	1.43804	1.30627	1.30528	1.55373	1.50745	1.68127	1.80018	1.9053
41	Jakarta	Indonesia	Rupiah	IDR	9716.402	9170.55	9144.191	9684.791	10390.18	9084.399	8778.087	9377.118	10437.13
42	Johannesburg	South Africa	Rand	ZAR	6.36645	6.77032	7.04951	8.27049	8.40681	7.31557	7.26408	8.20977	9.64595
43	Kiev	Ukraine	Hryvnia	UAH	5.0996	5.04195	5.03507	5.25565	8.06982	7.9492	7.98556	8.08214	8.15443

(*Continued*)

Appendix 3: (*Continued*)

No.	City	Country	Currency	Currency Code	Year 2005	2006	2007	2008	2009	2010	2011	2012	2013
44	Kuala Lumpur	Malaysia	Ringgit	MYR	3.78604	3.66707	3.43666	3.33366	3.52257	3.21854	3.05971	3.08764	3.14979
45	Kuwait	Kuwait	Dinar	KWD	0.29201	0.29021	0.28429	0.26892	0.2882	0.28685	0.27634	0.28013	0.28387
46	Lexington	United States	Dollar	USD	1	1	1	1	1	1	1	1	1
47	Lima	Peru	Nuevo sol	PEN	3.29648	3.27456	3.1286	2.92315	3.00936	2.82453	2.75346	2.63708	2.7032
48	Lisbon	Portugal	Euro	EUR	0.80486	0.79653	0.73053	0.68325	0.71886	0.75533	0.71891	0.77812	0.75278
49	London	Great Britain	Pound	GBP	0.5502	0.54318	0.49972	0.54565	0.6405	0.64754	0.62364	0.63098	0.63891
50	Los Angeles	United States	Dollar	USD	1	1	1	1	1	1	1	1	1
51	Luxembourg	Luxembourg	Euro	EUR	0.80486	0.79653	0.73053	0.68325	0.71886	0.75533	0.71891	0.77812	0.75278
52	Lyon	France	Euro	EUR	0.80486	0.79653	0.73053	0.68325	0.71886	0.75533	0.71891	0.77812	0.75278
53	Madrid	Spain	Euro	EUR	0.80486	0.79653	0.73053	0.68325	0.71886	0.75533	0.71891	0.77812	0.75278
54	Manila	Philippines	Peso	PHP	55.05343	51.28437	46.11587	44.43856	47.54909	45.06548	43.29744	42.18737	42.46212
55	Melbourne	Australia	Dollar	AUD	1.31219	1.32774	1.19473	1.19721	1.27908	1.08907	0.96903	0.96592	0.96795
56	Mexico City	Mexico	Nuevo peso	MXN	10.89151	10.9068	10.92797	11.1625	13.50034	12.63027	12.44312	13.15599	12.76189
57	Miami	United States	Dollar	USD	1	1	1	1	1	1	1	1	1
58	Milan	Italy	Euro	EUR	0.80486	0.79653	0.73053	0.68325	0.71886	0.75533	0.71891	0.77812	0.75278
59	Minneapolis	United States	Dollar	USD	1	1	1	1	1	1	1	1	1
60	Montevideo	Uruguay	Peso	UYU	24.48676	24.09789	23.44716	20.85531	22.51947	20.01705	19.27826	20.25497	20.43429
61	Montreal	Canada	Dollar	CAD	1.21128	1.13414	1.07402	1.06702	1.14048	1.03013	0.98913	0.99962	1.0299
62	Moscow	Russia	Rouble	RUB	28.30122	27.17623	25.57252	24.87792	31.74015	30.37403	29.40309	31.06076	31.85876
63	Mumbai	India	Rupee	INR	44.11288	45.32374	41.34948	43.46796	48.34151	45.72445	46.66326	53.51056	58.5864
64	Munich	Germany	Euro	EUR	0.80486	0.79653	0.73053	0.68325	0.71886	0.75533	0.71891	0.77812	0.75278
65	Nairobi	Kenya	Shilling	KES	75.62614	72.22191	67.33987	69.25628	77.28301	79.28755	88.86955	84.40002	86.09498

(*Continued*)

Appendix 3: (*Continued*)

No.	City	Country	Currency	Currency Code	Year 2005	2006	2007	2008	2009	2010	2011	2012	2013
66	New Delhi	India	Rupee	INR	44.11288	45.32374	41.34948	43.46796	48.34151	45.72445	46.66326	53.51056	58.5864
67	New York	United States	Dollar	USD	1	1	1	1	1	1	1	1	1
68	Osaka/Kobe	Japan	Yen	JPY	110.1786	116.3429	117.7851	103.3671	93.60092	87.73297	79.701	79.83711	97.58821
69	Oslo	Norway	Krone	NOK	6.44517	6.41065	5.85843	5.64848	6.28591	6.04571	5.60593	5.81836	5.87697
70	Paris	France	Euro	EUR	0.80486	0.79653	0.73053	0.68325	0.71886	0.75533	0.71891	0.77812	0.75278
71	Perth	Australia	Dollar	AUD	1.31219	1.32774	1.19473	1.19721	1.27908	1.08907	0.96903	0.96592	0.96795
72	Pittsburgh	United States	Dollar	USD	1	1	1	1	1	1	1	1	1
73	Prague	Czech Republic	Koruna	CZK	23.96354	22.57376	20.29005	17.06787	19.03237	19.09727	17.68393	19.56179	19.55566
74	Pretoria	South Africa	Rand	ZAR	6.36645	6.77032	7.04951	8.27049	8.40681	7.31557	7.26408	8.20977	9.64595
75	Qingdao	China	Yuan	CNY	8.19238	7.97309	7.60789	6.95021	6.83151	6.76805	6.46338	6.30932	6.14854
76	Quito	Ecuador	US Dollar	USD	1	1	1	1	1	1	1	1	1
77	Reykjavik	Iceland	Krona	ISK	62.88375	69.93396	64.05549	88.05067	123.7447	122.1333	116.0775	125.1255	122.1445
78	Rio De Janeiro	Brazil	Real	BRL	2.43421	2.17605	1.94659	1.83718	1.99859	1.7592	1.67429	1.95538	2.16117
79	Rome	Italy	Euro	EUR	0.80486	0.79653	0.73053	0.68325	0.71886	0.75533	0.71891	0.77812	0.75278
80	San Francisco	United States	Dollar	USD	1	1	1	1	1	1	1	1	1
81	Santiago	Chile	Peso	CLP	559.511	530.5965	522.2463	523.6846	558.4423	510.0648	483.7583	486.3013	495.2821
82	Sao Paulo	Brazil	Real	BRL	2.43421	2.17605	1.94659	1.83718	1.99859	1.7592	1.67429	1.95538	2.16117
83	Seattle	United States	Dollar	USD	1	1	1	1	1	1	1	1	1
84	Seoul	South Korea	Won	KRW	1024.381	954.9017	929.592	1101.672	1275.677	1156.559	1107.758	1126.288	1094.469
85	Shanghai	China	Yuan	CNY	8.19238	7.97309	7.60789	6.95021	6.83151	6.76805	6.46338	6.30932	6.14854
86	Shenzhen	China	Yuan	CNY	8.19238	7.97309	7.60789	6.95021	6.83151	6.76805	6.46338	6.30932	6.14854

(*Continued*)

Appendix 3: ***(Continued)***

No.	City	Country	Currency	Currency Code	Year 2005	2006	2007	2008	2009	2010	2011	2012	2013
87	Singapore	Singapore	Dollar	SGD	1.66446	1.58869	1.5068	1.41473	1.45378	1.36265	1.25716	1.24941	1.25101
88	Sofia	Bulgaria	Leva	BGN	1.57553	1.55828	1.43028	1.33403	1.40551	1.47735	1.40612	1.52188	1.47287
89	St Petersburg	Russia	Rouble	RUB	28.30122	27.17623	25.57252	24.87792	31.74015	30.37403	29.40309	31.06076	31.85876
90	Stockholm	Sweden	Krona	SEK	7.47889	7.37193	6.75614	6.5968	7.64365	7.20368	6.49319	6.77232	6.51365
91	Suzhou	China	Yuan	CNY	8.19238	7.97309	7.60789	6.95021	6.83151	6.76805	6.46338	6.30932	6.14854
92	Sydney	Australia	Dollar	AUD	1.31219	1.32774	1.19473	1.19721	1.27908	1.08907	0.96903	0.96592	0.96795
93	Taipei	Taiwan, China	New dollar	TWD	32.17025	32.52509	32.86105	31.54304	33.03176	31.49157	29.40221	29.57319	29.6962
94	Tel Aviv	Israel	New shekel	ILS	4.48806	4.45648	4.10864	3.58426	3.92724	3.73258	3.57748	3.85422	3.60976
95	Tianjin	China	Yuan	CNY	8.19238	7.97309	7.60789	6.95021	6.83151	6.76805	6.46338	6.30932	6.14854
96	Tokyo	Japan	Yen	JPY	110.1786	116.3429	117.7851	103.3671	93.60092	87.73297	79.701	79.83711	97.58821
97	Toronto	Canada	Dollar	CAD	1.21128	1.13414	1.07402	1.06702	1.14048	1.03013	0.98913	0.99962	1.0299
98	Vancouver	Canada	Dollar	CAD	1.21128	1.13414	1.07402	1.06702	1.14048	1.03013	0.98913	0.99962	1.0299
99	Vienna	Austria	Euro	EUR	0.80486	0.79653	0.73053	0.68325	0.71886	0.75533	0.71891	0.77812	0.75278
100	Warsaw	Poland	Zloty	PLN	3.23606	3.10249	2.76508	2.40946	3.11423	3.01739	2.96516	3.25446	3.15896
101	Washington DC	United States	Dollar	USD	1	1	1	1	1	1	1	1	1
102	Wellington	New Zealand	Dollar	NZD	1.42039	1.54209	1.36046	1.42546	1.59647	1.387	1.26527	1.23519	1.21878
103	Zurich	Switzerland	Franc	CHF	1.24631	1.25289	1.20004	1.0824	1.08495	1.04236	0.88659	0.93774	0.92673

Source: Calculated from daily average exchange rates obtained from the Bloomberg Terminal